THE STORY OF THE
1st BATTALION CAPE CORPS
(1915-1919).

BY

CAPTAIN IVOR D. DIFFORD,
Quartermaster, 1st Cape Corps, 1915-1919.

With an Introduction by
The Rt. Hon. John X. Merriman, P.C., M.L.A.

WITH PHOTOGRAPHS, SKETCHES AND MAPS.

The Naval & Military Press Ltd

Published by
The Naval & Military Press Ltd
5 Riverside, Brambleside, Bellbrook
Industrial Estate, Uckfield, East Sussex,
TN22 1QQ England

Tel: +44 (0) 1825 749494
Fax: +44 (0) 1825 765701
www.naval-military-press.com
www.military-genealogy.com

In reprinting in facsimile from the original, any imperfections are inevitably reproduced and the quality may fall short of modern type and cartographic standards.

LIST OF PRINCIPAL ILLUSTRATIONS.

	PAGE
Colonel Sir W. E. M. Stanford, K.B.E., C.B., C.M.G. (Honorary Colonel)	Frontispiece
Lieut.-Colonel G. A. Morris, C.M.G., D.S.O. (Officer Commanding)	Frontispiece
The First Officers of the Battalion	Frontispiece
Major C. N. Hoy, D.S.O. and Bar (Second in Command) ...	Frontispiece
Major C. G. Durham, D.S.O.	Frontispiece
The Cape Corps Recruiting Committee	17
Sir Harry Hands, K.B.E. (Chairman, Recruiting Committee) ...	19
Some Members of the Recruiting Committee	21
Captain W. G. Gunningham (Adjutant, 1915/16)	31
Group of Instructors and European N.C.O.'s at Simonstown ...	34
Departure for East Africa	42
Late 2nd Lieutenant J. C. Hosack	62
Major F. E. Bradstock, D.S.O., M.C.	86
Late Captain (acting) T. M. Hoffe	110
Late Lieutenant I. A. M. Guest	144
Late 2nd Lieutenant J. McNeil	146
Late Lieutenant C. F. Abbott	146
Late Lieutenant W. Power	148
Enemy machine gun captured in a bayonet charge, 8th November, 1917	150
Captain J. H. Tandy, M.C. (Adjutant, 1917/19)	159
Officers at Kimberley, March, 1918	168
Aerial photo of Kh. Jibeit	206
Late Major W. R. Cowell, D.S.O.	211
Late Captain J. V. Harris, M.C.	211
Late Lieutenant A. N. Difford	213
Late Lieutenant Gordon White	213
Late Lieutenant G. R. Barnard	215
Late 2nd Lieutenant A. E. J. Antill	215

	PAGE
Late 2nd Lieutenant J. S. Dreyer	217
Late 2nd Lieutenant C. A. Vipan	217
Field guns captured from the Turks, September 18/20, 1918	220
160th Brigade Staff	230
Officers who joined on Mobilisation still serving at date of Armistice	234
The Concert Party	238, 281
The Battalion on Parade in Egypt, June, 1919	250
The last Parade, Maitland, 5th September, 1919	252
Officers in Egypt, June, 1919	255
Warrant Officers in Egypt, June, 1919	257
Warrant Officers and Sergeants in Egypt, June, 1919	259
Major W. J. R. Cuningham (O.C. Reserve Half Battalion)	261
Officers, Reserve Half Battalion, June, 1918	263
Return of the Reserve Half Battalion to South Africa, June, 1919	283, 287
Captain F. Burger (O.C. Machine Gun Company)	291
The Machine Gun Company	294
Major W. P. Anderson	297
The Flag Presentation, October 12th, 1916	299
The Band at Mustapha	330

LIST OF MAPS.

	PAGE
British (part of) and German East Africa (shewing the whole East African War Area, 1914-18)	44
Illustrating Battalion's advance from British East Africa to Moshi	46
Illustrating Battalion's advance in German East Africa from Kahe to Morogoro	64
Illustrating Rufiji River operations	78
Illustrating operations against Ober-Lieutenant Naumann's Force	108
The Enemy's position on Luita Berg (Ober-Lieutenant Naumann)	112
Illustrating operation against Lieutenant Zingel's Force	128
Wanjoki position (Lieutenant Zingel)	134
Illustrating operations in the Lindi Area	152
Palestine	192
Map of the front at El Mugheir (near Jerusalem)	208
Square Hill (Palestine front)	224

TO MY COMRADES OF THE 1st CAPE CORPS, AND TO THE MEMORY OF THE FOUR HUNDRED AND FIFTY OFFICERS AND MEN OF THE BATTALION WHO GAVE THEIR LIVES DURING THE GREAT WAR (1914-8), "TILL THE DAY OF THE LAST GREAT GATHERING."

I. D. DIFFORD.

CONTENTS.

	PAGE.
INTRODUCTION.—By the Right Honourable J. X. Merriman, P.C., M.L.A.	
FOREWORD	
CHRONOLOGICAL SUMMARY	
CHAPTER I.—The Cape Coloured Man in Earlier Wars. (Period 1795—1842). By Mr. W. R. Morrison	1
CHAPTER II.—The Cape Coloured Man in Earlier Wars. (Period 1846—1896). By Mr. W. R. Morrison	9
CHAPTER III.—Recruitment of the Cape Corps. By Mr. A. Eames Perkins	18
CHAPTER IV.—Mobilisation at Simonstown. (Period 21st October, 1915, to 9th February, 1916)	29
CHAPTER V.—In East Africa. (Period 10th February to 14th December, 1916)	45
CHAPTER VI.—The Rufiji River Campaign. (Period 12th December, 1916, to 21st March, 1917)	79
CHAPTER VII.—The Detachment in the Coastal Area between Dar-es-Salaam and the Rufiji River. (Period 1st December, 1916, to August, 1917)	98
CHAPTER VIII.—Guerilla Operations after Major Wintgen's Force. (Period 17th April to 21st June, 1917)	101
CHAPTER IX.—The Naumann "Stunt." (Period 10th July to 1st October, 1917)	107

	PAGE.
CHAPTER X.—THE ZINGEL "STUNT." (Period 26th July to 27th September, 1917)	127
CHAPTER XI.—OUR MOROGORO DEPOT IN GERMAN EAST AFRICA. (Period February to December, 1917)	138
CHAPTER XII.—TWO MONTHS' HARD WORK IN THE LINDI AREA. (Period 20th October to 16th December, 1917)	143
CHAPTER XIII.—IN THE UNION OF SOUTH AFRICA. (Period 25th December, 1917, to 3rd April, 1918)	167
CHAPTER XIV.—IN EGYPT. (Period 19th April to 15th July, 1918)...	176
CHAPTER XV.—OUR SHARE IN GENERAL ALLENBY'S GREAT VICTORY IN PALESTINE. (Period 16th July to 31st October, 1918)	188
CHAPTER XVI.—IN EGYPT. (Period 1st November, 1918, to 5th September, 1919)	237
CHAPTER XVII.—THE RESERVE HALF BATTALION	262
CHAPTER XVIII.—OUR MACHINE GUNNERS	288
CHAPTER XIX.—THE REGIMENTAL DEPOTS IN SOUTH AFRICA	298
CHAPTER XX.—SPORT AND ATHLETICS	309
CHAPTER XXI.—AFTERWORD—THE CAPE CORPS GIFTS AND COMFORTS COMMITTEE—COLOURED TROOPS REST HOUSE, CAPE TOWN—VOCATIONAL TRAINING—THE GOVERNOR-GENERAL'S FUND—CAPE CORPS' MEMORIAL FUND—REGIMENTAL BAND—PENSIONS—THE FUTURE	322

APPENDIX.

Explanation of Abbreviations	334
Officers, Nominal Roll of	337
Officers, Record of Active Service of	341
Other Ranks, Nominal Roll of	349
The Roll of Honour	425
The Honours List	438
Copies of Letters and Telegrams of Congratulation, etc.	441
Courses passed at Schools of Instruction	448

THE STORY OF THE 1st CAPE CORPS

Photo by]   *[The Gilham Studios, Pretoria.*
COLONEL SIR WALTER E. M. STANFORD, K.B.E., C.B., C.M.G.
Honorary Colonel, 1st Cape Corps.

THE STORY OF THE 1st CAPE CORPS.

Photo by]   [*The Middlebrook, Studio, Kimberley.*
LIEUT.-COLONEL GEORGE ABBOTT MORRIS, C.M.G., D.S.O.
Officer Commanding 1st Battalion Cape Corps throughout its existence
(October, 1915—September, 1919).

THE STORY OF THE 1st CAPE CORPS.

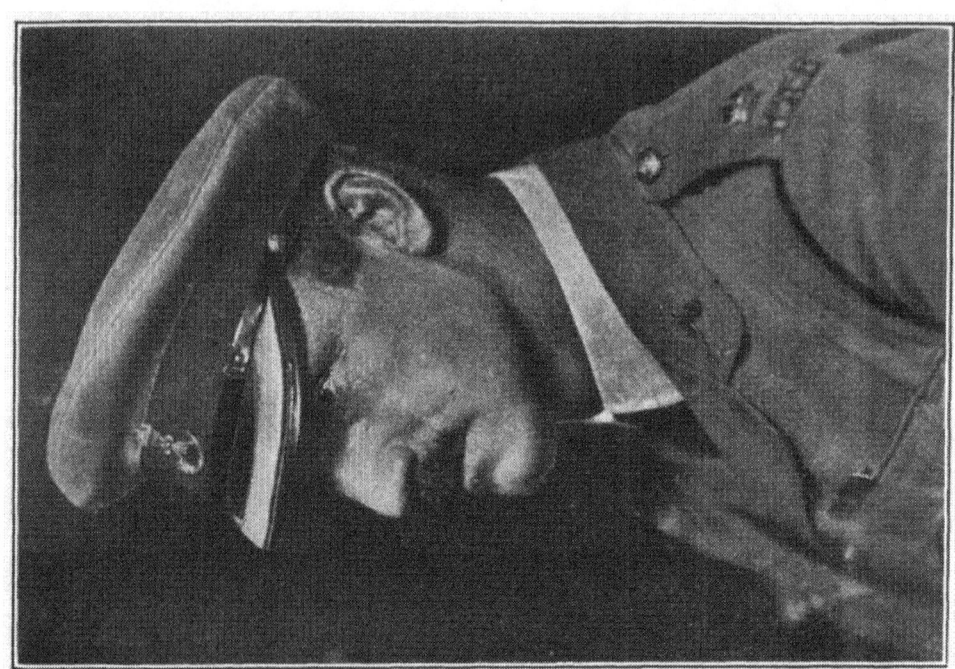

Major C. G. Durham, D.S.O.
Photo by [Leon Levson, Cape Town.

Major C. N. Hoy, D.S.O. and bar.
Second in Command of the Battalion (several times acted as O.C. during Lieut.-Colonel Morris' absence in hospital, etc.)

THE STORY OF THE 1st CAPE CORPS.

THE FIRST OFFICERS OF THE BATTALION TAKEN WITH MAJOR-GENERAL THOMPSON (G.O.C. SOUTH AFRICA) AND LIEUT.-COLONEL FINCH (G.S.O.I.) AT THE CASTLE, CAPE TOWN, IN JANUARY, 1916, SHORTLY BEFORE EMBARKATION FOR EAST AFRICA.

Top row: Lieutenant J. V. Harris, 2nd Lieutenant S. W. Whitaker, 2nd Lieutenant H. Edwards, 2nd Lieutenant T. P. Rose-Innes, 2nd Lieutenant D. K. Pearse, 2nd Lieutenant G. C. Macintosh, Captain A Earp-Jones (Chaplain). Second row: Captain H. G. Warr, Captain J. E. Robinson, Lieutenant F. Burger, Lieutenant F. C. Hallier, Lieutenant D. W. Robertson, Lieutenant W. J. R. Cuningham, Lieutenant J. M. Michau, Lieutenant J. Arnott, D.C.M., 2nd Lieutenant F. Murchie, 2nd Lieutenant W. W. Procter, Lieutenant J. E. Dennison (Signalling Officer), Captain I. D. Difford (Q.M.R.), Lieutenant C. E. Stevens. Third row: Captain R. M. Robb, S.A.M.C., Captain L. Campbell (O.C. Marchine Guns), Captain F. J. Bagshawe, Major C. G. Durham, Lieut.-Colonel G. A. Morris (Officer Commanding), Major-General Thompson (G.O.C., South Africa), Lieut.-Colonel Finch (G.S.O.I., South Africa), Captain W. R. Cowell, Captain W. G. Gunningham (Adjutant), Captain F. E. Bradstock, Captain W. P. Anderson. Fourth row: 2nd Lieutenant F. W. C. Stanford, Lieutenant S. Ashley, Lieutenant J. H. Tandy, Lieutenant B. Boam (Paymaster), Lieutenant S. Youart. Insets: 2nd Lieutenant E. J. Rackstraw, Lieutenant W. W. Alexander, 2nd Lieutenant R. Wilson. Absent on duty: Major C. N. Hoy (Second in Command).

INTRODUCTION.

By the Rt. Hon. J. X. Merriman, P.C., M.L.A.

I have been asked by Captain Difford to say a few words by way of introduction to the valuable record which he has compiled. I do so with pleasure, though, thanks to Mr. W. R. Morrison, Mr. Eames Perkins, and to Captain Difford himself, little remains to add to what they have said so ably. Mr. Morrison has done well to trace the origin of the idea of the formation of the Cape Corps as a successor to the Pandours of the old Dutch days, and to the Cape Corps of the old Hottentot days, which was merged after the war of 1851-54 into the European regiment known as the Cape Mounted Rifles, a smart and expensive corps which will not soon be forgotten by those who are old enough to remember the *Noctes Ambrosianæ* for which their mess was renowned at Grahamstown, Fort Beaufort, and Kingwilliamstown.

The mutiny of a large part of the old Cape Corps and of the Kafir Police in 1851 disinclined the idea of training non-Europeans as regular soldiers, though it is only fair to add that in most of our native outbreaks there has never been any reluctance to employ natives, possibly on the old maxim *Divide et impera*, to fight our battles under European leaders.

Mr. Rhodes, as Mr. Morrison reminds us, went a step further in the same direction when he organized a force of what are known as Cape Boys to fight Rhodesian battles in Mashonaland. Excellent service they rendered and a good character they earned for courage and discipline on that occasion. Prejudice, however, stood in the way of following the example of the French in raising a non-European Force either for police or for military service.

The present volume is a worthy record of another experiment in the same direction, and it deserves careful study by all those who are interested in the future of South Africa.

When, after the campaign that ended in the conquest of German South-West Africa, General Botha, who had opportunities of seeing the good service rendered by our "Cape Boys" in various capacities in the field and their behaviour under discipline, determined on raising a contingent under European officers to form part of the Force destined to share in the task of the conquest of German East Africa, he took a bold, and, as all readers who study Captain Difford's story of their fortunes must agree, a wise step.

No collection of men ever showed more zeal, devotion to duty, or discipline than the Cape Corps. Emphasis of that statement is to be found in every step from their training camp at Simonstown, the universal testimony of the different captains who commanded the various transports, as to the discipline, the obedience and the cleanliness of this hitherto untried material under circumstances that are often very trying even to disciplined troops, and to testimony from many other sources.

On the field of action, at first in the difficult task of transport and on the lines of communication, and afterwards when in the fighting line in the deadly Rufiji Valley and the swamps on the coast, and the various engagements with the elusive enemy—everywhere and on all occasions there was the same manifestation of duty, discipline, and character which show the material we have here in South Africa when we learn how to handle it.

On all occasions the Cape Corps, both officers and men, bore themselves with a steadfastness that did them infinite credit. In East Africa it was a case of hard solid endurance in the very depth of misery and squalor, without any of the "pomp and circumstance of glorious war." Far different was the scene in Egypt and Palestine, where the Cape Corps had an opportunity of perfecting itself in discipline and in all the modern arts of war, and of testing its fighting mettle alongside the men of many countries.

Captain Difford gives a straightforward picture of the finish of the campaign, and of the sacrifice in life that the final effort cost. Those who follow his narrative will have no reason to feel ashamed of the part played by the coloured contingent sent from South Africa or the record they brought back from the Holy Land.

We can only trust that the lessons they learned, and the example they set of discipline, endurance, and sacrifice to duty may be of inestimable service to all races in dealing with the many problems that lie before us in South Africa.

By all who take an interest in those problems a great debt of gratitude is due to Captain Difford for the pains that he has taken in the compilation of this volume.

JOHN X. MERRIMAN.

FOREWORD.

THE purport and object of this story is to place on record the good service rendered by Officers and men, but particularly the men, of the 1st Battalion Cape Corps for King and Empire, and especially for South Africa, during the great World War.

The reasons for this Story must be obvious. Every Regiment worthy of the name and with a record worthy of perpetuation aspires to its written story or history, and those who read this book will surely agree that the 1st Cape Corps is worthy.

There is, however, a more important reason. The formation of the 1st Cape Corps in 1915 was an experiment. True—as will be seen from the very interesting Chapters 1 and 2 which Mr. W. R. Morrison of the Editorial Staff of the *Cape Times* has so kindly written—Cape Coloured men have done excellent service for over a century in South Africa's many wars and minor campaigns. But the latter were very small fry in comparison to the recent great world upheaval. There were many in South Africa who were opposed to the enrolment of Cape Coloured men in the armed Forces of the Empire: some on principle, others who doubted the ability of the men to make good under the tremendously exacting conditions of modern warfare, and others again—and there were many of these latter—by reason of blind and most unreasoned prejudice.

It is but natural, therefore, now that happily the War is over and the Cape Coloured man has proved himself worthy and capable up to the full expectation of his friends—if indeed not beyond that—that the story of his service should be told. The Cape Coloured Community and their many friends have the right to expect that much.

The Coloured Community of South Africa is a considerable percentage of the population. A very large majority have been useful law abiding and loyal citizens, and when the Great War broke out and surprised an astonished world they at once came forward with urgent requests that their loyalty might be proved and translated into action. A large number of Cape Coloured men participated in the German South-West African Campaign as Artillery and Transport drivers, motor drivers and mechanics, as Officers' servants, and in various other non-combatant capacities, and performed much useful work. But it was not until September, 1915, that official sanction for the enrolment and mobilisation of the Cape Coloured man into a separate Infantry Battalion—to be known as the Cape Corps—for oversea war service, vastly delighted the whole Coloured Community of South Africa and their friends. The result of that service is related to the best of the ability of the writer in this Story. It will be for the reader to judge whether the service rendered was worthy or otherwise.

The writer had the privilege and the good luck to serve with the 1st Cape Corps throughout its career—in fact had a longer period of service with the Battalion than any other officer or man—from its inception in October, 1915, until practically the last man had been demobilised towards the end of last year.

THE STORY OF THE 1st CAPE CORPS.

When, therefore, the suggestion was made that he should write the history of the Battalion the task was accepted as an obvious duty, not only with pleasure but also with alacrity. There will not doubt be many short comings in this book. Of that the writer is fully conscious. To those who have been on active service the reasons will be obvious and should need no apology. To those who have not it may be pointed out that active service conditions do not afford much opportunity for journalistic or literary excursions. Little time is available for the keeping of diaries or memoranda or taking notes. The writer had no intention of penning this story until several months after the Armistice, and did not therefore keep a diary or take notes. Access has, of course, been had to the official records and to the Battalion's War Diary, but those documents by no means supplied all the necessary facts or information. The Diaries and occasional notes of several Officers and N.C.O.'s of the Battalion have been of much assistance, and for the rest he has had to rely on the memory of brother officers and on his own.

The net result is a story which it is believed supplies a substantially accurate record of the doings of the 1st Cape Corps during a period of four eventful and most interesting years—a story which it is hoped will be read with some interest by the friends and relatives of ex-members of the Corps and by the Coloured Community of South Africa generally, and perhaps by not a few of their fellow South Africans of European descent—as well as by some of the many officers and men of other forces, formations, corps, etc., with whom the Battalion came into contact at various times in East Africa, Egypt, and Palestine.

The Rt. Hon. John X. Merriman, P.C., M.L.A., has very kindly written an introduction to this story. That introduction cannot fail to be read by all who peruse these pages with very great interest, and the sound advice he offers with regard to the future must surely be earnestly borne in mind by all responsible men in South Africa.

It seems quite unnecessary to add that Mr. Merriman's splendid tribute to the work done by the 1st Cape Corps will be vastly appreciated by all ranks of the Battalion. Every officer and man, one may certainly assure Mr. Merriman, will in consequence bear himself with greater pride and endeavour in the future to prove himself worthy of such high praise.

In addition to tendering his thanks to Messrs. W. R. Morrison and A. Eames Perkins of Cape Town, for the very interesting chapters which they have so kindly contributed to this book, the writer desires also to gratefully acknowledge the valuable assistance he has received from a large number of Officers and N.C.O.'s of the Battalion, and particularly from the following, viz.: Lieut.-Colonels Morris and Hoy; Major Cuningham; Captains Jardine, Tandy, and Earp Jones; Lieutenants R. Feetham, M.L.A., and S. V. Samuelson; R.Q.M.S. Betts; C.Q.M.S. de Vartek; Sergeants Alies, La Vita, Berry, Arendse; and Corporal J. Armstrong.

The Officer i/c Records, Imperial Service Contingents, at Pretoria (Lieut.-Colonel F. G. Harvey) and the Cape Corps Paymaster (Captain W. H. Smith) have greatly assisted by very kindly supplying much valuable information from their records, and, last but not least, Mr. Alfred J. Parsons, C.E., of Cape Town, has been at great pains to draw several maps and illustrations which surely cannot fail to prove interesting beyond the ordinary.

It may be as well to point out that this Story has been written primarily for the ex-members of the Unit and their friends and relations.

It therefore necessarily includes much detail and record which can interest only those readers, and which the casual reader will no doubt pass by.

I. D. DIFFORD.

CAPE TOWN, OCTOBER 21ST, 1920.

CHRONOLOGICAL SUMMARY.
1915 to 1919.

1915.

September 20th.	Decision to raise the Cape Corps arrived at.
October 21st.	Recruiting for the Cape Corps authorised by the Director of War Recruiting, Pretoria, and commenced.
October 25th.	Recruiting Campaign opened at the City Hall, Cape Town.
	Captains Gunningham and Difford; Lieutenants Anderson, Dennison, and Lever opened the Mobilisation Depôt at Noah's Ark Camp, Simonstown.
	First batch of recruits (from Carnarvon) arrived at the Depôt at Simonstown.
November & December.	Large numbers of recruits report at the Depôt.
December 6th.	Total of men attested and in Depôt at Simonstown exceeds One Thousand.
December 12th.	Recruiting ceases owing to required complement having been obtained.

1916.

January	Battalion takes the field for three days' field training on Red Hill, Simonstown.
February 9th.	Battalion embarks at Cape Town Docks on H.M.T. "Armadale Castle" for East Africa.
	Strength: 32 Officers, 1,022 other ranks.
February 17th.	Battalion arrives at Kilindini Harbour (Mombasa), British East Africa, and entrains for Kajiado.
February 18th.	Arrival at Kajiado.
February 23rd.	Departure from Kajiado for Longido West (on German East African Border).
March 2nd.	Arrival at Longido West.
March 7th.	In action for first time at Ngare Nanjuki Swamp.
March 19th.	Arrival at Moshi.
March to June.	On Lines of Communication duty at Moshi, Taveta, Unterer Himo, Aruscha Road, etc.
June 1st to 15th.	Battalion concentrates at Tsame, South of the Pare Mountains, and becomes Divisional Troops (1st East African Division) under Major-General A. R. Hoskins.
June 23rd.	Battalion Headquarters now at German Bridge.
June 25th.	Battalion leaves German Bridge by detachments to participate in the advance south to the Central Railway at Morogoro.
July 10th to August 3rd.	Battalion Headquarters at Kangata.
July 27th.	Major Hoy leaves Kangata with one Company on patrol duty to Manga.
August 1st.	Regimental Depôt in South Africa transferred from Simonstown to Woltemade III.

THE STORY OF THE 1st CAPE CORPS.

August 14th.	Manga patrol rejoins.
September 2nd.	Arrival at Morogoro.
December 12th to 14th.	Battalion leaves Morogoro with Force Reserve for Rufiji River Campaign.
December 25th.	At Dutumi.

1917.

January 2nd.	Forced march of flying column (Half Battalion) under Lieut.-Colonel Morris, to the Rufiji River (31 miles).
January 3rd.	Flying Column crosses Rufiji River at Kipenio.
January 29th.	Kibongo fight. Battalion's first big scrap. Signal victory, but many casualties. Major Durham with "A" Company attacks and captures Nyakisiki.
February 26th.	Enemy attack on Nyakisiki driven off.
March 2nd.	Lieut.-Colonel Morris's column in action at Tindwas and on Matarula Road. Enemy driven off.
March 12th.	Remnants of the Battalion leave Rufiji River area.
March 21st.	Arrival at Morogoro.
April 17th.	Major Hoy leaves Morogoro with four hundred men for Kiromo area operations.
June 21st.	Major Hoy's Detachment reaches Morogoro from Kiromo.
July 10th.	Lieut.-Colonel Morris leaves Morogoro with half the Battalion for Aruscha via Dar-es-Salaam, Kilindini and Moshi, to go in pursuit of Enemy Force under Ober-Lieutenant Naumann.
July 26th.	Major Hoy with four hundred men leaves Morogoro for Dodoma, to go in pursuit of Enemy detachment under Lieutenant Zingel.
September 2nd.	Lieutenant Zingel unconditionally surrenders his Force to Major Hoy at Tschogowali.
October 1st.	Naumann capitulates to Lieut.-Colonel Morris at Luita Berg.
October 2nd.	Naumann's Force lay down their arms unconditionally.
October 4th.	Battalion concentrates at Dodoma after Naumann and Zingel stunts.
October 9th.	Battalion returns from Dodoma to Morogoro.
October 17th to 19th.	Battalion leaves Morogoro for Campaign in Lindi area.
October 19th and 20th.	Embarkation at Dar-es-Salaam for Lindi.
October 21st.	Arrival at Lindi.
October 26th.	Battalion marches from Lindi to join Column Three at Njangao.
November 5th.	Column Three advances against the Enemy from Njangao.

THE STORY OF THE 1st CAPE CORPS.

November 6th.	Column Three engages Enemy at Mkungu. Cape Corps heavily engaged and suffers many casualties.
November 7th and 8th.	Engagement at Mkungu continues.
November 8th.	Enemy forced to retire. Cape Corps get in with the bayonet and capture Machine Gun.
November 9th to 19th.	Enemy continue to retire, fighting strong rearguard actions daily.
November 18th.	Large Enemy Hospital surrenders to Cape Corps at Nambwindinga's. On this day we fired our last shot in East Africa.
November 19th.	Thirty Europeans and Seventy-eight Enemy Askari surrender to Cape Corps at Kitangari.
November 22nd.	At Mwiti Mission.
November 24th.	Arrival at Massassi.
November 26th.	At Nairombo.
November 28th.	Return to Massassi.
December 7th.	Battalion marches from Massassi *en route* to Lindi, Dar-es-Salaam and South Africa.
December 13th.	Arrival at Lindi.
December 15th.	Regimental Depôt in South Africa transferred from Woltemade III. to Kimberley.
December 16th.	Battalion leaves Lindi.
December 17th.	Arrival at Dar-es-Salaam.
December 20th.	Departure from Dar-es-Salaam per H.M.T. "Caronia" for Durban.
December 25th.	Arrival at Durban.
December 25th to January 9th, 1918.	Officers and men ex East Africa in Convalescent Camps, at Jacobs Camp (Durban), Potchefstroom, and Kimberley.

1918.

January and February.	Officers and men, ex East Africa, on recuperative leave in the Union.
February and March.	Battalion concentrates again at Kimberley.
March 31st.	Battalion leaves Kimberley.
April 3rd.	Arrival at Durban and departure for Egypt.
April 19th.	Arrival at Suez.
April 20th.	Arrival at Kantara.
April 20th to May 21st.	At Kantara.
May 21st and 22nd.	Move to El Arish (Sinai Peninsula).
May 22nd to July 15th.	In training at El Arish.
July 15th to 16th.	Departure from El Arish for Palestine Front.
July 22nd.	Battalion joins 160th Brigade (53rd Division, XX. Corps) at Rham Alla.
September 18th.	General Allenby's great Palestine Push begins.

THE STORY OF THE 1st CAPE CORPS.

September 18th (Evening).	Cape Corps capture Dhib Hill.
September 19th.	Cape Corps capture Square Hill.
September 20th.	Battalion heavily engaged at Kh Jibeit and receives temporary set back and heavy casualties. On this day, we fired our last shot in Palestine.
September 26th.	Battalion leaves Palestine Front.
October 11th to 30th.	Battalion at Ramleh.
October 30th.	Battalion leaves Palestine for Egypt.
November 1st.	Arrival at Alexandria.
November 1st to March 12th, 1919.	Battalion at Alexandria.

1919.

March 12th to May 31st.	Battalion and Reserve Half Battalion assist in quelling Egyptian Rebellion.
May 18th.	The Reserve Half Battalion leaves Suez for South Africa.
June 9th.	Reserve Half Battalion reaches Durban and is demobilised there during the succeeding fortnight.
July 15th.	Battalion leaves Alexandria for Suez.
July 16th to August 6th.	At Suez.
August 6th.	Battalion leaves Suez for South Africa.
August 29th.	Arrival at Durban.
September 4th and 5th.	Arrival at Cape Town, reception at City Hall by His Excellency the Governor-General (Viscount Buxton), The Prime Minister (General Smuts), the Administrator Cape Province (Sir Frederic de Waal), and The Mayor (Mr. W. J. Thorne).
September 5th to 8th.	Battalion is demobilised at Dispersal Camp, Maitland, near Cape Town.

CHAPTER I.

THE CAPE COLOURED MAN IN EARLIER WARS.
(Period 1795-1842). By W. R. Morrison.

INTRODUCTORY. "PANDOURS." SERVICES AGAINST THE BRITISH. FIRST BRITISH CAPE CORPS. BATAVIAN REPUBLIC SERVICE. CAPE CORPS ESTABLISHED BY SIR DAVID BAIRD. OPERATIONS AGAINST NAHLAMBE, 1811. SLACHTERS NEK, 1815. PATROLLING THE FRONTIER, 1816-1818. MAKANA WAR, 1819. FRONTIER OPERATIONS, 1820-1834. MACOMO CAMPAIGN, 1834-5. NATAL, 1842.

FOR considerably over a century the coloured manhood of South Africa has rendered military service in the defence of the country. From 1795 to the present day, in the innumerable native wars and disturbances, coloured men have borne their share. In the more recent campaigns, subsequent to 1854, their service, whilst not combatant, has been of great value and in the transport organisation they have proved a valuable auxiliary, but it was not until the great world war, now happily at an end, that they had the opportunity of showing their value as fighting material on a similar footing to their European brethren in arms, and the services they have rendered in that great conflict have been of the greatest value and won the highest encomiums of their commanding generals and officers. The story of their doings, however, in that connection will be fully set forth in succeeding chapters. My task is to place on record the story of their contribution to the defence of South Africa from the earliest period. Existing records, in this connection, are scant and generally inaccessible, yet sufficient exist to provide an exceedingly interesting chapter in colonial history and one entirely creditable to the coloured community.

The only satisfactory method of dealing with this record, in order that a just measure of appreciation may be arrived at, is to arrange the various military services in chronological order and in this sequence it will be seen that, in the earlier period, but very few years passed without a coloured corps being engaged in one or other of the warlike operations against the natives which were such a feature in the history of the Cape in the early and mid-nineteenth century.

Throughout the whole story of the coloured men and their military service there appears to be considerable confusion as to the exact constitution of the various corps. The very earliest references undoubtedly deal with Hottentots only, and it is probable that in the Pandours Corps there were very few other than Hottentots. From 1800 onward coloured men of mixed descent were undoubtedly recruited and by 1817 it is reasonably certain that the bulk of the men in the regiment were of mixed descent.

The late Mr. Theal implies that the regiment was always purely Hottentot and that the recruiting of coloured men could not have taken place until about 1837 or thereabouts. This assumption is at variance with known facts and the idea that there were very few Cape coloured men before 1819 appears to be based on wrong premises. The difficulty, however, has been to find out when the coloured element in a regiment was dominated by the European and when it disappeared. Careful study of the available records and authorities goes to show that up to 1854 the C.M.R. was still a partly coloured regiment, but after that date it became purely European. It also appears that between 1817 and 1854 there was a gradual, and in the early years a very gradual, enlistment of Europeans. Thus from 1817 to 1830 the Cape Corps or C.M.R. may be said to have been a coloured corps. From 1830 to 1840 the greater portion of the regiment was coloured, and from 1840 to 1854 there was a percentage of coloured soldiers in the regiment.

In the various accounts of skirmishes I have been careful to record only those where the participants were known to be coloured, and in alluding to the various names of the regiment, which are apt to be misleading, I have inserted (Cape Corps) in order to leave no doubt in the matter.

Among the names which occur in the lists of officers of the regiment from the earliest times are many which are marked upon colonial history, whilst an interesting feature is the predominantly Scottish element. In 1805-6 the name of H. Lichtenstein, the celebrated explorer, occurs as surgeon, and also in the same period Baron von Boucheuroder. Then under the British command appear the well-known names of Lieut.-Colonel John Graham, Major Cuyler, C. L. Napier, J. Sutherland, the Rev. A. A. van der Lingen (chaplain), W. W. Harding, A. Stockenstroom, J. van Ryneveld, Colonel H. Somerset, H. D. Warden, Bisset, and J. Buchanan, whilst the names of officers commemorated to-day as place names are A. B. Armstrong and W. Cox (Forts Armstrong and Cox).

From 1854 coloured men took part in various native wars, but not, so far as can be ascertained, excepting in the case of the Matabele campaign of 1896, as a recognised corps, consequently the regimental history may be said to have terminated in the year mentioned, though, as has been pointed out, they took part in many of the later campaigns in non-combatant capacities.

To this day the name of the Cape Corps is perpetuated in various towns such as Grahamstown, Kingwilliamstown, Pietermaritzburg, etc., where the words Cape Corps Barracks or Cape Corps Lines commemorate the share the coloured men took in the earlier campaigns.

1795 The first official cognisance of the use of coloured men, either Hottentots or of mixed descent, in a military capacity would appear to have been in 1795 when Commissioner Sluyskens embodied a corps of "Pandours" and used them in his operations against the British. The corps was one hundred and thirty-eight strong at this period. On August 7th, 1795, the English drove away a small detachment stationed at Kalk Bay. A couple of ships were anchored to command the Muizenberg encampment, and an attack, covered by the fire from the ships, ended in the flight of the garrison under Colonel de Lille, the English pursuing them until repulsed by a party of Pandours under Captain Cloete, some loss being sustained on both sides. It would appear that the Pandours were particularly active at this time and parties of them constantly annoyed the English outposts.

On September 1st a number of the Pandours complained bitterly of the ill-treatment their wives and children received from the burghers, whilst they themselves were risking their lives in the field. Sluyskens conciliated them by increasing their pay to two shillings a month. As a last resource the harassed Commissary endeavoured to raise a strong force of Pandours, but before this eventuated the capitulation occurred.

At this period the uniform consisted of a short scarlet jacket with yellow collars and cuffs and trimmed with a kind of white lace, blue cloth trousers with a black and red stripe and a round felt hat.

THE STORY OF THE 1st CAPE CORPS.

After the capitulation efforts were successfully made to induce the coloured levies to enter the British service, for in April, 1796, it is recorded that a number of coloured men presented themselves at the quarters of the Light Infantry Brigade under Major King at Stellenbosch. At first these men were employed as cooks, but their number increased and they were embodied into a corps under Lieutenant John Campbell of the 98th Foot with a sergeant of the same regiment. Additional officers and N.C.O.'s were attached and the corps was stationed at Hout Bay. The men were enlisted for one year and provided with arms, clothing and rations and the munificent sum of sixpence a week in money. Their service was for the interior of the Colony, and the primary object of their enlistment would appear to have been in connection with the refusal of the burghers at Graaff-Reinet to take the oath of allegiance to King George III.

They are next referred to in March 1799, when a detachment was sent to Graaff-Reinet to suppress the rebellion there. They were under the command of Brigadier-General Vandeleur, who took a strong detachment of dragoons and a party of the coloured Pandours overland from Cape Town. Parties also left on board the "Star" and the "Hope" and landed at Algoa Bay. When the news of their arrival spread a large number of Hottentot apprentices came to the conclusion that the strife was between their own people and the Dutch and deserted from their former masters and repaired to the British camp. About one hundred of these men were enlisted in the regiment, which so discouraged the farmers that they abandoned their ideas of resistance and surrendered. **1799**

In 1799 the Cape Corps, under General Vandeleur, took part in the operations against the Kaffir chiefs N'dhlambi and the rebellious Hottentots.

In 1800 the men were formed into a regiment under the command of Lieut.-Colonel King, with Major D. Campbell as second in command. Their headquarters were at Groenekloof, near Cape Town, detachments being stationed at Graaff-Reinet and Port Elizabeth. **1800**

From 1801 to 1803 the regiment, with the exception of the mounted men, was employed on the frontier, and on the handing over of the Colony to the Batavian Republic in 1803 the men were taken into the Dutch service. The regiment was quartered at the Government farm Rietvlei on the Cape Flats, and when handed over consisted of two hundred and fifty privates, thirty corporals, and seventeen drummers, in receipt of rations and very small pay. **1801** **1803**

From 1803 to 1804 the records are silent in regard to the regiment, but in February, 1804, the last European regiment at the Cape was sent to Batavia, where troops were urgently required, and to make up the deficiency General Janssens increased the Pandours first to five hundred and then to six hundred men. The uniform at this period was blue with scarlet facings. **1804**

The troops opposed to Sir David Baird, whose force arrived on January 3rd, 1806, consisted of the 22nd Battalion Infantry of the Line, 5th of Waldeck, 1st Hottentot Light Infantry, 9th Jagers, 5th Artillery, one squadron of Light Dragoons, a small body of Horse Artillery, the field train, Malay artillery and the Burgher Militia, in all between two and three thousand men. The Hottentot Infantry rendered good service on this occasion and one of the subsequent articles of capitulation set forth that the battalion of Hottentot Infantry should march to Simonstown with the Batavian troops and should be allowed either to return to their homes or engage in the British service. There were three hundred and forty-three men in the regiment and, as the British forces were inadequate, Sir David Baird directed Major Graham to take as many into the British service as could be persuaded to enlist. The majority, like "Barkis," proved willing, and the following proclamation was issued:— **1806**

"January 13th, 1806. Whereas I find it expedient for His Majesty's service that a corps of Hottentot infantry be raised as soon as possible, I do, therefore, notify all magistrates and other inhabitants to direct and encourage all Hottentots immediately to report to the Castle, where Major Graham will be ready to receive and to form them into a corps, which will be paid and subsisted on the same footing as His Majesty's other troops of infantry."

The regiment formed was five hundred strong under Lieut.-Colonel Graham, with headquarters at Wynberg, a detachment of fifty being sent to Fort Frederick (Algoa Bay). The regiment was named the Cape Regiment (Cape Corps) and may be looked upon as marking the inception of the C.M.R., although in its full European signification the C.M.R. may be said to have commenced as such after the disbandment of the F.A.M.P. in 1879. The full muster was given as five hundred rank and file to be subsequently increased to eight hundred, with one company stationed at Graaff-Reinet and another on the frontier.

With a view to removing any possible cause for attachment to the Batavian cause the Republican colours of the uniform—red and blue—were discarded and Sir David Baird caused the uniform to be altered to green with black facings and round felt hat with green tuft.

From this date more information is available and the records of the regiment become fuller.

1807
1809 During these years the regiment traversed the greater part of the Colony, collecting various bodies of Kaffirs and removing them beyond the boundary of the Great Fish River.

1810 In this year five companies were employed on this duty on the frontier under Major Lyster, who at that time commanded the regiment, Colonel Graham being in command of the whole force on the frontier.

The first Kaffir war of any consequence in the history of South Africa broke out in this year. The campaign consisted of the operations in the Zuurveld under Colonel Graham against the chiefs Ndhlambe, Cungwa, and others who insisted on remaining within the Colonial borders and would not desist from plundering the colonists. The British force was in three divisions, the right under Landdrost Stockenstroom, the left under Landdrost Cuyler, and the centre under Captain Fraser. A detachment of the Cape Corps under Major Prentice crossed the Sundays River on Christmas Day and encamped at Commando Kraal, whence parties were sent to mark the roads through the Addo Bush. That work completed, the bush was scoured, and while some burghers and a party of the Cape Corps were moving to the top of the Addo Pass a number of Kaffirs jumped up and threw their assegais, killing Fieldcornet Greyling and wounding two others. The Cape Corps thereupon entered the bush and a sharp skirmish ensued which ended in the Kaffirs retreating.

In these operations, after Landdrost Stockenstroom had been treacherously murdered by the Kaffirs whilst he was parleying with them, Major Fraser with a detachment of the Cape Corps marched to the scene of the murder. On the road the party was ambushed but escaped the snare and attacked the natives, killing fifteen of them. The detachment succeeded in recovering the bodies of Mr. Stockenstroom and his comrades.

In consequence of the threatening attitude of the Kaffirs, headquarters were established at Grahamstown, the Cape Corps being located on the site of Fort England (Lucas Meyer's old farm), and the regiment was distributed in small parties along the frontier. In all twenty-two posts were established, some of which were afterwards occupied by British soldiers, the men of the Cape Corps being found more fitted for patrol and scouting duties.

An interesting sidelight on the Cape Corps at this period is afforded in "The Journal of a Resident in India," by Maria Graham, published in 1813, in the course of which she says: "They are orderly and well behaved as soldiers. They are remarkably honest and their Colonel told me that in the five years he had been with them he never saw one of them take deliberate revenge. Their dispositions are extremely cheerful and at the same time they have a surprising degree of naïveté. A sergeant and his party being appointed to guard some French prisoners on their march from Simonstown to Cape Town had to cross a rivulet swollen so as to be high. The sergeant made some of his men stand on one side and some on the other and ordered them to fire on the first Frenchman who should stoop in the water, saying that they were sailors and lived as well below the water as on land and if they once got into their own element they would never see them again. . . . The Colonel's cottage is close to the parade on the edge of the hill of Wyneberg. The men are extremely fond of him and call him father."

Sir John Cradock increased the corps to eight hundred in order to relieve the burghers who were garrisoning the frontier, but this action resulted in the withdrawal of some of the European troops. There was at that time considerable opposition to the regiment being maintained, and the Imperial Government was urged to disband them and replace them with a battalion of Europeans. The Imperial authorities consented to this, but, owing to the inconvenience attending the step, the disbandment was postponed. During this and the succeeding year the regiment was continuously engaged on the frontier under Major Fraser. **1814**

During this year occurred what is known as the Slachter's Nek rebellion. Frederick Bezuidenhout has refused to appear before the landdrost on a charge of ill-treating a Hottentot, and threatened to shoot the messenger if he approached near his premises. A warrant was issued, and the messenger was authorised to call in the nearest military force. The messenger applied to Lieutenant Rosseau (Boschbergpost, now the village of Somerset), who, with twenty men of the Cape Corps, entered the Baviaan's River Poort towards the residence of Bezuidenhout. The whole story of this determined but misguided man is too well known to need repetition and too little understood, or perhaps rather too wilfully misunderstood, to necessitate its telling again. Suffice it to say that Bezuidenhout, after a desperate defence, was shot. Eventually certain of the farmers of the Somerset and Tarka districts rose in arms and Major Fraser proceeded to the scene of action. Colonel Cuyler, who was then commandant of the frontier, arrived shortly afterwards and surprised the rebel farmers who were busily engaged in discussing their plans. **1815**

After the death of Bezuidenhout his brother, relatives and neighbours assembled at the funeral and engaged to avenge the deed. They entered into negotiations with the Kaffir chief Ngqika with the avowed object of expelling the British troops from the frontier. Fortunately their plans miscarried, and the British received timely intimation of all that was transpiring.

After many unsuccessful attempts to dissuade the rebels from their course of action, various military operations were undertaken. A portion of the rebels surrendered, but Bezuidenhout and his followers retired from the fastnesses of the Baviaan's River to the Winterberg, immediately bordering on Kaffirland. Here Major Fraser with a detachment of the Cape Corps surrounded them in a deep kloof where they were come upon while outspanned. Rejecting all offers of surrender, Bezuidenhout and the others took up a position behind their wagons and maintained a regular skirmish, killing one of the Cape Corps and wounding another. It was not until Bezuidenhout was shot and Faber wounded that the whole party was made prisoners. The sad but necessary ending to the tragedy has nothing to do with the purposes of this narrative and is also sufficiently well known for no useful purpose to be served by reiteration.

A detachment was, during the year, separated from the regiment and attached to the Royal Artillery as drivers.

In October, 1815, two hundred men of the regiment were marched to Kaffirland under Captain Boyle to recover stolen property from the Kaffirs.

In March of this year the establishment was ten companies, each of three sergeants, two corporals and fifty soldiers. **1816**

THE STORY OF THE 1st CAPE CORPS.

1817   Throughout this year the regiment was employed in patrolling the Fish River Bush and repelling incursions of the Kaffirs.

In April three hundred men under Major Fraser accompanied Lord Charles Somerset on his visit to Gaika, and the friendly relations then established led to the strength of the regiment being reduced, and subsequently in September of the same year the regiment was disbanded and a new regiment was raised called the Cape Corps, consisting of ninety-eight cavalry and one hundred and sixty-nine infantry, commanded by Major George Sackville Fraser with five other commissioned officers. The new corps was much less expensive to maintain than its predecessor and apparently consisted of a few Europeans, coloured men and Hottentots.

In October three signallers of the regiment, returning from the Kowie, were waylaid and murdered by Kaffirs.

1818   On January 8th Major Fraser entered Kaffirland with an armed force of sixty men of the Cape Corps and recaptured stolen cattle from T'slambie's tribe.

1819   Next occurred the Makana war. Makana, called by the colonists Linksh and by the Kaffirs Nxeli (left-handed), was one of those extraordinary characters who appear occasionally, possessed of great strength of mind. He aimed at moulding a nation into form. He was a hero among the natives and his memory is revered by them to-day. Makana speedily found himself at the head of a force of nine thousand men.

On the morning of April 22nd Captain Wiltshire was inspecting a detachment of the Cape Corps when he was apprised of the approach of Makana's force. The Colonel, with an escort of the men, galloped off to observe Makana's movements. He came unexpectedly upon the enemy and only the fleetness of his horse saved him. Preparations had been made to receive the Kaffirs, and in the engagement which ensued, at a critical moment Captain Boezae of the Hottentot levies with one hundred and thirty of his men, rushed forward to meet the enemy along the river bank from the old Cape Corps barracks. The onset was checked. The guns opened a destructive fire of grape, and wild panic ensued. The fleeing enemy were pursued by Cape Corps cavalry for a short distance.

With the surrender of Makana the war ended. In this action, which saved Grahamstown, the whole of Makana's force of nine thousand was met by three hundred and fifty European troops and a small detachment of the mounted men of the Cape Corps under Sergeant-Major Blakeway. The casualties inflicted on the enemy were over two thousand killed. The conduct of the Cape Corps on this occasion called forth the approbation of Lieut.-Colonel Wiltshire.

In May two troops of cavalry and four companies of infantry of the Cape Corps advanced into Kaffirland and remained there till September, when the Kaffirs were completely subdued.

In October the regiment was increased to twenty-three officers and four hundred and fifty N.C.O.'s and men. Not quite one-third were cavalry, but horses were provided for the majority of the others, so that they could serve as mounted infantry, an exceedingly early reference, it may be noted, to the use of mounted infantry. From the Genadendal records it appears that on July 9th Captain Rawstone wrote, in reference to fifty men recruited from that place: "that the men were obedient and behaved so well that their conduct was placed as an example before the regiment."

1823   Two troops were added to the regiment for defence on the frontiers. The regiment consisted of two hundred and sixty cavalry and two hundred and fifty infantry under the command of Colonel G. S. Fraser.

THE STORY OF THE 1st CAPE CORPS.

In October Major Henry Somerset succeeded to the command. The regiment assisted in reprisals for thefts of cattle by the Kaffirs. The force engaged in these operations, which were highly successful, consisted of the cavalry of the regiment and two hundred burghers. The result of these operations caused a cessation of the thefts for a considerable period.

1824 The regiment was constantly engaged on the frontier in repelling raids by Kaffirs, and besides numerous successful encounters to their credit, succeeded in recapturing six thousand head of cattle.

1827 In December, as a measure of retrenchment, the infantry of the regiment was disbanded by order of the Secretary of State, and the cavalry, two hundred and fifty strong, was thereafter called the C.M.R., although the terms Cape Corps, Cape Mounted Regiment, and Cape Mounted Rifle Regiment were all used simultaneously. The regiment was formed into three companies of mounted riflemen under a major with headquarters at Fort Beaufort.

1828 The Ordinance 50 of 1828: "For improving the condition of the Hottentots and other persons of colour," was promulgated in this year. Professor Cory says in this regard: "The Cape Corps should have been an object lesson to those who moved in the matter of the removal of all restraint from these people and abandoning them to their worst enemies—themselves. The Hottentots who composed the regiment and were under the necessary military discipline, proved themselves useful and exemplary members of the community."

During a long and eventful period they had shown they were not incapable of endurance and fatigue. That the restrictions to which they had to submit had had a salutary effect on them, and being withal excellent shots and possessing more than ordinary courage, they had been of immense service in the bush warfare peculiar to this country. The Cape Corps probably did more for the Hottentots than all the proclamations and ordinances.

1834 From 1828-1834 the regiment was continuously employed on the frontier and in Kaffirland, under Colonel H. Somerset, repelling attacks, recapturing cattle and patrolling the frontier.

1835 Space forbids any account of the causes which led to the Kaffir war of 1834-5 (the Macomo campaign). During its progress many incidents are recorded entirely creditable to the Cape Corps. Thus, in December, 1834, a sergeant and six men had been detached from a party under Lieutenant Sutton, to capture cattle from the natives to be held as ransom for stolen horses. The sergeant captured his cattle. Meanwhile Lieutenant Sutton's party was hotly engaged. The sergeant's men rejoined the party with difficulty and the small force endeavoured to make good their retreat to Fort Beaufort in face of overwhelming numbers. At the very crisis of their fate, when they were on the point of being overpowered by numbers, a rescue party from the fort put a different complexion on matters and the Kaffirs were driven off.

At headquarters, Colonel Somerset, with a detachment of the Cape Corps, routed a considerable force of the enemy near Roode Draai, killing sixteen.

On January 10th, 1835, it was decided to create a diversion by entering Kaffirland. A force consisting of seventy-six English, ninety burghers, and forty of the Cape Corps under Major Cox, 75th Regiment, was despatched with this object. In an engagement some thirty Kaffirs were killed and much cattle was recaptured. On their return the force entirely destroyed the great kraal of Tyali near Block Drift on the Chumie River, and arrived at the New Post, where they joined one hundred and forty men of the Cape Corps under Major Burney. The order issued on this occasion said: "If the regularity and discipline which are observable in regular troops were not conspicuous in the body which formed this expedition, yet the alacrity to act and the submission to obey were features strongly prominent during the whole of this harassing duty."

After the savage murder of Brown and Whittaker by the Kaffirs, Major Lowen, with a detachment of Cape Corps, proceeded to the scene of the tragedy. The mixed patrol of which Brown and Whittaker were the leaders was, after their murder, commanded by Piet Lowe, formerly of the Cape Corps, and the prudence and determination shown by him were marked by his promotion to the rank of ensign in the newly-raised levies.

In the Committy's Drift and Trumpeters Drift skirmishes coloured men bore their share.

In an action on April 7th under Colonel Smith in which three companies of the Provisional (coloured) battalion were engaged under the immediate command of Captain Crause, Sergeant Cobus was shot by the enemy.

In the storming of the Buffalo Mountain position these men bore the brunt. The ascent was only possible by the men pulling each other up by their muskets. The fastness was defended by six hundred chosen warriors under Dushanie. Thirty-seven enemy were killed and many wounded, whilst four thousand head of cattle were captured. A deserter from the Cape Corps was captured in this engagement and his life was spared on his giving valuable information.

Indeed there is hardly a skirmish or engagement during this trying time in which the Cape Corps, or Provisional Battalion, did not take a prominent part until the termination of hostilities.

1842 On January 14th, 1842, Captain J. C. Smith, of the 27th Regiment, was appointed as Commandant of Natal with the small force of two hundred men and two field pieces. The force marched overland and reached its destination on May 12th. In a contemporary account of this march appears the following: "The evening we came here we saw the haughty Dutch banner was displayed on the fort at the harbour as large as life. But the next morning the captain, the engineer officer, with all the Cape Corps and a few of the artillery went down to the port and hauled down the rebel flag and hoisted the British Union of old England and spiked the gun alongside of it—a six-pounder. Ever since our arrival in Natal the whole of the men are obliged to wear their accoutrements the whole night and keep their arms alongside of them. The duty is very hard here. We have thirty-six men and two officers and a bugler for outlying picket, and an advance picket of the Cape Corps."

Later on, on May 9th, preparations were made for action. A message was sent to the Dutch Commandant to come in person, but he refused, so "the captain ordered out all the Cape Corps, one gun, six rockets and one hundred infantry." The force proceeded to the village of the Dutch Commandant and there ensued a conference in which the Commandant was given fifteen days in which to come to a resolution. Thereafter followed the various actions between Captain Smith's small force and the Boers, until the arrival of the "Southampton" and "Conch" with much-needed relief on June 25th. In the course of these operations, exclusive of the disastrous attack on Congella on June 23rd, the casualties were one sergeant and two privates of the 27th killed and one Cape Corps.

The inscription on one of the old tombstones in Durban Cemetery, still standing in 1888, read: "Sacred to the memory of Privates A. W. E. Wessels and C. Jacobus, C.M.R. (Cape Corps), who were killed in action at Port Natal the 28th June, 1842."

CHAPTER II.

THE CAPE COLOURED MAN IN EARLIER WARS.
(Period 1846-96). By W. R. Morrison.

WAR OF THE AXE, 1846-7. BOOMPLAATS, 1848. KAFFIR WAR, 1851-2. SIR HARRY SMITH'S MEDAL. OPERATIONS AGAINST SANDILLI AND KRELI, 1852-1854. MATABELE CAMPAIGN, 1896.

IN March, 1846, the War of the Axe broke out. Certain prisoners *en route* from Fort Beaufort to Grahamstown were rescued by Kaffirs. Two of the prisoners were handcuffed to other prisoners—British subjects—and these latter were murdered by the Kaffirs and their comrades freed by the arms of the murdered men being struck off with an axe. Hence the War of the Axe. A conference took place at Block Drift between the Lieutenant-Governor and the Gaika chiefs. The Kaffirs intended treachery but no collision occurred. After some delay troops were ordered to enter Kaffirland, and two columns were formed, one under Colonel Somerset and the other under Colonel Richardson. After occupying Sandilli's deserted kraal the troops took the field in three columns, with the centre column under Major Armstrong, and the three columns under Colonel Somerset were the mounted Cape Corps.

In the course of a charge Booy Davies and Witbooy Klein were killed. A camp formed at Burns Hill had been attacked and cattle taken by the Kaffirs. A squadron of Cape Corps and of the 7th Dragoons were sent to recapture the cattle. An engagement ensued in which Captain Bambric of the 7th Dragoons was killed and, in the dense bush, our men were beaten back. In the affair at Chumie Hoek, whilst the camp was moving from Burns Hill, thousands of the enemy poured down from the mountains. The Kaffirs made such a vigorous attack on the centre wagons that the defending escort was driven back on the main body. The Kaffirs cut loose the oxen and blocked the road. The whole of Colonel Richardson's wagons (fifty-one in number) were abandoned.

Eventually the Cape Corps and artillery cleared the bush after heavy fighting and gained the open and reached camp. Lieutenant Boyes, on the same day on special duty with ten men of the Cape Corps, had to fight their way through dense masses of the enemy and five of the ten were killed or wounded.

The camp was attacked several times and the following day was moved to Block Drift, the enemy attacking during the whole of the movement. Just as the rearguard was leaving the camp Corporal Telmachus of the Cape Corps and one man galloped up. They were all who were left of an escort which had started from Victoria Post to follow the troops with despatches from H.E. Sir P. Maitland. The corporal with six men was met by a body of Kaffirs whom he charged, but lost two men. He then mistook the captured wagons for the British camp and lost two more men, and reached Chumie with two horses wounded. Then followed the action at Chumie Fort during which the ammunition of the rearguard was exhausted. Volunteers were called for from the cavalry, when the 7th Dragoons and Cape Corps stepped to the front and on foot replaced the rearguard.

The result of the action was that the Kaffirs were driven back and camp was formed at Block Drift. Meanwhile the Kaffirs passed on into the Colony and overran Lower Albany. In the affair of the Kowie Bush an officer was leading his men up the bed of the river where the channel gave a bend. The officer was about to step across the river to the bend when a man of the Cape Corps pulled him back, saying, "Wacht, baas." At the same time he put a forage cap on the end of a stick and held it at the exact spot where the officer was going to step. Instantly twenty bullets riddled the cap. "Nouw, baas, gaat aan," said his preserver. They went on and found fifty Kaffirs in the water, all of whom were killed.

During the siege of Fort Peddie in the early part of the campaign a relief column with supplies was sent out from Grahamstown. (A detachment of the Cape Corps was in this.) From Committy's Drift to Breakfast Vlei the road wound up the heights of the Fish River. The convoy extended along some miles of the narrow bush road when the column was attacked by Kaffirs, who held a ledge of rock in the bush in such a position that they could not be outflanked. Lieutenant Armstrong, with a troop of the Cape Corps and a troop of Dragoons, dashed forward and captured the position. There was stiff fighting all through the bush, and it took three hours to fight a way through to the open. Eventually Fort Peddie was relieved.

In the battle of the Gwanga a force, including two squadrons under General Somerset, was moving after the relief of Peddie and found the Kaffirs in the open. The 7th Dragoons, artillery and Cape Corps in column of route formed troops and squadrons. The Dragoons opened out to allow the guns through to come into action. Then the 7th formed line on each flank of the guns and charged, the Cape Corps, forming line in extended order, charged in succession to the Dragoons. The Cape Corps went through the broken mass of Kaffirs in one long line. The cavalry wheeled and recharged the enemy, who fled in disorder, more than six hundred being killed in the action. The only time, it may be added, the Kaffirs were ever really caught in the open.

1847 In May came the affair of the Goolah Heights. An escort was proceeding under one Sergeant (Crawford) and ten men of the Cape Corps with two wagons for Need's camp with supplies. They fought a very stiff engagement in the bush with a large hostile force within three miles of their destination. Just as the party's ammunition was exhausted a despatch party of twenty Cape Corps came at full speed and saved the day. Many Kaffirs were killed. The patrol received the special thanks of the Commandant of the forces for their gallant action.

The Cape Corps were also engaged at the Beeka Mouth.

Sandilli having been captured, desultory operations were continued against Kreli until 17th January, 1848, when peace was concluded with the latter by the new Governor, Sir H. Smith, who shortly before had released Sandilli.

1848 For some years before the arrival of Sir Harry Smith in November, 1847, there had been fighting between the emigrant farmers, who had migrated north of the Orange River, and the natives to whom the territory belonged. The chiefs had called upon H.M. Government for assistance. Soon after his arrival Sir Harry Smith met several of the emigrant leaders at Bloemfontein. Eventually Sir Harry Smith proclaimed the Queen's sovereignty over the territory between the Orange and the Vaal Rivers. The party opposed to this policy organised a force and demanded the withdrawal of the British resident and the garrison. Without means of adequate resistance the resident complied. Sir

Harry Smith then ordered up troops from the eastern frontier and proceeded personally to superintend the operations. The force crossed the Orange River in August, 1848, and moved towards Bloemfontein. On the way they found the insurgents massed at Boomplaats. On 29th August the advance was commenced, headed by fifty men of the Cape Corps with strict orders not to fire, Sir Harry Smith believing that the Boers would not fire on him. As soon as the advance guard got under the hills fire was opened on them and the men were forced to retire, leaving a dozen killed and wounded. On this the Boers came from behind the hills and the Cape Corps advanced towards them. The whole action lasted three hours, the first hour being a very hot one. The number of our killed and wounded was fifty out of a total force of six hundred.

The General Order gave the number of enemy casualties at three hundred, a number much exaggerated. In the Government notice of 9th September, 1848, appears the following:—" On reaching the summit of the Pass the enemy made a bold, though fruitless, effort to maintain their position, but the C.M.R. (Cape Corps) drove them from their position and they fled in the utmost disorder."

Sir Harry Smith subsequently presented two members of the advance guard with the medal for bravery, of which mention is made at a later stage. It is apparent from the accounts of the battle that His Excellency had a very narrow escape on the occasion of this action with the advance guard, and probably owed his preservation to the members of the advance guard of the Cape Corps.

Molitsane, in Basutoland, having killed Fingoes and taken their cattle, Major Warden determined to attack them, and on September 20th, 1850, sent Captain Bates to deal with the matter. The official report on the subject says: " Captain Bates, with the Cape Corps, headed by Captain Bramley, here made a pretty charge which, being immediately followed up by six rounds from the guns, created sad dismay among the enemy: by midday three thousand four hundred and sixty-eight head of cattle were captured and fifteen Korannas and Bataung were killed and a good many wounded." **1850**

In 1850 came the mutterings of the storm from Kaffirland and in April, 1851, hostilities again broke out, to last, without interruption, for two and a half years. Within the circumscribed limits of this chapter it would be impossible to detail all the actions in which the Cape Corps were engaged, but during this trying period they earned unstinted meed of praise. It is from the records a little difficult to find out exactly from what date the Cape Corps or C.M.R. began to lose its " coloured " association and by the admission of European recruits to gradually become the F.A.M.P., and subsequently the C.M.R. of recent years. During the war under review, at any rate, the regiment was in its initial stages wholly, and later partly composed of coloured men. There would also appear to have been a very lax habit in regard to the naming of the regiment in despatches, it being indiscriminately called the C.M.R., Cape Corps or C.M. Horse at one and the same time. **1850/1**

On May 3rd, 1851, Sir Harry Smith, in dealing with the Amatola mountain affair, states: " The conduct of every man of the Cape Corps has been exemplary."

In General Orders dated 3rd May, 1851, dealing with this affair the D.Q.M.G. says: " The C.M.R. (Cape Corps) made a most gallant charge in which it is reported three deserters fell by their hands. In thus recording the severe part of the conflict it must be borne in mind that Captain Robertson (an officer of the Cape Corps in command of Armstrong's Horse) with Ensign Kingsley, C.M.R. (Cape Corps), supported by a detachment of C.M.R. (Cape Corps) under Lieutenant Boyes, most actively succeeded in capturing three hundred and sixty head of cattle; the enemy very daringly attempted the recapture, but these gallant fellows preserved their prize and were victorious before the support reached them, while in another part of the field a detachment of C.M.R. (Cape Corps) under Ensign Stoddert, made a successful inroad and captured some cattle most gallantly."

On May 1st, 1851, the return of the troops at the Cape of Good Hope shewed the distribution of the Regiment: In the field on the frontier, C.M.R. (Cape Corps) under Lieut.-Colonel Somerset, eleven officers, twenty-two subalterns, six staff, fifty-four sergeants, thirteen drummers, seven hundred and seventy-seven rank and file and six hundred and ninety-one horses.

At Cape Town.—One sergeant, five men.

Queen's Fort.—Two captains, two subalterns, two sergeants, one drummer, sixty-eight men.

Natal.—Two subalterns, two sergeants, one drummer, forty-five men.

Fort Hare.—One field officer, two captains, five subalterns, three staff, fifteen sergeants, seven drummers, two hundred and twelve men and three hundred and thirty horses.

Fort Beaufort.—One field officer, nine men.

Fort Brown.—One subaltern, one sergeant, eight men, nine horses.

Grahamstown.—One captain, one staff, two sergeants, forty-three men and twenty-five horses.

Fort Peddie.—One subaltern, two sergeants, twenty-four men and eighteen horses.

Trumpeters Drift.—One subaltern, one sergeant, fifteen men and sixteen horses.

Whittlesea.—One captain and four men.

Kingwilliamstown.—Two field officers, one captain, nine subalterns, one staff, twenty-three sergeants, five drummers, two hundred and sixty-nine men and three hundred and fourteen horses.

Fort Cox.—Seven men and seven horses.

Fort White.—One subaltern, one sergeant, eighteen men and nineteen horses.

Fort Glamorgan.—One sergeant and three men.

Fort Murray.—Nine men and eight horses.

Fort Grey.—Twelve men and ten horses.

In a despatch from Sir Harry Smith dated 6th May, 1851, he says: "The C.M.R. (Cape Corps) whose defection has been the subject of such deep regret have well returned to their duty and are now ready to encounter any of Her Majesty's enemies."

May 17th, 1851, in a despatch from "Toise's Kraal," Colonel MacKinnon says: "Some mounted Kaffirs appeared on our right and I directed Ensign Lucas to charge them with a detachment of forty of the Cape Corps. This service was well carried out and several Kaffirs cut off and killed." He continues: "After dark I was joined by Lieut.-Colonel Napier with the cavalry, in possession of three hundred head of cattle. One hundred of these had been captured by a party of the Cape Corps under Lieutenant Stoddert and the remainder by the Mounted Levy and by a sergeant's party of the Cape Corps.

On May 30th, 1851, Colonel MacKinnon states: "On descending the Chumie Valley I was joined by the detached parties of the Cape Corps under Lieutenants Goodison and Stoddert. They had in a very gallant and spirited manner captured three hundred head of cattle and killed nine Kaffirs. I cannot conclude this report without reverting to the gallant and efficient conduct of the Cape Corps. These men have now had an opportunity of witnessing the state of destitution and misery to which their former comrades who deserted to Sandilli are reduced."

The desertions above mentioned refer to the rebellion at Theopolis.

On 30th June, 1851, occurred the action at Mekuatling in which a body of the Cape Corps took part.

In August of the same year the Natal Government offered a force of two companies of the 45th Regiment and one officer and twelve Cape Corps to join H.M. Forces engaged in the sovereignty.

A company of the Cape Corps or C.M.R. was stationed at Maritzburg, having marched up to that place with the 45th after the relief of Captain Smith at Durban. At Fort Napier to this day a portion of the old fort is still known as the Cape Corps lines.

The first request for European recruits for the Cape Corps would appear to be that contained in Sir Harry Smith's despatch to the Secretary of State of July 5th, 1851, wherein he says: "I hope that some drafts from regiments of cavalry or recruits may also be on their way to join the C.M.R. (Cape Corps)."

On July 14th, 1851, Major Donovan, Cape Corps, reports that the Basutos attacked Sikonyela who was crossing the country under an escort. The Major chased the enemy into a mountain which his force ascended and drove the enemy before them, capturing an immense number of cattle. A six-pounder gun, supported by a detachment of the Cape Corps under Ensign Somerset, were hard pressed by the enemy for many hours and escaped with difficulty.

On August 20th, 1851, further desertions by the Cape Corps in Grahamstown caused Sir Harry Smith again to urge that European recruits should be secured.

On August 15th, 1851, Major H. D. Kyle, Fort Cox, reporting on a patrol action says: "I made depositions to keep the enemy in check, in which I was much aided by the spirited movement of a detachment of the Cape Corps. Among the killed on the enemy's side were observed deserters from the Cape Corps."

Captain H. T. Vialls, Fort Peddie, reporting on another patrol action, says: "The Cape Corps were of the greatest service to me and I cannot speak too highly of their conduct."

On August 25th, 1851, a Court of Enquiry assembled at Grahamstown to enquire into the desertion of six members of the Cape Corps with their arms and ammunition. The finding of the Court was that the six men, Andries Hans, Stephanus Jantjes, Piet Stoffel, Adam Adonis, P. Bier and Afrikander Hendricks, had deserted on account of the report which had been spread among the men that they were to be disarmed and given over to the Fingoes.

In September, Lieutenant Salis was with a patrol engaged in looking for the deserters. The patrol wounded and captured Afrikander Hendricks, whilst two others, one being Jantjes, were shot by a patrol on August 30th.

On September 9th, 1851, Colonel Fordyce marched to the Kroome Bush with a strong patrol, on which occasion the Fingo levies failed. Colonel Fordyce says: "The detachment of the Cape Corps did that duty admirably, with the greatest cheerfulness and activity." In this action the Cape Corps suffered casualties one killed and one wounded.

September 5th. A strong force under Colonel MacKinnon was engaged in clearing the fastnesses of the Fish River Bush and Committy's Hill, and again the Cape Corps were complimented on their behaviour.

On September 11th, in similar operations, Lieut.-Colonel Eyre says: "It is with much pleasure I am able to report on the admirable conduct of the Cape Corps under Captain Campbell." One Cape Corps was killed in this skirmish.

In General Orders No. 165, 17th September, 1851, the following occurs: "Lieut.-Colonel Eyre has been most conspicuous in this Kaffir war and never did his personal gallantry, and that of the bold 73rd regiment shine with greater lustre than on this occasion, and to which Major Armstrong (his officers and soldiers) in command of the C.M.R. (Cape Corps) and a detachment of his horse most nobly contributed."

1851 On October 16th, 1851, the regiment, under the command of Major-General Somerset, was returned as four field officers, nine captains, twenty-two subalterns, seven staff, fifty-three sergeants, thirteen drummers, seven hundred and ninety-three men and eight hundred and forty horses.

General Order No. 183, October 21st, 1851, dealing with the operations in Waterkloof and Blinkwater, says: "The conduct of Captain Carey of the C.M.R. (Cape Corps) and his squadron, who three times charged through the enemy's skirmishers with great success, attracted the notice of the troops." Again, General Order 191, 8th November, 1851, says: "The C.M.R. (Cape Corps) stationed at Waay Plaats equally well deserve the thanks of the Commander in Chief."

Dealing with the question of recruits for the regiment the Secretary of State on September 19th, wrote: "After the close of the present war it appeared that since the defection at Kingwilliamstown and the readmission into the ranks of the men who were on that occasion deprived of their arms, the conduct of the Cape Corps has been such as to justify the expectation of its fidelity thenceforward and of the continuance of those good services for which the regiment had been previously distinguished in all the operations in the field. The Commander in Chief would be of opinion that it should be maintained. His Grace would advise that in the event of cavalry being deemed essential at the Cape, the Cape Corps should be succeeded by one of Her Majesty's regiments of cavalry. His Grace is of opinion that a coloured corps composed partly of Hottentots and partly of Englishmen is not likely to prove an efficient body." Whilst a despatch from Lord Grey, dated 30th December, says: "Drafts of four hundred and sixty-four men will be sent to replace the men from the regiment living in the Colony, whom the Commander in Chief has instructed you to allow to volunteer for service in the Cape Corps of Mounted Riflemen."

It is interesting to recall that possibly the rarest, and certainly the most sought after medal by collectors, is the medal awarded by Sir Harry Smith to members of the Cape Corps for gallantry and distinguished conduct. The issue of this decoration certainly evidenced the high opinion formed by Sir Harry of the Cape Corps, and as a distinction the medal may be said to be unique. Thirty only were awarded, and to-day only two of these have been traced, one being in the collection of Colonel Murray, and the other fittingly in the collection of Major William Jardine, himself an officer of the regiment during the 1914-8 war.

Sir Harry Smith on the occasion of his return from Fort Cox to Kingwilliamstown was much pleased with the bravery shewn by several members of the coloured corps. He was particularly impressed with their behaviour when his escort of members of the Cape Corps had to run the gauntlet through a country swarming with enemies. Members of the escort were among the recipients of the medal, and a few were also awarded for Boomplaats.

The description of the medal is as follows :—

Obverse lion statant regardant upon a wreath of laurel. Below: 1851.

Reverse in raised letters: "Presented by His Excellency Sir H. G. Smith, Bart., G.C.B., to . . . ., C.M.R., for gallantry in the field."

THE STORY OF THE 1st CAPE CORPS.

The name of the recipient was engraved in a space left blank for the purpose. The ribbon worn was the Sutlej ribbon, chosen no doubt in remembrance of the part played by Sir Harry Smith in that battle.

An extract from the Genadendal records shows that in December, 1851, two men from that place, Lodewijk Kleinhaus (sergeant) and Johannes Jass (sergeant major) were decorated with these medals.

On the recall of Sir Harry Smith in 1852, General Sir George Cathcart was appointed to succeed him and arrived in the Colony on March 31st, 1852.

In a despatch dated 31st March, 1852, giving a general survey of conditions at the Cape, Sir George Cathcart says: "With regard to the dissatisfaction of a large portion of the Hottentot population, this has not been by any means so general as has been supposed and as Colonial prejudice would still represent it to have been. Nothing could have been more satisfactory than the conduct of the Cape Corps generally, with the exception only of those who deserted at the outbreak."

1852

In December, 1852, in the operations against Sandilli, Kreli, Macomo, and Mosesh, the Cape Corps bore their accustomed share and on December 23rd, after the action against the Basutos at the Berea, the General Order states: "His Excellency marked with admiration the gallant bearing of the detachment of the C.M.R. (Cape Corps) under Lieutenant Gough."

In this action the regiment had five privates killed, one N.C.O. and three privates wounded.

In May, 1854, Sir George Cathcart left the Colony at peace, a condition which had not prevailed for many years.

From 1854 onwards in the Gaika-Galeka operations of 1877-8 and in the Basuto and Zulu wars of 1879-80 and in the various small campaigns right up to the Anglo-Boer War and the subsequent Natal native rebellion, no coloured regiment would appear to have existed, though references are frequent to their services in various non-combatant capacities, principally in connection with transport, but in the Matabele Campaign of 1896-7 the Cape Corps was revived.

Sir Thomas Scanlen, writing to General Gordon in this year, said: "We have in the districts further back coloured persons in considerable numbers who could be depended upon as fully as the Colonists generally. If a force drawn from this class could be raised, say five thousand, we should have confidence in them, and I think they could be more cheaply maintained, would be more amenable to discipline and order and less liable to desert than mild youths sent out by the emigration agents in London."

1882

In June, 1896, came the Matabele campaign, when Major Robertson, an old officer of the Royal Dragoons, recruited in various portions of South Africa a strong contingent of Cape boys for service in Matabeleland and Mashonaland. The Cape Corps, as it was again called, rendered yeoman service and took part in many and hard-fought fights. A few contemporary extracts from the despatches of Baden-Powell and others will perhaps afford the best indication of the value of their services. Thus in July, dealing with the operations at Myati, some fifty miles north-east of Bulawayo, Colonel Baden-Powell says: "Colonel Plumer took a column out there—nearly eight hundred strong—and after a clever and most successful night march surprised the enemy at dawn in a desperate-looking kopje stronghold called 'Taba Sika Mamba.' There was some tough fighting and the newly arrived corps of Cape boys, much to everybody's surprise, shewed themselves particularly plucky in storming the kopje."

1896

On another occasion in the campaign in the Matoppos, he says: "It was delightful to watch the cool businesslike way Robertson brought his boys along. They floundered through the boggy stream and crawled up the smooth dome-shaped rocks beyond, and were soon clambering among the kopjes, banging and cheering."

THE STORY OF THE 1st CAPE CORPS.

"It is laughable to watch a Cape boy prying into a cave with his long bayonet held out before him as if to pick some human form of winkle from his shell. Suddenly he fires into the smoke which spurts from the cave before him. Too late, he falls, and then tries to rise; his leg is shattered. A moment later three of his comrades are round him, they dash past him and disappear into the hole; two dull thud-like shots within, and presently they come out again jabbering and gesticulating to each other, then they pick up the injured man by his arms and drag him out into the open and, leaving him there for the doctor's part to find, they are quickly back again for further sport. At one moment they appear like monkeys on unexpected points of rock, at another like stage assasins creeping round corners and shooting—or being shot." Similar instances can be multiplied indefinitely, for the Cape Corps wrote their name large over the campaign. Commendation of their bearing will also be found in the works of Colonel Plumer and Major Alderson. The Corps was disbanded in December, 1896, and this was the last occasion when a Cape Corps served as a destructive regiment in South Africa until after the outbreak of the Great World War, when the 1st Battalion Cape Corps was mobilised for service in East Africa. The story of their deeds there, and later in Palestine, is set forth in the succeeding chapters of this book.

THE STORY OF THE 1st CAPE CORPS.

Photo by]   THE CAPE CORPS RECRUITING COMMITTEE.   [*Zadik & Co., Cape Town.*

Sitting (left to right): Mr. J. B. Lindley, C.M.G., Colonel T. J. J. Inglesby, Colonel Sir W. Stanford, K.B.E., C.B., C.M.G., Sir Harry Hands, K.B.E., Mayor of Cape Town, Colonel R. Stuart Solomon, Lieutenant-Colonel Divine, Mr. Advocate M. Alexander, M.L.A.

Standing: Captain T. M. Rawbone, Mr. P. C Ryan, Captain W. D. Hare, Mr. H. J. Stodel, Major W. Jardine, Mr. M. J. Fredericks, Mr. A. E. Perkins, Mr. J. Currey, Mr. H. Hartog.

Absent from group: Sir John Graham, K.C.M.G., Major G. B. van Zyl, M.L.A., Rev. Geo. Robson, Canon S. W. Lavis, Rev. W. L. Clementson, Dr. A. Abdurahman. M.P.C., Dr. J. Abdurahman, Captain Peter Davidson, Captain Rev. Caradoc Davies, Mr. L C. Serrurier, Mr Frank Aitcheson. Mr. R. R Brydone.

CHAPTER III.

RECRUITMENT OF THE CAPE CORPS.

By Mr. A. Eames Perkins.

I HAVE been asked by the Author of this Volume to write "something" relative to the recruitment of the Cape Corps.

It may be said at once that there are two gentlemen who could have undertaken this task with greater credit. I refer to Colonel Sir Walter Stanford, Chairman of the Cape Corps War Recruiting Committee, and to Colonel T. J. J. Inglesby, one of its valued members. Both were associated with the movement from its commencement, both keenly interested in the possibility of the Coloured man as a fighter able to share with the white man the privilege of taking part in the Great War, and both particularly well qualified to lead such a movement.

There were times when, as we all know, the Mother Country was almost pathetically calling to her sons to come forward voluntarily in the cause of humanity and Empire. Men were stirred as they never were before, and perhaps never will be again.

The appeal got hold of the Coloured man and gripped him, and with the help of his many friends strong representations were made to the Union Government to give him his chance.

But it was only on General Botha's return from the German South-West African Campaign that those earnest representations were seriously considered.

The acceptance of the principle that the Coloured man should be allowed to become a soldier took concrete form in the month of September, 1915, when the Imperial Army Council accepted the offer of the Union Government to raise an Infantry Battalion of Cape Coloured men for Service oversea.

A telegraphic despatch was received in Cape Town from the Director of War Recruiting at Pretoria (Sir Charles Crewe) asking Senator Colonel the Hon. Walter Stanford, Sir John Graham, Dr. A. Abdurahman, the Mayor of Cape Town (Mr. Harry Hands), Colonel T. J. J. Inglesby and Mr. Eames-Perkins (Hon. Secretary of the Cape Town War Recruiting Committee), to meet him to discuss the formation of a Cape Coloured Regiment.

The formation of such a Unit was entirely in the nature of an experiment. A section of the people of the Cape Province resented the idea of raising such a force for employment in the fighting line. On the other hand there were many who resented the exclusion of such an organised force from the German South-West Campaign, and saw no valid reason now why the Coloured man should not be given an opportunity to serve his King and Country and follow in the footsteps of the white men and coloured races throughout the Empire then flocking from all its corners to take part in the great struggle for human freedom.

The Empire was calling for men, more men. The Cape Coloured man asked for and was given his chance, and a new chapter in the history of the Coloured people of the Cape opened.

THE STORY OF THE 1st CAPE CORPS.

SIR HARRY HANDS, K.B.E.
Mayor of Cape Town, and for some time Chairman,
Cape Corps Recruiting Committee.

THE STORY OF THE 1st CAPE CORPS.

Prudence demanded that a very high standard should be aimed at, and it was decided that only men of exceptionally good character, between the age of 20 and 30, minimum height 5 ft. 3 in., chest measurement 33½ in., unmarried and without dependents of any description, should be accepted for service in this unit.

On enrolment the Coloured man became an Imperial soldier, under the Army Act, for the period of the War and six months afterwards, or until legally discharged, with Imperial rates of pay, viz. :—

	s.	d.	
Sergeant	2	4	per diem.
Sergeant Cook	2	10	,,
L.-Sergeant	2	0	,,
Corporal	1	8	,,
Bugler, Piper, or Drummer	1	1	,,
Private	1	0	,,

and with Pensions and Gratuities as for the British West Indian Imperial Service Contingent.

The foregoing details and instructions having been determined, the Cape Corps War Recruiting Committee was formed, with Headquarters at Cape Town, for the purpose of enrolling Coloured men for active service with the Battalion of the Cape Corps.

Colonel Grey (Commissioner of Police), Major G. A. Morris of the Natal Carbineers (Special Service Squadron), Captain J. C. Berrange, and Captain H. G. Wilmot were mentioned in connection with the Command.

The mantle fell upon Major George A. Morris, son of Mr. J. W. Morris, a former Transkeian Magistrate.

Major Morris was duly gazetted as Lieut.-Colonel and Officer Commanding the Cape Corps on October 5th, 1915.

The following gentlemen accepted the responsibility of a seat on the Cape Corps Recruiting Committee, viz. :—

Senator Colonel Walter Stanford, C.B., C.M.G., Chairman; Major G. B. Van Zyl, M.L.A., Vice-Chairman; Mr. A. Eames-Perkins, Hon. Secretary. Colonel T. J. J. Inglesby, V.D.; Lieut.-Colonel John Hewat, M.L.A.; Lieut.-Colonel F. W. Divine; Captain W. D. Hare; Sir John Graham, K.C.M.G.; Sir Frederick W. Smith, Kt., J.P.; Rev. Canon Lavis; Rev. George Robson; Advocate Morris Alexander, M.L.A.; Mr. J. W. Jagger, M.L.A.; with the following leaders of the Cape Coloured community, viz.: Dr. Abdurahman, M.P.C.; Mr. H. Hartog; Mr. P. Ryan; Mr. M. J. Fredericks; Mr. J. Currey. NOTE.—Several other gentlemen joined this Committee later and Sir Harry Hands, K.B.E. (Mayor of Cape Town) became Chairman of the Committee—*vice* Colonel Stanford who went to Pretoria to become Director of War Recruiting— and Canon S. W. Lavis, Vice-Chairman. (*Vide* Illustration, page 17.)

The Cape Corps War Recruiting Committee had the good fortune to secure the services of Sergeant-Major Samuel Hanley Reynard as a member of the Staff. No choice could have been better. His cheerfulness and conscientious performance of his work throughout the Recruiting Campaign won the esteem and respect of all who came in contact with him. Though a veteran he never flinched in carrying out of his very arduous duties.

During especially busy times the assistance of the Boy Scouts was asked for, and they never failed to answer the call made on them. Valuable assistance was willingly given, and the boys who were detailed to the Recruiting Committee by the Secretary of the Boy Scouts' Association well earned the War Certificate that the performance of their duties at the City Hall entitled them to.

THE STORY OF THE 1st CAPE CORPS.
MEMBERS OF CAPE CORPS RECRUITING COMMITTEE.

Mr. A. Eames-Perkins.

Photo by]　　　　　[J G. Horsfall, Cape Town.
Canon S. W. Lavis.

Colonel R. Stuart Solomon.

Photo by]　　　　　[Payne's Studios, Cape Town.
Mr. H. Hartog.

THE STORY OF THE 1st CAPE CORPS.

A large crowd of Coloured men and women gathered outside the Recruiting Station at the City Hall, Cape Town, in the early morning of 25th October, 1915, aroused into action by announcements in the Press that the Coloured man's opportunity was now open to him. The crowd surged into the Vestibule when the doors opened at 10 o'clock, and it became necessary to erect barriers and to provide a squad of Police before the men could be handled. To witness the inauguration of this circumstance of significance many prominent personages, Civil and Military, visited the Recruiting Station, including the General Officer Commanding in South Africa (Major-General C. W. Thompson) and his Staff.

Captains W. R. Cowell and C. G. Durham, Officers of the 1st Cape Corps, with Colonel T. J. J. Inglesby and Lieut.-Colonel Divine, members of the Recruiting Committee, had charge of the proceedings. By noon well over a hundred recruits had passed through the hands of the Military Medical Officers, but only a small percentage succeeded in passing the very strenuous test imposed. As a result of the first day's recruiting twenty-two men were entrained at Cape Town for Simonstown, where the Mobilisation Camp for the reception of the enlisted men had been established, there to receive their first instruction from competent instructors and to have instilled into them habits of discipline, etc., as well as to meet their future comrades who were journeying from such places as Stellenbosch, Worcester, Port Elizabeth, Kimberley, and the Mission Stations of Saron and Mamre, etc.

Considering the strenuous conditions of enlistment laid down the first day's result was not unsatisfactory, but there were some who had got their "tails up." "The pay was insufficient"!! "There was no separation allowance"!! To ventilate those views a meeting of Coloured men was held on the Grand Parade, and no blame could be attached to the women who kept a strict watch on the actions of the men who supported them. Though, as a matter of fact no men were accepted for service in cases where there were dependents, and the Officers of the Cape Corps and the members of the Recruiting Committee zealously guarded instructions to that effect from Headquarters. And no wonder! They were not out to pauperise women and children.

There could be no burking the fact that at Cape Town the class of man required was holding back, and this reluctance to come forward was due solely to the question of no separation allowances and the insistence that there should be no dependents. Reports from other recruiting centres for the Cape Corps in this connection were illuminating; for example:—Worcester was asked to supply 60 men; that number was obtained in one day. Port Elizabeth provided 31 men out of 45 required. Johannesburg was only asked to supply 30 recruits, and those left for Simonstown on the day recruiting for Coloured men opened. Kimberley's quota was 50 men, and they were secured also in one day and were entrained for Simonstown.

In addition, other country places intimated that they could supply a certain number of men, while districts which had already furnished their quota expressed willingness to add to the number already secured, and the Mission Stations at Saron and Mamre each volunteered to furnish a company.

The Mother City of Cape Town found itself in this peculiar position that while she had taken the lead in expressing the desire for Coloured men to serve in the War, it seemed that the Coloured residents of the Peninsula would be ill represented in the first coloured fighting force to be established, whilst places other than Cape Town collared the honour. One loop hole in this peculiar situation presented itself, viz.:—the Governor-General's Fund. But all hopes in that regard was quickly dispelled by the definite instructions of the Director of War Recruiting that no man with dependents would be accepted. Indeed, it was hardly a fair request to make that the Governor-General's Fund should provide for dependents.

The very real grievance *re* pay and allowances was immediately tackled by the Recruiting Committee, and in November, 1915, Colonel Inglesby and Mr. Brydone were deputed to go to Pretoria to endeavour to obtain better conditions, whilst Colonel Stanford, the Chairman, and the members of the Recruiting Committee in force waited upon General Smuts in Cape Town in the same pressing connection. Meanwhile a slight concession was made by the Governor-General's Fund, viz.: that they would give assistance in special cases, when brought to their notice.

It was about this time that the Cape Corps Gifts and Comforts Committee came into being. Later this committee became affiliated to the South African Gifts and Comforts Committee and did splendid work in supplying comforts for the men of the regiment.

"I have been informed," said Lord Buxton at the Recruiting Conference held at Pretoria on November 14th, 1915, "that the successful operations in German South-West Africa have had a great moral effect in the European sphere of operations and caused great depression in enemy circles. The successful subjugation of German East Africa will bring about even greater moral effect to the advantage of our side all the world over."

To take part in that subjugation of the enemy's outposts Lieut.-Colonel Morris was now busy training his men at the camp at Simonstown, which, notwithstanding the many difficulties encountered, was steadily swelling its population.

"They are as keen as mustard," said their Commanding Officer, "and in their spare time are drilling on their own," so that when His Excellency the Governor-General, accompanied by Major-General Thompson, inspected the Cape Corps at Simonstown on the 30th November, 1915, they were complimented by him on their smart and soldierly appearance and workmanlike bearing.

That outside forces were in fullest sympathy with the men of the Cape Corps were shown by many thoughtful incidents. Two may be given.

"Tango" was enrolled. He was a smart Airedale terrier presented by Master Jack Ashley of Belville as a mascot to the 1st Cape Corps. In the proverbial canine fashion he wagged himself into the affections of officers and men alike during his short stay at the camp at Simonstown, and Lieut.-Colonel Morris, in expressing his thanks to the juvenile donor, wrote: "I am sure that he will bring us luck." "Tango," when the Battalion embarked for East Africa, was called upon to show the stuff he was made of, for the Commander of the "Armadale Castle" was compelled to refuse to allow him to embark. With the persistence of his kind, however, "Tango" found another way of circumventing official opposition. A flying leap from the quay landed him on deck among his pals and the ship's Commander had no heart to eject him.

The following letter speaks for itself :—

Wellington.

"Dear Sir,

I am a coloured woman. It is a very little money that i send this is the money for the Cape Corps fund which i buy flowers from my own money and sell out again. I think it is very little but it will help too, my husband is gone to the front."

(Signed) (Mrs.) D.S.

A postal order for fifteen shillings was enclosed.

During the months of October, November, and December, 1915, very strenuous work was done by the Recruiting Committee to enable the full complement of men (about one thousand and twenty) to be secured. The methods employed varied. Bands, Street Parades, Meetings in outlying Suburban Districts, Speeches at Bioscopes, Stirring Posters, Press Notices (the value of which cannot be over estimated) all had their turn. Ours was, of course, the job to induce those who were hanging back for various reasons to come to the recruiting stations. Once there the conditions were fully explained to the men, and the presence on duty of officers and non-coms in the smart uniform of the Cape Corps swept away all hesitation, if there were any, and made them all long to emulate those who had already joined as soldiers of the King. Having made up their minds they were then invited to interview the selection officers appointed by Lieut.-Colonel Morris.

These had their tables in the vestibule of the City Hall, Cape Town, and with drafts continually arriving from other centres, were kept pretty busy.

The officers in charge were Major Durham (a strict disciplinarian) and Captain Cowell (a kindly and just officer and beloved by his men, who later made the great sacrifice). They accepted or rejected the men. The accepted men were then passed on to the inner room (Reception Hall) for medical examination.

I remember one particularly strenuous morning. The vestibule was a busy hive with the hum of many voices, and, a not particularly savoury odour of old clothes—clothes that reeked with the sweat of hot and honest daily toil. The folding doors from the Reception Hall opened and a waft of sweet music floated through. The City Orchestra in the Main Hall was rehearsing. Instinctively drawn to breathe the music's divine message, I was met by the Military Medical Officer, stethoscope in hand. He came to invite me to witness between sixty and seventy coloured men stripped for examination. These men had just previously been handed over to him. Then I realised that the clothing makes (or mars) the man. Now, lined up and smiling, naked to the world, they were fine specimens of strong brawny manhood. So splendidly developed were many of them that it might have been a parade of prize fighters, and, ugly in physiognomy as many of them undoubtedly were, their smiles revealed dentures that many a woman would have sacrificed a good deal to call her own. It is perhaps needless to say that every one of those men passed as medically fit for active service. They were attested and sent to the camp right away.

Early in December, 1915, the Cape Corps was nearing its full complement, and recruiting definitely closed on 12th December, 1915.

At that date the nett result of the recruitment for the Cape Corps was one thousand and sixteen men. Considering the difficulties in regard to pay and allowances, which all the efforts of the Recruiting Committee had so far failed to get altered, it did vast credit to the young coloured man without encumbrances and shewed quite clearly the spirit that was in him to assist his country in time of need.

On the world's day of rejoicing, Christmas Day (1915), the Camp at Simonstown was thrown open to relatives and friends of the men of the Cape Corps, and full advantage was taken of the concession.

Amongst the old time customs, plum puddings and music and bands were provided and dancing and joviality took place as though no red war existed and in spite of the gloomy news that trickled through over the cables. It was just for the day, the work with all its seriousness and earnestness, was for the morrow.

Mr. Harry Hands (the Mayor) in his message to the citizens of Cape Town clearly gave the key note in reference to the position as it was at that time.

"We are on the eve of Christmas," he said, "and at the end of another year, a year of war, and, for many hundreds and thousands of human beings, of suffering and sadness, a year in which death has taken a heavy toll of the

Empire's manhood. From many a home in the Peninsula loved ones who have gone forth at the call of duty will be absent this Christmas. There must therefore, be a note of sadness in our greetings, but we can still find comfort in the old, old message. Seventeen months of war have not shaken our confidence and our conviction that right must prevail, and though we may be sore let and hindered we shall endure to the end, and the end will be victory."

In January, 1916, with the full complement of recruits secured, courtesies were exchanged between the Senior Officers of the Cape Corps and the members of the Cape Corps War Recruiting Committee in the form of simple luncheons at the Camp at Simonstown and at the Civil Service Club at Cape Town. The main reason for those proceedings was to wish "God Speed" and "Good luck" on the eve of departure on the one hand, and on the other the expression of thanks (none of course were needed) to the Recruiting Committee for what they had accomplished.

When the Cape Corps' embarkation date arrived, very naturally the South African Military Command did not take any chances. A smoke-screen was thrown over the movement of all troops. That notwithstanding, a great crowd assembled at the docks at Cape Town, and all the approaches thereto, to witness the departure of the Battalion for East Africa on 9th February, 1916.

It was a true South African summer's afternoon. Three train loads of men steamed into the Docks, direct from Simonstown to the ship's side.

H.M.T. "Armadale Castle" was waiting to receive the Officers and men of the Cape Corps. The embarkation was speedily and smartly accomplished. Many a mother strained with tears of pride in her eyes to get a glimpse of her son; many a young Coloured woman, who had a very particular interest in her newly-made soldier friend, moved in the crowd in the hope of a last farewell.

With the Band playing martial airs and the men leaning over the great ship's side anxious for a last good-bye, and the sun shining upon a sea of helmets and dark skinned faces and flashing upon the trappings of the uniforms, it was difficult to believe that these were the same men, who only a few months before had come to enlist at the City Hall, many ill-clad and anything but smart.

The transformation was so complete. Straight, and smart and smiling, with boots, buttons, and equipment polished to a turn, they were a fine workmanlike body of healthy men, and for cheerfulness, dignity of bearing, and soldierly appearance the Officers in Charge would not have been easy to beat in any regiment.

Then, God Save The King, every one stood to attention, and the great Troopship steamed majestically away (I fancy "Tango" barked). As evening came she dwindled to a speck on the sea, and finally vanished from sight.

The Cape Corps had gone on the great adventure, taking with them the hearts and the hopes of thousands of their kinsfolk in the Union. The reputation of the Coloured community of South Africa was in their hands.

The Recruiting Committee could rest on its oars until casualties and disease thinned the ranks of the departed warriors and a new recruiting Campaign was ordered to fill the gaps.

It became evident soon after the departure of the "Armadale Castle" that a number of the men of the Cape Corps had left women and children dependents unprovided for, notwithstanding the care that had been exercised by the Selection Officers and the Recruiting Committee. It was unthinkable that these should be left to suffer. The situation was taken in hand at once by the Recruiting Committee, and a list of married men with dependents prepared. Commercial establishments who had employed such men before enlistment were approached, and guarantees obtained in most cases that half civil pay would be given to proved dependents, until Military separation allowances were secured.

THE STORY OF THE 1st CAPE CORPS

The New Year (1916) was scarcely one month past when General Smuts took charge of the East African Campaign. From that time calls for reinforcements for the Cape Corps were frequent, with the authorisation that married men could be accepted for Service, and that Separation Allowances would be paid upon the following basis, viz. :—1s. 1d. per diem to wives, and 2d. per diem for each child under the age of 16, or in cases of widowless and motherless children, 4d. per diem. Proved Dependents of unmarried men were placed on the same scale, always provided that the soldier allotted to the dependent half his pay. This placed recruitment for the Cape Corps upon a better footing, more especially as grants from the Governor-General's Fund were left entirely in the hands of the local Committees of that Organisation.

The foregoing may, it is hoped, convey some idea of the activities of the Cape Corps War Recruiting Committee in the earlier stages of the Recruiting Campaign as well as of the feeling held by that body relative to the care of the families of the enlisted men, during their period of active service.

Frequent calls came later from the Director of War Recruiting, Pretoria, for men, more men, who, by dint of hard work and the beating up of Suburban and outlying districts, never failed to materialise. For instance, during the period 27th February to 27th April, 1917, 1,457 Coloured men were attested for the Cape Corps, whilst a large number were turned down as unfit for Active Service.

In all, during the Recruiting Campaign, 6,000 men were enrolled for the 1st Cape Corps, and 2,000 for the 2nd Cape Corps.

Other Coloured units were formed, of a different character to the Cape Corps it is true, but all useful in their different spheres, and all dovetailing and harmonising into the great fighting machine of the Empire. For instance, the Cape Corps War Recruiting Committee were requested to find one thousand men for the Cape Coloured Labour Battalion, with reinforcements as required, whilst they were interested in and consulted with reference to the formation of the South African Native Labour Contingent, in which ten thousand men were enrolled.

In addition, the Recruiting Committee were called upon to supply Coloured men to the S.A. Artillery (Drivers and Leaders) and for the Cape Auxiliary Horse Transport Companies, etc., etc.

The exact total figures of Coloured men obtained by the Cape Corps Recruiting Committee are not before me at the present time, but it is certain that they were in the neighbourhood of twenty-five thousand, over rather than under. It is in my opinion a fair calculation to make that 4 to 1 of the men who presented themselves for enrolment were turned down as medically unfit, and if this basis is correct, it shows the handling of one hundred thousand Coloured men.

Amongst the rejected there was genuine disappointment and not a little grumbling. Many such men, especially the younger ones, hung about the recruiting station for weeks hoping by hook or by crook to be allowed to go, while the spectacle of their "pals" in the smart uniform of the Cape Corps heightened their misery at being left behind.

Every post brought letters from men in the country districts, bitterly complaining that the medical officer either did not know his job, or that he had mistaken their case.

Covering some ten closely written pages, smatterings of English and Dutch, a Coloured boy at Clanwilliam, 19 years of age, bemoaned his fate because he was two inches under the regulation height to enable him to join the Cape

Corps. He begged to be allowed to join as a bugler; he knew that he could get one cheap if the money was sent to buy it, and, he added, "God would bless the Recruiting Committee."

Besides the actual recruiting of Coloured men, the Recruiting Committee took upon its shoulders other matters closely connected with the men enrolled. For instance:—The obtaining of maternity grants relative to children born after the soldier's enlistment.

The question of free Education for Coloured children during the soldier's period of active service.

The remission of the fee for the Marriage Certificate—it being a regulation that this must be produced before Separation Allowance could be claimed or assessed.

Medicine and Comforts for Sick wives and children of soldiers.

The witnessing of the Signature on Military Cheques for monthly allowances in order to satisfy Banking requirements, etc., etc.

A batch of from thirty-five to forty coloured women, some with babies at the breast, others leading ragged and bare-footed children by the hand—little things that the soldier of the Cape Corps had left behind him to be cared for by the country whose freedom he was helping to keep intact—came to the recruiting station one slack morning. Sergeant-Major Reynard was pounced upon in the vestibule of the City Hall. He stood their fury and anger like the good old soldier that he is until explanations were possible.

When order was restored out of the chaos, they were invited to appoint one of their number to interview the writer in an inner room.

It was not hard to enter into the feelings of these women. Their separation allowances as has been stated were very small, just enough to provide food to keep them and their children alive and with no hope of putting anything by to meet an unforeseen emergency. However, they were content to suffer the hardships that white and coloured alike were called upon to bear at that time.

But the least delay in the payment of the allowances due created more difficulties than they were prepared to endure. A delay of some days had already taken place in the arrival from the Paymaster of the usual monthly draft, and the children were without food. They had already applied to the Paymaster of the Cape Corps, but he was powerless to assist them in their trouble, and had to explain that there would be a further delay of three or four days—due entirely to the change of office from one centre to another. The Cape Corps Gifts and Comforts Committee found the matter was one that did not come within their scope, and no tangible result accrued as the result of an application to the local Secretary to the Governor-General's Fund. Finally the Cape Corps War Recruiting Committee was approached as described.

The writer's own application to the then Secretary of the Governor-General's Fund shared the same fate as the women's appeal, and it became necessary to bring the full force of the Recruiting Committee into action. The result was entirely successful, and each family or individual went away with a sufficiency to tide over the awkward period. The women were satisfied and even grateful and dispersed to their various homes in outlying parts of the Cape Peninsula. The same method was adopted in cases where difficulties arose with landlords, who either wished to eject dependents of soldiers on account of the men being on active service, or to increase the rent on threat of ejectment if they did not agree to pay.

In fact there was no genuine grievance connected with the dependents of the enlisted men, which the Recruiting Committee was not compelled to redress.

There were, of course, some strange incidents connected with the recruiting of the coloured units. The following may be cited:—

THE STORY OF THE 1st CAPE CORPS.

Private John Jacobs of the 1st Cape Corps had, by good fortune—or otherwise—obtained leave of absence from his Regiment during a lull in its activities, and found himself in the Cape Peninsula. Resultant upon his good—or evil—fortune he took it upon himself to form fresh attachments and responsibilities in domestic life.

The sequel to this visit was revealed in a letter, businesslike in its brevity and very much to the point, to the Hon. Secretary Recruiting Committee, as follows:—

"Hon. Sir,

I married John Jacobs a week ago. He has gone back. We have ten Children. Please let me know how I stand.

Yours truly, ..."

On a tour of the Eastern Province of the Cape quite recently the writer had the good luck to have as a companion on the journey an ex-officer of the Cape Corps who had served in the East African campaign and in Palestine. During the journey opportunity was afforded of hearing something of the doings of the Cape Corps in the actual fighting line, some of which no doubt will be set down in this volume. That officer's praise of his men, of their manly courage and pluck, of their discipline and cheerful endurance in times of hardship and difficulties, served to confirm the reports one had heard of the splendid work and behaviour of the men in camp, on the march, or under fire.

At most of the stations at which the train halted, coloured men stepped out from somewhere, and, in their working clothes, stood to attention and saluted—they were so obviously glad to see their old officer, and to have the opportunity to refresh in a few words their memories of the time when they had served under him in the Great War.

It was the same in many of the places we visited during the tour. There was generally some coloured man who halted in his work to salute the officer, notwithstanding that both wore civilian clothes. Indeed, on the train by which we travelled, an ex-member of the Cape Corps brought us our nightly bedding, and the chef's coloured assistant in the dining-car tendered his respectful greetings and was recognised.

On some of the farms visited at which ex-officers of the Cape Corps had entered into possession, the servants, the farm hands, and those employed in other capacities were all, wherever possible, returned soldiers of the Cape Corps. In some of the towns ex-officers of the Cape Corps who had embarked upon new ventures since release from service employ men in their offices who have seen service in the Battalion. This continued association in civil life of European officers and Coloured ex-soldiers who served under them during the Great War is of course only natural and may in course of time evaporate and become only a memory. But what seems to be forced upon one is that this sympathetic understanding and respect between the white officer and the coloured man who served with and under him, if fostered in some way, should prove of inestimable value to the State.

South Africa, we are told, is a land that is merely scratched upon the surface. Could not some semi-military body be formed from what is left of the Cape Corps for its greater development?

CHAPTER IV.

MOBILISATION AT SIMONSTOWN, PERIOD 21ST OCTOBER, 1915, TO 9TH FEBRUARY, 1916.

OFFICIAL sanction having been given, recruiting commenced simultaneously in various parts of the Union on 25th October, 1915. The recruiting was done by officers already gazetted to the Battalion, and Lieut.-Colonel Morris, who was gazetted 5th October, 1915, left two weeks later on a tour of the recruiting stations to interview the various Cape Corps Recruiting Committees that had been formed.

The initial recruiting stations and officers were:—

Cape Town	Captain W. R. Cowell.
Paarl	
Wellington	Captain C. G. Durham.
Worcester	
Carnarvon	Lieutenant J. M. Michau.
Kimberley	Captain L. Campbell.
Prieska	Lieutenant H. G. Warr.
Port Elizabeth	Lieutenant G. C. Macintosh.
Oudtshoorn	Lieutenant D. W. Robertson.
Mossel Bay	

A tribute must be at once paid to the whole-hearted solid good work done by the various Recruiting Committees, composed both of Europeans and coloured men. The Cape Town Recruiting Committee was especially in earnest, and the names of some of the most active and enthusiastic members of that body must certainly be recorded, viz., the then Mayor of Cape Town (Harry Hands, Esq.), Senator Colonel the Hon. W. E. M. Stanford, C.B., C.M.G., Canon S. W. Lavis, Colonel R. Stuart Solomon, Colonel T. J. J. Inglesby, Major G. B. van Zyl, Messrs. A. Eames Perkins, H. Hartog and C. Currey.

The camp selected for the mobilisation and training of the Corps was at Simonstown, just above the Noah's Ark Battery, about two and a half miles from the railway station. No more unsuitable site could have been selected. During the three and a half months prior to the departure of the Battalion for East Africa the south-east wind blew violent gales four or five days a week, the ground had a pronounced slope, in fact from the lower to the top end of the camp necessitated a strenuous climb, and it was extremely rough and stony.

There were sufficient wood and iron buildings in the camp to provide an orderly room and office, officers' and mens' messes, camp medical hut, quartermaster's stores, etc., but the strong winds blew stones and pebbles against the iron buildings with such force that the proper conduct of office work, lectures, etc., was well nigh impossible.

Officers and men were accommodated in bell tents, which constantly blew down. The parade ground was on the slope, extremely rough and stony, and exposed to the full blast of the south-easter, and instruction was carried on under the greatest possible difficulty. After a few days officers and instructors had lost their voices, and, as time was all important, the above factors constituted a very severe handicap indeed.

The first recruits to arrive in the camp were a batch of nine recruited by Lieutenant Michau at Carnarvon. Prior to that several officers had reported, the first to do so being Captain W. G. Gunningham (Adjutant), Captain I. D. Difford (Quartermaster), Lieutenant J. E. Dennison (Signalling Officer), Lieutenant C. J. Lever (Paymaster), and Lieutenant W. P. Anderson. All these officers had seen service in the Anglo-Boer war and in the South-West African campaign and were thus qualified to set about their respective duties without delay.

Recruits underwent a preliminary medical examination at the recruiting stations, but immediately on arrival at the depôt were subjected to a more thorough and careful medical overhauling by Captain Cecil J. Impey, S.A.M.C., who had been posted to us for duty until a Battalion Medical Officer was appointed.

It had been decided that the Battalion should be recruited, clothed, fed, and paid by the Union Defence Department, acting for and on behalf of the Imperial authorities, to whom all charges were debited, but that the training and discipline should be controlled by the Imperial authorities, the Officer Commanding being responsible to the G.O.C. South African Military Command at the Castle—then Major-General C. W. Thompson, C.B., D.S.O. That officer took the greatest possible interest in the Corps, as did his G.S.O.I., Lieut.-Colonel Finch. The latter had been invalided from the command of the 4th Battalion Middlesex Regiment on the western front, and his experience and advice were therefore up-to-date and of the greatest possible assistance to Lieut.-Colonel Morris and his officers. Major-General Thompson paid several visits of inspection and Lieut.-Colonel Finch gave two or three lectures to the officers. No two men could have rendered more sympathetic assistance to the Corps in the trying days of its infancy and inexperience than did the two officers named. Lieut.-Colonel T. E. Fowle, D.A.G., also rendered us every possible assistance in his power.

It was difficult at that time to find a sufficiency of competent and experienced instructors in the Union. Major-General Thompson succeeded however in getting together a very good body of men, partly Union Defence Force Warrant Officers and N.C.O.'s; and partly Imperial men (R.E. and R.G.A.), and, in order to fully equip them for their duties, the majority of the instructors were themselves put through a brief refresher course of instruction at Wynberg Camp, before reporting for duty at Simonstown. Sergt.-Major James Alexander Windrum (Permanent Force Staff, U.D.F.), was placed in charge of the training and instructors, and had at one time as many as forty of the latter under his supervision. Windrum proved an ideal man for the task. He was very keen, hardworking, and very much of a martinet. To him, and to the rapid standard of efficiency to which he very soon brought his staff, was very largely due the remarkable progress made by the recruits. The men were put through the same syllabus of training as those recruited in the United Kingdom for the Western Front.

It has to be remembered that a very large proportion of the pupils were raw recruits in the most literal acceptance of the term, in fact, probably less than five per cent. had previously handled a rifle or knew a step of drill. Yet the result of a few weeks' training was literally astounding. Lieut.-Colonel Morris and his officers and every other rank of the 1st Cape Corps fully acknowledges, and is more than glad—nay, anxious—to testify to the great debt the Battalion owes for their later achievements to Sergt.-Major Windrum, and in a lesser degree to his staff of instructors.

THE STORY OF THE 1st CAPE CORPS.

C.S.M. P. A. DANIELS (1).

"THE LONG AND THE SHORT OF IT."
Captain J. M. Michau, 6 ft. 5 ins.; and
and Captain J. V. Harris, M.C., 5 ft. 2 in.

R.Q.M.S. F. W. E. BETTS, D.C.M.

CAPTAIN W. G. GUNNINGHAM.
(First Adjutant.)

THE STORY OF THE 1st CAPE CORPS.

It was with deep regret that all past and present officers and men of the 1st Cape Corps learned that Sergt.-Major Windrum died at Wynberg Military Hospital on Sunday, 30th November, 1919, after a long illness.

The choice of his officers was left by the authorities to Lieut.-Colonel Morris. Subjoined to this chapter is appended a report by Major-General Thompson on the unit prior to its embarkation for East Africa, and it were more appropriate for the historian to draw attention to the reference therein to the original officers of the battalion than to make any comment of his own.

It was understood, if not actually promised in writing, that the choice of his officers should remain with Lieut.-Colonel Morris so long as the 1st Cape Corps continued in existence. With very few exceptions the original officers selected had served through the South-West African campaign, and, those who were old enough, without exception, in the Anglo-Boer war also. They were therefore of the right stamp, *i.e.*, men who had volunteered at once to do their plain and simple duty, and had not been driven into the field by "white feather" or "drive out the slacker" campaigns.

Owing to the fact, however, that the previous experience of nearly all the officers had been in mounted corps, it was necessary for them to undergo a course of training as infantrymen before they were capable of undertaking their duties or instructing the rank and file. For that purpose, with the exception of specialists such as the machine gun and signalling officers, adjutant, and quartermaster, who had been selected by reason of previous experience, all the officers underwent a course of a few weeks' special instruction at Wynberg Camp under Major Leslie Cox. They returned to Simonstown loud in praise of Major Cox and his staff and greatly benefitted by their experience.

Tribute has been paid to the splendid work done by Sergt.-Major Windrum and his instructors, but it is only fair to the men to say that they had most extraordinarily willing and pliable material to work upon. Practically every recruit who came into camp seemed to be obsessed with the idea that the good name and fame of the coloured community of the Union of South Africa rested mainly on his individual keenness, hard work, good conduct, and ability to rapidly absorb the lessons which it was desired to impart to him. The outcome was a most extraordinary keenness which resulted in very rapid progress being made. The men's day commenced—it was summertime—at 5 a.m., with physical drill and bathing parades and continued, with breaks at meal hours only, until sundown. Lectures and class-room instruction were wisely blended with practical demonstration on the parade ground, so that the men should not become too tired or too bored to assimilate the knowledge endeavoured to be imparted to them.

Notwithstanding the long and tiring day, and it was tiring owing to the boisterous winds, the men were so keen that even after their evening meal they kept hard at it until first post, at unofficial parades, rehearsing and coaching one another in drill, handling arms, etc., on the rough ground of the mountain side above the camp.

One man—an officer's batman—was asked to name the numerous different parts of a rifle. He correctly named and explained thirty odd parts, and explained, but could not name, another thirty odd parts. He knew something about the remaining parts and excused himself for lack of *complete* knowledge by saying that he had only had *one* lesson from an instructor and a pal had given him another lesson.

The men were placed in squads of from twelve to twenty each under an instructor, and as training progressed the squads were formed into advanced, partially trained, and awkward squads (i.e., raw recruits), and as the various squads mastered their drill they were issued with arms and taught the mechanism and parts of a rifle and, having mastered that, were sent in companies of two hundred, under their own officers, to the Woltemade ranges for three weeks to be put through their musketry course. A percentage of the men was also instructed in field engineering, bridge building, the use of the bomb, signalling, pioneer and medical work, etc., and later on when the companies were formed these men were distributed as equally as possible and had to impart their knowledge to their colleagues. A machine gun section was also formed (four guns) and placed under the command of Captain Lindsay Campbell, who had had previous experience as a Brigade M.G. Officer in South-West Africa. There was great eagerness to get into that section, and right through the career of the unit it was most remarkable with what ease and speed the men learned to handle the Maxim (and later the Vickers) gun and the keenness and pride they took in their section. Later on the machine gunners did some exceptionally good work under Captain Frans Burger, to which reference is made in subsequent chapters.

The training through which the men were put was so severe and the medical inspections so thorough and searching that quite a number of men were discharged within three months as physically unfit for service or as unlikely to become efficient soldiers.

Not the least noteworthy fact in the early stages of the unit, indeed the fact remained throughout, was the quite exceptional adaptability of the material upon which the Corps was built. Machine gunners, signallers, pioneers, bridge builders, motor drivers or mechanics, cooks, butchers, etc., or what not, for any or every job for which it was necessary to find suitable and likely men— the same were always forthcoming with previous civilian experience likely to quickly fit them for the particular job or task required. Later on in East Africa it became almost a tradition that the Cape Corps were the handy men of the Force who could always be called upon to tackle any odd job successfully.

When authority was first issued for recruiting to commence, four single companies only was the intention, *i.e.*, just over five hundred men. These were, however, obtained in little more than a month, and authority was at once given for an increase of two hundred and fifty men, and later further authority came to bring the battalion up to four double company strength, *i.e.*, one thousand and fifty-six of all ranks. But the clothing and equipping of these men was greatly delayed owing to the blundering of someone in authority at Pretoria who forgot to advise the Quartermaster-General's branch of the increased establishment. Consequently, instead of a man being equipped right off, the job took two or three months, the unfortunate individual receiving a toothbrush one day and a bootlace the next and so on.

The conditions of service at first laid down were single men, between the ages of twenty and thirty years, and without dependents and at Imperial rates of pay (one shilling per day) and no dependents' or separation allowances. Whoever was the responsible authority evidently knew very little of the requirements of a battalion in the field, or of the economic position and status of the coloured community in the Union of South Africa. In fact, if it had been intended to prevent or hinder the Corps from becoming *un fait accompli* no surer handicap to recruiting could have been devised. It says much for the loyalty, patriotism and enthusiasm of the coloured community that recruits came forward at all. Later on certain concessions were made in response to very strong representations made to the then Union Minister of Defence (Lieut.-General J. C. Smuts) by a deputation from the Cape Town Recruiting Committee, headed by their chairman, Colonel Walter E. M. Stanford, who later on became honorary colonel of the regiment. The age limit was extended both upwards and downwards (eighteen to thirty-five) and a percentage of married men were allowed and separation allowances and pensions to their next of kin granted,

THE STORY OF THE 1st CAPE CORPS.

A GROUP OF INSTRUCTORS AND 1ST CAPE CORPS N.C.O.'S (EUROPEAN) TAKEN AT SIMON'S TOWN IN JANUARY 1916.

Left to Right—BACK ROW: Staff Sgt. I. Lorenza (C.G.A.), Instructor; Staff Sgt. N. O. Harvey (1361), 1st Cape Corps; Bugler Sgt. van Bonde (C.P.R.); Pay Sgt. J. J. Bam (U.D.F.) Pay Corps; Staff Sgt. ——; Staff Sgt. F. J. Shipp (1350) 1st Cape Corps; Staff Sgt. M. C. Cassidy (1050) 1st Cape Corps; Staff Sgt. —— (R.G.A.); Staff Sgt. Salida (U.D.F.) Instructor; Staff Sgt. Taylor (R.G.A.) Instructor; Staff Sgt. C. Richardson (1365) (U.D.F.) Instructor; Staff Sgt. J. J. Greenhead, 1st Cape Corps.

MIDDLE ROW: Staff Sgt. J. Howard (R.G.A.) Instructor; Staff Sgt. G. H. Pepper (1362) 1st Cape Corps (Armourer); Staff Sgt. Kullin (C.G.A.) Instructor; Staff Sgt. Justis (C.G.A.) Instructor; R.S.M. G. Forsyth (1141) 1st Cape Corps; S.M. Instructor J. Windrum (U.D.F.); R.Q.M.S. J. Hosack (1137) 1st Cape Corps; Pay Sgt. W. Mills (U.D.F.) Pay Corps; Staff Sgt. Keohane (U.D.F.) Instructor; Sgt. T. C. Adams (1139) 1st Cape Corps; Sgt. C. Holstock (R.G.A.) Instructor.

FRONT ROW: Staff Sgt. I. Clenell (1053) 1st Cape Corps; C.S.M. W. T. Wigman (1051) 1st Cape Corps; Staff Sgt. Clonke (C.G.A.) Instructor; Staff Sgt. F. W. Betts (1049) 1st Cape Corps; Sig. Sgt. H. Martin (1282) 1st Cape Corps; Staff Sgt. D. A. Patterson (1052) 1st Cape Corps; Sgt. J. Hart (1275) 1st Cape Corps; Platoon Sgt. R. A. Cloke (1138) 1st Cape Corps.

but the latter were even then, to say the least of it, ridiculously inadequate, being at West Indian Army rates, which displayed a colossal ignorance of the difference between a West Indian native and the Cape coloured man.

Recruiting however at once took a great spurt and before the end of the year, *i.e.*, within ten weeks from the start, one thousand men were already in the camp at Simonstown training for all they were worth.

Several questions suggest themselves with regard to the original conditions, *e.g.*:—

Where was the experience, the steadiness and the control to come from, and the stamina required for the tremendous exertions that were to be demanded from the Battalion later on under conditions known to exist, or which should have been known to exist, in East Africa, or in any other part of the world for that matter, under modern active service conditions?

Where was the commanding officer to get his senior N.C.O.'s from,—men likely to exercise leadership, control, restraint, coolness, and discipline and set the example that in the main only old and wise heads are capable of setting?

Long afterwards, in fact not until early 1918, did Lieut.-Colonel Morris and his friends and supporters, after a good deal of agitation and strenuous uphill work and appeal to the Union Parliament, succeed in obtaining more or less adequate separation allowances and pensions, and even then there was considerably less than more about it.

When thirteen hundred men had finally passed the medical officers and been duly attested, recruiting was stopped for the time being, but began again in a few months as soon as the tremendous wastage from fever in East Africa began to be realised in the Union—and continued practically without cessation until the middle of 1918.

As soon as progress was sufficiently advanced to enable a battalion parade to be held, Major-General Thompson, accompanied by Lieut.-Colonel Finch, took the first inspection, whilst shortly afterwards His Excellency the Governor-General, Viscount Buxton, came down to inspect us and later on again paid a more informal visit to watch the training actually in progress, the course of the same not being interrupted during his visit.

Brigadier-General H. A. D. Simpson-Baikie, C.B., C.M.G., accompanied by several of his staff officers and by Brigadier-General Sir Charles Crewe, then Director of War Recruiting (U.D.F.), also inspected the battalion and afterwards expressed his entire approval of what he had seen and also his astonishment that so much had been effected with a lot of raw recruits " in such an incredibly short space of time." Lieut.-General Sir Horace L. Smith-Dorrien, G.C.B., G.C.M.G., D.S.O., was to have taken the last-mentioned parade, the same having been arranged by Major-General Thompson by wireless before he reached Cape Town, but Sir Horace disembarked seriously ill and returned to England as soon as he was well enough, without having assumed duty. Consequently Brigadier-General Simpson-Baikie acted as his deputy.

The battalion was also inspected by Admiral King Hall, commanding His Majesty's Naval Station at Simonstown.

Having completed their training as far as possible in the limited time at their disposal (by Christmas time orders had been received that the corps was to embark for East Africa early in February) the battalion took the field for the first time (towards the end of January, 1916) on the plateau above Simonstown to Cape Point for three days' field training and manoeuvres. Major-General Thompson, Lieut.-Colonel Finch and the District Staff Officer (Major Hodgson, U.D.F.) spent one of these days with us, and it was understood that the G.O.C. expressed himself quite satisfied with what he had seen. In fact, in passing the unit as fit to take the field and ready for active service, he put in a report which caused much gratification to Lieut.-Colonel Morris and his officers and the various recruiting committees and other friends who had the welfare of the Battalion at heart. (Copy of the report is subjoined to this chapter.)

Lieut.-Colonel Morris had selected as his second in command Major Charles Norman Hoy, who had been a squadron commander in the Natal Carbineers in the South-West Africa Campaign. Owing to private affairs occupying his time Major Hoy was not able to report for duty until November 3rd, but when he did arrive he very promptly made his presence felt. He remained with the battalion until he was invalided to the United Kingdom owing to a breakdown in his health in March, 1919. It is not too much to say that the fine record later earned by the 1st Cape Corps was in a large measure due to the keenness and energy, insatiable capacity for hard work, and soldierly qualities of Major Hoy. In course of time he was awarded the D.S.O. and bar, and was twice mentioned in despatches, and if ever man earned those honours, he was that man. Throughout the twenty-two months spent in East Africa he was never a day off duty except for three weeks in hospital after being wounded in action at Hatia, 8th November, 1917.

Our Paymaster, Lieutenant C. J. Lever (*ex* Natal Carbineers) left us in December to take another appointment and was succeeded by Lieutenant (later acting temporary Captain) Barnett Boam. The latter went with us to East Africa and was quartered at Nairobi for a few months. He was then sent back to the Union and continued his duties at Cape Town, with short spells at Kimberley and Durban until early in 1919, when he resigned his commission and was succeeded by Captain W. H. Smith.

The original intention of the Director of War Recruiting after consultation with Lieutenant-Colonel Morris, was that the R.S.M., R.Q.M.S., Company Sgt.-Majors, Platoon Sergeants, Orderly Room Sergeants and Medical Sergeants, etc., should be European, in view of the fact that it was too much to expect coloured men to train on from raw recruits to efficient senior sergeants in the short period of less than four months. It was not possible to obtain the requisite number of European N.C.O.'s before leaving for East Africa, but a certain number were attested and it was decided that the balance should be drawn in East Africa, from the South African Infantry already there, as soon as possible after our arrival. The following were appointed before leaving Simonstown:—

R.S.M. Harrington Robert Bircham (Permanent Force Staff, U.D.F.), (21.10.15).
R.Q.M.S. James Charles Hosack (29.10.15), (late Natal Carbineers).
C.S.M.'s: William Thomas Wigman (1.1.16), (late Natal Carbineers).
    D. A. Paterson (1.1.16).
    M. C. Cassidy (1.1.16).
    J. J. Greenhead (15.1.16).
Signalling Sergeant H. Martin (10.1.16).
Machine Gun Section Sergeant Jesse Howard (No. 20030, 84th Co. R.G.A.), (5.2.16).
Medical Sergeants, etc.:
    Sergeant Frederick John Shipp (16.12.15).
    Sergeant Thomas Allen Forrest (16.12.15).
    Lance-Corporal Andrew Henry (27.10.15).
    Private Jones (27.10.15).
    Private P. M. Grant (27.10.15).
Orderly Room Sergeant Frederick William Betts (28.10.15).
Armourer Sergeant G. H. Pepper (P.F.S., U.D.F.) (6.1.16).

C.Q.M.S.'s:
  Robert Andrew Cloke (4.12.15).
  J. Clennell (1.1.16).
  Jackson Hart (ex 9th S.A.I.) (11.1.16).
  N. O. Harvey (1361) (22.1.16).

(Note.—The above four men handed over on 1st February, 1916 to coloured Q.M. Sergeants and became Staff Sergeants additional to establishment.)

Platoon Sergeants:
  T. C. Adams (29.11.15).
  D. R. Ogilvie (19.1.16).
  A. H. B. Lee (1.2.16).
  C. Richardson (1365) (1.2.16).

Attached for Pay purposes:
  Staff Sergeant William Thain Mills (21.10.15, discharged 5.2.16).
  ,,   Johannes Justinus Bam (24.12.15).
  ,,   A. Goodwin (6.1.16).
  ,,   Ephraim Harris (2.2.16).

R.S.M. Bircham returned to duty with the Defence Department after a couple of months and was succeeded by George Forsythe on 1st January, 1916.

R.Q.M.S. J. C. Hosack received his commission on 4th December, 1915, but ten days later reverted at his own request and resumed his original duties, taking over from Frank W. Grey, who had succeeded him. Grey (the well-known South African cricket umpire, by the way) left at once to take a position in the South African Records Office at Nairobi, B.E.A.

Several of the coloured men shewed, however, during the short period of training, such a remarkable aptitude for absorption of the military spirit and of the essentials necessary to the evolution of a good N.C.O., that within a year the C.O. found it possible to eliminate the European N.C.O.'s with two exceptions and carry on with coloured N.C.O.'s. In fact, when, on 3rd April, 1918, the battalion embarked for Egypt, Sergt.-Major Shipp (Medicals) was the only European N.C.O. to accompany us. This was highly satisfactory, as the men very naturally preferred non-commissioned officers selected from amongst themselves. It was a great incentive for every man to fit himself for promotion by every means within his power, and it was an equal pleasure to the C.O. and officers, and to friends of the experiment of the formation of the Corps and to the whole coloured community of the Union of South Africa and their well-wishers, to find that there could be found within the men's own ranks soldiers possessing the necessary qualifications and fully capable and willing, nay eager, to accept the responsibilities and many onerous duties devolving and encumbent upon a good warrant officer and sergeant.

It has been said that the power to make or mar a regiment lies in the hands of the Adjutant and R.S.M., but those best able to judge will testify that—however good the Adjutant and R.S.M.—without a good standard of N.C.O's throughout a unit nothing really great can be achieved. In fact, as has been very truly said, "The N.C.O. is the backbone of the British Army."

It will no doubt prove of interest to record the names of the coloured N.C.O.'s originally appointed, viz.:—

First Provost Sergeant: William Thomas McLeod (111) 24.10.15.
First Transport Sergeant: J. W. Peake (138) 24.10.15.
First C.Q.M. Sergeants: P. F. Heeger   (21) 25.10.15
                        A. J. Daniels (13) 25.10.15.
                        C. D. Sasse   (209) 28.10.15.
                        A. J. Hendricks (1067) 7.12.15.

THE STORY OF THE 1st CAPE CORPS.

First Sergeant Shoemaker: J. J. Petersen (943) 6.12.15.
First Pioneer Sergeant: J. C. M. Paulsen (432) 13.11.15.
Transport Sergeant: Simon February (1357) 19.1.16.
First Bugler Sergeant: J. G. Brown (228) 22.11.15.
Machine Gun Section: Sergeant S. W. Dunn (1134), 17.12.15. (was transferred to Headquarters as Sergeant in charge Scouts, 29.2.16.)
First Sergeant Cook: J. H. Jacobs (5) 25.10.15.

Sergeants:
Name	No.	Date
A. J. Daniels	(28)	24.10.15.
A. C. L. Felton	(169)	25.10.15.
W. Koetenberg	(39)	25.10.15.
P. Daniels	(1)	25.10.15.
C. le Grange	(143)	27.10.15.
H. E. Smith	(146)	27.10.15.
H. J. R. Heber	(145)	27.10.15.
E. du Plessis	(137)	27.10.15.
C. A. Ruiters	(132)	27.10.15.
A. Olieslager	(182)	27.10.15.
C. Calvert	(152)	27.10.15.
H. May	(127)	27.10.15.
J. D. Samson	(219)	28.10.15.
F. Hendricks	(225)	28.10.15.
S. J. Fredericks	(255)	30.10.15.
J. P. Carolissen	(280)	1.11.15.
S. F. Lakey	(105)	1.11.15.
C. Veldsman	(284)	1.11.15.
J. G. Brown	(228)	1.11.15.
M. J. Abrahams	(318)	3.11.15.
P. D. Schoor	(480)	15.11.15.
J. Lock	(609)	27.11.15.
L. la Fleur	(758)	1.12.15.
W. F. Barbier	(875)	4.12.15.
F. N. de Jongh	(873)	4.12.15.
H. D. le Roux	(904)	6.12.15.
J. W. Langford	(905)	6.12.15.
H. W. Herman	(978)	7.12.15.
J. Karele	(1038)	8.12.15.
P. Karstens	(1031)	8.12.15.
R. E. Henry	(327)	20.12.15.

Sixteen men with some rudimentary musical knowledge were selected in November to be trained as buglers, and by the end of the year were able to blow the principal calls.

On the 22nd December, Acting Sergeant de Vries (No. 7) was accidentally shot. This was our first casualty; but, alas, only the first of several hundred.

Whilst at Simonstown Lieutenant Frank Collings Hallier was married on January 16th to Miss Whiteside. The ceremony took place in one of the huts converted into a chapel for the occasion, and the reception took place in the officers' mess. Several of the senior officers furnished the customary guard of honour and crossed swords in time-honoured fashion to form an archway for the happy pair to pass through on leaving the temporary chapel.

Everything passed off with more than the usual gaiety and éclat customary on such occasions and was a most pleasant and charming interlude to the steady routine of training.

Photo by]   [U.H.T.

THE BATTALION ON PARADE AT SIMONSTOWN, JANUARY, 1916, PRIOR TO INSPECTION BY BRIG.-GENERAL SIMPSON BAIKIE.

Photo by]   [Miss B. Pilgram.

DEPARTURE OF THE BATTALION FROM CAPE TOWN FOR EAST AFRICA PER H.M.T. "ARMADALE CASTLE," 9TH FEBRUARY, 1916.

Photo by]   [U.H.T.

IN TRAINING AT SIMONSTOWN.—BAYONET FIGHTING.

Photo by]   [U.H.T.

FIELD TRAINING AT SIMONSTOWN, JANUARY, 1916.

THE STORY OF THE 1st CAPE CORPS.

There was not much time for games, sport or athletics during our strenuous period of mobilisation and training at Simonstown. A few of the officers certainly found time for an occasional game of cricket at Newlands and Lieutenant Dudley Pearse scored 145 in a club match for the Western Province Cricket Club. But it was not all work and no play, as the Cape Corps Gifts and Comforts Committee arranged several concerts in camp and the efforts of the ladies and gentlemen artistes were vastly appreciated by all ranks. Further reference will be made later on in this book to the truly splendid work done on our behalf by the abovementioned most energetic Committee to whom we can never be sufficiently indebted.

About the end of January orders were received that the Battalion would embark for East Africa on H.M.T. "Armadale Castle" on the 9th February. This information gave great pleasure and at the same time forced everybody to work overtime completing final preparations. We left Simonstown in three special trains, and within an hour of the arrival of the last train at the quay side in Cape Town Docks the embarkation had been completed.

It may here be recorded that the officers who proceeded to East Africa when the battalion embarked to take the field for the first time were:—

Officer Commanding ...	Lieut.-Colonel G. A. Morris.
Second in Command ...	Major C. N. Hoy.
Adjutant	Captain W. G. Gunningham.
Quartermaster	Captain Ivor D. Difford.
Machine Gun Officer ...	Captain Lindsay Campbell.
Signalling Officer ...	Lieutenant J. E. Dennison.
Transport Officer ...	Lieutenant J. Arnott, D.C.M.
Chaplain	Captain Rev. A. Earp-Jones.
Paymaster	Lieutenant B. Boam.

"A" Company.
  Officer Commanding: Major C. G. Durham.
  Second in Command: Lieutenant D. W. Robertson.
  Platoon leaders: Lieutenant W. J. R. Cuningham.
       ,,   F. C. Hallier.
       ,,   F. C. W. Stanford.
       ,,   W. W. Procter.

"B" Company.
  Officer Commanding: Captain W. R. Cowell.
  Second in Command: Captain W. P. Anderson.
  Platoon leaders: Lieutenant J. V. Harris.
       ,,   S. Youart.
       ,,   G. C. Macintosh.
       ,,   D. K. Pearse.

"C" Company.
  Officer Commanding: Captain F. J. Bagshawe.
  Second in Command: Captain H. G. Warr.
  Platoon leaders: Lieutenant F. Burger.
       ,,   J. H. Tandy.
       ,,   F. Murchie.
       ,,   S. W. Whitaker.

"D" Company.
  Officer Commanding: Captain F. E. Bradstock.
  Second in Command: Captain J. E. Robinson.
  Platoon leaders: Lieutenant S. Ashley.
       ,,   H. Edwards.
       ,,   J. M. Michau.
       ,,   T. P. Rose-Innes.

THE STORY OF THE 1st CAPE CORPS.

The embarkation was a record and Lieut.-Colonel Morris was very highly complimented by the Embarkation Staff Officer and other Dock officials on the remarkable speed and smoothness with which it had been effected.

The coloured community of the Cape Peninsula gave us a magnificent send-off. The scene on the wharf beggars description. The men were in great spirits and the enthusiasm tremendous. The "Armadale" pulled out about 5 p.m. on February 9th, and reached Kilindini in seven and a half days.

As we were the only unit on board, except for two or three details, there was ample room for everybody, and for parades, sports, physical exercises, etc. The ship's captain, Commander Geary Hill, and all his officers did all they could to assist in making the voyage a pleasant one. Commander Hill himself entered with great enthusiasm and keenness into our sports and games and taught the officers several new physical drill "stunts." Prior to disembarkation he informed our C.O. that he had been trooping for over a year and that this voyage had been the most pleasant of the lot. He also paid very high tribute indeed to the discipline of the battalion, and was emphatic in declaring that no other troops had conducted themselves so well or had left his ship in such a state of cleanliness and good order.

When the battalion left Simonstown there were about two hundred partially trained recruits in the Depôt. Captain C. E. Stevens was left in command of these, with Lieutenant W. W. Alexander and 2nd Lieutenants E. J. Rackstraw and R. Wilson to assist him. His instructions were to forward drafts of not less than fifty at a time as soon as the men became qualified and efficient.

LIEUTENANT F. C. HALLIER'S WEDDING AT SIMONSTOWN.
JANUARY 16TH, 1916.

THE STORY OF THE 1st CAPE CORPS.

Photo by] [B. Pilgram.
Departure for East Africa, 9th February, 1916.

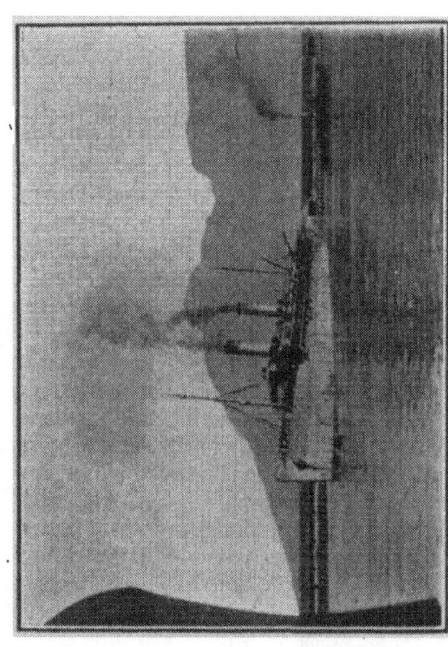

Photo by] [B. Pilgram.
H.M.T. "Armadale Castle" leaves with Battalion for East Africa, 9th February, 1916.

"Good-bye" to Cape Town, 9th February, 1916.

Photo by] [B. Pilgram.
Crowd waving "Au revoir" to Battalion on board H.M.T. "Armadale Castle," Cape Town Docks, 9th February, 1916.

THE STORY OF THE 1st CAPE CORPS.

Report on the Cape Corps by Major-General Charles W. Thompson, C.B., D.S.O., G.O.C. South African Military Command:—

It may be of interest to record briefly the steps taken to raise and train the Cape Corps.

The decision to raise the Corps was arrived at on September 20th, 1915, recruiting commenced on October 25th, and the instructors arrived on November 8th.

ORGANIZATION.—The Cape Corps is organized on the Imperial four company basis with an establishment of thirty officers and nine hundred and ninety-five other ranks.

RECRUITING.—This cannot be said to have started with a boom. The conditions were Imperial pay and no dependents' allowances. The recruits obtained in the Peninsula were at first of poor physique, were not of the best class, and also did not come forward in any considerable numbers. The recruits from up-country, and especially Kimberley, were of a much better stamp. Later on concessions were made as to pay and dependents' allowances and the stamp of recruit at once improved as did also the flow of numbers.

OFFICERS.—Lieut.-Colonel G. A. Morris was placed in command, and he was, I believe, given absolute discretion as to the nomination of the officers for the Battalion. Whatever the method of recruiting the officers the result has been that they are an exceptionally good and hard-working body.

TRAINING.—The officers, without exception I think, had all served previously in mounted corps and had little knowledge of infantry drill. Many of the instructors that were sent down from up-country were similarly situated, and all the instructors that were supplied locally from the R.G.A., the R.E., and the C.G.A. were, from the nature of things, not experts in infantry training.

To rectify this state of things, and while the Corps was still mainly occupied in recruiting, equipping and generally shaking down in their new surroundings, classes were formed at Wynberg under experienced instructors, and all the officers and instructors were put through a very strenuous course of infantry work commencing with squad drill and physical training, and gradually working upwards. These courses lasted four weeks. The result was immediately apparent when the instructors got to work on their squads, for all then worked on a system. Each instructor had about twelve men in his squad. The hours of work were 7 a.m. to 12.15 p.m. and 2 p.m. to 5.45 p.m., but later on, owing to the heat, no outdoor work took place between 11.30 a.m. and 4 p.m. The first few weeks were entirely devoted to instilling discipline into the ranks, and for this purpose close order drill and physical drill was the medium. Gradually the Corps received its arms and in due course each company was put through a modified course of musketry. At a later stage each company was exercised in company field firing. When the musketry course was completed it became necessary to form the various specialists, and selected men were formed into machine gun sections, signallers, pioneers and first aid, etc. Each lot was instructed under specialist officers and N.C.O.'s and their future time was almost wholly devoted to their special duties. These classes have now attained a very fair measure of efficiency, and, considering the limited time at their disposal, may be pronounced as good. This term especially applies to the Pioneers, most of whom in civil life were artisans, etc., and so readily assimilated the training given by the 47th Company R.E.

GENERAL REMARKS.—It may, I think, be fairly said that considering the short time available for training, the Cape Corps has made remarkable progress and has attained a very creditable state of efficiency. This is due in the first place to the great zeal of the Commanding Officer, Lieut.-Colonel Morris. He is an ideal man for the job and has thrown all his energy into his work. He has been most ably seconded in his efforts by his officers, all of whom without exception have worked their best and hardest. Each of the four companies will have at least three white N.C.O.'s in addition to its own white officers, and the machine gun section has two white instructors. The weak point in the regiment is the coloured N.C.O. Three months ago they were recruits the same as the other men, and they were chosen for their stripes according to their standing in civil life and according to their ability to read and write. Naturally they have not as yet much hold on the men, nor are they themselves sufficiently proficient in their military duties to breed confidence in themselves and in those under them. They are coming on, however, and if only the Corps can be given a successful "blooding." I feel pretty confident that it will "find" itself.

Finally it gives me pleasure to testify to the good conduct of the Corps. Of serious crime there has been none, and minor crime has chiefly arisen from inability of the untutored coloured mind readily to grasp the essential requirements of discipline.

(Signed) CHAS. THOMPSON,

Major-General.

Cape Town,
9th February, 1916.

[NOTE.—Major-General Thompson's reference to the original coloured N.C.O.'s is interesting in view of the wonderful progress made by those men after less than twelve months' military training (*vide* Chapter V.).—EDITOR

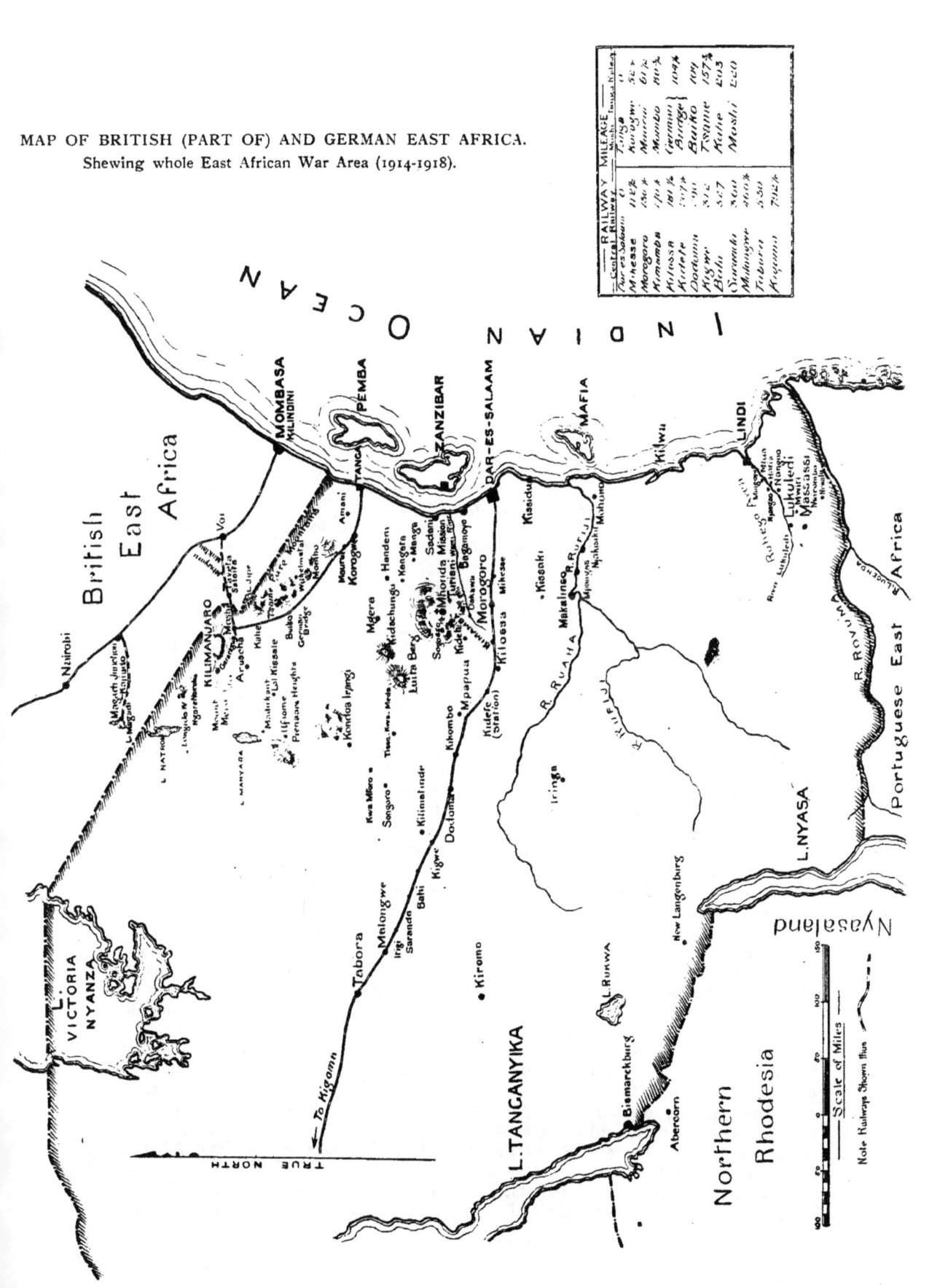

MAP OF BRITISH (PART OF) AND GERMAN EAST AFRICA.
Shewing whole East African War Area (1914-1918).

CHAPTER V.

IN EAST AFRICA—PERIOD 17TH FEBRUARY TO 14TH DECEMBER, 1916.

DISEMBARKATION in East Africa took place at Kilindini, the harbour for Mombasa, and before dark on the day of arrival (17.2.16) the battalion in two troop trains was en route to Kajiado, in British East Africa, near the northern border of German East, and then railhead on the branch line to Lake Magadi, leaving the main line from Kilindini to Nairobi at Magadi junction. This journey occupied about thirty hours, and afforded us our first impression of the wonderful scenery and luxuriant foliage of East Africa. During the journey we got our first view of Kilimanjaro, that magnificent snow-capped mountain which towers, the highest peak in the African Continent, 19,350 feet above sea level. For four or five months we were not to lose sight of this great leviathan whose sublimity and ineffable grandeur impressed itself upon one more and more indelibly with every passing day.

Our arrival in British East took place very shortly before Lieut.-General J. C. Smuts took over the supreme command there from Major-General M. J. Tighe, and just after the South African Infantry and Field Artillery, who had preceded us East by a few weeks, had covered themselves with glory at Salaita Hill near Taveta, the gateway to German East.

At Kajiado we came under the orders of Post Commandant Colonel Walter Kitchener, elder brother of Earl Kitchener of Khartoum, who succeeded to the title when his great brother was drowned in the "Hampshire" a few months later. Here Lieutenant F. Burger was transferred to the Machine Gun Section with which he remained until the battalion was demobilised. Later he assumed command of the section and with it did much valuable work.

Major Hoy and Sergeant Betts rejoined at Kajiado on February 20th. They had left us at Simonstown shortly before embarkation to interview the Officer in Charge of Records, Pretoria, re various records, confusion having arisen owing to several men having given their names, or the names of their next of kin and addresses, etc., incorrectly when attesting.

After a few days at Kajiado, where we were inspected by Major-General J. M. Stewart, C.B., commanding 1st Division, orders were received to proceed to Longido West, our advanced post in German territory. Having drawn the necessary transport (mules) we moved off at sundown on the 23rd February, taking charge of a supply convoy of some seventy wagons. This journey of seventy-four and a half miles via Bissil, Ol Ekunoni, Kidongai and Namanga, occupied eight days, including three days' halt at the last named place.

At Lone Hill, between Kidongai and Namanga, Major Durham was left behind on lines of communication duty with two hundred men (two platoons each of "A"' and "B" companies) and Captain Warr on the same duty with the same number of men (two platoons each of "C" and "D" companies) at Namanga. At Longido West we remained from March 2nd to 5th, and there joined Major-General Stewart's (now Sir J. M. Stewart) 1st East African Division, being allocated to Brig.-General Sheppard's 2nd Brigade—in which were also the 25th Royal Fusiliers, 129th Baluchis, and 29th Punjabis. Two batteries of S.A.F.A., under Major Lorch (now (D.S.O.), were Divisional Troops.

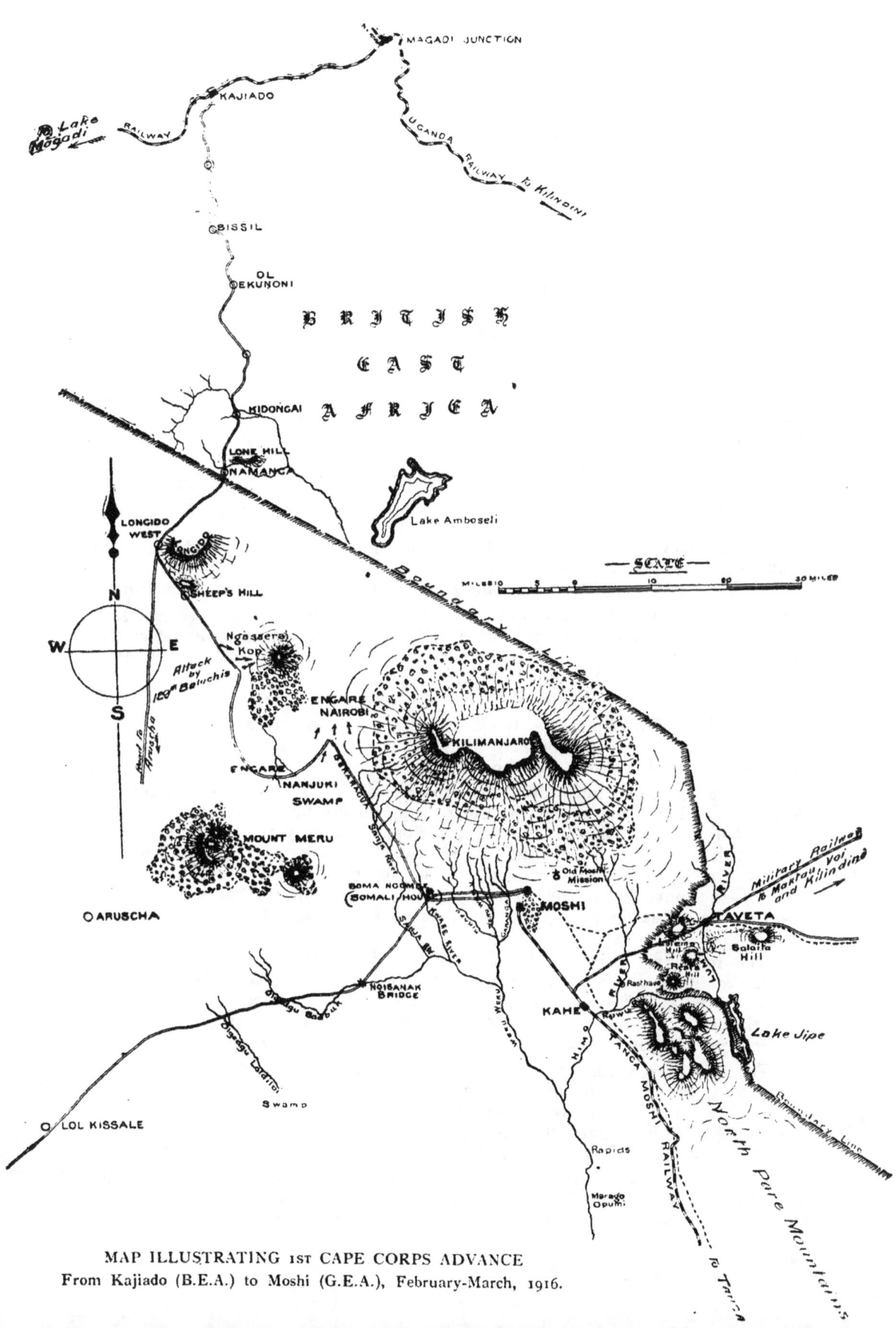

MAP ILLUSTRATING 1st CAPE CORPS ADVANCE
From Kajiado (B.E.A.) to Moshi (G.E.A.), February-March, 1916.

On March 5th the whole force moved on to Sheep's Hill (seven miles), concentrated there and moved off in the evening for Ngare Nairobi en route for Moshi round Kilimanjaro, approaching Moshi from the south-west.

The intention was a forced march, driving the enemy before us, to co-operate with our main forces, under Lieut.-General Smuts, who were advancing on Moshi via Maktau and Taveta, over the eastern and southern slopes of Kilimanjaro. The object of capturing Moshi was to secure the railhead of the Tanga-Moshi railway and to drive the enemy southwards in the direction of the central railway (Dar-es-Salaam through Tabora to Lake Tanganyika at Kigoma).

The first objective in General Stewart's advance was the enemy fortified post of Ngare Nairobi. A half company under Lieutenant Hallier (Cape Corps) was despatched on the afternoon of March 4th on the main road towards Aruscha. The object was to mislead the Hun that a strong force was advancing that way by dragging bushes drawn by oxen in order to create a great dust, and induce the enemy to leave their fortified post at Ngare Nairobi to attack the supposed force.

The main column then advanced after dark on 5th March from Sheep's Hill, and marched all night to attack Ngare Nairobi from Ngasserai (twelve miles distant), but thick thorn bush and sansiviera (indiginous sisal) in places caused the position to be considered impregnable.

It was, however, decided to attack as far as Ngasserai Kop, and the 129th Baluchis, supported by artillery, were detailed to do the job. They were successful after a hot little skirmish, in which they sustained a few casualties.

It was well that our main advance was not continued from Ngasserai Kop along the direct road to Ngare-Nairobi as further on the enemy had a wonderfully prepared position, which would almost certainly have proved impregnable, and in any case would have caused us very heavy casualties. This was the position burnt by Captain Cowell a few days later (*vide* page 49).

Whilst the Baluchis were attacking Ngasserai Kop the main column went on and turned in a south-westerly direction when two miles beyond the Kop with the object of making a flanking attack via Ngare Nanjuki swamp.

Advancing from Sheep's Hill General Stewart's Division formed a column several miles long, and it was the Cape Corps' misfortune to act as rearguard, behind the whole Divisional Transport. This was a very trying march as the transport was continually stopping for several minutes at a time. The distance covered to Ngare Nanjuki Swamp was approximately thirty miles, and we were on the move for sixteen hours with only a halt of two hours during the night. There was no water, but more than a sufficiency of sand and extreme heat.

The following morning (March 7th) the 129th Baluchis and Cape Corps (about six hundred strong) advanced across the flat under Colonel Hannyngton, C.M.G., D.S.O., Officer Commanding 129th Baluchis, to attack Ngare Nairobi from that side, but this plan was frustrated by the enemy flooding the flat and swamp from the river flowing at the foot of the kopje.

The brigade remained all day at Ngare Nanjuki swamp and we were forced to camp for the night on the flat about two miles from Ngare Nairobi. Here the battalion got their first baptism of fire. At about eleven p.m. four prisoners were brought in by a Baluchi patrol.

These prisoners gave us information upon which it was decided to act at once, and Lieutenant Harris was accordingly sent back with a platoon to reconnoitre and report upon the enemy fortified position near Ngasserai Kop, mentioned above, and to attack and capture the position if possible.

THE STORY OF THE 1st CAPE CORPS.

Photo by] [J.H.T.

TRANSPORT DIFFICULTIES—LONGIDO-MOSHI SAFARI.
TRANSPORT DIFFICULTIES—LONGIDO-MOSHI SAFARI.
"C" COMPANY'S CAPTURED DONKEYS.
A.T. CARTS ON SAFARI.

A CAMP SCENE AT KIDONGAI.
TRANSPORT DIFFICULTIES—LONGIDO-MOSHI SAFARI.
OUR CAMP AT LONGIDO WEST.
A CAPE CORPS PATROL UNDER MAJOR HOY

Harris had just got outside our pickets, proceeding north, when the enemy opened fire on our camp from the south-east.

The men behaved with exemplary coolness, taking up their positions in the trenches quietly and calmly. Orders had been given that fire was not to be opened except under instructions from an officer, and those orders were implicitly obeyed and the men lay in the trenches (dug before they bivouaced for the night) with bayonets fixed ready for any emergency, but nothing happened as the Baluchis let off a few shots and the enemy, probably a small number, finding we were ready for them, cleared. Whether they had any casualties is not known. We had none. By their behaviour that night the men fully satisfied their officers that they could be relied upon in action. The fact that this was a night attack emphasised the men's coolness and steadiness. It was presumed that the enemy who attacked our camp were the same party as Harris had been sent out to attack.

Early next morning (March 8th) the Baluchis moved off to rejoin the Brigade, who were marching on Geraragua, and at the same time Captain Cowell was sent out in support of Harris with the remainder of "B" company and to clear up the country towards Ngasserai. In the course of their advance they crossed the Ngare Nairobi Kop and arrived at Ngasserai after a very hot and waterless march. A supply convoy came in there from Sheep's Hill without water and had to send their animals down to the Nanjuki swamp to water, a journey which occupied nearly twelve hours to and fro. Captain Cowell then helioed for water, which was sent out from our camp and met him on the road next day.

The next day he returned to Ngare Nairobi, en route burning the aforesaid German position (vacated) in the bush, which he found to be extraordinarily strongly fortified.

After Cowell had left camp dust clouds seemed to indicate that the enemy had got in behind and cut him off from the main body. Fortunately the scare turned out to be nothing worse than a herd of giraffe on the move.

The Cape Corps then advanced to attack Ngare Nairobi, but met with no opposition—the enemy having evidently cleared during the night. We occupied the kopje and remained there five days in order to establish and protect lines of communication, and to establish supply parks at various points, and to open the way for the supply columns and the 2nd line transport of the fighting forces. Captain Cowell had reported all clear within a few hours of going out, and the supply column (under Captain Devenish Meares) then moved up and established a park on the flat across the river just below our camp.

During the advance on Ngare Nairobi Major Hoy, with one orderly, followed Captain Cowell and preceded the main body to reconnoitre the road for our transport. After going a short distance he saw through the bush what appeared to be mounted men following Cowell's spoor. Anxious that he should not give a false alarm, he followed these men and twice looked at them through his glasses, only turning back to warn the C.O. when he was convinced that his first suspicion was correct. The C.O. was duly informed and all speed was made to occupy Ngare Nairobi, which our scouts had reported unoccupied. It was suspected that Cowell's party would be attacked in the rear at a favourable opportunity and considerable anxiety was entertained until a helio message from him was received from Ngasserai notifying his safe arrival there. It was later learned that the supposed mounted men were large buck whose curiosity impelled them to follow Cowell's spoor.

A similar incident happened (also during the advance on Ngare Nairobi) to No. 12 Platoon of "C" campany, who were leading the advance. Everybody was of course very much on the *qui vive* and orders were to rush the position and consolidate. Machine gun emplacements were being prepared when suddenly the Colonel shouted: "There they are!" On our right flank could be seen galloping towards us what looked exactly like a squadron of mounted men with a screen of scouts and flanks out. The leaders halted under a tree, apparently to hold a consultation, and there was much excitement on the hill in anticipation of an attack, until strong field glasses disclosed the fact that "the enemy" was a big herd of gemsbok.

The long grass and bush were, of course, primarily responsible for the deception.

Thus we learned the lore of our new terrain.

Three days after we had occupied Ngare Nairobi Major Durham rejoined from Lone Hill with his two companies. He had been sniped at on the way but had no casualties. The line of communication and supply position having been established the brigade moved from Geraragua via Boma Ngombe (Somali House) to Moshi, taking a road which debouched to the right and leaving behind the whole of their mounted men to follow later. At the same time Major Hoy took "C" company under Captain Bagshawe to relieve the men left at Geraragua and escorted a supply convoy there. During this march our men saw their first aeroplane. We had not been told that the enemy were without aircraft and it was some time before this one could be recognised as British.

On arrival at Geraragua Major Hoy found that the mounted men and artillery of the division had retired on that place after a skirmish with an enemy party proceeding from Kampfontein to Moshi.

As there was only a small party of the 129th Baluchis, under Major Crawford, available to accompany the mounted men and guns, Major Hoy detailed two platoons (Lieutenant Michau's and Lieutenant Murchie's) of "C" company, under Captain Bagshawe, to reinforce that column until it gained touch with the Division which was then at Boma Ngombe (Somali House).

Captain Bagshawe returned with his men to Geraragua the same evening, having seen nothing of the enemy, who had evidently cleared in all directions as they were not encountered again before we reached Moshi.

The battalion moved up to Geraragua on March 13th and joined Major Hoy's detachment there.

Whilst at Geraragua the Brigade Supply Officer visited a neighbouring farm and found and buried there the dead body of an E.A.M.R. man who had been stripped naked by the enemy and left lying in the sun.

The next day "B" Company went out road repairing and on March 15th we left Geraragua for Moshi clearing a road through the Geraragua forest and taking charge of a supply convoy of forty wagons. These, of course, were additional to our own ten wagons. From here our troubles commenced. There had been, and continued to be, a good deal of heavy rain—no Scotch mist but tremendous and long continued downpours—and the roads and river crossings became one long succession of quagmires. The enemy had dug deep holes, cut down and laid trees across the roads, filled the river beds with broken bottles and adopted every conceivable fair or unfair method of delaying our advance.

We were now approaching the Kilimanjaro watershed and every few miles met with rivers, spruits and streams, delightfully cool and refreshing from the snow clad peak, but the very devil for a column encumbered with ox transport. At every crossing there was a drop of several feet into the river bed and an equal ascent on the far side. After one or two wagons had negotiated a passage the state of slush and slide may as well be imagined as described, and to make matters worse the oxen were quite raw and untrained, and the sole qualification for their job of the majority of the transport drivers and natives seemed to be a capacity for raucous shouting and an ability to use their damnable whips with frequent and fiendish cruelty. The result was that the majority of wagons became stuck in mid-stream and were only extricated by double hitching the teams and by man-handling. At some of the worst crossings it was only with thirty-two oxen to a wagon, aided by the almost superhuman efforts and patience of forty or fifty men striped to the waist, that the wagons were got through. Most days three or four such rivers had to be negotiated and the expenditure of time and labour involved in getting fifty wagons through each one was almost incredible. The men, however, for the most part thoroughly enjoyed themselves and tackled their herculean tasks with rare good will. Great boulders rolled into the river beds by the fleeing enemy was another heavy handicap.

The weather during this march was typically tropical, *i.e.*, when it did rain it did so in no half measure, and when it did not the sun shone with the maximum of power and added greatly to the tax on the stamina of both man and beast. However, after four days of this sort of thing Moshi was reached. On Sunday, March 19th, a tired but happy and triumphant Battalion marched into that place at 8 p.m., the men singing as if under the impression that they had reached the Promised Land.

It is reported that when the battalion was marching through the streets of Moshi someone asked General Stewart what unit it was coming in, and that the reply was: "There is only one battalion in my command that can sing after that march, and that is the Cape Corps."

During the march from Kajiado to New Moshi only seven men had fallen out and those few were the result of ill-fitting boots and not of physical breakdown. Before we could cross the Sanja River "C" Company had to repair the road and drift, a task involving several hours' hard labour.

After leaving Boma Ngombe the guides misled and landed us into a swamp, which caused twelve hours delay and required abnormal exertions by all concerned to get the transport through.

The scenery during the march from Bissil to Moshi was glorious beyond description, the foliage and flowers being luxuriant and the grass fresh and green, and in the distance always that glorious snowclad Kilimanjaro—a sight worth journeying half over the world to see—appeared to watch us like a giant sentinel, whilst away to the west another great peak, Mount Meru, almost as lofty, acted as a foil to her big sister.

For the most part the bush was very thick, but in places there were stretches of open park-like country abounding with game. Numerous natives were met with, all friendly disposed and anxious to surrender and to sell us furniture, etc. (looted from the surrounding farms), and fruit and other farm produce.

The roads were for the most part quite good, except at the drifts and where destroyed by the enemy. To give an idea of the difficulties of negotiating some of the drifts, it may be stated that it occupied from two to three hours to get the transport through more than one, and our progress some days did not average one mile per hour. On one occasion a mule driver in a panic let go the reins and jumped and was only dragged from under the wheels in the nick of time by the conductor.

Our transport conductors on this march, by the way, were H. B. Stricker and A. E. Lowe, both well known Johannesburg "Soccer" footballers—two splendid fellows. They worked like Trojans, and it was with great sorrow that we heard before the end of the year both had succumbed to the dread blackwater fever.

The trek from Longido West had occupied three weeks and had proved most valuable alike to officers and men. Much needed experience had been gained of entirely new conditions, and of the handicaps and hardships of campaigning in a tropical country and of the fighting and trekking through thick

Photo by]   *[J.H.T.*
KIKAFU BRIDGE.

Photo by]   *[J.H.T.*
A CAPE CORPS BLOCKHOUSE AT UNTERER HIMO IN THE SWAMPS.

WERU-WERU BRIDGE.

bush. The men, however, had been splendid and earned grateful thanks and very high praise from the Supply Convoy Officers. The greater the call the greater was the response and already the men had clearly absorbed the true spirit of the British army, which accepts every additional task and hardship with increased cheerfulness, not to say grim humour.

On arrival at Moshi we learned that the main force under Lieut.-General Smuts had entered that place without opposition six days previously (March 13th) and had left in the direction of Kahe, which they took a week later.

On March 22nd, at 3 a.m., Lieutenant Cuningham, with No. 2 platoon, left for Store Camp, towards Kahe, escorting an ammunition column and marched twenty-five miles in sixteen hours.

The next day we were told that the G.O.C. had decided that no further operations in this direction would be attempted until after the rains—two or three months—and we accordingly became line of communication troops with our headquarters at New Moshi.

It was of course inevitable that somebody should do the dull grind of L. of C. work, but we had been passed as ready for the field by the G.O.C., South Africa, before leaving Cape Town and everybody was greatly disappointed that we were not to get our chance at once in the firing line. However, it was no doubt an honour to be selected to do this most important work as upon the maintenance and guarding of the roads, drifts and bridges depended the welfare, indeed the lives, of General van Deventer's mounted division at Kondoa Irangi.

The G.O.C. himself had his headquarters at Old Moshi, an old slave trading and mission station about 1,500 feet above the plain on the slopes of Kilimanjaro and about five miles from our camp.

Lieut.-Colonel Morris was then appointed Post Commandant of Moshi, with Lieutenant Cuningham as his Post Adjutant (9.4.16) and later Staff Captain, and Lieutenant Youart as A.P.M. (22.3.16). Meanwhile Major Hoy assumed temporary command of the battalion.

On March 23rd, Major Durham arrived with his detachment (four hundred and twenty-one all ranks) from Ngare Nairobi, and all ranks in camp now numbered one thousand and nine. These reinforcements were heartily welcomed as line of communication and garrison duties were now becoming exceedingly arduous. Every vulnerable point had to be occupied by a company, platoon or smaller body, guns to be posted, trenches dug, etc., etc.

Early in April Captain Bagshawe with "C" Company and two platoons of "D" was sent to garrison Taveta, and at the same time half of "B" Company was sent to occupy Rasthaus, and to guard the line being constructed from Taveta, through the Himo river swamp, to Kahe. Shortly afterwards Captain Bagshawe and his detachment at Taveta were posted along this line to build and occupy block-houses. This proved a most trying ordeal as the swamp was putrid and fever infested, and the rains now incessant. One block-house was absolutely surrounded by water. The men began to go down wholesale with fever, the daily average sick parade being about fifty per cent., and this detachment had after two weeks to be relieved by "A" Company, who fared no better. Indeed by the end of April full half the battalion were in hospital or sick in the lines.

Simultaneously with the above duties road and bridge making and mending had also to be undertaken towards Kondoa Irangi.

Lieutenant Ashley and his platoon were sent to the Garanga River, Lieutenant T. P. Rose-Innes to Weru Weru River, Lieutenant Procter to Kikafu, Captain Robinson a few miles further on, and Captain Warr to Sanja River. Meanwhile Lieutenant Harris and his men mended a section of the railway from Moshi to Kahe, and then repaired the road between Weru Weru and Kikafu, constructed a light line and built a pulley bridge.

C.Q.M.S. P. Caster (392).

Lieutenant Ashley's Blockhouse at Garanga River Bridge, May, 1916.

Men of 12 Platoon ("C" Co.) at Unterer Himo. Private Cronje (with axe), Privates Pienaar and Harding (standing), Privates Mason and Hendricks (sitting).

1st Cape Corps Detachment Camp at Tanga, November, 1916.

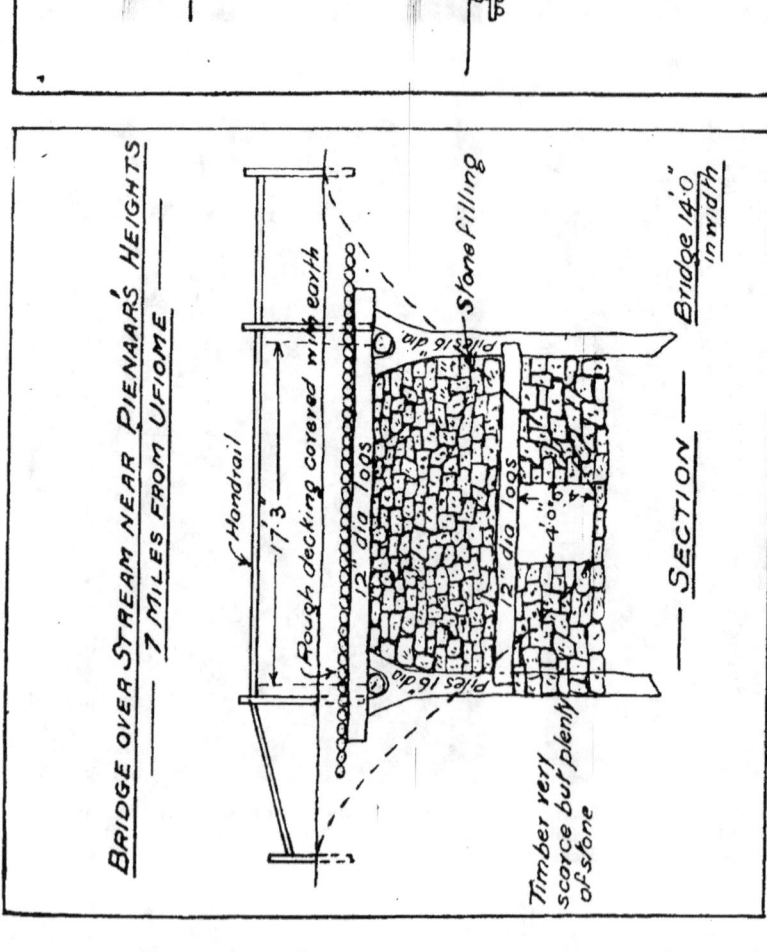

This laborious work was cheerfully done under most trying weather conditions, heavy rains alternating with extreme heat. Sergeant J. Karele (1038) and Private Henry Hoffmeister (902) (later promoted sergeant) deserve to be mentioned for exceptionally good work done in this connection.

In April, Captains Bradstock and Robinson were sent out with small parties to reconnoitre the country in the direction of Lolkissale, with the object of finding a better road to Kondoa Irangi and Aruscha. They had a very trying time owing to heavy rains and thick bush, and were nearly cut off by the enemy, but nevertheless succeeded in handing in a report which was of much value to the I.G.C.

Whilst on this "stunt" Captain Bradstock had an amusing experience. He went on a road reconnaissance near the Sanja River, taking two men with him. The enemy were reported in the vicinity and, crossing a drift over the Noisanak River, Bradstock thought he saw their tracks. He kept a sharp look-out and suddenly heard talking. He lay low and, telling his men not to move a muscle, crept forward to reconnoitre. He had not gone far when the voices came nearer. He dropped flat fearing that his chance of freedom was vanishing, but hoping for the best. Suddenly there was a great outburst of jabbering, and Bradstock knew to his great relief that "the enemy" were monkeys.

Lieutenant Wilson went out about the same time and constructed a bridge over the Sanja River (*vide* illustration, page 55). This was a well done job on which Lieut.-Colonel Morris was complimented by the authorities. In fact, at this time the battalion was doing a great deal of tremendously hard and useful work and might well have been an engineer or pioneer corps. The adaptability of the men and their previous all-round experience and particularly the training in field engineering done at Simonstown, proved of great value now, and Lieut.-Colonel Morris was more than once complimented by Brig.-General Edwards, D.S.O., Inspector-General of Communications, East African Forces.

Early in April Lieutenant Arnott was appointed Railway Transport officer at Moshi, and continued to act in that capacity for several weeks until we left the Moshi area. The railway from Taveta to Kahe junction was completed during the last week in April, and it then became possible to transport stores, rations, etc., by rail direct from Kilindini via Voi, Maktau, Taveta and Kahe to Moshi, an immense saving of time and labour, particularly as it was then the middle of the rainy season and transport difficulties had been immense.

Motor lorries frequently took three or four days to get by road from Taveta to Moshi (thirty miles). At first, owing to the swampy nature of the ground between Taveta and Kahe, heavy rolling stock could not be utilised and a small train was improvised consisting of a Studebaker (1912 model) motor car engine mounted on a light trolley and drawing four similar light trolleys, of which Private I. M. Adams (No. 207) was the driver. This train made one, on rare occasions two, journeys per diem each way.

Having assisted to make and repair this branch line, build blockhouses, repair bridges, guard the line and occupy the blockhouses and also provide the R.T.O. and engine driver, the 1st Cape Corps may justly claim to have performed most useful work in opening up communications from Kilindini to Moshi and, via Kahe, east towards the coast in the direction of Tanga, in which area our forces were now located until such time as weather conditions permitted the following up of the enemy southwards towards the Central Railway.

The weather at this time was so bad that, but for this most opportune through rail communication, our forces in this area would have fared ill indeed, if they had in fact not actually starved.

THE STORY OF THE 1st CAPE CORPS.

Photo by]   *[I.D.D.*
C.Q.M.S. Caster (392) loading Q.M.R.'s Stores at Moshi for Kahe, June, 1916.

Musketry Practice at Tanga, November, 1916.

Kilimanjaro (the highest eminence on the African Continent) from Mbuyuni.

At the end of the first week in May the rains abated somewhat, and on Sunday the 14th, the first church parade for five weeks was possible, to the infinite delight of our Padre, who had had a decidedly idle month.

When "C" Company returned to Moshi after their deadly experience in the Himo and Lumi river swamps, Major Hoy took them out to join "D" Company on outpost duty on the Aruscha road, and the two companies were placed under command of Captain Bradstock, who became Post Commandant at Lolkissale.

Lieutenant Arnott, who had been Transport Officer for the past six months, was now transferred to the Machine Gun detachment and took charge of the Rexer gun squad. Our transport was handed in soon after arrival at Moshi and when it was returned to us later on at German Bridge, Lieutenant Cloke became transport officer.

On May 20th orders came that the 1st Division, which had been encamped at Kahe for some weeks, was moving coatswards and that we were to concentrate three hundred and fifty men at that place by noon next day. This was a most difficult proposition as there were about six hundred men out on the Aruscha Road, one hundred and twenty at Rasthaus, and one hundred and thirty in hospital.

However, a supreme effort was made. A special train was sent to Rasthaus to fetch Captain Cowell and the men there fit to go forward, and all available mechanical transport was commandeered and sent out on the Sanja-Lolkissale road to collect officers and men. The task was not rendered easier by the necessity for selecting, in an hour or two in darkness, absolutely fit men, owing to the fact that the division anticipated forced marches and considerable opposition. Nevertheless one hundred and twenty-five men were deposited at Kahe two hours before the appointed time, fifty later the same day, one hundred and thirty next morning, and the balance the following day. Only twenty-five men were now left in camp at Moshi, which place, however, remained our depôt in East Africa for another two months or more. Captain Anderson who had been seriously ill, and who had been in charge of our rest camp at Old Moshi (see below), for some time remained behind in command of this depôt until towards the end of July.

The three hundred and fifty men concentrated at Kahe were placed under the command of Captain Cowell and left on May 23rd as divisional troops to the G.O.C. in the advance down the Pangani River and on Wilhelmstal.

Cowell was first sent out to occupy a place named "Rapids" on the flank of the advance, but, owing to the enemy's rapid retreat, plans were altered and the detachment carried on with the division to Marago Mikwajuni, where they cleared an aviation landing ground. From there Cowell was ordered to take his detachment back to Kahe (forty miles), the force having to be reduced owing to scarcity of rations.

On May 31st orders were received for an establishment of sixty-four porters for the Machine Gun Detachment to replace the pack mules. This was a great relief to the O.C. M.G.detachment as the mules (small Abyssinians and the concentrated essence of every kind of mule vice) had caused endless trouble. These porters were very raw, but later became most efficient and useful (*vide* M.G. section chapter).

About the same time as the above-mentioned concentration at Kahe took place we were allowed to establish a Rest Camp at Old Moshi, on the slopes of Kilimanjaro, about one thousand five hundred feet above the plain, and here officers and men recovering from fever were sent for a week or more to recuperate. It was very much cooler there than down below and the results of the rest were very soon apparent, indeed, it was surprising that other units did not follow our example.

THE STORY OF THE 1st CAPE CORPS.

During the first fortnight in June the battalion began to concentrate at Tsame, south of the Pare mountains on the Moshi-Tanga railway a few miles east of Kahe, having now been transferred from lines of communication to become divisional troops under Bt.-Colonel (temporary Major-General) A. R. Hoskins, C.M.G., D.S.O., now commanding 1st East African Division. This concentration took some days as a large number of officers and men were still on outpost duty on the Aruscha road and could not all be relieved at once. On Thursday, June 8th, Major Furse (Bishop of Pretoria), who had arrived on a visit to South African units, consecrated the military burial ground at New Moshi, where up to that time seven of our men, viz., Private van Haarte, M. (1081), Private Visagie, Jacob (383), Corporal Jozaffe, Gabriel (458), and Privates Moody, J. (268), Cotton, R. (3), Groep, M. (1268), and Francis, D. (263) had found their last resting place. All our available men in camp, about two hundred and fifty, paraded for the ceremony under Major Hoy.

On Sunday, 18th June, a large consignment of comforts—the first—arrived from the Cape Corps Gifts and Comforts Committee in South Africa. Needless to say they were most gratefully received and appreciated. Many more such consignments followed at intervals during the next three years and all were equally welcome.

By the 23rd June, Battalion Headquarters had been moved south-east to German Bridge on the Pangani River, where Lieut.-Colonel Morris became Post Commandant and Major Hoy assumed temporary command of the battalion.

On June 25th Major Hoy left German Bridge with all available men (about three hundred and twenty) to join up with Divisional Headquarters, marching via Palms, Makayo, Mkalomo, Luchomo, Mbagui and Handeni to Lukigura Bridge, almost due south towards the Central Railway. At this time Captain Bradstock was Post Commandant at Wilhelmstal, having with him Lieutenants Edwards and Stanford and one hundred men, whilst Captain Bagshawe held a similar position at Mombo, having with him Lieutenants Pearse and Murchie and one hundred men. Lieutenant Robertson with fifty men was at Palms, a post fifteen miles south from German Bridge. Colonel Morris had with him at German Bridge, the writer, Lieutenant Rackstraw and one hundred men; the remainder of the battalion—some five hundred men—being in hospital at Moshi and Maktau, etc. Within the next two weeks, however, several officers and some three hundred and fifty men came forward and were sent on to join Major Hoy at Lukigura River Bridge. When Lieut.-Colonel Morris took over Post Commandant's duties at German Bridge he found about seven thousand troops in camp, the same being details of practically every unit in the Division, and Departmental units, *i.e.*, R.E. Ordinance, Supplies and Transport (animal and mechanical), Post and Telegraph Corps, Stationary Hospital, etc.

During our advance from Moshi by stages to Kahe, Tsame, Mombo, German Bridge, and Wilhelmstal, the battalion, being divisional troops, had not had contact with the enemy, but our main force were constantly in touch with them. After the Salaita Hill battle, the fall of Moshi, the series of actions at Reata, Latema Hills and Ruwu river, which gave us the complete and undisputed possession of a very large and important area, the Hun evidently came to the conclusion that we were too strong for him and retreated south and east into the Usambara mountains, and, when driven from there, south towards Handeni, and later on towards the Central Railway at Morogoro. He did not, however, allow us all our own way, in fact put up strong rearguard actions all the way.

THE STORY OF THE 1st CAPE CORPS.

A Captured Photo.
THE "KOENIGSBERG" SINKING THE BRITISH MERCHANTMAN "CITY OF WINCHESTER."

Photo by]   *[U.H.T.*
CAPTAIN H. WARR DIRECTING MOTOR DESPATCH RIDERS AT KIKAFU.

SALAITA HILL, GERMAN EAST AFRICA.

BRITISH MONITOR AT ZANZIBAR.

THE STORY OF THE 1st CAPE CORPS.

In the work of clearing the Usambara mountains and sweeping the enemy from our lines of communication after our thrust at Msiba, the 2nd East African Infantry Brigade, under Lieut.-Colonel (temporary Brig.-General) J. A. Hannyngton, C.M.G., D.S.O. (129th Baluchis) bore the brunt of the fighting.

Here a brief reference must be made to the splendid work done by all the South African units during the past four or five months. The infantry had done work at Salaita Hill and elsewhere which, when the very short period of training they had had before leaving South Africa is borne in mind, was literally astonishing. The men of the 2nd East African Division performed prodigies of valour and endurance under (temporary) Major-General J. L. van Deventer in the forced march on and capture of Kondoa Irangi, and the holding of it against determined attacks, under circumstances of great difficulty in regard to supplies, medical comforts, etc., until Lieut.-General Smuts' advance on Lukigura forced the enemy to abandon his positions before Kondoa in order to concentrate in defence of Morogoro.

Lieut.-Colonel Stanley S. Taylor and the South African Field Artillery under his command did splendid work at Kondoa Irangi, and Lieut.-Colonel Taylor himself added greatly to the laurels he had won when in command of the Transvaal Horse Artillery in South-West Africa. In the words of General Smuts, " In the story of human endurance this campaign deserves a very special place and the heroes who went through it uncomplainingly, doggedly, are entitled to all recognition and reverence."

About this time several of our men whilst in detail camps along the Lines of Communication had performed fatigue duties in various Base and Stationary Hospitals, where they so pleased the medical officers and nursing sisters that a special request was made for a number of Cape Corps men to be seconded for duty with the medical services in hospitals where coloured men and natives were patients. This was done on 26th June, the men detailed being of course those needing a rest from hard marching.

Before Major Hoy and his detachment left German Bridge for Lukigura the battalion were issued with ox transport to replace the mules which had been withdrawn shortly after our arrival at Moshi. These oxen were untrained and gave endless trouble and caused much delay all the way to Morogoro. In fact, even when the latter place was reached two months later it had been impossible to get the beasts to pull together as teams. Large numbers died and the majority of the survivors were so weak that the lot of the Transport officer was most unenviable.

At German Bridge, in addition to ox wagons, we received a number of light two-wheeled carts known as A.T. carts, similar to those used in the hill country in India. These were drawn by two or four oxen or mules and proved most useful.

On arrival at Lukigura during the first week in July, Major Hoy was at once ordered to take the battalion back some twenty miles to Kangata and garrison that place, the reason being that an enemy force from Tanga was reported to be advancing on Handeni (between German Bridge and Kangata, about fifty miles from former place and twenty-five from Kangata) and the 2nd Infantry Brigade, under Brig.-General J. A. Hannyngton, C.M.G., D.S.O., was turned back to intercept them.

In passing through our section of the road Brig.-General Hannyngton despatched Captain Bradstock with a company to search the neighbouring villages and scour the country. They met with no opposition, finding the natives well disposed, and accordingly returned to camp.

Whilst at Lukigura our men had their first experience of shell fire. The enemy had some 4.1 guns, taken off their destroyed cruiser " Koenigsberg," posted on a hill overlooking our Division's camp (which consequently became

THE STORY OF THE 1st CAPE CORPS.

Late 2nd Lieutenant J. C. Hosack, killed at Mssinga, East Africa, 20th July, 1916.

Photo by] [Zadik & Co., Cape Town.
Captain I. D. Difford, Quartermaster.

known as Shell Camp) and indulged in the nasty habit of dropping shells into the camp at irregular hours, day and night. The damage done was negligible, but existence in Shell Camp was not enviable, resembling too closely that of a mole.

Simultaneously with the above move Lieut.-Colonel Morris came on from German Bridge to Handeni to become Post Commandant at the latter place, having Captain Robinson with one hundred of our men as garrison there. A chain of posts was now established every few miles between Handeni and Lukigura, our section being from the last named place to six miles north of Kangata. Lieutenant Michau's platoon was at the northern end of our line (known as refilling point) and Lieutenant Harris' platoon at the southern end (Massinga), where they were constantly sniped at by the enemy and worried by lions. The enemy had commenced to cut the wires and lay road mines between Handeni and Kangata and our forces had several casualties. Their plan was to creep up to the roads during the night, lay the mines, and retire, with disastrous results to the first wagon or motor lorry passing that way next morning, and those of us whose duties took us to and fro on these roads were more than glad to reach camp with whole skins. This necessitated all night patrols who marched just off the road in the wet grass. It need hardly be said that this was anxious work enjoyed by no one.

One patrol sent out from Kangata had a lucky escape. Lieutenants Tandy and Arnott, with Lieutenant Birkett (I.D.), and twenty men went out with a Rexer gun on a long patrol to reconnoitre a certain position. When a few miles from their objective spies brought in news that the place was strongly held by about two hundred of the enemy. They accordingly decided that discretion was the better part of valour and returned to camp.

The country between Handeni and Lukigura was positively beastly. The men suffered severely from fever and dysentry, flies were an abomination, and the Tsetse fly created havoc with the transport, horses, mules and oxen dying literally by hundreds, if not thousands, and the jigger, or burrowing flea, was by no means the least of our troubles.

That horrible little insect particularly infested old camping grounds and became an absolute nightmare. The female settles on the feet and eats her way into the flesh, where she lays an egg, usually under the toe-nails. If not removed at once a swelling is caused and when, as frequently happened, a man had twenty such bites on his foot it may well be imagined that his marching powers were much curtailed. The local natives were expert at removing the egg sack with a pin or needle, but did not always use a clean instrument and, in the absence of antiseptics, results were not always satisfactory.

Snakes also abounded here as in most other parts of East Africa and we were very fortunate in having no fatal results from snake bite, although officers and men more than once found the reptiles curled in their blankets in the morning. A young python shared Captain Murchie's tent one night on detachment duty, but as he had the men's rum issue in his care that night there may have been ulterior motive in the creature's presence.

Whilst at Kangata we had our first casualty amongst our officers, 2nd Lieutenant J. C. Hosack being accidentally shot at Massinga post before dawn on July 20th by one of our own pickets. Hosack was returning with a party of men from an all-night patrol on the look-out for enemy mine-layers. Our picket was an Indian one and, owing to some error, had evidently not been warned that a patrol was on the road, and accordingly acted on instructions to fire on sight, that being necessary in view of the activity of the mine-layers. Except our patrols no traffic was allowed along these roads during darkness. This most unhappy incident was a great grief to the whole battalion, Jimmy Hosack being beloved by all ranks.

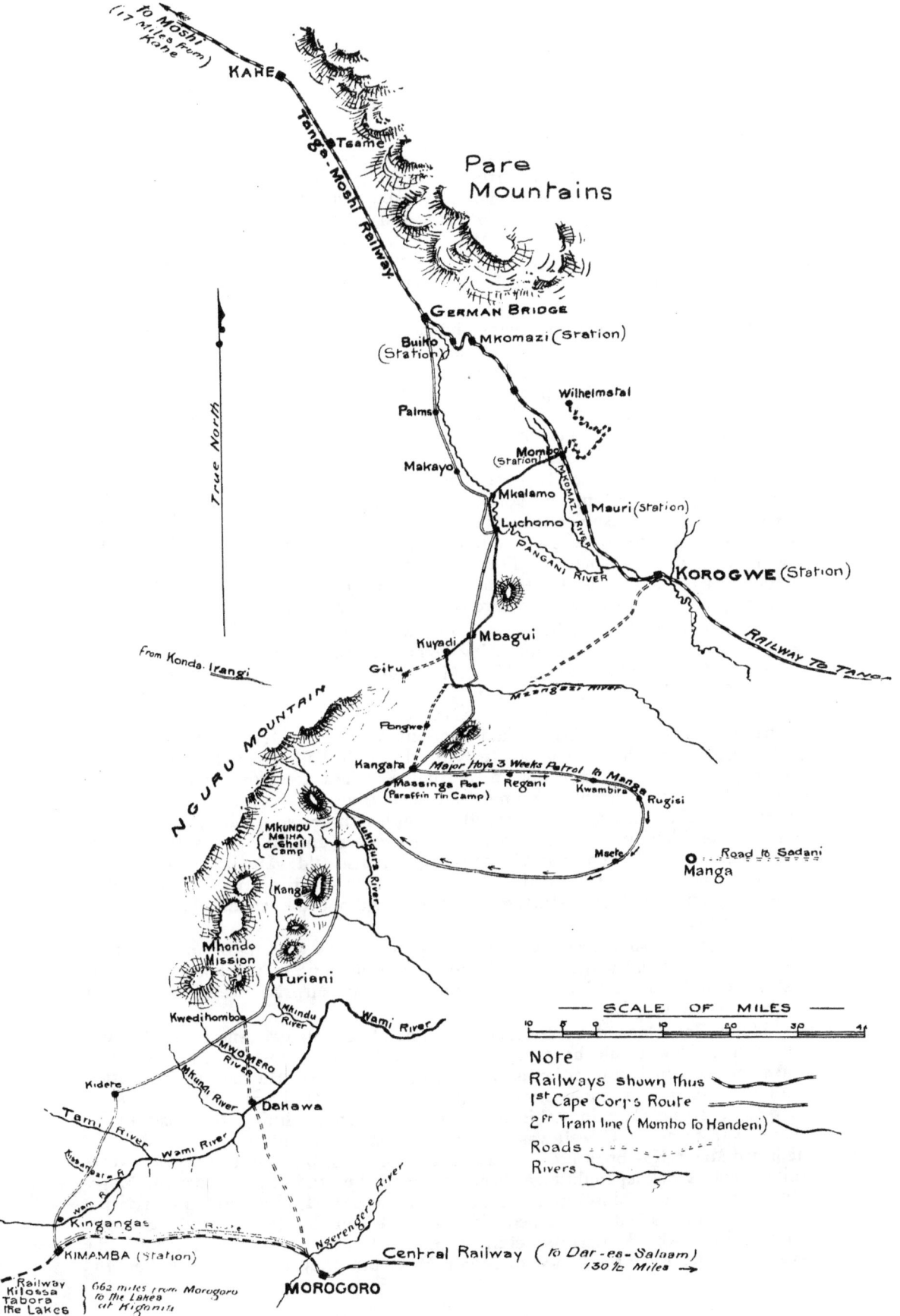

MAP ILLUSTRATING THE BATALLION'S ADVANCE IN GERMAN EAST AFRICA.
From Kahe (Tanga-Moshi Railway) to Morogoro (Central Railway), June-September, 1916.

Massinga Post where Hosack fell had been an enemy petrol store, but one of our aeroplanes having located it with a bomb, all that was left was a huge collection of empty tins. Henceforth the camp was known to us as Paraffin Tin Camp, and many officers and men of the battalion will long remember it, some by reason of the plague of jigger fleas, and other—Lieutenant Robertson's detachment—for a night attack on the post by lions. This latter incident would afford amusing reading, but unfortunately so many different stories of the affair were related that the real truth was in this case at least not readily ascertainable.

Additional pests in this area were the inevitable mosquitos—hordes of them—snakes, scorpions, spiders, the latter usually large and particularly formidable looking tarantulas, and ants. The latter were of two kinds, the white ant which lived on one's food, apparel, or ground sheets, eating great holes in the latter articles, and the red ant (known as the soldier ant), a fierce and fiery pest which attacked one's person.

General Louis Botha, on a visit to the South African Forces in East Africa, passed through our camp at Kangata shortly before the end of July to visit the most advanced troops, and extraordinary precautions were taken to keep the enemy mine-layers in subjection. The day before he passed through Private Demos (No. 220) located a mine and, though inexperienced in their handling, dug it out and demolished it. For this act he was deservedly awarded the Military Medal, and thus gained the coveted honour of being the first man of the Cape Corps to receive an award during the great war.

On Thursday, July 27th, Major Hoy was sent east from Kangata on a three days' patrol with the following officers, viz., Captains Cowell and Robinson; Lieutenants Arnott, Ashley, Macintosh, Pearse, T. Rose-Innes, Tandy and two I.D. Officers (Lieutenants Percival and Birkett) and a detachment of two hundred men. Their instructions were first to attack the enemy party of which Lieutenants Tandy and Arnott had brought in news a few days previously (*vide* page 63) and then to co-operate with the 40th Pathans and clear up the country round Manga, direction east from Kangata towards Sadani on the coast, before the Division's imminent advance from Lukigura. This job was expected to take three days but actually occupied three weeks and, but for the assistance of friendly natives, who provided carriers and sold them food, they would have starved. The party's native guide also did valuable work, being very keen and clever. During the night of the first surprise attack he led three different parties to their respective objectives without the enemy being aware of their presence.

This guide also helped very much by telling us which of our Jumbis (porters) to trust and which not. On his suggestion one of the suspect Jumbis was kept under a guard during the night of the surprise attack mentioned in the next paragraph.

Major Hoy planned a simultaneous night attack on two enemy posts and, with a little luck, would have captured the entire posts, instead of a few men and some arms and ammunition as was actually the case. He took up a position with the Rexer gun under Lieutenant Arnott well in front of the enemy's pickets, and sent Captain Robinson to make a detour, lining the road in V-shape, whilst Captain Cowell was to attack a post half a mile further on directly he heard Major Hoy open fire. Considering the thick bush and darkness everything went as well as could have been expected, but the enemy between Major Hoy and Captain Robinson were so surprised and scared, that instead of retiring by the footpath as had been hoped, they scattered on the flanks in all directions leaving food, kit, documents, etc., behind. Captain Cowell expected the enemy to offer some resistance to Major Hoy, but they fled helter skelter and he had to attack with the bayonet sooner than he expected. The enemy simply faded into the bush, leaving behind their food and kits and a few prisoners and rifles. Several men were wounded but got away in the thick bush and darkness. Important papers were captured and forwarded to G.H.Q.

The officer in charge of the enemy posts, who was one of their chief Intelligence Officers, got away in his pyjamas.

Shortly after the above attack Major Hoy got into touch with Lieut.-Colonel Mitchell, commanding 40th Pathans, who instructed him to report with his detachment at Manga as soon as possible.

They reported the same evening and the following day the whole column moved out under Mitchell to attack the enemy position.

Our intelligence agent reported that the enemy were strongly entrenched about two miles away, and that the approach thereto was grassy. The grass and bush proved so thick that two hours were occupied in getting into deploying position and it was impossible to advance in extended order. The men had literally to drag themselves through the undergrowth. Lieutenant Tandy, who had one part of the attacking line, was much concerned when he lost touch with a handful of his platoon (who had got into the support line) but he was somewhat consoled when the 40th Pathans machine gun officer told him that he had lost a double company.

After about an hour's hard work our scouts reported that the enemy had cleared the night before and that only a few men remained. They fired a few shots and then disappeared into the bush.

On August 1st the G.O.C. passed through our camp at Kangata and, in a brief interview with Lieut.-Colonel Morris informed him that we were to be increased by two double companies, i.e., from four to six double companies, or approximately from ten hundred and fifty-six to fifteen hundred men. This was an unique establishment authorised especially for the Cape Corps owing to the number of recruits coming forward. It is a great pity that another battalion was not at once authorised and placed under the command of Major Hoy. A second battalion was in fact formed several months afterwards. Lieut.-Colonel Flindt was gazetted first C.O. of the 2nd Battalion, but only retained the command for a few weeks. On his resignation the command was given to Lieut.-Colonel J. G. B. Clayton, M.C. (who had done good service in South-West Africa with the 12th Citizen Battery and in East Africa with the XIth S.A.I. and on the Staff). Under Clayton the 2nd Battalion did good work in Central Africa with General Northey's force for several months during the latter half of 1917 and early in 1918. About May, 1918, they were disbanded and the majority of the officers released from service. A few of the officers and all the men were transferred to the 1st Battalion and a number of them arrived in Egypt in time to see service on the Palestine front.

Lieut.-General Smuts also informed our O.C. that recruits were to come forward from the Union at the rate of ten per centum per mensem and that we were likely to be on the move again shortly.

On August 3rd Brig.-General Hannyngton returned with his brigade from the reconnaissance to the east of the Korogwe-Handeni road. On Saturday, August 5th, Lieut.-Colonel Morris left Kangata with all available men and marched through Massinga Post to Lukigura. Captain Anderson was left behind at Kangata in charge of our sick, about two hundred, who were comfortably housed in large, airy bandas (huts built of reeds and dried grass, etc.), which the C.O. had caused to be erected for their accommodation.

Fortunately only one night was spent at Lukigura, the Division leaving for Kimbe to make a wide flanking movement in order to endeavour to turn the enemy's left flank at Mohonda Mission and clear them out of the Nguru Mountains. The Field Artillery, however, could not get through that way owing to bad roads, so the Cape Corps were sent back the following day with them, and two days later left to escort them through Msiha (or Makindu: Shell Camp) along the main road through Kanga camp to Turiani, where the whole division concentrated again.

When the battalion left Lukigura to go forward Lieut.-Colonel Morris had less than two hundred and fifty of all ranks with him, the balance, nearly one thousand, being scattered as follows: Two hundred with Captain Youart on lines of communication at Korogwe (Tanga-Moshi line), two hundred with Major Hoy still out on the Manga "stunt," two hundred or more unfit at Kangata with Captain Anderson, fifty at Massinga Post, and the remainder in various hospitals along lines of communication, some as far back as Moshi, Voi, and even Nairobi, whilst about fifty had by then been invalided back to South Africa.

Between August 10th and 14th, however, Major Hoy and all officers and men with him rejoined. On August 16th news came through that the enemy had got away from our pursuit across the Mkindu River, afterwards blowing up the bridge. This was a great calamity, as it was common knowledge that the G.O.C. had completed his plans for thoroughly surrounding them. Those on the spot knew full well why the expected coup did not materialise. To blame others, however, is not the purpose and province of this book. Suffice it to say that if Smuts had not been let down the German East African campaign would have been over before the end of the month.

At Turiani the 25th Royal Fusiliers, the Gold Coast Regiment and the Cape Corps were sent forward to rebuild the bridge over the Mkindu River, and the Division then concentrated again at Ruhungu (or Kwedihombo), where the G.O.C. laid his plans for the attack on Morogoro.

Major-General Van Deventer's Division advancing east from Dodoma on the central railway had meantime reached Kilossa, and the enemy were entrenched in force on the far side of the Wami River. The Cape Corps were then sent forward with instructions to effect a junction with Van Deventer's force at Kimamba, seventeen miles east of Kilossa, but on reaching the Tami River were ordered to wait there as Van Deventer had been held up at Kilossa. Meanwhile our main force had advanced across the Wami River and were driving the enemy before them in the direction of Morogoro, Brig.-General Shepperd's brigade being sent out on the left flank to endeavour to cut off the enemy to the south and east of Morogoro.

When Van Deventer had driven off the enemy at Kilossa we moved on and effected junction with him at Kimamba, on the Central Railway, and the following day received orders to go on to Morogoro, where we arrived on Saturday, September 2nd. For the first week we were camped on the flat north of the railway and experienced much discomfort owing to the swampy nature of the ground and heavy rains. A move across the line and about five hundred feet up the mountain side to the old German askari barracks was, however, a great improvement, and there we spent three passably comfortable months. The rest gave Captain McNeil an opportunity of pulling the Battalion's health together, and by working overtime he effected wonders before the next move orders were received. He was very much aided by the fact that the men were quartered in substantial buildings.

During the past three months, *i.e.*, since leaving German Bridge, we had been continuously on short rations, sometimes receiving only half the scale laid down, sometimes a quarter, and occasionally none at all. When the latter happened, however, it was generally possible for the O.C. to purchase sufficient from the surrounding friendly natives to sustain life. At the same time this food scarcity was a very serious matter for troops weakened by dysentry and malaria, and it can never be known how many deaths recorded as due to those

THE STORY OF THE 1st CAPE CORPS.

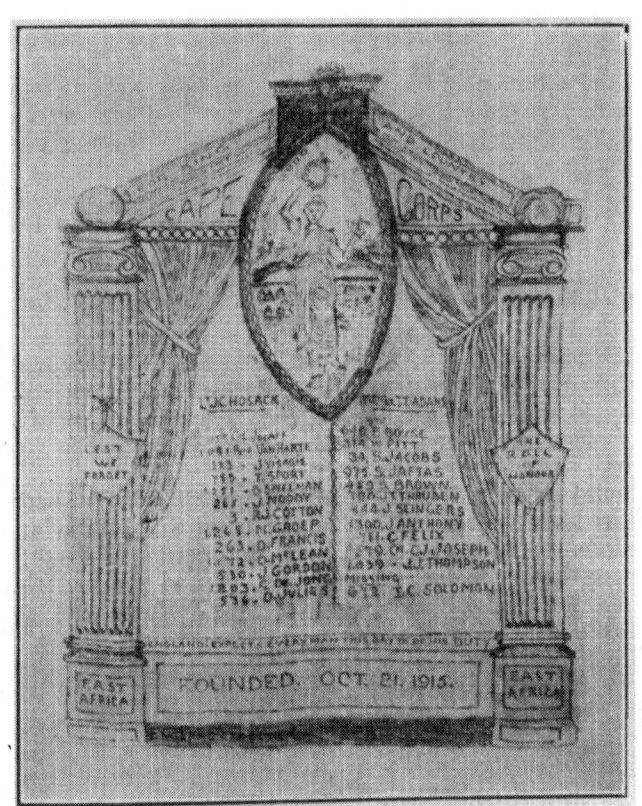

OUR FIRST ANNIVERSARY ROLL OF HONOUR.
Designed and drawn at Morogoro by R.Q.M.S. Betts on the lining of a sugar ration bag with a carbon pencil.

two causes were really attributable to starvation or malnutrition. Full army rations are quite good enough for healthy men, but invalids badly needed hospital diet, which was at that time practically unobtainable.

Shortly after reaching Morogoro we ceased to be divisional troops, being transferred to the 2nd Brigade of the 3rd East African Division commanded by Major-General Coen Brits.

On Thursday, September 7th, the British possession and occupation of Morogoro was impressed upon the local inhabitants, native as well as Hun, by the official hoisting of the Union Jack in the Market Square with appropriate ceremonial and dignity, all troops within reach being paraded for the occasion.

On October 15th Major Hoy left, accompanied by Captain Tandy, for Tanga, via Dar-es-Salaam, to take charge of and train some six hundred men who had gathered there *ex* hospitals and old lines of communication posts, etc. Captain Youart had moved from Korogwe to Amani and thence to Tanga with over two hundred men, and all men discharged from the base hospitals had also been concentrated there. In addition, Captain Stevens had arrived there from the Union via Kilindini towards the end of August with fifty-one men, Lieutenant Hallier with fifty-three more on 12th October, and 2nd Lieutenant W. S. Heaton with fifty-four men on November 7th. The men were trained and brought to a high state of efficiency, and the extended order work learned by some of the new recruits stood them in very good stead later on. As soon as a troopship was available they were brought by sea from Tanga to Dar-es-Salaam on H.M.A.T. "Himalaya."

On October 21st we held an all-day sports meeting to celebrate the first anniversary of the formation of the regiment. All the usual athletic and military events were included in the programme and, the weather being splendid, a most enjoyable day was spent. The day ended with a most successful concert and a large number of officers and men from other units at Morogoro were our guests at both functions.

Here it should be noted that Dar-es-Salaam had been occupied on 6th September by our forces advancing along the coast via Sadani and Bagamoyo. Rail communication between the coast and Morogoro could not, however, be established at once, owing to lack of rolling stock and the fact that the enemy had blown up all the bridges and culverts. This railway had evidently been constructed regardless of cost. It was, of course, metre gauge, its formation width being three and a half metres on embankments and three metres in cuttings, and the bridges, culverts, station buildings, etc., were all first-class structures of splendid workmanship, good stone being always used. There were workshops at Dar-es-Salaam, Morogoro, Kilossa, Dodoma, and Tabora, and at Dar-es-Salaam and Morogoro electric power plants. There were wells at many stations and telephones at all. There had been travelling cranes on the line and two inspection coaches. The locomotives were the product of five different German firms and the passenger and goods wagons of both the two-axle and bogie truck type and the goods wagons of ten and twenty-ton (metric) loading capacity. The wires were carried on Mannesmann tubes, increased in height in the giraffe country. At Kilo 86 there was a bridge four hundred and eighty-eight metres in length, with a clear opening of four hundred metres spanning a deep ravine. This had been entirely destroyed, and with it a great quantity of rolling stock, including several engines which had been run on to the bridge before the charge was ignited. The crazy folly and waste of war was very forcibly brought home to one by that dump of once valuable engines, etc., now a mere mass of twisted and useless old iron at the bottom of the ravine. But vain regrets for what might have been being of no avail, the South African Pioneer Corps, under Lieut.-Colonel J. H. Dobson (General Manager, Johannesburg Tramways) tackled the job of repairing the line with magnificent energy and such success

THE STORY OF THE 1st CAPE CORPS.

Photos by]   *[J.H.T.*

A LECTURE ON MACHINE GUNS BY CAPTAIN F. BURGER.
HUN DESTRUCTION ON THE CENTRAL RAILWAY.

A TRACTOR LOAD ON THE CENTRAL RAILWAY.
ON SAFARI. A MID-DAY HALT—NAUMANN STUNT.
(See Chapter IX.)

DISEMBARKING FROM TUG AT LINDI.
(See Chapter XII.)

Photo by]   *[J.H.T.*

GENERAL LOUIS BOTHA AND LT.-GENERAL SMUTS IN CAR AT KANGATA SPEAKING TO LT.-COLONEL MORRIS (STANDING).

that towards the end of October the line was through. A wide deviation of two or three miles overcame the impossibility of replacing the big bridge at Kilo 86 above mentioned. Rolling stock was *en route* from India and also so much as could be spared by the British East Africa Railway Company was sent from Kilindini, but pending the arrival of the latter Lieut.-Colonel J. G. Rose improvised trains out of our big Reo motor lorries by fixing to them railway wheels and axles very considerately left at Morogoro by the enemy, and using a Reo lorry engine as the propelling force. These trains consisted of an engine and three or four tractors, each capable of carrying from ten to fifteen tons, and did the journey from Dar-es-Salaam to Morogoro in twelve hours.

The effect of this on the supply position can readily be appreciated as, until rail connection was established, all supplies had to come by road from Korogwe via Handeni. This, under the most favourable conditions, occupied three days, but frequently took a week or more, owing to heavy rains and the collapse of the temporary bridges. The maximum lorry load by road was only three tons, and the strain on the cars and drivers, owing to the bad roads, was so great that the service was in grave danger of breaking down altogether.

On the 18th October information was received that the 3rd Division was to be disbanded and that the majority of the South African units were to be returned to the Union. The authorities had come to the conclusion that the country was more or less impossible for European troops and therefore intended to finish the campaign with coloured and native units as far as possible. Of the latter there was a large number available, viz., several battalions each of Indians and King's African Rifles, a Nigerian brigade, the Gold Coast Regiment, West African Rifles, Indian artillery, and ourselves.

The disbandment of the 2nd S.A. Mounted Brigade commenced at once, but one regiment was formed out of fit men of the brigade and attached to the 1st Mounted Brigade of the 2nd Division under Major-General J. L. van Deventer. On October 25th we were posted to Force Reserve under Brig.-General P. S. Beves (later C.B., C.M.G.), who gave us a very hearty welcome and reception.

On November 6th Brig.-General Beves, accompanied by his Staff, inspected the battalion on the ground we had cleared for our sports on the 21st ultimo. The inspection lasted two hours and was a very thorough and searching one, especially in respect of the machine gunners and signallers, who were put through firing and signalling tests respectively. It was understood that the Brigadier expressed himself as entirely satisfied with what he had seen.

About this time an appreciable percentage of the battalion were still in such a poor state of health that, in order to eliminate the unfits before the next move, a special medical board visited our camp and boarded all invalids. The result was that four officers and one hundred and thirty-seven other ranks were declared temporarily unfit for further tropical service and ordered to be returned to South Africa as hospital ship accommodation became available. It was well that this was done, as the Rufiji River operations, then on the tapis, were carried out during the rainy season and in one of the worst fever areas in the whole country. It is certain that if those one hundred and forty odd officers and men had gone to the Rufiji a good many would have never returned.

At the end of October the Brigadier informed our C.O. that the advance to the Rufiji River was expected to commence the next week, but it proved to be actually six weeks later before we moved. During the intervening period a number of the abovementioned one hundred and forty-one officers and men "boarded unfits," whose departure by hospital ship was delayed, recovered sufficiently to go forward, and it must be recorded greatly to their credit that scarcely a man wished to be sent back, in fact there was great anxiety to be re-boarded and declared fit.

THE STORY OF THE 1st CAPE CORPS.

On November 18th Lieut.-Colonel Morris went to Zanzibar on ten days' leave and, Major Hoy being still at Tanga, Major Cowell assumed temporary command of the battalion.

When the C.O. returned he brought the news on reliable authority that we were to proceed to Egypt at the end of the East African campaign. This was good news indeed and everybody hoped more fervently than ever for the termination of the present campaign.

Shortly after arrival at Morogoro we had handed in our ox transport and been issued with mules, but the deaths from disease of the latter, and the officers' chargers as well, were very heavy and it was not surprising that the G.O.C. had decided practically to eliminate mounted troops for the future. Not even the British Imperial Exchequer could long stand the loss of valuable animals at the rate of actually hundreds (in the whole force) per diem. The wastage of horse flesh in some of the mounted regiments had averaged very nearly one hundred per cent. per month.

On December 5th, Major Hoy with Captain Tandy and Lieutenants Youart, Murchie and Hallier and three hundred men arrived from Tanga via Dar-es-Salaam, and on the same day Major Durham arrived at Dar-es-Salaam from South Africa with the following officers, viz. :—Captains W. J. R. Cuningham, W. Jardine and Gordon C. White; Lieutenants H. Coates, R. Feetham, Ivor Guest, A. A. Hayton, T. E. James, A. Leslie, M. Potgieter and H. R. Thornton and one thousand and fifty men. These officers and men came on to Morogoro at once by special trains, and by December 10th we had nearly two thousand men in camp. Captain Gordon White voluntarily reverted to Lieutenant at his own request immediately on arrival at Morogoro, this being the only possible way to correct a mistake by the Union Defence Department in erroneously gazetting him captain on his appointment to the battalion and thus promoting him over the heads of some twenty officers who had been in the field with the battalion for several months.

On December 12th, the move south towards the Rufiju River began, Major Hoy leaving in the afternoon for Kissake with about seven hundred and fifty men ("B" and "C" Companies) and the C.O. followed on the morning of the 14th with seven hundred and seventy men of "A" and "D" Companies. The total marching out strength of the battalion, including machine gun porters, officers' servants, transport drivers and other followers exceeded one thousand seven hundred men.

Captain Jardine remained at Morogoro as O.C. Force Reserve Depot, having with him Lieutenants Potgieter and Guest (as acting Adjutant and Q.M.R., respectively) and all unfit men. Captain Difford and Lieutenant Pearse also remained behind and were invalided to South Africa on December 18th. 2nd Lieutenant N. F. Howe-Browne was later on appointed acting Q.M.R. during Captain Difford's absence.

The battalion travelled very light, viz., one A.T. cart per Platoon and fourteen A.T. carts for ammunition, Q.M.R., Signallers, Medicals, Headquarters and Machine Gun section. Pack Mules for reserve ammunition. One pack donkey for two officers for kit. One pack donkey per Company Officers' mess.

During the period covered by this chapter, the following promotions and changes in personnel, etc., took place :—

At Bissil, February 24th, Captain Campbell was admitted to hospital as the result of a severe kick from one of his pack mules, and Captain Bradstock took charge of the Machine Gun Section during his absence of several weeks.

At Kidongai, on February 26th, the Battalion Scouts were organised and Sergeant S. W. Dunn (1134) placed in charge, the others being :—Lance-Corporal J. Haynes (315), Lance-Corporal H. Johnson (474), Privates L. Rudolph (18), H. Jassen (104), J. Burger (243), J. Visagie (383), P. Adams (1307), A. Africa (675), P Carolus (1177) J. Moodie (268), J. Swartz

THE STORY OF THE 1ST CAPE CORPS.

Photo by] [Sergeant H. W. Herman, Kimberley.
C.Q.M.S. A. J. HENDRICKS, D.C.M. (1067).

FATHER AND SON
Private F. Rensburg (3430), father; Private F. Rensburg (2987), son.

SERGEANT-MAJOR F. J. SHIPP (MEDICALS).

Photo by] [J. G. Horsfall, Cape Town.
SERGEANT D. A. WILKINSON (1253).

THE STORY OF THE 1st CAPE CORPS.

(331), J. Langeveldt (1279) and J. Sauls (332). These men having been duly trained were then distributed between the four companies.

At Namanga, on February 28th, Lieutenant J. Arnott, Transport Officer, rejoined with officers' chargers, which he had been to Kilindini to fetch, these having come from South Africa on another vessel.

Corporal H. Stockenstroom was transferred to us from 5th S.A. Infantry on March 1st and posted to "A" Company as Platoon Sergeant. On March 1st, twelve men who had qualified as signallers were granted proficiency pay. These included No. 825 Lance-Corporal Alies, J., who afterwards became Signalling Sergeant and the Signalling Officer's right hand man for over two years.

At Geraragua, on March 14th, the following European N.C.O.'s reported to us for duty and were posted Platoon Sergeants, viz.: Sergeants B. E. Scott, C. M. O'Driscoll (1188), C. S. H. Gardner (6876) and A. G. Sumner.

At the beginning of April our first draft of fifty-one other ranks arrived from the depôt (Simonstown) under Lieutenant W. W. Alexander, and a day or two later (5th April) Lieutenant R. Wilson and forty-eight other ranks.

Private Marthinus van Haarte (1081), who died in hospital at Moshi (24.3.16), was the first of many to succumb to fever during our stay at Moshi (March-June, 1916), and before we left there several deaths had occurred and a number of men had been invalided back to South Africa.

On May 12th 2nd Lieutenant E. J. Rackstraw arrived from South Africa with a draft of one hundred men.

On May 13th Major Durham left for South Africa to take over command of our Regimental Depot, and Captain W. P. Anderson succeeded to the command of "A" Company. Two weeks later Captain R. M. Robb, S.A.M.C. (who on joining in the previous November had stipulated that he could only remain on service for six months) left us to return to South Africa, handing over his medical duties to Captain R. P. McNeil, S.A.M.C., who remained with us for eighteen months and did magnificent service throughout, gaining the Military Cross in the following January. On May 26th, Lieutenant R. Wilson was seconded to the Works Department for engineer duties (road and bridge making, etc.).

During the last week in May, several men were invalided to the Union of South Africa including two European N.C.O.'s, viz.: C.S.M. Cassidy, M.C. (1050), and Sergeant Lee, A. H. (1371) who did not return to the battalion, and C.S.M. Paterson, D. A., followed them on 21st June. Platoon Sergeant Craigen, W. (1439) took the latter's place as C.S.M.

Private I. C. Solomon (672) disappeared from a patrol sent out from Lembani on June 6th. It is presumed that he was 'got' by a lion as he was never seen or heard of again and was declared "missing."

On June 16th, Lieutenant F. C. Hallier was invalided to the Union of South Africa and Lieutenants W. W. Procter and S. W. Whitaker were transferred to the King's African Rifles. The vacancies were filled by the promotion of the following European N.C.O.'s to be 2nd Lieutenants, viz.: R.Q.M.S. J. C. Hosack, C.S.M. R. A. Cloke, Platoon Sergeant C. S. H. Gardner. Cloke's promotion did not actually go through orders, however, until June 30th, and in the interim he acted as R.Q.M.S., vice Hosack promoted, handing over duties of R.Q.M.S. on last named date to Sergeant J. Wilkes (1443) (European).

At German Bridge, on June 23rd, Lieutenant Harland S. Bell, with ninety-seven other ranks, joined up from our South African depôt. Lieutenant Bell having handed over his draft was transferred immediately to the East African Political Department.

On July 3rd, Pay Sergeant E. Harris (European) was transferred to the South African Pay Corps. Platoon Sergeant T. C. Adams (1139) (European) died at Moshi on July 8th from septic poisoning after several weeks illness and intense suffering borne with great fortitude.

To fill the vacancy caused by 2nd Lieutenant Hosack's death, C.S.M. W. T. Wigman (1051) was promoted 2nd Lieutenant on 21.7.16.

Captain F. J. Bagshawe left us on 14th September to join the Political Service, and Captain H. G. Warr succeeded to the command of "C" Company, whilst Lieutenant W. J. R. Cuningham received the vacant Captaincy and was promoted a Company Commander (thus jumping one step, viz., 2nd in command of a company). At the same time Sergeant-Major N. F. Howe Browne (from Despatch Riders) joined us and was promoted 2nd Lieutenant, vice Cuningham.

A week later our Adjutant, Captain W. G. Gunningham, followed Bagshawe to the Political Service. Captain Bradstock became Adjutant and Captain J. E. Robinson took Bradstock's place as Officer Commanding "D" Company. At the same time R.Q.M.S. Wilkes was seconded to the S.A.S.C. (M.T.) and Orderly room Sergeant F. W. Betts was promoted R.Q.M.S. (22.9.16). Three weeks later Wilkes returned and was then transferred to the Regimental Depot (S.A.).

THE STORY OF THE 1st CAPE CORPS.

On September 26th, Captains Anderson and Cuningham left to return to South Africa, the former to take over command of the Depot at Woltemade III., and the latter to take command of a company at the Depot and bring them forward at once.

In September, at Morogoro, the following subalterns received their captaincy: Lieutenant D. W. Robertson (21.9.16) vice Major Durham, transferred to Depot (S.A.); Lieutenant F. Burger (21.9.16) vice Captain Gunningham to Political Department. Lieutenants J. E. Dennison and J. H. Tandy (27.9.16) vice Captains Anderson and Cuningham, transferred to Depot (S.A.), and at the same time C.S.M. Greenhead (1338) was transferred to King's African Rifles. Captains Dennison, Burger and Tandy became 2nd in command of "A," "B" and "D" companies, respectively.

On September 30th, Staff Sergeant R. Akehurst (1438) (European) was transferred to the A.P.M.'s staff at Morogoro and became gaoler there. On October 10th Corporal R. A. Thompson (3695) was transferred to us from 5th S.A.H. and became 2nd Lieutenant and Signalling Officer vice Lieutenant Dennison, promoted.

At Morogoro, in October, Armourer Sergeant G. H. Pepper was invalided to the Union, and Corporal J. H. van Rooyen (1270) was promoted Sergeant and Acting Armourer. Van Rooyen had been trained and received his certificate at the School of Instruction at Morogoro. His case furnished one more proof of the fact that if properly trained the Cape coloured man was fully capable of filling all the non-commissioned officers' ranks in the battalion. Indeed, this fact had so fully impressed itself on the Commanding Officer that before the end of the year he had replaced all the European N.C.O.'s by coloured men, with the exception of the R.S.M., R.Q.M.S. and Medical Staff Sergeant,—those Europeans who had not already been invalided back to the Union (quite a number) being transferred to other units. In this connection the following promotions went through orders on 11th November at Morogoro with effect from 18.9.16:—

No. 1092 Acting C.S.M. D. Twynham to be C.S.M. "B" Company.
No. 111 Acting C.S.M. W T. McLeod to be C.S.M. "C" Company,
No. 152 Acting C.S.M. C. Calvert to be C.S.M. "D" Company;

the below-named European N.C.O.'s having been invalided to South Africa and taken on strength of our Depot there, viz.:—

No. 1053 C.S.M. Clennell,
No. 1361 S. Sgt. N. O. Harvey,
S. Sgt. A. G. Sumner;

Photo by] [I.D.D.
HEADQUARTERS SWAHILI SERVANTS AND KITCHEN AT MOROGORO.

OUR CAMP AT KAHE.

THE STORY OF THE 1st CAPE CORPS.

and the following transferred to the Carrier Corps, viz. :—
>No. 1180 Staff Sgt. M. O. Driscoll,
>Staff Sgt. B. E. Scott.

At Morogoro, the following officers joined up in connection with the increased establishment from four to six double companies which had now been duly authorised, viz :—

>Lieutenant H. Walton from S.A.I. Reinforcements (30.10.16).
>Private T. Bain (4921) from 9th S.A. Horse and promoted 2nd Lieutenant (30.10.16).
>Lance-Corporal Edgar Stubbs from 6th S.A.I. and promoted 2nd Lieutenant (30.10.16).
>Corporal George Horseman (246) from 4th S.A. Horse and to be 2nd Lieutenant (14.11.16).
>Trooper A. F. Bourhill (5363) from 5th S.A. Horse and to be 2nd Lieutenant (13.11.16).
>Private E. H. Browne (534) from 4th S.A. Horse and to be 2nd Lieutenant (15.11.16).

On October 27th Captain Campbell was invalided to South Africa and Captain Burger assumed command of the Machine Gun section, of which he continued in command until the battalion was finally demobilised in September, 1919.

On the 6th November Captain H. G. Warr was seconded for employment in the Political Department and placed on the Supernumerary list and Lieutenant J. M. Michau received his captaincy to complete establishment, and became 2nd in command of "D" Company on 1.12.16., vice Captain Tandy transferred to 2nd in command "B" Company, vice Captain Burger to Machine Gun section.

During November Lieutenants Arnott, Alexander and Edwards and ninety-four other ranks were invalided to South Africa. At the beginning of December, 2nd Lieutenants Wigman and Heaton were transferred to the Machine Gun section and Lieutenant Gardner was placed in charge of ammunition, the Machine Gun section establishment having been increased from eight to twelve guns.

On December 10th R.S.M. George Forsythe (1141) left us and Staff Sergeant R. Akehurst (1438) returned to us from A.P.M.'s staff at Morogoro and became R.S.M., and Sergeant C. A. Ruiters (132) C.S.M. On December 10th, 2nd Lieutenant Howe Browne was appointed Assistant Adjutant and on December 13th Lieutenant R. Wilson rejoined from the Road Corps.

Photo by] [A. L. Pepper, Cape Town.
CAPTAIN ALAN EARP-JONES (CHAPLAIN).

Photo by] [Sydney Taylor, Cape Town.
CAPTAIN S. ASHLEY.

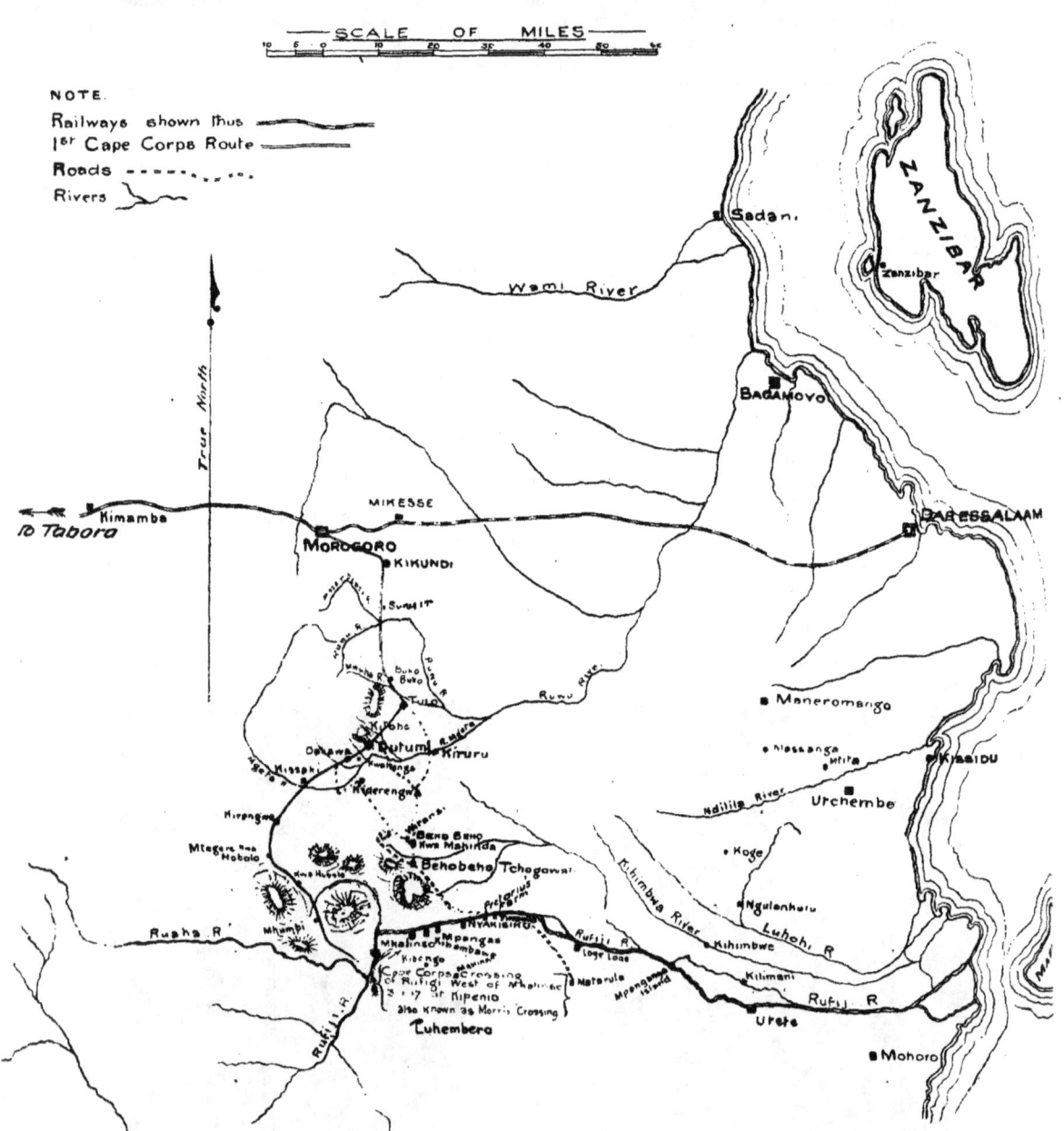

MAP ILLUSTRATING OPERATIONS ON THE RUFIJI RIVER (GERMAN EAST AFRICA).
December, 1916, to March, 1917.

CHAPTER VI.

THE RUFIJI RIVER CAMPAIGN (12TH DECEMBER, 1916, TO 21ST MARCH, 1917).

MAJOR HOY left Morogoro on the afternoon of December 12th with "B" and "C" Companies and two machine gun sections, in all approximately seven hundred and fifty of all ranks. Captains Cowell and Cuningham commanded "B" and "C" Companies, respectively. The respective seconds in command were Captains Tandy and Dennison.

The remainder of the battalion, under Lieut.-Colonel Morris, marched out of Morogoro in pouring rain on the morning of December 14th, accompanying Force Reserve, under Brig.-General P. S. Beves, C.B.

"A" Company was under Major Durham with Captain Robertson as second in command.

Captain Robinson commanded "D" Company and Captain Michau was his second in command. All ranks of the battalion numbered over fifteen hundred, or with porters, native servants, etc., about seventeen hundred.

With the exception of two or three who were provided with Abyssinian mules all officers were on foot. Horses could not exist in the Rufiji River swamps.

Our transport consisted of A.T. carts drawn by mules and donkeys. These were utilised as far as Kissaki. From there animal transport became impossible owing to the bad roads and unhealthy nature of the country. Mechanical transport was also out of the question south of Kissaki, and man power (native porters) became the sole means of conveying munitions, rations, etc.

Although our six double company establishment had been authorised in November, the necessary reorganisation was not possible before we left Morogoro, owing to the non-arrival in time of sufficient officers from the depôt, and the four companies therefore marched out of Morogoro each about three hundred to three hundred and twenty-five strong.

The battalion, in fact, never at any time during its career went into action more than four companies strong, the two extra companies, when formed later on, remaining in reserve in our various depôts, first at Morogoro, afterwards at Kimberley (March to July, 1918) and finally in Egypt and Palestine (August, 1918, to May, 1919).

The route taken from Morogoro to the Rufiji River was practically due south to Kissaki, via Summit, Tulo, Dutumi and Dakawa.

Captain Dennison was left at Tulo with Lieutenants White and Bain and one hundred and forty-four riflemen of "C" Company on December 18th, with instructions to hold that post, which he took over from Major James of the 29th Punjabis.

The rain which began on leaving Morogoro continued with few and brief fine intervals until the battalion straggled back to that place towards the end of March a weary and fever-stricken remnant of the proud regiment that had marched out full of hope of high endeavour three months earlier.

THE STORY OF THE 1st CAPE CORPS.

Photos by]   [*J.H.T.*
PORTERS CARRYING BERTHON BOATS FOR OUR CROSSING OF THE RUFIJI RIVER.   OUR NATIVE STRETCHER BEARERS.

Photos by]   [*J.H.T.*
OUR CRACK GAME SHOT, CAPTAIN J. E. ROBINSON, WITH A VICTIM IN EAST AFRICA.   MAJOR C. N. HOY AND CAPTAIN R. P. McNEIL, S.A.M.C., AT DUTUMI   A CAPE CORPS DETACHMENT UNDER MAJOR HOY CROSSING THE RUWU RIVER.

THE STORY OF THE 1st CAPE CORPS.

Major Hoy reached Dutumi on the evening of December 19th and the next day took over from Lieut.-Colonel R. A. Lyall of the Kashmir Rifles, who had been in that position for some weeks and had contrived to keep the place out of sight of the enemy's guns. Duties there were strenuous. Fires were not permissible and special arrangements had to be made by night to feed those on outpost duty. We had two field guns and, though we were subjected to continuous sniping and shelling, the enemy did not succeed in locating our camp or the guns.

Christmas day was spent at Dutumi, where dinner consisted of bully beef and biscuits, and none too much of that.

It rained all day and the following day, on which the battalion left Dutumi at 5.30 a.m., leaving Major Durham with six hundred men of "C" and "D" Companies to garrison that place, and reached Dakawa five hours later. There Captain Cuningham took command of "A" Company vice Major Durham.

Here a patrol, under Lieutenant Murchie, exchanged shots wth the enemy at Kwahongo, in which Sergeant M. J. Abrahams (318) was severely wounded.

For three days we rested, waiting for our Forces to take up their respective positions, and then, on December 30th, made an early morning march into Kissaki, where we learned the dispositions for the coming offensive and the objective aimed at, namely, the ejection of the enemy from his trenches on the Mgeta River and the seizure of the passages of the Rufiji River.

On December 30th, Captain Jardine, from Morogoro, joined Major Durham at Dutumi as second in command, and the same day the following casualties occurred during skirmishes there, viz.:—

Killed: Private A. Harts (1369).

Wounded: Private A. Cornelius (80), dangerous; Corporal C. J. Petersen (1129), severely.

On Old Year's Day Lieut.-Colonel Lyall with the 4th Column, consisting of a Nigerian battalion with two 2.95 inch guns, and the 2nd Kashmiris, was lying at Kiruru; Force Reserve, under Brig.-General Beves, at Kissaki; the 2nd Brigade, under Brig.-General S. H. Sheppard, D.S.O., at Dakawa and Kissaki; and the Nigerian Brigade, under Brig.-General F. H. B. Cunliffe, C.B., C.M.G., at Dutumi. That night a portion of Sheppard's brigade was sent forward to execute a tactical flanking movement in the direction of Wiransi. At 4 a.m. on New Year's Day, Beves crossed the Mgeta River and at daybreak the Nigerians commenced to move southwards.

The G.O.C. directed and controlled operations from an observation post on Dutumi Hill.

The burning of the huts at Kiruru by Lyall at 7.30 a.m. on New Year's Day was the signal for everyone to engage the enemy, and everyone did so successfully. Sheppard got in with the bayonet on the north bank of the Wiransi River, and the Baluchis and Punjabis greatly enjoyed themselves, as they disturbed the enemy at breakfast and at the end of the day were happy and heavy with loot. The Nigerians, backed up by the Howitzer battery and 15-pounders and 4.1 inch naval guns, rushed their positions, whilst Lyall cut the enemy's line of retreat and captured a 6 inch Howitzer at Kiderengwa.

Our 4.1 inch naval guns opened on the enemy position at Dutumi at 11 a.m. the same morning.

Force Reserve were not in action that day, but the next day moved on a few miles beyond Kirengwe, whilst Lyall pushed on from Kiderengwa to Beho-Beho-Kwa-Mahinda and Sheppard was in action at Wiransi.

On January 1st our forces captured a number of European and Askari prisoners and a quantity of very useful loot. The hospital hut at Wiransi was in our hands and the German graveyard told its tale of European loss by fever.

"ON SAFARI" IN EAST AFRICA, CROSSING A RIVER.

CAPE CORPS AT THE RUFIJI RIVER, JANUARY, 1917.

(*A captured photo.*)
ENEMY WORKING ONE OF THE GUNS OF THE CRUISER "KOENIGSBERG" (DESTROYED BY OUR FORCES) ON THE RUFIJI RIVER.

THE STORY OF THE 1st CAPE CORPS.

At Kwa Mahinda, Sheppard and Lyall joined forces on January 2nd and advanced south to Beho-Beho-Tchogowali, where they became heavily engaged. Here it was that Captain Frederick Courtenay Selous, the great African hunter and explorer, was killed on his 65th birthday, gallantly leading his company of the 25th Royal Fusiliers, and there he lies buried under a tamarind tree with a few gallant members of the Legion of Frontiersmen.

On the afternoon of that day Sheppard and Lyall were held up at Kibambawe, and the G.O.C. accordingly instructed Beves, who had already marched ten miles that day, to push on a flying column to force a passage of the Rufiji River higher up at Makalinso. For this enterprise Lieut.-Colonel Morris was ordered to take five hundred men of his battalion, a section of the 1st Kashmir Mountain Battery, the Faridkot (Indian) Pioneers, four machine guns and six Berthon collapsible boats, the whole column being led by scouts under the famous Major Pretorius, D.S.O. This officer had been a trader and hunter in German East Africa for some time before the war. He had a farm close to Nyakisiki and therefore knew well every inch of this particular area. He had very quickly made a name as the greatest scout on the British side and earned the D.S.O. A few months earlier at Morogoro he had organised and trained the African Scouts Battalion who were composed of Askari captured from the enemy.

The flying column moved off at 2 p.m., January 2nd, and marched for twelve hours without a halt.

It is difficult to relate with sufficient realism the details of that march, especially the latter part of it in complete darkness, the strain of cutting and clearing a road for the guns, the sweating porters straggling along under the weight of the boats—three of them reeled out of the ranks and dropped dead by the roadside—the ceaseless vigilance exercised by the scouts, the instant readiness of the machine gunners and porters, the absence of lights, smoking or talking.

At 2 a.m. (3rd January) the column had covered close on thirty miles and an hour's halt was called within three miles of the crossing at Makalinso which Pretorius reported that he thought was held by the enemy. It was accordingly decided to cross two and a half miles west at Kipenio. Just as dawn broke the river bank was reached and the column dug in at once, the guns were posted and the Berthon boats rapidly assembled under cover of the forest.

Each boat carried a rower and two men. Lieutenant Harris was detailed to take the first party of twelve men across, having with him in his boat Sergeant Wilkinson (1253) and Private Bird (51).

There was great anxiety and tension as it was impossible in the half light to see if the enemy was entrenched and waiting for us on the south bank, and a few rifle shots would have sunk a boat. However, the rapidity of the forced march had evidently surprised the enemy, who was unsuspicious of our presence so near. The first boat got across safely and the two passengers scrambled out and up the bank and dug themselves in as quietly and rapidly as possible, while the rower rushed his boat back for another load.

This operation was repeated in absolute silence until the whole detachment was across and dug in on the south bank.

It should be mentioned that before the first boat was launched Pretorius deliberately rode along the bank to draw the enemy's fire if he were there, and the mountain guns were concealed in the bush covering the opposite bank and ready to plaster the enemy with shell if he opened fire.

By 7 a.m. Lieut.-Colonel Morris was able to report by wire to the Brigadier that his whole column was across and entrenched on the south bank of the river. The column had marched thirty-one miles, carried the boats, dragged the guns, cut the road, laid a telephone wire as they advanced, crossed the river and dug themselves in on the far side in seventeen hours. This was the biggest marching feat performed in East Africa up to that time (the Cape Corps excelled it themselves more than once later on) and brought a congratulatory wire from the G.O.C. to Lieut.-Colonel Morris: "On your brilliant achievement," whilst Reuter's correspondent wrote: "The Cape Corps are a credit to South Africa, and particularly to Cape Town."

When across the river our signallers rendered valuable assistance by tapping the enemy's telephone connections which helped greatly in locating their various posts.

Brig.-General Beves then moved up slowly and camped on the north bank of the river opposite us, where Captain Robertson had been left with one company.

During the first night in this camp a herd of hippopotami charged through our camp causing much excitement and alarm, it being at first thought that the enemy had surprised us. They did little damage except to stampede our cattle who cleared into the bush and only three or four out of a couple of dozen were recovered. This was a very serious loss as our meat ration was already short.

The following evening information was received that the enemy was still picketing the Makalinso Crossing, so at midnight Captain Cuningham, with Lieutenants Harris and James and one hundred men, was sent to attack them. This they successfully accomplished, killing, wounding or capturing the lot—six Europeans, thirty Askaris, and a large number of porters—without suffering any casualties themselves. They reached the enemy post at dawn and before they were observed had actually crept up close enough to see the Hun officers walking about in their pyjamas and having baths. Our men got in with the bayonet to their great delight, and created an absolute panic. Major Pretorius led and guided the above party.

On January 7th Beves, with Force Reserve, crossed at Kipenio.

Von Lettow was still holding up Sheppard's brigade at Kibambawe and sent a force to attack Beves on the south bank at Makalinso. But he was defeated and driven off by the 6th S.A. Infantry, under Lieut.-Colonel Molyneux, supported by the 1st Kashmir Mountain Battery, who pumped shells into the enemy with such telling effect that in a couple of hours he was compelled to evacuate his position and retire eastward along the river.

The 6th S.A.I.'s casualties were only one killed and a few wounded.

The Cape Corps, after their strenuous work of the past few days, were held in reserve, being detailed to protect the flanks of the 6th S.A.I., and did not come into action that day.

Force Reserve were then ordered to return to our original crossing at Kipenio, west of Makalinso, which became known as Morris' Crossing.

On January 5th, Major Pretorius' scouts had captured a large quantity of medical stores and telephone equipment on the south bank of the river.

Sheppard's fight at Kibambawe lasted two days (January 7th and 8th). His own camp was on the north bank of the river, where he had two field guns taken from the enemy, one, the howitzer, captured by Lyall near Kiruru and another found abandoned.

A battery of S.A. Field Artillery, under Major Gordon Grey (later D.S.O., M.C.), was supporting Sheppard. The latter's camp was under rifle and machine gun fire from the south bank, and a party who had managed to cross the river had to resist a determined attack by the enemy, who had evidently rallied and had brought up two field guns.

On January 9th, the whole force was camped on the south bank of the river, except two hundred and fifty of the Cape Corps, under Captain Robertson, on the north bank.

THE STORY OF THE 1st CAPE CORPS.

Thus, in little more than a week of wonderfully precise and effective operations, we had driven the enemy out of his strong positions on the Mgeta River, inflicted heavy casualties upon him and captured much valuable loot and medical stores. After an advance of thirty-five miles on a thirty mile front we had installed ourselves, with very light casualties, upon the south bank of the Rufiji and forced the enemy to retire south and east.

This was the last operation under the personal command of Lieut.-General Smuts and was remarkable for its swiftness, complete effectiveness and certainty, and for its strategic importance. It was a pity that Smuts could not remain to finish off Von Lettow and his gallant army, but he was needed for more important work elsewhere; so, having delayed his departure to the last moment in order to carry the campaign as far as possible, he handed over to Major-General A. R. Hoskins, C.M.G., D.S.O., and returned to South Africa.

On January 10th, Major Durham brought up his two companies from Dutumi, and Captain Jardine took over the command from Captain Robertson of the detachment on the north bank. The battalion then got a week's much needed rest. On January 13th, Private H. de Goede (2958) died of wounds (accidental) at Dutumi.

The enemy did a good deal of mine laying about this time, but Major Pretorius soon afterwards stalked and captured the chief culprit with all his murderous impedimenta.

On January 17th, the Nigerians who had arrived two days before via Kipenio were in action at Mkindu and at 6.30 a.m. that day Lieut.-Colonel Morris with a column marched out from Mkalinso to assist the Nigerians by attacking the enemy position at Mpangas in order to enable Sheppard's brigade to cross at Kibambawe.

The column consisted of twenty-nine officers, six hundred and eighty-five other ranks and six machine guns of 1st Cape Corps, 1st Kashmir Mountain Battery, a cable section, and a section of 2nd S.A. Field Ambulance, with necessary porters, etc.

Captain Jardine was left with a detachment of the Cape Corps to garrison Mkalinso.

On the night of the 17th and 18th we had a very trying march over the Hame escarpment, great difficulty being experienced in getting the mountain guns, the cable section and the loaded porters down the escarpment. A detour occupying several hours had to be made in order to get into position to attack Mpangas from the south.

During the morning of the 18th, contact was effected with the 130th Baluchis (Sheppard's brigade).

At daybreak on January 19th Major Durham was sent from Kibambawe with "A" Company and two machine guns and half a Kashmir Battery to attack the enemy post at Nyakisiki which the main force had evacuated, retiring south towards Utete.

The remainder of the Cape Corps, under Lieut.-Colonel Morris, proceeded to Mkindu at 10.30 a.m. on the 19th to reinforce the Nigerians. From there we could hear Durham engaging the enemy towards Nyakisiki. In the afternoon Lieut.-Colonel Morris was instructed to attack Kibongo, four miles further on and about three miles south-east of Mkindu towards Luhembero, with a force consisting of three companies of the Cape Corps (four hundred and twenty-eight rifles and four machine guns) under Major Hoy, the 2nd Nigerians under Major Uniacke, and two Kashmir mountain guns under Major Cole.

We marched at 4.30 a.m. (January 20th) and at dawn bumped into the enemy, estimated about eight hundred strong, who were on the move to attack

THE STORY OF THE 1st CAPE CORPS.

Photo by] [Sydney Taylor, Cape Town.
CAPTAIN WM. JARDINE.

LEFT TO RIGHT: SERGEANT E. BREUIDENHOUT (2775), PRIVATE D. G. KOLBEE (1027), SERGEANT MacTHOMAS (366).

Photo by] [Zadik & Co., Cape Town.
CAPTAIN J. E. ROBINSON, OUR BIG GAME SHOT.

Photo by] [J.H.T.
MAJOR F. E. BRADSTOCK, D.S.O., M.C. AND BAR.

the Nigerian brigade. The Cape Corps were leading and detailed to open the attack. Within five minutes a very hot engagement was in progress, our men going into action in great style.

The Cape Corps deployed in bush formation; two platoons each of "B" and "C" Companies were in advance under Lieutenants Bain, Youart, Harris and Stubbs. Lieutenants Rackstraw and Ashley, each with a platoon of "D" Company, were on the left and right flanks, respectively.

Captain Burger and Lieutenant Heaton each with two machine guns, supported the right and left flanks, respectively. Captain Bradstock was in charge of the firing line and Captain Robinson in support with two platoons of "D" Company (Lieutenants Cloke and Hayton).

The 2nd Nigerians were in reserve.

After advancing about one thousand yards we forced the enemy to evacuate his front line; continuing to advance we attacked the enemy's second line trenches, about three hundred rifles and four machine guns, with their left resting on a small hill, entrenched. Both sections of our machine guns and the mountain guns now came into action, and we strengthened our flanks in anticipation of the usual attack on them. This was done none too soon, a determined attack on the right being driven off. During this Ashley was severely wounded and some casualties took place amongst the men. Hayton then took over the right flank whilst Cloke reinforced the left, which was extended by Rackstraw's platoon being brought into line, and was also strengthened by Vickers guns just in time to defeat a determined attack from that side, in which we lost two killed and several wounded.

The action became very hot and general between nine and ten o'clock when the advance was ordered, and Captain Burger sent Hayton with a section of his platoon to attack the hill which was the pivot of the enemy's position. Hayton succeeded, and Burger's guns and the remainder of "B" Company were at once rushed on to the hill and dug in under hot fire. The enemy were now reinforced and twice counter-attacked strongly but were driven off with the aid of the mountain guns.

Captain Bradstock was severely wounded in organising the position on the hill, the defence of which was then handed over to Captain Robinson, whilst Captain Tandy took charge of the firing line.

When the two platoons of "D" Company in support had been thrown in to assist in the defence of the hill a company of the 2nd Nigerians was sent to Major Hoy to act in the support line.

The last enemy counter-attack was driven off at 11.45 a.m., and by 12.20 p.m. the new line was completed.

As all our men had now been in action for several hours Lieut.-Colonel Morris asked for reinforcements.

The 1st Nigerians, who had made an excellent march the previous night, were at dawn across the road by which the enemy opposing us were expected to retire.

Information was then received by Brig.-General Cunliffe that the enemy opposing Lieut.-Colonel Morris had been reinforced, and he accordingly ordered the latter to dig in and sit tight, and at the same time sent the 1st Nigerians to attack the enemy from their left rear.

The latter were, however, already retiring and escaped the Nigerians by clearing in a south-westerly direction through the bush.

By 13.30 hours the Nigerians had joined forces with Lieut.-Colonel Morris.

At sixteen hours the 1st Nigerians were left to hold the ground won and the 2nd Nigerians and the Cape Corps returned to camp at Mkindu, having been in action eleven hours throughout a very hot day.

We drove the enemy off three different ridges during the day.

There was no water, same having to be brought up from three miles back in chaguls (canvas water bags) by porters. Our casualties were four men killed and two officers and eight men wounded, of whom two subsequently died. Lieutenant Allen (I.D.) was also killed.

Killed.
  Private C. Allison (3142).
  Private J. Franks (2039).
  Private J. Geduld (2763).
  Private Z. Frans (2552).

Wounded.
  Captain F. E. Bradstock.
  Lieutenant S. Ashley.
  Private A. Jacobs (2143), severely.
  Private J. Langeveldt (1279).
  Private D. Poole (2370), severely.
  Private C. Petersen (2388), slightly.
  Private A. W. Philander (2593), slightly.
  Private A. Paulsen (820), severely.

Died of Wounds.
  Sergeant J. P. Tembe (1966).*
  Lance-Corporal J. Bredenkamp (1859).‡

  *At Mkindu, 22.1.17.
  ‡At Morogoro, 20.2.17.

S./SGT. F. J. CAIRNS, M.M. (1144), (Medicals).

Throughout this action the men behaved splendidly, in fact it was our first chance, the great opportunity that for twelve months past we had lived for. Lieut.-Colonel Morris had an anxious day, as we were up against a much superior force. But he had his reward on return to camp. Wires of congratulation came from the Brigadier (Beves) and from the 6th S.A.I., and the G.O.C. expressed himself as greatly pleased.

Brig.-General Cunliffe specially asked that the burial of our dead might be delayed until he could be present, and next day (January 21st) attended with all the Nigerian officers, and after the funeral asked our O.C. to parade the men away from the graveside in order that he might personally congratulate and compliment them on their bravery and morale under fire.

The enemy's casualties must have been very heavy, but were unknown to us. They always buried their dead when time permitted, if not, carried them and the wounded away.

Captain Bradstock and Captain McNeil (S.A.M.C.) received the Military Cross for their good work that day. Captains NcNiel and Earp-Jones (Padre) and Sergeant Cairns (medicals) went into action under heavy machine gun fire in order to evacuate the wounded. Sergeant Cairns (1144) received the Military Medal, as did also Private le Brun (1179), machine gunner.

The Machine Gun section, under Captain Burger, was much in evidence throughout the day and Captain Burger was highly pleased with the result of his men's first real test in action. Others who did excellent work that day were Corporals Stemmers (1148) and Fredericks (829) of the medical section, and Sergeant Johaar (160) of the machine gunners.

Captain Earp-Jones' good work was by no means confined to this particular day, not to any other particular day, week or month, for that matter. For three years he was always on the spot when we were "on the job," helping the wounded, carrying equipment or rifles of sick men, and making himself generally useful as only a padre can.

A few days later the Nigerians attacked the enemy further south, and by brilliant work gained their objective and captured two machine guns. Their own casualties were light, but being over keen they pursued the retreating enemy and bumped into a vigorous counter attack from which they suffered severely, their losses in officers and European warrant officers and N.C.O.'s being very heavy.

Meanwhile, Major Durham with "A" Company and two machine guns and supported by two field guns of the Kashmir Mountain Battery, had been in difficulties at Nyakisiki. He was sniped at directly he left Kibambawe (January 19th) and this continued all the way, until shortly before reaching Nyakisiki he was heavily attacked by superior numbers. He could not dislodge the enemy, so sent for reinforcements and hung on till next morning. During the night help arrived from Sheppard in the shape of men from the 130th Baluchis and 30th Punjabis, and with their aid and with the assistance of the two naval guns (4.1 inch) from Kibambawe, which participated in the attack at fourteen thousand yards range, Durham advanced and reached his objective, the enemy retreating south.

A valuable capture here was a Base Hospital, well equipped with medical comforts, etc., which were most useful as we were very short of those as well as rations and other necessaries.

In the hospital were five German ladies (nurses), sixteen German whites, and about two hundred blacks sick and wounded.

Major Durham's casualties during this scrap were:—

Wounded: Private N. Hendricks (1460).
Private J. Crewe (2884).
Private J. September (1612).

Having received orders to keep in touch with the enemy at all costs, Major Durham sent out Captain Robertson on January 21st with a platoon, and Lieutenant Wigman with two machine guns to reconnoitre. Robertson re-established touch with the enemy about two miles east of Nyakisiki and then returned to camp.

Lieutenant Feetham was then sent out with forty men to maintain touch with the enemy and to take up a position as a night post, and Captain Robertson with seventy-five men and a machine gun supported him. Feetham sent back three men to report, one of whom, Private W. Trantrall (1197) was killed by a mine.

On January 24th Lieut.-Colonel Morris' force returned to Kibambawe.

Durham was then instructed to advance from Nyakisiki towards Loge Loge, but as the result of an aeroplane reconnaissance report, was told to return to Nyakisiki. This was lucky for him as the next day an intelligence report stated that the camp he had vacated the previous night had been heavily fired on. He then remained and garrisoned Nyakisiki.

During the advance on the last named place Sergeant Schoor (480) particularly distinguished himself as N.C.O. in charge of skirmishers. He did valuable work in locating the enemy and thus prevented his party being outflanked. He also dug up several road mines at night, for which he received the personal congratulations of Sheppard. Later on Schoor got the D.C.M. for other good work.

The rains were now very heavy and continuous and greatly restricted operations during the next two weeks, which will be chiefly remembered for the number of fever cases, men being admitted to hospital at the rate of thirty or forty per day.

On January 26th, Captain Jardine with Lieutenants Murchie, Stanford, Walton, Coates, Wilson and Potgieter and one hundred and sixty-two men,

Captain R. P. McNeil, M.C., S.A.M.C.

reached Kibambawe from Makalinso and Lieutenant Bain returned to that place with a party escorting naval motor launches. On January 27th the 6th S.A. Infantry returned to Kibambawe.

On January 29th, Captain Jardine left Kibambawe to reinforce Major Durham at Nyakisiki, taking with him Lieutenant Stanford and a platoon of " A " Company.

At Nyakisiki Captain Jardine took command of " A " Company having with him Lieutenants Stanford, Hallier, James and Feetham.

At the end of January Sheppard's brigade received orders to return to Morogoro, leaving the Nigerians (Brig.-General Cunliffe) and Force Reserve (Brig.-General Beves) to continue the campaign.

On February 1st, Captain Jardine prepared an aviation landing ground at Nyakisiki. (Captain Waller landed with the first aeroplane in this aerodrome a week later and incidentally broke his propeller in alighting.)

On February 4th a German officer came in to Nyakisiki under a white flag to report that Captains Bridgman and Moon, R.N.A.S., had come down in the Rufiji River. The former was drowned and the German officer handed over his watch and other personal property. His body was later on removed and re-interred at Zanzibar.

On February 4th, Captain Robinson with one hundred and sixty men crossed to the north bank of the river with the African Scouts Battalion, under Major Montgomery, to endeavour to mop up a roving party of the enemy. They found the difficulty of getting through the swamps so great that they returned to camp on learning that the enemy had evacuated the post.

On February 6th, the G.O.C. and Brig.-General Sheppard arrived at Nyakisiki to inspect our camp and defences there.

On February 7th the 6th S.A. Infantry left for Morogoro and South Africa to be disbanded, and Beves' brigade now consisted of the 30th Punjabis and ourselves.

The rains now became so heavy and persistent that all idea of continuing active operations for the present had to be abandoned and Force Reserve were ordered to move to the only bit of high ground in the vicinity, at Mpangas, and to dig in and build bandas and make themselves as comfortable as might be there for the rainy season. Mpangas was surrounded by water on three sides, but its proximity to the river bank was important as supplies were then coming down the river on motor boats brought by road to Makalinso from Mikesse on the Central Railway.

If drier than the surrounding country Mpangas was no less dominated by mosquitos, Tsetse and blue flies, and in fact outside the nether regions it would not be easy to find a more undesirable place in which to exist.

Fever and dysentery were now causing such havoc in our ranks that our C.O. obtained permission to send all the worst cases back to Morogoro to recuperate, and accordingly on February 9th Major Hoy left with Captain Michau, Lieutenants Stanford and Thompson, taking a number of sick with him and picking up others en route.

Major Hoy also took with him details of the 6th S.A.I. and 30th Punjabis and a number of redundant porters. They had a most trying march back to the railway owing to continuous rains and lack of rations. The men were as nearly starved as men could be. Major Hoy found a detachment at Tschogowali who had marched eleven miles (as hospital patients) on half a pound of rice per man, and next morning were started on a march of fourteen miles on half a biscuit and a cup of milk (tinned of course) per man.

Another party were started on a march of thirteen miles with no food whatever. After a protest they received two biscuits each.

There was a most comfortable hospital at Morogoro, the 15th Stationary from Gallipoli, which was located just above our old camp on the mountain side, and there our sick were most carefully and kindly tended, and, when more or less restored to health, handed over to Major Hoy to take further care of. By the end of February over a thousand men had gone back to Morogoro and less than three hundred were left with Lieut.-Colonel Morris at Mpangas.

Our depôt at Morogoro had been moved across the spruit and the men were under canvas again, and, as the heavy rains still continued, experienced much discomfort. Major Hoy divided the camp into two sections, fits and unfits. The former was much the smaller, consisting chiefly of recent arrivals from South Africa and a few who had not been down to the Rufiji. These men were kept hard at work training, whilst the larger number of unfits, who were incapable of any effort, were merely rested and built up by careful attention to diet, which was very necessary after nearly three months of semi-starvation on the Rufiji. The sick parades at Morogoro at that time exceeded one hundred per diem, chiefly fever, and a word of praise must be given to Captain Heygate, R.A.M.C., for his splendid care and attention.

On February 10th, Major Durham left Nyakisiki for Kibambawe, leaving Captain Jardine in charge of the first-named place. Captain Jardine was visited next day by Brig.-General Beves who complimented him on his defences, remarking "They are like a bit of Flanders." Captain Jardine obtained permission from Beves to employ one hundred Shenzis (natives) to remove the bush round his camp, and with their aid he cleared a circle giving him a clear field of fire of two hundred yards in all directions in case of attack.

On February 16th the G.O.C. (General Hoskins) again visited Nyakisiki.

On February 20th, Lieutenants Harris and Cloke arrived at Nyakisiki with twenty-five men and a machine gun to reinforce Captain Jardine. Harris returned to Kibambawe two days later, and the following day Lieutenant Potgieter joined Captain Jardine. The latter was then having an anxious time as his spies expected the enemy to attack Nyakisiki in force and their patrols were becoming aggressive.

On February 21st, the following laconic entry appeared in the Padre's diary: "Mpangas, Ash Wednesday: Christmas puddings turned up. Glorious dinner!!" So that if nearly two months late the Christmas cheer was none the less appreciated.

On February 24th our spies reported that an enemy Wangoni company had arrived at Tindwas, a few miles lower down the river, and that night the force at Nyakisiki stood to arms all night.

After Major Hoy had left Mpangas things were quiet for some days, but on February 24th a report was brought in that about fifty of the enemy were at Pretorius' farm, about five miles from Nyakisiki, and that strong reinforcements were expected. Lieut.-Colonel Morris was accordingly given a column consisting of one hundred and fifty Cape Corps, one hundred 30th Punjabis, and two Kashmir mountain guns, and ordered to clear them out. The column left Kibambawe on 25th February, under Major Cole (Kashmiris), Lieut.-Colonel Morris and Major Durham going down the river by motor boat.

On reaching Nyakisiki intelligence was brought in that the enemy had been reinforced by three companies and six machine guns and that they intended to attack that place at midnight under the impression that it was held by a small garrison only.

Preparations were at once made to attack, but Cole's column was delayed by rains and swollen streams and could not get through that night. About ten p.m. Captain Youart, Lieutenant Bain and thirty-eight men managed to wade or swim through the swamps, thus increasing the garrison to about one

THE STORY OF THE 1st CAPE CORPS.

hundred and fifty. At 4.20 a.m. the garrison stood to arms and when the enemy attacked at 4.30 a.m. they met with a very warm reception and were driven off in a couple of hours. The enemy's attacking strength was two Wangoni companies, the 26th and 27th Schutze Companies and six machine guns. Our casualties were two only.

During this fight our sick who were in hospital were so keen on participating that they actually crawled forward into the trenches and took a hand in the game.

Major Cole got through the swamps a few hours later, and at 11.30 a.m. reached Nyakisiki with a company of the 30th Punjabis, under Captain Wilson. Lieutenant Gray and two guns of the Kashmir Mountain Battery and a signal section, R.E.

Meanwhile, Lieut.-Colonel Morris had been ordered to wait for the 2nd Nigerians who were being sent down the main road to Nyakisiki to reinforce him.

On February 28th, Captain Downes, R.G.A., and Lieutenant Dolier reached Nyakisiki with two naval twelve pounders (these guns were ex H.M.S. "Pegasus"—destroyed a year or more previously by the "Koenigsberg") and a 4.5 Howitzer.

The 2nd Nigerians, under Major Uniacke, reached Nyakisiki on March 1st and Lieut.-Colonel Morris' column advanced against the enemy at Tindwas at 2 a.m. next morning, making a wide detour to endeavour to outflank them.

After a twelve hours non-stop march through very dense and swampy country, during which the men were frequently up to their middles in water, the column got astride the Matarula road and dug in behind the enemy. The Nigerians were meanwhile advancing along the main road to Pretorius' farm.

The enemy resisted for a while, but, losing some killed and wounded, very soon cleared off in all directions through the bush where it was impossible to follow them, and leaving behind their killed and wounded.

The whole column occupied and bivouaced at Tindwas that night, and the next day (March 3rd) marched to Pretorius farm and on to Nyakisiki.

On March 4th the column returned to Mpangas, leaving Captain Jardine and his men to follow next day, after handing over the camp at Nyakisiki to the 30th Punjabis.

On March 10th, Captain Robertson with Captains Youart, Earp-Jones, Lieutenant Murchie and one hundred and forty unfit men returned to Morogoro, leaving only one hundred and fifty-six men in camp at Mpangas with Lieut.-Colonel Morris, of whom ninety-four were sick.

On March 12th the remnant of the battalion, still further depleted by sickness during the past two days and numbering little more than one hundred, marched out of Mpangas en route to Morogoro.

Many men fell out sick by the way, and on March 21st Lieut.-Colonel Morris marched into Morogoro with seventy half-starved men (five officers and sixty-five other ranks), the meagre remanant of a battalion of over fifteen hundred fit officers and men who had left for the Rufiji campaign three months and one week earlier. Such were the ravages of disease in the rainy season in the fever and dysentery stricken areas of East Africa.

The past few months proved to be the most strenuous that the battalion experienced during their whole four years on active service. Much harder marching was in store for us a few months later in the chase after Naumann and Zingel, and we saw much heavier fighting in the Lindi area in the following November and in Palestine in September, 1918, but for general hardship and discomfort, semi-starvation and the ravages of disease, the Rufiji campaign stood alone—indeed one questions if any of the millions who took up arms between

1914 and 1918 on behalf of the British Empire, endured much greater hardships than those who campaigned on the Rufiji River in 1916-17. During the thirteen weeks the battalion participated in those operations they were never once on full rations, seldom indeed on half rations. Quarter rations, varied by none at all many days, was their normal portion.

The only animal transport ever possible was pack donkeys, and even they died in such numbers that they had soon to be abandoned in favour of native porters.

From Mikesse, on the Central Railway, for a distance of about thirty miles to Summit on the top of the plateau overlooking the low country towards the Rufiji, mechanical transport was utilised, but the difficulties of those convoys were almost beyond description and the Army Service Corps (Mechanical Transport) drivers who were responsible for the service were heroes all. Every man of them deserved a D.S.O. They had to fight nature in a mood that very few who will read these lines have ever experienced and will scarcely believe.

The cars became stuck up to the tops of the wheels in mud and slush, and often had to remain so all night. Frequently the drivers were lifted out of their cars by natives and carried back to the nearest clearing station, suffering from fever or dysentery, and many of those who managed to force their way through with their loads had to be lifted from their cars utterly exhausted and seriously ill.

From Summit to the river the rations, ammunition, and other war stores were conveyed by porters, except of course across the rivers and wider spruits, where pontoons and motor launches were employed. The natives were organised into squads, and each squad covered a section of approximately six miles. The stores were made up into fifty-pound loads, which of course were carried on the head. On the return journey the porters carried back the sick and wounded. The rations were chiefly bully beef, mealie meal and rice. A few oxen were driven down to the river, but had to be slaughtered at once before the tsetse fly killed them. The condition of the mealie meal and rice on arrival may better be imagined than told. The natives were naked and odoriferous. When resting they sat on their loads, which were also, of course, exposed to the pouring rain, and consequently reached their destination in a state of ferment, hot and sour. But it had to be eaten, the alternative was starvation. On many a day a man's ration consisted of two tablespoonsful of rice and the same of mealie meal, on many another day less than that or nil.

When at Mpangas Captain Robinson, who was a first-class shot, was detailed for special duty to shoot game for the brigade, several porters being told off to assist him to bring in his bag.

The lot of the poor devils of porters was a completely unenviable one. They were by no means robust and vigorous at the best of times. In peace their womenfolk performed the bulk of the domestic manual labour. Practically naked, they toiled with their loads through torrents of rain, slimy, sticky clay and mud often to their middles, and sometimes up to their necks in it. They died like flies and more than one provided a meal for a greedy " croc " lurking in the swamps. Of the cruelty of it all there could be no two opinions, but the alternative was—what? Such is war: *Cui bono?*

Our wounded and grievously sick had an appalling time. The worst cases were carried in canvas hammocks, slung on bamboo poles, by the porters who staggered, slipped, and stumbled along by day and night. Then a forty or fifty mile journey in a motor lorry, jolted and bumped almost to death in an agony of suffering. And only the worst could be carried.

THE STORY OF THE 1st CAPE CORPS.

Many with high temperatures and disease wracked frames fit only for the softest of beds and the best hospital diet and comforts, dragged their weary way on foot one hundred and fifty miles to the railway, endeavouring to eat the same hard tack as the fit men, resting and sleeping, or trying to sleep at the roadside when and where they could. The task of the medical officer and stretcher bearers was not rendered easier by the desire of the men to carry on at all hazards. Men in the first stages of dysentery and fever were so keen to get on that their N.C.O.'s had to keep a careful watch and force them to report sick, and on the march a very careful lookout had to be kept to prevent men, often partially paralysed, blind or delirious, from getting into the bush to lie down and escape from the sun. That was, of course, fatal as the whole column would pass on leaving the man to die of starvation or be taken by lions. When a man fell out on the march his half-section had to be told off to remain with him until a passing ambulance or porters could pick him up.

In standing camps men would be missed when their turn came for duty or a move was on, and a search would probably locate them in the bush half a mile or more from camp with a temperature of 104 or thereabouts.

It may be mentioned that the present rainy season was the worst that had been experienced for nine years. The Rufiji River rose fifteen feet in places and flooded the surrounding country for miles.

Roads which were dry when we marched to the Rufiji in December were so swamped in February and March that native porters were actually taken by crocodiles on the roads and hippopotami roamed about in places where two months earlier there had been no spoor or other indication that such amphibians were to be found there.

Before the men had been in the Rufiji area long their clothing and boots wore out and could not be replaced owing to transport difficulties. Many men were in rags, one or two even wearing towels round their middles in lieu of shirts or shorts, and the Battalion eventually arrived back at Morogoro in a deplorably dilapidated condition.

It was the intention of the authorities to send the Battalion to join the Central Force operating round Bismarckburg and Lake Tanganyika, under General Northey, as soon as we had reorganised and recovered sufficiently from our Rufiji experiences. Before we were ready for that, however, unexpected developments necessitated the retention of our services nearer at hand, and from May to the end of September we were engaged in the rounding up and capture of small marauding parties of the enemy under Wintgens, Naumann and Zingel, who had broken back across the Central Railway and carried on a guerilla warfare round Aruscha and Kondoa Irangi.

Our crossing of the Rufiji River on January 3rd, west of Makalinso, greatly disturbed the hippos. They were very curious, particularly a foolish young calf which persisted in popping up near the boats, emitted a frightened bellow, and disappeared again. The old cow was much perturbed at the antics of her young and approached the boats in a distinctly hostile attitude more than once. As the river was full of crocodiles as well as hippopotami, the men did not altogether enjoy their morning's boating.

During the period covered by this chapter the following promotions and changes in personnel took place :—

R.S.M. Akehurst was invalided back to Morogoro from Dutumi and R.Q.M.S. Betts received promotion to fill the vacancy, whilst Staff Sergeant Shipp (medicals) became acting R.Q.M.S. Shortly afterwards Betts went to hospital and Shipp then became acting R.S.M. also. Lieutenant Howe Browne, Assistant Adjutant and A/Q.M.R. had also gone to hospital, so Shipp had a tremendous task, in fact in his own words he was Quartermaster-General. But whatever his title and however manifold his duties, it must certainly be recorded that he carried them out with wonderful cheerfulness, energy and ability.

Major Cowell left Makalinso on January 15th, evacuated to hospital, and did not return to the Rufiji River.

On January 21st, Captain Tandy became acting Adjutant (vice Captain Bradstock wounded) and retained the appointment, with the exception of one or two brief intervals noted below, until he was demobilised in June, 1919. Captain Bradstock resumed duty as Adjutant (4.6.17.) but was admitted to hospital with a broken ankle on June 24th, and Lieutenant Hoffe then took over and held the appointment until his death (23rd September, 1917), whereupon Captain Tandy succeeded him and continued to fill the position until his demobilisation.

Captain Tandy only had three weeks illness during the whole period of his field service and got through a tremendous amount of hard and valuable work, which in due course earned him the Military Cross and the Belgian Croix de Chevalier de l'ordre de la Couronne.

Lieutenant J. V. Harris received the vacant Captaincy created later by Captain Bradstock's evacuation to South Africa (7.2.17).

During January and February Captains Cowell and Bradstock (wounded), Lieutenants S. Ashley (wounded), and T. Rose-Innes; 2nd Lieutenants A. Leslie and H. R. Thornton and three hundred and forty-three men were invalided to South Africa per hospital ship.

During the Rufiji campaign disease took toll of from forty-five to fifty lives, including those who were invalided back to Morogoro and died there. During March five officers and two hundred and ninety-one other ranks were invalided to South Africa per hospital ship, and the following officers, viz.: Lieut.-Colonel Morris, Captains Robinson, Robertson, Youart and Harris, Lieutenants Murchie and Stanford; Staff Sergeant Shipp; C.S.M.'s Calvert and Ruiters; C.Q.M.S. Hendricks and twenty-eight other ranks, proceeded on a month's leave to the Union on March 23rd.

Conductor C. F. Abbott (S.A.S.C.) received his commission as 2nd Lieutenant on March 29th and joined up at Morogoro. Before the end of the year he lost his life at Mkungu when in charge of our Stokes Trench Mortars.

On March 30th, Staff Sergeant S. H. Rose-Innes was transferred to us from S.A. Field Ambulance and promoted 2nd Lieutenant. On April 3rd, Lieutenant Arnott returned from South Africa, bringing with him 2nd Lieutenants A. N. Difford and G. R. Barnard and one hundred and thirty-seven other ranks. Difford and Barnard had received their commission during the same week, and it is sad to record that both those fine young officers lost their lives in Palestine the next year.

On April 10th, Lieutenant Walter Power came to us from South African Infantry Reinforcements.

On April 15th, Private F. Fillies (982) was missing at Morogoro. He was never seen nor heard of again and death was accordingly presumed.

On April 16th, Captain H. G. Warr, who had been acting as Assistant Political Officer at Morogoro, returned to regimental duty.

THE STORY OF THE 1st CAPE CORPS.

After the foregoing chapter had been written Von Lettow's book on the East African Campaign from the enemy point of view appeared.

It cannot be said that the author appears always to be strongly imbued with the desire to place Truth on a pedestal, unless perchance a more charitable reason may be suggested. Frequent attacks of malaria have several times recently been claimed in the criminal courts to have induced loss of memory. Von Lettow admittedly suffered severely from fever. Possibly when he penned the chapter on the Rufiji River operations he was the victim of a bad attack.

For example, he says that our crossing of the river at Kipenio, west of Makalinso, on January 3rd, 1917, did not take him by surprise. The absurdity of such a statement is its own refutation. Our crossing would not have been possible had Von Lettow been aware of our coming. He was not such a fool as to allow several hundred men with machine guns to cross a river in small boats, two in a boat, if he could have prevented them.

Our crossing had serious consequences for the enemy, and Von Lettow would have at once fully realised that if the possibility of our crossing had occurred to him.

After crossing the river our signallers tapped the enemy's field telephone wire and gained valuable information which enabled us to make considerable captures. Would that have happened if Von Lettow had been aware of our whereabouts? Such nonsense is unworthy of him.

Further on in the same chapter he says that our troops reached the Rufiji "exhausted and unfit for further operations."

The facts with regard to Force Reserve, of which the Cape Corps was one unit, are these. When we had established our bridgehead on the south bank of the river at Kipenio we had three days' rations in hand and were ready to continue the advance. It was originally intended that Force Reserve should at once proceed east along the south bank to take the enemy on the flank at Kibambawe and thus assist General Sheppard to cross with his Brigade further east.

This move was delayed owing to the receipt of reports that an enemy force was advancing eastwards from the Mahenge area to reinforce Von Lettow at Kibambawe. There is no doubt that the original intended move would have been very successful.

The report of enemy movement from Mahenge proved to be unfounded, and Force Reserve advanced to attack the enemy and support Sheppard, but found that the former had retired and that the latter had crossed the river.

The whole of our Forces were across the river by the 8th January. We continued a vigorous offensive for several weeks and defeated the enemy in two or three pitched battles and several smaller engagements. We drove them in headlong retreat a considerable distance from the river southward into the swamps, and finally left them in March in the deadliest swamps of the whole territory, there to stew in their own juice through the worst of the rainy season.

If that was the work of exhausted and unfit troops, it was well for Von Lettow that he was not called upon to face fit and fresh troops.

There are statements in other chapters in Von Lettow's book which might be controverted did it come within the scope of this story to do so

"A FRIEND IN NEED."
H.M. HOSPITAL SHIP "OXFORDSHIRE."

CHAPTER VII.

THE CAPE CORPS DETACHMENT IN THE COASTAL AREA, BETWEEN DAR-ES-SALAAM AND THE RUFIJI RIVER. PERIOD 1ST DECEMBER, 1916 TO AUGUST, 1917.

BY the 1st December, 1916, Captain C. E. Stevens had reached Dar-es-Salaam from Tanga with a draft en route to join up with the battalion then at Morogoro.

On arrival at Dar-es-Salaam he assumed command of all Cape Corps details in the vicinity (*ex* hospital, etc.) and was awaiting train accommodation to take them to Morogoro.

At that time application was made by the I.G.C. for three hundred men of the battalion to assist in lines of communication duties in the Dar-es-Salaam area and also to form the nucleus of a coastal column which was in course of organisation. Lieut.-Colonel Morris agreed, with the approval of higher authority, that Captain Stevens and his men, with the addition of the requisite officers and men from Major Durham's draft which had just arrived from South Africa, should be detailed for this duty.

Captain Stevens accordingly took command of three hundred men and Major Durham detailed Second-Lieutenants Leslie and Thornton to assist him. Duties commenced at once, posts having to be provided at various places on the road south to Maneromanga along which an enemy column was moving.

Captain Stevens remained in charge at Dar-es-Salaam, Thornton was sent to No. 3 post about eleven miles south, and Leslie to No. 4 post near Maneromanga.

Except for a little sniping nothing unusual occurred and at the end of December S.A.I. details took over the posts, when a column under Lieut.-Colonel N. H. M. Burne, D.S.O., moved south to attack the enemy.

Captain Stevens' command was then concentrated to form the nucleus of a coast column under Major Logan of the Loyal North Lancashire Regiment. This column embarked on H.M.T. "Barjora" on January 5th, 1917, and, sailing "under sealed orders," proceeded down the coast to Kissidu, which was at that time believed to be held by about two hundred of the enemy. The Cape Corps detachment consisted of Captain Stevens, Lieutenants Leslie, Thornton and Dormehl, and some three hundred and fifty other ranks, with one machine gun. (The last named officer was attached from the S.A.I. Forest Cutters section).

H.M. ships "Challenger" and "Mersey" and three armed whalers accompanied the column to support the landing in case of opposition. On arrival at Kissidu Lieutenant Thornton, in charge of a platoon in three boats, was first towed in shore by motor launch, but the launch broke down in the breakers and the boats remained tossing about in the surf for three hours.

Lieutenant Dormehl with a platoon then proceeded in open boats, and Lieutenant Leslie with eighty other ranks followed in an armed whaler. Landing was difficult and dangerous as the surf was very heavy and the men had to wade ashore from the boats. The landing was, however, unopposed and in due course the whole column managed to reach the shore and occupy the evacuated enemy camp.

Major Logan and Captain Stevens disembarked next morning and at once set up a small naval portable wireless station which enabled communication to be established with the gunboats.

On the following day (January 9th) the column was reinforced by the 75th Mafia (Arab) Rifles from Zanzibar.

In the meantime Lieut.-Colonel Burne's column had moved south and a week later (January 15th) orders were issued to Major Logan that a demonstration was to be made against a village named Utchembe, about twenty-eight miles from the coast, which was said to be held by the enemy, and patrols were sent out to keep in touch with them. Owing to delay in delivery of the orders to Major Logan, the same did not reach him until the night before the day on which the demonstration was to be made. Captain Stevens with Lieutenants Leslie and Kettle (of the British West India Regiment) and one hundred and eighty of the Cape Corps and a machine gun were despatched immediately.

Their orders were to make a demonstration in rear of the enemy's position at Mtita, which was to be attacked by a column operating from Massanga at three o'clock the same afternoon (January 17th).

The detachment left camp at 2 a.m. (January 17th), waded through the river near camp, and marched right through to Utchembe which was reached at 4.30 in the afternoon. No opposition was met with, the enemy having evacuated Mtita.

Captain Stevens occupied and held Utchembe for three days and then returned to Kissidu, leaving Leslie with a platoon to hold and patrol the Utchembe area.

Two or three days later Leslie had orders to return to Kissidu and in doing so passed through country where British troops had not been seen before. They were heartily welcomed by the headmen of the various villages and received gifts of fruit, etc. Many headmen accompanied Leslie back to Kissidu in order to pay their respects to the "headman" of the column (Major Logan).

A few days later later Major Logan and Lieutenant Dormehl had unfortunately to be invalided back to Dar-es-Salaam.

From Kissidu the Cape Corps detachment marched by easy stages inland to Massanga which they reached without having encountered the enemy who were reported to be retiring on Ngulankulu.

A naval patrol was then sent to the mouth of the Rufiji River to locate certain posts said to be held by the enemy, but as these were found to have been evacuated it was decided to divide the column, which now consisted of detachments of the Cape Corps and of the Mafia Rifles (under Lieutenant Smith).

The Cape Corps proceeded to Koge to join Lieut.-Colonel Burne, whilst Lieutenant Smith took the Mafia Rifles to the mouth of the Rufiji River.

From Koge Lieutenant Leslie was evacuated to Dar-es-Salaam sick.

The day after arrival at Koge the Cape Corps detachment were attached to a column under Lieut.-Colonel Willans, D.S.O., which moved out at once to advance against Mpanganya, an island on the Rufiji, at that time strongly held. Owing to the swampy nature of the ground progress was very difficult, but Mpanganya was eventually reached (February 4th) and the place shelled. The result was not known but our fire was not returned. The next day Captain Stevens was ordered to return with his men to Kihimbwe, from which place patrols were sent out daily.

On one of these patrols Lieutenant Thornton came upon an enemy stern-wheeled steamer moored on the opposite bank of the river. As it was found impracticable to attempt the capture of this vessel Captain Stevens took out a party of men with a machine gun on February 7th to disable her. Fire was opened at long range and many hits registered, but the occupants—four in number so far as could be seen—escaped into the bush.

In the attack on this steamer (named the "Tomondo") acting-Sergeant January (2895) and Corporal Strydom, T. J. (311) did good work. Reports afterwards established the fact that the boat had been holed and beached.

Captain Stevens remained at Kihimbwe from February 6th to March 25th, patrolling the surrounding country. This was a most unhealthy job as the country was one long swamp and the patrols were always knee-deep or more in water, with the result that fever and rheumatism were rife.

On March 25th the advance was continued south of the river through Killimani to Utete, where Major Leach of the 25th Fusiliers was in command of a large area of the country on the banks of the Rufiji. At Killimani Captain Stevens commenced a survey of the channel of the river in order to assist in piloting our river flotilla to Mpangas, but before he had completed the job he was evacuated sick to Dar-es-Salaam.

Lieutenant Walton took over the detachment from Stevens on April 3rd and proceeded to Mpanganya, about sixteen miles further up the river, which he garrisoned with forty men for three or four months, during which period the detachment was greatly depleted by evacuations to hospital.

Mpanganya was a big supply depôt and large stores of supplies had been accumulated there for the service of our forces operating to the south. The enemy were reported to be in the vicinity but did not attack the place, which, having regard to the immense value and quantity of the stores at stake, appeared to shew a great lack of dash and enterprise on their part.

Captain Wilson, D.S.O., who was the river Transport Officer, moved constantly up and down the river in an armed motor launch and probably assisted to scare the enemy off.

Eventually all the stores were removed and Lieutenant Walton then returned to Utete with his men and took over command of some sixty of our men who had been left there with Major Leach by Captain Stevens. A Sergeant and twelve men remained at Mpanganya in a German house converted into a fort.

Another twelve men were sent up the river to form a post at Upangese. About a month later, owing to the continued retirement of the enemy, the river posts were abandoned and in August Lieutenant Walton collected his men at the two river posts and marched up to Kimambawe. There he crossed the river and returned to the central railway via Tulo and Summit and entrained for Dodomo, which was then Battalion Headquarters. The men with Walton had been seven months on the Rufiji and were greatly debilitated by fever and dysentery. A number had to be left behind at every stopping place where medical attention was possible and eventually Walton's strength on reaching Dodoma was some sixty odd, out of over three hundred who had left Dar-es-Salaam with Stevens at the beginning of the year.

CHAPTER VIII.

Guerilla Operations after Major Wintgen's Force. Period April 17th to June 21st, 1917.

BEFORE the next task allotted to the 1st Cape Corps is described it is necessary, in as few words as possible, to state the then strategical position of the British and hostile forces in East Africa at the end of February, 1917. The enemy had been driven into the south-eastern corner of German East Africa, and the British held a line roughly as follows: From Kilwa-Kiswani on the coast running in a westerly direction south of the Rufiji River to a point north of Mahenge, then north-west to Iringa and south-west through Lepembe and Ssongea.

The line was lightly held by small posts and by the striking forces then preparing for a further, and, it was hoped, final advance.

At the end of February General von Lettow Vorbeck conceived, and proceeded to translate into action, a diversion which cost us heavy expenditure in personnel and material. He despatched Major Wintgens from the Mahenge area with a column variously estimated at from eight hundred to twelve hundred rifles, with fifteen to twenty machine guns and two field guns (one pounders), with orders to break through the British lines and to invade the territory to the north-west.

The latter area had been cleared by the British and Belgian forces and was now held only by political officers and their staffs and by police posts.

The Hun raiders first moved west and came in contact with Brig.-General Northey's Force, based on Lake Nyassa. Being roughly handled by a column of that Force, Wintgens broke north-east from near Lake Rukwa, followed closely by a column of Nyassaland and Rhodesian native troops under Lieut.-Colonel Murray, D.S.O.

The 1st Cape Corps were fated to spend the next six months in dealing with Wintgens and his command.

By the 1st of April Lieut.-Colonel Morris and a number of officers and men had gone on leave to South Africa, and a much larger number of officers and men had been invalided to the Union after their Rufiji River hardships. Major Hoy was in command of the remnants of the battalion at Morogoro, where officers and men were being "nursed" and put through a period of quiet training during the lull in active operations.

Orders were suddenly received early in April that a detachment might be required to proceed to Bismarckburg, via Tabora and the Lakes, for service in that area. Preparations for that enterprise were well in hand and every possible officer and man was being mobilised when that order was substituted by another instructing Major Hoy to proceed at once with all availables to Itigi (Kilo 632) on the Central Railway, and there to report to Lieut.-Colonel P. H. Dyke, D.S.O., commanding 130th Baluchis, who had been appointed O.C. operations against the enemy raiders.

On April 17th Major Hoy left Morogoro with a detachment of four hundred rifles and four machine guns. The detachment was organised into two companies under Captains Arnott and Hallier respectively. The other officers on the "stunt" were Lieutenants Bain, Guest, Hayton, Heaton, Horseman, Power, Stubbs, and 2nd Lieutenants Abbott, Barnard and Difford. Captain Tandy left Morogoro a week later to join the detachment as adjutant. The machine guns were under Lieutenants Guest and Heaton.

Two days after arrival at Itigi Major Hoy with his No. 1 company under Captain Arnott went "on safari" to the south-west, en route to Kiromo about ninety miles distant.

They formed the nucleus of the Kiromo column, which a few weeks later came under the personal command of Lieut.-Colonel P. H. Dyke, D.S.O. Kiromo was reached on April 27th after a very trying march, the water being frequently up to the men's knees (it was the middle of the big rains), but not a man fell out sick by the way.

At this time Wintgens was travelling in a north-easterly direction closely followed by Lieut.-Colonel Murray, whose column did some splendid marching.

The 1/6th K.A.R. (late African Scouts Battalion), under Major Montgomery, M.C., were already holding Kitunda Mission, about forty miles to the south-west. The African Scouts Battalion were Askari captured from the enemy and trained by Major Pretorius, the famous scout, at Morogoro towards the end of 1916. A story was current at the time that an N.C.O. of the battalion deserted to the enemy with the nominal roll. This greatly alarmed the men, as they anticipated that they would be hung if re-captured.

Major Hoy's orders were to deny the enemy access to the Kiromo area, where food was plentiful, and, if opportunity arose, to strike. An immediate attempt was made to effect communication with Montgomery. That was not successful, and on April 24th it was learned that he had evacuated Kitunda and retired towards Sikonge Mission in the direction of Tabora.

The second company of the Cape Corps under Captain Hallier, accompanied by a section of B/120 Indian Field Ambulance under Captain H. H. King, I.M.S., reached Kiromo on April 30th. (Note.—Our own medical officer, Captain McNeil, and his staff were busy looking after our own sick at Morogoro.)

Captain Tandy reached Kiromo a day or two after Captain Hallier's company. He marched down from Itigi to Kiromo with two men and about ten machine gun porters, and escorted a ration convoy of about two hundred and fifty pack donkeys. These donkeys, like those we had later on in the Lindi area, were, to employ a vulgarism, "the absolute bally limit."

Five donkeys were allocated to each native driver. The loads were placed in nets with large meshes and then lifted on to the pack saddles. The drivers could not pack or adjust the loads properly. When one donkey dropped his load and was having it adjusted all the others would stand and gaze and each in turn would drop his load. Before the first trek it took a whole morning to get the packs loaded.

Brig.-General W.F. S. Edwards, D.S.O., I.G.C., now took charge of the operations against Wintgens and made his headquarters at Tabora.

At Kiromo a number of important bura buras (improved paths) met from the surrounding districts, affording us moderately good going south-west to Kitunda, west to Kwa Madereka (where the paths intersected the bura bura Kitunda-Tabora), south-east towards Kidete, north-east towards Saranda, and north towards Itigi.

Kiromo was thoroughly entrenched and organised for defence by Major Hoy, and he also threw out strong fixed patrols with orders to scout in the direction of possible hostile approach. In that work every assistance was rendered by the local natives, the Wanyamwezi, the largest tribe in East Africa, hardy, brave, and the best porters in the country.

THE STORY OF THE 1st CAPE CORPS.

Photo by] [J.H.T.
OFFICERS ON THE KIROMO STUNT.
Captain Stradling, Carrier Corps.   Captain H. H. King, I.M.S.

Photo by] [J. G. Horsfall, Cape Town.
SIGNALLING SERGEANT J. H. ALIES (825).

During the first week or two at Kiromo numbers of the men went down with fever, and outpost duties were found with much difficulty.

Kiromo was in touch by wire with Lieut.-Colonel Dyke at Itigi and the wire was extended under the protection of our patrols towards Kitunda. Giraffe caused much trouble by constantly damaging the wires, and the regular maintenance of communication in the circumstances reflected great credit upon the linemen.

Our intelligence agents furnished us with daily reports, and as our column was the means of communication with Lieut.-Colonel Murray, it was no uncommon sight to see Major Hoy and Captain Tandy busy at midnight decyphering code telegrams. In fact our daily code work during the chasing of Wintgens, Naumann, and Zingel, described in the two succeeding chapters, was greater than during the whole of the remainder of the life of the 1st Cape Corps.

Major Hoy wished to occupy Kitunda, fearing that the enemy would do so on hearing that Major Montgomery had evacuated the place, but was ordered not to leave Kiromo. About the 12th May news was received from our patrols that the enemy were approaching Kitunda and on the 15th they occupied the mission there. By this time the men were benefitting from the better climate, which was much less enervating than Morogoro, and fever became less of a handicap. Captain King was unremitting in his care and everyone was made to build himself a sleeping shelter over his trench. The food, too, was excellent, fresh meat and vegetables being readily procurable from the natives.

The country round Kiromo was parklike and very pretty. The natives were prosperous and their cattle and crops in fine condition. As soon as the men had shaken off the fever some good, steady work was done at Kiromo. A bayonet fighting course was fixed up and much useful practice obtained.

After remaining at Kitunda a few days Wintgens evacuated the mission again, moved north-west, and entrenched himself on the bank of the Ruhawa River. He left some British prisoners from Northey's force and eight of his own men sick at Kitunda, and sent a note asking Major Hoy to send for them. A Red Cross party under Lieutenant Power accordingly went out and returned three days later with the patients and prisoners.

Touch was now gained with Lieut.-Colonel Murray, who reported that he was ready to attack the enemy at Ruhawa River, and would do so if it did not interfere with General Edwards' plans. Major Hoy at once asked permission to close in, but was not allowed to do so as it was feared that the enemy might break away and back to Kiromo. If Murray had been allowed to attack, supported by Major Hoy, it is quite possible that Wintgens would have been dealt a very effective knock. The enemy seemed to be of that opinion as they quickly evacuated their position and moved north to Sikonge Mission, and Murray then occupied Kitunda Mission, whence he eventually rejoined his own Force (Northey's), and Brig.-General Edwards was left to deal with Wintgens.

About this time a troop of K.A.R.M.I. under Lieutenant Kelly joined Major Hoy to assist in patrol work, and on May 20th Lieut.-Colonel P. H. Dyke, D.S.O., arrived at Kiromo with two hundred rifles of the 30th Punjabis and took command there, and that Force became known as Dyke's Column.

About May 15th Major Hoy was instructed to clear a site for an aerodrome and work was commenced at once east of Kiromo Village. The job was completed after ten days' hard graft and with the assistance of the 30th Punjabis, but the aerodrome was never used as the enemy cleared north, evidently bent on crossing the Central Railway.

Shortly after Dyke had assumed command Major Wintgens was captured by a Belgian patrol near Gombe. He was ill and with a hospital party, having separated from his command in order not to delay them. Wintgens was taken a prisoner to Tabora and his late command devolved upon Ober-Lieut. Naumann, his adjutant.

On May 26th the Cape Corps detachment was ordered to proceed from Kiromo towards Itigi, but at their first camp after leaving Kiromo were instructed to make a forced march to Ikuru-Kwa-wamba which was reached at 5 p.m. on May 28th.

At eight o'clock that night a wire was received from Dyke, who had gone on to Itigi, enquiring how soon Major Hoy could reach Kilo 699, on the Central Railway, some thirty miles distant. After a study of the map a reply was sent: "About noon the day after to-morrow." The detachment marched at dawn next morning, moving along the old slave route in a north-westerly direction, and reached their destination within half an hour of the appointed time. The men had marched eighty miles from Kiromo in four days and finished fit, strong, and smiling. Only one man—a malaria chronic—fell out on the march, notwithstanding intense tropical heat, meagre rations, and very rough going over old elephant tracks.

From Kilo 699 the detachment entrained at once for Malongwe, where they were destined to remain several weeks.

Naumann and his force broke across the Central Railway two miles west of Malongwe (Kilo 737) about two days before we reached there, and had gone north. The Cape Corps detachment could not at once be made use of to follow owing to a shortage of porters.

Naumann was being closely followed by a battalion of the Nigerians to whom two detachments of the Cape Corps, under Lieutenant Stubbs and 2nd Lieutenant Abbot escorted ration convoys. That involved a total march of two hundred and fifty miles to the Sibiti River and back, which was accomplished without a single man falling out.

Naumann succeeded in getting away from the Nigerians, and Lieut.-Colonel Dyke, who hurried out with another column from Tabora, just missed intercepting him owing to receiving wrong information deliberately given by natives. Having administered a knock to the Belgians, Naumann made himself scarce and was next heard of making north-east with Aruscha as his evident objective.

Major Hoy was appointed Post-Commandant at Malongwe and was entrusted with the organisation and despatch of the ration convoys to our troops who had followed Naumann northwards. Lions were numerous round Malongwe and forced us to keep very much on the alert.

On June 21st, Major Hoy was ordered to take his detachment back to our depôt at Morogoro where at the station he met Lieut.-Colonel Morris who had just arrived from South Africa with a large draft.

Three weeks later Lieut.-Colonel Morris with half the battalion left Morogoro for Aruscha via Dar-es-Salaam and Kilindini to go in pursuit of Naumann, whose capture he eventually accomplished at the end of September after the strenuous chase described in the next chapter.

Officers and men who did good work during the period embraced by this chapter were:—

    Captain H. H. King, I.M.S.
    Captain Stradling, M.C., Carrier Corps, who was in charge of our porters.
    Lieutenant Horseman who did splendid work in disciplining our porters and instilling into them a knowledge of camp sanitation.
  C.Q.M.S. Davids, J. L. (97) who acted as detachment Quartermaster.
  Sergeant Alies, J. H. (825) and his signallers who were the medium for the transmission of all messages and did exceptionally well, particularly Private Drury, F. (1272) (later killed in action 8th November, 1917).

THE STORY OF THE 1st CAPE CORPS.

Whilst at Malongwe, before returning to Morogoro, Hoy's detachment were able to fraternise with the Belgian battalions stationed there, and an excellent spirit of cameraderie very soon existed between our officers and those of the Belgian Force. Major Bataille, who was in command of our Allies, was a keen soldier whose Force later on did excellent work in the advance on Mahenge.

Photo by] [J.H.T.
BAYONET FIGHTING COURSE, KIROMO.

Photo by] [J.H.T.
COLONEL P. H. DYKE, D.SO.,
WITH CAPTAIN HAMILTON,
M.C., ON HIS LEFT.

MACHINE GUN PORTERS ON SAFARI.

AT SARANDA STATION

CHAPTER IX.

The Naumann "Stunt"—Period July 10th to October 1st, 1917
(*vide* Map page 108).

EARLY in July, 1917, the enemy force under Ober-Lt. Naumann mentioned in the previous chapter, was reported to be making for Aruscha. The object was clearly to create a diversion, do as much damage as possible, embarrass the G.O.C. by forcing him to detach a large force to round them up, and to string out long and expensive lines of communication. The enemy's strength was on July 1st said to be about eight hundred rifles and fourteen machine guns.

The Cape Corps was one unit selected to go in pursuit and subsequent events were to prove that the G.O.C.'s confidence in us was not misplaced.

On July 10th, Lieut.-Colonel Morris received orders at Morogoro to select five hundred picked men and proceed at once to Dar-es-Salaam. The order was received at 8 p.m. to entrain at midnight. The station was two and a half miles distant and very little transport was available to convey officers' and men's kit, ammunition, etc., to the station. But promptly at midnight the half battalion, consisting of the fittest men of "A," "B" and "C" companies, left Morogoro. The actual marching out state was twenty officers, five hundred and twenty-six other ranks, one hundred and nine machine gun porters, twenty-seven stretcher bearers and other followers and four machine guns.

On arrival at Dar-es-Salaam, Lieut.-Colonel Morris was ordered to proceed at once to Mombasa, entrain for Moshi and from there march at once to meet the enemy, and at all costs prevent him from capturing Aruscha.

Dar-es-Salaam was reached at 9 a.m. on 11th July, and six hours later the Cape Corps, accompanied by a medical unit known as B/120 Indian Field Ambulance, under Captain H. H. King, embarked on H.M.T. "Tuna."

Kilindini was reached at 10.30 a.m. July 12th. During the voyage Private Fredericks, M. (3191) was washed overboard and drowned.

At Mombasa we were issued with five motor cars to carry out rations, etc. and entrained in the afternoon for Moshi via Taveta, where our C.O. had instructions to enroll his own porters.

At Taveta it was found that the railway was being repaired so the train was taken for Sanja River, but at Weru Weru Bridge the engine became derailed and toppled over a bank, injuring a few men slightly. The track was destroyed, and as it was not possible for the train to proceed to Railhead at Sanja, a shunting engine was procured and the train taken back to Moshi, where two days were spent in collecting porters and completing the necessary organisation.

On the morning of July 15th, Major Cowell marched out to Aruscha with "A" company, and in the afternoon "C" company, under Captain Tandy, entrained for Sanja River Railhead, which was reached the same evening. Here Captain G. Botha, S.A.S.C., was left to establish a supply depôt for Lieut.-Colonel Morris' column. Lieutenant Feetham was also left at Sanja River with fifteen men to establish a Rest Camp for the column, to take charge of the camp at Sanji River, and also to act as a guard over the Supply Depôt.

[Note.—The subsequent movements of Lieutenant Feetham and his men are recorded at the end of this chapter, *vide* page 122.]

THE STORY OF THE 1st CAPE CORPS.

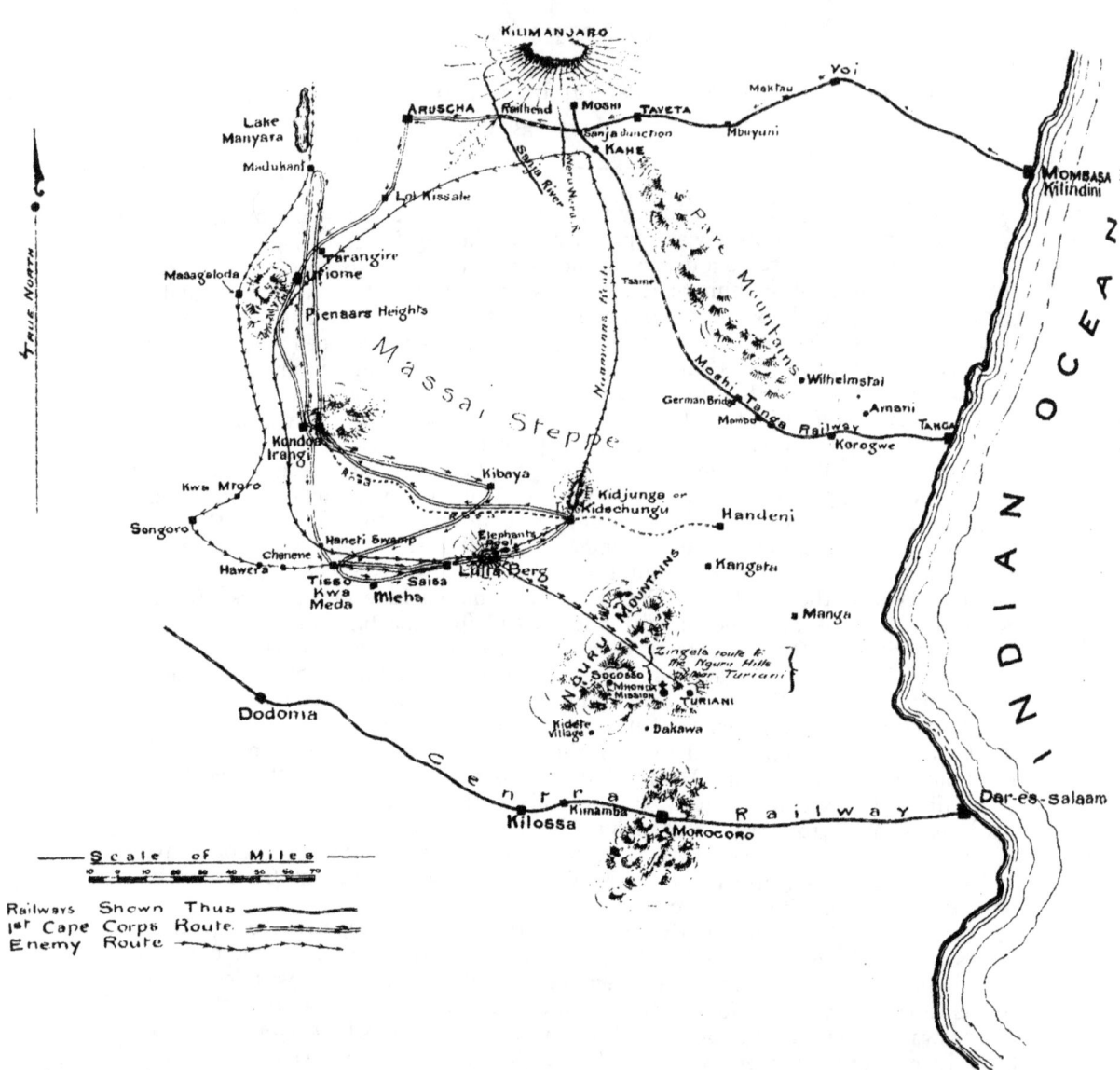

MAP ILLUSTRATING ROUTE TAKEN BY COLUMN UNDER LIEUT.-COLONEL MORRIS, D.S.O., IN OPERATIONS RESULTING IN CAPTURE OF ENEMY FORCE UNDER OBER-LIEUTENANT NAUMANN.
Period 15th July to 1st October, 1917.

The next morning "C" company set out to march to Aruscha. Their guide took them in exactly the contrary direction and, although much questioned, persisted that he was right. He was replaced by a porter who knew the way and "C" company joined "A" company at Magi ya Chai and the whole column reached Aruscha—thirty-six miles—on July 18th.

Fifteen miles out of Aruscha the District Political Officer, Major Browne, reported to Lieut.-Colonel Morris as his Intelligence officer. The officers with our C.O. on this "stunt" were: Major Cowell (2nd in command), Captains Harris ("A" company), Tandy and Arnott ("C" company), Lieutenants Stanford, Cloke, Feetham, Stubbs and Pillans ("A" company); T. P. Rose-Innes, Heaton, Barnard and Potgieter ("C" company); S. H. Rose-Innes (A/Q.M.R.), Thompson (signalling officer), Botha and Guest (machine guns), and Captain McNeil (M.O.).

The first duty on arrival at Aruscha was to reorganise the defences as thoroughly as possible. Information was then received to the effect that the enemy were in the neighbourhood, but on learning that Aruscha was strongly held had passed down the eastern side of Lake Manyara, through Madukant, past Masagaloda, and were making south in the direction of Kondoa Irangi.

We therefore made for Kondoa Irangi via Lol Kissale and Ufiome. At Lol Kissale the water supply was put in order. On arrival at Kondoa Lieut.-Colonel Morris came under the command of Lieut.-Colonel P. H. Dyke (130th Baluchis) who had been placed in charge of all operations north of the Central Railway. Lieut.-Colonel Dyke made Dodoma his headquarters. Kondoa was reached on August 6th and the column hurried on at once via Heneti Swamp to Tisso-Kwa-Meda, the enemy having already passed that place travelling east. Kondoa Irangi was held by Lieutenant A. Difford and forty men who had been sent up from Dodoma. Our sick and footsore men were left with him and his fittest men taken to replace them. Later on Lieutenant Difford handed over to Captain Arnott and joined up with the column.

Our first march from Kondoa was twenty-one miles without a halt to the nearest water. After passing Masagaloda the enemy travelled well west of Kondoa through Kwa-Mtoro, then west to Songoro, south-east to Hawero, and east through Chenene, Tisso-Kwa-Meda, Mleha and on to Saisa. At Tisso-Kwa-Meda the K.A.R.M.I., under Captain A. T. Miles, who had been sent after Naumann from Dodoma, and de Jager's scouts, under Major H. de Jager, were attached to Lieut.-Colonel Morris' column, and orders were received to form a flying column by eliminating all but the fittest men, and to hang on to the enemy until they were forced to make a stand. By this time four out of five ration cars had broken down and porters had to be utilised, motor despatch riders being sent on in advance to warn the next supply dump to have the loads ready.

At Tisso-Kwa-Meda certain partially trained local native troops, known as Ruga-Ruga, were attached to the column as scouts. Two or three were usually attached to the advance, flank and rearguards. They got on well with our men and seemed to appreciate their position of responsibility, though some no doubt hankered after the freer life of an independent scout.

An all-night march of twenty-two miles from Tisso-Kwa-Meda brought the column to a camp near Saisa which the enemy had just left. After a short halt we moved on again and the K.A.R.M.I. got into touch with their rearguard. At Saisa the enemy were so hard pressed that they destroyed and abandoned two light Hotchkiss pom poms (one pounders) and three machine guns, and also left behind large quantities of ammunition.

From Saisa they continued east to Luita Berg where our column was only three hours behind them. Here intelligence was brought in that the enemy had split into two parties and had fled in different directions under Naumann

Photos by]   [*The Bower Studios, Durban.*
ACTING CAPTAIN THOMAS MITCHELL HOFFE.
(Acting Adjutant 24/6/17 to 23/9/17). Died at Dodoma, 23rd September, 1917.

and Zingel, respectively. The last named had the smaller party (about one hundred and fifty rifles with necessary followers), but it was eight hours before Lieut.-Colonel Morris was able to discover that fact.

Zingel proceeded south-east towards the Nguru Hills, and Naumann north-east towards Handeni. As the whole object of our pursuit was to drive the enemy south and across the Central Railway, our C.O. decided to follow Naumann and sent a party of K.A.R.M.I., under Lieutenant Batchelor, to keep in touch with Zingel, pending the arrival of another Cape Corps flying column, under Major Hoy, which was sent out from Dodoma by the O.C. operations against Naumann.

Two hours after leaving Saisa we heard that the enemy had camped thirty-five miles east of Luita Berg at Elephant Pool, the only water for many miles around. We followed, intending to attack them at once as we also wanted that water. After an all night march we arrived at nine in the morning to find that the bird had flown an hour earlier, our M.I. getting contact with their rearguard. We followed in the afternoon and the M.I. were again in touch. Early next morning we were again on the move and at 3 p.m. reached the enemy's camp just after they had cleared, leaving freshly cooked food, which was very acceptable.

Next day we followed close on their heels. Naumann took a circular route in the hope of putting us off the trail, and eventually broke off towards the Tanga-Moshi railway and took up a very strong position in the mountains, slightly to the north of the Kondoa-Handeni road. We had evidently brought him to bay, and at Kidschungu, near Talama, we got to grips and after an engagement drove them off. Our casualties were two killed and several wounded (none of these were Cape Corps men).

The enemy then bolted north over the Massai Steppe towards Kahe junction. At this stage we had marched between one hundred and fifty and one hundred and sixty miles through waterless country, in seven days, during the last three of which we had outrun our supplies and lived on the country, the nearest depôt being one hundred miles away. A halt of twenty-four hours was therefore called to enable rations to be brought up by motor car from Kondoa Irangi.

Lieut.-Colonel Morris then pointed out to higher authority that the enemy had cleared in the direction of our fortified posts at Aruscha, Moshi, and Handeni, and also that they could not live long on the country on the Massai Steppe. Permission was accordingly given to us to return to Kondoa in order to get north of the enemy again. On August 22nd we returned to Kidschungu, met our rations, reduced our strength according to orders, and marched back to Kondoa. There information was received that the enemy had attacked Kahe, captured a train, and then cleared across the Steppe again in the direction of Lol-Kissale, with the apparant intention of making for the Lakes.

At Kondoa Lieutenant Percy Bredell (S.A.S.C.M.T.) reported for duty with fifty Hup cars, which had been sent to increase our mobility. From here Captain T. M. Hoffe (adjutant) was sent in by car to Dodoma ill with pneumonia, from which unfortunately he never recovered. His loss was a sad blow as he was both a very able and a very popular officer. (He died in Dodoma hospital on September 23rd.)

On August 30th the column moved on again (north) and, with the assistance of the Hups, reached Pienaar's Heights, near Ufiome, next day. "C" company marched through from Kondoa to Pienaar's Heights (twenty-seven miles) in thirteen hours. There instructions were received to proceed to Lol-Kissale, but hearing that an enemy party had crossed the main road at Tarangire, Lieut.-Colonel Morris decided to make for Madukant, at the same time sending on Major Cowell with a party of eighty men of "C" company in the cars to endeavour to effect a surprise.

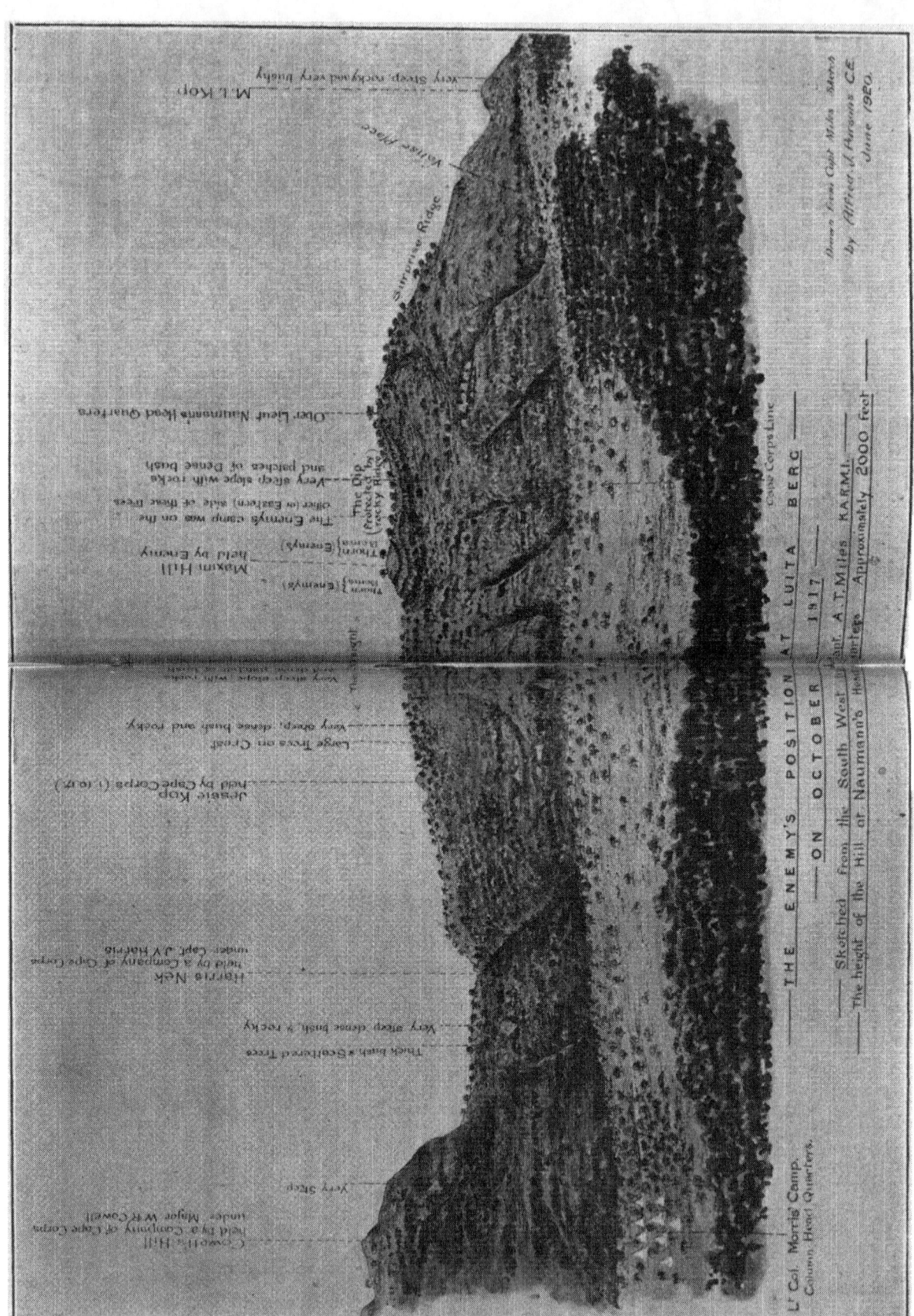

Major Cowell reached Madukant by moonlight about three hours after the enemy. The latter opened fire and our men got out of the cars to reply, but the enemy bolted and the cars could not follow owing to bad roads. Had his guide had a better knowledge of the country Major Cowell would in all probability have effected a coup, but as it was the enemy had the advantage of position, being on a flanking kopje with machine guns covering the road. Responsibilty for the cars also handicapped Major Cowell, and without them he was immobile, having only four porters to carry the machine guns.

This enemy party, under one Broeckmann, did not attempt to return to the main body under Naumann, but cleared northward over the mountains by forced marches towards Lake Manyara. They were in a badly disorganised state and would have lost all their porters, who endeavoured to escape during the brush with Major Cowell's party but were prevented by the Wambugwe natives at Madukant who attacked them and forced them to return to Broeckmann. This party subsequently surrendered to the K.A.R. on October 10th at Umbulu, in the Aruscha neighbourhood, about fifteen miles south-west of Lake Manyara, where Captatin F. J. Bagshawe, late of ours, now D.P.O. Aruscha, helped to effect their surrender.

Major Cowell received instructions to wait for the remainder of our column, which then entered Madukant (September 3rd). An unconfirmed report was brought in that Naumann was also making for the same place but, probably hearing that we were in possession, he cleared south towards Dodoma. We followed to Kondoa where instructions were received to proceed to Kibaya. Here it should be noted that early in September Lieut.-Colonel Dyke was given command of Force Reserve at Kilwa, and handed over the control of the operations against Naumann about September 6th at Dodoma to Colonel Tytler (Indian Army).

It was expected that the enemy would make for Handeni and arrangements were made to follow them by car. The intention was to push forward a hundred men in cars for some distance, and whilst the cars returned for another hundred, the forward party carried on by marching, and so on until the whole column was concentrated at Handeni. Captain Harris took the first hundred men and Major Cowell the second.

Meanwhile Lieut.-Colonel Morris proceeded by car to Dodoma to discuss the situation with Colonel J H. Breytenbach (late O.C. 10th S.A. Horse) who had taken over charge of all operations north of the Central Railway from Colonel Tytler. The result of the "council of war" was that it was agreed that Captain Harris with half a company should occupy Kibaya and that the remainder of the column should concentrate at Tisso-Kwa-Meda in anticipation of a break back by the enemy towards the Massai Steppe.

Whilst at Dodoma Lieut.-Colonel Morris heard that the enemy were making for the water at Saisa near Luita Berg. Instructions were therefore sent out by despatch riders to Captain Harris and to Major Cowell who was following him, to turn south at once and try to reach the water first, heading the enemy off. Harris who had left Kondoa on 19th September was now forty miles from that place and Major Cowell twenty. The latter did a splendid forced march of eighty miles in three days and got round to the west of Luita Berg. Meanwhile the 10th S.A.H. under Lieut.-Colonel Threlfell (since deceased) had been sent out from Dodoma and came up towards the south side of Luita where they exchanged shots with the enemy's patrols and outposts.

About the same time Captain Harris crossed the nek between the eastern and western kopjes of Luita Berg and made for the waterhole at the eastern end. Before he had gained his objective, however, he was ambushed. The enemy allowed his men to pass and then opened with machine guns on his porters in the rear. The result was a panic amongst the latter who dropped their loads

THE STORY OF THE 1st CAPE CORPS.

Photo by] [J.H.T.
NATIVE WOMEN KNEADING NATIVE CORN AT KONDOA IRANGI FOR LIEUT.-
COLONEL MORRIS' COLUMN.

Photo by] [Late Major W. R. Cowell.
2ND-LIEUT. R. A. THOMPSON (SIGNALLING OFFICER) GETTING IN TOUCH
WITH A K.A.R COLUMN AT LUITA BERG. MAJOR BRETT, D.P.O,
STANDING BY.

and bolted, losing all their ammunition, rations and kits. Harris at once turned back and, after a gallant skirmish which lasted some hours, and in which his men behaved splendidly, got his wounded safely away and recaptured everything, except the officers' kits which was subsequently burned by Naumann the night before he surrendered.

The officers with Captain Harris that day were Lieutenants Stanford, Botha, Stubbs and A. Difford. When subsequently asked if he could name any of them for especially good work, Captain Harris' reply was, in effect, that it was a case of *primus inter pares*: (consequently no one got mentioned).

Our casualties in this affair were:—
Wounded:
Private Jaftha, J. (1320) seriously.
Private Peters, T. (3424) severely.
Private Klink, G. (3431) slight.
Also seventeen porters killed or wounded.

When Major Cowell arrived at Luita he was ordered to drive the enemy off the western on to the eastern kopje, which he duly did.

Meanwhile, Lieut.-Colonel Morris had returned from Dodoma to Tisso-Kwa-Meda, where, on the 22nd September, he learned of Harris' encounter the previous day. He accordingly proceeded with the remainder of his column with all speed, via Mleha (along the excellent road constructed by Major Cadiz, D.P.O., Dodoma) to Saisa.

Our column had now been increased by the arrival of the 4th/4th K.A.R., under Lieut.-Colonel Lilley, from Handeni, and two squadrons 10th S.A.H. from Dodoma, whilst the Cape Corps, which had been reduced to about two hundred and fifty owing to men gone sick and footsore, etc., gained an accession in strength by the timely arrival of Major Bradstock with one hundred reinforcements.

On September 29th, Major Hoy and Captain Cuningham joined up from Dodoma.

There now seemed for the first time a real probability that Naumann was at last thoroughly cornered and would require all his skill—not inconsiderable—and a good deal of luck to extricate himself.

The enemy were entrenched on the eastern slope of Luita Berg, and by continually moving the 10th S.A.H. on the north and the K.A.R.M.I. on the south side of the mountain, Lieut.-Colonel Morris held them to their position until the arrival of reinforcements from Dodoma. He was also able to reduce his original perimeter of thirty miles to half of that, as well as to strengthen the cordon, which on September 30th was complete, with all troops in very close touch. The whole perimeter was connected by telephone, thanks to some very hard work, in which Lieutenant Ambler, R.E. (signals) assisted.

Our dispositions at this time were as follows: Lieut.-Colonel Morris' headquarters on the southern side of the Nek between the two kopjes, with the K.A.R.M.I. and de Jager's scouts in reserve to the south; Cape Corps under Major Bradstock, south; 4th/4th K.A.R., east; 10th S.A.H., north; Cape Corps under Major Hoy, west.

The 24th Indian Mountain Battery, which had reinforced us from Dodoma and been held in reserve for a few days, shelled the enemy's position from September 27th to 30th. Naumann afterwards admitted to two killed, fourteen wounded and several porter casualties as a result of this shelling, and also that he had to dig in under fire and was without food for forty-eight hours.

Everybody was now kept fully on the *qui vive*, patrolling their allotted fronts day and night, and under orders to exercise the utmost vigilance to prevent the enemy breaking through. The water supply was a most difficult proposition as every drop required had to be brought some ten to twelve miles from Saisa by porters carrying it in chaguls or paraffin tins, which had been sent out from Dodoma for the purpose.

On September 30th the Cape Corps on the western perimeter seized the Spitz Kop on the western end of the enemy's hill and patrolled right up to the "machine gun point" where the enemy had very strongly fortified a shoulder of ground with a Boma (fence) and machine guns. Captain Harris took command here and dug in right across the hill.

The height of Luita Berg was about two thousand feet, of which the top was two hundred feet of sheer precipice. The distance round the eastern kopje was about twelve miles. The enemy held the only path to the water at the eastern end, which Captain Harris had failed to reach.

The main road along the southern slopes of the Berg was held by the enemy and we had to cut a path by compass through dense thorn bush between the Cape Corps and the K.A.R. and for communication between the various attacking units. Paths had also to be cut through the bush in towards the hill to enable us to attack.

A general attack had been planned to take place at 9 p.m. on September 30th, but two hours before that time Naumann sent down an envoy under the white flag to negotiate with a view to surrender.

A 4.5 inch Howitzer arrived from Dodoma on September 30th, but before it could be brought into action Naumann's envoy had arrived and Lieut.-Colonel Morris at once sent a reply by Captain Wilson, D.S.O., and wired for Colonel Breytenbach to come out from Dodoma.

At 10 a.m. on October 1st, Lieut.-Colonel Morris received Naumann, who capitulated, and on the following day his force came down the mountain and surrendered. Their strength was fifteen Europeans, one hundred and sixty-five Askari, about four hundred porters, fifty head of oxen and a few donkeys.

Colonel Breytenbach was present at our headquarters at the surrender, but refused to take same, saying that as Morris had done all the hard work, he should have the honour of the victory.

A copy of Naumann's letter to Lieut.-Colonel Morris and translation of the same is subjoined to this chapter.

The European prisoners were taken into Dodoma by car, under escort of the 10th S.A.H., and the Askari were marched in under the ciceronage of the Cape Corps and then railed to Tabora for internment.

Naumann had chosen Luita Berg for his final stand on account of the dense bush and the lack of water for miles around. In two and a half months our column had covered over eleven hundred miles, three-fourths of it on foot. The health of the force had been on the whole excellent, with the exception of a certain amount of recurrent fever and a good many sore feet, as was to have been expected. The keenness and determination of all ranks concerned in the chase contributed materially to its successful termination.

Lieut.-Colonel Morris received the C.M.G. as his award for the thoroughly satisfactory manner in which he had disposed of Naumann and his marauders.

The surrounding natives, whose loyalty had been very marked, greatly welcomed the capture. As may well be imagined they had been considerably disturbed.

In Lieut.-Colonel Morris' report "to higher authority" on the operations, the following passage is worthy of quotation :—

"I was much impressed with the equipment of the German Askari, who carried no weight. Each man had an attendant porter, who also was not over-loaded, and every man had his own light portable tent. I am sure that these are factors which kept the Askari fit and enabled him to march so extraordinarily well, and I consider that my own Infantry did

THE STORY OF THE 1st CAPE CORPS.

Photos by]   *[J.H.T.*

OBER-LIEUTENANT NAUMANN WITH HIS WHITE AND BLACK SERGEANT-MAJORS DISCUSSING TERMS OF SURRENDER.   COLONEL BREYTENBACH AND LT.-COLONEL MORRIS AT LUITA BERG AFTER SURRENDER OF NAUMANN.   MAJOR F. W. BRETT AND MAJOR CADIZ, TWO HELPFUL POLITICAL OFFICERS AT LUITA BERG.

Photo by]   *[J.H.T.*

NAUMANN'S PORTERS AFTER SURRENDER.

C.Q.M.S. J. L. DAVIDS (97) AND SERGEANT J. WALKER (3132).

wonderfully well in holding on with such heavy equipment as they were burdened with."

Our men's packs, with spare clothing and rations, their ammunition and rifles, etc., weighed in all (including clothing worn on the person) over fifty pounds.

The following officers and other ranks were brought to the notice of higher authority by Lieut.-Colonel Morris for good work done in these operations:—

Lieut.-Colonel Lilley, 4/4 K.A.R.
Lieut.-Colonel Threlfell, 10th S.A.H.
Major Browne, D.P.O., Aruscha.
Major Brett, D.P.O., Kondoa Irangi.
Captain H. P. Creswell, D.A.D.M.L.
Captain Bresler, 10th S.A.H.
Captain H. H. King, B/120 I.F.A.
Captain A. T. Miles, K.A.R.M.I.
Lieutenant G. Kelly, K.A.R.M.I.
Lieutenant Batchelor, K.A.R.M.I.
Lieutenant Malan, 10th S.A.H.
Lieutenant P. Bredell, O.C. Hup Convoy, S.A.S.C.M.T.
Lieutenant Ambler, R.E. (Signals).
Lieutenant Hamman (I.D.)
Lieutenant B.Rosen, M.D. Riders.
5853 Sergeant J. W. Houitt, M.L.B.
2090 Acting Sergeant C. G. Brooke, E.A.M.T.C.
Corporal T. J. Hanna, M.L.B.
4101 Lance-Corporal Jama Awad, K.A.R.M.I.
3603 Driver G. J. Smith, S.A.S.C. (M.T.)
Major W. R. Cowell, 1st Cape Corps.
Captain J. H. Tandy, 1st Cape Corps.
Captain J. V. Harris, 1st Cape Corps.
980 Corporal F. Schroeder, 1st Cape Corps ⎫ recommended for prompt
829 Corporal H. J. Fredericks, do. ⎬ awards.
269 Lance-Corporal J. Ruiters, do. ⎭

Captain Miles and Lieutenants Batchelor, Hamman and Percy Bredell (of Boksburg) subsequently received their reward in the shape of a Military Cross.

Major Browne and Lieutenant Hamman, our Intelligence officers, did exceptionally good work throughout the operations, and Major Brett, D.P.O. (Kondoa Irangi), also lent valuable aid.

Officers and men of the battalion who received honours and awards in connection with these operations were:—

C.M.G.:—
Lieut.-Colonel Morris.
Diploma Chevalier de l'ordre de la Couronne (Belgian):—
Captain Tandy.
Mentioned in Despatches:—
Captain Harris.
Captain Tandy.
Sergeant Alies, J. H. (825).
Sergeant February, M. (92).
a/C.S.M. Scullard, J. (1363).
Military Medal:—
Corporal F. Schroeder (980).
Corporal H. J. Fredericks (829).
Belgian Decoration Militaire (2nd Class):—
Corporal Manuel, P. (71).

THE STORY OF THE 1st CAPE CORPS.

Our Motor Despatch Riders.

Lieutenant Percy Bredell, M.C. The Officer i/c Motor Convoy.

Left to right: Colonel Brytenbach, Captain A. T. Miles, Lieut.-Colonel Morris, Captain McNeil, and Major Cowell.

Enemy Prisoners leaving Luita Berg by Motor Car.

THE STORY OF THE 1st CAPE CORPS.

Photos by] [J.H.T.

K.A.R.M.I. ON SAFARI.
ENEMY ASKARI N.C.O.'S.
CAPTAIN McNEIL LOOKING FOR MOSQUITOS.
K.A.R. WATCHING PARADE OF NATIVE WOMEN CAPTURED WITH NAUMANN AT LUITA BERG.

A BOER FAMILY LEAVING ARUSCHA.
NAUMANN'S NATIVE WOMEN CAMP FOLLOWERS.
OUR SIGNALLERS AT WORK AT LUITA BERG.
LT.-COLONEL MORRIS STANDING AT BACK.
INSPECTION OF CAPTURED ENEMY KIT AT LUITA BERG.

C.Q.M.S. Davids, J. (97) and Sergeant Lavita, W. H. (1127) also did very good work on this "stunt."

The Hup convoy did great work, in fact without them it is doubtful if we should have succeeded in effecting Naumann's downfall. When not in use to transport the troops they assisted by giving the porters and their loads a lift. The porters very soon became wise to this and instead of carrying on waited on the roadside with their loads on the chance of securing a joy-ride.

Our porters did splendid work throughout this chase, carrying out their most strenuous tasks with grim determination. They were very keen to be in at the death and were vastly delighted at the final capture, the only fly in the ointment being our failure to capture more cattle.

Lions caused the column a good deal of trouble and excitement at different times. One night at Tisso-Kwa-Meda they got two of our donkeys, and the night before the fight at Kidschungu three of them drove in our outposts. Two nights later Sergeant Ross and five men, whilst returning to Kondoa, were tackled and Private L. Williams (2470) was mauled to death. They had failed to keep their night fires burning. Another night a K.A.R.M.I. man on horse guard was driven up a tree and had to remain there until morning.

COPY.

Copy of a letter addressed by Ober-Lieut. Naumann to Lieut.-Colonel Morris asking for a conference.

LUITA, 30 Sept., 1917.

AN DEN KOMMANDIERENDEN OFFIZIER
DER BRITISCHEN STREITKRAEFTE
BEI LUITA.

Ich ersuche Sie mir mitzuteilen, ob Sie damit einverstanden sind, sich mit mir am 1. Oktober 1.J. Zu einer Ihnen passenden Zeit ich schlage vor 10 Uhr Vormittag auf der nach Soisa fuehrenden Strasse zu einre Unterredung zu treffen. Ich bitte im Falle Ihres Einverstaendnisses dem Ueberbringer des Schreibens den Ort und die Zeit naeher zu bezeichnen.

Der kommandierende Offizier der Deutschen Streitkraefte auf Luitaberg.

(Sgd.) NAUMANN,
Oberleutnant.

(Translation of the above.)

LUITA, 30th Sept, 1917.

To the Commanding Officer
of the British Forces
at Luita.

I request you to inform me whether you are agreeable to meet me on the 1st of October at an hour suitable to your convenience,—I propose 10 a.m.—on the road leading to Soisa in order to have a conference with you.

I ask you in case you agree to describe to bearer of this letter the location and the time of the conference.

The O.C. of the German Forces on Luita Berg.

(Signed) NAUMANN,
1st Lieutenant.

[NOTE.—Lieut.Colonel Morris' reply to the above was: "No Conference—unconditional surrender."]

MOVEMENTS OF LIEUTENANT FEETHAM'S DETACHMENT.

(vide page 107).

When Lieutenant Feetham was left at Sanja River Railhead, a section of Indian Field Ambulance (B120), under Sub-Assistant Surgeon Gupta, was left with him to care for the sick. Men discharged from Hospital at Moshi reported to Feetham and the fits were sent forward to join the Column.

On the 2nd August, on orders received from Lieut.-Colonel Morris, Feetham left Sanja River for Lol Kissale with a dozen men and two wagons, in order to join the Column on its way south. On arrival at Lol Kissale, three days later, he was met with a message from Lieut.-Colonel Morris, dated 2nd August, reading as follows:—" Column proceeding Kondoa, impossible you overtake us, collect all men possible, join me Dodoma via Kilindini and Dar-es-Salaam." Feetham accordingly returned with wagons to Sanja River, collected about seventy men from hospital at Aruscha and elsewhere, and reported to G.H.Q., who instructed him to " Move complete to Korogwe."

The detachment left Sanja River for Korogwe on the 12th August; strength, one officer, sixty-four N.C.O.'s and men, and the Indian Field Ambulance Section. Quartermaster-Sergeant Heeger was appointed Acting Sergeant-Major of the detachment, and served in that capacity until they rejoined the Battalion at Massassi on November 24th.

The detachment arrived at Korogwe on the 13th August.

At Korogwe, Feetham's duties were to take measures to protect the place in case any of Naumann's Force should attack in that direction. He took up his quarters on a hill two miles outside the town on the Handeni Road, overlooking the road bridge across the Pangani, and sent pickets to two Railway bridges in the neighbourhood. Within a few days additional troops (K.A.R.) were concentrated at Korogwe, and news came of the engagement between Lieut.-Colonel Morris' Column and Naumann at Kidschungu on the Kondoa-Handeni road.

On the 23rd August the detachment left Korogwe for Kahe Bridge, with orders to guard the bridge, which had been destroyed by the enemy in their retreat more than a year ago, and had just been restored and re-opened for traffic after eight months' work. Naumann, after the engagement at Kidschungu, had disappeared northwards into the Massai Steppe, and as he was reported to be carrying a quantity of dynamite it was expected that he would try and destroy railway bridges on the Tanga line, of which Kahe Bridge was the biggest and most tempting.

The strength of the detachment on arrival at Kahe Bridge on August 24th was, Cape Corps, one officer, fifty-one N.C.O.'s and men, I.F.A. section and thirty-eight porters. On the afternoon of August 28th one of Feetham's patrols brought in runners with a message from Lieutenant Hamman, the Intelligence Officer who was following up Naumann through the Massai Steppe, to the effect that Naumann's Force would arrive on August 29th or 30th at a place about 15 miles from Aruscha Tschini, and that from there he would send a strong patrol to Aruscha Tschini for the purpose of collecting food. This message was despatched to G.H.Q., and late that night a detachment of 4/4 K.A.R.'s (a recently raised Battalion) under Captain King, was sent up the line to Kahe, and Feetham, with thirty Cape Corps, was ordered to accompany two K.A.R. platoons, on the morning of the 29th August, to Aruscha Tschini (about five hours' march from Kahe) in order to lie in wait for Naumann's patrol. The bulk of this detachment, Lieutenant Stuart with sixty K.A.R. and Feetham with twenty Cape Corps, left Kahe early on the morning of the 29th, Lieutenant Stuart, 4/4th K.A.R., being in command. Captain King followed up later with a baggage guard of ten Cape Corps and ten K.A.R. and porters.

About two and a half hours' march from Kahe, Stuart's Force, to which the twenty Cape Corps under Feetham acted as advance guard, arrived on the banks of a tributary of the Pangani, a strong stream about thirty yards wide. The question then arose whether to ford the river at that point or to march two hours up stream to find a plank bridge, the existence of which was reported by local natives. It was decided to cross at the ford. After another two and a half hours' march the Cape Corps' advance guard, just as they were at last approaching the outskirts of Aruscha Tschini, sighted an enemy picket with which they exchanged shots as the picket made a hasty retreat through the bush.

THE STORY OF THE 1st CAPE CORPS.

Photo by] [Aziz & Dores, Alexandria.
SERGEANT J. D. LOUW (1621).

Photo by] [Chas. Leonard, Kimberley.
SERGEANT (A/C.S.M.) J. P. CARROLLISSEN (280).

Photo by] [H. W. Herman, Kimberley.
C.Q.M.S. W. H. LA VITA (1127).

Photo by] [Fred Bourne, Cape Town.
SERGEANT P. HENDRICKS (223).

It was clear that Naumann was in advance of Lieutenant Hamman's time table. Cape Corps and K.A.R. scouts were sent out, and it appeared from their reports that the enemy was holding Aruscha Tschini in force. Lieutenant Stuart, seeing that he had been forestalled and could not carry out the plan of lying in wait for the enemy patrol, decided to withdraw; he was not strong enough to attempt the capture of Aruscha Tschini by assault, and the position of his small force in the bush, without supplies and some distance from the river, was obviously a precarious one. The Cape Corps were ordered to act as rearguard during the withdrawal.

Shortly after the decision to withdraw had been taken, a party of the enemy advanced and opened fire on the position which the Cape Corps were holding to cover the retreat of the main body. The attack was quickly beaten off without casualties on our side. It was subsequently reported by a prisoner that the Germans had one white man and three Askaris wounded in this scrap and the previous encounter with the picket. The withdrawal was then safely accomplished, and Captain King's party were met about a mile and a half from the scene of the scrap.

Captain King then sent out a patrol to find out what the enemy were doing, and withdrew the remainder of his men across the river. The ford was re-crossed just before nightfall, and the detachment bivouacked for the night close to the river on the Kahe side.

During the night August 29th/30th Captain Sims, R.E., arrived from Kahe bridge with a Cape Corps' Escort under Sergeant Heeger, and brought the news that an enemy party had that afternoon seized Kahe Junction (about six miles from Kahe in the direction of Moshi) and captured two trains. As Kahe bridge had been left with only a small garrison of sick men Feetham marched his Cape Corps men back there early on the morning of the 30th, but found the enemy had made no attempt on the bridge. Kahe Junction was also ascertained to be clear of the enemy.

Subsequent enquiry shewed that the sequence of events was as follows:—Naumann, doubtless by night marches, had moved much more rapidly than was expected. Instead of reaching on August 29th or 30th the place about a day's march from Aruscha Tschini whence he was to send his patrol to that place, he had arrived at Aruscha Tschini himself with his main body late on the evening of the 28th. His total force at Aruscha Tschini was reported to consist of fifteen Europeans, about two hundred Askaris, and as many porters, and he had at least one serviceable maxim.

Early on the morning of the 29th, when Lieutenant Stuart was starting out from Kahe to Aruscha Tschini, Naumann had sent out from the latter place a patrol consisting of four white men and between fifty and sixty Askaris in the direction of the railway line. This party took the path by the plank bridge, about the time that Stuart's Force crossed the river at the ford. Had Stuart happened to choose or to have been guided to the bridge instead of crossing at the ford he would almost certainly have met the enemy patrol in the bush, and would have been able to stop their game. As it was, in the hide and seek conditions of bush warfare, the two parties missed.

The enemy reached the railway near Kahe Junction, stopped two trains, of which they burned one containing bombs and other military stores, killed several native passengers, shot the stationmaster at Kahe Junction, captured three British officers who were passengers in one of the trains, and also a Cape Corps sergeant, Smith, C. J. (3160), (the latter made good his escape the same night by slipping away in the bush) and then cleared out again. Hearing a garrison was at the bridge they avoided that point, and marched back to Aruscha Tschini on the night of the 29th, taking the same path by which they had come—by the plank bridge.

Early on the morning of the 30th, Naumann's whole Force left Aruscha Tschini.

The enemy with whom Lieutenant Stuart came into contact on the afternoon of the 29th was therefore Naumann's main body, less the patrol of sixty which had been sent to the railway, a much stronger force than that which Stuart had at his disposal.

While Sergeant Smith was a prisoner, before he was marched off by his captors from Kahe Junction, one of the European N.C.O.'s with the German Force dealt him a severe blow in the back with the butt of a rifle, which resulted in his detention in hospital for some weeks.

Lieutenant Feetham remained to garrison Kahe Bridge until September 12th, when he was relieved by a K.A.R. detachment, and left via Sanja River for Aruscha where he arrived on September 15th. His strength, after evacuation of sick to hospital at Tanga, was then forty-four other ranks and one F.A. section. On arrival at Aruscha practically all the men went down with fever, owing to the change to the higher altitude, and Feetham was therefore unable to carry out the order received from Lieut.-Colonel Morris to march to Kondoa Irangi to rejoin.

On October 10th the detachment left Aruscha via Sanja River for Kilindini. It was detained at Kilindini waiting for transport until November 13th, when it left per H.M.T. "Barjora" for Lindi, where it arrived on November 16th—strength, one officer, seventy-two rank and file.

From Lindi the detachment marched inland to Massassi and rejoined the Battalion there on November 24th.

Photo by] [J G. Horsfall, Cape Town
C.Q.M.S. P. F. HEEGER (21).

CHAPTER X.

The Zingel "Stunt," period 26th July to 27th September, 1917
(vide map, page 128).

WHEN Lieut.-Colonel Morris left Morogoro on July 10th for Aruscha via Dar-es-Salaam in order to go in pursuit of Captain Naumann, Major Hoy was left in command at Morogoro.

A fortnight later Major Hoy received orders to proceed at once with all fit men to Dodoma and from there to co-operate with Lieut.-Colonel Morris' column, acting under orders of the O.C. operations against Naumann, Colonel P. H. Dyke, D.S.O., whose headquarters were at Dodoma.

The detachment was known as Cape Corps Column No. 2. They left Morogoro by train for Dodoma on July 26th and consisted of " D " Company, a composite company of " A," " B," and " C " Company details, under Captain Michau, a signal section under Sergeant Alies, four machine guns, and six Lewis guns.

The officers who left Morogoro with Major Hoy were Captains Michau, Earp-Jones, Pearse, and Edwards, Lieutenant Horseman, and 2nd Lieutenant McNeil, and other ranks numbered three hundred and ninety-three.

Three days before the detachment left Morogoro Lieutenant Difford had been sent with his platoon by rail to Dodoma and thence by motor car (seventy miles) to Kondoa Irangi to strengthen the small garrison there.

On July 24th Captain Burger, Lieutenants Hayton and Howe-Browne, and 2nd Lieutenant Abbott, with sixty three men, one hundred and eighteen machine gun porters, four Maxim guns, and four Lewis guns, had left Morogoro by rail for Dodoma. Lieutenant Howe-Browne was detailed to act as staff officer to Colonel Dyke at Dodoma.

Captain Burger left Dodoma by motor car on July 27th with twelve men, thirty-five machine gun porters, and two Maxims to join the garrison at Kondoa Irangi, of which he was to assume command. Major Hoy's detachment detrained at Dodoma (two hundred and forty miles from Dar-es-Salaam) on July 27th and remained there five days, during which period a section of No. 2 S.A. Field Ambulance (Captain Ingle and eight other ranks) and Captain Stradling, M.C. (Carrier Corps) with some two hundred and fifty porters joned the detachment.

On July 31st the detachment entrained for Saranda, seventy miles further west. At Saranda considerable work had to be done as the enemy, who were active to the north, had cut our communications with Ssingida and Makalama, where we had established small posts under the respective political officers.

Lieutenant Howe-Browne was sent to Ssingida with fifteen men, and thirty-seven rank and file to strengthen the post at Makalama. Men unfit to march were, of course, selected for those duties.

The Cape Corps detachments in the Dodoma area were then designated as follows:—

Major Hoy's command: Detachment No. 5.
Captain Burger's command (Kondoa Irangi): Sub-Detachment " A."
Lieutenant Howe-Browne's command (Ssingida): Sub-Detachment " B."

MAP ILLUSTRATING OPERATIONS OF 1st CAPE CORPS DETACHMt Under Major Hoy, D.S.O., resulting in capture of Lieutenant Zingel's Force
Period July 26th to ... mb.. 2nd, 1917.

On August 1st an enemy patrol, reported as four whites and fifty Askari, attacked Lieutenant Howe-Browne's post at Ssingida but were driven off with a few casualties. Our casualties were a few porters wounded.

Whilst at Saranda our railway engines stood always with banked fires ready to move at a few minutes' notice, and scouts and patrols were kept continuously out to the north, as the enemy were seeking a safe crossing of the railway to the south in an endeavour to rejoin their headquarters then at Mahenge.

At Saranda a motor lorry which had been converted for use on the railway was armoured by Lieutenant McNeil with material found in the engine shed and with sand bags, and was used for patrolling the line and to take scouts and patrols to their jumping-off points.

Captain Burger with fourteen other ranks and two Maxim guns and thirty-five porters joined the detachment at Saranda from Kondoa Irangi on August 3rd, and on the same day Intelligence Agent Cottar with ten native scouts. He left at once by motor car for Songoro and returned in the evening with four enemy porters who had deserted. The latter gave information to the effect that the enemy's strength was two officers, thirty European other ranks, and three hundred Askari with a pom-pom and twelve machine guns.

On August 4th the detachment was reinforced by the arrival from Dodoma of two Indian officers and ninety-five rank and file of the Bharatpur (Indian) Infantry. Our strength in porters had at this time been increased to six hundred and fifty-five, and our machine gun porters and other African followers to a total of one hundred and fifty-six.

On August 5th Lieutenant Bain joined the detachment from Morogoro with two men and thirty-one machine gun porters, and two days later Captain Robinson and R.S.M. Betts, who had been on sick leave to South Africa, also arrived from Morogoro.

On August 8th Major Hoy received orders to move to Bahi, where the enemy was expected to attempt to cross the line, but later the same evening the detachment was ordered to return to Dodoma, where they went into camp and remained six days. Whilst there Major Bradstock, Lieutenants Gardner and Leslie, 2nd Lieutenants Samuelson and Colson, and forty-four rank and file joined up from Morogoro.

The officers with Major Hoy were now Major Bradstock, Captains Robinson, Michau, Pearse, Edwards, and Earp-Jones, Lieutenants Bain, Colson, McNeil, Horseman, Gardner, Leslie, Howe-Browne, and Samuelson. Lieutenant Bain, who had been sent out from Saranda on August 7th by motor car to Mpondo, thirty miles north-east, to locate the enemy, returned to Dodoma on August 10th. He reported that the enemy had shot several natives who had declined to act as porters, as well as several old porters who were no longer of any use to them. Also that they had carried off numbers of women for immoral purposes and that all the natives were escaping to the hills when news of the enemy's approach reached them.

On August 13th Lieutenant Bain and eight rank and file left for Kigwe station to endeavour to round up a few enemy Askari reported near there, and the next day Sergeant Hector left by rail for Gulwe with seventeen other ranks and proceeded from there by motor car to garrison Mpapua.

On August 14th Major Hoy's detachment proceeded by rail from Dodoma to Kidete, thirty-two and a half miles east, where they remained for three days awaiting orders, and meanwhile patrolling the surrounding country.

During these three days the men lived in the train with banked fires maintained on the engine ready for an instant move.

On August 17th orders were received to proceed to Kimamba, thirty-seven miles nearer to Morogoro, which was reached the same evening.

Information had reached Colonel Dyke at this time that Naumann's force had broken into two parties, and that Lieutenant Zingel, with the 26th Field Company, had left Saisa in a south-easterly direction heading for the Nguru Hills, where ample food would be obtainable and in which were many well-watered valleys.

The task of chasing Zingel was delegated to Major Hoy's detachment, with orders to at all costs prevent him breaking east, and if possible to bring him to battle and destroy or capture his whole party.

Lieutenant Zingel had been District Commissioner at Morogoro under the German régime, and it was natural that he should make for a district which he knew well and where he expected to be looked up to by the natives. In that, however, he was to be greatly disappointed, as the natives helped us in every possible way, supplying scouts and porters, cattle and grain.

Major Hoy's detachment left Kimamba early on August 18th and marched all day past Rudewa and on to Kinganga and Kissangata (fourteen miles).

The strength of the column was 1st Cape Corps, sixteen officers, three hundred and forty-four rank and file; one hundred and twenty-three machine gun porters and followers; 2nd S.A. Field Ambulance, one officer, six other ranks, thirty-one stretcher-bearers; Carrier Corps, one officer, one N.C.O., and four hundred and eighty-nine porters; S.A.M.D.R. (motor despatch riders), two; S.A.S.C.M.T. (motor car drivers), two.

On August 19th, shortly before the column reached the Wami River, the Akida from Mamboja came in with a following and reported that he had just escaped capture and that the enemy had looted and burned his village. He also brought information that they were then camped at Mberega. Major Hoy sent out native intelligence agents to glean the latest information and made an all-night march from Kifwe to Njangalo with the object of attacking, but did not succeed in getting touch with the enemy.

The composite company was sent from Njangalo to Kidete on the Kimamba-Kwedihombo road on August 20th, and the remainder of the column followed the next day on orders from Dodoma.

At Kidete it was learned that the enemy had cleared north on the western side of the Ngulu Hills via Talagwe and was threatening to break east through Mhondo Mission above Turiani. We followed at once to counter this move, "D" Company going forward by motor convoy to Magubugubu and Lieutenant Bain being sent forward to act as intelligence agent and glean the latest information.

The column reached Mwomero on the 22nd and Kwedihombo on the 23rd, having then marched about eighty-four miles in five days. There news was received that no sign of the enemy had been seen about Mhondo Mission, and a day's much-needed rest ensued, pending receipt of later news from our intelligence agents. Meanwhile a supply dump was established at Kwedihombo.

At midnight information came in that the enemy were at Muscat Mission in the hills to the west of Mhondo Mission. At daybreak on the 24th Major Bradstock left Kwedihombo with "D" Company (about one hundred and twenty-five strong) and four Maxim guns under Lieutenant Abbott for Mhondo Mission and at the same time Captain Michau was sent with the composite company to Mkundi, a village at the bottom of the valley which practically divides the Nguru mountains from north to south. Major Hoy remained at Kwedihombo to keep in touch with headquarters at Dodoma and to arrange the convoy or rations, etc. Bradstock's orders were to prevent the enemy from breaking east and to try to drive them south down the Mkundi Valley into the arms of Captain Michau's Company. He was also to endeavour to impress the enemy with his strength by arming his porters with sticks and marching them with him.

Captain Michau marched to Nyumi village five miles north of Mkundi, but when Major Hoy joined him there he was withdrawn to Mkundi to wait for the enemy and Major Hoy returned to Kwedihombo.

On the morning of the 25th the Nguru Hills were reported clear of the enemy and Colonel Dyke ordered Major Hoy to return with his column to Morogoro and Major Bradstock was notified to that effect by runner.

All preparations were completed on the 26th for the return of the detachment to the Central Railway, when in the afternoon Major Bradstock reported that the enemy had been located in the vicinity of Muscat Mission and that he was making dispositions to attack them. Later in the afternoon intelligence was received that the enemy were moving south down the Buruma Valley and Major Hoy at once wired for permission to continue his operations, which was of course granted.

Meanwhile Major Bradstock had set out Lieutenant Power with his platoon by a steep mountain path leading direct from Mhondo to Muscat, and with the remainder of his company proceeded north-east to get round north of the enemy and endeavour to drive him south. The enemy, finding Power blocking their way from Muscat to Mhondo, cleared west and Bradstock followed to attack. He missed the main body by half an hour but came up with and attacked the porters and captured thirty of them and their escort, with about one hundred loads of ammunition and supplies. The European N.C.O. in charge and two Askari were captured, five Askari killed and the remainder dispersed in the bush.

Bradstock's energetic action left Zingel with very little ammunition or food, except livestock, so he headed for Wanjoki, an isolated hill near Sogossa Mountain, and, driving his cattle with him, strongly entrenched himself.

It was obviously not his policy to stand and fight, but equally obviously Major Hoy had made the pace such a cracker that he had no alternative but to make a stand and hope for the best.

Bradstock followed the enemy to Wanjoki, but was not strong enough to attack or surround him.

On receipt of this news Major Hoy sent word to Captain Michau to hurry on to Nyumi, and followed there himself. At Nyumi on the afternoon of the 27th Major Hoy, having gleaned a thorough knowledge of the vicinity and paths from the local natives, divided his force into two parties. Captain Michau was sent with seventy-two riflemen and two Lewis guns to Kilama to the west of the hills so that he could drive Zingel back if he attempted to break through an opening in the mountains at Tschogowali village to the south-west.

At the same time Major Hoy, with the remainder of his men, marched north up the Mkundi Valley until midnight. Just at sundown Sergeant Dunn (1134) captured an enemy Askari who had been one of the enemy convoy escort when Major Bradstock attacked them.

Major Hoy now held the south and west end of the hills and Bradstock was instructed to get between the enemy and Muscat Mission to prevent him escaping north.

At dawn on the 28th Major Hoy continued his advance northwards, and during the morning came in sight of the enemy's position on Wanjoki, and it was decided to surround him that night if possible.

The column hid in the bush for the rest of the day and moved on again at dusk, and at 10 p.m. reached Tschogowali village, where Michau and his men rejoined a little later.

At this time the whole column had been reduced to little more than three hundred rifles, so many men having fallen out with sore feet. The average daily march had been from fifteen to eighteen miles through mountainous

country, over roads so bad that porterage was the only means of transport. Even the motor despatch riders had to be substituted by native runners.
Having outrun his supplies, Major Hoy had to rely on purchases of cattle and native corn from the surrounding villages.

Owing to the smallness of our force for purposes of attack, the most careful dispositions had to be made to prevent the enemy from getting through our cordon. Major Hoy made a sand map in the dry bed of a stream of the country and paths surrounding Wanjoki, as given by our scouts and guides, and in that way a very good idea of the terrain was obtained.

At midnight on the 28th Captain Michau was sent with Lieutenant Leslie and fifty men with two Lewis guns to occupy Urandi Nek, south-west of Sogossa Hill. Captain Pearse, with thirty-five men, was sent north of Sogossa Hill to join up with Bradstock's right and Lieutenant Colson, with a platoon and two Lewis guns was sent to Magesula Ridge to block the only path affording a way of escape between Michau's right and Bradstock's left. Major Hoy remained at Tschogowali to direct operations, having with him only a few sick men and our porters.

By 11 a.m. on the 29th Captain Michau had seized Urandi Nek after a skirmish with the enemy in which he captured four Askari and had three men wounded.

To reach the top of the nek necessitated a very strenuous climb; the men had to pull themselves up by the long grass which was very dry and slippery and liable to give way; a false step meant a heavy fall, and one man who took a toss was in hospital for some time in consequence. To have got up safely with machine guns was some feat and considerably astonished the enemy, who were about half a mile distant. They promptly opened fire, to which Michau vigorously replied, and, taking cover, held on to the position.

On the top of the nek twenty enemy porters were surprised and captured. They gave valuable information about the enemy's position which faced east towards Major Bradstock.

On the night of the 29th the enemy attempted to get through a nek held by Lieutenant Power, but were driven back.

From Urandi Nek Captain Michau sent Lieutenant Leslie with twenty men to occupy another bit of high ground overlooking Wanjoki. He reached his position after a two hours' stiff climb and was immediately fired on. He replied with his Lewis gun and put a machine gun out of action, and continued in action until dark. As Michau held his position very precariously Lieutenants Edwards and Samuelson, with forty men and two Lewis guns, were sent up from Major Bradstock's party to reinforce him.

On August 30th Lieutenant Batchelor, with ten men of the K.A.R.M.I., joined the column to assist in patrolling and scouting.

Having now completed and consolidated his position, Major Hoy moved his headquarters from Tschogowali to Urandi Nek on September 1st, and then took Lieutenant Batchelor, his intelligence officer, and Sergeant Dunn, his chief scout, on foot on a personal tour of inspection of all his positions. This was a physical feat involving many hours of strenuous climbing to and fro.

The enemy were holding the water and our positions were so exposed that for five days all food and water had to be carried up to the firing line at night.

Everything possible had to be done to convince the enemy that our strength was greater that it actually was, and to this end on September 1st all Maxim and Lewis guns were distributed about the permeter and a few minutes' hot fire opened on the enemy with all ordnance. More could not be done owing to shortage of ammunition. Food was also getting scarce, and as time was being wasted by desultory fighting, Major Hoy decided to send an ultimatum to the

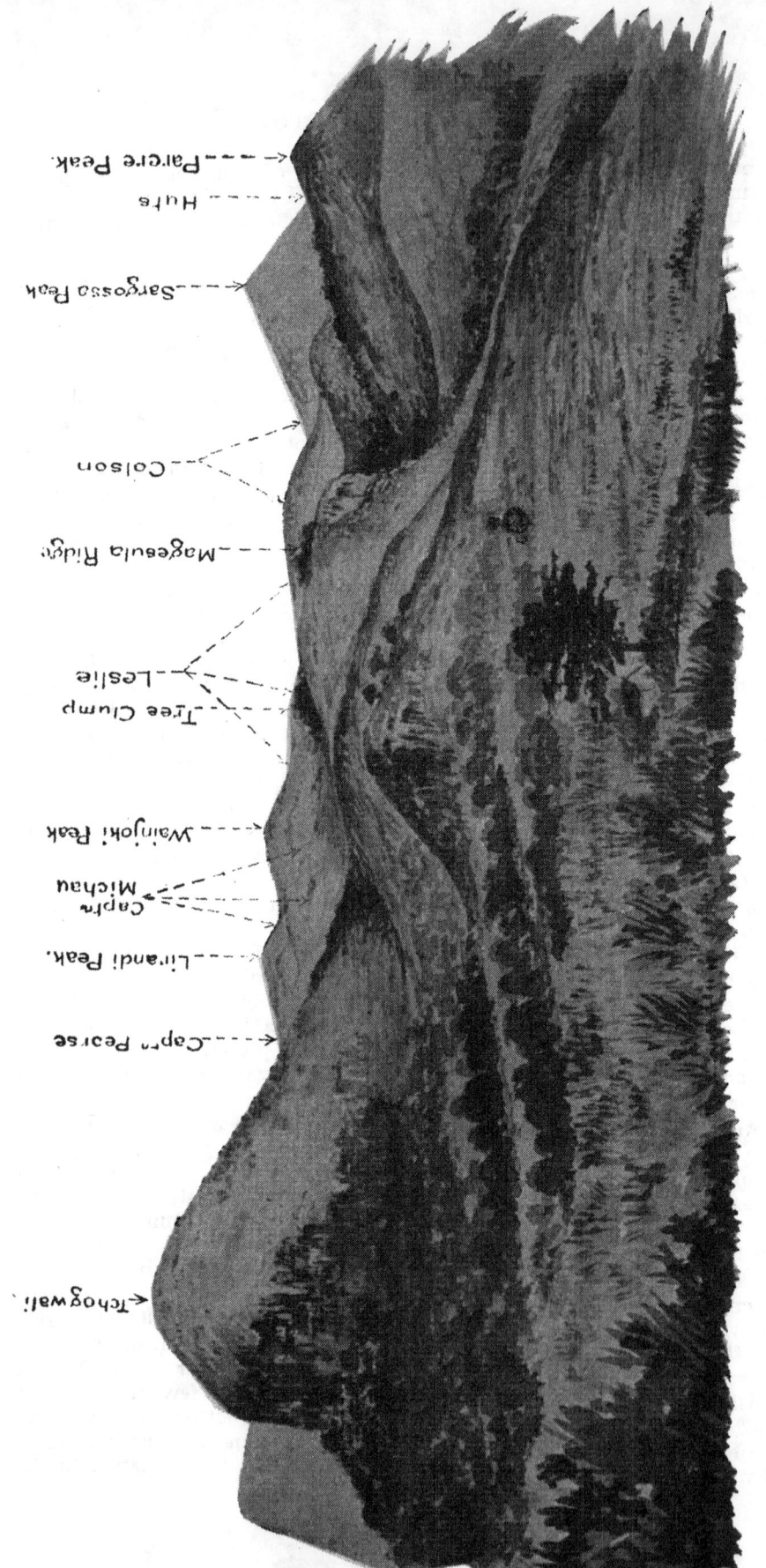

WANJOKI POSITION, AS SEEN FROM TSCHOGOWALI CAMP. 2nd SEPTEMBER. 1917.

Drawn by Alfred J. Parsons, C.E.
From a sketch by Lieut. R. Colson.

enemy demanding unconditional surrender, failing which he would attack from all positions on the night of Sunday, September 2nd.

Lieutenant Leslie was accordingly sent up on the morning of the 2nd under a white flag, accompanied by a bugler (Corporal Cozett). He met a European sergeant who took the message to Zingel. The latter came down and wished to discuss terms, but on Leslie declining, he agreed to surrender unconditionally. He made a request that his men should be allowed to march out of their position with their arms, which they would hand over immediately in front of Michau's trenches. Believing he was dealing with an honourable enemy, Major Hoy agreed to this, but when he went up with Leslie shortly afterwards to take the surrender it was found that, as usual, a German officer's word could not be relied on and that Zingel had burnt all his arms. As, however, his whole force had been made ineffective and were prisoners, no official cognisance was taken of this Hun characteristic breach of faith.

The total number who surrendered were two officers (Lieutenant Zingel and Captain Wolff, M.O.), seven European N.C.O.'s, eighty-eight Askari, twelve Ruga Ruga, one hundred and ninety porters, twenty-six women, numerous boys, a few mules and donkeys, twenty cattle, two machine guns, and thirty-five thousand rounds of ammunition. The remaining machine guns and all the rifles and equipment were burned.

The strength of the Cape Corps with Major Hoy on the day of the capture was fifteen officers, two W.O.'s, and three hundred and twenty other ranks, of whom some seventy-five were in hospital or unfit for duty.

After the enemy had surrendered Leslie took them down to Tschogowali Mission, where they spent the day and night. Next day (September 4th) Lieutenant Colson and his platoon started off on foot to escort the prisoners into Morogoro, which they reached on September 9th. The remainder of our column rested at Tschogowali Mission all day September 3rd. Here Major Hoy was knocked up by overwork and want of sleep, which brought on an attack of fever and necessitated his being carried on a stretcher for two or three days.

The next day we marched to Kalama village, where Major Bradstock and his command rejoined. Continuing, the column returned to Nyumi, Mkundi, and Magubugubu.

Here on September 7th an urgent call for one hundred men was received from Dodoma. They were sent at once, some per motor convoy and the remainder on foot.

The next day Captain Burger joined the detachment with fifty rifles and two Maxim guns, having marched from Morogoro via Kwedihombo and Mhondo Mission.

Major Bradstock left Magubugubu with his company on September 9th to support a squadron of 10th S.A.H., under Captain Green, who were rounding up stray enemy Askari round Mberega. From there Bradstock eventually joined up with Lieut.-Colonel Morris' column at Luita Berg after a most trying march through an arid area.

Major Hoy had received orders to march back to Morogoro with his column, but these were cancelled. The receipt of the order was delayed by a giraffe carrying away the telegraph wires—result a futile march of twenty miles.

From September 10th to 23rd the column patrolled the country to and fro between Nyumi, Mkundi, Magubugubu, Kwedihombo, Weru, Mhondo Mission, Kidete, and Kitaka, in case Naumann's force—then being pursued by Lieut.-Colonel Morris' column from Kondoa Irangi to the east towards Luita Berg—broke that way. Four days were spent at Mhondo Mission, where the thoroughly tired men got a most welcome rest and, what was even more necessary, ample food. Goats, pigs, fruit, eggs, etc., were readily procurable from the natives and at prices that would have gladdened the hearts of the harassed housewives of the Union to-day, pigs, for example, at three rupees (four shillings) each.

At Magubugubu on September 18th Lieutenant H. Walton reported with seventy-five reinforcements *ex* Dodoma.

On reaching Kidete on September 20th word was received that an enemy party was active in the Talagwe area and had had a skirmish with some K.A.R.M.I. Major Hoy decided to get this party and did a forced march of forty miles to Kalama, west of the Nguru Hills. On arrival there it was learned that the information was entirely false, the skirmish having taken place between two British patrols in thick bush, and the detachment, after a day's rest, marched back towards the Central Railway.

By September 23rd it was clearly established that Naumann had been completely bottled up at Luita Berg. Major Hoy at once received orders to return to the Central Railway at Kimamba, his jumping-off place six weeks earlier. The railway was reached on September 27th and the party at once entrained for Dodoma, arriving there the same evening.

Thus ended a most satisfactory little " stunt " which greatly pleased higher authority and earned Major Hoy and all ranks under his command much eulogy. Some of the marches, judged by distance alone, would have done credit to a corps of long-distance walking champions. Add the weight carried by the men (forty to fifty pounds), the heat, dust, bush, long grass, gradients and rough roads, the shortage of food and water, the need to keep always absolutely on the alert, the duties necessary on arrival in camp, such as pickets, guards, fatigues, etc., and the whole completes a splendid tale of effort, endurance, and devotion to duty.

Major Hoy got a bar to his D.S.O. as his most thoroughly well-earned reward for this capture. Major Bradstock, Captain Michau, and Lieutenant Bain were mentioned in despatches, and other awards were the D.C.M. to Sergeant S. W. Dunn (1134) and Sergeant H. W. Abrahams (278).

Dunn did splendidly throughout as chief scout. He had made a study of the native lingoes, which he had so thoroughly mastered that he was granted extra duty pay as an interpreter. Some of his work was worthy of a first-class intelligence officer.

Captain Ingle, S.A.M.C., and his section of the S.A. Field Ambulance attached to the column, did sterling work throughout, as did Lieutenant Batchelor during the last few days.

Lieutenant Horseman was adjutant to Major Hoy from July 26th until the column returned to Dodoma, and got through a great deal of hard work most efficiently, whilst Lieutenant Leslie was commended by Major Hoy for specially good work during the final operations leading up to the capture.

Acting Armourer Sergeant J. van Rooyen (1270) acted as quartermaster sergeant to this column and was highly praised for his solid good work.

Sergeant Benjamin (164) distinguished himself in Major Bradstock's attack on the enemy's rearguard near Muscat Mission, capturing one European, two Askari, and several porters.

Lance-Corporal Beukes (100) and six men, whilst escorting ration porters to Major Bradstock, were tackled by a patrol of three whites and twenty Askari, but kept the enemy at bay and got the rations safely through. For this and other good work during the operations Beukes received the Belgian Decoration Militaire (2nd class) and was mentioned in despatches.

Corporal Nefdt (1085) who was in charge of the advance guard when Captain Michau got in touch with the enemy on Urandi Nek on August 29th behaved very well under fire and kept his party well under control.

THE STORY OF THE 1st CAPE CORPS.

Private Marsh (3140) carried despatches to and fro three or four times a day between Urandi Nek and Urandi Hill for two or three days. Every journey was under fire, but this did not seem to disconcert him in the least.

Bees gave the column trouble more than once, and in the final attack on Wanjoki the enemy's machine gun fire, whether by design or accident, disturbed some hives above our trenches. The desired panic did not eventuate. Mosquito nets were brought into requisition, and those without wisely preferred bee stings to machine gun bullets.

Our casualties during the Zingel stunt were very light, viz.:—

Killed:

Private A. Davids (3496), at Kwedihombo, 26.8.17.
Private R. Johnson (2434), accidentally at Sogosso Hill, 30.8.17.
Private J. van Aarde (1395), accidentally at Sogosso Hill, 30.8.17.

Wounded:

Private G. Fortuin (1724)
Private J. Plaatjes (989) } near Mgere, 29.8.17.
Private A. Africa (353)

Photo by] [Sergeant Alies.
"On Duty."

Photo by] [J.H.T.
RAILWAY STATION, DAR-ES-SALAAM.

CHAPTER XI.

OUR MOROGORO DEPÔT IN GERMAN EAST AFRICA, FEBRUARY TO DECEMBER, 1917.

MOROGORO was our Depôt in East Africa from the date of our first reaching there (2nd September, 1916) until December 15th, 1917, when all officers and men then remaining there entrained for Dar-es-Salaam to join up with the battalion from Lindi en route for final departure from East Africa.

After his return from the Rufiji River on the 16th February, Major Hoy was in command at Morogoro until Lieut.-Colonel Morris arrived from the River, and when the latter went on leave to South Africa on March 23rd, Major Hoy again took over for a brief period prior to going on the Kiromo 'stunt.' Captains Burger and Bradstock in turn then had short spells in command until Lieut.-Colonel Morris' return from leave, and when the latter proceeded on the Naumann 'stunt' in July, Major Hoy again assumed command for a brief period before going 'on safari' after Zingel.

During April, R.S.M. Betts and one hundred and seventy-two other men were invalided to South Africa, and during May Captains Difford, Cuningham, Jardine, Warr, Stevens, Lieutenant Wigman and one hundred and sixty-four other ranks.

On May 16th, Captain W. R. Cowell received his majority vice Major Durham transferred to K.A.R., and Lieutenant S. Ashley got his third star, vice Cowell promoted. Second Lieutenant S. H. Rose-Innes took over the duty of acting Quartermaster until Captain Difford's return in September.

The following decorations and mentions were announced in June:—

D.S.O :—Lieut.-Colonel Morris, for good work done in the Rufiji River area.
D.S.O.: Major Hoy
M.C.: Captain F. E. Bradstock } for good work done at the
M.C.: Captain R. P. McNeil (S.A.M.C.) } Kibongo fight in January.
Order of the Crown of Italy (silver medal): Captain J. E. Robinson, for general good work in the Rufiji area.
Order of the Crown of Italy (bronze medal): Sergeant J. G. Berry (1135), for general good work.
Order of the Crown of Italy (bronze medal): Sergeant P. Hanmer (862), for general good work.
Medaille Militaire (French): C.S.M. W. T. McLeod (111), for general good work.
Mentioned in Despatches:
  Lieut.-Colonel Morris.
  Major Hoy.
  Captain F. E. Bradstock.
  R.S.M. Forsythe, G. (1141).
  C.S.M. McLeod, W. T. (111).
  C.S.M. Calvert, C. (152).

During June, the following officers returned from South Africa (leave or hospital): Major Cowell, Captains Michau, Harris, Earp-Jones, Lieutenants Botha, Edwards, Pearse, Stanford and T. Rose-Innes.

THE STORY OF THE 1st CAPE CORPS.

Lieutenant Edwards brought with him thirty-eight men per H.M.T. "Kyarra," and Major Cowell eight officers and five hundred and forty-seven other ranks per H.M.T. "Chow Tai." Of these latter, two hundred and thirty-three were old hands rejoining from leave or hospital, and the remainder recruits from the depôt.

With Major Cowell to report for duty was Second Lieutenant J. McNeil, who had received his commission on May 10th.

During June, the following were promoted acting Captains vice other officers invalided, viz.:—

    Lieutenant J. Arnott, D.C.M., from 17.4.17.
    Lieutenant D. K. Pearse, from 18.6.17.
    Lieutenant F. C. W. Stanford, from 18.6.17.
    Lieutenant H. Edwards, from 18.6.17.

Second Lieutenant H. R. H. Thornton, whilst in the Union, was released from service "permanently unfit," 7.6.17.

On June 22nd, Lieutenant R. Wilson was boarded out as "medically unfit for further service."

On June 26th, Captain F. E. Bradstock, M.C., was promoted Major by special authority of the War Office in view of the increase of the battalion from four to six double companies.

On July 1st, Part II. orders contained the following announcements, viz.:—

C.S.M. Twynham, D.F. (1092) to be acting R.S.M. vice R.S.M. Betts (European) invalided to South Africa (13.4.17) and C.Q.M.S. Sasse, C.D. (209) to be A/R.Q.M.S. vice A/R.Q.M.S. Shipp (European) invalided to South Africa (24.3.17).

The Warrant officers and N.C.O.'s of the battalion were for the time being therefore entirely coloured men. Both Betts and Shipp returned later on, but the former had to be finally invalided out before the end of the year.

During June, eighty-eight other ranks were invalided to South Africa.

On July 1st, Lieutenant T. M. Hoffe became acting Captain vice Captain Youart, invalided.

On July 21st, Part II. orders recorded:—

To be Lieutenant within establishment, Second Lieutenant C.S.M. Pillans (from unattached list E.A.P.F.) (23.6.17); to be Second-Lieutenants (within establishment) Mr. R. Colson and Mr. S. V. Samuelson (2.7.17).

On July 3rd, Lieutenant G. C. White and one hundred and twenty-nine other ranks were evacuated to South Africa per hospital ship "Oxfordshire."

On August 1st, ex R.S.M. Forsythe, G. (1141) and sixty-one other ranks were evacuated to South Africa per hospital ship, and Lieutenant Hayton left a few days later on special leave.

The following returned from South Africa during August: Captains J. E. Robinson and D. W. Robertson, Lieutenants F. C. Hallier and E. J. Rackstraw, Second Lieutenants Gardner and Leslie and twenty-three other ranks, and Second Lieutenants Colson and Samuelson joined up.

During September, Lieutenant Cloke and twenty-nine other ranks were invalided to South Africa, and on the 26th September, the following officers rejoined from leave or hospital (South Africa), viz: Captains I. D. Difford, W. J. R. Cuningham; Lieutenants Murchie, Wigman and Bourhill and two hundred and sixteen other ranks with them, and the following recently commissioned officers joined up, viz.: Second Lieutenants E. B. Bloxam, M. S. Davies, J. S. Dreyer, F. I. Girdwood, E. Rose-Nel, G. L. Ware.

Captain Cuningham's draft travelled from Durban to Dar-es-Salaam on H.M.T. "Anglo-Egyptian." They were three weeks en route, owing to delays

R.Q.M.S. C. D. SASSE (209).

SERGEANT HARRY SILJEUR (349).

SERGEANT A. M. ADAMS (48).

COOK-SERGEANT S. FEBRUARY (1357).

at Beira and Kilwa. The Commander of the troopship was most eulogistic on the subject of the general good conduct of this draft and the exceptional state of cleanliness into which they got and maintained his vessel.

After the ill effects of the Rufiji operations had worn off the health of the battalion improved vastly, and the total number of deaths from disease in East Africa, period 1st May to 31st October, 1917, was only twenty-three. This was due chiefly to the care taken by the O.C. and staff of No. 15 Stationary Hospital, Morogoro (our own M.O., Captain McNeil, was "on safari" most of the time), and by Major Hoy in our depôt there after the patients had been discharged from hospital.

At the end of September there were only a couple of hundred more or less unfit men at Morogoro, Lieutenant James being O.C. Depôt. Another two hundred men, also unfit, were at Dodoma, under Captain Pearse, and the balance of the battalion still out after Naumann and Zingel. These latter, however, all mobilised at Dodoma during the first week in October and returned to Morogoro in three special trains, October 9th to 11th, leaving only hospital patients at Dodoma.

On October 6th, Major Bradstock was sent from Dodoma to Morogoro to organise and take charge of training there. All the more recently joined subalterns were sent to him as soon as possible, and a large number of N.C.O.'s and men also went through a course of training. These officers and men also attended bombing, Lewis gun, and other classes at the Morogoro School of Instruction and Artillery School. Time was limited, but between October the 7th and 17th many valuable lessons were learned and much useful knowledge imparted, all of which was to bear fruit later on.

The period from October 10th to 17th was a particularly busy one for all ranks, but especially so for the Quartermaster and his staff, the whole battalion —now about fifteen hundred strong—having to be practically reclothed and re-equipped. That done satisfactorily, thanks to the very ready help of Captain Joyce, A.O.D., the battalion entrained again, twelve hundred odd strong, in four special trains, October 17th to 19th, for Dar-es-Salaam en route to Lindi in order to participate in the operations in that area.

Captain Hallier left us at Dar-es-Salaam on October 20th (seconded to the Political service) and Lieutenant Ware was sent for from Morogoro to complete establishment.

Six officers and one hundred and thirty-two other ranks, all unfit, remained behind at Morogoro, the majority recovering from sore feet after their recent prodigious marching feats. Captain Robinson was left in charge, and with him Captains Robertson and Stevens, Lieutenants Colson, Bloxam, Coates and Pillans.

There were also the following at the places shewn, viz.:—

	OFFICERS.	O.R.	TOTAL.
In Hospital (Morogoro)	2 (Captain T. P. Rose-Innes; Lieutenant Potgieter)	100*	102
Convalescent Camp (Morogoro)	—	40*	40
At Dodoma (on lines of communication)	—	16	16

THE STORY OF THE 1st CAPE CORPS.

	Officers.	O.R.	Total.
At Dodoma Hospital	1 (Lieutenant Bain)	120*	121
At Dar-es-Salaam (on lines of communication)	—	10	10
At Kilindini (awaiting ship to Lindi)	1 (Lieutenant Feetham)	60	61
	4	346*	350*

*Approximately.

During the period March to December, 1917, the following men died and were buried at sea, between Durban and Dar-es-Salaam, viz.:—

Private Roberts, M. (2656) of dysentery, March 28th.

Private Hamet, F. (1918) of pneumonia, May 13th.

Private May, J. (2916) of dysentery, June 7th.

Private Grovell, J. (3710) was declared missing on November 16th and death accepted.

The Morogoro depôt was finally closed on December 15th, 1917, when Captain Robertson took all officers and men there to join up with the Battalion at Dar-es-Salaam for final departure from East Africa.

Base Commandant's Office, Dar-es-Salaam.

British Hospital at Dar-es-Salaam

CHAPTER XII.

Two Months' Hard Work in the Lindi Area, period October 20th to December 16th, 1917.

THE battalion, over twelve hundred strong, left Morogoro for Dar-es-Salaam in four special trains between Wednesday, 17th and Friday, 19th October.

On the last train were also B/120 Indian Ambulance, which had been with us on the Naumann 'stunt' and was to accompany us to Lindi. Captain H. H. King, O.C. B/120 left us at Dar-es-Salaam, and all ranks much regretted the separation for a first-class M.O. who was also a good soldier and a good comrade. Captain Hill took over command of B/120 and soon became one of us.

On October 19th our Machine Gun and Stokes Trench Mortar and Bombing sections and some of the Medicals left for Lindi via Zanzibar on H.M.T. "Pemba." The battalion embarked on H.M.T. "Salamis" on Saturday, October 20th, reached Lindi twenty-four hours later, and disembarked next day. Whilst aboard the "Salamis" the second anniversary of the formation of the Cape Corps was celebrated with due ceremony.

Captain Gardiner, commander of the "Salamis" was greatly pleased with the conduct of the Corps whilst aboard his ship and remarked to our O.C. that it was a great treat to carry such a cheery body of troops. There were several senior and staff officers aboard, and the senior officer complimented Lieut.-Colonel Morris on the command of such a happy and fit regiment.

We remained at Lindi five days waiting for our donkey transport, disembarkation of which was delayed owing to shortage of lighters. During this short period no less than ninety-one men were admitted to hospital.

On Friday afternoon, October 26th, the battalion left Lindi to march to Njangao, where we were to join up with our brigade. Our marching out state was approximately twelve hundred 1st Cape Corps, one hundred and thirteen B/120 I.F.A., and six hundred porters, the latter being Machine, Lewis, and Stokes gun porters and first line porters (*i.e.*, for ammunition, rations and water), officers' servants, etc.

In addition we had as 2nd line transport Captain H. N. Hoyer (R.A.S.C.) with the necessary complement of conductors and native drivers and three hundred and twenty donkeys. These donkeys were hopelessly raw and unbroken. They frequently got lost in the bush, and stampeded when meeting the motor convoys, barged into trees and knocked off their loads, and generally behaved as only a donkey does, whilst the native drivers were about on a par with the donkeys.

The trek south-west to Njangao, via Mingoyu, Mtua, and Mtama occupied five days, a distance of seventy-five miles through picturesque country. At Njangao we came under the orders of Brig.-General H. de C. O'Grady, commanding No. 3 Column. (There were four columns co-operating in this area.)

Lieut.-Colonel Morris left us at Mtua on October 28th to assume command of No. 4 Column, taking with him Lieutenant S. H. Rose-Innes as his A.D.C., and Major Hoy assumed command of the battalion.

Photo by] [Thomas Brothers, Klerksdorp.
LATE LIEUTENANT IVOR A. M. GUEST, KILLED IN ACTION AT MKUNGU, EAST AFRICA, 6TH NOVEMBER, 1917.

Major Cowell became acting Second in Command and the Company Commanders were:—

"A" Major Bradstock.
"B" Captain Harris.
"C" Captain Cuningham.
"D" Captain Michau.

(Note.—On November 9th, when Major Bradstock became acting Second in Command for a few days Captain Pearse commanded "A" Company, and when Captain Michau was wounded Captain Edwards took over command of "D" Company.)

Column 3 remained at Njangao for six days. Whilst there, Lieutenant English, R.A.M.C., joined us to assist our M.O.

Lieutenant Horseman was attached to Column Headquarters from November 3rd, to act as Staff Captain to the Brigadier.

The other units in Column 3 were the composite battalion K.A.R. (2/2 and 2/4) under Lieut.-Colonel Gifford, a Stokes Trench Mortar section, the ammunition column, a signal section with an escort of twenty-five Nigerians under Captain Baldwin, B/126 Indian Field Ambulance under Captain Howard (since deceased), and the A.P.M. and his staff.

Column 3 marched at 3 p.m. on November 5th to endeavour to envelope the right flank of the hostile position at Mahiwa from the south, and to form a junction to the rear of the enemy with the Nigerian brigade operating from the north, our first objective being through Kambona to Chinemena. Our donkey transport did not, of course, go forward with the advance, but several hundred more porters were handed over to us and our total strength in porters and other followers was at this time approximately twelve hundred, under an officer and two European sergeants. Many of these porters had recently been recruited and were a most undisciplined lot. They were of very inferior physique, lazy, and cowardly. Their officer was incapable of controlling them and the consequence was endless trouble and worry.

At this time the latest Force Intelligence reports estimated the enemy's southern forces, under von Lettow Vorbeck at twenty-three companies, with a maximum strength of four hundred whites, including convalescents, three thousand Askari, fifty-six Machine guns, two large (ex cruiser "Koenigsberg") naval and three small (field) guns.

Of the above twenty-three companies, seven and one howitzer and two small guns were believed to be in the Mahiwa area, three or four companies in the Natsho-Mlausi area, and the remainder in the area Lukuledi-Ruhego.

A battalion of Column 2 was to attack at Natsho on November 7th, and Column 1 and the remainder of Column 2 were to be concentrated at Lukuledi. Simultaneously Column 4 was to demonstrate against the enemy from the east, and the Nigerians were to effect junction with Column 3 on the Massassi road to the rear of the enemy's position.

In the advance from Njangao on November 5th, Lieutenant Ware's platoon ("D" Company) was detailed as bodyguard to the Brigadier.

The column halted for the night at Chinemena and carried on before dawn next day. The Cape Corps were leadng, "B" Company in advance. At 4 a.m. they flushed a strong enemy outpost and just at dawn encountered an enemy patrol returning to their camp and captured three porters who gave useful information. Our position was reached by a patrol of Sergeant H. W. Abrahams (278) and two men of "C" Company sent out to locate the main road. Abrahams found the road and a cable running along it, which he promptly cut with his Jack knife. At the same time he saw an enemy platoon marching towards him in column of route with their officer leading. Just then

THE STORY OF THE 1st CAPE CORPS.

LIEUTENANT W S. HEATON, M.C.

C.S.M. C. A. RUITERS (132).

LATE 2ND LIEUTENANT J. McNEIL, DIED OF WOUNDS AT MKUNGU, EAST AFRICA, 7TH NOVEMBER, 1917.

LATE LIEUTENANT CHARLES FREDERICK ABBOTT.
Killed in action at Mkungu, Lindi Area, 6th November, 1917.

Lieutenant Rose-Nel emerged from the bush with his platoon. Abrahams signalled to him to keep back under cover, but was too late and the enemy opened fire. Their attack at first was on the advance and right flank ("C" Company). Lieutenant Guest and his machine gun team were put out of action at once and their gun was no man's property for about four hours.

The Nigerian's advance had been held up by the enemy and as they were not at the rendezvous, Major Kraut, the enemy commander, was able to concentrate on O'Grady's Brigade (column 3). His attack was on our right from the east and gradually increased in intensity as he first swung round to the north and then to the west.

In the afternoon the enemy worked round to attack the left flank of the column whilst maintaining pressure in front. "D" Company, which had been held at Column Headquarters, was at once brought up to reinforce the left flank, linking up with "C" Company's left. Severe fighting took place and Captain Michau sent for our Stokes Mortars.

Lieutenant Abbott was immediately killed whilst mounting a gun. Lieutenant J. McNeil and his platoon ("D" Company) were sent up to reinforce "B" Company, but McNeil was immediately wounded (he died next day).

"A" Company on the right flank did not meet with quite such determined opposition, but one platoon under Lieutenant Colson, supporting "B" Company got it hot, Colson being severely wounded. "D" Company from the commencement were in a very warm corner. Lieutenants Power and Ware were ordered by the Brigadier to take a certain ridge. They did so, but Power lost his life. Captain Michau and Lieutenant Samuelson were both wounded and Captain Edwards took over the Company, he and Lieutenant Ware being the only unwounded officers of "D" Company before midday.

The enemy fought desperately on our left flank, charged with the bayonet three times and got within thirty yards of our line, and it was only the steadiness and coolness of "D" Company which prevented them from enveloping us on that side. Lieutenant Samuelson fought his platoon splendidly and received the M.C. (prompt award).

Meanwhile "B" Company (Captain Harris) were obliged to call on "C" Company for reinforcements and Lieutenant Heaton's platoon was sent up, getting into position under very heavy fire. Lieutenant Heaton's leadership earned him the M.C. (prompt award).

Lieutenant Leslie's platoon joined up on the left of "B" Company and shortly afterwards "D" Company linked up with Heaton's left and our line became consolidated.

The bush hereabouts was very dense and in places it was not possible to see the enemy at two hundred yards distance, consequently machine gun fire was somewhat disconcerting.

At about 3 p.m. the enemy brought up their 4.7 inch naval gun and 4.1 inch howitzer and opened on us, and about the same time the heavy fire of the enemy who were trying to outflank us caused a panic amongst our porters who bolted into the thick bush and dropped their loads. The majority of them turned up during the night without their loads at the column's 2nd line transport camp located about three miles back under our Quartermaster. This caused us heavy loss in ammunition, not to mention rations, water, officers' kits, etc. Fortunately the porters recovered their nerve somewhat when out of range of shell fire and next day most of them were induced to return to the front with such of their loads as it had been possible to recover.

Heavy fighting continued all the afternoon (November 6th) without decisive result and at dark our advance was withdrawn about fifty yards to occupy a ridge for the night, with the exception of Lieutenant Heaton's platoon which

THE STORY OF THE 1st CAPE CORPS.

LATE LIEUTENANT WALTER POWER.
Killed in action at Mkungu, November 6th, 1917.

SERGEANT P. D. SCHOOR, D.C.M. (480).

C.S.M. J. SCULLARD (1363).

R.S.M. C. CALVERT, D.C.M. (152).

remained out in an advanced position until about 4 o'clock next morning. Our right remained in *statu quo*, the Stokes mortars were on the left, under Major Bradstock, and "A" and "D" Companies in the rear. Everybody dug in and consolidated positions for the night, during which there was heavy rain.

Our wires to the rear had been cut by an enemy patrol during the afternoon.

C.S.M. C. Calvert (152) and Sergeant Henry Damon (1465) received the D.C.M. (prompt award) for their magnificent courage and example to their comrades this day. Sergeant H. W. Abrahams (278) "C" Company and Sergeant Swartz (331) "D" Company, who was in charge of his Company's Lewis gun section, also did admirably.

In addition to killed and wounded already mentioned, the following casualties also occurred on the 6th, viz. :—

Wounded :—
Captain R. P. McNeil (slight).
Lieutenant Samuelson (head).
Lieutenant Botha (slight).

Killed :
Private G. Arends (956).
Private L. Botes (3714).
Private W. Feder (1535).
Private D. W. Tennant (3187).
Private D. Africa (3489).
Private J. Davids (1037).
Private J. Houtsammer (586).
Private J. Watney (3272).
Private J. Abrahams (2372).
Corporal F. Schroeder, M.M. (980).

Died of Wounds : Private J. Niekerk (253).

Forty-six other ranks wounded and thirteen missing.

Lieutenants Wigman, Ware and Girdwood were also slightly wounded, but as they did not return to the dressing station they did not appear in the official casualty list.

This was the severest day's fighting the battalion had experienced to date, and the magnificent conduct of the men under heavy shell and machine gun fire at close range was a source of much gratification to all concerned.

Desultory fighting continued until 3 a.m. on the 7th and, after a couple of hours break, began again and continued all day. The enemy had failed to surround us as they had apparently hoped, and for the next thirty-six hours appeared to be irresolute whether to attack again vigorously or to retire. Their searching shell fire was, however, very accurate, dropping into our trenches on both right and left flanks. Shelling continued all day and two attacks from the west were beaten off.

Early in the morning Lieutenant Barnard was sent out on our front with twenty men, and Sergeant Abrahams with a patrol of six men. Barnard got into action at once and very soon was himself brought in badly wounded.

At this time the 3rd/4th K.A.R. from column 4 were sent to reinforce us and remained with our column for two or three days.

Early on the morning of the 7th the Nigerian battalion who had joined up on our right were heavily engaged on the main road on the right flank of O'Grady's Brigade whither they had been guided by a Cape Corps patrol under Sergeant Abrahams (278). The remainder of the Nigerian Brigade had a comparatively quiet day and Brig.-General O'Grady returned to headquarters at Njangao in the afternoon to confer with Brig.-General Cunliffe, commanding the Nigerian Brigade.

Photo by] [Zadik & Co., Cape Town.

ENEMY MACHINE GUN CAPTURED IN A BAYONET CHARGE BY 1ST CAPE CORPS AT HATIA, GERMAN EAST AFRICA, NOVEMBER 8TH, 1917 (WAS PRESENTED TO THE CITY OF CAPE TOWN BY LIEUT.-COLONEL MORRIS, OFFICERS, N.C.O.'S AND MEN OF THE BATTALION AND NOW STANDS IN THE VESTIBULE OF THE CITY HALL, CAPE TOWN.)

THE STORY OF THE 1st CAPE CORPS.

As a result of this conference plans were made for an advance. The Nigerian Brigade was ordered to push the enemy out of his trenches at dawn on the 8th, after which O'Grady's Brigade, with the Cape Corps in advance, was to take up the running and proceed towards Nangoo.

Unfortunately the Nigerians were unsuccessful in this attack and received one hundred and ten casualties in their attempt. The enemy were fighting very determinedly at this stage, obviously endeavouring to prevent the Lindi Force from reaching Nangoo before their troops opposing our Kilwa Force had retired south of that point. New dispositions had accordingly to be made and as a result, about 2.30 p.m. on the 8th, the Cape Corps were warned that they would be relieved in their sector by the 2/2nd K.A.R. and that they were to attack the enemy's right, debouching from Brigade Headquarters.

While the relief was in progress the enemy opened a hot attack on the Cape Corps sector and Major Hoy decided to remain in position and report for instructions to Brigade Headquarters. As a result further K.A.R. reinforcements were detailed and eventually about 4 o'clock p.m. the relief was completed and the Cape Corps concentrated for attack. They proceeded to Brigade Headquarters, where final instruction were received and deployment for attack was effected at once.

"C" Company, under Captain Cuningham, had pride of place and orders were to push right through the enemy trenches in a westerly direction with the bayonet and then, having reorganised, turn half right to the north and cut the main Lindi-Massassi road behind the enemy. The terrain was slightly undulating park lands with occasional tropical thickets.

About four hundred yards from Brigade Headquarters our scouts encountered enemy posts, which were driven in and the advance pressed. Another four hundred yards and the main enemy trench line was encountered and the firing line met determined resistance from rifle and machine gun fire. "C" Company pressed on with great gallantry doing heavy execution, and Lieutenant Heaton's platoon captured a machine gun and accounted for the whole of its crew. This gun may be seen to-day in the vestibule of the City Hall, Cape Town.

At this point Major Hoy was wounded in the foot and was compelled to hand over at once to Major Bradstock, who commanded the support company. Later on Major Cowell took command as soon as he was made aware of the position. As Second in Command he had been advancing with the rear companies.

Our advance was carried on without cessation, except for momentary pauses under brisk fire to adjust our alignment, until the top of the rise was reached (about one mile), and for the first time for three days we had the pleasure of seeing the enemy on the run.

During the day Major Cole brought up the Kashmir Mountain Battery and heavily plastered the enemy's right flank, being assisted by our Stokes mortars. They did great execution, a number of bodies, European and Askari, being seen during our advance next day, when the enemy's retreat was so precipitate that they had no time to bury their dead.

About the time Major Hoy was wounded the enemy attempted to get round on our left flank. Our machine guns quickly put that right and the advance continued. Captain Murchie and Lieutenant Leslie were sent ahead with two platoons of "C" Company to reach and straddle the main road, which they did and got into touch with the Nigerians at Hatia Mission—the enemy retiring south-west along the main road to Nangoo. There our advance ceased for the time being and we camped for the night.

On the 7th and 8th our casualties were much lighter than on the 6th.

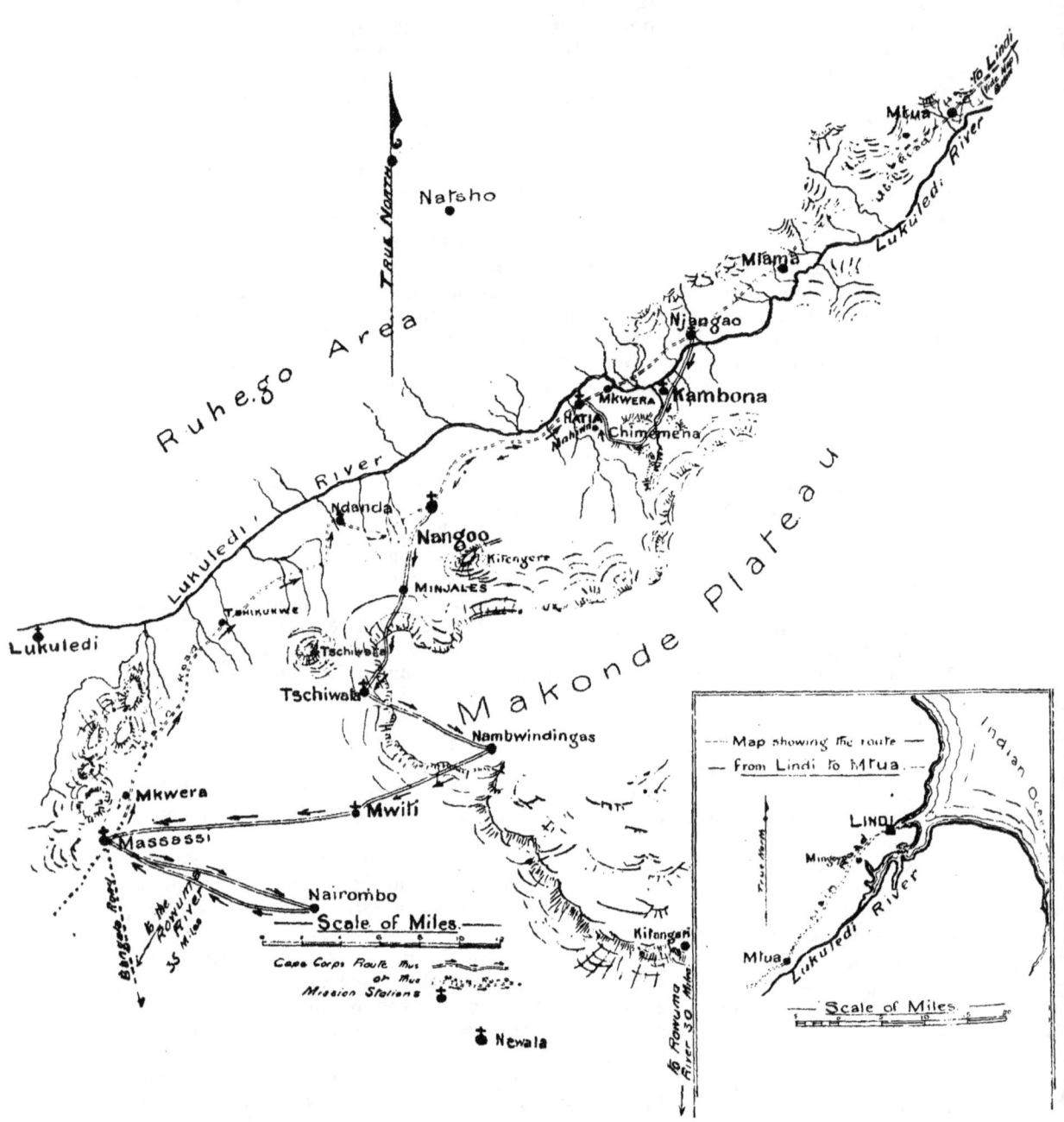

MAP ILLUSTRATING 1ST CAPE CORPS ROUTE DURING OPERATIONS IN THE LINDI AREA
(OCTOBER TO DECEMBER, 1917).

Second Lieutenant McNeil died of wounds in the B/126 I.F.A. clearing station on the 7th. On the 8th, Signaller F. Drury (1272), one of the cheeriest men in the battalion, was killed in the advance and Privates D. Mouton (2337) and D. October (441) died of wounds at Mikware. Lieutenant E. Rose-Nel (slightly), Sergeant D. Hector (977) and five men were also wounded in the advance.

Private J. Stuurman (1514), one of the Quartermaster's escort, was wounded on the 8th and died next day. R.Q.M.S. Sasse (209), C.Q.M.S. Reagon (1143) and Private W. MacKenzie (1573) attended to this man and carried him to cover under heavy fire.

On the 9th November the retreating enemy were followed along the main road to Nangoo. The column was held up for a time by the arrival of a white flag party from von Lettow with the impertinent request that we would forward their private letters. This was no doubt a ruse to gain time for the main body to get away. Anyway, the envoys were sent to our rear to post their own letters so that any information they had gleaned could not be communicated to their C. in C.

On the 9th, Major Cole's Kashmiri's, a S.A. Field Artillery Battery under Major Gordon Grey, M.C., and a 4.1 inch naval gun, posted near the Nigerian's headquarters on the main road, greatly aided us. That day three men on the flank were slightly wounded in an encounter with an enemy patrol to the right of the main road.

On the 10th, the S.A.F.A. Battery passed us to get nearer to the retreating enemy, and on the same day C.S.M. Daniels (No. 1) (wounded) and twelve other men who had been missing since the 6th, turned up.

It was expected that the enemy would stand again and fight, but they continued to retreat, fighting strong rearguard actions all day on the 9th and 10th. The K.A.R. were leading our advance on those days and the Cape Corps had a comparatively easy time except our Stokes gunners who were in the firing line and did good execution. On the 11th we were leading again, " C " Company in front in the attack on Nangoo, which was delayed for some time owing to water shortage. All water had to be brought up in chaguls by porters, from seven miles back. When the Brigadier had personally seen the leading company's water bottles filled he allowed the advance to proceed. Strong resistance was anticipated, but did not materialise. Dense bush and intense heat caused the march to be a very trying one, but the enemy continued to retreat and Nangoo was entered without opposition.

On arrival at Nangoo a Cape Corps patrol of one and twenty was at once sent out towards Ndanda to get in touch with our Brigadier-General Hannyngton's Force operating from Kilwa. This they succeeded in doing and returned to camp reporting "all clear," thus linking up our Kilwa and Lindi forces.

A feature of our advance from Hatia to Nangoo had been the number of casualties inflicted on our rear by enemy snipers concealed in the thick bush.

At Nangoo the enemy left behind a hospital with a European M.O. and one white and twenty-seven Askari patients. The majority of these latter had evidently been wounded by bombs from our aeroplanes. Two hours after entering Nangoo a K.A.R. patrol of Ridgway's column came in from Ndanda direction (west).

The column rested at Nangoo on November 12th and 13th. On the first named day Lieut.-Colonel Morris returned and took over the command of the battalion again.

Our strength in porters had by this time been reduced to about eight hundred and fifty, of whom three hundred and fifty were first line (*i.e.*, for Vickers and Lewis guns, and ammunition for same, signalling equipment and stretcher bearers) and five hundred second line (known as Shenzis) (for reserve ammunition, rations, water, etc.), and officers' servants, etc.

On November 14th our Intelligence officers reported that the enemy had retired towards Kitangari, about twenty miles south. His main body was holding Tschiwata Mission at the foot of the escarpment to the west of the Makonde Plateau.

Brig.-General Hannyngton (column 1) was attacking Mwiti, with the Cavalry working on a wider circle to their south, and two battalions of the Nigerians and Column 2 were in position in or about Tshiwada.

On the evening of the 13th, the K.A.R. advanced again, going south to Minjales and up the escarpment (a strenuous climb of some two thousand feet) to the top of the Makonde plateau. The reasons for this were: (1) to prevent the enemy main force at Tshiwata from getting on to the plateau, (2) to prevent an enemy airship which had left the Turkish coast from landing on the plateau.

(This airship never arrived though it actually left Turkey and was seen over the Sudan).

On the morning of the 14th, Lieut.-Colonel Morris left Nangoo with "C" and "D" Companies for Minjales, towards Tschiwata, where he waited for Major Cowell and "A" Company, under Major Bradstock, and next day climbed the escarpment. At Tschiwata the big enemy hospital surrendered to Major Bradstock. In the hospital were approximately two hundred and sixty Europeans and seven hundred Askari sick or wounded.

Captain Harris followed the column from Nangoo on the 15th with "B" Company. The whole of the column (less "B" Company) concentrated on top of the escarpment early on the 15th and moved on again. The 2/2 K.A.R. were in advance and the objective was to cut the Tschiwata-Mwiti main road. As soon as the K.A.R. reached the road (about 9.30 a.m.) they got into action and a stiff engagement developed and continued all day, during which we turned and started to push the enemy down the Mwiti road. About noon the enemy tried to envelop the K.A.R. right flank and Captain Cuningham was sent on to link up and reinforce them. Here Sergeant Abrahams (278) again did good patrol work.

Towards evening the column formed a perimeter, with the K.A.R. in front and Cape Corps in the rear, and bivouaced for the night. The enemy were dug in only one hundred and fifty yards from us.

During the day the 2/2nd K.A.R. had had very heavy casualties, the 2nd in command and eight other officers and about one hundred and fifty other ranks being killed or wounded.

During the night of the 15th the enemy retired about a mile and a half. Next morning at dawn we were at them again, Cape Corps in advance, "D" Company in front, Captain Edwards on the right flank and Lieutenant Ware on the left. Captain Arnott and Lieutenant Hayton had been temporarily posted to "D" Company to replace casualties on the 6th instant.

The enemy continued to retire fighting all the way and inflicted some casualties on us, including Lieutenant Girdwood, wounded (for the second time within ten days). One porter (machine gun) was killed and several wounded. A sniper who was a crack shot troubled us for a while, but during the morning Lieutenant Ware severely wounded and captured him.

During the afternoon Lieut.-Colonel Morris took "A" and "C" Companies round on the left flank and nearly brought off a coup. The enemy saw him just in time to save themselves by breaking off the engagement and clearing through the bush. The column thereupon continued to advance and pushed on about a mile where we again became heavily engaged and fought on until dark when perimeter was formed with the Cape Corps in advance and K.A.R. in the rear.

Sniping and bombing continued all night, the enemy being entrenched only about two hundred yards distant. At midnight six men, Lance-Corporal Manuel (3128), Privates Adonis (2855), Williams (1935), Moses (2509), Pritchard (3777) and Taylor (3237) were sent out bombing and got right up to the enemy trenches before throwing two bombs each. The enemy opened fire and Private Adonis was wounded. The reason of this patrol was to induce the enemy to waste ammunition which they duly did, the whole line blazing away for several minutes..

At dawn (17th November) we found the enemy had so placed a machine gun as to sweep the main road into our camp. This resulted in several casualties including the Brigade Major (Major Dowding) killed, and Captain Hill, O.C. B/120 I.F.A. wounded (shot through the jaw). Several other casualties occurred from this and also from enemy shell fire during the day, our reserve ammunition dump having a very narrow escape from shell fire. The machine gun was evidently directed by observation to fire at anyone crossing the road and it was difficult to get our porters to understand this.

Early in the morning we sent out a contact patrol, so called, of course, because their object was to locate and draw the enemy's fire. They were away five hours, eventually returning through our rear and bringing back useful information. They had exchanged shots and bagged an enemy picket. The bush was so dense that this patrol lost its way for some time and it was not until our artillery opened that they were able to locate their position.

Names of patrol: Corporal Holland (120); Privates Amos, J. (2550), Bartes, W. (2022), Frans, S. (3062), and Limini, A. (3068), all of "C" Company.

"B" Company, under Captain Harris, joined up from Nangoo in the morning. Fighting continued all day. About noon "B" Company was sent out to the right flank of "D" who were leading the advance.

The Nigerians then came up on Harris' right and endeavoured to envelope the enemy's left, but they retired and about three hundred yards further on the column halted for the night, the Cape Corps taking left half of the perimeter and the K.A.R. the right.

Just before dark Lieutenant Wigman was sent out with his platoon to endeavour to push the enemy off a bit. He got in touch and engaged them but was forced to withdraw to avoid being surrounded. The bush was so thick that he was able to pull out without the enemy being aware of it and the latter continued to scrap amongst themselves for at least half an hour before they discovered their mistake. Wigman had Sergeant Schoor (480) and Private Janeker (3814) wounded.

During the day Lieutenant Difford rejoined, ex Lindi hospital.

Sniping continued all night and at daybreak (November 18th) Lieut.-Colonel Morris took out "A" and "C" Companies to try to get round the enemy's left flank. They were held up by a bush fire and the enemy cleared, setting alight to the grass with the wind in our direction to retard our advance.

The Brigadier then sent orders to "A" and "C" Companies to return to the road, join up with "B" and "D" Companies and push on towards Nambwindinga's, where the enemy was known to have a big hospital. Von Lettow Vorbeck was also believed to be there with his main force. We reached the hospital at 11 a.m., less than six hours after von Lettow's rearguard had passed through, retreating hurriedly.

Major Bradstock took the surrender of the hospital where he found twenty-two Hun officers, two hundred and fifty European other ranks and about six hundred Askari, and numerous women, porters, servants, totos (boys), etc. The majority of the prisoners were fit men who had had enough of war, or rather of being kept continuously on the run before our relentless pursuit. It was said that the previous night von Lettow's men had practically mutinied and that the ex-Governor of German East, von Schnee, and von Lettow had almost come to blows. Von Schnee and the majority contended that it was murder to continue such a forlorn hope. Von Lettow told him and the surrender party to go to the devil and invited the bitter-enders to carry on. About two hundred and fifty Europeans and one thousand Askari agreed and bolted with von Lettow towards the Rovuma River on the Portuguese border.

Captain Pearse was sent out with a platoon to cover the hospital in case of treachery during the above surrender, and got engaged with von Lettow's retiring rearguard.

At the hospital we released twenty-five British, five Portuguese, and two Belgian officer prisoners whom von Lettow had been compelled to leave behind. One of the British officers was Captain H. Wallis, M.C. (8th S.A.I.), who afterwards joined us.

Having taken over the hospital, prisoners, etc., the Cape Corps returned to a good camping site about a mile back, and the remainder of the brigade came up.

Column three did not follow von Lettow, as they were urgently in need of rest after their hard work of the past fortnight, and furthermore it was expected that our other columns would get him. But von Lettow prove too elusive, and for three or four days it was not known what direction he had taken. This was another illustration of the difficulties of campaigning in bush so thick that two Army Corps might be camped within a mile of each other without knowing it.

Our column therefore rested at Nambwindingas for three days (November 19th-21st). On the 19th Major Humann (at one time a Judge of the Martial Court and an ex-Acting Governor) surrendered to Lieutenant Hayton who was on outpost duty.

On the same day Captain Robinson and Lieutenants Bloxam, Coates, and Pillans arrived from Morogoro to replace officer casualties on the 6th instant.

On November 20th Lieutenant Stubbs was sent out with two men under a white flag with a letter to von Lettow from the G.O.C. (Lieut.-General van Deventer). He came up with the enemy about sixteen miles away at Kitangari, where thirty Europeans and seventy-eight Askari surrendered to him, including the Commander and several officers of the late German cruiser "Koenigsberg" (blown up by our forces at the mouth of the Rufiji River). Stubbs returned to camp to report, and next day two companies of the K.A.R. went out to bring in the prisoners.

On the 21st Lieutenant Rose-Nel was sent out with his platoon to bring in another party of the enemy who had surrendered. Those and Lieutenant Stubbs' captures were hand over to Lieutenant Coates and his platoon to escort to Tschiwata and deliver to responsible authority there.

Whilst camped at Nambwindingas our patrols scoured the country in the vicinity and brought in large quantities of abandoned arms, ammunition, machine guns, etc.

By this time it had become clearly established that our operations since the 6th November had been highly successful in all directions. The enemy had been continuously on the run for a fortnight and was approaching demoralisation. Since October 1st we had killed or captured over sixteen hundred Europeans in the Lindi area, and there is no doubt whatever that the extraordinary thickness of the bush had alone saved von Lettow from surrender or annihilation.

During the past fortnight column 3 had had a very strenuous time. General O'Grady was very much handicapped by the smallness of his force. A third battalion would have been of the greatest possible assistance. His two battalions were not up to full strength and had to take the advance on alternate

THE STORY OF THE 1ST CAPE CORPS.

Photos by] [J.H.T.
OUR STRETCHER BEARERS AND MACHINE GUN PORTERS ON SAFARI, LINDI AREA.

CHANGING GUARD AT MASSASSI.

Photos by] [J.H.T.
MAJOR W. P. COWELL AND A FRIEND AT MASSASSI.

MAJOR COWELL'S FAMOUS "IMPESHI" (COOK-BOY).

THE C.O.'S CHAUFFEUR, PRIVATE J. FARO (2564).

days. The result was that the battalion in reserve was called upon to assist in flanking movements and other sudden calls and neither got a day's rest for fourteen days. A third battalion could have executed strong and wider flanking movements simultaneously with the frontal attacks, and as the enemy could not afford to waste either man power or ammunition, he would have been kept more on the run than was actually the case.

On the 21st November column 3 were under orders to proceed due south to attack Newala, which was held by the enemy. Shortly before the time fixed to march, however, news came through of the surrender of that place with a bag of one hundred and twenty-six more whites and numerous Askari prisoners.

On Thursday, November 22nd, the column marched to Mwiti Mission, awaited orders there for forty-eight hours, and then proceeded west to Massassi. This was a very trying trek of some eighteen miles. At Mwiti, on November 24th, Lieutenant Feetham and his platoon arrived from Kilindini.

We reached Massassi at midnight, 24th November, remained there twenty-four hours, and then got orders to move fifteen miles south-east to Nairombo by a forced march. From there Lieutenant Hayton was sent out with twenty-five men escorting a signalling patrol to Huwu, and was away three or four days, whilst Lieutenant Difford and his platoon proceeded to Luatala to bring in the prisoners, approximately thirty whites, two hundred and fifty Askari, four hundred porters, and two hundred women, who had surrendered there a few days previously.

On November 26th the brigade (less Cape Corps) left Nairombo, direction south to Newala near where the enemy had been located, and the Cape Corps was ordered to march down the river due south to attack Tafel, who was operating on the left flank. Half an hour from camp, however, we were recalled, as news had come through that Tafel with ninety-six Europeans, one thousand two hundred and twenty-six Askari, and some two thousand porters had surrendered to Brig.-General Hannyngton's column near Newala.

On November 28th we (Cape Corps) marched back to Massassi where we found our second line transport (donkeys) had arrived from Njangao, much to the satisfaction of all ranks. Not that there was any consuming desire to resume acquaintance with the donkeys, but they meant kit bags and a change of clothing.

Shortly before this date Lieut.-Colonel Morris had represented to higher authority that his battalion had had over twenty months' continuous service in East Africa and borne their full share of the heat and burden of the day, and that owing to the ravages of disease all ranks were badly in need of an entire rest. The reply was the appointment of a Medical Board, which sat at Massassi on November 29th and two following days. The report of the Board evidently confirmed our C.O.'s contentions, as within a week we were under orders to proceed to Dar-es-Salaam at once for embarkation to South Africa.

Our last shot in East Africa proved to have been fired on November 18th in the attack on Nambwindingas. During the advance to the last-named place from Hatia Mission (November 9th to 18th) we suffered a number of casualties, but had inflicted two or three times as many on the enemy.

Privates S. Janaker (576) and S. Lewis (2898) were killed on November 16th, and the following died of wounds, viz. :—

    Private D. Smouse (2100), November 10th.
    Private C. Starkey (3100), November 16th.
    Private A. George (165), at Ndanda, November 27th.
    Private W. Behr (3111), at Dar-es-Salaam, November 21st.

Thirty-one men were wounded during the above period and there were also several casualties amongst our porters, stretcher-bearers, officers' servants, etc.

Photo by] [W. Waston Robertson, Pietermaritzburg, Natal
LIEUTENANT S. V. SAMUELSON, M.C.

Photo by] [The Middlebrook Studio, Kimberley.
LIEUTENANT E. P. STUBBS, M.C.

R.Q.M.S. C. D. SASSE (209) (SEATED) AND C.Q.M.S.
A. J. REAGON (1143)

CAPTAIN J. H. TANDY, M.C.
Adjutant, 21st January to 23rd June, 1917, and
September, 1917, to May, 1919.

Our total casualties for the month of November, 1917, were:—

	Killed.	Died of Wounds.	Wounded.
Officers	3	1	10
Other ranks	13	8	80
Total	16	9	90

Honours and awards received during these operations were:—

D.S.O.
    Major Cowell.

M.C.
    2nd Lieutenant S. V. Samuelson (prompt award).
    2nd Lieutenant W. S. Heaton (prompt award).
    Captain J. V. Harris.
    Captain J. H. Tandy.
    Lieutenant E. P. Stubbs.

Mentioned in Despatches.
    Lieut.-Colonel Morris.
    Major Bradstock.
    Captain I. D. Difford.
    Captain H. Edwards.
    Captain J. H. Tandy.
    Captain J. V. Harris.
    Captain J. M. Michau.
    Lieutenant W. Wigman.

D.C.M.
    C.S.M. C. Calvert (152), (prompt award).
    Sergeant H. Damon (1465), (prompt award).
    C.S.M. D. J. Brown (9).
    Sergeant P. D. Schoor (480).
    Sergeant I. W. Arendse (607).
    Sergeant J. Swartz (331).
    Corporal Carelse (688).

M.M.
    Sergeant H. W. Abrahams, D.C.M. (278).
    Lance-Corporal M. C. le Roux (161).

Mentioned in Despatches.
    C.Q.M.S. J. Davids (97).
    C.Q.M.S. W. H. la Vita (1127).
    C.Q.M.S. P. Heeger (21).
    C.Q.M.S. A. J. Hendricks (1067).
    C.Q.M.S. A. J. Reagon (1143).
    Pioneer Sergeant J. C. M. Paulsen (432).
    Sergeant W. S. Samuels (504).
    Lance-Corporal G. Charles (594).
    Lance-Corporal E. Beukes (100).
    Private C. Bailey (1373).
    Private P. Matawana (400).
    Private C. Joseph (2133).
    Private A. Fortuin (592).
    Private J. Adams (1220).
    Private H. J. Symes (842).
    Private F. Gallant (1731).
    Private A. Marsh (3140).
    Private J. Harold (1917).

THE STORY OF THE 1st CAPE CORPS.

Photo by]   *[I.D.D.*
LINDI, G.E.A., OCTOBER, 1917.

Photo by]   *[G. Horseman.*
THE LAST ENEMY BIG GUN (HOWITZER) BLOWN UP AND ABANDONED AT NAMBWINDINGAS, MAKONDE, PLATEAU, G.E.A., IN NOVEMBER, 1917.

THE STORY OF THE 1st CAPE CORPS.

On November 29th news reached Massassi that von Lettow had crossed the Rovuma River into Portuguese East Africa. This necessitated road repairs for our mechanical transport in the direction of the river, and "A," "B," and "C" Companies spent three days on that job on the Bangalla road.

On November 30th an entire reorganisation of our Forces took place. The result, so far as it affected us, was our transfer from column 3 to Force Reserve, to the command of which Lieut.-Colonel Morris succeeded on December 1st. At the same time he became Post Commandant of Massassi, and Major Bradstock O.C. Detail Camp. As Major Hoy was still in hospital recovering from his wound, Major Cowell assumed command of the battalion.

On December 6th Lieut.-Colonel Morris was evacuated to hospital with enteric fever. He was several weeks at Mingoyu (near Lindi) and did not leave East Africa until the 23rd January.

In our advance from Hatia to Massassi we came upon the last two "Koenigsberg" 4.1 inch guns, which the enemy had managed to retain up to that period. Both guns had been rendered useless before being abandoned. They had no doubt been of assistance in delaying our advance somewhat, but it is questionable whether the employment of the requisite porterage (six hundred per gun) and the labour involved in the conveyance of their rations was an economically sound proposition for a retreating force in such country.

Quite a feature of the past month had been the splendid work done by the machine gun porters (*vide* chapter xviii.) and stretcher-bearers, especially under fire. Ten of these porters were mentioned in despatches as having received monetary awards for their bravery and coolness in action. The Shenzi porters, on the other hand, were not a success, but the fault did not lie so much with the individual as with the collective lack of training and discipline.

On December 5th the most welcome order was received that the battalion were to leave in forty-eight hours to march to Lindi and proceed thence to Dar-es-Salaam for re-equipment and immediate return to South Africa. Captain Arnott was at once sent off by motor car to collect all men in the various hospitals and clearing stations between Massassi and Lindi, so that few as possible should be left behind. Men fit enough to march did so, and the sick were taken by the returning empty motor convoys.

The next day Captain Difford also went ahead to Lindi by motor car and caught the first boat to Dar-es-Salaam in order to draw equipment and assist Major Hoy, who was there, to make the necessary arrangements for final departure.

It should be recorded that our supply organisation during the Lindi operations was first rate. Full rations were the rule not the exception.

On December 6th all officers and men extra-regimentally employed returned to duty. Our Vickers and Lewis guns were handed over to the 1st/2nd K.A.R., and our machine gun porters, stretcher-bearers and all surplus Shenzis were returned to the Carrier Corps.

In orders that day a copy of the following cable from the War Office to the G.O.C.I.C., East Africa, appeared:—

"On the occasion of your driving the last remaining enemy force from German East Africa the War Cabinet desire to congratulate you and all forces under your command upon your recent successes, which during the past four months have resulted in the capture of six thousand prisoners, and the conquest of nearly fifty thousand square miles of hostile territory.

"The determined endurance of your troops, who have had not only to overcome the resistance of a determined enemy but the difficulties of a tropical and roadless country, has been beyond praise."

On December 7th at 6.30 a.m. the battalion, under command of Major Cowell, marched out of Massassi, homeward bound. The route taken was via

THE STORY OF THE 1st CAPE CORPS.

Photo by]   *[The Middlebrook Studio, Kimberley.*
CAPTAIN TREVOR P. ROSE-INNES.

Photo by]   *[J. G. Horsfall, Cape Town.*
SERGEANT S. D. JANSEN, D.C.M. (1614).

Photo by]   *[A. J. Bini, Claremont.*
C.Q.M.S. A J. REAGON (1143).

Photo by]   *[The Monochrome Studio, Durban.*
SERGEANT E. B. GEORGE (1566).

Ndanda, Nangoo, Njangao, Mtama, Mtua, Mingoyu, and Lindi, the last-named place being reached on December 13th.

Major Bradstock remained behind at Massassi pending receipt of confirmation of his transfer to the 1st/2nd K.A.R. which had been arranged.

It is noteworthy that the marching out strength from Massassi was only some four hundred and fifty of all ranks, as against approximately twelve hundred who had taken the field from Lindi six weeks earlier. The casualty list accounted for one hundred and fifteen of these (killed and wounded) so that practically six hundred and thirty men, or an average of over one hundred per week had been admitted to hospital, chiefly, of course, with malaria.

At Lindi a number of hospital dischargees were taken on strength, all remaining porters were handed over to Carrier Corps, and the Stokes trench mortars to Ordnance.

On December 16th the battalion embarked on H.M.T. "Tuna," reached Dar-es-Salaam on the following day, and marched to the detail camp. The next two days were very busily filled re-equipping and in preparations for departure.

On the afternoon of December 19th the battalion was inspected by the G.O.C., Major-General J. L. van Deventer, who made complimentary reference to the good work done by the Corps since their arrival in East Africa.

Early on December 20th we embarked on H.M.T. "Caronia" and sailed the same evening for Durban. Our embarkation was hopelessly muddled, with the result that a large quantity of kit was left behind. The kit taken on board did not fare much better. It was most carelessly slung into the hold, five decks down, and got considerably damaged in the process. The baggage of the Cape Corps, of the 10th S.A.H., 7th S.A.I., and of sundry details was all mixed up and access could not be had to it during the voyage.

Several officers had only the clothing in which they stood for a four days' voyage. The Union was reached during the Christmas holidays, which meant further delay before they could purchase a change. The men were more fortunate as they were able to draw upon the Quartermaster to replace their losses.

Our departure from East Africa was tinged with regret at having to leave behind Major Bradstock, M.C. (transferred to K.A.R.), and Captain Hallier (seconded to Political Service). The former was one of the original Company commanders and greatly loved and respected by all ranks, and Hallier was a most conscientious and good soldier. The Battalion suffered a distinct loss in the transfer of those two officers.

Thus ended over twenty-two months' continuous service in East Africa. We had landed at Kilindini on February 16th, 1916, very much of an experimental and untried unit. We left Dar-es-Salaam on December 20th, 1917, with a reputation of which every one of us had ample reason to feel thoroughly proud. That fact was fully established by the G.O.C.'s farewell address to us at Dar-es-Salaam, and by the numerous wires and letters of congratulation (*vide* appendix) received from time to time from Force, Column, and Brigade commanders under whom we had served, and from various other highly-placed officers with whom we were brought into contact. The honours and awards list (*vide* appendix) is perhaps the most eloquent testimony to the men's calibre, capacity, and courage.

Whatever success had been achieved had no doubt been due to the keenness and *esprit de corps* of all ranks and to the intense loyalty to their Commanding Officer. Other units in other theatres of war had no doubt far heavier casualty lists, but very few can have undergone more continuous hardships. The long list of death from disease tells its own sad tale.

The men were called upon at times for tremendous efforts, but the greater the call the greater the response. They were always cheerful and willing, never groused, and possessed a keen sense of humour which overcame almost every difficulty. The officers soon learned to have the greatest confidence in the men, well knowing that it would not be misplaced. The hotter the corner the more sure of them one became.

Reference is made to the machine gun porters (mostly Kavirondo) in another chapter. They did grand work and were particularly fine in action. A number of those who were with us in the Lindi area had been in the field with us for twenty months and had become much attached to the officers and men of the machine gun section. They were well disciplined and knew more than the rudiments of drill.

On two different occasions a porter carrying a gun slipped crossing a stream, but on each occasion by a gymnastic feat the man managed to land on his back and, with his hands, held up the gun to save it from damage.

At Hatia a machine gun porter armed only with a panga (bush knife) chased and captured an enemy Askari. For this feat he received a monetary award.

Our stretcher bearers were imbued with the same spirit and equally attached to the battalion.

During our fight along the Mkonde plateau (November 14th to 18th) they had a good deal of dangerous work to do. But they were imperturable. When under heavy machine gun and rifle fire they always remained quiet until the word " stretcher bearers " was passed along. Then they would creep forward without hesitation and do their job efficiently and quietly. They had been well trained by Captain McNeil and followed his magnificent example when in action.

Nor were the officers' Swahili servants, in their own sphere, less valuable. Every officer had one, and a few occasionally two, of these " warriors." They became much attached to their own particular " baas," and several became quite efficient " safari " cooks. On one occasion the late Major Cowell's well known " Impishi " carried the soup stock-pot eighteen miles on his head, and half an hour after arrival in camp, at midnight, surprised headquarters mess with a dish of steaming hot soup.

On another occasion when there was a sudden alarm, several of these Swahilis rushed outside the perimeter where their officers were resting and brought all the kit to a safe place. One of these same boys later had a rare mix-up with a strange native who was trying to " pinch " his master's " bivvy " sheet. Many of them were very sad when we had to discharge them the day before we finally left East Africa, and the attachment was often mutual. Several of us would gladly have retained our Swahili servants as valets for life.

During the period the battalion were in the Lindi area the following promotions and other matters affecting personnel have to be recorded :—

Lieut.-Colonel Morris, whilst temporarily detached for duty to act as Commander of Column 4 (October 26th to November 12th), was graded as A.A.G. with temporary rank of Colonel.

Lieutenant (acting Captain) J. Arnott to be Captain *vice* Captain J. E. Dennison released from service (17.7.17).

Lieutenant A. Buchanan (8th S.A.I., attached 2nd Stokes Battery) was attached for duty (8-23.11.17) *vice* Lieutenant C. F. Abbott killed in action.

During November the below named received commissions as 2nd Lieutenants to replace officer casualties on the 6th idem, viz. :—

November 7th, No. 11332 Private C. A. Vipan (6th S.A.I.)
November 7th, No. 10609 Private E. W. Templer (6th S.A.I.)
(These two officers reported for duty on November 9th.)
November 17th, Staff Sergeant A. S. Gibson, S.A. Forces.
(Reported for duty 1.12.17.)

THE STORY OF THE 1st CAPE CORPS.

On October 11th, C.S.M. D. Twynham (1092) became acting R.S.M. *vice* R.S.M. Betts invalided to South Africa.

During October, Lieutenants Thompson and E. H. Browne and forty-two other ranks were invalided to South Africa, and during November Captains Michau and Stevens; Lieutenants Rackstraw, Leslie, Colson, Bain, Potgieter and one hundred and fifty other ranks.

On November 29th, a draft of one hundred and seven other ranks arrived at Dar-es-Salaam from South Africa.

On December 16th, Major Bradstock was transferred to the King's African Rifles, and Captain W. P. Anderson received the vacant majority.

Acting Captain F. C. Hallier became Captain *vice* Anderson promoted, and Acting Captain D. K. Pearse became Captain *vice* Captain Hallier, seconded to Political Department. Lieutenants Wigman, Heaton and Barnard were invalided to South Africa on December 19th.

During the voyage of the "Caronia" from Dar-es-Salaam to Durban, Private Beit, G. (3483) died of cerebral malaria and was buried at sea (December 23rd).

The officers of the battalion who returned to the Union on board the "Caronia" were: Major (Acting Lieut.-Colonel) C. N. Hoy, D.S.O., Major Cowell, Captains Tandy, Difford, McNeil, Earp-Jones, Burger, Robinson, Robertson, Cuningham, Arnott, Harris, Edwards, Pearse, Murchie, T. Rose-Innes, Stanford; Lieutenants Botha, Bloxam, Bourhill, Coates, Davies, Difford, Dreyer, Feetham, Gardner, Gibson, Girwood, Hayton, Horseman, James, Pillans, S. Rose-Innes, Rose-Nel, Samuelson, M.C., Stubbs, Templer, Vipan and Ware.

All of those, except Captain Robertson, had taken part in the Lindi operations, as had also the following who were evacuated by hospital ship from Dar-es-Salaam, viz.: Lieut.-Colonel Morris, Captain Michau, Lieutenants Barnard, Colson, Leslie, Wigman, Heaton, M.C., Rackstraw.

Our total casualties in East Africa during our whole period of service there (17th February, 1916, to 20th December, 1917) were:—

	Officers.	Other ranks.	Total.
Killed in action	4	19	23
Died of wounds	1	12	13
Died of disease and accident	1	126	127
Total deaths	6	157	163
Wounded in action	12	94	106

Whilst in different parts of East Africa our sick and wounded were at different times admitted to the S.A. Field Ambulance commanded by Lieut-Colonel Girdwood. The result was always satisfactory, every possible care and attention being devoted to the patients. All ranks will always gratefully remember Lieut-Colonel Girdwood and his subordinates.

After the battalion had finally left East Africa the following officers and men who had remained behind there returned to the Union, viz.:—

Per hospital ship:
Lieutenant Walton (30.12.17).
Lieut.-Colonel Morris (23.1.18).
Seventy-four other ranks (during December).
One hundred and six other ranks (during January).

Per troopship:
Twenty-four details in January, ex hospital, etc.
Fifteen details in February.

Lieutenant N. F. Howe-Browne remained in East Africa on special duty and on 2nd February, 1918, was seconded to the Political Department there.

CHAPTER XIII.

(IN THE UNION 25TH DECEMBER, 1917 TO 3RD APRIL, 1918.)

H.M.T. "Caronia" docked at Durban at 9 a.m. on Christmas day (1917). Our first greeting was a most satisfactory one in the shape of the following War Office cable in the morning paper:—

"The experiment of forming a combatant force of the coloured population of the Union of South Africa has been amply justified by the good opinion formed of the Cape Corps by the G.O.C. in Chief, East Africa, where this unit has rendered constant and valuable service since taking the field early in 1916. The capacity of the officers and the zeal of the rank and file reflect the utmost credit on all concerned with the organisation and training of the Corps, and on the loyal population from which it was recruited. It is the desire of the Army Council to afford the Cape Corps a further opportunity of service in another theatre, and the Union Government has accordingly been requested to reorganise the Corps with that object on its return from East Africa, after all ranks have had a period of rest and recuperation to which their services entitle them."

As soon as the local officials came on board we were informed of the arrangements made for our disposal. These were, three hundred men to entrain at once for Potchefstroom and a like number for Kimberley, and the remainder, approximately six hundred, to go into Jacobs Camp near Durban. All ranks were then to be quarantined for a period of ten days during which every man's blood was to be tested for malaria symptoms. If the test registered two negatives the individual was to be allowed to proceed on a month's recuperative leave. Those who could not register the desired negatives were to remain in quarantine until they could do so. The reason why we were not all to be kept together was said to be lack of the necessary accommodation, medical officers, and facilities in any one place. Two special trains were ready to take the Kimberley and Potchefstroom detachments north at once. The "Caronia" was expected to dock three hours earlier than she actually did. When the delay was discovered no attempt was made to alter the time of departure of the specials. There was no time to get the bulk of the kits out of the holds and our disembarkation was consequently as much a muddle as our embarkation had been, and the majority who went north had perforce to travel without their kit.

As soon as the gangways were in position a large quantity of Christmas cheer, the gift of the Cape Corps Gifts and Comforts Committee, was placed on board. Needless to say this act of thoughtful kindness was greatly appreciated by all ranks.

The first special train left the Point (Durban Harbour) at 10 a.m. for Kimberley. There were seven officers and three hundred men ("A" Company and Headquarters) on board, Captain Tandy being O.C. train. Half an hour later Captain Cuningham left with "C" Company and the Machine Gun section, three hundred in all, for Potchefstroom, and our Acting C.O., Major Hoy travelled by the same train to report at Pretoria. After lunch Major Cowell with "B" and "D" Companies went by special train to Jacobs Convalescent Camp,

THE STORY OF THE 1st CAPE CORPS.

Photo by] [*The Middlebrook Studios, Kimberley.*

OFFICERS OF THE BATTALION AT THE DEPÔT, KIMBERLEY, MARCH 1918, BEFORE EMBARKATION FOR EGYPT.

Back row (left to right): Captain B. Boam (Paymaster), Lieutenant A. A. Hayton, Captain J. Arnott, D.C.M., Lieutenant A. Leslie, Lieutenant S. H. Rose-Innes, Lieutenant R. A. Cloke, Captain D. W. Drew, S.A.M.C., 2nd Lieutenant C. A. Vipan, Captain J. W. Bouwer, S.A.M.C., 2nd Lieutenant R. Colson, 2nd Lieutenant E. W. Templer, 2nd Lieutenant E. B. Bloxam, Lieutenant H. C. Manley (Signalling Officer).

Middle row: Captain A. Earp-Jones (Chaplain), Lieutenant G. W. de Villiers (Depôt Adjutant), Lieutenant D. F. Botha, Lieutenant G. R. Barnard, Lieutenant E. P. Stubbs, M.C., Lieutenant G. C. White, 2nd Lieutenant M. S. Davies, 2nd Lieutenant J. S. Dreyer, 2nd Lieutenant F. I. Girdwood, Lieutenant G. Horseman, Lieutenant E. J. Rackstraw, and Lieutenant S. V. Samuelson, M.C., Lieutenant B. H. Moin, 2nd Lieutenant A. S. Gibson, Lieutenant T. E. James, Lieutenant A. N. Difford.

Bottom row: Captain F. Burger (O.C. Machine Guns), Captain D. K. Pearse, Captain J. E. Robinson, Captain I. D. Difford (Q.M.R.), Captain J. M. Michau, Major W. J. R. Cuningham, Major C. N. Hoy, D.S.O., Lieut.-Colonel G. A. Morris, C.M.G., D.S.O., Major W. R. Cowell, D.S.O., Major W. P. Anderson (O.C. Depôt), Captain D. W. Robertson, Captain S. Youart, Captain J. H. Tandy, M.C. (Adjutant), Captain H. Edwards, Captain T. P. Rose-Innes, Captain J. V. Harris, M.C.

Absent from group: Captains W. Jardine and F. Murchie, Lieutenants R. Feetham, M.L.A., C. S. H. Gardner, W. T. Wigman, A. S. Ross and G. A. Woods, M.C., 2nd Lieutenant C. R. Lambe.

half an hour from Durban. The special trains to the north were held up for half an hour at Pietermaritzburg and the men regaled with tea, cakes, and seasonable cheer by the Mayor and Corporation of the Natal capital, whilst the officers were equally well looked after by charming ladies.

When Major Cuningham's detachment reached Johannesburg they were met by the Mayor (Mr. T. F. Allen), several other councillors, and leading citizens at Braamfontein Station. The Mayor extended a hearty "welcome home" to officers and men and congratulated them in the name of the Witwatersrand, the Reef, and the Transvaal upon their splendid record and service in East Africa. Major Cuningham suitably responded.

On arrival at our Kimberley depôt (De Beers No. 3 Compound) Captain Tandy's detachment met with an unpleasant surprise. During the holidays there had been some street rowdyism culminating in passages of arms between the men in the Regimental depôt and the local hooligans. A great deal of capital was made by certain sections of the community out of what was really nothing but a storm in a teacup. The true facts of the case, as far as it was possible to ascertain them, were briefly as follows: The Cape Corps depôt had been moved from Woltemade III. (near Cape Town) ten days before Christmas. Prior to that the Cape Auxiliary Horse Transport Corps Depôt had been located at Kimberley for some time. At that time they were badly disciplined and in consequence had upset a section of the local inhabitants. On the other hand there is no doubt that the presence in their midst of a large number of coloured men wearing the King's uniform, and not averse to showing that they were proud of it, was an offence to many of the young slackers of the town.

When the Cape Corps arrived at Kimberley from Woltemade the O.C., Major Anderson, was informed by the Chief Inspector of Police that the Beaconsfield hooligans intended to "have a go" at his men during the holidays. On Christmas Eve the rowdyism duly broke out and was repeated on a smaller scale the following evening, but thanks to strong handling of the situation by Major Anderson and to the good sense and discipline of the men, serious trouble was averted.

Acting on the principle that prevention is better than cure, Major Anderson was instructed by the District Staff Officer, U.D.F., to send his men (including the three hundred who had just arrived from East Africa) out of the town over the New Year holidays, and the whole depôt accordingly camped out at Riverton for three days. They were without tents and the weather unfortunately proved cold and wet, and officers and men consequently spent a miserable New Year. The recent arrivals from East Africa, having come direct from a tropical summer, suffered severely and were justly indignant at having to undergo this unnecessary hardship. The discipline and restraint of the Cape Corps under severe provocation was beyond praise. (This matter is referred to again in Chapter XIX.)

On arrival at Pretoria on December 27th, Major Hoy (Acting Lieut.-Colonel) was ordered to proceed at once to Kimberley to investigate and report.

[NOTE.—Lieut.-Colonel Morris it will be remembered had been left behind in hospital in East Africa.]

On Major Hoy's report and undertaking to hold himself responsible for their good behaviour the men were at once brought back from Riverton. The day following the arrival of the detachments of the battalion from East Africa in their respective camps, officers and men underwent their first blood test and a second test was taken about a week later. During our stay in those camps we were put on special diet, being given such luxuries as fresh eggs and milk. This was absolutely necessary after the hard work and privations of the past twenty-two months. As a result of this treatment the majority picked up wonderfully and

THE STORY OF THE 1st CAPE CORPS.

C.S.M. K. HUTCHINSON (710), D.C.M.

C.S.M. M. J ABRAHAMS (1483).

Photo by] [Grant Bros., Cape Town.
SERGEANT J. C. WATERWICH (869).

SERGEANT J. H. CARELSE (916).

quite a fair percentage obtained two negatives at once, and by the 10th January quite fifty per cent. had been sent away to their homes on a month's recuperative leave. Those who could not pass the test were subjected to further treatment and dieting and by degrees about another twenty per cent. got a clean bill of health. The remainder were transferred to hospital at Kimberley and, sooner or later, discharged therefrom as permanently unfit for further war service.

Between the 15th and 20th February the majority of those on leave had returned to the depôt at Kimberley, which about that time began to assume an extraordinarily busy aspect. Re-organisation, re-equipment, training, etc., was taken in hand in deadly earnest in order to prepare the battalion for its next adventure—the advance into Egypt—which was to take place as soon as possible.

During the period 20th February to 20th March some twenty officers and about eighty other ranks proceeded to the Gunnery School at Potchefstroom for refresher courses in Lewis and Vickers gunnery, bombing, etc. Several signallers attended the Signalling School at Potchefstroom, of whom eighteen passed out " classed as signallers."

About this time the establishment of the battalion was reduced from six to four double companies and the following increased establishment authorised to accompany the battalion to Egypt, viz.: a Reserve Half Battalion, to consist of two double companies with the necessary officers. A Major was to be appointed to command one company and also to command the Reserve Half Battalion. Two subalterns of the R.H.B. were to act as transport officer and signalling officer for the battalion. Two subalterns, twenty-five other ranks and four machine guns were added to the Machine Gun section as a reserve. A medical officer was to be appointed to the R.H.B.

Lieutenant C. S. M. Pillans was released from service on 13th February " on ceasing to be employed with Imperial Service Contingents."

On February 21st, Captains Tandy and Michau returned to East Africa to give evidence in a court martial case at Dar-es-Salaam. Lieutenant James acted as Adjutant until Captain Tandy returned.

Lieutenant B. H. Moin (10th S.A.I.) was transferred to the battalion (machine gun section) on 21st February, 1918.

Major Hoy returned from ten days' leave on 1st March and resumed command of the battalion.

Captain R. P. McNeil, M.C., S.A.M.C., resigned his commission on February 15th, and, on March 2nd, Captain D. Drew, S.A.M.C., reported to replace him.

Every officer and man in the battalion heard of Captain McNeil's decision with the greatest regret. For eighteen months in East Africa he had done magnificent work and the men had learned to have the greatest affection for and confidence in him.

Captain C. E. Stevens relinquished his commission (by decision of Medical Board) 28th February, 1918.

The following officers were released from service on relinquishing their temporary Imperial commissions on the dates shewn (by decision of Medical Board) viz. :—

        Lieutenant G. L. Ware (5.3.18).
        Lieutenant E. Rose-Nel (16.3.18).
        Lieutenant H. Walton (19.3.18).
        Lieutenant H. Coates (23.3.18).

The last two named were very keen hard working officers who had done considerable service with the Battalion and their departure was regretted by all ranks.

The battalion was honoured on March 14th by a visit of inspection from His Honour the Administrator of the Cape Province, Sir N. F. de Waal, K.C.M.G. Sir Frederic afterwards addressed the parade and expressed his pleasure at the smartness of the men. He also very highly complimented the battalion on their good service in East Africa and wished us luck and a similar record in Palestine.

Mr. H. C. Manley was gazetted Lieutenant and Signalling officer on March 16th (*vice* Lieutenant R. A. Thompson seconded to Political Department, East Africa, December 23rd, 1917).

Whilst at Kimberley every officer and man was inoculated against enteric fever and small pox.

On Sunday, March 24th, a most impressive farewell parade service was held at the Kimberley Cathedral. This was very largely attended by relatives and friends, it being our last Sunday prior to leaving for Egypt.

Captain J. W. Bouwer, S.A.M.C., reported for duty on 24th March and was attached to the R.H.B.

Lieut.-Colonel Morris returned from leave and assumed command of the battalion on March 25th, but four days later, having been medically boarded temporarily unfit, handed over the command again to Major Hoy.

Captain W. J. R. Cuningham was promoted Major, and to command the Reserve Half Battalion on 25th March. The month of March proved an exceptionally busy time for all ranks. The end of the month found the battalion thoroughly re-organised and ready to take the field again. The health of all ranks, too, had very considerably improved.

Shortly before the end of the month it was announced that embarkation for Egypt would take place at Durban early in April, but that owing to lack of accommodation on the troopship the Reserve Half Battalion would have to remain at Kimberley for the time being.

The battalion left Kimberley in three special trains on Sunday, March 31st, arrived at Durban on April 3rd, embarked on H.M.T. "Magdalena" next morning and sailed the same day.

At Durban Lieutenant G. A. Woods, M.C. (ex 7th S.A.I.) and Lieutenant A. S. Ross (ex 4th S.A.H.) reported for duty.

Thirty-two other ranks had to be taken off the ship at the Point as there was no room for them on board. They returned to the depôt at Kimberley under Lieutenant A. S. Ross.

The embarkation strength was thirty-seven officers and nine hundred and fifty-seven other ranks. The officers who embarked were: Major C. N. Hoy, D.S.O., Major W. R. Cowell, Captains I. D. Difford, J. H. Tandy, A. Earp-Jones, D. Drew (S.A.M.C.), J. E. Robinson, F. Burger, D. W. Robertson, J. M. Michau, J. V. Harris, S. Youart, H. Edwards, D. K. Pearse, T. P. Rose-Innes, Lieutenants D. F. Botha, E. B. Bloxam, G. R. Barnard, R. Colson, R. Cloke, M. S. Davies, J. S. Dreyer, A. N. Difford, G. Horseman, A. A. Hayton, A. S. Gibson, F. I. Girdwood, A. Leslie, E. J. Rackstraw, S. H. Rose-Innes, E. P. Stubbs, E. W. Templer, S. V. Samuelson, M.C., C. A. Vipan, G. C. White, G. A. Woods, M.C., H. C. Manley.

The Reserve Half Battalion had been brought up to full strength before the battalion left Kimberley and there were also two or three hundred men in the depôt under command of Major Anderson. There were also a considerable number of men in hospital at Kimberley, of whom many had to be discharged as "medically unfit for further war service."

THE STORY OF THE 1st CAPE CORPS.

Top row, left to right: LIEUTENANT LESLIE, LIEUTENANT GIRDWOOD, CAPTAIN BURGER, LIEUTENANT STUBBS, CAPTAIN PEARSE, LIEUTENANT MOIN. Seated, left to right: LIEUTENANT TEMPLER, LIEUTENANT BOTHA, LIEUTENANT HORSEMAN, LIEUTENANT CLOKE, CAPTAIN ROSE-INNES, LIEUTENANT HAYTON, AT SCHOOL OF INSTRUCTION, POTCHEFSTROOM, FEBRUARY, 1918.

Photo by] [*The Middlebrook, Studio, Kimberley.*
CAPTAIN D. DREW, S.A.M.C.

ENTRAINING AT KIMBERLEY FOR EGYPT, APRIL, 1918

Captain Arnott was detailed for duty at the hospital as Orderly officer (for 1st Cape Corps) to assist the Medical Officer in charge (period February 15th to March 31st, 1918). Captain Arnott was then himself released "medically unfit." Captain Arnott was the senior officer of the battalion in years, but one of the youngest in vigour, keenness and energy. He had done very good work in East Africa, enduring hardships with the best, and all ranks bade him farewell with very real regret.

During the months of January to March, whilst so many of the men were on leave in the Cape Peninsula, Captain W. Jardine was detailed for special duty there to maintain discipline and to look after the men's interest generally. In that capacity he rendered equally good service in the interests of the battalion and of the individuals.

SIGNALLER DRURY
(1703).
Killed in action, 8th November, 1917.

THE ADMINISTRATOR (SIR N. F. DE WAAL) ADDRESSES THE OFFICERS AT KIMBERLEY.

THE STORY OF THE 1st CAPE CORPS.

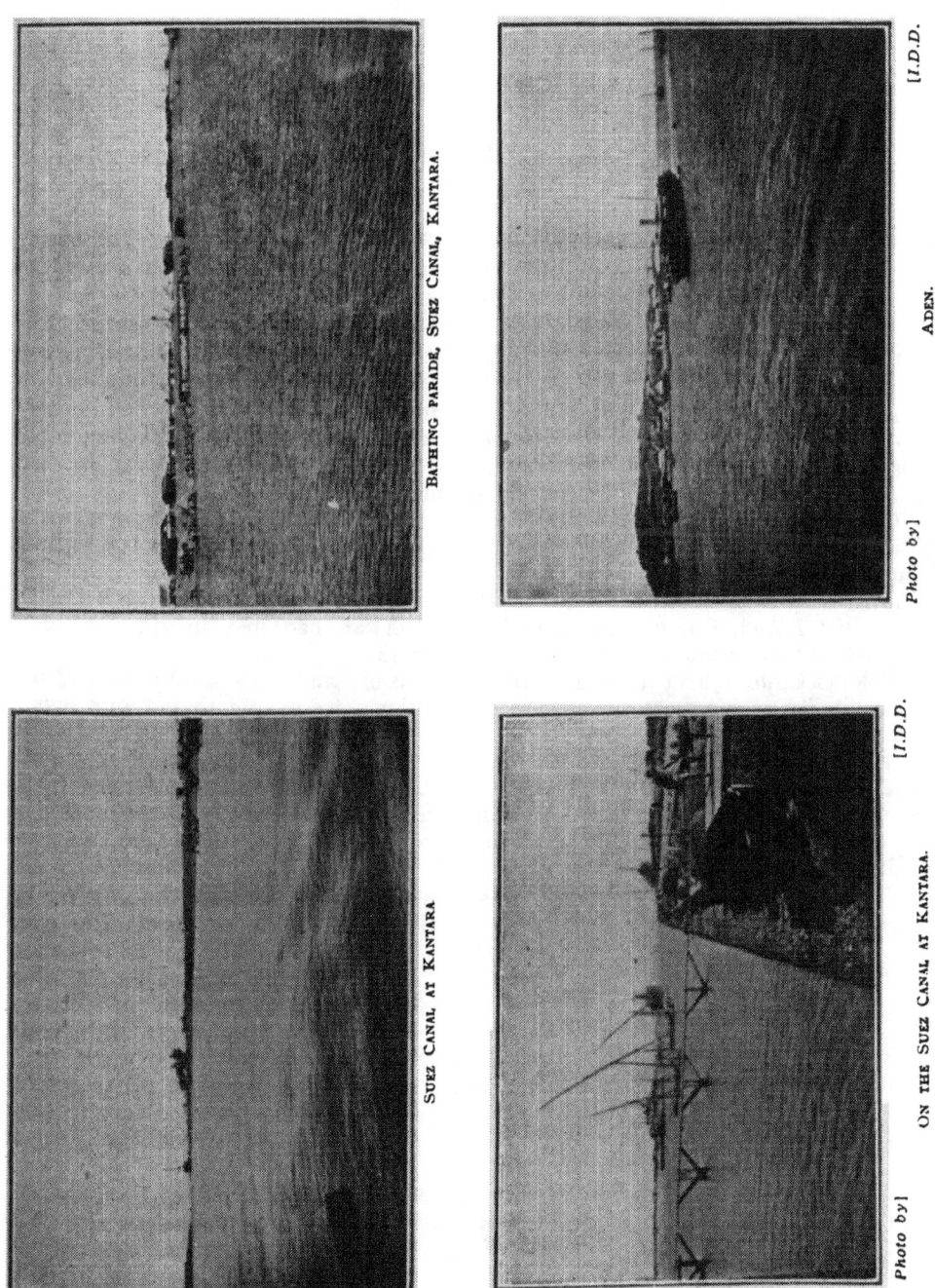

Bathing Parade, Suez Canal, Kantara.

Photo by] Aden. [I.D.D.

Suez Canal at Kantara.

Photo by] On the Suez Canal at Kantara. [I.D.D.

CHAPTER XIV.

In Egypt—Period 19th April, 1918, to 15th July, 1918.

THE "Magdalena" reached Port Suez on Friday, April 19th. The battalion disembarked in fifty minutes and left at once by special train for Kantara, on the Suez Canal, midway between Suez and Port Said.

The master of the "Magdalena" signed the voyage report as "satisfactory," and the chief officer reported that there had been fewer shortages and breakages of mess utensils than on any voyage since the vessel had been trooping.

Kantara was reached at 2.30 a.m. on April 20th, and we marched across the Canal at once to our allotted camp—a very hot and sandy spot. Tents, cooking utensils and other stores were drawn without delay and after a long and tiring day everybody was more or less settled down by nightfall.

On arrival at Kantara every N.C.O. and man was paid the sum of five shillings, a generous and much appreciated gift from the Cape Corps Gifts and Comforts Committee.

Our camp at Kantara adjoined the Indian Base Depôt, of which the O.C. was an old friend, Colonel Cunningham, whom we had met in East Africa whilst he was commanding the 1/101st Grenadiers.

Colonel Cunningham gave us a hearty welcome and very kindly extended the hospitality of his mess to our officers until we were able to get our own going.

Very soon after our arrival at Kantara our C.O. realised that we were soldiering under very different conditions to those which had obtained in East Africa. A thousand men, all practically fit, unattached to any Corps or Division, and unknown, did not seem to count for much here (in East Africa even a hundred fit men would have been a valuable asset to any column).

It was learned that an endeavour was being made to retain the unit for lines of communication work, which was a most discouraging prospect after over a year in the front line in East Africa. Lieut.-Colonel Hoy at once drew up and forwarded to G.H.Q. a memorandum giving a resumé of the battalion's past record, its personnel, training, service, and honours won in the field. This apparently had the desired effect, for within a few days orders were received for the commencement of intensive training with a view to the battalion taking its place in the front line. At the same time all ranks fully realised that before attaining our desire we should have to undergo very searching and thorough tests. This proved an immediate incentive to increased keenness and put every man on his mettle.

In accordance with instructions the battalion had arrived in Egypt without equipment of any sort—not even rifles and Web equipment—merely in the clothing they stood in. Orders were of course at once received to draw rifles and Web equipment. It was found that in Egypt the rifle was considered very much the primary factor for infantrymen, and that men were expected to have passed their musketry course before being considered of any value. It was also expected that fifty-five per centum should have come forward having a working knowledge of the Lewis gun, and that every man should be acquainted with

THE STORY OF THE 1st CAPE CORPS.

Kantara Station.

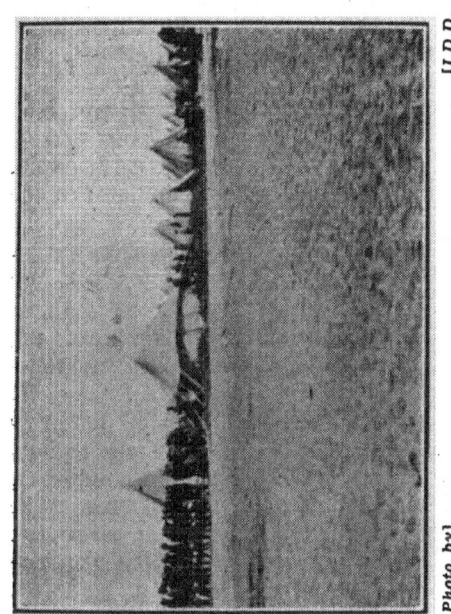
Photo by] Marking Mess Tins at Kantara. [I.D.D.

Captured Enemy Guns at Kantara.

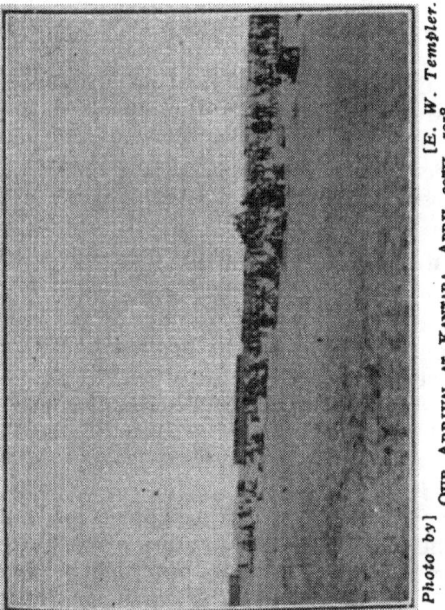
Photo by] Our Arrival at Kantara, April 20th, 1918. [E. W. Templer.

the characteristics of and be able to use the Mills Burrows hand grenade. Bayonet fighting and physical drill were also considered training essentials, and games requiring quick thought and action were encouraged to develop activity. Certain physical " stunts " had to be carried out at the double, a bayonet assault course was to be given to every man, and men taught to jump obstacles with fixed bayonets.

In musketry, men were to be taught to thoroughly understand and read the back sight, and faulty trigger pressing—the cause of so much poor marksmanship—was to be rigorously checked. Unless the men were of good mental capacity they were to be eliminated, the maxim being " fools cannot become soldiers."

Recruits for the Machine Gun Company were, of course, to be well grounded in the Vickers gun, and a good percentage were to be trained as signallers.

Officers were expected to know how to use the Compass and Protractor, the Lewis gun and its characteristics, the bomb (hand grenade) and its advantages, and to have a good knowledge of musketry, map-reading, sketching, and topography generally, etc.

Briefly, we very soon discovered that, although we had learned much in East Africa, there was a vast deal more to assimilate in Egypt. It was equally soon learned that there was far more system and method about the conduct of the Egyptian and Palestine campaign than there had been in East Africa. The departmental services, ordnance, supplies, etc., were very much more up-to-date and well organised, and the hospitals and medical services generally were infinitely superior. In a word, we had left the amateur stage behind us and were by way of becoming professionals.

A period of intensive training was foreseen, involving much hard graft, but all ranks tackled the task with a will, feeling that the satisfaction of knowing that we should be more or less masters of our craft would surely be our reward.

Training was commenced in earnest two days after reaching Kantara, and continued without cessation for the next month.

A week after arrival we were inspected by Brig.-General A. H. Lloyd, C.B., C.M.G., M.V.O., Acting I.G.C., P. L. of C., who expressed himself pleased with the clean and smart turn-out of the parade and the steadiness of the men under arms.

The result of this inspection was the receipt of orders (May 11th) to draw equipment as laid down for war establishment.

On April 26th, Sergeant J. G. Berry (1135) proceeded to Alexandria for duty at Records Office (G.H.Q. 3rd Echlon) there. He remained there until the battalion left Egypt in August next year.

On May 2nd, Captain J. E. Robinson was admitted to hospital. He returned to duty a few weeks later; but very soon had to be re-admitted to hospital. He was never well in Egypt, in fact should never have left South Africa. After a long spell in hospital in Egypt he returned to South Africa via United Kingdom on the 18th August, per hospital ship, and was finally released from service, medically unfit, on the 8th April, 1919.

On May 3rd we were called upon to furnish a prisoner of war escort of fifty-four men. (There were thousands of Turkish prisoners in Kantara at that date who had to be escorted daily from and to their camp to carry out their allotted labours in various parts of the area). For several days afterwards we found prisoner of war escorts, sometimes as many as eight to ten officers and four hundred other ranks being called upon, but on May 11th the B.G.G.S. (training) visited us and found that training was being interrupted by those duties, which were consequently taken over by another unit.

THE STORY OF THE 1st CAPE CORPS.

Photo by] [I.D.D.
R.S.M. W. E. RUTHERFORD AND SERGT.-MAJOR F. J. SHIPP AT EL ARISH, JUNE, 1918.

Photo by] [Captain A. Earp-Jones.
RETURNING FROM INSPECTION BY BRIG.-GENERAL LLOYD AT KANTARA, MAY, 1918. CAPTAIN ROBINSON LEADING "B" COMPANY.

Photo by] [B. H. Moin.
A FAMILIAR LANDMARK. THE MOSQUE AT KANTARA (SUEZ CANAL) IN 1918.

A CRICKET GROUP.
Lieutenant H. W. Taylor, M.C., R.A.F.; Captain I. D. Difford, 1st Cape Corps; Major G. A. Faulkner, D.S.O., R.F.A.; Captain J. H. Tandy, M.C., 1st Cape Corps, at Alexandria, May, 1918.

Turkish prisoners at Cairo.

Continental Hotel, Cairo. [I.D.D.]

Interior of El Azhar Mosque, Cairo.

Kasr-el-Nil Bridge over Nile, Cairo. [I.D.D.]

THE STORY OF THE 1st CAPE CORPS.

On May 12th orders were received to be prepared to proceed to El Arish as soon as equipping was completed. The original intention was that we were to go to Mex, near Alexandria, for further training in the same depôt as the B.W.I. Regiments, but on Lieut.-Colonel Hoy making representations to the authorities as to the inadvisability of that, orders were given for us to establish our own depôt at El Arish.

On May 13th, C.S.M. Rutherford, W. E. (290121) (2/7th Northumberland Fusiliers) reported for duty as battalion R.S.M., our C.O. having decided that our R.S.M. must be a man with experience of modern warfare as practised on the western front.

On May 18th, Lieutenant Cloke (transport officer) and thirty-one other ranks were sent to the R.A.S.C. Animal Transport School at Ludd, and a number of men were sent to the Signalling School (at the G.B.D.) Kantara.

Captain Chadwick, the officer in charge of signalling instruction at the G.B.D., was a very good friend to us. He assisted and advised our signalling officer and throughout our stay in Egypt took the greatest pains with and interest in our signallers.

Before leaving Kantara, officers' chargers were drawn and a portion of the prescribed establishment of a battalion's transport, i.e., G. S. wagons, travelling kitchens, water carts and mules. The balance of the latter was issued to us later at Ludd.

Whilst at Kantara bathing parades, route marches, and several football matches supplemented the more technical syllabus of training, and tended greatly to increase the men's stamina and physical fitness.

On May 21st, the battalion proceeded in two special trains to El Arish to establish our depôt there and to continue training. El Arish is on the Mediterranean coast about eighty miles east from Kantara. It had been our army headquarters in the Sinai Peninsula prior to our attacks on Gaza and Beersheba (in 1917).

General Sir Edmund Henry Hynman Allenby, G.C.B., G.C.M.G., took over supreme command of the E.E.F. on June 28th, 1917. He captured Beersheba on October 31st and Gaza on November 7th of that year. Prior to his arrival there had been two costly and futile attacks on Gaza, mainly due to underestimation of the enemy's strength and his formidable defences. El Arish at the time of our arrival was still an important military centre.

It was our advanced R.O.D. workshops and depôt. There was also in the area a big School of Instruction and a very large Convalescent and Rest Camp, to which men were sent from the front for rest and recuperation. (There were over two thousand officers and men in the camp in May, 1918.)

Others in El Arish at the time were a large R.A.S.C. depôt, the 360th (Water company) R.E., detachments of the Imperial Camel Corps and the Camel Transport Corps, the 43rd Casualty Clearing Station, the Scottish Horse Field Ambulance, Army Postal and Telegraph Units, and the 204th (Calcutta) Battery R.G.A. The latter, who were old East African friends of ours, had two big guns mounted to protect the place from attack from the sea.

El Arish village was some two miles inland. The army were located on the sea board on a frontage of four or five miles. The climate was magnificent and the sea-bathing unequalled. The water was so warm that it did not bring out malaria as cold sea water always did, and our two months at El Arish effected a wonderful all-round improvement in health. The "snap" and vigour so absolutely essential, but which had been impossible in East Africa, soon returned, and henceforward was a marked feature of the battalion's work.

Our camp was within three hundred yards of the sea and delightfully situated amongst date palm groves. Officers (except a few seniors who had Bell

Photo by] [*I.D.D.*
UNION DAY SPORTS AT EL ARISH, 1ST JUNE, 1918.
CAPTAIN J. V. HARRIS, M.C., JUDGING THE HIGH JUMP.

Photo by] [*I.D.D.*
CAPTAIN TANDY AND GUIDE IN THE TEMPLE OF OSIRIS, NEAR GREAT PYRAMID, CAIRO.

Photo by] [*I.D.D.*
SERGEANT I. W. ARENDSE (607) TAKING THE HIGH JUMP AT EL ARISH, JUNE 1ST, 1918. CAPTAINS MICHAU AND HARRIS, M.C., JUDGING.

(Left to right) LATE LIEUT. G. C. WHITE, CAPT. I. D. DIFFORD, LIEUT. S. H. ROSE-INNES, LATE LIEUT. A. N. DIFFORD AT EL ARISH.

THE STORY OF THE 1st CAPE CORPS.

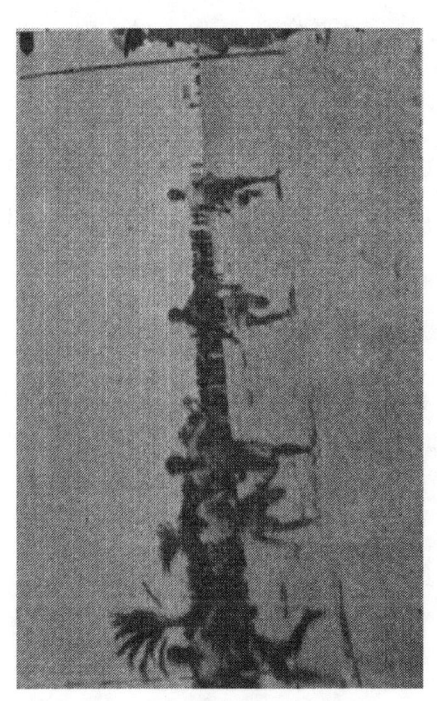

Photo by] [U.H.T.
BATTALION SPORTS AT EL ARISH, 1ST JUNE, 1918. FINAL 100 YARDS RACE.

Photo by] [I.D.D.
SUEZ CANAL AT KANTARA.

Photo by] [I.D.D.
WATER CARTS AT Q.M.R.'s STORE, EL ARISH.

Photo by] [I.D.D.
TRAM ROUTE TO THE PYRAMIDS, CAIRO.

THE STORY OF THE 1st CAPE CORPS.

The Battalion Reviewed at El Arish, June, 1918. The March Past.

To the Lines at El Arish, June 1918.

Training at El Arish—Trench Digging. Late Captain J. V. Harris, M.C., in centre directing.

Q.M.R.'s Stores at El Arish.

tents) and men were housed in bivouac tents, which were very small and uncomfortable. That, however, did not deter the training in the least, and during the next two months all ranks put in a tremendous spell of hard work, which commenced at daybreak and continued till dusk and after.

Vickers, Stokes and Lewis gunnery, musketry, bombing, trench warfare, physical drill, bayonet fighting, etc., were carried on without intermission, equal attention being paid to theory and practice.

Coincident with the work done at El Arish nearly all the officers and N.C.O.'s and about twenty per cent. of the men went to Schools of Instruction in various parts of the country. The senior and machine gun officers went to the Imperial School at Zeitoun (Cairo). Bombing, trench warfare, scouting and Lewis gunnery were learned by subalterns, N.C.O.'s and men at the El Arish School, under Lieut.-Colonel Synott; signalling at Kantara East; bayonet fighting and physical drill at Mustapha (Alexandria); gas warfare at Rafa; transport work at Ludd and cookery at Ismailia. Several subalterns also took the platoon officers' course at the El Arish school.

Practically all the officers and the majority of the men passed their courses well. (There were no officer failures). In the case of a number of the men it was found that the written examinations were a stumbling block. This was proved by the fact that men who could read and write well obtained better percentages than others who were far better in practice and application. If all the men had been able to express themselves freely and fluently (in English) they would have done a good deal better, as the instructors with one accord commented on their practical knowledge, their keenness and attention at lectures, and their rapid and instinctive grasp of essentials.

Lieutenant A. N. Difford headed a big officers' class at El Arish in trench warfare and bombing. He gained ninety-eight per cent. of marks and was classified as "D" (distinguished), a rare honour which earned him a personal letter of congratulation from General Allenby.

On May 28th, Second Lieutenant A. M. McVey (1st Garrison Battalion Northants Regt.) arrived from the Gas School at Rafa and spent a month with us instructing officers and men in the theory and practice of gas warfare and the methods of protection against it.

On Saturday, June 1st, an all-day regimental sports meeting was held to celebrate Union Day (May 31st). This proved a most enjoyable break to the steady routine of training.

On June 1st, Corporal W. Reeson (1/5 Suffolk Regt.) and Sergeant Pilley (1/5 Essex Regt.) reported for temporary duty as Lewis gun and bombing instructors, respectively.

On June 6th, Major Ackworth (G.S.O. 2) from headquarters, P. L. of C., spent the day in camp. He expressed satisfaction at the zeal with which training was being carried out.

On June 10th, Lieut.-Colonel Hoy assumed command of El Arish area in addition to his regimental duties.

On June 13th, Bt. Lieut.-Colonel (temporary Brig.-General) E. N. Broadbent, C.M.G., D.S.O., K.O.S.B., I.G.C., P. L. of C., inspected the battalion on parade and complimented the C.O. on the work being done.

On June 28th, an excellent report was received from the O.C., R.A. Signal School (G.B.D.) Kantara East, with reference to the good work, keenness and conduct of N.C.O.'s and men whilst undergoing instruction there. The following did exceptionally well, registering over ninety per cent. of marks, viz.:

Photo by]   [S. H. Rose-Innes.

LEFT TO RIGHT: LATE CAPTAIN J. V. HARRIS, M.C., LATE LIEUTENANT GORDON C. WHITE, CAPTAIN D. K. PEARSE, AND LATE LIEUTENANT ARCHIE DIFFORD AT KANTARA, MAY, 1918.

Photo by]   [S. H. Rose-Innes.

LIEUTENANTS GORDON WHITE AND ARCHIE DIFFORD AT KANTARA, BOTH LATER KILLED AT EL MUGHEIR.

CORPORAL C. CARELSE (1348), SERGEANT J. C. M. PAULSEN (432), AND CORPORAL J. OLIVER (846).

Photo by]   [I.D.D.

MAJOR (ACTING LT.-COLONEL) C. N. HOY, D.S.O. In command of the Battalion in Egypt (April-August, 1918).

Private Jacobs, D. (1146) headed the class with ninety-seven per cent.
Sergeant Alies, J. H. (825).
Corporal Joyce, A. (574).
Private Wyngaard, H. (1409).
Private Williams, W. T. (436).

Lieutenant Cloke and his men returned from the R.A.S.C. Animal Transport School at Ludd shortly before the end of the month. They brought back a report from the O.C. School to the effect that they had passed the course at the head of the list and that their conduct during training had been of the highest possible standard and a credit to their Battalion.

At the end of June when the majority of officers and men had returned from the schools, the benefits of the courses of instruction were obviously most marked.

The commandants of all the schools remarked on the keenness and good behaviour of all ranks.

On July 9th notification of an early move to Ludd and subsequently to the 20th Army Corps for service at the front was received.

On July 10th the musketry refresher courses of all ranks were completed. Though hurried, the courses had been most beneficial.

Captain Difford went to hospital on July 13th and was away from duty for over two months.

On the night of July 15/16th the battalion entrained for Ludd in two special trains.

During the training at El Arish the need of officers was greatly felt. With so many away at schools of instruction, and others still subject to recurrent attacks of fever, training was much handicapped. Had it not been for the very good work done by many of the senior N.C.O.'s, the position would have been most difficult. No reserve officers arrived in Egypt for four months after the battalion.

The eight weeks of training at El Arish were all too short for most of us, though the majority worked harder than ever before in their lives. Double the period would have been none too long for all there was to be learned. However, we were considered "up to standard" and were wanted in front, so forward it was, and every man must have gone forward fully conscious of the fact that he was a far better equipped, efficient, and more knowledgeable soldier than when he landed in Egypt three months before. The C.O. too, one feels sure, was quietly confident that his battalion, granted reasonable fortune, would not let him down when the supreme test came.

During the period covered by this chapter it is highly satisfactory to record that there were no deaths in Egypt from disease.

At Kantara, on May 5th, Armourer Staff Sergeant G. Giles (R.A.O.C.) reported for duty as Armourer Sergeant, and Acting Armourer Sergeant J. H. van Rooyen (1270) handed over to him.

When the battalion left El Arish for Ludd, Captain Burger remained behind to carry on the training of his Half Machine Gun Company. His strength was four officers and some one hundred other ranks. The officers were Lieutenant D. F. Botha, and 2nd Lieutenants M. S. Davies, F. I. Girdwood and E. W. Templer.

CHAPTER XV.

THE 1ST CAPE CORPS' SHARE IN GENERAL ALLENBY'S GREAT VICTORY.
PERIOD JULY 16TH TO OCTOBER 31ST, 1918.

ON arrival at Ludd, on July 16th, Lieut.-Colonel Hoy was informed that the battalion had been allotted to the 160th Infantry Brigade, 53rd Division, XXth Corps. The XXth Corps was commanded by Major-General (temporary Lieut.-General) Sir Philip W. Chetwode, Bt., K.C.B., K.C.M.G., D.S.O. The 53rd Division was commanded by Major (temporary Major-General) S. F. Mott, C.B. The then commander of the 160th Infantry Brigade was Bt. Lieut.-Colonel (temporary Brig.-General) V. N. L. Pearson, D.S.O. (2/10th Middlesex Regiment).

All ranks were fully impressed with the honour and privilege of allocation to such famous commands and were determined to prove worthy of the confidence placed in them.

The other units of the 160th Brigade at the time were the 1st/7th Royal Welsh Fusiliers, the 1st/17th (Loyal) Indian Infantry, the 1st/21st Punjabis, and the 160th Light Trench Mortar Battery.

The 53rd Division consisted of the 158th, 159th, and 160th Infantry Brigades, and the following divisional troops, viz.:—

53rd Divisional Cyclist Company.
265th Brigade R.F.A. (A, B, and C Batteries).
266th Brigade R.F.A. (A, B, and C Batteries).
267th Brigade R.F.A. (A, B, and 439th Batteries).
53rd Divisional Ammunition Column.
436th and 437th (Welsh) Field Companies, R.E.
72nd Company, 3rd Sappers and Miners.
53rd Divisional Signal Company, R.E.
53rd Divisional Machine Gun Battalion (No. 158, 159, and 160 Companies).
1st/155th Pioneers.
53rd Divisional Train (No. 246, 247, 248, and 249 Companies R.A.S.C.).
53rd Mobile Veterinary Section.

The Division was composed originally of Territorial battalions, and landed in Egypt from Gallipoli as a Territorial Division. It took part in the advance from the Suez Canal, the first and second battles of Gaza, and eventually joined the XXth Corps on its formation in August, 1917.

Certain British battalions were withdrawn and others amalgamated or disbanded between June and August, 1918, and their places taken by Indian units and the 1st Cape Corps.

Major-General S. F. Mott, the Divisional Commander, was well known nearly twenty years ago on the Western Province Cricket Ground at Newlands (Cape) when Captain S. F. Mott, the Rifle Brigade.

When the Cape Corps joined the 160th Brigade Lieut.-Colonel (temporary Brig.-General) J. W. Walker, D.S.O., T.D., R.F.A. (T.F.), was commanding the Divisional Royal Artillery.

THE STORY OF THE 1st CAPE CORPS.

Jerusalem from Damascus Gate. [E. W. Templer.

Mosque of Omar, Jerusalem. [E. W. Templer.

The Kaiser's Clock Tower, near Jaffa Gate, Jerusalem. [E. W. Templer.

General Allenby with Allies' Attachés at Jerusalem.

Having drawn transport, the battalion left Ludd on July 19th and marched via Latron and Biet Nuba, south-east in the direction of Jerusalem, to a camp at Ain Arak known as Ranger's Corner, which was reached during the evening of July 21st.

Lieutenant G. R. Barnard died suddenly of malignant cerebral malaria on July 22nd at Ranger's Corner, to the great grief of the whole battalion. From the Rham Alla graveyard, where he was buried, those who were able to attend the funeral obtained their first distant view of Jerusalem.

On July 22nd we moved to a new camp near Rham Alla, where our reception by the Division and Brigade was most cordial. The Divisional and Brigade Commanders, senior departmental officers, and others, called at once and everyone was most anxious to assist and shew us the ropes. On arrival at our first camping site with the 160th Brigade the 1/7th R.W. Fusiliers had already pitched tents ready for our officers.

The expected great Palestine Push was evidently some weeks ahead, and all ranks were glad to hear of the probability of further opportunity for the continuation of training.

When we arrived the 160th Brigade were taking their turn out of the front line. (At that time each brigade, after a period in the front line, spent a month a few miles behind the line training and resting.)

The Rham Alla area was said to be malarial, but it did not prove so for us. Nevertheless our sick parades began to grow to an alarming extent before the end of the month. The men suffered severely at first from diarrhœa and later on from influenza.

During the four weeks we remained at Rham Alla opportunity was afforded to every officer and man to visit Jerusalem. Leave parties marched from Rham Alla every two or three days, and the men were accommodated in a leave camp at Jerusalem. Needless to say the opportunity was taken full advantage of and all ranks greatly enjoyed their good fortune. Guides were provided and every facility afforded to the men to see as much as possible in the time at their disposal, and to learn a good deal more than they knew before of the wonderful historical associations of Christendom's most holy city.

During the period from July 23rd to August 18th we carried on strenuous training at Rham Alla.

The divisional and brigade commanders closely supervised and carefully tested our field work.

Rham Alla is twelve miles as the crow flies from Jerusalem. A light railway connected the two places before the big advance. This railway was twenty miles in length owing to the hilly nature of the country. It was specially constructed for the big push and was a wonderful engineering feat.

At Rham Alla Lieutenant Leslie was appointed Assistant Adjutant, Lieutenant Samuelson, M.C., Bn. Intelligence Officer, and Lieutenant Woods, M.C., Bn. Lewis Gun Officer.

Here it may not be out of place to briefly set forth the position of the contending armies in Palestine at this time. After the surrender of Jerusalem (December 9th, 1917) General Allenby found that any further advance northwards was out of the question for the time being. Roads had to be constructed and the improvement of communications in the forward areas to be attended to. Stores, supplies, and munitions had to be accumulated and until the railway had reached a point considerably nearer the front, this was a difficult task, and one rendered still more difficult by frequent spells of wet weather. Moreover, it was necessary before any further advance could be made, to drive

THE STORY OF THE 1st CAPE CORPS.

Photo by]   On the Military Railway near Jerusalem.   [I.D.D.

Photo by]   Jerusalem—Mount of Olives in background.   [E. W. Templer.

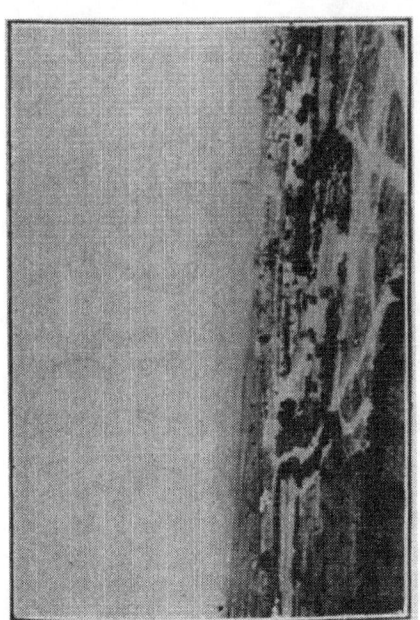

Photo by]   Ramleh (Ludd). The rear Base for the Big Push.   [E. W. Templer.

Photo by]   Shadouf (ancient well) between Ludd and Jaffa.   [E. W. Templer.

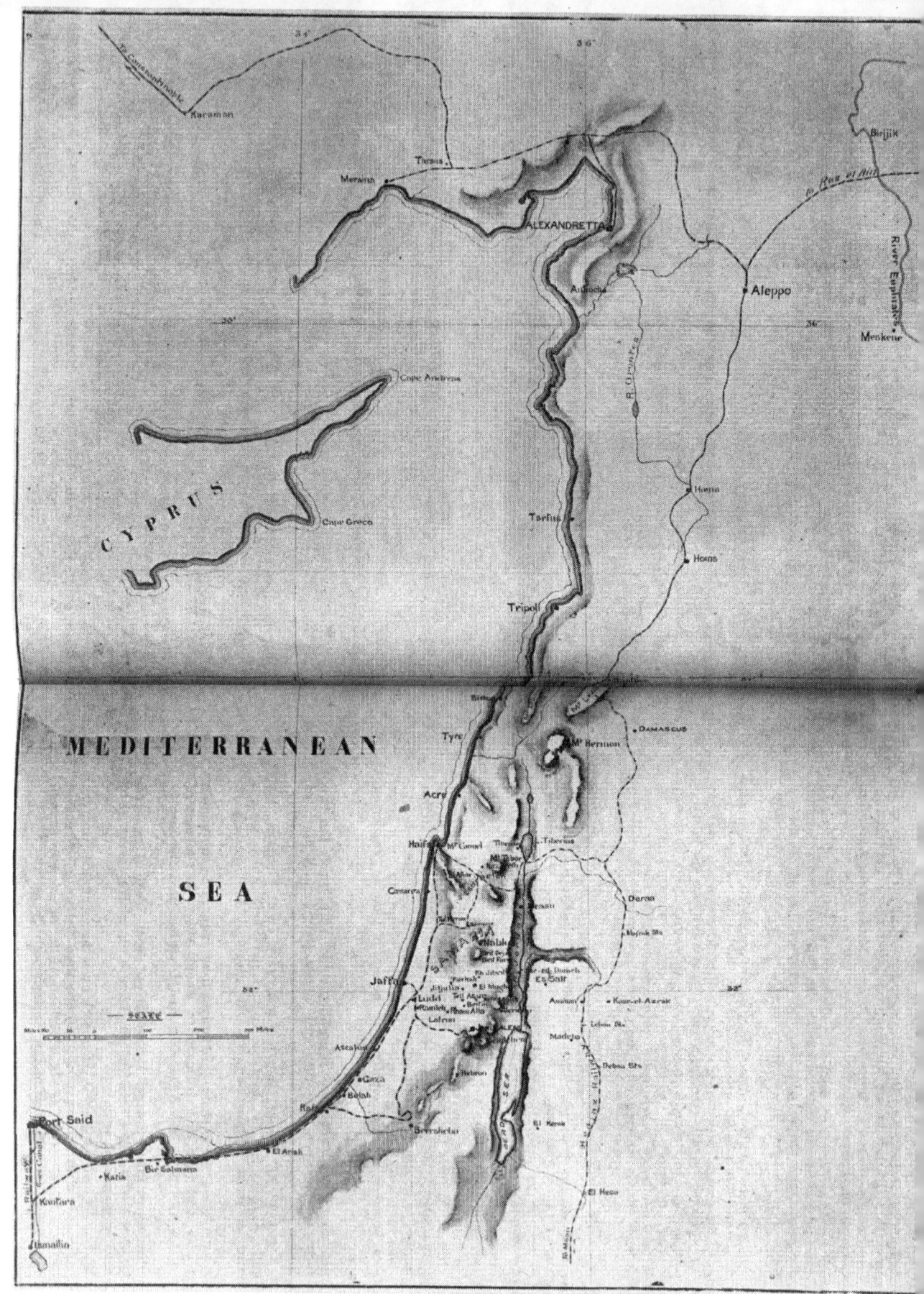
PALESTINE

the enemy east across the Jordan and thus render our right flank secure. That was accomplished during the latter half of February, 1918, Jericho being occupied on February 21st. During March, the 20th and 21st Corps cleared the Jordan Valley sufficiently to enable operations to be carried out against the Turkish line of communications to the Hedjaz.

The passage of the Jordan was negotiated under fire, March 22nd/23rd, and during April operations were directed against Es Salt and Amman, about fifteen miles due east of the Jordan. Es Salt was occupied, but could not be held owing to the enemy's strength and the fact that they brought up large reinforcements.

General Allenby accordingly withdrew his army across the Jordan on May 4th, and for the next few months was not in a position to renew the offensive owing to the reorganisation of his forces. British troops were at this time urgently required for the Western front and a heavy call was made upon the E.E.F. During the first fortnight of April the 52nd and the 74th Divisions embarked for France, and before the end of the month nine Yeomanry regiments, five and a half Siege Batteries, ten Infantry battalions and five Machine Gun Companies had been withdrawn from the line preparatory to embarkation for France.

In May, a further fourteen British battalions were withdrawn, and during July and the first week in August another ten British battalions left. The Yeomanry regiments were replaced by Indian Cavalry sent from France, and the British battalions by Indian battalions from India. These latter had, however, not seen service during the present war, and a great deal of reorganisation and training was the natural corollary.

The adoption of a policy of active defence was therefore necessary, during which only various minor operations and a number of raids could be carried out.

The last Indians to arrive had been incorporated into divisions early in August, and General Allenby thereupon decided to make his big push about the middle of September. He would have preferred to allow the new troops further opportunities to accustom themselves to the prevailing conditions before calling upon them to embark on the anticipated arduous operations on a large scale. The rains, however, usually commence at the end of October, rendering the plains of Sharon and Esdraelon impassable for transport, and further delay was impossible.

Before Allenby's great advance took place (September 18th, 1918) the two armies were facing one another from the coast (about eleven miles north of Jaffa) to the Jordan and Dead Sea on a front of between fifty and sixty miles.

Our 21st Corps, under Major General (temporary Lieut.-General) Sir Edward S. Bulfin, K.C.B., C.V.O., held the coastal and Sheik Abbas sectors with headquarters at Jerisheh (near Sarona) and advanced headquarters at Sabieh.

The 20th Corps headquarters were at Jerusalem from January to the middle of September, 1918, and were then advanced to Rham Alla. To the east of the 20th Corps the Australian and Anzac Mounted Divisions held the line to the Jordan.

On the 11th August, Lieut.-Colonel Morris arrived from South Africa and resumed command of the battalion, and (Acting) Lieut.-Colonel Hoy reverted to Major and second in command again.

On the night of August 19th our Division took over the front line from the 60th Division. We were to the right of the Jerusalem-Nablus (Shechem in biblical history) road, about ten miles north of Rham Alla. Curiously enough we faced the 53rd (and 26th) Division of the Turkish 20th Corps.

THE STORY OF THE 1st CAPE CORPS.

The 160th Brigade marched to the Dar Jerir bivouac area at night (August 19th) and took over from the 181st Brigade of the 60th Division the following evening. The route taken was from Rham Alla—Home Counties road—east of Beitin to Mary Cross.

The Cape Corps took over from the 130th Baluchis, with whom we had already seen service in East Africa.

In taking up positions companies had to march two hundred yards apart and other usual necessary precautions against enemy aircraft action had to be taken. We occupied four positions as follows:—

Fusilier Ridge ("C" Company under Captain Michau).
Ide Hill ("A" Company under Captain Harris).
Kh Abu Felah ("B" Company under Captain Edwards).

with "D" company under Captain Robertson in reserve at Tay Wady, and the whole under command of Captain Robertson. Battalion headquarters were close to Tay Wady.

The quartermaster and his staff with stores, etc., were at Mary Cross, half a mile from the brigade forward supply dump, and the transport officer, with our wagons, etc., was seven miles back towards Rham Alla, at Wady Dougal, out of sight of enemy observation.

Our Division was about fifteen miles due north of Jerusalem and occupied a front of about fifteen miles from Fusilier Ridge facing north-east to the hills above the Jordan Valley. The country was very rough, stony, and hilly, even precipitous in places. Trenches could not be dug and our defences consisted of sangars, stone and sand bag parapets and barbed wire.

All movement during the day was limited to the irreducible minimum. Rations and water had to be brought up to the front line under cover of darkness. Our observation and snipers' posts were, however, kept fully employed during the daytime.

Enemy aircraft came over hurriedly at rare intervals, but did not disturb us much as they were completely dominated by our own. In fact, as a new unit to this sort of warfare, we were very vastly impressed by the wonderful feats of the R.A.F. Their work was marvellous. They literally played with and seemed to delight in worrying the enemy flyers.

Rations and water were brought up to us by camels, which were controlled by the brigade camel officer. For water convoy purposes each camel carried two fanatis (small lead tanks, capacity ten, twelve and a half or fifteen gallons each). This water was taken from a reservoir near Mary Cross. The daily water supply for a battalion was fifty-two full fanatis.

At this time the enemy positions were dominated by our artillery, due to the fact that we held higher positions, and also because our observation was infinitely superior. For sniping purposes twelve pounders captured from the enemy and known as "pip squeaks" were used. For more important work the artillery's main weapon was the 5.9 inch Howitzer. Our observation and sniping posts were connected by telephone with battalion and brigade headquarters, and also with the artillery.

The battalion first came under enemy shell fire on August 18th and were continually so for a month, even when in reserve at Cheshire Ridge. Though disconcerting and annoying it was ineffectual so far as we were concerned, chiefly owing to strict attention to orders to keep out of sight during daylight hours.

On August 21st our ranks were becoming seriously depleted owing to an epidemic of Spanish influenza, and the forward positions were being held by sixty men instead of full company strength of over two hundred and twenty. Consequently fresh dispositions had to be made.

The 1/7th R.W.F. took over Abu Felah from " B " Company, whose fit remnants joined the skeleton of " A " Company at Ide Hill. " D " Company handed over to one hundred men of the 1/7th R.W.F. at Cheshire Ridge and their " fits " reinforced " C " Company at Fusilier Ridge.

By August 23rd the effective fighting strength of the battalion had been reduced to two hundred and ninety-seven owing to the ravages of influenza. The front line was accordingly handed over to the 1/7th R.W.F. and the battalion went into reserve, taking over brigade reserve headquarters at Cheshire Ridge during the night of August 23/24th, and the influenza patients were isolated.

A feature to be noted at this period was the good fellowship and comradeship which marked our relations with other units of the brigade. Officers and men were on the best of terms with the Royal Welsh Fusiliers and also with the Indian units.

The 1/17th Indian Infantry had fought with us in the Lindi area (East Africa) and our patrols going through their lines at night employed the Swahili language. This was not only interesting but most useful, as many of them could not speak English and none of us Hindustani. Moreover, the Swahili lingo would have been Greek to the enemy, if perchance any of their spies contrived to sneak into our lines. In particular Lieutenant Samuelson, our intelligence officer and his scouts, found the Swahili medium most useful on numerous occasions.

Although in reserve, and despite influenza, the next few weeks were by no means a period of idleness. All fit ranks had to apply themselves to training with undiminished thoroughness. The company training attack scheme, compass marching, Lewis gunnery, gas and bayonet drill were practised with the most intensive application. A number of men were sent to the divisional forward Lewis gun school for a four days course and lectures were also attended. At these classes and lectures new methods of fighting were taught and the men practised the new " stunts " which were to be adopted in the forthcoming attack.

On September 4th, all battalion commanders were summoned to divisional headquarters and informed of the scheme for the impending big push, and the respective positions each would have to take on the given day were indicated. The C.O.'s of each battalion were the only persons let into the secret and they were then ordered to find similar positions and country behind our lines and rehearse their " stunts." Rehearsals at first took place daily and later on at night, the whole being practised over a distance of six and a half miles over rough, stony ground and deep Wadys (valleys and dry river beds).

A week before the imminent advance company commanders were informed of the plan of campaign, and after the battalions had rehearsed separately for a few days the whole brigade rehearsed together.

Early in September the influenza epidemic diminished appreciably and the battalion were able to devote themselves to rehearsals of the tactical scheme with the maximum of energy. These rehearsals were carried out with strict attention to detail and were most thorough in every respect.

The Company that was to lead the attack on the given day always did the same at rehearsal. In fact, this was the case even with platoons and sections.

From September 10th to 17th the battalion headquarters officers, the company commanders and all other officers who were to participate in the attack did daily personal reconnaissance from our front line trenches, and spent hours studying the respective positions which they had to take.

THE STORY OF THE 1st CAPE CORPS.

Photo by]   [Capt. D. Drew.
GREEK CHURCH ON MOUNT OF OLIVES, JERUSALEM.

SITE OF THE TEMPLE OF SOLOMON AT JERUSALEM.

Photo by]   [E. W. Templer.
THE HOLY SEPULCHRE, JERUSALEM.

Lieutenant Samuelson, our intelligence officer, took nightly patrols as near as possible to the enemy's positions and Sergeant Steyn, J. (947) and Private Sindon, H. (2339) did good work at night in going over the ground over which we were to advance and taking the time from place to place.

On Sptember 6th, Captain Jardine arrived with a draft of one hundred and forty-four other ranks from the depôt at El Arish.

On the 14th September administrative instructions were received with regard to the coming operations. The officers were to be dressed exactly like the men (in serge) and were to discard Sam Browne belts in favour of Web equipment similar to that worn by the men. The men were to move as light as possible, discarding their packs and haversacks. They were to carry sixty rounds of ammunition, one hand grenade, two water bottles and one day's iron rations. Greatcoats were not to be worn, but as it was to be night fighting, every man was to wear a white armlet. The enemy were accustomed to wear greatcoats at night. This made it possible for instructions to be issued that any man wearing a greatcoat and not wearing a white armlet could safely be obliterated.

The men had, of course, been taught to observe strict silence and to use the bayonet—in fact, no firing was to be done without special orders to that effect.

In addition to clothing actually worn the total weight carried into action by every man was thirty-one pounds. This included rifle, ammunition, extra (full) water bottle, etc.—in fact everything.

On the night of September 15th, our Transport moved up from Wady Dougal and took cover just behind our line, where they collected the men's greatcoats, packs, haversacks, and other surplus kit. Blankets were dumped at the brigade dump.

On the night of September 16th the battalion moved up to an olive grove, about one and a half to two miles from the starting point for the attack.

On the same night Captain T. P. Rose-Innes arrived from the depôt with the following officers: Lieutenant Ross and 2nd Lieutenants Antill, W. J. Buchanan, Hirsch, Hollins, Lambe and Solomon and one hundred and sixty men.

Our tents were left standing in our old camp at Cheshire Ridge to mislead the enemy into believing that we were still there. During the 17th everyone had to keep under the trees in case of enemy aircraft observation.

Full instructions had been issued for the use of light signals as an emergency by commanders of front line posts for communication with artillery and brigade and battalion headquarters in the event of the failure of other means of communication. The use of coloured lights by the enemy was to be at once reported, so that our own light signals might be changed if necessary.

The artillery plan and programme for the attack had been worked out in most minute and precise detail and copies of same furnished to all officers who needed to know same.

Our artillery consisted of:—
  Five batteries (each six guns) 18 pounders.
  Three batteries (each 4 guns) 4.5 Howitzers.
  One battery (four guns) 6 inch Howitzers.

Before detailing the plan of attack of the 160th brigade a brief reference to the general situation on the whole front on the 18th September and the general plan of the offensive may, perhaps, prove of interest.

At the beginning of September, General Allenby estimated the strength of the 4th, 7th and 8th Turkish armies at twenty-three thousand rifles, three thousand sabres and three hundred and forty guns. The 4th army—six thousand rifles, two thousand sabres and seventy-four guns—faced our forces in the Jordan valley. The 7th army held a front of some twenty miles astride the

THE STORY OF THE 1st CAPE CORPS.

Photo by]   *[J.H.T.*
"STUNT" PRACTICE.

Photo by]   *[J.H.T.*
"STUNT" PRACTICE.

Kh Jibeit.   Square Hill.
AERIAL PHOTO OF KH JIBEIT.
(Taken 1st September, 1918.)

Photo by]   *[J.H.T.*
STUNT PRACTICE, PALESTINE FRONT.

Jerusalem-Nablus road with seven thousand rifles and one hundred and eleven guns, whilst the 8th army front extended from Furkhah to the sea and was held by ten thousand rifles and one hundred and fifty-seven guns.

In addition the garrison of Mann and the posts on the Hedjaz railway north of it consisted of some six thousand rifles and thirty guns.

The enemy's general reserve, only three thousand rifles and thirty guns in strength, was distributed between Tiberias, Nazareth and Haifa. His total strength amounted to some four thousand sabres, thirty-two thousand rifles and four hundred guns, representing a ration strength south of the line Rayak-Beirut of one hundred and four thousand.

General Allenby had at his disposal two Cavalry Divisions, two Mounted Divisions, seven Infantry Divisions, an Indian Infantry Brigade, four unallotted battalions and the French detachment (the equivalent of an Infantry brigade with other arms attached), a total in the fighting line of twelve thousand sabres, fifty-seven thousand rifles and five hundred and forty guns. He thus had a considerable superiority in numbers, especially in cavalry, over the enemy, who were known to be short of reinforcements—in fact, it was known that there had been considerable friction between the Turks and Germans in this connection.

General Allenby was anxious to gain touch with the Arab forces (our Allies) east of the Dead Sea, but was unable to do so so long as the enemy controlled the Jordan crossing at Jisr-ed-Dameh, which enabled him to transfer troops from the west to the east bank. The defeat of the 7th and 8th Turkish armies would give us the control of this crossing and would also leave the enemy's 4th army isolated, if it continued to occupy the country south and west of Amman.

General Allenby, therefore, determined to strike a blow west of the Jordan, where the whole Turkish army in that area was enclosed in a rectangle forty-five miles in length and only twelve in depth.

All the enemy's communications to Damascus ran northward from the eastern half of this line, converging on El Afule and Beisan some twenty-five miles to the north. Thence his communications ran eastward up the valley of the Yarmuk to Deraa—the junction of the Palestine and Hedjaz railways. Thus El Afule, Beisan and Deraa were the vital points of the enemy's communications. If they could be seized his retreat would be cut off.

The two former were within reach of our cavalry if the infantry could break through the enemy's defensive positions and create a gap for the cavalry to pass through. Deraa was within reach of mobile detachments of the Arab army, who could at least disorganise all traffic, even if they could not hold the railway junction.

It was essential that the cavalry should reach their destinations before the enemy could make his escape, or before he could man the passes in the hills of Samaria, or their extension towards Mount Carmel, which had to be crossed before the Plain of Esdraelon and the Valley of Jezreel could be reached by us.

For this reason General Allenby decided to make his main attack in the coastal plain rather than through the hills north of Jerusalem, where the ground afforded the enemy positions of great natural strength. In addition the coastal route would enable the cavalry to pass through the hills of Samaria at their narrowest point, thus ensuring greater speed and less likelihood of being checked. The rationing of a large force of troops in the plain also presented fewer difficulties.

The main difficulty lay in concealing the withdrawal of two cavalry divisions from the Jordan Valley, and in concentrating secretly a large force in the coastal plain.

THE STORY OF THE 1st CAPE CORPS.

To prevent, if possible, the decrease in strength in the Jordan Valley being discovered, Maj.-General Sir Edward Chaytor, K.C.M.G., C.B., A.D.C., was ordered to carry out a series of demonstrations with the object of inducing the enemy to believe that an attack east of the Jordan was intended, either in the direction of Madeba or Amman.

The enemy was thought to be anticipating an attack in these directions and every possible step was taken to strengthen his suspicions. At this time a mobile column of the Arab army, accompanied by British armoured cars and a French mountain battery, was assembling at Kasr-el-Azrak, fifty miles east of Amman. The real objective of this column was the railway north, south, and west of Deraa. Should the concentration of this column be observed it was hoped that the demonstrations by Chaytor's Force would strengthen the enemy's belief that a concerted attack on Amman was intended.

Sir Edward Chaytor's Force consisted of the Anzac Mounted Division, the 20th Indian (Imperial service) Infantry Brigade, the 38th and 39th Bns. Royal Fusiliers and the 1st and 2nd Bns. B.W.I. Regiment.

Whilst the concentration in the coastal plain was nearing completion, the enemy's railway communications at Deraa were attacked by the Royal Air Force, and by the mobile column of the Arab army, which, after concentrating at Kasr el Azrak, fifty miles east of Amman, had moved into the Hauran.

The railway line and station buildings at Deraa were damaged by the Royal Air Force on September 16th and 17th. On September 16th the Arab column, which had been joined by the Shalaan sections of the Rualla, Anazeh, and by a number of Druses, attacked the Hedjaz railway, fifteen miles south of Deraa, destroying a bridge and a section of the railway. On the following day the line was attacked both north and west of Deraa, extensive demolitions being carried out. As the result of these demolitions all through traffic to Palestine ceased, and a considerable quantity of transport, which had been intended for the Hedjaz, was diverted to bridge the break in the railway.

The day before the September advance the enemy intelligence service issued a disposition map, which was later captured in the headquarters of the Yilderim army group at Nazareth. The information embodied in this map was quite in accordance with the enemy's air service reports that " no essential changes had taken place in the distribution of the British forces." No change was shewn. The move of the 60th Division into the 21st Corps area, and the concentration of the cavalry on the coast, not to mention the alteration in the front of the 10th and 53rd Divisions, were passed unnoticed. The latter was apparently considered as being in reserve to the sector lately occupied by the Desert Mounted Corps.

The 6th Poona Division (then in Mesopotamia) was shewn as being within ten miles of the front line. The position of our general headquarters was not shewn, and that of the 21st Corps headquarters was placed eleven miles from where it was actually to be found. The French troops in the line were queried as Italians.

On 18th September General Allenby's preliminary concentration was complete. The divisions detailed for the main attack, *i.e.*, the 60th, 7th, 75th, 3rd, 54th and the French contingent, had actually taken up their positions, the troops previously holding the coastal sector having closed up on their own flanks to make room for them.

The cavalry were concealed in the orange and olive groves, two divisions immediately north and east of Jaffa, and one (the Australian Mounted Division) near Ludd; all were within easy reach of the positions of assembly which they were to occupy during the night 18th/19th September. On the right the 10th and 53rd Divisions had closed in their outer flanks, west and east respectively, leaving their centre from Kefr Malik to Jiljulia covering the main Jerusalem-Nablus road to be occupied by "Watson's Force," a composite detachment formed from the 20th Corps cavalry regiments, two pioneer battalions, and the 20th Corps reinforcement camp.

Now to return to matters of more immediate concern to this narrative.

The operation orders for the 160th Brigade read as follows:—

"The Brigade will make a night march and break through the enemy works on Wye Hill and advance along the watershed east of the Wady Samieh to Dhib and Square Hills with the object of entering the enemy's main line defences at Valley View and about El Mugheir from the rear of those works."

The 159th Brigade were on the left of the 160th with the 158th behind them. The 1/17th (Loyal) Indian Infantry were to act as the advance guard for the 160th Brigade. Their objective was to secure the crossing of the Wady Samieh for the troops following, then to call for the artillery bombardment to commence on Sh-el-Azier and Valley View and to advance close under the bombardment, and, when it lifted, to assault Wye Hill. One company was then to follow the Cape Corps and mop up certain enemy defences. The remaining three companies were on entering the front line works, to turn left and right, mop them up, and then picket the flanks of the advance.

The Cape Corps were to follow the 1/17th Infantry, pass through them and march along the watershed to take Dhib Hill, Chevron Hill, Crest Hill, End Hill, and Square Hill, pickets being dropped en route to protect the right of the advance. Smoke shells were to be fired on the forward slopes of Dhib Hill to serve as a guide. On arrival at Dhib and Square Hills the battalion were to be responsible for protecting the right flank of the brigade against counter attack from the east, north-east and north, and touch was to be gained with the left Lewis gun detachment of the 17th Infantry who were to follow the Cape Corps and relieve them on Chevron and Crest Hills. When the 1/7th R.W.F. signalled the capture of Hill 2362, detachments were to be pushed forward to seize Kh Jibeit. The 1/7 R.W.F. were to follow immediately behind the Cape Corps until they could disengage to the left of Dhib Hill, when they were to march direct on Tongue Hill. When the bombardment of Valley View ceased they were then to push along the track to El Mugheir, their special objectives being Sh-el-Azeir, El Mugheir, Boulder Boil and Hill 2362.

The 21st Punjabis were to follow immediately behind the 1/7th R.W.F. during their attack on Sh-el-Azeir and eventually to concentrate at the northern end of Valley View.

The following precautionary measures were adopted in case the brigade or any of its component battalions were heavily reversed: One Colonel per brigade remained in reserve at brigade headquarters, and from each battalion the following: One company commander, and from each company the junior captain and one subaltern and as many N.C.O.'s as would be necessary to help reorganise in case of heavy casualties. (These precautions subsequently proved a godsend in the case of the 1st Cape Corps.)

Under the above scheme Lieut.-Colonel Morris remained at brigade headquarters until the afternoon of September 19th and Major Hoy commanded the battalion.

On our intelligence maps (of which, of course, every company commander received a copy) the enemy's machine gun posts, water, headquarters, etc., were clearly marked. At 11 a.m. on the 18th September, Lieut.-Colonel Morris personally explained the plan of action, and emphasised the importance of the work to be done, to all ranks, a platoon at a time. The men's keenness when

THE STORY OF THE 1st CAPE CORPS.

Cheshire Ridge.

Field Guns Captured from the Turks by 1st Cape Corps at Square Hill, September 18/20, 1918.

Medicals at Stunt Practice, Palestine Front.

A Village in Palestine.

they understood that a big job was on hand was intense, and men who had been reporting sick for days past suddenly forgot their ailments. The battalion sick parade actually fell from sixty to three in one day.

Each company took two Lewis guns into action, with the ammunition for same carried in magazines by men, and the remaining eight guns were to follow under the battalion Lewis gun officer, together with ammunition on pack mules at dawn next day. One platoon was detailed to carry eleven miles of telephone wire for the signallers, the same having to be laid as we advanced,—no easy job in the dark over rough and stony country.

To denote the positions we had to take in sequence our artillery dropped a smoke shell every five minutes on to the positions, in case we lost our way in the dark over ground which had been reconnoitred by aircraft only. These smoke shells proved extremely useful in indicating directions.

The disposition of the 160th Brigade previous to the issue of the above operation orders was the line from and including Fusilier Ridge, Ide Hill, Kh-abu-Felah, and Round Hill (all held by Royal Welsh Fusiliers), Cardiff Hill, Bubbly Knoll, The Warren, Rock Park, Pear Hill (all held by 17th Loyal Infantry), Morris Hill, Kubbet-en-Nejmeh (held by 21st Punjabis) with the Cape Corps in reserve at Cheshire Ridge. Brigade Engineers under Major Campbell, M.C., occupied a strong post on the lower slopes of Chipp Hill on the Strand road.

Brigade headquarters were at Drages Hill, immediately behind Cheshire Ridge. Our forward supply dump with motor transport (R.A.S.C.) were at Mary Cross, at the junction of Home Counties road and the Strand road; main supply dump at Rham Alla; the Camel Corps with thousands of animals were at Dar-Jerir; Machine Gun headquarters were at Tell Asur, behind Tinto Hill, whence machine guns were distributed to battalions just previous to the start. Aerodromes were situated twenty or thirty miles behind the scene of operations.

On the evening of September 17th, the whole of the fighting strength of the brigade congregated at and near Wady Dar Jerir, behind Rock Park and Pear Hill, leaving only skeletons to hold the line.

Animal transport (reserve ammunition, reserve Lewis guns, water, transport, etc.) gathered at a point behind El Munatir and near to Morris Hill, thence to be ready to move forward first down Wady el Akhraf and then into Samieh Wady.

Artillery batteries had a few days previously moved by night right forward to the reserve line on to and within easy distance of the good road leading down the Strand into Tay Wady and Wady-el-Kola.

Patrols of the 17th Loyal Infantry under Captain Hammond, M.C. (killed subsequently on the 20th) on the night previous to the push penetrated into enemy positions far beyond previous limits and ascertained that the Turks had no "forward strong posts," but had outposts at the heads of the valleys leading up to their main works.

On the same night Major Hoy took the battalion intelligence officer and Private Sinden (a scout equal to the best) on a patrol, to examine the ground and ascertain the best descent to be made by the battalion the next night to the "meeting" point of the whole brigade in Wady Samieh (no man's land). They also took "times," that is timed distances from starting to meeting points, and also took bearings with a strongly illuminated compass. Major Hoy left nothing to chance and wanted to see everything himself before starting.

During the daytime of the 18th September troops were ordered to have a thorough rest. The men of the Cape Corps spread themselves out under the numerous olive trees and indulged in such rest as fatigues, and arms, ammunition, water, and emergency ration inspections would permit. A venturesome

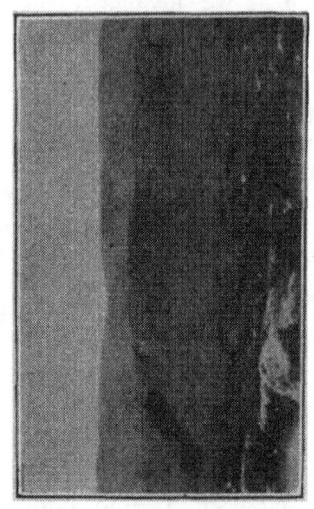

Kh Jibeit Position shewing Shell Holes.

Dhib Hill (captured by 1st Cape Corps, 18th September, 1918).

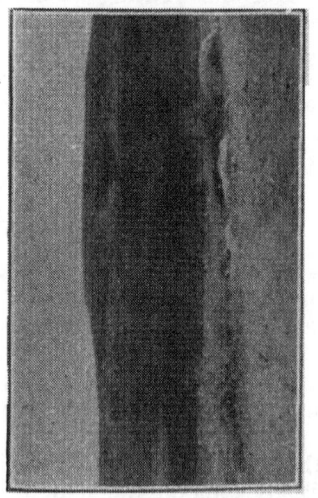

Square Hill (captured by 1st Cape Corps, 18-19.9.18).

Photo by]   A Rest at Dhib Hill.   [U.H.T.
Left to right: 2nd Lieutenant Hirsch, Lieutenant Horseman, Major Cowell, Lieutenant Stubbs.

Aerial Photo of Square Hill, Kh Jibeit, etc., taken 1.9.18.

Turkish aeroplane, at a height of some ten thousand odd feet, travelled at full speed homewards, chased by a couple of Britishers, and caused some of the men to open one eye and exclaim in disgust, " Hij is bang." (" He is afraid.").

An extract from an officer's diary says: "Between rests the men sang, made their wills, said their prayers and washed their teeth!! At the immediate prospect of a scrap at close quarters they were high-spirited and full of vim."

Just at sundown the battalion assembled and moved off to a point at Pear Hill, not under enemy observation. Immediately after dark, guided by Major Hoy and the intelligence officer, we moved forward in column of fours over the sky-line and descended the heights, over stony and precipitous country to the meeting point in the Samieh Wady. The order of the companies was "B" (Major Cowell), "A" (Captain Harris), "D" (Captain Robertson), "C" (Captain Youart) with headquarters staff and signallers immediately behind the leading company. The M.O. with his staff and stretcher bearers followed in the rear.

The brigade mustered silently at Wady Samieh without mishap or disturbance from enemy fire, although the place was fully exposed in daytime. Here rather a tedious hour was spent, first getting the brigade into formation and position and the separate battalions into their own formation. Half an hour before the brigade again pushed on Captain Hammond, M.C., with two platoons of Indians under Indian officers, went forward to mop up the outposts at the heads of the valleys on either side of our line of advance in Usk and Wye Wadis. This was duly done and caused the enemy to send up alarm rockets. The line of advance was out of Samieh Wady over the highest point between Usk and Wye Wadis, which necessitated a precipitous climb of twelve hundred feet.

Much to our surprise and delight we were allowed to proceed right through Samieh Wady, and it was not until we approached Wye Hill (the 17th Infantry's objective) that any fire was opened on us. At this time the enemy, too late, put down a barrage into Samieh Wady, disturbing our transport.

The approach to Wye Hill was most precipitous, and to-day one wonders how we reached the top. Consequent upon this fact a short delay was necessary in order to enable the slowest of the men to catch up to the more vigorous. Colonel Fagan, D.S.O., in command of the 17th Infantry, rightly decided, therefore, to delay calling for the barrage until such time as he was sure that the whole brigade was up the hill and closed up. At 10 p.m. (zero hour) he asked for the barrage and after twenty minutes bombardment of Wye Works his battalion attacked with great dash and took the position in a few minutes. Colonel Fagan and his regiment were under machine and rifle fire the whole time and took eighty odd casualties in capturing the hill (including Colonel Fagan himself) which they did at the point of the bayonet, capturing forty or fifty prisoners and seven machine guns.

Immediately following the capture of Wye Hill the Cape Corps went on, " B " Company leading, towards Hill 2260 and Chevron Hill. After a five minutes' barrage " B " Company seized those objectives and, after short bombardments, Crest and End Hills also, whereupon "A" Company took Dhib Hill without opposition. The 1/7th R.W.F. then turned west to attack Valley View and El Mugheir, and " D " Company went on to attack Square Hill, which was found to be strongly held. A barrage of five minutes having been put down " D " Company got the hill after some machine gun opposition, and " C " Company was sent up to reinforce them before dawn next morning. They consolidated the position and, all the night's objectives having been gained, the brigade consolidated to await the next move.

The operations just described had taken from 6.45 p.m. (18th) to 4 a.m. (19th).

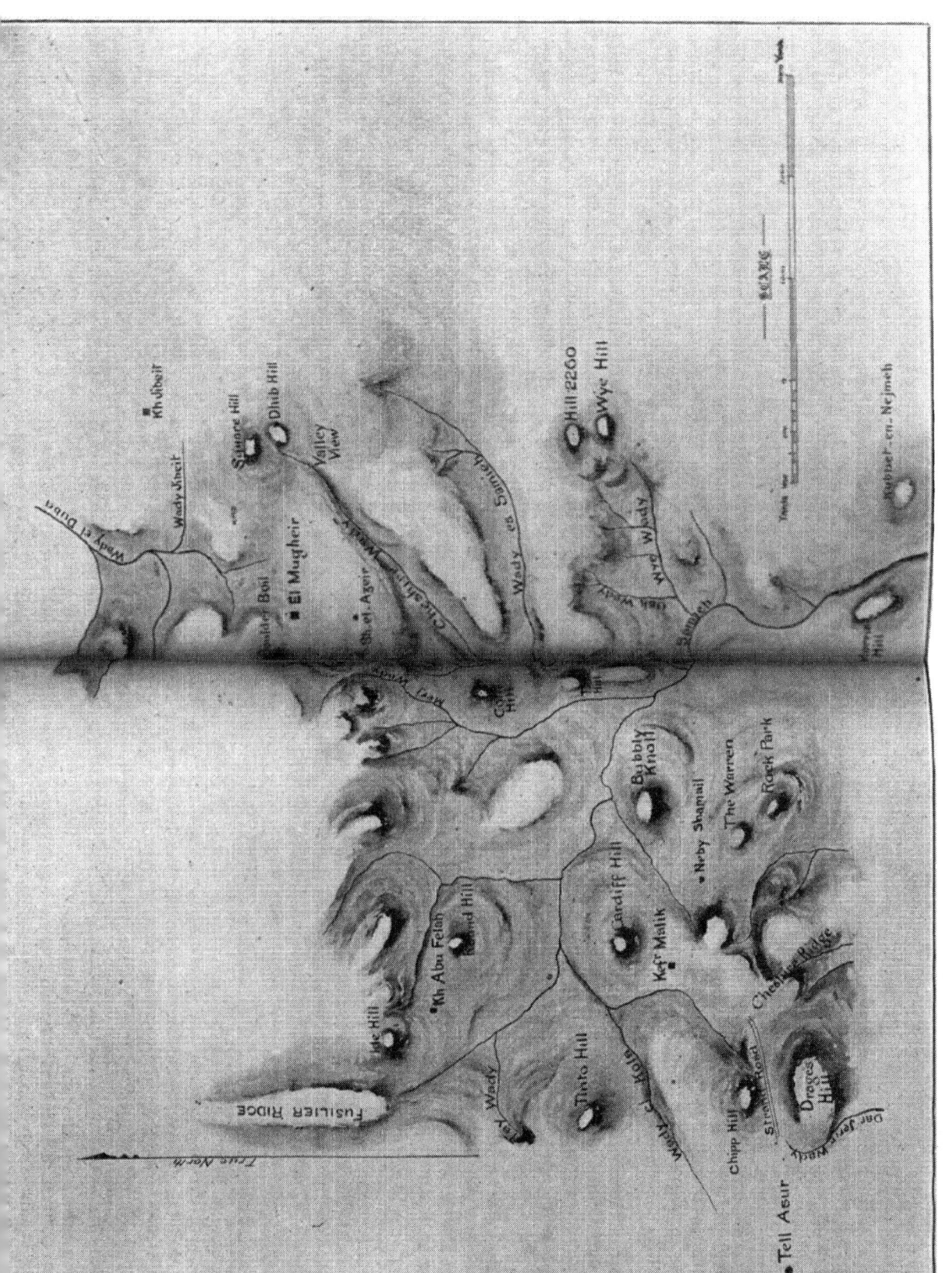

MAP OF THE FRONT ON THE JERUSALEM-NAIUS ROAD NEAR THE VILLAGE OF EL MUGHEIR.

Shewing the positions at Square Hill, Kh Jibeit, etc., attacked and captured by 1st Cape Corps and other units of the 160th Brigade (53rd Division XX Corps), September -20th, 1918.

The enemy made one fairly persistent counter-attack on Square Hill, but our men did not reply to their fire which gradually subsided.

The work during this night was practically all done with the bayonet. The strictest silence had been enjoined and the men carried out orders implicitly. Owing to the over-keenness of three men who tried to capture about twenty-five of the enemy on their own, a nice little coup was missed that night on Square Hill. If the three had waited for the headquarters reserve platoon to get into position the whole twenty-five might have been captured.

The original intention was for "D" Company to take Dhib Hill and "A" Company Square Hill. The hills were however mistaken in the moonlight and as Captain Robertson was "well in" to Square Hill by that time "A" Company were sent to cut across and tackle Dhib Hill. No time was lost in the change of plan.

Lieutenant Dreyer and his platoon ("C" Company) were sent about this time to cut off any enemy breaking through from Dhib Hill to Valley View.

The capture of Dhib Hill and El Mugheir was an important factor in the whole plan of operations from the sea to the Jordan. It was on high ground commanding the road from the Jordan Valley whence enemy reinforcements would come, and was the pivot from which the whole attack would then swing round on to the first main objective, Beisan. Furthermore, a strong offensive would, it was hoped, lead the enemy to suppose that this was the point of our main attack and thus induce him to draw reinforcements from the coastal area (his right flank) and afford our cavalry the desired opportunity to break through there.

The capture of Square Hill was effected about 4 a.m. on September 19th and the signal was at once given (at 4.30 a.m.) by a tremendous thunder of guns right along our front to the sea. After an intense bombardment of fifteen minutes the infantry deployed for action and the main coastal attack was fully launched before dawn.

Our signallers did very fine work during the advance on Dhib and Square Hills. They kept right up with the advance and in communication with brigade headquarters and the artillery.

The line was several times broken by the enemy's barrage but was immediately repaired.

During the night of September 18th the 1st Cape Corps captured one hundred and eighty-one prisoners. Lieutenant Samuelson handed over eight officers and one hundred and twenty-three other ranks to the prisoner's guard, and Sergeant February (92) and twenty men of "C" Company captured forty-three others including two officers. The circumstances of the latter capture are well worthy of record. February and his men were assisting our signallers, who were laying their line on our left flank nearest the enemy. When they saw the enemy party advancing they chucked down their wire and, shouting, went for them with the bayonet. The forty-three, evidently believing a large force was advancing, "hands-upped," and February and his twenty men got the lot. For this and other good work that night Sergeant February deservedly got the D.C.M.

Sergeant February had altogether thirty men with him. At each temporary halt they were used as a headquarters reserve platoon.

On the same night at Square Hill Lance-Corporal Thimm (3713) and the Lewis gun sections of "C" and "D" Companies captured an enemy field gun. They were on the flank and saw the gun moving down a road. They at once got into action at three hundred yards range and shot down all the mules except one. The gun team were all killed, except one sergeant who escaped. This gun was brought into camp the following evening and was the first gun captured on the Palestine front during Allenby's great push. It is now in

Photo by] [Zadik & Co., Cape Town.
THE LATE CAPTAIN JAMES VAUGHAN HARRIS, M.C.
Killed in action at Kh Jibeit, Palestine, 20th September, 1918.

THE LATE MAJOR WILLIAM RALPH COWELL, D.S.O.
Killed in action at Kh Jibeit, Palestine, 20th September, 1918.

THE STORY OF THE 1st CAPE CORPS.

Pretoria, with another one mentioned below, until such time as it can be placed with the 1st Cape Corps Memorial which is to be erected at Cape Town in due course.

For this bit of good work Lance-Corporal Thimm was promoted Corporal.

Another gun was put out of action on the northern slopes of Square Hill about the same time, and we got it when we advanced towards Kh Jibeit next day.

The night of the 18th September was our first encounter with the Turks in Palestine (except patrol and outpost skirmishes). The men fought with magnificent spirit and dash and were clearly determined to prove that a Cape Corps man was more than a match for Johnny Turk. Our casualties that night were very light, viz.: Killed: Lance-Corporal Visagie, S. (139); Wounded: Private Gobey, S. (1479).

About 10 a.m. on September 19th our Brigadier made a redistribution of his forces, which resulted in our "A" and "B" Companies concentrating at Dhib Hill. They then handed over the Hill to the 21st Punjabis and moved down behind Square Hill in the afternoon, where they were held in reserve. Throughout the day there was continuous sniping and enemy shelling but nothing material transpired. The enemy shelled us intermittently with high explosive and shrapnel. Our casualties during the day were, Killed: Private Jonkers, J. (3891); Private Groep, G. (1698); Wounded: Private Hahman, D. (2363).

Captain Robertson, early on the morning of the 19th, reported by runner from Square Hill to battalion headquarters (then at Dhib Hill) that "there was a big retirement of the enemy in the Jordan Valley northwards."

This information confirmed our confidence that we should be free from attack on our right flank. Our left flank we could see for miles and were in helio communication with the prominent positions of El Mugheir and Boulder Boil and the nearer peaks of Hindhead. Thus, our flanks being perfectly secure, we were only faced with the difficulty of holding the enemy, who, to cover retirement, had all mustered at Kh Jibeit, immediately in front of us at a distance of about seven hundred yards and covered on both flanks, i.e., by Gallows Hill on the south-west and Outpost Hill on the east.

Here a reminder is necessary that all we had to do was hold on and keep as many of the enemy as possible busily engaged opposing us. The break through and advance was to come from the coastal area, swinging round on us —the pivot.

The next divisional move seemed to us to be obvious, i.e., to extend our advance along the high commanding ground at Hindhead, which was lightly defended, if at all.

Such a move would have caused an immediate retirement from Kh Jibeit, otherwise the whole force would have been cut off from the possibility of retirement on Domeh. But for some reason, of which we were unaware, it was decreed otherwise, and the Cape Corps was ordered to storm and capture the isolated and strong position of Kh Jibeit. It was isolated because we could not possibly draw in support from the flanks owing to the nature of the terrain on either side.

On September 19th the men turned in early thoroughly tired out. After dark, Lieutenant Hirsch brought up a camel convoy with water and rations and Lieutenant Woods, M.C., came up with his eight Lewis guns. At about 9 p.m. Corporal Ruiters, M.M. (269) went out with a patrol to ascertain the approximate strength and exact position of the enemy. They did a very dangerous job thoroughly, returning about midnight with valuable information.

THE STORY OF THE 1st CAPE CORPS.

Photo by] [Levson, Ltd., Johannesburg.
THE LATE LIEUTENANT GORDON CHARLES WHITE.
Died (at Gaza, 17th October, 1918) of wounds received in action at Kh Jibeit, Palestine, 20th September, 1918.

Photo by] [The Bower Studio, Durban.
LATE LIEUTENANT A. N. DIFFORD, KILLED IN ACTION AT KH JIBEIT, PALESTINE, 20TH SEPTEMBER, 1918.

At about 9 p.m. that night, Lieut.-Colonel Morris, who had taken over command of the battalion from Major Hoy during the afternoon, received orders to advance on Kh Jibeit before dawn next morning and to have and to hold it by 7.30 a.m., and all preparations were at once made.

Kh Jibeit was a stronghold situated on three apparently small hills running parallel to the ridge we held at Square Hill, with the main enemy position on the middle hill. Enfilade and oblique machine gun and rifle fire could be brought down on either flank from the main position. The approaches to the position were over a flat wady, affording no cover or protection to attacking troops. The length of the position was approximately fifteen hundred yards and the average breadth of it four hundred yards. The enemy right flank rested on an extensive flat, and the left flank on hilly country where no reconnaissance had been made by our troops. Enemy strength immediately opposing us was not known, but was not regarded as considerable. Supports in large numbers were, however, it was certain, at Domeh, four miles in the rear. About two thousand yards behind the enemy position there was also a battery of artillery, which could support the garrison at Kh Jibeit. (It was ascertained afterwards that five hundred supports had been brought up from Domeh on the evening of the 19th September).

Before the attack our position was this: "D" Company held the sangars and trenches of the "forward" slopes of Square Hill and had good observation of the enemy position and all approaches. "C" Company was in immediate support of "D," under complete cover from enemy machine gun and rifle fire and also from enemy observation. "A" and "B" Companies were resting in support some four hundred yards in the rear in the valley separating Dhib Hill from Square Hill.

One company of the 1/7 R.W.F., under Lieutenant Jones, held Knib Knoll some five hundred yards to our left rear.

Besides our company Lewis guns in the front line we had also two Vickers machine guns there and two others (four altogether) on Dhib Hill, all covering the approaches to our position on Square Hill. Lieutenant Woods, M.C., in command of the reserve Lewis guns, also had his guns forward ready for emergency.

The two machine gun posts (forward and rear) were connected up by telephone and were all under the command of Lieutenant Riley, M.G. Corps. Telephone connection was also established between regimental and brigade headquarters, and between the forward observation officer and the artillery batteries some miles in the rear. The F.O.O. was Lieutenant Forrest, R.G.A. (of Zululand).

Major Hoy's written plan of attack, made on the 19th and approved of by Brig.-General Pearson, was this: The general plan of attack was to assault and capture the main enemy defences in the centre by attack in enfilade from the enemy's right flank. The attack was to be of a surprise nature timed for 3 a.m. under cover of darkness. It was to be supported by an artillery bombardment of five minutes, intended to damage the enemy's defences and shake the morale of the defending troops, and to keep down their fire until the assaulting troops were close up and ready to go in with the bayonet as soon as the artillery fire lifted.

The western flank was to be our main point of attack by two full Companies, "A" and "B," under Major Cowell, D.S.O. Their mission was to attack in depth the extreme western flank and gradually, under "dead ground," which would be available after our first rush across the wady, then assault and capture the centre. One platoon of "C" Company, under Lieutenant Bloxam, was to advance straight ahead to protect our right flank. This turned out to be one

Photo by] [The Gilham Studios, Pretoria.
THE LATE 2ND LIEUTENANT A. E. J. ANTILL.
Died 21st September, 1918, of wounds received in action at Kh Jibeit, Palestine, 20th September, 1918.

Photo by] [The Bower Studio, Durban.
THE LATE LIEUTENANT G. R. BARNARD.
Died at Rangers Corner, near Rham Alla, near Jerusalem, 22nd July, 1918.

of the most strongly fortified of the enemy's positions, though we were not aware of it at the time. Large caves on the far side of the hill afforded splendid protection against our shell fire.

Careful planning ensured that the best use of artillery and smaller offensive weapons would be made. In other words the co-operation of all arms formed a most important factor in the plan of attack as arranged between the Brigadier and Major Hoy. The company commanders, with Major Hoy, had previously made a careful eye study of the ground to be covered and of the enemy position from good observation posts on Square Hill. Aeroplane photographs of the enemy defences enabled a reproduction of those defences to be laid out for examination before the attack.

That was the general plan of attack adopted by Lieut.-Colonel Morris, and it seemed good, as everything had been most carefully planned and studied.

From this point it has sadly to be recorded that things went hopelessly agley. It appeared that we had over-reached our artillery barrage, except the 60 pounders. The barrage had to be cut out and an attempt made with the 60 pounders to give us battery fire on the hill. This was unsuccessful and was called for again. Meanwhile the precious minutes were slipping by towards the dawn, and our men were straining at the leash waiting for the definite orders which seemed as if they would never come. Major Cowell received his orders from Lieut.-Colonel Morris at 4 a.m., but some confusion arose owing to an earlier order reaching Cowell shortly afterwards. The latter order had been delayed owing to the runner losing his way and getting into the enemy's lines. Finally, about 5 a.m., the order was given to attack at once without artillery preparation. Everyone knew full well what that meant, as it would be daylight before we could get to grips. Officers who fully realised the position shook hands with others standing by who were not going in.

"A" and "B" Companies went in in platoon depth as follows:—

"A" Captain Harris, O.C.
    No. 1 Platoon, Lieut R. Cloke.
    No. 2 Platoon, Lieutenant A. Difford.
    No. 3 Platoon, Lieutenant Gordon White.
    No. 4 Platoon, Sergeant Jansen (1614).

"B" Major Cowell, O.C.
    No. 5 Platoon, Lieutenant Stubbs.
    No. 6 Platoon, Lieutenant Rackstraw.
    No. 7 Platoon, 2nd Lieutenant Vipan.
    No. 8 Platoon, Sergeant J. D. Ross (2619).

Immediately the advance started it was met with terrific machine gun fire and casualties at once became very heavy. Lieutenant Stubbs was the first officer hit immediately he went "over the top."

They pushed on, however, ignoring the enemy's fire and reached the spur of their position on Gallows Hill considerably thinned by casualties. Lieutenant White was hit before he got down the slope on our side into the Wady.

Our men charged with the bayonet and a very hot hand to hand fight took place in which the men used their hand grenades with good effect. We captured two machine guns and twenty prisoners. The latter were at once utilised to carry out our killed and wounded. The Turks were then reinforced and the fighting became even more fierce. Major Cowell was mortally wounded and called Harris to his side to hand over to him and to say goodbye, and the latter was instantly killed whilst shaking hands with Cowell. About the same time Lieutenants Difford and Vipan were also killed.

At this stage Lieut.-Colonel Morris, having been twice wounded at battalion headquarters, was taken to the dressing station and handed over command to Major Hoy.

THE STORY OF THE 1st CAPE CORPS.

Late 2nd Lieutenant C. A. Vipan, killed in action at El Mugheir, Palestine, 20th September, 1918.

Photo by] [Ravenscroft, Malmesbury, C.P.
Late 2nd Lieutenant J. S. Dreyer, killed in action at El Mugheir, Palestine, 20th September, 1918.

As the enemy was being heavily reinforced "C" Company was pushed out to attack the enemy's left flank and capture Outpost Hill and thus take the pressure off the other flank. They suffered heavily but accomplished their task. Lieutenant Dreyer was killed and Lieutenant Antill mortally wounded here. Lieutenant Rackstraw was wounded the first time crossing the Wady and twice more half way up the hill on the west side. He and all our other wounded in that vicinity lay out all day, as it was sacrificing life needlessly to send out the stretcher bearers, so hot was the enemy's fire.

Meanwhile "D" Company in reserve was still holding our most important position, viz.: Square Hill. They were also receiving casualties, being only seven hundred yards from the enemy.

The enemy were now heavily shelling us and strongly counter attacking and Lieutenant Webber, M.C. (R.A.F.) flew down to within fifty feet of us and dropped a message to say that large reinforcements were coming up (from Domeh). He also delivered the same message from the air by megaphone to brigade headquarters and, as "A" and "B" Companies had lost seven out of eight officers, they were ordered to retire on Square Hill. Lieutenant Cloke was wounded just then and the two Companies were left untirely unofficered. The retirement had, therefore, to be conducted by N.C.O.'s. It was carried out in the most orderly and admirable manner, in the same formation in which the platoons went in, the men continuing to fight a rearguard action during the retirement.

Lieutenant Webber, R.A.F., rendered great assistance in covering the retirement by splendid Lewis gun work at a low altitude during which he came under heavy rifle and machine gun fire. This most gallant officer was killed next day whilst similarly engaged elsewhere.

"C" Company also retired in good order and when they got back Captain Youart was the only officer of "A," "B" and "C" Companies who was not a casualty.

This retirement won great admiration on all sides and commanding and senior officers who were watching operations from neighbouring heights were loud in their praise, both of the attack and the retirement—more particularly the latter.

Reuter's account of the attack said:—

"The deployment of "A" and "B" Companies was carried out with great speed and precision in open column of platoons. They advanced with great determination and dash, crossing the Wady through a hail of rifle and machine gun fire. The position was then assaulted and a number of prisoners captured. The attack was continued to the final objective, but a strong counter attack drove back our now scattered formation. The withdrawal of our whole line was then necessary and it was carried out in good order and rapidly. The attack of "C" Company on the eastern flank was also carried out with determination. Captain Youart was ordered to retire when it was found that our main attack had failed. An aeroplane (Lieutenant Webber, M.C.) greatly assisted our retirement."

By 8.30 a.m. the remainder of "A" and "B" Companies had taken up a defensive line near Square Hill and Lieut.-Colonel Murray sent a company of the 21st Punjabis to the foot of Square Hill to assist if necessary. At this time our artillery were on the move and did not reply to our calls for a barrage.

At 10 o'clock a.m. the whole battalion (strength now ten officers and three hundred and fifty other ranks) was concentrated at Square Hill.

After our retirement the enemy put down a heavy barrage on Square Hill, which they kept up for some hours.

About midday our artillery heavily shelled the enemy's positions for some time and at 2 p.m. put down a heavy barrage. The latter was a preliminary to our counter attack which was allotted to the 1/17th Infantry who had been in support of us during the morning. Our barrage caused a regular panic in the ranks of the enemy who could be plainly seen running about without their rifles.

Our men were very keen to have another go but were not allowed to owing to shortage of officers and their heavy work during the morning. The men's disappointment was very great, but the Brigadier was of course absolutely right in sending in a fresh battalion rather than one which had already fought for hours in a hot sun.

The 1/17th Infantry found their task comparatively easy and suffered very few casualties,—in fact, they found that the enemy could not withstand our heavy barrage and had already commenced to retire.

Owing to the brilliant success of Allenby's push all along the line, and particularly because of the rapidity of the cavalry advance in the coastal area, the 53rd Division did not again come into action.

Cavalry warfare, assisted by aircraft, armoured cars and other mobile weapons, ensued for the next week—the infantry meanwhile resting on their laurels—until the final rout and surrender of the entire enemy forces on this front.

Our casualties on the morning of the 20th September were unfortunately heavy, viz. :—

	Officers.	Other ranks.	Total.
Killed	5	38	43
Died of wounds	2	6	8
Wounded	6	95	101
Prisoner	—	1	1

Total : Fifty-one killed, one hundred and one wounded and one prisoner.

The proportion of officers killed was, it will be noticed, unusually heavy, viz. : one to less than seven. This was, of course, to be expected in daylight fighting at close quarters, the officers being readily picked off. Fighting was sometimes hand to hand. In fact, encounters with fists and sticks actually took place.

Particular mention must be made of a few men for exceptionally good work on the 20th, though where all performed prodigies of great valour distinctions may perhaps seem invidious. The killed need no eulogy. They died gallantly doing their duty.

The fact that their task was herculean, if not impossible, did not deter them for an instant. "Their name liveth for evermore."

Though the period of General Allenby's great victory—one of the greatest of all time—extended over several days, September 20th was the great day which decided the issue. It was a great day—great for the Empire, great for South Africa and the coloured races thereof, and the greatest day in the history of the 1st Battalion Cape Corps. If September 20th, 1918, will ever be remembered by us as a day of great sadness, it will also the more surely be recalled as one of greater glory.

Lieutenant Woods, M.C., did exceptional work in going into exposed positions to rescue our wounded. The enemy were seen to be mutilating and robbing the wounded left on the field, and wounded men crawling to cover were being sniped. Extraordinary efforts had therefore to be made to evacuate them speedily. In this work Lieutenant Woods and Private van Wyk, A. (629) worked together and were most conspicuous. They had already got four men to safety when van Wyk was shot through the heart as they put down the fifth man under cover. Van Wyk was a very stout fellow, in fact absolutely fearless. Earlier in the day he had twice carried a message across the flat to Major Cowell and brought back replies under a murderous fire. This had to be done as the signallers were shot down if they shewed themselves to use the flag or helio.

Reproduced by the Gilham Studio, Pretoria, from a snapshot.
FIELD GUNS CAPTURED FROM THE TURKS AT SQUARE HILL, NEAR JERUSALEM, 18TH TO 20TH SEPTEMBER, 1918, BY 1ST BATTALION CAPE CORPS.

THE STORY OF THE 1st CAPE CORPS.

When Van Wyk returned the first time after getting through the enemy's lines to Major Cowell he asked for bombs to take back and have a go "on his own." Van Wyk was the best of the headquarters "runners." All did very fine work, Privates Fick (3358) and Fortuin (2041) were only excelled by Van Wyk, whose case was in reality one of "better than the best."

The signallers did great work throughout the day, making desperate endeavours to maintain communication between the firing line and battalion headquarters,—an almost impossible task owing to machine gun fire, sniping, etc.

C.Q.M.S. Davids, J. L. (97) "C" Company, was much in evidence all day bringing up ammunition and evacuating the wounded from the front line. This N.C.O. had been mentioned in despatches for good work in East Africa, and recommended on another occasion. He had the great gift of rising to a great occasion. In East Africa his company commander reported that he was always "on the job" when the day was hottest and the trek longest and cheerful hard work and example of especial value.

C.S.M. Hutchinson, K. F. (310) although wounded in the head, carried on splendidly. When all the officers were casualties he took a platoon to protect "C" Company's flank and cover their retirement. For this he earned the D.C.M.

During the retirement of "C" Company from Outpost Hill Lance-Corporal W. Hutchinson (2796), brother of the C.S.M. just mentioned, observed the enemy mutilating and robbing our wounded. On his own initiative he remained behind and with his Lewis gun covered these unfortunate men for some hours until the attack of the 17th Infantry in the afternoon. The first that battalion headquarters knew of this was the arrival of one of Hutchinson's gun team for more ammunition.

It is noteworthy that the C.Q.M. Sergeants of "A" and "C" Companies went with their companies into the firing line. C.Q.M.S. Hoffmann ("A" Company) was killed.

Sergt.-Major Shipp, F. J. was indefatigable in tending the wounded.

The following honours and awards were gained by the battalion during the period 18th to 20th, viz.:—

    Military Cross:
        Lieutenant E. J. Rackstraw.
    Mentioned in Despatches:
        Lieut.-Colonel Morris, C.M.G., D.S.O.
        Major Hoy, D.S.O.
        Captain D. W. Robertson.
    D.C.M.:
        C.S.M. Hutchinson, K. (310).
        Sergeant February, M. (92).
        C.Q.M.S. Hendricks, A. J. (1067).
        Sergeant Jansen, S. D. (1614).
        Lance-Corporal Hutchinson, W. (2796).
    Military Medal (prompt award):
        Lance-Corporal Ruiters, J. (269).
    Mentioned in Despatches:
        C.Q.M.S. Hendricks, A. J. (1067).
        A/C.S.M. Scullard, J. (1363).

During the period September 18th to 20th the work of the 113th Combined Field Ambulance was greatly appreciated by all ranks of the battalion. Major Green, M.C., Captains Hill and Dagleish and all their subordinates were unremitting in their care and attention to our wounded. (Captain Dalgleish was attached to us for duty later on when Captain Drew went on leave).

THE STORY OF THE 1st CAPE CORPS.

Photo by] [Dorothy Duffus, Cape Town.
LIEUTENANT E. J. RACKSTRAW, M.C.

Photo by] [Zadik & Co., Cape Town.
CAPTAIN D. W. ROBERTSON.

Photos by] [E. Peters, Cape Town.
SERGEANT M. A. S. LA FLUER (747).

SERGEANT H. J. HOFMEISTER ((902)

THE STORY OF THE 1st CAPE CORPS.

In General Allenby's despatch to the Secretary of State for War on the operations, September 18th to 20th, the following passage occurred:—

"The 1st Cape Corps and the 1/17th Infantry (Indian) particularly distinguishing themselves."

These were the only two individual units of all those under his supreme command from Jaffa to the Jordan mentioned by the G.O.C. in Chief in the above despatch.

Lieut.-General Sir Philip Chetwode, our Corps Commander, in his report to General Allenby after the fight used these words: "and the Cape Corps fought like tigers." (For further reports, copies of letters of congratulation, etc., in reference to our share in the Palestine Push *vide* appendix.

All ranks greatly regretted that our Machine Gun Half Company, under Captain Burger, did not get into action in Palestine. They were attached to the 53rd Divisional Machine Gun Battalion and it was the intention of the Divisional Commander to give them the opportunity of supporting their own battalion in action if possible, but they had not come up the line from Ludd in time to take a hand on September 18th to 20th. They were much disappointed. They had trained with exemplary keenness and thoroughness and could scarcely have failed to make good.

All ranks of the Cape Corps actually in the line, September 18th to 20th, were approximately one thousand. Of those exactly four hundred ("A," "B" and "C" Companies) went into action at Kh Jibeit on the morning of September 20th, and one hundred and fifty-two became casualties. The remaining six hundred were composed of "D" Company (in reserve at Square Hill), ninety-seven on transport duties, headquarters (runners, Q.M.R.'s staff, etc.) and men doing various battalion and brigade duties such as guards, escorts, etc.

Of these "D" Company and headquarters runners and signallers were also in action during the day.

Our casualties were heavier than those of any other unit on the Palestine front during the great advance.

During the night of the 18th September, the 160th Brigade practically took prisoner the entire 163rd Turkish brigade opposed to them. The enemy's brigades at this time were much depleted and scarcely exceeded fifteen hundred.

Here a few extracts from General Allenby's despatch on the the operations may be quoted:—

"The way in which the preliminary concentration was carried out and concealed from the enemy was one of the most remarkable achievements of the whole operations.

"A hostile aeroplane reconnaissance on September 15th reported as follows: 'Some regrouping of cavalry units apparent on the enemy's left flank, otherwise nothing unusual to report'; and this at a time when three cavalry divisions, five infantry divisions and the majority of the heavy artillery of the force were being concentrated between Ramleh and the front line of the coastal sector, no less than three hundred and one guns replacing the normal seventy. Prisoners from the coastal plain and the lower foot-hills of the Judæan range say that they had been told that the British would make a big attack about the 18th, but they had so often been given the same warning that no attention was paid to this one.

"That the enemy chief command were uncertain as to which part of the front would be attacked is indicated by the fact that nowhere were troops grouped in reserve where they could make an effective counter-attack.

PLAN OF SQUARE HILL AT 10 A.M., 19/9/18, AFTER CAPTURE OF THE HILL BY 1ST CAPE CORPS. SHEWING DISPOSITIONS OF "C" AND "D" COMPANIES.

THE STORY OF THE 1st CAPE CORPS.

Photos by]   [J.H.T.

LIEUTENANT G. R. BARNARD'S GRAVE AT RHAM ALLA.

HEADQUARTERS RUNNERS, SEPTEMBER 18TH-20TH, 1918.

A BIVOUAC AT CHESHIRE RIDGE.

BRIG.-GENERAL F. H. BORTHWICK, D.S.O.

RETURNING FROM PALESTINE TO EGYPT. ON THE MARCH FROM EL MUGHEIR TO LATRON, OCTOBER, 1918.

CAPT. T. W. CORBETT, M.C., BRIGADE MAJOR, 160TH BRIGADE.

BANDMASTER LINSELL IN A NEW ROLE. CUTTING THE MAJOR'S HAIR.

"But, to take the main attack as a whole, the hackneyed expression that 'it went entirely according to plan' is quite inadequate; the pace at which the infantry broke down the opposition and the cavalry got through and away exceeded the most sanguine hopes.

"It must be remembered that the 53rd Division were operating in a most difficult country, also on this day (September 20th) they were attacking prepared, and often wired, positions.

"The enemy in this portion of the field were not disorganised and were able to oppose a stout resistance to the advance. The country is broken and rugged, demanding great physical exertion on the part of the troops and preventing the artillery keeping pace with the infantry. Nevertheless good progress was made.

"Shortly after our cavalry had taken El Afule, a German aeroplane arriving from the north landed in the aerodrome, the pilot being quite unconscious of the fact that the place was in the hands of the British.

"In a word, a boldly conceived and ambitious cavalry scheme had been carried out to the letter, and all lines of retreat west of the Jordan denied to the enemy."

The concentration in the coastal plain was carried out by night and every precaution taken to prevent it becoming apparent to the enemy. Full use was made during the day of the many grooves round Ramleh, Ludd, and Jaffa. The chief factor in the secrecy maintained was, however, the great supremacy of the R.A.F. The process of attrition had been going on for months. During one week in June one hundred aircraft crossed our lines. At the end of August the number had been reduced to eighteen. So many were shot down during the next two weeks that only four crossed our lines during the period of concentration. The enemy were clearly in ignorance of Allenby's intention to attack in the coastal plain, as on the morning of the 19th September when the attack was launched his dispositions were normal.

East of the Jordan the activities of the R.A.F. and the mobile column of the Arab Army had so damaged the Hedjaz railway and Deraa Station that all railway communication with Palestine ceased by September 17th.

The attack in the coastal plain on the morning of the 19th September was a complete success. On the right, in the foothills, the French Tirailleurs and the Armenians of the Legion d'Orient advanced with great dash. The 3rd (Lahore), the 60th, and the 75th Divisions overwhelmed the enemy opposing them. The 60th Division turned north-east towards Tul Keram, leaving the coast clear for the operations of the Desert Mounted Corps.

The 60th Division and the 5th Australian Light Horse Brigade, with a composite regiment of Chasseurs d'Afrique and Spahis attached, captured Tul Keram on the night of September 19th. Bodies of troops, guns, motor lorries, and transport of every description were endeavouring to escape along the road towards Messudie and Nablus. The road followed the railway up a narrow valley and there the R.A.F. and the Australian Flying Corps caused great havoc. The road was blocked and inextricable confusion ensued, from which there was no escape, and a large amount of transport, guns, etc., fell into our hands.

The 13th Cavalry Brigade of the 5th Cavalry Division, riding across the Plain of Esdraelon, entered Nazareth at 5.30 a.m., September 20th. Nazareth was the site of the Yilderim General Headquarters. The G.O.C., the German General Liman von Sanders, managed—but only just—to make his escape in a motor car. His papers and some of his staff were taken.

The 4th Cavalry Division rode into El Afule at 8 a.m., 20th September.

THE STORY OF THE 1st CAPE CORPS.

Photo by] [E. W. Templer.
CRUSADERS TOWER AT LUDD.

Photo by] [E. W. Templer.
DAMASCUS GATE, JERUSALEM.

Photo by] [J.H.T.
GORDON WHITE'S GRAVE AT GAZA.

Photo by] [Capt. D. Drew.
THE TOWER OF THE FORTY MARTYRS AT RAMLEH.

THE STORY OF THE 1st CAPE CORPS.

The enemy's resistance was broken on September 20th, and next day the 5th Australian Light Horse Brigade, with the French Cavalry leading, entered Nablus from the west.

Within thirty-six hours of the commencement of the battle all the main avenues of escape remaining to the Turkish VIIth and VIIIth armies were closed and all organised resistance ceased. Everywhere the disorganised enemy were in flight, relentlessly pursued by the Royal Air Force. The road to Beisan passed through a narrow gorge. The head of the flying column was heavily bombed, drivers left their vehicles in a panic, wagons were overturned, and very shortly the road was completely blocked.

After the 21st September there was practically no further infantry action—certainly none of importance—but for some time we were busily engaged in clearing the battlefield, collecting and marching in prisoners, making roads, developing water supplies, and performing the innumerable other duties that remain to be done after a swift advance.

General Allenby's advance continued for another month. The principal events of the same were:—

By the evening of September 22nd the important crossing of the Jordan at Jisr-ed-Dameh had been seized by the New Zealand Mounted Rifles Brigade and the 1st Battalion B.W.I. Regiment. Next day the same force occupied Es Salt (east of the Jordan). On September 23rd the XXth Corps Cavalry captured on one stretch of road less than five miles in length eighty-seven guns, fifty-five motor lorries, and eight hundred and forty-two vehicles. On September 23rd Acre and Haifa fell and Chaytor's force captured Amman (east of the Jordan) on September 25th, and the same day five thousand prisoners and twenty-eight guns were taken, the railway seized some miles north, and the 5th Cavalry Division moved to Nazareth preparatory to the advance on Damascus. There was an interesting race for the latter place. The IVth Turkish Army were hurrying north in the vain hope of getting there before Chaytor's force could effectively bar their retreat, but on their right flank the Hedjaz Army had done much to delay the retreat by the destruction of railways and bridges. It was possible that the bulk of the IVth Army might have got through in time to organise some sort of defence against the cavalry but for the destructive activities of the Arab Camel Corps and armoured cars under Lieut.-Colonel T. E. Lawrence, C.B.

The R.A.F. also did much to enable the Australian Mounted Division and the 5th Cavalry Division to get a good start.

Deraa was entered unopposed on September 27th.

The 14th Cavalry Brigade and the Sherefian troops entered Damascus on October 1st, to find that no enemy administration had survived in such a form as to enable it to undertake the task of capitulation.

On September 30th at Damascus the Turks and Germans had a brisk fight over the distribution of vehicles for further flight. Satisfactory numbers on both sides lost their lives in this fight. This was probably the biggest scrap between the Turks and their Prussian friends, but German corpses all along the line of retreat told their own tale.

In Gilead Chaytor's force located the remnants of the Turkish IVth Army at Kastal on September 29th. Four thousand prisoners (five hundred sick), twelve guns, and thirty-five machine guns were taken, bringing Chaytor's captures during the operations of his Force as a separate entity to over ten thousand prisoners, fifty-seven guns, and one hundred and thirty-two machine guns, also large quantities of rolling stock, ammunition, etc.

The 7th (Mereut) Division (XXIst Corps) left Haifa on October 3rd, marched along the coast, crossed the Ladder of Tyre, and reached Beirut on October 8th, being received with great joy by the populace of Tyre and Sidon.

THE STORY OF THE 1st CAPE CORPS.

160TH BRIGADE STAFF.
(Standing): Lieut. Hett, Signal Officer; Capt. R. Jebb, M.C., Staff Capt.; Lieut E. W. Alderson, M.C.
(Sitting): Capt. T. W. Corbett, M.C. and Bar, Brigade Major; Brig-Gen. F. H. Borthwick, D.S.O. and Bar;
Capt. F. Miller, M.C., Bde. Transport Officer.

Continuing their march along the coast the XXIst Corps occupied Tripoli on October 13th and reached Homs two days later. The relentless pursuit continued, and Aleppo was entered on October 25th.

The next objective was Alexandretta, but before that could be taken the Turkish Empire had crumbled to the dust and the coming into force of the Armistice between the Allies and Turkey on October 31st brought Allenby's armies to a standstill.

The Desert Mounted Corps alone had captured forty-six thousand prisoners during the operations.

During their advance along the coast the 5th Cavalry Division had covered five hundred miles between September 19th and October 26th, and captured over eleven thousand prisoners and fifty-two guns. Aleppo was three hundred miles from our front line before the big push commenced. Between September 18th and October 26th seventy-five thousand prisoners were taken, of whom over two hundred officers and three thousand five hundred other ranks were Germans or Austrians. Three hundred and sixty guns were captured and the transport and equipment of three Turkish armies. In addition to the prisoners actually taken, many hundreds fled northwards, a mass of individuals without organisation and without transport, whose only motto was *sauve qui peut*. The enemy's casualties will probably never be known, but must have been exceedingly heavy.

In the early phases of the operations the enemy hastily abandoned all their material and equipment in a mountainous area of over two thousand five hundred square miles, and were then chased for three hundred miles, leaving dead and wounded, hospitals, and an incredible quantity of material and equipment, etc., all along the road. The captures included over eight hundred machine guns, two hundred and ten motor lorries, forty-four motor cars, some three thousand five hundred animals, eighty-nine railway engines, and four hundred and sixty-eight carriages and trucks. Those were the serviceable or repairable numbers; the smashed and destroyed figures were equally large.

No greater debacle had ever before been experienced by a defeated army

Here one must revert to the operations of the 53rd Division after the capture of Khan Jibeit (September 20th). The Division continued to advance at midnight and on September 21st the 158th Brigade seized Kh-Birket-el-Kusr, and the 159th Brigade captured Kusrah. By nightfall the Division had reached Beit Dejan and Beit Furik, having dislodged the enemy from positions of great natural strength and driven the remnant fifteen miles across most difficult country on to the cavalry patrols of the Desert Mounted Corps.

The 160th Brigade were not in action after September 20th. The prisoners captured by the 53rd Division during the operations were: Officers, eighty-six (seventeen wounded); other ranks, eleven hundred and nine (two hundred and twenty-two wounded); guns, nine; machine guns, fifty. Of these the 160th Brigade took over six hundred prisoners, four guns, and thirty machine guns.

Gas warfare did not take place during General Allenby's great Palestine victory. It was said that the enemy proposed the disuse of that dirty low down method of warfare. The reason was, of course, obvious. They had not the necessary paraphernalia. However, notwithstanding that the advantage would have been with us as we had ample supplies of gas and other requisites, the G.O.C. in Chief readily agreed, gas warfare having always been anathema to the British principles of making war and had only been adopted on the Western Front in retaliation.

On the afternoon of September 21st the 1st Cape Corps moved to El Mugheir and, until the 26th of the month, were engaged in salvage operations on the battlefield and in road making.

THE STORY OF THE 1st CAPE CORPS.

On September 24th a draft of eleven officers, viz.: Captain W. P. Anderson, Lieutenants Hillary and Reunert, 2nd Lieutenants Adamson, Brown, D. Buchanan, Hall, Louw, Macfarlane, Whitfield, and Wheelwright, arrived from Kantara direct from South Africa, and on September 27th one hundred and thirty-two other ranks from our depôt at El Arish.

On September 26th the battalion left El Mugheir and marched back fifteen miles to Tel Asur. Captain Jardine was left at Q.3, three miles south-west of El Mugheir, in charge of the 160th Brigade Pioneers.

On September 29th at Tel Asur a battalion parade service took place to the memory of our fallen comrades.

The first week of October was occupied in salvage work, reorganisation, and training.

On October 9th the battalion moved back from Tel Asur to Mary Cross, under orders to march via Latron to Ramleh. At Mary Cross we met our brigade and marched to Ain Arak (Ranger's Corner). The next day we reached Latron, and on the following day (October 11th) Ramleh. The same day two drafts (total one hundred and fifty other ranks) reported at Ramleh from the depôt at El Arish. Sixty-seven men fell out sick on the march from Tel Asur to Ramleh, of whom twenty-six were admitted to hospital. These figures were better than those of the other units of our brigade.

On October 14th the battalion was inspected by the G.O.C. 53rd Division. On the same day Captain Murchie and one hundred and fifty other ranks reported from the depôt at El Arish.

During October training and reorganisation continued without ceasing.

On October 17th news was received of the death that day from wounds (received September 20th, 1918) in hospital at Gaza of Lieutenant Gordon White. He was expected to recover, but suddenly collapsed. He was a most popular officer and his demise was a very great grief to all ranks.

A battalion sports meeting was held at Ramleh on our third anniversary (October 21st).

At the end of October the 53rd Division were ordered to Alexandria. We marched from Ramleh to Ludd and entrained on October 30th for Kantara, and next day proceeded from there to our destination. Our strength when leaving Ludd was twenty-three officers and one thousand and forty-five other ranks.

On arrival at Alexandria the 160th Brigade camped at Mustapha, a suburb about five miles from Alexandria and served by a tram and train service. The remainder of the Division were located at Sidi Bishr and Hadra, nearby suburbs.

During the period July 16th to 31st October the following matters affecting the personnel of the battalion should be noted.

On July 18th Armourer Sergeant G. Giles (R.A.O.C.) (No. A/1951) returned to his unit and Armourer Staff-Sergeant S. Baxter (No. A/2168) reported for duty from R.A.O.C., Kantara.

Lieutenant S. V. Samuelson, M.C., was appointed Battalion Intelligence Officer on July 28th.

Lieut.-Colonel G. A. Morris, C.M.G., D.S.O., having arrived from South Africa, took over command of the battalion on August 11th.

Lieutenant G. A. Woods, M.C., was appointed Battalion Lewis Gun Officer on August 12th.

In August the 160th Brigade won the Divisional Inter-Brigade Competition for Lewis gun assembling (blindfold).

Private H. Meyer (476), B Company, won the second prize.

On August 13th Lieutenant Cloke handed over the duties of Transport Officer to Lieutenant Horseman.

Sergeant-Cook S. February (1357) passed twenty-first out of a class of seventy-six examined at the school of cookery, Ismailia, in July.

Captain J. E. Robinson was evacuated to United Kingdom per hospital ship on August 18th.

Lieut.-Colonel Morris was admitted to hospital on August 20th, and on the same day one hundred and thirty-two other ranks (influenza). Lieut.-Colonel Morris was discharged from hospital on August 25th.

Lieutenant Leslie was appointed Assistant Adjutant on August 25th.

R.S.M. Rutherford was admitted to hospital on September 7th and was away from duty for some weeks, during which period C.S.M. Calvert (152) once more acted as R.S.M. When Rutherford was discharged from hospital he was sent to the Reserve Half Battalion to assist in the training. He remained with the R.H.B. until he returned to his own unit in January.

On September 23rd Lieutenants Rose-Innes and Horseman were admitted to hospital and Lieutenants Wigman and Gibson became A./Q.M.R. and Transport Officer respectively.

About the end of September, Brig.-General F. H. Borthwick, D.S.O. and Bar, took over Command of our Brigade (160th) from Brig.-General V. N. L. Pearson, D.S.O. Here also it may be noted that during Brig.-General Pearson's absence on leave, for a week or two in August, Lieut.-Colonel H. Harker, D.S.O., 1st/7th R.W.F., acted as our Brigadier.

On the 3rd October results of recent examinations at Schools of Instruction were published. Very few failures were recorded. Lieutenant Leslie passed the musketry course as a first-class instructor and 2nd Lieutenant Antill (since killed in action) took a first-class in the scouts course. His report was marked " Good in all subjects."

Lieutenant A. Leslie was promoted Acting Captain *vice* Captain J. V. Harris, M.C., killed in action, on October 5th.

On October 12th Private J. Williams (4250), who had been reported " killed in action " on September 20th, was found to be with the Staffordshire Yeomanry.

The following brigade figures of men who fell out on the march from Mary Cross to Ramleh (October 9th-11th) are interesting, viz. :—

1st Cape Corps	67
1/17th Infantry	79
1/7th R.W.F.	132
21st Punjabis	202

2nd Lieutenant J. L. Hollins died in hospital at Alexandria on October 15th.

During the period covered by this chapter deaths from disease were the comparatively small number of fourteen, one officer (Lieutenant G. R. Barnard) and thirteen other ranks. Private W. van Rooy (1641) was drowned in the canal at Kantara (16.9.18).

GRAVES OF OFFICERS AND MEN OF 1ST CAPE CORPS WHO FELL AT KH JIBEIT, 20.9.18.

Photo by] [J.H.T.
JAFFA GATE, JERUSALEM.

THE STORY OF THE 1st CAPE CORPS.

Photo by] [*Aziz & Dores, Alexandria, Egypt.*

OFFICERS WHO JOINED THE BATTALION ON MOBILISATION IN 1915-16 AT SIMONSTOWN AND STILL ON SERVICE WITH THE BATTALION IN 1919 AFTER THE ARMISTICE.

Captain J. H. Tandy, M.C., Captain H. Edwards, Captain A. Earp-Jones, Captain S. Youart, Captain F. Murchie, Captain D. K. Pearse, Lieutenant E. J. Rackstraw, M.C., Captain D. W. Robertson, Major C. N. Hoy, D.S.O., Lieut.-Colonel Morris, C.M.G., D.S.O., Major W. J. R. Cuningham, Captain J. M. Michau. Absent from group on duty: Major W. P. Anderson, Captains I. D. Difford, and T. P. Rose-Innes.

THE STORY OF THE 1st CAPE CORPS.

General Allenby's Inspection of 53rd Division at Alexandria, 2nd December, 1918. Lieut.-Colonel Morris riding at head of 1st Cape Corps.

[Captain S. Youart.
General Allenby taking the Salute at his Inspection of the 53rd Division at Alexandria, 2nd December, 1918.

[J.H.T.
Men preparing for daily leave-out from Camp at Mustapha, Alexandria.

[J.H.T.
160th Brigade Staff at General Allenby's Inspection, Alexandria, 2nd December, 1918.

Photo by]   *[Sergeant Alies.*
THE SALUTING BASE, MOHAMED ALI SQUARE, ALEXANDRIA, FOR GENERAL ALLENBY'S REVIEW OF 53RD DIVISION, 2ND DECEMBER, 1918.

Photo by]   *[Sergeant Alies.*
HOUSE AT MUSTAPHA RESERVED AS A "HOLIDAY HOME" FOR THE EX-CROWN PRINCE OF GERMANY.

GENERAL ALLENBY AND STAFF AT ALEXANDRIA, DECEMBER 2ND, 1918.

CHAPTER XVI.

PERIOD 1ST NOVEMBER, 1918, TO 5TH SEPTEMBER, 1919. (a) IN EGYPT (1.11.18 TO 6.8.19). (b) RETURN TO SOUTH AFRICA AND DEMOBILISATION AT MAITLAND, 6TH AUGUST TO 5TH SEPTEMBER, 1919.

THE Battalion arrived in Egypt from Ludd in three special trains on November 1st, 1918. Detrainment took place at Sidi Gaber Station, a few miles from Alexandria, and the Battalion at once proceeded to a camp at Mustapha on the sea front about four miles from the town. It was understood that the 53rd Division would proceed oversea very shortly and that we should embark with our Brigade. The Dardannelles was stated to be our probable destination, in order to join the Army of Occupation in Turkey.

On November 10th Lieut.-Colonel Morris had sufficient recovered from his wounds received on the 20th September to obtain his discharge from hospital and resume command of the Battalion. On the day of the signing of the Armistice with Germany (November 11th) we were notified that the Battalion would not proceed oversea with our Division, but would return to South Africa for demobilisation at the earliest opportunity. After the signing of the Armistice strictly military duties and training were ordered to be modified somewhat and educational schemes and recreational training undertaken.

On November 12th a cable was received from Viscount Buxton, Governor-General of South Africa, to the effect that the War Office had approved, as from 1st August, 1918, of increased separation allowances for dependents of other ranks of the Battalion. This announcement was naturally the cause of much joy in camp.

On November 18th the competitive scheme for training in drill and sports, etc., was inaugurated in accordance with the scheme laid down by G.H.Q. for all units in the E.E.F., and on November 23rd inter-platoon football competitions commenced.

On 19th November we received news that our old enemy, Von Lettow Vorbeck had surrendered in East Africa, consequent upon the signing of the Armistice. The date and place of surrender was November 14th on the Chambezi River, south of Kasama.

By the end of November the men had practically recovered from the strain and hardships of the previous few months and the general health of the Battalion was very good.

On December 2nd General Allenby inspected the 53rd Division at Alexandria. Very large crowds witnessed a splendid military display in grand weather. Our C.O. was complimented by the G.O.C. on the splendid marching and steadiness of the Battalion on parade. Our parade strength was twenty-four officers and nine hundred and five other ranks. The G.O.C. 53rd Division complimented all unit commanders on the excellent turn out and stated that General Allenby, in addition to asking him to thank all unit commanders and staffs for the smart turn out, had also requested him to convey to all ranks his thanks for their recent splendid work in Palestine. Our Corps Commander also wired to the Divisional Commander conveying the G.O.C.'s appreciation of the splendid appearance of the Division on parade.

THE STORY OF THE 1st CAPE CORPS.

Photo by] The Kasr-el-Nil Bridge over the Nile at Cairo. [Sergeant Alles.

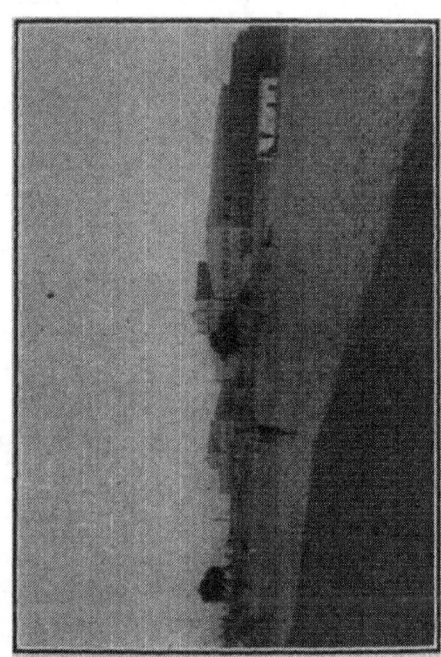

Photo by] Barracks at Mustapha. [Sergeant Alles.

Friends in Need.

Photo by] Our Concert Party. [B. P. Mosenthal.

THE STORY OF THE 1st CAPE CORPS.

On December 8th regimental schools were opened under the educational training scheme, and about two hundred men attended. Captain Earp Jones and Lieutenant H. Louw and several N.C.O.'s and men undertook duty as lecturers. At the same time thirty-seven men were attached to the R.A.O.C. for pioneer and technical trade training. On December 11th twenty-eight men were sent to No. 644 M.T. Company to be trade tested as motor drivers and mechanics.

December 17th was observed throughout the E.E.F. as a general holiday and day of thanksgiving for the success of the allied arms in the war.

On December 21st the Battalion took fourth place in the Divisional cross country race.

On Christmas Day a message of goodwill was published in Orders from Their Majesties the King and Queen, who particularly sent their greetings to the sick and wounded.

On Boxing Day Battalion sports were held. Throughout the month of December the competitive training scheme by companies was continued. In December, G.R.O. No. 4796 announced: "ACT OF GALLANTRY. The C. in C. desires to place on record his appreciation of the gallant conduct of Private Williams, J. (2297), Private Cornelius, R. (486), Private Franz, H. (2705), and Private Bannister, H. (4348) of the 1st Cape Corps on their courageous efforts to save a comrade from drowning whilst bathing in the sea at Gaza on December 2nd, 1918."

During this period men were allowed to visit the Graeco-Roman Museum at Alexandria, a privilege taken advantage of by many. On December 31st warning was received of probable early return to South Africa. The Battalion continued to be ready for embarkation at very short notice for the next ten weeks, but owing to lack of an available transport there was nothing doing.

On January 3rd the Battalion concert party, which had been formed under the supervision and direction of Captain Edwards, gave its initial performance and showed much promise. Captain Edwards received much assistance in training and organising the concert party from "The Welsh Rabbits," the concert party of the Welsh Fusiliers, which was perhaps the best of several concert parties in the E.E.F.

For results of Battalion competitions (drill, etc.) held during the period 1st December to 5th January see Chapter XX.

On January 8th permission was received from G.H.Q. to retain and take home to South Africa the two field guns captured from the enemy at Square Hill on the previous September 19-20th.

On January 11th our Machine Gun Company, under Captain Burger, rejoined the Battalion from the 53rd Division Machine Gun Battalion in view of our expected early repatriation.

On January 13th the regimental schools were closed for the same reason. On January 22nd the Battalion won first and second prizes for best turned-out man at our Brigade assault-at-arms.

On January 23rd the Drum and Fife Band was sent to do duty with the R.H.B. at El Arish.

As the result of the 160th Brigade assault-at-arms eliminating competitions the Battalion represented the Brigade at the Divisional assault-at-arms (held 28th January) in several competitions. *Vide* Chapter XX.

Our Brigade (160th) earned most points at the above assault-at-arms and took the first (Brigade) prize.

On February 3rd the regimental schools were re-opened. On the same day a consignment of tobacco and cigarettes, soap, sweets, etc., was received from the Cape Corps Gifts and Comforts Committee (South Africa) and distributed amidst much enthusiasm.

THE STORY OF THE 1st CAPE CORPS.

Photo by]   SIDI-GABER MOSQUE.   [Sergeant Alies.

Photo by]   BAND PRACTICE AT MUSTAPHA.   [Sergeant Alies.

Photo by]   THE MEDICAL SECTION AT MUSTAPHA.   [Capt. D. Drew.

THE LATE MAJOR W. R. COWELL, D.S.O., KILLED IN ACTION 20/9/18.

THE STORY OF THE 1st CAPE CORPS.

On February 6th the G.O.C. 53rd Division presented the medals which had been won at the assault-at-arms on the 28th ultimo.

About the middle of February information was received that the Battalion would embark on H.M.T. "Kildonan Castle" at the end of the month, but that vessel was delayed for some time owing to the coal strike in England.

The regimental schools were again closed on 21st February in view of our expected early repatriation, but this latter proved to be another false alarm.

On February 25th Major Hoy left camp to proceed on a lecturing tour to various stations in the E.E.F. His subject was the late enemy territory of German East Africa and the possibilities of settlement there.

Major Anderson (who had just received promotion, dated 21.9.18, *vice* Major Cowell, killed in action) assumed duty as acting second in command, *vice* Major Hoy.

On February 26th the men who had been undergoing training at the Ordnance Depôt and at the 644 M.T. Company and all other men on command returned to camp to be ready for embarkation.

On February 28th Lieutenant M. S. Davies won the quarter-mile Army championship race at the E.E.F. sports at Cairo.

On March 10 "A" Company won most events at a Battalion sports meeting.

During the period November 20th to the end of February, Battalion Inter-Platoon Rugby and Association football competitions were held and were the cause of keen rivalry and much interest and enthusiasm.

Early in March, when the Battalion were daily expecting and anxiously hoping for embarkation orders to return home to South Africa, signs of unrest became manifest in Egypt owing to the arrest and deportation of Saad Pasha Zaghlul, Vice-President of the Legislative Assembly and leader of a new Nationalist Party, and three of his chief confederates. (A note more or less fully explaining in detail the situation in Egypt at that time will be found subjoined to this chapter.)

Demonstrations and strikes and other forms of disturbances became frequent, and the unruly element in the country districts commenced destroying the railways and other communications, and murdering, looting, and pillaging, etc.

All available troops in the E.E.F. had at once to be mobilised to maintain order, and the Battalion's embarkation orders were again postponed.

On March 12th the Battalion was ordered to be in readiness to proceed at short notice to any scene of unrest in or around Alexandria.

On March 12th it was published in orders that the War Office had decided that the men of the Battalion were entitled to receive the same scale of proficiency pay as British units of the Imperial Forces from 29th September, 1917, in terms of the Army Order of that date, and also that our men would receive war gratuity on demobilisation on the same scale as British units of the Empire's Army. These substantial concessions were, of course, only fair and just, and had also been thoroughly well earned, but they were none the less for that vastly appreciated by all ranks.

On March 17th a flying column of three officers and one hundred other ranks were detailed to be in instant readiness to move to the scene of any disturbance. and "C" Company were sent to Sidi Gaber Tram Station to assist in keeping order there. At the same time "B," "D," and Composite Companies were sent into Alexandria, but returned to camp in the afternoon. On this day no less than seven hundred and thirty-seven of all ranks were actually out of camp on various duties in connection with the disturbances.

On the last mentioned date the Battalion were posted to the 158th Brigade owing to the demobilisation of the 160th Brigade for repatriation. The next day "B" Company took over duty at Alexandria to keep the strikers in order, and our Lewis guns, which had been handed in in anticipation of embarkation, were

THE STORY OF THE 1st CAPE CORPS.

Photos by]   [Captain S. Youart and J.H.T.

GENERAL ALLENBY'S INSPECTION OF 53RD DIVISION AT ALEXANDRIA, 2ND DECEMBER, 1918.
GENERAL ALLENBY AND STAFF AT ALEXANDRIA, 2ND DECEMBER, 1918.
INSPECTION BY GENERAL ALLENBY AT ALEXANDRIA, 2ND DECEMBER, 1918.
SERGEANT DRURY'S SQUAD—WINNERS BEST TURNED-SQUAD, BATTALION SPORTS, MUSTAPHA.
THE BAND AT MUSTAPHA.
PRACTISING BAYONET FIGHTING AT MUSTAPHA.
AN ALARM RACE.
L.-CORP. BETHANIE'S LEWIS GUN SECTION, "C" COMPANY.

redrawn from Ordnance. On the same day Lieutenants Davies and Girdwood and thirty other ranks (machine gunners) joined the 53rd Machine Gun Battalion at Sidi Bishr for duty.

On March 18th "A" and "D" Companies, each one hundred and fifty strong, were posted at various stations on the main line between Alexandria and Cairo as far as the Nile to protect the station buildings and patrol and guard the line. The main line had been damaged and communication with Cairo interrupted more than once, and the narrow gauge Delta railway had also suffered. Major Anderson was in command at Teh-el-Barud in charge of No. 1 Sub-Section, which comprised all stations south of Damanhour, and Captain Burger at Kefr-el-Dawar in command of No. 2 Sub-Section, comprising all stations north of Damanhour. Captain Burger had with him four officers and one hundred and sixty-nine men, of whom one hundred and one were from the Composite Company and the remainder details from "A," "C," and "D" Companies. Damanhour was at the time the headquarters of the 158th Brigade to which the Battalion was now attached. There were six stations in No. 1 Sub-Section, including two detached posts at Aft and Dessouk, at the former of which was situated the pumping station which supplied Alexandria with water. This post was under Lieutenant Hall. In No. 2 Sub-Section were seven stations in charge respectively of (1) Lieutenant W. J. Buchanan, (2) Captain Pearse, (3) Beida, Sergeant Parkins, (4) Kefr-el-Dawar, Lieutenant Samuelson, M.C., (5) Sergeant Raubenheimer, (6) Lieutenant Lambe, (7) Sergt.-Major Wilkinson. Lieutenant Botha was R.T.O. at Damanhour and Lieutenant Macfarlane acted as Supply Officer at the same place. Mounted infantry were distributed along the line under the command of Captain Williams, R.G.A. Rebel snipers were very troublesome, paying particular attention to night patrols. Three men were wounded in the Kefr-el-Dawar district, viz.: Private Jones, M. (3884), Private Jafta (725), and Private Silver, J. (5172). The M.I. offering easier targets, had six or seven casualties.

On March 19th trouble was expected at the docks, and two officers and one hundred men were held in readiness to proceed there at a moment's notice by motor lorries, which were sent to our camp to stand by in case of need. In addition to the above duties various small guards of from ten to twenty men, each under one or two officers, had to be found daily for duties in and around Alexandria at vulnerable places such as the Headquarters Alexandria district, the tram station and sheds at the railway terminus, and suburban stations, etc. The Battalion, in fact, had a very strenuous time, which was not at all appreciated, "mob warfare" being little to the liking of either officers or men.

On March 24th a plan to poison all guards in and around Alexandria was discovered. The scheme was to put opium or poison into fruit and sell same to the guards all over the town on the same day. The object was to steal the rifles of the various guards.

During the night, March 30th-31st, Captain Robertson took out a search party of five officers and two hundred and fifty other ranks to collect concealed arms from the surrounding villages. They returned to camp the following afternoon with a large haul of blunderbusses and other antiquated weapons which were subsequently burned. Captain Robertson was assisted by Australian cavalry who had been sent to assist in the search and to patrol the surrounding villages. On April 8th a company was sent to picket and patrol the town and to prevent the strikers intimidating the workers and to stop demonstrations. Captain Robertson was in command of this company, which consisted of four officers and one hundred and seventy men of "C" Company and the balance from "A" and "B" Companies. They left camp at daybreak in eight motor lorries.

THE STORY OF THE 1st CAPE CORPS.

A Detachment of the Battalion Present Arms at General Allenby's Inspection at Alexandria, 7th May, 1919.

Photo by]   "On Leave."   [Sergeant Alies.
R.S.M. Calvert, D.C.M. (152), and C.Q.M.S. Hendricks, D.C.M. (1067), at Zeitoun.

Photo by]   [J.H.T.
Inspection by General Allenby, Alexandria, May, 1919.

At this time men were not allowed out of camp, except on duty, after 7 p.m., and officers had strict injunctions to carry revolvers at all times. Officers and men were also not allowed to go about singly.

On April 10th four officers and two hundred and fifty other ranks were on duty at Alexandria Railway Station. On April 12th and 13th seven officers and two hundred and seventy-eight other ranks took over guard duties at No. 1 Prisoner of War Camp at Sidi Bishr, and the Battalion also found the guard at the electrical works in Alexandria for ten days, and between April 12th and 15th the remainder of the Composite Company who had been in camp were sent to reinforce our Damanhour detachment.

At this date no troops were allowed in Alexandria, except on duty, after 6 p.m., and officers and men were warned to go about in parties of not less than four. Men not on duty, and therefore not armed, had to carry entrenching tool handles as a protective measure. On April 19th all guards were doubled and the next day two officers, one hundred other ranks and two Lewis guns were sent to protect the Ordnance Depôt at Gabarri.

Monday, April 21st, was the Festival of Shem-el-Nessim and extra special instructions were necessary to avoid conflict between the Army and the celebrants of the festival.

On April 22nd our guard of a full company at the P.O.W. Camp at Sidi Bishr was relieved, but four days later we again took over that duty.

On April 26th Lieut.-Colonel Morris assumed temporary command of the 158th Brigade during the absence of the Brigadier. Lieut.-Col. Morris was away on that duty for four weeks, during which period Major Anderson acted as O.C. Battalion and Captain Robertson took over the detachment command from the latter at Teh-el-Barud.

On April 27th Lieutenant M. S. Davies won the Lawn Tennis Singles Championship of Alexandria.

On April 30th no less than twenty-four officers and eight hundred and seventy other ranks were on outpost and detachment duty.

During the heaviest work in connection with the Riots many men were on duty two nights out of three, and even the Band had to be pressed into service.

The health of the Battalion had been very good since the New Year, and all ranks were vaccinated and innoculated against cholera.

On May 7th the G.O.C. inspected the troops at Mustapha. Major Anderson, Captain Michau, Lieutenant Leslie and one hundred and fifty men were on parade at this inspection—all other officers and men were on command.

By May 10th the duties devolving upon the Battalion were so numerous and heavy that four officers of the 4/5th Welsh Fusiliers had to be attached to us for duty, viz.: Lieutenants A. G. Harding and W. G. Phillips, and 2nd Lieutenants J. G. Thomas and E. Williams.

Early in May, as more serious trouble was anticipated, the two companies guarding the railway were concentrated at Teh-el-Barud, about two hours by rail from Alexandria, under the command of Captain Burger.

Early in May Major Anderson was detailed to proceed to Suez to assume command of the Reserve Half Battalion and take them to South Africa.

On May 15th he left Mustapha with Captains Robertson, Tandy, and Youart, and Lieutenants Colson and Manley and three hundred ("Headquarters," 15; "A," 17; "B" 30; "C," 20; "D," 205; and "Composite," 13) other ranks. They joined up with the R.H.B. at Suez next day and sailed for South Africa on H.M.T. "Tambov" on May 18th. The embarkation strength was thirteen officers and nine hundred and ninety-eight other ranks. (See also Chapter XVII.)

THE STORY OF THE 1st CAPE CORPS.

Photo by] [*The Gilham Studios, Pretoria.*
CAPTAIN A. LESLIE,
Adjutant, May–September, 1919

"C" COMPANY SERGEANTS IN EGYPT.
Back row (left to right): Sergeants H. Damons, D.C.M. (1465), J. Walker (3132), MacThomas (366), H. Smith. Sitting: C.Q.M.S. J. L. Davids (97), C.S.M. K. Hutchinson (310), Sergeant J. Scullard (1363). Floor: Sergeant Pat Thomas (1122).

PRIVATE SAMPIE (584), "A" COMPANY.
Best turned-out man in Brigade competition at Alexandria, January, 1919.

Photo by] [*Sherwood, Durban.*
CAPTAIN D. K. PEARSE.

THE STORY OF THE 1st CAPE CORPS.

On May 17th Lieutenant D. F. Botha left us to join the E.S.O.'s Staff at Suez (Army of Occupation).

Early in June the unrest subsided considerably, and the arrival of the Army of Occupation troops from England about the middle of the month enabled the Battalion to be relieved of all duties in view of expected early embarkation for South Africa.

During the whole period of the disturbances is was dangerous for officers or men to move about unarmed or alone.

It was impossible to distinguish friend from foe amongst the natives, and the snipers generally managed to have a wide canal between themselves and their intended victims.

For the most part their ammunition was slug, which increased the sniper's chance of hitting his mark.

In the area protected or patrolled by the Cape Corps only two fatal casualties occurred, two Australian troopers being killed near Teh-el-Barud, but in other parts of Egypt numerous murders of officers and men took place.

The worst case was the hold-up by the mob of a train between Luxor and Cairo, and the cold blooded murder of several nursing sisters, officers and men in circumstances of revolting violence and outrage. On several different occasions both in Cairo and Alexandria and elsewhere it was necessary for the troops to fire on the mob and strikers, and numbers of the latter were killed and wounded.

Extreme measures were, of course, only taken where they were absolutely unavoidable. The rank and file of the Cape Corps got on well with the loyal section of the inhabitants during the disturbances, as in fact they did throughout their sojourn in Egypt.

Early in June the Battalion was again warned for embarkation on the 14th of the month, but it was exactly a month later before definite move orders were actually received.

In June the Divisional Cricket League Competition came to a victorious conclusion from the Battalion's point of view.

Our team won the league, and Sergeant Alies (825) and 2nd Lieutenant F. C. Adamson won bats presented for the highest batting averages. Sergeant Alies averaged 45.75 and Adamson 27.75. These bats and medals to the winning team were presented on Orders Parade on June 20th, and the Divisional Commander congratulated our team on the fine sporting spirit which they had at all times displayed.

On June 25th the following officers, who had applied for service with the Army of Occupation in Egypt, left camp to take over their new duties, viz. : 2nd Lieutenants W. D. Wheelwright, W. I. Brown and E. W. Templer, who were posted to the 1/4th Essex Regiment at Cairo.

On June 30th the following honours and awards were published in orders for exceptional service during the operations in Palestine in the previous September, viz. :—

Military Cross :
    Lieutenant E. J. Rackstraw.
D.C.M. :
    C.S.M. Hutchinson (310).
Mentioned in Despatches :
    Lieut.-Colonel G. A. Morris, C.M.G., D.S.O.
    Major C. N. Hoy, D.S.O. (and Bar).
    Captain D. W. Robertson.
    A/C.S.M. A. J. Hendricks (1067).
    Sergeant J. Scullard (1363).

THE STORY OF THE 1ST CAPE CORPS.

Photo by] [E. W. Templer.
IN COURTYARD OF MOSQUE OF EL AZHAR, CAIRO.

MOHAMED ALI STATUE AND SQUARE, ALEXANDRIA.

Photo by] [I.D.D.
H.M.T. "TAMBOV" EMBARKING BATTALION FOR REPATRIATION,
AT SUEZ, 6TH AUGUST, 1919.

THE STORY OF THE 1st CAPE CORPS.

At long last, on July 13th, came definite and final orders that the Battalion would leave Mustapha Camp for Suez for repatriation within forty-eight hours.

On July 15th Captain Murchie, who had volunteered for the Army of Occupation, left for Kantara to assume his new duties in the General Base Depôt there.

Owing to the lack of cabin accommodation on our troopship, the "Tambov," five officers had to proceed for repatriation to South Africa via the United Kingdom. Those who volunteered were Captains Burger and Pearse, Lieutenants Moin, Wallis, M.C., and D. Buchanan. They left Mustapha on the 16th July for embarkation at Port Said.

The Battalion left Mustapha per special train on July 15th, under orders to embark at Suez next day, but on arrival there it was found that the "Tambov" needed to be dry docked at Alexandria for repairs.

The Battalion accordingly remained in the Transit Camp at Suez for three weeks pending the return of the "Tambov."

Lieutenant Max Davison, who had seen several months' service in Egypt with the 334th Battery R.G.A., returned to South Africa with the Battalion. He had been attached to us for some weeks waiting for repatriation.

During our stay at Suez two or three cricket matches were played against the Somerset Light Infantry stationed there and the inter-company competition, commenced at Mustapha, was concluded. This latter was won by Headquarters, who beat "A" Company in the final.

Whilst at Suez our band was in great request, playing several times in the town, at the French Club, and at the Hospital and Indian Detail Camp.

Embarkation finally took place on August 6th, the "Tambov" leaving in the afternoon for Cape Town.

Durban was reached on August 29th after an uneventful voyage during which the only stop had been a call of a few hours at Aden.

The "Tambov" remained at Durban for two days, which afforded the opportunity for a civic welcome being given to the Corps on the day of arrival.

The Battalion disembarked at 9 a.m., and, headed by the band, marched through the town to Albert Park, where they were received by the Deputy Mayor (Mr. Councillor J. Coleman), Colonel Molyneux and a number of prominent citizens, in the presence of a large crowd, in which the local coloured community was naturally well represented.

Mr. Coleman, having stated that the Mayor of Durban had gone to Pretoria to attend General Louis Botha's funeral obsequies, expressed the very great pleasure it gave him to welcome Lieut.-Colonel Morris and his officers and men back to South Africa.

On behalf of the burgesses of Durban he expressed appreciation of the services of the 1st Cape Corps and told them that they had made a great reputation wherever they had been and also behaved in an exemplary manner.

They were men who, like the lamented General whom all South Africa was mourning that day, had offered their all for the Empire.

Mr. Coleman referred to the fact that the men of the Cape Corps were amongst the first to take up arms on behalf of King and Empire, and he reminded those present that a large number of the men had been over four years in the field and had seen service in German East Africa, Egypt and Palestine, and that many had also served in various capacities attached to units of the South African Forces which had conquered German South-West Africa. The public having given three cheers for the regiment, Lieut.-Colonel Morris, in a brief reply, thanked the Deputy-Mayor and citizens of Durban for the very hearty welcome accorded to his men.

Having referred to the great loss South Africa had sustained by the lamented death of Louis Botha, in whom the Cape Corps had always had a staunch friend,

THE STORY OF THE 1st CAPE CORPS.

Photo by]   *[Aziz & Dores, Alexandria, Egypt.*
THE BATTALION ON PARADE AT MUSTAPHA CAMP, ALEXANDRIA, EGYPT, JUNE, 1919.

Photo by]   *[Aziz & Dores, Alexandria, Egypt.*
THE BATTALION ON PARADE AT MUSTAPHA CAMP, EGYPT, JUNE, 1919.

THE STORY OF THE 1st CAPE CORPS.

Lieut.-Colonel Morris said that his regiment had done their best to uphold South Africa's reputation in the East, not an easy task owing to the great reputation of the South African Brigade and the South African Heavy Artillery, who had preceded them in Egypt.

The men, having returned the compliment by loudly cheering the Deputy-Mayor and citizens, were then entertained to tea and refreshments by the Cape Corps Comforts Committee.

Shortly afterwards the Battalion fell in and marched back to the "Tambov," which continued her voyage to Cape Town the following afternoon.

On September 1st a meeting of Officers was held in the Saloon of the "Tambov" to decide as to the disposal of the balance to credit of the Regimental Fund. It was unanimously decided that the available surplus should be transferred to the Cape Corps Memorial Fund (vide Chapter XXI.).

The following Memorial Sub-Committee was elected, viz.: Lieut.-Colonel Morris, Major Cuningham, Captain Jardine, 2/Lieutenant Hirsch, A/C.S.M. Wilkinson (1253) (Headquarters), Sergeant Bredenkamp (979) ("A" Company), Corporal Kolbee (1027), Privates January (1210) and J. Muller (1621).

On September 2nd Lieut.-Colonel Morris published in Orders a farewell message to Officers and men of the Battalion.

In bidding all ranks good-bye he thanked them for their loyalty and the cheerful manner in which they had carried out their arduous duties during the past four years and wished one and all success and prosperity in their civilian life.

He told the men that their splendid work in the field had gained the admiration of the whole of South Africa and that the European population would take greater interest in them than ever before.

"We all hope," continued Colonel Morris, "that this will mean that conditions as a whole for Coloured men in South Africa will be greatly improved." He counselled the men to behave after demobilisation in such a modest and orderly manner as to gain greater appreciation for the good work that had been done.

In conclusion he reminded the men that their old Officers would always take an interest in their welfare, and be ready at all times to give them advice and such assistance as lay in their power.

The "Tambov" reached Cape Town on the afternoon of Thursday, September 4th, too late for disembarkation to take place that day and the same was accordingly postponed until the next morning.

The programme arranged for the welcome home of the Battalion included a review and inspection on the Grand Parade by His Excellency the Governor-General, Viscount Buxton.

Unfortunately most inclement weather almost entirely spoiled the proposed ceremony.

The Battalion left the troopship shortly after 9 a.m. by train to Monument Station, where they detrained and marched via Adderley Street and Darling Street to the Grand Parade.

Nothwithstanding the weather a large crowd of citizens and many prominent personages had assembled on the Parade to welcome the returned warriors.

His Excellency the Governor-General was accompanied by Brig.-Gen. H. S. L. Ravenshaw, C.M.G., G.O.C. South African Military Command, by his A.D.C. and A.D.C. in waiting, by His Honour the Administrator (Sir Frederic De Waal), the District Staff Officer (Colonel Hodgson), and the Honorary Colonel of the Regiment (Colonel Sir Walter E. M. Stanford, K.B.E., C.B., C.M.G.). Others present were, the Mayor of Cape Town (Mr. W. J. Thorne), local members of Parliament and many other well known men.

THE STORY OF THE 1st CAPE CORPS.

Photo by]   [*Fisher's Studio, Maitland.*

THE LAST PARADE. AT THE DISPERSAL CAMP, MAITLAND, 5TH SEPTEMBER, 1919. AN OFFICER OF THE DEMOBILISATION STAFF (CAPTAIN KEOHANE) ADDRESSING THE MEN PRIOR TO DEMOBILISATION.

THE STORY OF THE 1st CAPE CORPS.

Just as His Excellency stepped forward to address the parade a very heavy storm of rain and hail broke over the ground, necessitating a hurried adjournment to the City Hall.

This was a disappointment to many in the crowd who were looking forward to the Ceremonial Parade movements in which the Battalion was known to excel. Owing to lack of space in the City Hall two Companies of the Battalion filed into the Drill Hall adjoining, where they were received by the Deputy Mayor (Mr. W. C. Gardener).

In the City Hall the men were addressed by Lord Buxton, the Administrator, the Prime Minister (General Smuts) and the Mayor.

Lord Buxton said that South Africa was grateful to the Battalion for what they had done in the Great War; they had carried out their work in action with courage, intelligence, and efficiency, and in the intervals between fighting they had always conducted themselves in a way which redounded to their credit.

The Mayor of Cape Town said that the citizens were conscious of the magnificent and heroic work which the Cape Corps had done, and referred especially to their share in General Allenby's great historic victory in Palestine.

General Smuts, speaking in Dutch, referred to the magnificent service to South Africa which the men had rendered, and stated that when in England recently he had received the most glowing accounts of their doings " You fought as well and as bravely as any other unit of the British Army," said the General, " and established a brilliant record for your Corps."

" You have attained a name of honour and on behalf of the Union Government I thank you most heartily for what you have done."

Sir Frederic De Waal said the men had come forward to befriend South Africa against the German menace. They had had their opportunity, and they had grasped it, and South Africa was very proud of them and he was pleased to give public testimony to the debt which South Africa owed to the Cape Corps. Colonel Sir Walter Stanford and Lieut.-Colonel Morris briefly replied on behalf of the Battalion.

Colonel Stanford reminded the men of the strong personal interest Lord Buxton had always taken in the Corps and said that they owed it to him that the Imperial Authorities had increased their Pensions and separation allowances. Lord Buxton had personally written to gentlemen in authority in England on their behalf.

Lieut.-Colonel Morris thanked the citizens for the magnificent welcome that had been accorded to them. They felt very honoured and proud. He also thanked the Gifts and Comforts Committee, especially the Ladies who had worked so hard for them for four years.

In conclusion he said that the South African Brigade had made a great reputation in Egypt in 1916 and that his Battalion had tried their best to maintain South Africa's reputation.

In the Drill Hall the Deputy Mayor (Mr. W. C. Gardener) welcomed the two Companies which had assembled there.

Lord Buxton also addressed these men and thanked them on behalf of His Majesty the King.

The Hon. F. S. Malan, speaking in Dutch, by request, thanked the men in the name of the Government of the Union of South Africa.

He trusted they would carry into civil life the discipline and good habits acquired on Service.

If they continued to put into practice the good conduct and discipline they had learned on service their example would be most valuable to their compatriots in this Country.

THE STORY OF THE 1st CAPE CORPS.

Major W. J. R. Cuningham thanked the Deputy Mayor for the splendid reception the City had given them. "They had seen many countries, but they were glad to be back in South Africa, which they all agreed was the best."

After cheers for His Excellency, the Deputy Mayor and the Hon. F. S. Malan and reciprocal cheers for the Corps, the men were entertained to tea and refreshments by the ladies of the Gifts and Comforts Committee.

Half an hour later the Battalion marched back to Monument Station and entrained for the Dispersal Camp at Maitland.

The actual strength of the Battalion on disembarkation from the "Tambov" was:

            Officers   23
            Other Ranks 1010

                                                 1033

Lieutenants Stubbs, Hillary, Woods, and Lambe disembarked at Durban and proceeded overland to the Dispersal Camp. Lieutenant Max Davison also disembarked at Durban.

On arrival at the Dispersal Camp no time was lost in demobilisation. Lieut.-Colonel G. Hurst, Officer Commanding, and his efficient staff of officers and N.C.O.'s despatched the men to their homes and destinations as speedily as the most impatient could have wished.

Every man was paid £3 on arrival at the Camp and £10 before he left to entrain for his home (the balance of pay due to the men was forwarded by post by the Paymaster within a few weeks, and some men had quite a substantial balance to draw, in some cases in excess of three figures).

Having handed in their Arms and Equipment the men were medically examined, and, if passed by the Board, were at once despatched by train to their homes, large parties in charge of an Officer, smaller parties under N.C.O.'s. Men who could not pass the Medical Board were sent at once to No. 1 General Hospital at Wynberg for treatment.

Within a week of arrival at Maitland every man, except the comparatively small number admitted to Hospital, had received his discharge papers and left for his home, and the 1st Cape Corps had ceased to exist.

During the next few months quite a number of men who had been sent from Egypt to the United Kingdom per Hospital Ships arrived at Cape Town from England, but before the end of the year practically every man had returned and been demobilised and very few were left in the Wynberg Hospital.

During the period covered by this Chapter the following promotions, changes in personnel, etc., took place:—

Major Hoy's health gave cause for anxiety shortly after our return to Egypt from Palestine. He was in Hospital from November 9th to 15th and again from 16th March to April 6th.

On the latter date he was invalided to the United Kingdom per Hospital Ship "Madras." That was the last we saw of our gallant and most popular Major. He returned to South Africa from England in June and proceeded at once to his home in the Standerton District.

Captain Anderson reported from duty as O.C. Depôt at El-Arish on November 28th, having handed over there to Major Cuningham.

Lieutenant A. Leslie left for a month's U.K. Leave on January 16th, and Lieutenant Woods, M.C., was appointed Assistant Adjutant during his absence.

Lieutenants Wigman and Gibson, R.Q.M.S. Sasse and S.M. Shipp proceeded on a month's U.K. Leave on March 3rd.

A/C.S.M. Hendricks, A. J. (1067) was appointed A/R.Q.M.S. vice Sasse.

THE STORY OF THE 1st CAPE CORPS.

Photo by] [*Aziz & Dores, Alexandria, Egypt.*
OFFICERS 1ST CAPE CORPS AT MUSTAPHA CAMP, ALEXANDRIA, EGYPT, JUNE, 1919.

Top row (left to right : Lieutenant B. H. Moin, 2nd Lieutenant W. I. Brown, Captain A. Earp-Jones (Chaplain), 2nd Lieutenant C. R. Lambe, Lieutenant C. Reunert, 2nd Lieutenant D. W. Wheelwright, 2nd Lieutenant B. P. Mosenthal, Lieutenant E. P. Stubbs, M.C., Lieutenant M. S. Davies, 2nd Lieutenant J. G. Hirsch, Lieutenant S. H. Rose-Innes, Lieutenant C. A. Hillary, 2nd Lieutenant H. Louw.
Second row (left to right) :- Lieutenant D. F. Botha, Captain J. W. Dalgleish, M.C., Captain A. Leslie (Adjutant), Captain H. Edwards, Captain J. M. Michau, Major W. J. R. Cuningham, Lieut.-Colonel G. A. Morris, C.M.G., D.S.O., Officer Commanding; Captain I. D. Difford (Q.M.R.), Captain F. Burger, Captain D. K. Pearse, Captain T. P. Rose-Innes, Captain F. Murchie.
Bottom row (left to right) : Lieutenant H. C. van Diggelen, 2nd Lieutenant E. W. Templer, 2nd Lieutenant F. C. Adamson, 2nd Lieutenant D. H. F. Buchanan.

On March the 10th the following promotions appeared in Orders :—

Captain W. P. Anderson to be Major from 21/9/18 vice Major W. R. Cowell, killed in action 20/9/18.

2nd Lieutenants S. V. Samuelson, M.C. and R. Colson to be Lieutenants from 2nd January, 1919.

On March 14th, Captain Rose-Innes who had been on duty with the R.H.B. for some time, rejoined.

2nd Lieutenant Mackenzie left on U.K. Leave on March 23rd, and was followed two days later by Captain Drew (Medical Officer).

To replace the latter, Captain J. W. Dalgleish, M.C., R.A.M.C., was attached to us from the 53rd Division. Captain Dalgleish remained with us during the remainder of our stay in Egypt and returned to South Africa with us on the "Tampov." He soon became very popular with Officers and men who parted from him with real regret.

When the Battalion was demobilised Captain Dalgleish had a spell of leave and duty in the Union and then left South Africa for England for demobilisation in December, 1919.

Lieutenant Leslie returned from U.K. Leave on March 26th.

Major Anderson was appointed Acting Second in Command (vice Major Hoy to Hospital) on April 1st.

It may here be noted that during April Brig-General James W. Walker, D.S.O., took over Command of the 53rd Division from Major-General S. F. Mott, C.B.

Captain Murchie, who was on duty with the R.H.B. for a month, returned to Camp on April 13th.

Captain Pearse assumed duty as " A " Company Commander on May 1st, vice Major Anderson promoted.

Captain Rose-Innes took Command of " B " Company on May 14th, vice Captain Robertson repatriated.

When Major Anderson left for Suez on May 15th, Captain Michau took over acting command of the Battalion as Lieut.-Colonel Morris was still absent on duty, and at the same time Lieutenant Leslie became acting Adjutant, vice Captain Tandy repatriated.

On May 17th the following Officers proceeded on U.K. leave, viz. :—

Lieutenant Horseman, 2nd Lieutenants W. J. Buchanan, Hall, and Macfarlane.

On May 18th Major Cuningham and Captain Difford, Lieutenants Hillary, Moin, and Van Diggelen and 2nd Lieutenants D. Buchanan and Brown and their batmen reported from R.H.B.

Major Cuningham assumed duty as second in command, Captain Difford resumed duty as Quartermaster, and Lieutenant Brown took over the Transport Officer's duty *vice* Lieutenant Horseman.

Lieutenant Leslie's promotion to acting Captain from 29th May appeared in Orders 30th May.

Lieutenant Wigman returned from U.K. leave on 21st June, and S.M. Shipp on June 30th.

Captain Edwards proceeded on U.K. leave on July 12th.

Sergeant J. Berry (1135) was promoted Colour Sergeant on July 27th, 1919.

THE STORY OF THE 1st CAPE CORPS.

Photo by]   [*Aziz & Dores, Alexandria, Egypt.*

LIEUT.-COLONEL G. A. MORRIS, C.M.G., D.S.O., MAJOR W. J. R. CUNINGHAM, CAPTAIN A. LESLIE (ADJUTANT), AND SENIOR WARRANT OFFICERS, JUNE, 1919.
Standing: C.S.M. J. Scullard (1363), C.S.M. D. Wilkinson (1253), C.S.M. D. J. Brown, D.C.M. (9), C.S.M. P. A. Daniels (1), C.S.M. C. A. Ruiters (132).
Sitting: A/R.Q.M.S. A. J. Hendricks, D.C.M. (1067), Major W. J. R. Cuningham, Lieut.-Colonel G. A. Morris, C.M.G., D.S.O., Captain A. Leslie (Adjutant), R.S.M. C. Calvert, D.C.M. (152).

THE STORY OF THE 1st CAPE CORPS.

Photo by]   [Aziz & Dores, Alexandria, Egypt.

LIEUT.-COLONEL G. A. MORRIS, C.M.G., D.S.O., Officer Commanding, MAJOR W. J. R. CUNINGHAM, CAPTAIN A LESLIE (Adjutant), with BANDMASTER C. LINSELL and WARRANT OFFICERS and SERGEANTS AT MUSTAPHA, ALEXANDRIA, EGYPT, JUNE, 1919.

Top row (left to right): Band Sergeant C. Grey (2539), Sergeant Poole (1888), Sergeant A. Parkins (3179), Sergeant E. L. George (1566), Sergeant S. D. Jansen, D.C.M. (1614), Sergeant H. Damons, D.C.M. (1465), Sergeant W. Raubenhiemer (2699), Sergeant W. Truter (1248), Sergeant J. D. Louw (1621), Sergeant H. W. Abrahams, D.C.M., M.M. (278), Sergeant H. Hofmiester (902), Sergeant J. Karele (1038), Sergeant P. D. Schoor, D.C.M. (480), Sergeant M. P. Thomas (1122), Sergeant P. Manuel (71).
Second row (left to right): Sergeant I. W. Arendse, D.C.M. (607), Sergeant W. Samuels (2230), C.Q.M.S. J. Davids (97), S./Sergeant F. J. Cairns, M.M. (1144), Sergeant W. H. Augustus (204), Sergeant J. Walker (3132), Sergeant S. J. Fredericks (255), Sergeant S. February (1357), Sergeant MacThomas (366), Sergeant E. Bezuidenhout (2775), Sergeant A. Thompson (1826), Sergeant A. P. de Vos (1072), Sergeant C. Carelse, D.C.M. (688), Sergeant W. Samuels (504), Sergeant J. Smit (1204).
Sitting (left to right): C.S.M. P. Daniels (1), C.S.M. J. Scullard (1363), A./R.Q.M.S. A. J. Hendricks, D.C.M. (1067), Bandmaster C. Linsell, Major W. J. R. Cuningham, Lieut.-Colonel G. A. Morris, C.M.G., D.S.O., Captain A. Leslie (Adjutant), R.S.M. C. Calvert, D.C.M. (152), C.S.M. C. A. Ruiters (132), C.S.M. D. J. Brown, D.C.M. (9), A./C.S.M. D. Wilkinson (1253).
Bottom row (left to right): Sergeant J. H. Yon (1472), C.Q.M.S. W. H. la Vita (1127), C.Q.M.S. A. J. Reagon (1143), Sergeant J. Bredekamp (979), Sig./Sergeant J. H. Alies (825), Sergeant J. Fitz (3143), Sergeant S. Maart (372), Sergeant J. Fillies (2504), Sergeant J. Locke (609).

THE STORY OF THE 1st CAPE CORPS.

Meanwhile the extremists were continuing to carry on an active propaganda in favour of continuance; at the same time they appealed for the support of the foreign residents and attempted to suborn the British troops. Strikes of railway employees were organised with considerable success and efforts continued to be made to intimidate all Government servants from remaining at their posts.

In effect the provinces of Egypt were in a state of rebellion. The Beduin in the west constituted a partially armed enemy, who might eventually number many thousands.

The situation, it will be seen, presents certain parallels both to the Indian Mutiny and to the Boxer rebellion. So far the behaviour of the Egyptian army and city and rural police has been all that could be expected. In many cases small detachments of police shewed considerable gallantry; in others they allowed themselves to be disarmed by overwhelming numbers.

One of the principal difficulties was to distinguish between the enemy and our friends.

Several cases of murders of defenceless Europeans had already occurred, and in order to secure the safety of the British and other foreigners scattered throughout the country, the most energetic measures to nip the movement in the bud were called for. A caution may be given against all spreading of alarmists reports. A movement of this nature could not be really formidable in face of modern arms of precision, and in view of the forces available.

The movement has several aspects, according to the character of the participants. Underlying all there is a genuine national movement of the Egyptians. The ignorant, however, and especially the Beduin, care little or nothing for Egypt. With them it is apt to turn into a pro-Turkish and particularly into a Moslem movement. The Turkish flag has already been hoisted on various marakis (court-houses) which have been captured by the rebels. There is also some indications of the movement taking on a fanatical Moslem character. In those cases the risk of life of the foreign residents in the outlying districts will be increased. On the other hand, the sympathies of the Copts, who form a fairly large proportion of the population, will be alienated, since they themselves will be exposed to massacre.

[Photos by
Private Lawrence, C. (756),
"B" Company.
Stripping Lewis Gun Competition (Blindfold) at Mustapha.

J.H.T.]
Leaving Mustapha Camp to assist in quelling the Riots at Alexandria, April, 1919.

Photo by] [Captain S. Youart.
A big British Gun at Jerusalem.

Photo by]   [Zadik & Co., Cape Town.
MAJOR W. J. R. CUNINGHAM.
O/C. R.H.B.

CHAPTER XVII.

THE RESERVE HALF BATTALION.

AS stated in Chapter XIII., the War Office, early in 1918, authorised the formation of a Reserve Half Battalion to the 1st Battalion. The Reserve Half Battalion was to be in substitution of the extra two double companies which had been specially sanctioned about eighteen months previously, and which ceased to exist concurrently with the coming into being of the Reserve Half Battalion.

The authorised establishment of the Reserve Half Battalion was:—

Two company commanders (one to be a Major and also to command the Reserve Half Battalion), two Captains (company second in commands), twelve subalterns (four per company, two for the reserve machine gun section, one Adjutant and one Quartermaster), a Medical officer and a Padre. Two Companies and a Machine Gun Section.

Two of the subalterns were to go forward with the battalion as Transport and Signalling Officers respectively. The total authorised establishment was eighteen officers and four hundred and seventy-three other ranks. The Padre, however, though authorised, was never appointed.

The Reserve Half Battalion came into being at our Kimberley depôt on the 13th March, 1918. Captain W. J. R. Cuningham was promoted Major on March 25th to command same, and organisation started immediately.

The following officers were appointed at once:—
  Adjutant, Lieutenant T. E. James.
  Quartermaster, Lieutenant W. Wigman.
  Medical Officer, Captain J. W. Bouwer, S.A.M.C.
  Officer Commanding " E " Company, Captain W. Jardine.
  Officer Commanding " F " Company, Captain F. Murchie.

At first there was a considerable shortage of officers, but by degrees several rejoined from hospital and others were appointed by the Union Defence Department, so that when the Reserve Half Battalion embarked for Egypt in July, Major Cuningham has his full complement.

Training was taken in hand without delay, the depôt instructional staff being assisted by a few experienced N.C.O.'s Major Cuningham had at his disposal.

When the battalion left Kimberley for Egypt at the end of March the Reserve Half Battalion moved out of No. 3 Compound (Kimberley) and went under canvas on an adjoining site, leaving the compound entirely to the Regimental Depôt.

Men rejoining from hospital were dealt with by the depôt for record purposes and then taken on Reserve Half Battalion strength. All recruits of course were also taken on depôt strength and also transferred to Reserve Half Battalion as required after a period of preliminary training. Major W. P. Anderson, who had been transferred from the 1st Cape Corps to the Union Defence Department, continued in command of the Depôt and the two commands were kept entirely separate.

THE STORY OF THE 1st CAPE CORPS.

OFFICERS RESERVE HALF BATTALION AT KIMBERLEY, JUNE, 1918.
(*Left to right, standing*).—Lieut. H. Wallis, M.C.; 2nd/Lieut. W. J. Buchanan; 2nd/Lieut. J. G. Hirsch; Lieut. C. S. H. Gardner; 2nd/Lieut. C. R. Lambe; 2nd/Lieut. B. P. Mosenthal; Lieut. A. S. Ross; 2nd/Lieut. A. E. J. Antill; 2nd/Lieut. R. R. Solomon.
(*Left to right, seated*).—Lieut. B. H. Moin; Lieut. R. Feetham, M.L.A.; Captain W. Jardine; Major W. J. R. Cuningham (O.C. R.H.Bn.); Lieut.-Colonel G. A. Morris, C.M.G., D.S.O. (O.C. 1st Cape Corps); Lieut. T. E. James (Adjutant); Captain F. Murchie; Captain J. W. Bouwer, S.A.M.C. (M.O.); Lieut. W. T. Wigman (Q.M.R.)

THE STORY OF THE 1st CAPE CORPS.

For the first few weeks Major Cuningham had to call on Major Anderson for instructors, owing to shortage of officers and N.C.O.'s. In this connection Staff-Sergeant Salida did exceptionally good work, as indeed he had done for the past two years in the Depôt. In five or six weeks very considerable progress was made, thanks in the main to Salida's efforts and energy.

On April 24th the Union Defence Department sent Staff-Sergeant Buxton and two others from Potchefstroom to assist in the training, and Salida was able to return to his duties in the Depôt. Training and organisation was then pushed on more energetically than ever for the next two months.

The regimental band, which had come into being in March, remained with the Reserve Half Battalion when the battalion embarked for Egypt, and under the very able tuition of Bandmaster C. Linsell, made such rapid progress that in less than three months were able to perform at various military functions at Kimberley.

The Reserve Half Battalion was inspected by Colonel Sir David Harris, K.C.M.G., V.D., at Kimberley, on May 24th.

Early in June preliminary warning of embarkation for Egypt was received. On Tuesday, June 18th, a farewell church parade at the Kimberley Cathedral was attended by the Reserve Half Battalion, all men in the Depôt, and all walking patients in blue from the hospital—a total parade strength of approximately thirteen hundred.

On June 22nd the Reserve Half Battalion entrained at Kimberley, arrived at Durban June 24th and sailed from there on June 27th in H.M.T. "Berwick Castle." All ranks on board the troopship numbered five hundred and sixty-two (twenty-one officers and five hundred and forty-one other ranks), which included approximately seventy left behind three months earlier by the battalion owing to lack of accommodation on their troopship.

Lieut.-Colonel Morris, who was prevented by illness from taking the battalion to Egypt in April, also embarked on the "Berwick Castle."

The officers with Major Cuningham were: Captains W. Jardine, F. Murchie and J. W. Bouwer (S.A.M.C.); Lieutenants R. Feetham, C. S. H. Gardner, T. E. James, O. R. Jeppe, B. H. Moin, A. S. Ross, H. Wallis, M.C., W. Wigman; Second-Lieutenants A. E. J. Antill, W. J. Buchanan, J. G. Hirsch, J. L. Hollins, C. R. Lambe, A. MacKenzie, B. P. Mosenthal and R. R. Solomon.

The "Berwick Castle" reached Port Teufik (Suez) on July 20th. Great heat was experienced during the latter part of the voyage and the men, being uncomfortably overcrowded, suffered a good deal. Concerts, boxing contests, and the band compensated much for the discomforts.

At Aden, when the ship coaled (July 12th/13th) General Beattie, the acting Governor, very kindly took Lieut.-Colonel Morris and several officers out to the trenches and explained the position on that front.

On arrival at Port Teufik the Reserve Half Battalion entrained at once for Kantara on the canal and, arriving there the same evening, proceeded to No. 2 Infantry Base Depôt. Training commenced again at once, despite intense heat, and the Quartermaster got very busy drawing arms and equipment, transport, etc.

Immediately after arrival at Kantara five officers proceeded to El Arish School of Instruction and twenty-five other ranks to the Signalling School at Kantara, where acting Corporal R. Burman (1108) did exceptionally good work.

Orders were received to move to the battalion's depôt at El Arish on August 4th, but Spanish influenza ruled otherwise and ten days isolation in a quarantine camp at Kantara supervened. By August 5th ten officers and nearly two hundred and fifty other ranks were in hospital with influenza. A week later, when the majority had recovered, a move was made to El Arish where Captain Burger and his Machine Gun Half Company were still busy training.

Photo by] [J. G. Horsfall, Cape Town.
C.Q.M.S. H. DE VARTEK (3481).

SERGEANT H. D. LE ROUX (904) and (4285).

Photo by] [I.D.D.
LIEUTENANT A. A. HAYTON AT EL ARISH.

Photo by] [I.D.D.
CAPTAIN D. W. ROBERTSON AND LIEUTENANT H. WALLIS, M.C., AT EL ARISH.

THE STORY OF THE 1st CAPE CORPS.

Lieut.-Colonel Morris left the Reserve Half Battalion at Kantara on August 9th to resume command of the battalion at the front.

At El Arish Major Cuningham at once got to work on intensive training according to the syllabus laid down for the E.E.F. As at Kimberley the shortage of officers and the lack of N.C.O.'s capable of instructing was a great handicap at first, but matters gradually improved as officers and N.C.O.'s returned from the Schools of Instruction.

The battalion was at this time in the line and officers and N.C.O.'s who came down to recuperate were able to assist greatly in the training by giving Major Cuningham the benefit of their recently gained experience.

Captain Burger left El Arish towards the end of August with the Machine Gun Company to join the Machine Gun Brigade at the front.

Influenza broke out again very shortly after arrival at El Arish and another spell of quarantine ensued. This prevented drafts being sent at once to the battalion, who were in urgent need of men owing to the prevailing pestilence. However, the salubrious climate of El Arish worked wonders, and on August 31st—not quite three weeks after arrival at El Arish—Captain Jardine went forward with the first draft, one hundred and forty-four strong. Other large drafts followed at frequent and regular intervals.

To enable as many officers and N.C.O.'s as possible to attend the various Schools of Instruction the working staff at El Arish was reduced to the irreducible minimum. This threw a heavy burden of work on those remaining, but they shouldered their task with great keenness and enthusiasm and training proceeded apace.

The proximity of the School of Instruction at El Arish proved most fortuitous, as it had been to the battalion two months earlier.

Lieut.-Colonel Synott, the commandant of the school, lent invaluable assistance and advice to Major Cuningham, as he had done earlier to Lieut.-Colonel Hoy.

The courses at the school were terminated by most realistic "stunts" to emphasise what had been taught, and to these, thanks to the courtesy of Lieut.-Colonel Synott, the Cape Corps were always welcomed.

Captain Rose-Innes took the second draft of nine officers and one hundred and seventy-two other ranks forward on September 10th.

On September 14th, Captain Anderson arrived at Suez from South Africa per H.M.T. "Palmacotta" with a draft of eleven officers and seven hundred and seven other ranks. The officers were:—

Lieutenants C. A. Hillary, L. C. Johnson, C. Reunert, Second-Lieutenants F. C. Adamson, D. F. H. Buchanan, W. I. Brown, R. L. Hall, H. Louw, P. Macfarlane, G. Whitfield, D.C.M., W. D. Wheelwright.

Captain Anderson left Kimberley on August 11th with eleven officers and seven hundred and twenty-five other ranks. At Durban, on August 13th, Second-Lieutenant G. Whitfield joined the draft and fourteen men were left behind (in hospital, etc.).

Thirteen officers and seven hundred and eleven other ranks embarked at Durban on August 17th. During the voyage two men died and were buried at sea, viz.: Private Smit, C. (4267) cerebral malaria, August 21st; Private Bantam, A. (5013) pneumonia, September 10th.

Lieutenant H. C. van Diggelen and two other ranks were disembarked at Aden (to hospital) and twelve officers and seven hundred and seven other ranks disembarked at Suez on September 14th.

Captain Anderson, after a good deal of trouble, had managed to get re-transferred from the Union Defence Forces to the 1st Cape Corps, but to do so had to drop a step in rank. This was a case of great injustice. Anderson had received his majority in the battalion in December, 1917, vice Bradstock

THE STORY OF THE 1st CAPE CORPS.

Photo by] [I.D.D.
SERGEANT PAULSEN ISSUING BEER AT EL ARISH, JANUARY, 1919.

Photo by] [I.D.D.
A DRAFT AT EL ARISH ABOUT TO LEAVE FOR THE FRONT, SEPTEMBER, 1918.

[I.D.D.
CAPTAIN J. W. BOUWER, S.A.M.C., WITH GROOM (PRIVATE KOLOMBE, 4676), AT EL ARISH, JANUARY, 1919

Photo by] [I.D.D.
OFFICERS, R.H.B., "AT HOME," ANNIVERSARY DAY (21ST OCTOBER, 1918) AT EL ARISH.

transferred. He was at that time in command of our Depôt at Kimberley. It was about then decided that the Depôt should be commanded by an officer of the Union Defence Forces and Major Anderson was accordingly transferred from the Cape Corps to the Union Defence Forces, but without his knowledge or consent. Five months elapsed before he could obtain his re-transfer, and meanwhile the promotion of Captain Cuningham had left no vacancy for a Major in the battalion.

Captain Anderson's draft arrived at Kantara on September 15th. Anderson himself and the officers with him except Lieutenant Johnson left four days later to join the battalion at the front in order to replace others at schools, in hospital, etc.

On September 18th, Captain Jardine proceeded from El Arish to Kantara to bring forward the men of Anderson's draft, but on arrival there he was instructed by wire to proceed at once to the front to join the battalion and accordingly handed over the draft to Lieutenants Hayton, Moin and Mosenthal who had been sent down from El Arish for the purpose. The draft reached El Arish on September 23rd.

On September 20th, Second-Lieutenant Brown and one hundred and forty-two other ranks left the Reserve Half Battalion for the front.

Next day news of the battalion's heavy casualties on September 20th reached the Depôt, and Lieutenants Jeppe and Wigman at once went forward, followed on September 27th by Lieutenant Gardner and one hundred and twelve men, and by fifty-seven more men on October 1st. By the latter date eighteen officers and six hundred and fifteen other ranks had gone forward from the Reserve Half Battalion to the battalion within thirty-one days. This more than entirely absorbed the original Reserve Half Battalion, but meanwhile large numbers from the battalion had drifted back to El Arish through hospitals, etc.

During September the strength of the Depôt at El Arish was once down to about two hundred, but, after the arrival of Captain Anderson's reinforcements, was never much below eight hundred. When the numbers in the Depôt exceeded six hundred the men were formed into three double companies, viz.: " E " under Captain Jardine (who had returned from the front); " F " under Captain James; " G " under Lieutenant (later Captain) Jeppe.

Lieutenants Moin and Wallis, M.C., continued at El Arish the training of the reserve machine gunners which they had commenced at Kimberley.

Captain Difford arrived in the Depôt from hospital at the end of August and remained with the Reserve Half Battalion for several months, having been medically classified as B.1 (lines of communication duty only). He took over duty on September 21st as Quartermaster Reserve Half Battalion from Lieutenant Wigman, who went forward to the battalion.

During the period 18th August to 12th October, twenty-four officers and seven hundred and fifty-one other ranks were sent forward from El Arish to join the battalion at the front.

On October 20th, Major Cuningham went forward to take over duty as second in command of the battalion and Captain Robertson arrived from the front to command the Reserve Half Battalion. Robertson only remained three weeks and then passed on the command to Major Anderson (November 11th).

After the signing of the Armistice (November 11th) the strictly military training at the Depôt was somewhat modified and more time given to games and recreation. Football, both Rugby and Association, were encouraged and inter-platoon competitions arranged. No. 17 Platoon (" E " company) captained by Sergeant M. J. Abrahamse (318) won both competitions.

On October 21st a most successful sports meeting was held to celebrate the third anniversary of the formation of the Cape Corps (for results *vide* Chapter XX.).

THE STORY OF THE 1st CAPE CORPS.

Photo by]   *[I.D.D.*
SHADOUF (NATIVE WELL) AT EL ARISH.

R.H.B. TRANSPORT PARADE AT EL ARISH.

Photo by]   *[I.D.D.*
R.H.B. SPORTS AT EL ARISH, DECEMBER 26TH, 1918.
FANCY DRESS COMPETITION.

Photo by]   *[I.D.D.*
SINAI POLICE AT EL ARISH, JANUARY, 1919.

The tendency to slackness following upon the armistice was combatted by every possible means. Route marches and parades in the morning were followed by football, cricket and bathing in the afternoon and frequent concerts in the evenings.

After the armistice, following the practice introduced throughout the E.E.F., a school was started in the Depôt and several men previously illiterate began rapidly to acquire knowledge of the three "R's." It was a great pity that the preliminary move order at Christmas time caused the closing down of the school and that the period of suspended animation which ensued prevented a re-opening.

Major Cuningham returned to El Arish and resumed command of the Reserve Half Battalion on November 26th, vice Major Anderson who rejoined the battalion.

A boat washed up on the beach near camp was repaired by the pioneers and a fishing party organised. Several good catches resulted. One day the use of a few hand grenades produced sufficient fish to feed two hundred and fifty men.

Towards the end of the year the Wady came down in flood, washing out the parade ground, but a better site was at once found on the football ground at the School of Instruction. The latter closed down early in December.

At the school farewell sports meeting after the final classes several men of the Reserve Half Battalion distinguished themselves. Lance-Corporal Hopley (5160) won the 100 yards and the obstacle race and was second in the mile. Corporal Sass (3772) was second in the 100 yards and Private Africa (517) second in the obstacle race. Lieutenant Moin on "the Bint" was second in the officers' jumping competition.

A few days before Christmas warning was given of early impending return to South Africa, but nothing came of it. This was the first of many false alarms and it was not until nearly three months later that the Reserve Half Battalion eventually left El Arish, and then it was not to return home but to do duty in Egypt.

On Boxing Day another most successful sports meeting was held and on New Year's Day a Marathon race was a huge success. Individual prizes subscribed for by the officers and a valuable company prize was given. (*Vide* Chapter XX.).

The course was about five miles along the beach and back to camp.

At the sports on Boxing Day quite the feature was the magnificent turn-out of the Depôt transport under Corporal Hankin, N. (4527). Prizes were given for the best turned out officer's charger, pack mule, and G.S. wagon and team. The judges (visiting officers) found great difficulty in awarding the prizes owing to the uniform excellence of the turn-out.

Colonel Parker, Governor of the Sinai Peninsula, who was one of the judges, stated that he had not seen a better transport parade in the E.E.F., or in twenty years' experience.

The squad under Sergeant Fisher (765) ("G" company) won the Guard Mounting competition at the Boxing Day Sports.

The regimental band came forward from South Africa with the Reserve Half Battalion, but after a few weeks at the Depôt went up the line to join the battalion. Soon afterwards the drum and fife band came from the battalion to El Arish and eventually returned to South Africa with the Reserve Half Battalion. Under Corporal Sylvester, H. (1055) they were of great assistance at the route marches, parades, guard mounting, etc.

Sergeant Paulsen (432) the battalion pioneer sergeant, was invalided to El Arish shortly after the arrival of the Reserve Half Battalion. With his assistance the Quartermaster organised a pioneer section which soon became most efficient,

THE STORY OF THE 1st CAPE CORPS.

Photo by] R.H.B. Camp at Fayed. [Captain I. W. Bouwer.

Photo by] Evening Prayer in the Desert. [Sergeant Alies.

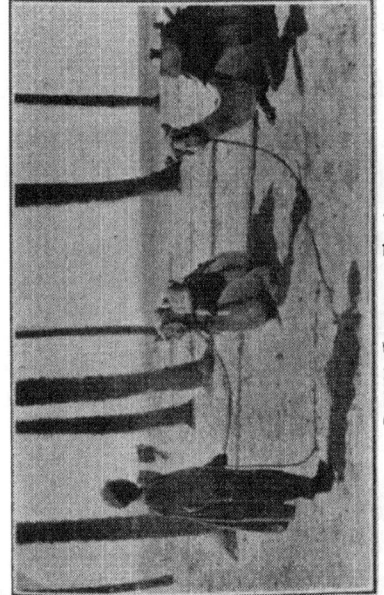

Riding Camels at El Arish.

Photo by] Native Gardens at El Arish. [I.D.D.

THE STORY OF THE 1st CAPE CORPS.

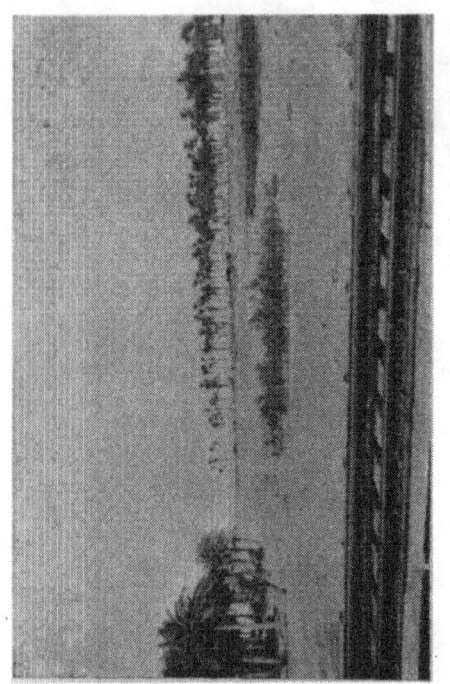

Photo by] [B. H. Moin.
THE "RIVER" OF EGYPT. THE WADI AT EL ARISH IN FLOOD. MILITARY RAILWAY TO PALESTINE IN FOREGROUND.

OFFICERS' LINES AT THE DEPÔT, EL ARISH. SANDBAGS AS PROTECTION AGAINST WIND.

Photo by] [B. H. Moin.
TEACHING THE YOUNG (LOCAL) IDEA. C.S.M RUITERS (WITHOUT HAT) ACTING AS M.C.

Photo by] [B. H. Moin.
MAJOR W. J. R. CUNINGHAM AT EL ARISH.

Photo by] B. H. Moin.
OWNER PICKING DATES IN PLANTATION AT EL ARISH, SINAI PENINSULA, OCTOBER, 1918.

Photo by] [I.D.D.
THE RATION ISSUER—A POPULAR PERSON.
LANCE-CORPORAL MEAS (4013) AT EL ARISH, DECEMBER, 1918.

Photo by] [I.D.D.
THE LOCAL HUSBANDMEN AT EL ARISH.

Photo by] [I.D.D.
MEN AT EL ARISH READY FOR DRAFTING.
Privates Bailey (3249), Lopsol (2138), Mannel (4741), Crowley (5251), and Frazer (5266).

THE STORY OF THE 1st CAPE CORPS.

Photo by]   The Wady comes down at El Arish, November, 1918.   [I.D.D.

Photo by]   In the Officers' Lines at El Arish, October, 1918.   [B. H. Moin.
Major Cuningham, Captains Bouwer and Murchie, Lieutenants Wallis, Hayton, Mosenthal and Mackenzie

Photo by]   R.H.B. Horse Lines at El Arish.   [B. H. Moin.

Photo by]   [Captain Bouwer.
Captain Jardine with Batman and Guide (Gad Michael Bay) in Egypt.

in fact, indispensable. They built kitchens for officers' and men's messes, stables and harness room for the transport, greatly improved the officers' mess accommodation, built a concert platform, made bricks and laid paths in the camp, etc. Before the Reserve Half Battalion left El Arish they had so much improved the camp that there was no other regimental depôt in the E.E.F. to compare with it. In fact, even the big depôts laid out and built by the R.E. were little better.

Captain Bouwer organised the sanitation of the camp on the most systematic and thorough lines and was equally efficient in his treatment of the camp sick.

After the operations on the Palestine front and the consequent imperative demand for reinforcements had ceased, the men of the Depôt were afforded the opportunity of visiting Jerusalem. Parties of thirty went there under an officer every few days, and afterwards Lieutenant Ross was temporarily stationed at Jerusalem to look after the leave parties.

There was a certain amount of rain, cold and high wind at El Arish during the winter (November to February) but on the whole the weather left little to be desired. The site of the camp in a palm grove and right at the water's edge was ideal, and the officers and men who were fortunate enough to spend some months there were lucky indeed.

Although there was no chaplain attached to the Reserve Half Battalion the spiritual welfare of officers and men was not neglected. El Arish was the headquarters of Anglican (Captain Backhouse) and Roman Catholic (Captain Amery) chaplains whose sphere of influence extended from Kantara to Ludd, and both reverend gentlemen contrived to hold church parades in our camp practically every Sunday.

On March 6th, Captain Edwards brought the battalion concert party (known as the "Peach Blossoms") to El Arish and gave two most enjoyable concerts, which were attended and greatly appreciated by all the troops in the area, as well, of course, as by the men in the Depôt.

Early in March ominous signs of unrest became apparent in Egypt, and no one was the least surprised when orders reached Major Cuningham to hold the Reserve Half Battalion in readiness to take a hand in maintaining order, and that meanwhile our return to South Africa would be delayed. A few days later orders to move into Egypt were received. The Depôt was at once closed and the Reserve Half Battalion left El Arish for Kantara on March 19th.

There we heard that rebellion had broken out and that the mob were blowing up the railways, attacking trains and murdering and pillaging all over Egypt.

Prompt corrective measures had already been taken and the task allotted to the Reserve Half Battalion was the protection of a section of railway some seventy miles in length between Suez and Ismailia. We left at once and established our headquarters on March 20th at Fayed Station, midway between the two places named.

Platoons were immediately posted at the various stations as under:—

    Nefisha and Serapeum: Lieutenant Rackstraw, M.C.
    Abu Sultan: 2nd Lieutenant Brown.
    Fayed: Headquarters (here were two hundred men and two machine guns). Major Cuningham; Captain Difford, Captain Bouwer (M.O.); Lieutenant Johnson (Adjutant), Lieutenant Moin (M.G.).
    Fayed Bridge: Captain Jeppe.
    Fanara: 2nd Lieutenant Whitfield, D.C.M.
    Geneffe: Lieutenant Hayton.
    El Gebel: Lieutenant Hillary.

THE STORY OF THE 1st CAPE CORPS.

Photo by]   *[I.D.D.*
LEFT TO RIGHT: LIEUTENANT L. C. JOHNSON, MAJOR CUNINGHAM, COLONEL PARKER, GOVERNOR SINAI PENINSULA; CAPTAIN STEWART, GOVERNOR, EL ARISH; CAPTAIN WM. JARDINE.

Photo by]   *[Captain J. W. Bouwer.*
LT.-COLONEL MORRIS, C.M.G., D.S.O., WITH MAJOR CUNINGHAM AND OFFICERS AT THE DEPOT, EL ARISH, FEBRUARY, 1919.

Photo by]   *[Captain J. W. Bouwer.*
COMPETITION BEST TURNED-OUT MAN AT DEPOT SPORTS, EL ARISH, JANUARY, 1919. SERGEANT BARBIER, W. F. (875), AND CPL. GOLIATH, F. (1032).

Photo by]   *[Zadik & Co., Cape Town.*
LIEUTENANT L. C. JOHNSON.
Cape Corps Records and Attesting Officer, December, 1916, to July, 1918. Adjutant, Reserve Half Battalion, 1918-19.

THE STORY OF THE 1st CAPE CORPS.

Photo by] [I.D.D.
R.H.B. Sports, El Arish, October 21st, 1918. Mule Race. Lieut.-Colonel Synnott and Major Swan (School of Instruction) Right Foreground.

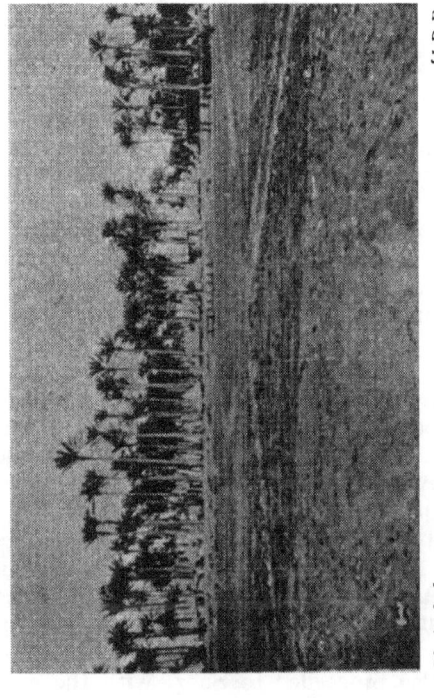

Photo by] [I.D.D.
Cape Corps Depôt at El Arish, September, 1918. Foreground is a Wadi (River Bed—Dry in Summer).

Photo by] [I.D.D.
On the Sweetwater Canal at Ismailia, April, 1919.
Note.—Ismailia was Attacked by the Enemy in 1917.

[Sergeant Alies.
The Sphinx and Great Pyramid at Cairo.

Shallufa : Captain James.
Abu Halab : Lieutenant Ross.
El Kubri : Lieutenant Gardner.

Lieutenant van Diggelen and Second-Lieutenant D. F. H. Buchanan acted as relieving officers.

For the next month all ranks were kept very busy. The line had to be patrolled day and night and all signalmen, lamp men, and permanent way repair parties guarded and supervised. Many of the railway officials were suspect and had to be closely overlooked.

The weather was excessively hot, varied by strong winds and dust storms, but that was the worst we had to contend with. No attacks were made on our section of the line, nor was there any sign of insurrection or insubordination, and by the end of April the situation was normal in the Suez-Ismailia-Kantara area.

Major Cuningham had a very strenuous month, having to be constantly up and down the line inspecting and over-seeing his section. Shortly after our occupation of Fayed the S.A. Field Artillery, under Lieut.-Colonel S. S. Taylor, C.M.G., D.S.O., travelled over the section en route to Suez to return to South Africa. We paraded at the various stations and gave them a hearty cheer as they passed through. This compliment was much appreciated by "our gunners" (*vide* Lieut.-Colonel Taylor's letter, see appendix).

On May 1st preliminary warning was received of early return to South Africa and the next day Captain James with three other officers and four hundred and five other ranks proceeded to Suez to await embarkation.

On May 4th the remainder of the Reserve Half Battalion were relieved and also proceeded to Suez, with the exception of two platoons under Lieutenants Ross and Gardner who carried on at Nefisha Lock and Fayed respectively for some days longer.

Private Matthys, B. (4730) was run over and killed by a train at Suez on May 7th.

On arrival at Suez the Reserve Half Battalion went to the British Transit Camp to await embarkation. On May 6th Major Cuningham with two hundred men and the necessary complement of officers moved to Arbain camp and temporarily took over various guards and other garrison duties in Suez. The remainder carried on in the British Transit Camp with Captain James.

On May 16th the following officers, viz. : Major Anderson, Captains Robertson, Tandy, Youart, and Lieutenants Colson and Manley with three hundred other ranks homeward bound, arrived from Battalion Headquarters (Mustapha-Alexandria). Major Cuningham handed over the Reserve Half Battalion (seven hundred and fifteen all ranks) to Major Anderson and the latter at once embarked with thirteen officers and nine hundred and ninety-eight other ranks on H.M.T. "Tambov," and left for South Africa on May 18th.

The officers who sailed with Major Anderson were : Captains Robertson, Tandy, M.C., Bouwer, Youart, James and Jeppe ; Lieutenants Ross, Rackstraw, M.C., Gardner, Hayton, Colson, Johnson and Manley.

Major Cuningham, Captain Difford and Lieutenants Moin, Hillary, and van Diggelen, and 2nd Lieutenants Brown and D. Buchanan and their batmen left Suez the same day to rejoin the battalion at Alexandria. 2nd Lieutenant Whitfield was left in hospital at Suez and was later evacuated to the United Kingdom per hospital ship.

Before leaving Fayed (May 4th) Major Cuningham received a most complimentary letter of farewell and thanks from Brig.-General A. H. O. Lloyd, commanding P. L. of C. headquarters, Ismailia (*vide* appendix).

THE STORY OF THE 1st CAPE CORPS.

Photo by] [B. H. Moin.
R.H.B. HEADQUARTERS AT FAYED, APRIL, 1919, DURING THE UNREST.

Photo by] [I.D.D.
CAMP AT MOASCAR, EGYPT, TAKEN FROM AEROPLANE.

Photo by] [B. H. Moin.
BEAUTY AND THE LATEST FASHIONS AT CAIRO.

In a sense the work done by the Reserve Half Battalion at Kimberley, at the depôt, El Arish and on the Suez line (period March, 1918 to May, 1919) was of secondary importance, in that no actual contact with the enemy took place. Nevertheless, most useful service was rendered and much valuable work accomplished. The training, which was extremely systematic and thorough, was reflected in the great achievements of the battalion, September 18th to 20th, 1918, in which a large number of the Reserve Half Battalion participated.

The great care taken of the men's health was a great factor in the numerical strength and fitness of the several drafts sent forward.

In a word, everything in connection with the Reserve Half Battalion was performed with the most punctilious conscientiousness and regard for the welfare and interests of the battalion by Major Cuningham.

In addition to the officers and men already mentioned in this chapter for work well done, the names of the following should be added, viz.:—

    R.S.M. Rutherford, W. E.
    C.S.M. Ruiters (132).
    C.Q.M.S. Caster, P. (392).
    C.Q.M.S. de Vartek, H. (3481).
    Sergeant Abrahams, H. W. (278).
    Sergeant Le Roux, H. (4285).
    Corporal Cupido, D. (406).
    Corporal Meas, C. (4013).
    Corporal Oersen, T. P. (5015).
    Corporal Preston, G. H. (1211).
    Corporal Livers, J. A. (2666).
    Corporal Timmins, W. J. (1414).
    Corporal Citto, A. (1718).
    Corporal Abrahamse, J. C. (6395).
    Corporal Stevens, T. (1006).
    Corporal Hussey, E. (605).
    Private Alexander, P. (1283).
    Private Wyngaard, H. (1409).
    Private Palm, A. C. (3145).

The "Tambov" with the Reserve Half Battalion on board arrived at Durban on Monday, 9th June. She was met by Mr. Oliver Lea, Chairman of the Reception Committee, and the ladies of the West Street Hut, who boarded the vessel and dispensed fruit, cigarettes, etc., which needless to say were gratefully accepted and appreciated.

After breakfast the Reserve Half Battalion disembarked and, headed by the municipal band and their own drum and fife band, marched to Albert Park where they were received by the Mayor of Durban (Mr. Thomas Burman, M.B.E., M.P.C.) who extended to Major Anderson and his officers and men Durban's welcome and congratulations. Speaking with obvious sincerity His Worship referred to the proud achievements of the 1st Cape Corps and the high standard of efficiency which they had reached. He was sure the lessons learned on service would help them in their future careers.

Present at the Park and supporting the Mayor were the Mayoress, the Executive Committee of the Ladies' Patriotic League, members of the local Cape Corps Gifts and Comforts Committee, Councillers Vernon Hooper (Deputy Mayor) and W. H. Lane, Lieut.-Colonel Giles, C.B.E. (Base Commandant) and other officers of the Durban Base, Mr. Oliver Lea and other members of the Governor-General's Reception Committee, Mr. W. P. M. Henderson (Town Clerk), Mr. C. S. Jameson, President of the Cape Corps Reception Committee, and Mr. A. S. Williams, Secretary of the Cape Corps Gifts and Comforts Committee (Cape Town) who had travelled to Durban to meet the men.

THE STORY OF THE 1st CAPE CORPS.

Photo by] [B. H. Moin.
VICKERS GUNS READY FOR THE REBELS AT FAYED CAMP, MARCH, 1919.
Sergeant Meyer, Gunners Ziervogel, Lakay and Fester.

Photo by] [Sergeant Alies
MEN ON SHORT LEAVE AT ESBEKIEH GARDENS, CAIRO.

Photo by] [B. H. Moin.
BATHING PARADE AT FAYED, APRIL, 1919

Photo by] [B. H. Moin.
THE CONCERT PARTY VISIT THE DEPÔT EL ARISH, FEBRUARY, 1919.
BACK ROW: Sergt. D. Wilkinson (1253), L/Cpl. S. A. Williams (1802), Lieut. S. H Roselinnes, Sergt. J. H. Von (1472), Lieut. C. R. Lambe, R.S.M. C. Calvert, D.C.M. (152), Pte. W. Stohrer (2124), Sgt. J. P. Carollissen (280).
FRONT ROW: Cpl. J. Martin (4086), Captain H. Edwards, Cpl. F. Frost (3393).

281

Major Anderson, having replied on behalf of the 1st Cape Corps, the men gave hearty cheers for the citizens of Durban and were then regaled with refreshments, fruit, cigarettes, etc., by the Patriotic League, acting on behalf of the burgesses of the City of Durban.

This most hearty "welcome home" by the Mayor and prominent citizens of Durban was in keeping with Durban's traditional reputation for hospitality to the King's soldiers, whether coming or going, but it was not on that account the less appreciated and esteemed by officers and men of the 1st Cape Corps, whether actually present that day or not.

From Albert Park the Reserve Half Battalion marched to Congella camp where demobilisation commenced without delay. The organisation at Congella camp for rapid demobilisation was most excellent. After arms and equipment had been handed in officers and men were medically boarded, and within a fortnight all ranks had left for their homes except the medically unfit—principally men who had recently had malaria—who were detained for treatment.

The Base Commandant (Lieut.-Colonel Giles, C.B.E.) and the Camp Commandant (Major Butler) expressed great satisfaction at the conduct of the men and the assistance they received from the officers, whilst the Camp Quartermaster wrote thanking Major Anderson for the manner in which stores and equipment, etc., had been handed in.

The Y.M.C.A. Hut at Congella camp was about to close when the Reserve Half Battalion arrived but was kept open for another month for their especial benefit. Fruit, cigarettes, etc., were issued to the men and the officials in charge could not do enough for the men's needs and comfort.

The Cape Corps Paymaster (Captain W. H. Smith) and the Records Officer (Captain Cooper) who had travelled from Cape Town to Durban to meet the Reserve Half Battalion had a strenuous time for some days. Both officers and their respective staffs most efficiently and expeditiously dealt with the men's pay and records.

The men were despatched from Durban in special trains, each under a regimental officer, to their various destinations. Lieutenant Rackstraw, M.C., took the first train load to Cape Town where a great reception awaited them. Dense crowds collected along the route from the railway station to the City Hall, the coloured community naturally turning out in full force.

After inspection at the station by Lieut.-Colonel C. N. Hoy, D.S.O. (who had just returned from Egypt via the United Kingdom) the Reserve Half Battalion were received at the City Hall by the Mayor (Mr. W. J. Thorne) who was supported by Colonel Sir W. E. M. Stanford, K.B.E., C.B., C.M.G. (Hon. Colonel of the regiment), Sir Harry Hands, K.B.E., Bishop Gaul, Canon Lavis, Colonels Devine, T. J. J. Inglesby, Trew and Hodgson, Messrs. Blackstone Williams, Eames Perkins, and many others.

After the Mayor had extended a very hearty welcome to the men and eulogised the deeds of the 1st Cape Corps, His Excellency the Governor-General, Viscount Buxton, arrived and addressed the men. He welcomed them as Governor-General on behalf of His Majesty the King and in the name of the people of the Union of South Africa. His Excellency made highly complimentary reference to duty well done which had helped to uphold the reputation of South Africa.

Having sympathised deeply with the relatives and friends of those who had given their lives in the great cause for Empire, Lord Buxton wished the men of the Cape Corps every success in their future lives. Having proved good soldiers he was sure the men were determined to prove equally good citizens.

Colonel Mentz, Minister of Defence, and Sir Harry Hands also paid tribute to the 1st Cape Corps and eulogised their services.

THE STORY OF THE 1st CAPE CORPS.

The Reserve Half Battalion disembarking at Durban for Demobilisation, June, 1919.

The Reserve Half Battalion marching to Albert Park, Durban, for Civic Reception, June, 1919.

R.H.B Disembarking at Durban for Demobilisation, June, 1919.

The Reserve Half Battalion disembarking at Durban for Demobilisation, June, 1919.

THE STORY OF THE 1st CAPE CORPS.

Photo by] [Captain J. W. Bouwer.
Officers and N.C.O.'s of G Company at El Arish.

Photo by] [I.D.D.
Nursing Sisters take a Course of Musketry at El Arish, October, 1918.

Photo by] [Captain Bouwer.
Nursing Sisters take the Musketry Course at El Arish, October, 1918.

Photo by] [I.D.D.
Rations arriving at El Arish Depot, September, 1918.

THE STORY OF THE 1st CAPE CORPS

During the period covered by this chapter the following promotions, changes of personnel, etc., took place, viz. :—

C.S.M. Twynham, D. (1192) who had been at Durban on recruiting duty returned to Kimberley and assumed duty as R.S.M. Reserve Half Battalion on May 16th.

C.S.M. Carollisen (280) succeeded Twynham as R.S.M. on June 26th.

During the voyage from Durban to Suez Private Joseph, A. (2459) died of pneumonia on July 11th and was buried at sea.

Sergeant Henry Siljeur (349) left the Reserve Half Battalion at El Arish on August 15th to join the record office staff at General Headquarters, 3rd Echelon, Alexandria.

Photo by] [I.D.D.
THE DEPÔT PIONEERS AT EL ARISH, NOVEMBER, 1918.
Top row (left to right): Private Van Wyk, C. (5128), Private Terblanche, S. (4984), Private Diedericks, J. (4736), Corporal Liver, J. A. (2666). Seated: Private Isaacs, D. (3432), Private Johnson, W. (2836), Sergeant Paulsen, J. C. M. (432), Private Carelse, J. (194), Private Dunn, T. (2708). On ground: Private Endley, W. L. (5059), Private Carelse, C. (1348).

Photo by] [I.D.D.
THE DEPÔT BUGLERS.
Privates Jackson (1714), Abdulla (2387), Brink (4583), and Dyson (662).

In August, Lieutenant R. Feetham, M.L.A., left Egypt for England to become Chairman of the "Southborough Committee,"—one of two reform committees appointed by the Secretary of State for India, to visit India and enquire under the presidency of Lord Southborough into certain questions connected with the Indian Constitutional Reforms then under consideration, and to provide material for the new Government of India Bill to embody those reforms. The Bill was passed by the Imperial Parliament and became law at the end of 1919.

Lieutenant James was admitted to hospital on September 2nd and Lieutenant H. Wallis, M.C., was appointed acting Adjutant.

On October 13th, Lieutenant Johnson succeeded Wallis and continued to act as Adjutant until the Reserve Half Battalion was demobilised eight months later.

On October 17th Lieutenant H. C. van Diggelen reported at El Arish ex hospital (Aden).

Corporal N. Hankin (4527) and five of his transport men proceeded to the R.A.S.C. Animal Transport School at Ludd on October 29th. They returned a month later with an excellent report.

Private R. Johnson (2280) was drowned whilst bathing at El Arish on November 2nd.

Captain Jardine who had returned from the front was appointed second in command of the Reserve Half Battalion on November 15th and Captain Rose-Innes assumed command of " E " company.

On December 12th, Armourer Staff Sergeant Papworth, R.A.O.C., was attached for duty and remained with the Reserve Half Battalion for some weeks.

On January 12th R.S.M. Rutherford, who had been on duty with the R.H.B. for several weeks since his discharge from hospital, left to rejoin his unit, 2/7th Northumberland Fusiliers, and C.S.M. Abrahams, M. J. (1483) became Acting R.S.M., R.H.B.

In January Lieutenant Wallis, M.C., was seconded for duty with Headquarters P.L. of C. (first at Ramleh, afterwards at Ismailia) and did not return to the R.H.B. until May 8th.

Early in March Captain Jardine proceeded to the United Kingdom on leave.

Captain Murchie relieved Captain Rose-Innes of the command of E Company on March 14th, and the latter rejoined the battalion. Captain Murchie returned to the battalion on April 11th.

During the march to the station at El Arish on March 19th, Private N. Koeberg (4988) fell out and died next day of heart failure.

Lieutenant Wallis proceeded to the battalion for duty on May 11th.

THE STORY OF THE 1st CAPE CORPS.

Return of the Reserve Half Battalion to South Africa for Demobilisation, Civic Reception at Albert Park, Durban, 9th June, 1919.

CHAPTER XVIII.

THE 1ST CAPE CORPS MACHINE GUNNERS.

WHEN the 1st Cape Corps came into being at Simonstown towards the end of 1915, a Machine Gun section (four guns) was authorised. The establishment of the section consisted of one officer and forty-five other ranks. The latter included two European staff sergeants (Sergeants N. O. Harvey and J. Howard), one sergeant (the first was S. W. Dunn, 1134), four lance-sergeants and one corporal.

Captain Lindsay Campbell, who had been a brigade machine gun officer in the South-West African campaign, was appointed to the command of the section. The guns supplied to the section at Simonstown and used throughout the East African campaign were Maxims.

Training commenced at Simonstown in November, 1915, but was carried on under difficulty owing to the lack of skilled instructors to assist Captain Campbell and the total absence of the usual appurtenances of a School of Musketry. However, the best possible was done under the circumstances, and when the battalion embarked for East Africa on the 9th February, 1916, the Machine Gun Section had achieved a considerable measure of efficiency.

On arrival in East Africa General Headquarters decreed that another officer should be attached to the Section. On February 25th, therefore, at Kajiado, Lieutenant F. Burger, who was a trained machine gunner, was transferred from No. 9 Platoon to the Machine Gun Section. Two days later Captain Campbell was admitted to hospital as the result of a kick from one of his refractory mules. During his absence (two months) Captain F. E. Bradstock was placed in temporary command of the Section with Captain W. P. Anderson and Lieutenant Burger as sub-section commanders. On Captain Campbell's return to duty Captains Bradstock and Anderson returned to Company duty.

Early in May thirty-two native porters were posted to the Section owing to the fact that the pack mules could not live in the area in which the Cape Corps then was.

During May Lieutenant J. Arnott with two Rexer guns was posted to the Section, but that particular weapon was shortly afterwards discarded by the authorities as unsatisfactory and the guns were returned to Ordnance.

At Tsame (June, 1916) a further eighty-four porters were added to the Section.

During the period of the battalion's service on lines of communication (March to June, 1916) the Machine Gun Section underwent continuous training and made rapid strides.

Lieutenant Burger was placed in immediate charge of the porters. They were raw at first and the lack of a language medium proved almost insuperable. The N.C.O.'s, however, revealed marked aptitude for mastering the local native tongues and in a few months the porters were brought to a state of efficiency and discipline which was the subject of favourable comment by those best able to judge.

In July, at Kangata, Lieutenant Alexander was attached to the Section, but before long was invalided to South Africa and did not return.

THE STORY OF THE 1ST CAPE CORPS.

Photo by] [E. W. Templer.
LIEUTENANT D. F. BOTHA (MACHINE GUN COMPANY).

LIEUTENANT M. S. DAVIES, MACHINE GUN COMPANY.
Lawn Tennis Champion of Alexandria, April 27th, 1919, won E.E.F. Quarter-mile Championship at Cairo, February 28th, 1919.

Photo by] [B. H. Moin.
CAPTAIN F. BURGER AT EL ARISH, AUGUST, 1918.

Photo by] [E. W. Templer.
CAPTAIN F. BURGER, O.C. MACHINE GUN COMPANY

THE STORY OF THE 1st CAPE CORPS.

On the 21st September, Lieutenant Burger was promoted Captain and to be second in command of "B" Company. A few weeks later Captain Campbell was invalided to South Africa and Captain Burger succeeded to the command of the Section.

On October 1st the two European N.C.O.'s were invalided to South Africa and replaced by coloured men (Sergeants Brown, D. J. (9), and Jacobus, D. C. 599).

At Morogoro, in November, 1916, the complement of guns was increased to eight, which of course entailed an increase in personnel and porters. Lieutenants Gardner, Wigman and 2nd Lieutenant Heaton were accordingly detailed to join the Section, but before they could materially assist Captain Burger, they had to be instructed in machine gunnery.

On December 11th, at Morogoro, the following Corporals were promoted Sergeants, viz.:—
  Johar, G. (160).
  Temmez, H. (439).
  Allison, J. (647).

The Machine Gun Section proceeded with the battalion to the Rufiji River area in December, 1916, and a section with four guns took part in the famous march to the Makalinso crossing on January 2nd, 1917 (*vide* Chapter VI. page 83).

Magnificent work was done by the machine gun porters that day and a number of them received monetary awards.

On January 20th, the Machine Gun Section received their baptism of fire at Kibongo. Two sections were in action that day, one under the immediate command of Captain Burger and the other under 2nd Lieutenant Heaton. By common consent they did splendid work. Captain Burger's section was mainly responsible for capturing a hill held by and of great importance to the enemy, and they also materially assisted in turning the enemy's flank and in repelling a counter-attack.

Private le Brun (1179) received the Military Medal for good work in this action.

Returning to Morogoro with the battalion in March, 1917, the Machine Gun Section were in like parlous state to them, owing to the ravages of fever. There were not sufficient fit men to man one gun and the porters were in similar plight, and the reorganisation of the whole Section became imperative.

To that end, Captain Burger forfeited a month's leave to South Africa, which had been granted to him. Lieutenant Ivor Guest was posted to the section, but at the time knew nothing about machine gunnery. By dint of great application, however, he so thoroughly mastered the mechanism of the gun in a few weeks that he was of immense assistance to Captain Burger. In two months Captain Burger was able to man twelve guns, an extra four having in the meantime been authorised and allotted to him.

Shortly afterwards Lieutenant Botha and 2nd Lieutenant Howe-Browne were posted to the Section, which rapidly improved in efficiency.

On June 30th, 1917, Sergeants D. J. Brown (9) and D. C. Jacobus (599) were promoted C.S.M. and C.Q.M.S., respectively.

Two sub-sections under Lieutenants Guest and Botha took part in the operations which culminated in the capture of Naumann's force by Lieut.-Colonel Morris, and one sub-section under Second Lieutenant C. F. Abbott (temporarily attached) was "in at the death" of Zingel's party.

Howe-Browne was not with the Section long owing to illness, but at the end of September Second Lieutenants M. S. Davies and F. I. Girdwood arrived from South Africa and joined Captain Burger's command, and from then onwards he had his full complement of officers, viz.: Lieutenants

Photo by] [H. W. Herman, Kimberley.
SERGEANT J. MEYER (1064), M.G. Co.

CAPTAIN F. BURGER,
O.C. Machine Gun Company.

SERGEANT I. W. ARENDSE (607), D.C.M.

A FEW MACHINE GUNNERS.
(Standing): Cpl. Smit, J. (1204); Pte. Carelse, C. (688); L.-Cpl. I. W. Arendse (607). (Sitting): L.-Cpl. Johnston, A. (2893); Pte. Felix, C. (1670).

Guest and Botha, 2nd Lieutenants Davies and Girdwood. A keener set of machine gunners would have been hard to find in East Africa than the four just named, and the Section made rapid strides in consequence.

During the operations in the Lindi area in November, 1917, the machine gunners were in action daily for a fortnight and emerged from the ordeal with great credit.

On November 6th, at Mkungu, Guest and three men were killed on one gun, and on the same day Botha and Girdwood were wounded. Guest's death was a great blow to Captain Burger and his men. By his untiring energy and zeal he set a splendid example.

On November 8th, when the battalion made a most successful flanking attack (*vide* page 151), the machine gunners did fine work and especially the sub-section under Davies, which kept pace with the Infantry and got into action simultaneously with them.

On that afternoon a machine gun porter, armed only with a panga (bush knife) chased and captured an armed enemy Askari. For that feat he received a monetary award and was presented by the Brigadier (General O'Grady) with a captured sword. Alas! this sword, of which he was inordinately proud, was stolen from him a few days afterwards.

Girdwood was wounded a second time on the Makonde Plateau (November 16th), but meanwhile Second Lieutenants E. W. Templer and C. A. Vipan (from S.A.I.) had been posted to the Section to replace casualties (Guest and Botha). When Botha returned to duty Vipan was transferred to company strength, but Templer remained with the Section until demobilisation. He immediately gained the confidence of his men and did excellent work during the continuation of the Lindi operations.

At Massassi, on the eve of the departure of the battalion from East Africa, the guns of the Machine Gun section were handed over to the K.A.R. One of the guns had been presented with twenty-seven others to the Imperial Government in 1901, by the State of Guernsey. That particular gun was temporarily put out of action one night on the Makonde plateau—the fusee-spring box being damaged. A letter informing the State of Guernsey of the fact was despatched to the Secretary to the Dominion. It was read to the State in session and evoked much interest. Captain Burger received a request that the damaged box might be sent to the State as a souvenir, and that was duly done.

The value of discipline and training was very forcibly illustrated by the conduct of the machine gun porters in East Africa. Captain Burger from the first was at pains to impress upon them the fact that they were Askari (soldiers), not labourers. They were drilled and treated as soldiers. The result was that in the Lindi operations their discipline, conduct, and bravery in the firing line was beyond praise. Under heavy fire they carried their guns into action, returned with empty belts and brought up reserve ammunition without flinching. Their only complaint was that the Cape Corps always wanted to fight and never gave them enough time to prepare their " Chakula " (food). Their grief was great when they finally had to part with their " Bwana umkuba " (big chief) (Captain Burger) at Lindi before our final departure from East Africa.

On the return of the battalion to South Africa in December, 1917, the Union Defence Department were in communication with the War Office with reference to the Machine Gun Section. The result was the authorisation of a provisional establishment of a Half Machine Gun Company and a Reserve Section.

This Half Company consisted of seventy-seven of all ranks, the officers being Captain F. Burger (commanding), Lieutenant D. F. Botha, and 2nd Lieutenants M. S. Davies, F. I. Girdwood and E. W. Templer.

THE STORY OF THE 1st CAPE CORPS.

From Kimberley, in February, 1918, the Half Company went to the gunnery school at Potchefstroom for a refresher course. At the conclusion of the course the majority of the men were classified as first class gunners and the instructors expressed the opinion that they were quite equal to the best of the European troops who had passed through their hands.

The Half Company was inspected prior to leaving Potchefstroom by Colonel Grant, Commandant of the Camp, who told them that they were the smartest turned out body of men he had inspected during his two years of duty at Potchefstroom.

The men's conduct had been such as to remove the prejudice which still existed at Potchefstroom and elsewhere against coloured troops, and there was no friction whatever with the European staff.

On April 3rd, the Half Company embarked at Durban with the battalion for Egypt.

Lieutenants B. H. Moin and H. Wallis, M.C., remained at Kimberley with the Reserve Half Battalion in order to train and bring forward the Machine Gun Reserve Section.

On arrival in Egypt the existence of the Half Machine Gun Company surprised the authorities there as there was no such other establishment in the Imperial Forces.

The guns issued to Captain Burger in Egypt were Vickers, of which his men had no previous knowledge. With their wonted keenness, however, they soon mastered the intricacies of the weapon, and when Lieut.-Colonel Pardoe, G.S.O., P. L. of C. inspected the Half Company at El Arish in June, 1918, he was astonished at the men's knowledge of a new gun. He reported that the Cape Corps machine gunners were quite fit to belong to the Machine Gun Corps and orders were received for the Half Company to be attached thereto at once for further training, and that they would eventually be increased to a full Company.

Captain Burger was then sent to the Imperial School of Instruction (M.G. wing) at Zeitoun (Cairo) where he passed two courses and received flattering reports from the O.C. School. The courses were:—
   (1) Tactical combination in action of all arms;
   (2) Combined course, Tactical and Technical handling of machine guns comprising topography, map and compass reading, etc.

After Captain Burger's return from the school all his officers in turn attended courses there to their own advantage and considerable benefit to the Half Company.

In August, 1918, by order of G.H.Q., E.E.F., the Cape Corps Machine Gun Company came into being. Special authority for the establishment of the Company was issued, the same to consist of a Headquarters and two sections of four guns each.

Headquarters consisted of one officer, one warrant officer, two sergeants and twenty-four other ranks. Each section of two officers, two sergeants and thirty-two other ranks. Total five officers, one warrant officer, six sergeants and eighty-eight other ranks, or in all exactly one hundred. A complete equipment of transport proportionate to the establishment was also authorised. (In detail: six officers' chargers, thirty draught horses, six wagons, L.G.S., one cooks' cart and one water cart).

On August 12th, Lieutenants Moin and Wallis and the Reserve Section arrived at El Arish from South Africa with the Cape Corps Reserve Half Battalion..

The Machine Gun Company at 'Sidi Bishr.

THE STORY OF THE 1st CAPE CORPS

Photo by [B. H. Moin.
RESERVE MACHINE GUNNERS AT EL ARISH, SEPTEMBER, 1918.

MACHINE GUNNERS TRAINING AT EL ARISH.
Captain Burger (standing) directing

Photo by [E. W. Templer.
53RD DIVISION MACHINE GUN BATTALION AT BEITUNIA, PALESTINE, SEPTEMBER, 1918. CAPE CORPS MACHINE GUN COMPANY NEAREST THE ROAD.

Photo by [B. H. Moin.
MACHINE GUN COMPANY'S CAMP AT EL ARISH, SEPTEMBER, 1918.

THE STORY OF THE 1st CAPE CORPS.

The Machine Gun Company were to have followed the battalion to the front as soon as their training was completed, but an outbreak of influenza supervened, and it was not until nearly two months after the battalion had gone forward that Captain Burger and his men were able to leave El Arish.

At Rham Alla, Captain Burger reported to the 53rd Battalion Machine Gun Corps (XXth Corps) commanded by Lieut.-Colonel Partridge, D.S.O., and were placed in Divisional Reserve during the operations 18/20 September.

A promise was made that the Company should, if possible, support the battalion in action, but, as recorded in a previous chapter, the latter did not engage the enemy after September 20th, and the opportunity was consequently not forthcoming. This was a great disappointment to all ranks of both the battalion and the Machine Gun Company.

After the termination of hostilities on the Palestine front the Company returned to Egypt with the 53rd Machine Gun Battalion, and continued to do duty with them.

Later, when orders were received to repatriate the 1st Cape Corps, Captain Burger and his men rejoined the battalion and the Company returned to South Africa with them in August, 1919.

Captain Burger himself returned to South Africa via the United Kingdom. Lieutenants Davies and Girdwood returned with their men, and Lieutenants Botha and Templer remained in Egypt on duty with the Army of Occupation.

Whilst at El Arish information was received of the award of the D.C.M. for services rendered in East Africa to C.S.M. Brown, D. J. (9), Corporal (later Sergeant) Arendse, I. W. (607) and Private (later Sergeant) Carelse, C. (688).

Sergeant Samuels, W. S. (504) did splendid work with the Machine Gun Section in East Africa in looking after and drilling the porters and controlling them when in action.

During practically the whole period of its existence, from the time of arrival in East Africa to its departure from Egypt, Captain F. Burger was identified with the Cape Corps Machine Gun Section (later half company and company) and was responsible for its efficiency. He did most thorough and conscientious work throughout and was mentioned in General Allenby's final despatch "for gallant and distinguished conduct during the war."

Photo by] [Scallan, Cape Town.
C.S.M. D. J. BROWN (9).

SERGEANT C. I. MILLER (126), M.G. COMPANY.

THE STORY OF THE 1st CAPE CORPS.

Photo by] [*Sydney Taylor, Cape Town.*
MAJOR W. P. ANDERSON.
O.C. Cape Corps Depôts in South Africa, 1st November, 1916, to 11th August, 1918.

CHAPTER XIX.

THE REGIMENTAL DEPÔTS IN SOUTH AFRICA. PERIOD 9TH FEBRUARY, 1916, TO DECEMBER, 1918.—(1) SIMONSTOWN, 9TH FEBRUARY, 1916, TO 31ST JULY, 1916. (2) WOLTEMADE III., 1ST AUGUST, 1916, TO 13TH DECEMBER, 1917. (3) KIMBERLEY, 15TH DECEMBER, 1917, TO 12TH DECEMBER, 1918.

WHEN the battalion embarked for East Africa on the 9th February, 1916, Captain C. E. Stevens was left in command of the Depôt at Simonstown. With him were Lieutenant Alexander, and 2nd Lieutenants Rackstraw and Wilson and approximately three hundred other ranks and a staff of some dozen instructors under Sergt.-Major Windrum.

Training was continued on exactly the same lines and syllabus as prior to the battalion's departure. Recruiting had been suspended for the time being.

During the period from March to June drafts were sent forward to the battalion in East Africa as follows:—

In March: Lieutenants Alexander and Wilson with two platoons.
In April: Lieutenant Rackstraw with a platoon.
In June: Lieutenant H. S. Bell with a platoon.
(Lieutenant Bell had joined at Simonstown early in April.)

Major-General Thompson and Lieut.-Colonel Finch continued to take the same interest in the training of the men as they had done from the inception of the battalion and were frequent visitors to the Depôt at Simonstown and later on at Woltemade.

The D.O.R.E. at Simonstown rendered great assistance with the training and instructed the officers in entrenching, bridge-building and field engineering generally.

About the middle of June, the Loyal North Lancashire Regiment arrived at Simonstown for a period of rest and recuperation after a long spell in East Africa. They took over the portion of our site above the main road and our camp was moved to vacant ground below the road. The C.O. Loyal North Lancs. at once interested himself in our training and detailed several of his most experienced N.C.O.'s to assist our instructional staff.

At that time H.M.S. "Kent" was stationed at Simonstown and Commander Bedford took the greatest possible interest in the work of the depôt. He presented to Captain Stevens, for the Depôt, a flag which had been flown from his ship in the battle of the Falkland Islands and sent his ship's band to play Lieutenant Bell's platoon from the camp to the station when they left for East Africa.

European Staff Sergeants Wilkes (1443) and Akehurst (1438) reported for duty at the Depôt in June. Both these men went forward to East Africa with Lieutenant Bell's draft.

At the end of June, Major Durham arrived from East Africa to assume command at the Depôt.

Staff Sergeant A. A. Hayton was promoted Second Lieutenant on July 1st and was appointed Depôt Adjutant and Quartermaster.

On or about July 21st, Captain Stevens left for East Africa with a platoon.

THE STORY OF THE 1st CAPE CORPS.

Flag Presentation, Cape Town, October 12th, 1916. The March Past. Brig-General Cavendish, C.M.G., takes the salute supported by the Mayor.

Flag Presentation by the Mayor of Cape Town (Councillor Harry Hands), Cape Town, October 12th, 1916.

Flag Presentation by the Mayor of Cape Town (H. Hands, Esq.), 12th October, 1916. Major Durham with back to camera. Lieutenant James with Colours Guard.

Flag Presentation, Cape Town, October 12th, 1916. Inspection by Brig.-General Cavendish, G.O.C. South Africa.

THE STORY OF THE 1st CAPE CORPS

On Saturday, August 1st, the Depôt was transferred from Simonstown to Woltemade III. This move was sanctioned by the authorities as the result of representations made by Major Durham that a great deal of time was being lost and training delayed by the necessity of sending the men all the way to Woltemade for their musketry courses.

In the Depôt at the time were some fifty trained men and approximately two hundred recruits. A special train took all ranks to Woltemade which was reached at noon. In five hours the ground had been levelled and the new camp pitched.

On Monday, August 3rd, a new recruiting campaign was commenced throughout the Union. This was urgently necessary in view of reports received of the heavy toll fever and dysentery were taking of the battalion's ranks in East Africa.

Major Durham, in addition to his duties at O.C. Depôt, became also Chief Recruiting Officer at Cape Town. He was assisted by Lieutenant Hallier, who had been invalided from East Africa, and by Lieutenant L. C. Johnson (Records Officer.) On the day that the new campaign opened Lieutenant Hayton was sent on a route march through Cape Town with one hundred men in order to stimulate recruiting.

A few days after the move from Simonstown to Woltemade Captain Lawrence, S.A.M.C., was detailed from the Alexandra Hospital, Maitland, to act as Depôt Medical Officer with a medical personnel of one staff sergeant and two privates.

During the month of August, the following gentlemen were gazetted to commissions in the 1st Cape Corps, viz.:—

Major W. Jardine (A.C.F.) to be Captain 1st Cape Corps; Gordon C. White, Esq., to be Captain 1st Cape Corps; Lieutenant M. Potgieter and Messrs. H. Coates and T. E. James to be Lieutenants 1st Cape Corps; and Messrs. G. W. de Villiers, R. Feetham, M.L.A., I. A. M. Guest, A. Leslie, H. R. Thornton, and Sergeant W. S. Heaton (Loyal North Lancashire Regiment) to be Second Lieutenants.

The recruiting campaign proved an unqualified success and within two months fifteen hundred men had been duly attested. The training of these men of course involved much overtime work by all the officers and instructional staff. Of the latter, Staff Sergeants Salida, MacKenzie and Hopkins did especially good work.

Splendid progress was made and by the end of October over one thousand of the men had been formed into four companies, viz., "E," "F," "G" and Depôt Companies, and were sufficiently advanced to be ready for drafting.

Meanwhile Lieutenant Hallier had gone forward with a platoon in September and 2nd Lieutenant Heaton with another in October.

In October the Mayor of Cape Town received for presentation to the battalion a regimental colour which had been worked by the ladies of Boksburg (Transvaal) as a compliment to the Officer Commanding (Lieut.-Colonel Morris) who was a resident of Boksburg at the outbreak of war. This flag was presented to Major Durham—who accepted it on behalf of Lieut.-Colonel Morris and men of the battalion—by the then Mayor of Cape Town (Councillor Harry Hands, Esq.) on the Grand Parade, Cape Town, on October 12th, 1916. This event was made the occasion for a grand ceremonial parade of all officers and all more or less fully trained men in the depôt (about nine hundred). The officers on parade were Major Durham (in command); Captains Jardine and White and Lieutenant Leslie (company commanders); Lieutenants de Villiers, Feetham, Guest, Hayton, James, Potgieter and Thornton.

THE STORY OF THE 1st CAPE CORPS.

Prior to the presentation the parade was inspected by Brig.-General Cavendish, C.M.G., G.O.C., South African Military Command, who was accompanied by his staff and the senior officers of the garrison.

The Mayor, in making the presentation, said that the flag had been worked by the Women's War Fund Committee of Boksburg and was presented by them as a compliment to Lieut.-Colonel Morris and several other officers of the regiment who were Boksburg residents, and as a token of their interest in the battalion and as a mark of their appreciation of the services the men were giving on their behalf and on behalf of South Africa and the Empire.

Mr. Hands also said he was sure that he was expressing the feelings of the residents of Boksburg, as he was his own and those of the citizens of Cape Town, in saying that wherever they were called upon to serve he knew the men of the battalion would strive to uphold the traditions of the old Colony and add fresh laurels to those which had been won by the Cape Corps in this war and by the old Cape coloured regiment in the past.

Lieutenant James with the Colour Guard then advanced to receive the flag and with it marched back to the battalion where it was received with "the present" and the National Anthem. The battalion then marched past General Cavendish.

The *Cape Times* described the flag presentation as "a most impressive and successful function," and stated that "the men gave an excellent display of marching with precision" .... "The handling of this body of men reflected the greatest credit on all concerned and the whole of the movements executed on the Parade can only be described as a wonderful exhibition."

After the presentation the Mayor entertained the officers at the City Hall and the Cape Corps Gifts and Comforts Committee fêted the men.

Shortly after the flag presentation, when there were some twelve hundred men in camp, twenty-four hours' notice was given for the removal of the Depôt to Sir Lowry Pass, but within a few hours that order was cancelled, and it was intimated that one thousand men would proceed from Woltemade to East Africa at an early date to reinforce the battalion in the field.

On October 31st, Captain W. P. Anderson arrived from East Africa in order to take command at the Depôt and to relieve Major Durham who was to take forward the men he had trained. With Anderson came Captain Cuningham to take command of one of Durham's companies and go forward with it.

Captain Anderson took over the partially trained men (some three hundred and fifty) and the Depôt and instructional staff, whilst Major Durham commanded the four companies of trained men.

On November 25th, Durham left for Durban with the following officers, viz.: Captains Cuningham, Jardine and White; Lieutenant Guest; Second Lieutenants Coates, Feetham, Hayton, James, Leslie, Potgieter and Thornton and one thousand and fifty rank and file in three special trains.

At Durban the troop trains were drawn up alongside the troopship H.M.T. "Miltiades," which left, as soon as embarkation was completed, for Dar-es-Salaam (November 28th).

During the period that Major Durham was O.C. Depôt he was greatly assisted by Lieutenant Hayton who worked night and day in the dual rôle of Depôt Adjutant and Quartermaster.

When Captain Anderson took over he had only one officer, Second Lieutenant de Villiers, to assist him run the Depôt, in which there remained after the departure of Major Durham's draft, some three hundred and fifty partially trained recruits.

The day after Durham left, Anderson, who still suffered much from malaria, was removed unconscious to Wynberg Hospital and 2nd Lieutenant de Villiers, then quite inexperienced, was left alone to run the Depôt. When Anderson returned from Hospital three weeks later he found that de Villiers had done splendid work, and there was much to be done after the departure of over a thousand men, in straightening up the camp, the records, Quartermaster's stores, etc.

De Villiers had organised a staff which may have been inexperienced, but was at least more than willing. Sergeant Lakey, S. F. (105) and Privates Adriaanse, A. (1194), Arendse, S. I. (1002), and Smith tackled the clerical and stores work with great energy and application and the instructional staff had continued their yeoman work, particularly Sergt.-Major Windrum and Staff Sergeants Salida, Hopkins and MacKenzie.

Some of the other instructors were not satisfactory, and as the authorities were not able to replace them by better men, Captain Anderson decided to organise a coloured instructional staff. For that purpose he selected a number of the most capable N.C.O.'s who had been invalided from East Africa and had reported at the Depôt from hospitals and convalescent camps. These men were given three weeks' special instruction by Sergt.-Major Windrum and at the end of that time were passed as qualified to instruct, and set to work.

This experiment proved so great a success that Captain Anderson was able to get rid of all the European instructors except Windrum, Salida, Hopkins and MacKenzie. Coloured instructors who became most efficient were Sergeants Andrews (3034), Wilkinson (1253), Peters (1604), Paul (3575), Paulse (625), Sass (3772), and Benjamin (164). The first three named became first-class and did invaluable work.

After Lieutenant Hayton's departure for East Africa there was no Depôt Quartermaster for some weeks, but eventually Anderson's urgent representations resulted in the appointment of Captain A. R. Noble by the Union Defence Department.

By March, 1917, Captain Anderson had got everything in the Depôt running smoothly and instruction proceeding apace, and he was accordingly authorised to recruit another five hundred men. A certain number of these recruits came from all over the Union, but by far the larger proportion were attested at the City Hall, Cape Town, by Lieutenant L. C. Johnson (Records Officer). As time was not so all-important as it had been during the previous recruiting campaign Mr. Johnson was able to exercise great care in selection and only the best type of man was enrolled.

During the early months of 1917, large numbers of men of the regiment who had been invalided from East Africa reported at the Depôt from hospital and also several officers from hospital and leave.

Towards the end of May, Major Cowell and eight other officers and five hundred and eighty-five men left the depôt for East Africa. All the officers and two hundred and thirty-three of the men had been in East Africa, the balance were recruits going forward.

At the end of May, Generals Cavendish (G.O.C., South African Military Command) and Hunter and their staffs paid a visit of inspection to the Depôt, accompanied by Lieut.-Colonel Morris, who was then on leave from East Africa. They spent some time in camp watching the training in progress and conversing with the recruits, and expressed entire satisfaction with the work which was being carried on.

In May the formation of a 2nd Cape Corps Battalion had been authorised, and early in June Captain Anderson was instructed to recruit five hundred men for that unit. These men were drafted into the Depôt and their initial training undertaken by Captain Anderson. That he had no difficulty in doing, as Sergt.-Major Windrum's staff of coloured instructors had been increased and also become thoroughly efficient.

THE STORY OF THE 1st CAPE CORPS.

Photo by]   *[Carl Adams, Cape Town.*
SERGEANT A. ADRIAANSE (1194).

Photo by]   *[J. G. Horsfall, Cape Town.*
SERGEANT M. J. ABRAHAMSE (318) AND
SERGEANT H. HEBER (145).

Photo by]   *[H. W. Herman, Kimberley.*
SERGEANT A. S. PARKINS (3179).

AN OFFICER'S BATH ON THE FIELD (SOMETIMES).

THE STORY OF THE 1st CAPE CORPS.

Lieut.-Colonel Flindt was appointed first C.O. 2nd Battalion, but was released from service after a few weeks duty, and handed over the command to Lieut.-Colonel J. G. B. Clayton, M.C.

Simultaneously with the latter appointment Captain Anderson was ordered to recruit another five hundred men for the 2nd battalion. That was very soon done, and no sooner were these men handed over to Lieut.-Colonel Clayton than authority was received to recruit five hundred men for the Cape Coloured Labour Corps then under the command of Lieut.-Colonel Vollie van der Byl in France.

About the same time Woltemade III also became the depôt for details of the Cape Auxiliary Horse Transport Corps then serving in France.

The 1st Cape Corps Depôt had, therefore, become a general Depôt for all South African coloured units, and there were at the end of July, 1917, over two thousand men under canvas at Woltemade. To handle that large number of men Captain Anderson had, excepting medical personnel, only two officers (Captain Noble and Lieutenant de Villiers) and three European instructors (Windrum, MacKenzie and Salida). The work devolving upon that small European staff demanded herculean labour from every one of them. Fortunately for them they received occasional assistance from officers reporting at the Depôt from hospital and leave whilst waiting to return to East Africa. The administrative and clerical work could not possibly have been efficiently performed by so small a number of Europeans had not the coloured men proved equal to rendering much capable assistance as clerks, instructors, and assistants to the Quartermaster. Numbers of the men did most valuable work. They took pride and interest in their duties and very soon became thoroughly competent and trustworthy.

Early in 1917 such large numbers of the 1st Battalion had been invalided from East Africa that a wing of the Alexandra hospital at Maitland had to be set apart for their reception, and there were at times as many as a thousand men there. These men received the greatest care and attention from the medical and nursing staffs. The Cape Corps Gifts and Comforts Committee arranged frequent concerts, entertainments and outings for the patients, who, when convalescent, were allowed out frequently on pass so that their lot under all the circumstances was not altogether unenviable.

About the end of July the following officers who had been gazetted to the 1st Battalion reported at the Depôt, viz.: Second Lieutenants E. B. Bloxam, J. S. Dreyer, M. S. Davies, F. I. Girdwood, E. Rose-Nel and G. L. Ware.

On August 24th, Captains Difford and Cuningham, who had been in hospital, left the Depôt to return to East Africa. Cuningham took with him the six new officers just above named, three officers ex hospital (Captain Murchie, and Lieutenants Wigman and Bourhill) and three hundred men, some of whom were old hand returning after sick leave, and other recruits.

At the end of August, 1917, the total strength of the 1st Cape Corps was approximately four thousand, distributed roughly as follows:—
    One thousand five hundred in the field in East Africa.
    One thousand in the Depôt in South Africa.
    One thousand in hospital.
    Five hundred on leave.

Early in December, 1917, orders were received that the Depôt was to be transferred to Kimberley, where the Cape Auxiliary Horse Transport Depôt had been moved some months previously.

During the whole period that our Depôt had been in the Cape Peninsula (February, 1916 to December, 1917) great assistance was rendered to the various officers in command at the Depôt by the majority of the senior staff officers of the garrison, both Imperial and U.D.F. The great interest taken in the Corps and the practical assistance rendered by Major-General Thompson and Lieut.-Colonel Finch have already been referred to.

Others who did all they could to advance the interests of the Corps were Lieut.-Colonel Fowle (D.A.G. The Castle), Lieut.-Colonel G. Hodgson (District Staff Officer, U.D.F.) and Lieut.-Colonel C. Gutsche, C.G.A. (O.C. Table Bay Defences).

The move to Kimberley was completed on 15th December, on which date all officers and men were established in No. 3 Compound, Kimberley, which had been kindly placed at the disposal of the Union Defence Department by the directors of De Beers Consolidated Mines, Ltd.

At the same time all patients at Alexandra Hospital, Maitland, were transferred to No. 5 General Hospital, Kimberley.

The advent of such a large body of coloured troops was obviously not to the liking of a certain section of the inhabitants of Kimberley, and a certain amount of trouble and disorder occurred during the Christmas holidays. Fortunately, strong handling of the situation by Major Anderson, and later on by Lieut.-Colonel Hoy, very soon restored order and tranquility. Mr. G. J. Boyes, the Resident Magistrate, and some of the more influential inhabitants of the Diamond Fields, notably the Bishop of Kimberley, the Mayor (Mr. Orr) and the Chairman of the Recruiting Committee (Mr. K. C. Elliott) lent valuable aid in calming the hooligan element in the town. The finding of the official enquiry, held by Brig.-General Collyer, who came down from Pretoria for the purpose, was that the 1st Cape Corps were in no way to blame for what had occurred.

Officers and men who did valuable work in keeping the men in order during this trouble were Lieutenant Lynch (2nd Cape Corps), Sergt.-Major Ruiters (132), Sergeant Adriaanse (1194), and Privates A. Jaftha (725) and Marthinus, S. (1014). (*Vide* also page 169.)

Major Anderson had only just got the Depôt at Kimberley into something like working order when the 1st battalion returned from East Africa. The first draft of three hundred reached Kimberley, under Captain Tandy, on December 29th, 1917, and during February and March nearly a thousand more arrived at Kimberley on return from the month's leave granted to them after they had passed through the convalescent camps at Potchefstroom and Jacob's Camp (Durban). (*Vide* Chapter XIII.)

All these men on return to Kimberley were taken on Depôt strength and then re-transferred to the 1st Battalion, which was busy mobilising for further oversea service (Egypt).

Major Anderson went on a month's leave in February, 1918, and during his absence Major Cowell assumed temporary command of the Depôt.

In March the 1st Cape Corps Reserve Half Battalion was formed and drew on the depôt for its required establishment (eighteen officers and four hundred and seventy-three other ranks).

The 1st Battalion left Kimberley for Egypt on March 31st, and the Reserve Half Battalion on June 22nd. With the departure of the latter only two or three hundred men remained in the Depôt, but numbers continued to rejoin daily for some weeks on discharge from hospital at Kimberley. Recruiting and training continued unabated, as it was expected that large drafts would be required by the battalion in Egypt.

When Major Anderson returned from leave he found that during his absence and without his knowledge or consent he had been transferred to the U.D.F. He at once pointed out that he had no desire to be or to remain an officer of the U.D.F. and requested his immediate re-transfer to the Cape

THE STORY OF THE 1st CAPE CORPS.

Corps. On August 1st, after four and a half months persistence, he succeeded in getting back to his regiment, but to do so had to revert to Captain's rank, his place in the battalion having been filled.

Lieutenant G. W. de Villiers, Depôt Adjutant, was also transferred from 1st Cape Corps to the U.D.F. (on February 14th).

After his return to the regiment Captain Anderson continued to be O.C. Depôt until 11th August, 1918, when he handed over to Major Ralph Morkel (U.D.F.) and left for Egypt with a draft of eleven officers and seven hundred and twenty-five other ranks. The officers were Lieutenants Hillary, Johnson, van Diggelen, and Reunert, Second Lieutenants Adamson, D. F. H. Buchanan, Louw, Macfarlane, Hall, Wheelwright and Brown. (At Durban Second Lieutenant Whitfield joined the draft and fourteen men were left in hospital).

Shortly after Anderson's departure for Egypt Lieutenant G. W. de Villiers applied for his release and left the Depôt on September 20th. De Villiers had been Adjutant and the O.C.'s right hand man at the Depôt for close on two years, during which time he had put in an immense amount of loyal hard work.

Captain J. Nel (U.D.F.) took De Villiers place as Depôt Adjutant.

Shortly before the Depôt closed Captain C. W. Smuts (U.D.F.) took over command of the Depôt from Major Morkel.

In October, 1918, the influenza epidemic which ravaged South Africa at that time wrought great havoc in the Depôt at Kimberley. Matters became so bad that the Depôt had to be closed for a time and the men sent on leave to their homes.

During the epidemic two officers and one hundred and fifty-eight men died at Kimberley.

The Officers were Lieutenants W. R. Smith and H. A. Rainier. Captain A. R. Noble and Lieutenants Pickering and H. Feinhols of the U.D.F. Camp Staff also died of influenza.

During the time that Major Anderson was in command of the Depôt at Kimberley he received great assistance and support from Lieut.-Colonel A. J. Taylor, C.M.G., D.S.O., O.C. troops, Kimberley district, and from the latter's successor Major Prins, M.C.

Colonel McKenzie (A.D.M.S.) and the medical staff at the Kimberley Hospital, viz.: Colonel Orford and Captains Wilkinson and Davis (Adjutant), did everything that was possible for the care and comfort of the large number of invalids who passed through their hands.

Others who took a great interest in the welfare of the men in the Depôt and assisted Major Anderson in every possible way were Colonel Sir David Harris, K.C.M.G., and Mr. K. C. Elliott, Chairman of the Recruiting Committee.

The Cape Corps Gifts and Comforts Committee at Kimberley were not less indefatigable than their colleagues at Cape Town had been in looking after the men and entertaining them. Messrs. Tobin, Jaftha, McLeod and Sass were always particularly to the fore in this connection.

The signing of the Armistice on November 11th, 1918, brought the *raison d'etre* of the Depôt to an end. The men on leave owing to the influenza epidemic were accordingly recalled and every man was demobilised as soon as possible and the Depôt finally closed on 12th December, 1918.

The Depôt had been in existence from first to last for close on four years, during which time over six thousand men of the 1st Cape Corps alone had passed in and out. Including the 2nd Cape Corps, the Cape Horse Auxiliary Transport Corps, and Cape Labour Corps, the figures were nearly ten thousand. Only those behind the scenes were aware of the immense amount of hard work which devolved upon the O.C. Depôt and his staff.

THE STORY OF THE 1st CAPE CORPS.

The splendid reputation made by the 1st Battalion Cape Corps in the field was due in very large measure to the loyal and energetic efforts of Major Anderson and the officers and N.C.O.'s on his staff.

Mention has been made of the hard work done in the earlier stages by Lieutenant Hayton and also of the good service of Lieutenant G. W. de Villiers, Sergt.-Major Windrum and Staff Sergeant Instructors Salida, Hopkins and MacKenzie. Others whose efficient work contributed in no small degree to the smooth working of the Depôt were: Captain A. R. Noble (U.D.F.) Depôt Quartermaster for nearly two years until his death from influenza on October 8th, 1918; Lieutenant L. C. Johnson (U.D.F.) Records Officer from 8th January, 1916, until his transfer to the Cape Corps and departure for Egypt (11th August, 1918); Second Lieutenant H. Feinhols (U.D.F.) who was appointed a Staff Sergeant when European N.C.O.'s were authorised for clerical work in the Depôt. He worked like a Trojan and was most painstaking. Feinhols received his commission early in September, 1918, and died of influenza a month later.

Sergt.-Major Cook (U.D.F.). This Warrant Officer was sent to Kimberley from the S.A.M.R. to be Camp Sergt.-Major at the Depôt. He carried out his duties in a most capable manner, as did the Depôt Q.M.S. R. H. Cannell and Staff Sergeants C. A. Johnson and Cryer.

The following officers of the S.A. Medical Corps did duty at the Depôt at different times, viz.: Major Ellis, Captains Hertzlet, Lawrence and Mason; all of whom deserve the sincere and grateful thanks of all officers and men who passed through their hands for the care, consideration, and satisfactory treatment bestowed upon them.

MEN OF MAJOR DURHAM'S DRAFT LEAVING WOLTE-
MADE III. FOR EAST AFRICA, NOVEMBER, 1916.

THE STORY OF THE 1st CAPE CORPS.

This chapter may well be closed with a quotation from a sub-leader which appeared in the *Cape Times* on October 13th, 1916, the day after the flag presentation recorded in this chapter:—

> "Major Durham and the officers of the Cape Corps are to be congratulated on the splendid appearance of the regiment yesterday afternoon on the occasion of the presentation of colours. We have had occasion in the past to refer to the good work of the regiment in East Africa, where the men have given evidence of their high efficiency in many capacities. Thus an officer who has had opportunity of observing them under many conditions in the field wrote quite recently: 'Men have gained honour and glory in the fighting line, but no regiment deserves greater admiration than the Cape Corps for the manner in which they have carried out their work.' Yesterday the public had the opportunity of seeing the newest recruits to the regiment. They have been drilling and training for a very few weeks, yet the general opinion yesterday was that veteran regiments could scarcely have made a better showing upon parade. The explanation is that the men themselves are extraordinarily keen on maintaining the good name the regiment had already earned. They have acquired a sense of *esprit de corps* to a surprising degree. They devote even their hours off duty to drill and military exercises. Moreover, they are thoroughly well officered by men who are as keen as themselves. The discipline has been excellent and the behaviour of the corps in camp beyond reproach. There are sound reasons for believing that the formation of the corps is likely to have a permanent and a very important influence in improving the general moral of the community from which it has been recruited."

That was independent impartial testimony in October, 1916, and subsequent reference to the files of the *Cape Times* and other journals of standing, at different times during 1917 and 1918, would clearly indicate that the views then expressed held good to the end.

FLAG PRESENTATION, OCTOBER 12TH, 1916, GRAND PARADE, CAPE TOWN.
"THE PRESENT."

CHAPTER XX.

SPORTS AND ATHLETICS, ETC.

THE Anglo-Saxon passion for athletics and field games and sports of all kinds was admitted by all the world to have been a material, if not indeed the vital, factor in the success of the British Armies in the Great World War. The valuable lessons learned on the playing fields of the Empire stood the Imperial Navy and Armies in great and powerful stead on many a terrible day in the mud of Flanders, in the sands and heat of Egypt, Palestine, and Mesopotamia and in the fever stricken swamps of East Africa and elsewhere, and in a lesser degree all our Allies owed their success more or less to the fact that during the years immediately prior to 1914 practically the whole civilised world had come to see the virtue of games and physical exercises of every kind and had fostered and encouraged them in every possible way.

As the War progressed and developed it was more and more recognised and admitted everywhere that robust and vigorous sports and pastimes were the best possible peace time training for the man who would provide the fighting strength of a nation in time of war.

Since the Armistice evidence has been forthcoming from all quarters that the value of and the desirability of encouraging games and field sports of all kinds has received world wide acknowledgement as a result of the experience of the previous four terrible years.

That is a fact on which the whole world may be congratulated, and the British Empire, as the Pioneers, in particular.

For some time prior to 1914 some were found to say that too much time was devoted in Britain, in particular, and in the Empire in general, to sports and athletics.

It is unlikely that much of that sort of nonsense will be heard again during the next generation or two.

Young men and maidens will be able to indulge in, and old men and women support and encourage out-door sport and games to the utmost limit of their capacity and their leisure without fear of cavil or carping criticism. For that let us be truly thankful.

During the actual progress of the War, however, a comparatively small proportion of the contestants had much time to participate in games or athletic recreations.

For the major portion of their three years and ten months' service as a unit the Cape Corps certainly had to leave such pleasures severely alone. After the Armistice, however, during the nine months spent in Egypt, before returning to South Africa, Officers and men had ample opportunity to indulge in cricket, football, athletics, etc., and in competitions with other Units of the E.E.F. greatly distinguished themselves.

During the mobilisation period at Simonstown (October, 1915 to February, 1916) the men had no time at all for games, but several of the Officers took part in a few cricket matches, at Newlands, Army vs. Civilians, and so on, and Captain Pearse played two or three times with success for the Western Province Cricket Club.

In a match at Simonstown for the Military against the troopship "Orbita" five officers played and all scored over 20, Major Hoy leading with 63, and Captain Difford took six wickets.

During twenty-two months in East Africa twice only did opportunity occur to participate in games.

At Morogoro on October 21st, 1916—the first anniversary of our mobilisation—an entirely successful all-day sports meeting was held.

The local war sheet, "The Morogoro News," edited by Reuter's representative with General Smuts' Forces, that gifted Pretoria journalist, Mr. Vere Stent, gave a very good account of that enjoyable day which is worth quoting *in extenso* :—

THE CAPE CORPS.

"The first anniversary of the formation of the Cape Corps was celebrated in Morogoro on October the 21st last by the holding of sports. Amongst many well-contested events, the blind boxing proved most popular and caused roars of laughter.

The tug-of-war was a splendid item, a battle royal between the company teams ending in "D" Company coming out as the winner.

An adjournment was made about 12 noon and the visitors were thus given an opportunity to look round. The discipline maintained everywhere was the subject of remark. Musical items were supplied by two talented members of the Corps and the old-time clown caused a deal of fun with his ready wit and lively antics.

A spread for the men and visitors, laid out on the ground, consisted of cakes, jam tarts and tea—not forgetting the Q.M.S.'s water bottle, which was passed to the visitors for inspection. After all wants had been attended to, the visitors selected a shady spot for a siesta.

About 2 p.m. the sports was continued. Amongst the items for the afternoon were guard mounting by squads, drill by squads, and best-dressed N.C.O. It was certainly an eye-opener to the visitors. The squads marched on to the grounds with the perfect bearing of soldiers and their movements were as laid down in the drill book.

In the guard mounting the winning squad was "D" Company "A" Team, and the best drilled squad was "D" Company. The competition was so keenly contested that the judge found it necessary to request extra movements to decide the winners.

The best-dressed N.C.O. was another tough problem for the judge's attention, and he spoke in the highest terms of praise of Sergt.-Major Forsyth and his staff for the manner in which they had paid every attention to detail. The porters' race was keenly contested, a good number taking part. A new feature of those sports was the scramble for coins and cigarettes. Last, but not least, was the Maxim gun competition, in which No. 2 Gun Team were hopelessly outclassed. It was quite apparent that they were young hands at the game.

The final brought forth the Q.M.S.'s water bottle again, which everyone duly appreciated, including the R.S.M. of the Flying Corps.

Another feed of jam tarts and other luxuries, then a tramp back to camp, and to duty, and a thoroughly enjoyable day's outing had drawn itself to a close, leaving in our minds the realisation that the white man's burden rested no longer wholly on his shoulders, that those for whom the burden had been borne were already taking their share of the weight.

THE STORY OF THE 1st CAPE CORPS.

The following is the list of events with results:—

Event	Winner
75 Yards Flat	Sergeant Hutchinson (310).
Reveille Race	Private Jooste (1259).
Guard Mounting	"A" Team ("D" Company).
Passing the Order Race	Signallers (Headquarters).
Best Concealed Sniper	Private Le Grange (473).
Rifle Exercises	"D" Company.
Long Jump	Corporal Adams (48).
Sack Race	Corporal Adams (48).
Putting the Shot	Corporal Adams (48).
Best Turned Out N.C.O. under rank of Sergeant	Corporal Peregrino (1413).
Apple and Bucket Race	Private Cornelius (80).
Blindfold Boxing	Private Fredericks (986) and L.-Corp. Bredekamp (1170).
Machine Guns into Action	Corporal Allison's (647) Team.
Tug-of-War	"D" Company.

Captain J. E. Dennison acted as a capable honorary secretary to the Sports Committee.

The al fresco "smoker" with which the Cape Corps concluded their anniversary celebrations on Saturday, the 21st October, was excellent; and those of us who were privileged to be there thoroughly enjoyed the evening.

Lieut.-Colonel Morris took the chair and the audience basked in the sunshine of his cheery good fellowship.

Lieutenant Edwards presided at the piano. We don't know if his performance was really worth writing home about, but to us the skill and sympathy with which he accompanied singers of all sorts through their meanderings, seemed amazing. With a wriggle of the body, a twisting of the neck and a bending forward of the head, he will change from the sublime to the ridiculous. He provokes tears and drys them up with laughter. Q.M.S. Sasse did not belie his great reputation. His versatility is remarkable. He is a musician, a conjurer, a mimic, a ventriloquist, a magician. No wonder the "Jumbo" suspected witchcraft when rupees were culled from the tail of his shirt. Sasse is a wizard. C.S.M. Calvert has a good refined voice. His parodies were priceless. Private Joseph's sack dance "Vas Traap," or whatever the name of the folk dance is, was greatly appreciated. "Aas Koek" and other cries of satisfaction, encouragement, and delight greeted his efforts. What a treat the girls would have had.

Sergeant Wilkinson is a finished artist. We should have liked to have heard more of him. He outWeldoned Weldon in his rendering of "P.C. 49." Private Thomas rolled quietly on to the platform and after a moment's hesitation gave vent to a great bellow. When we had recovered from our fright, we began to listen and to watch him. No hall could contain him. He is too boisterous. In the open his thunder and lightning efforts are good. He gets his effect by brute force, without, however, the usual concomitant. Like the milkmaid in the song, his face is undoubtedly his fortune. That kind of fortune avails one very little though on active service, and no doubt he welcomed the special prize awarded him by Lieut.-Colonel Morris for the best turn of the evening."

On Easter Monday, 1917, a garrison sports meeting was held at Morogoro in which two or three officers and several men competed. Second Lieutenant A. N. Difford, from scratch, won the open 100 yards.

After our return from East Africa at the end of 1917 the men who were located in the convalescent camp at Jacobs, near Durban, for a few weeks played a couple of games of cricket against the local coloured teams, and at Kimberley in March, 1918, officers and men found very occasional opportunity for cricket and lawn tennis.

On arrival in Egypt, during our first month spent at Kantara on the Suez Canal, cricket and football once a week relieved the routine of intensive training. Kantara was at that time a very big Base camp and boasted a splendid sports ground, with pavilion, tennis courts, and ample room for cricket and football.

On May 13th, 1918, our officers beat the Yeomanry Depôt at cricket by 97 runs. Captain Tandy was in great form with bat and ball.

THE STORY OF THE 1st CAPE CORPS.

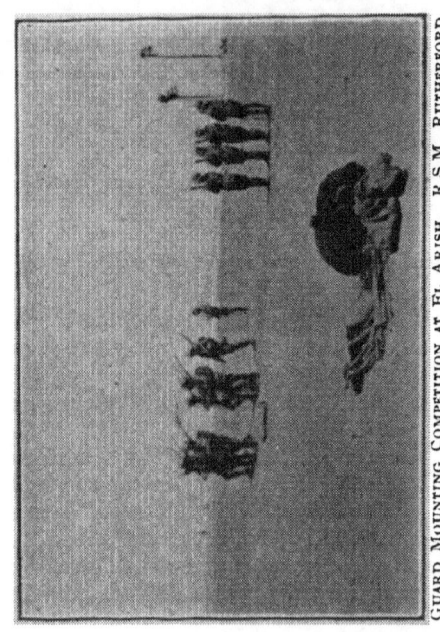

Guard Mounting Competition at El Arish. R.S.M. Rutherford taking notes.

Photo by] [Sergeant Alies.
The Battalion Rugby XV. which beat R.E. at Rondpoint.

[I.D.D.
Photo by] Union Day Sports at El Arish, 1st June, 1918.
Finish of Relay Race.

Photo by] [Sergeant Alies.
Headquarters Rugby XV. at Mustapha.

After we had lost three wickets for 20 (all scored by Gordon White), Tandy and Pearse added 147 in about an hour—Tandy hit 3 sixes and 9 fours and Pearse a six and eight fours.

The full scores were:—

1ST CAPE CORPS.	
Capt. D. K. Pearse, c Chorley, b Morgan	67
Lieut. A. N. Difford, c & b Chorley	0
Lieut. S. H. Rose-Innes, b Chorley	0
Lieut. G. C. White, st Taylor, b Chorley	20
Capt. J. H. Tandy, c Paige, b Belshaw	82
Capt. I. D. Difford, b Chorley	13
Lieut. M. S. Davies, b Chorley	2
Capt. J. M. Michau, c & b Chorley	1
Lieut. D. Botha, b Paige	14
Lt.-Colonel C. N. Hoy, not out	16
Lieut. S. V. Samuelson, c Earle, b Morgan	9
Extras	0
Total	224

YEOMANRY BASE DEPOT.	
Lieut. Morgan, c Tandy, b White	54
Pte. Chorley, c & b Samuelson	13
Lieut. Adamson, run out	5
Lieut. Broadbridge, b Samuelson	7
Lieut. Evans, c Pearse, b Tandy	2
Lieut. Paige, b Tandy	9
2nd Lieut. Belshaw, b Tandy	3
Sergt. Taylor, b White	22
Pte. Smith, b White	0
L.-Corpl. Earle, c & b Tandy	11
Lieut. Creery, not out	0
Extras	1
Total	127

For the Yeomanry Depôt Chorley took 6 wickets for 60 runs, Morgan 2 for 46, Paige 1 for 17, and Belshaw 1 for 27. Smith, Earle and Creery also bowled and had 19, 23 and 32 runs scored off them but took no wicket.

For the Cape Corps Tandy took 4 wickets for 43 runs, White 3 for 11, and Samuelson 2 for 33. Pearse also bowled and had 40 runs scored off him but took no wicket.

During our period of training at El Arish (May 22nd to July 14th, 1918) time was found for one or two games of cricket and an all-day sports meeting on June 1st to celebrate Union Day (May 31st). The nursing sisters and practically all the officers and men of other units in the area were our guests that day and expressed themselves as entirely satisfied with a very enjoyable day.

Captain Difford was chairman of the Sports Committee and Lieutenants Colson and Girdwood laid out the sports ground to everyone's satisfaction.

The events and results were:—

Event 1.—GUARD MOUNTING (Teams of 7).
Sergeant Wilkinson, D. (1253).
Private Koopman, F. (2414)
Private Sheldon, E. (967).
Private Lawrence, C. (756).
Private Whiteman, F. (1968).
Private Matawana, P. (400).
Private Basson, J. N. (3438). All "B" Company.

Event 2.—100 YARDS FLAT RACE.
Heat 1.—1, C.S.M. Hutchinson, K. (310), "C" Co.
2, Pte. Carelse, C. (688), Maxims.
Heat 2.—1, Pte. November, P. (1555), "C" Co.
2, Pte. Damons, J. (3593), Maxims.
Heat 3.—1, L.-Corpl. Fitz, J. (3143), "C" Co.
2, Sergt. Adams, A. (48), "B" Co.
FINAL.
1, C.S.M. Hutchinson, K.
2, Pte. Carelse, C.
3, Pte. November, P.

Event 3.—SACK RACE.
Heat 1.—1, Pte. Meas (4012), "A" Co.
2, Pte. Carstens (2739), "A" Co.
3, Pte. Dyason, R. (662) Headquarters.
Heat 2.—1, L.-Corpl. Isaacs, J. (3126), "C" Co.
2, Pte. Wolhuter, G. (1103), Headqrtrs.
3, Pte. Deers, A. (3189), "A" Co.
Heat 3.—1, Pte. Fredericks, A. 3250), "A" Co.
FINAL.
1, Pte. Fredericks, A.
2, L.-Corpl. Isaacs, J.

Event 4.—THREE-LEGGED RACE.
1, Pte. Davids (3823) and Pte. Seibritz 2918), "C" Co.
2, Pte. Oliver (1685) and Pte. Cottle (4383) "A" Co.

Event 5.—LONG JUMP.
1, L.-Corpl. May, F. (3416), "B" Co., 15 ft. 4 ins.
2, L.-Corpl. Fitz, J. (3143) "C" Co., 14 ft. 7 ins.
3, L.-Corpl. Mintoor, D. (807), "B" Co.

Event 6.—220 YARDS FLAT RACE.
Heat 1.—1, Pte. Carelse, C. (688), Maxims.
2, L.-Corpl. Fitz, J. (3143) "C" Co.
Heat 2.—1, Pte. Damons, J. (3593), Maxims.
2, Pte. May (3416), "D" Co.
Heat 3.—1, Pte. November, P. (1555), "C" Co.
2, Pte. Franz (3665), Maxims.

FINAL.
1, Pte. Carelse, C.
2, Pte. November, P.

Event 7.—MULE RACE.
1, L.-Corpl. Thimms, E. (3713), "D" Co.
2, Pte. Bailey, D. (3456), "A" Co.

Event 8.—HIGH JUMP.
1, L.-Corpl. Fitz, J. (3143), "C" Co., 4 ft. 11 ins.
2, Pte. Carstens (2739), "A" Co., 4 ft. 9 ins.
3, Corpl. Arendse, I. W. (607), Maxims, 4 ft. 7 ins.

Event 9.—POTATO RACE.
1, Pte. Sheldon, E. (1010), "D" Co.
2, Pte. Campher, B. (3278), "A" Co.
3, L.-Corpl. May, F. (3416), "B" Co.

Event 10.—BOMB THROWING (Long Distance).
1, Pte. Kerspey, A. (1306), "B" Co.
2, Pte. Harridine, L. (2764), "C" Co.
3, Pte. Damons, J. (3593), Maxims.

Event 11.—BOMB THROWING (Accuracy).
(Teams of four from each company.)
1, Headquarters—Ptes. Williams, F. (719), Ward, P. (1249), Turner, J. (2328), and
2, Machine Gunners—Corpls. Arendse, I. W. (607), Armstrong, J. (1303), Strydom (311), and Pte. Herring, G. (3529).

Event 12.—OFFICERS' RELAY RACE, 225 Yards.
(Each competitor to run 75 yards.)
1, Machine Gunners—Lieuts. D. F. Botha, M. S. Davies, and E. W. Templer.
2, Headquarters—Capt. J. H. Tandy (Adjt.), Capt. A. Earp Jones (Chaplain), and Lieut. A. Hayton (Lewis gun officer).

Event 13.—COMPANY RELAY RACE.
(Teams of four.)
1, "C" Company—C.S.M. Hutchinson (310), L.-Corpls. Fitz, J. (3143), Isaacs, J. (3126), and Pte. November, P. (1555).
2, "A" Company—Ptes. Aries (2107), Carstens, V. (2739), Wanza, A. (768), and Isaacs, J. (1920).

Event 14.—TUG-OF-WAR.
(Teams of eight from each company.)
1, Headquarters—Sergts. February, S. (1357), De

THE STORY OF THE 1st CAPE CORPS.

Vos, A. P. (1072), Ptes. Attwell, H. (3414), **April**, S. (3843), Bailey, C. (1373), Henry, E. (2834), Sharpley, P. H. (1892), and Ward, P. (1249).
2, " C " Company—Sergts. Thomas, M. (366), Scullard, J. (1363), Ptes. Misselbrook (2582), Moses, W. (3509), Smith, C. (3017), Haradien, L. (2764), Phillips, P. (4340), Watson R. (11).

Event 15.—BOOT RACE.
1, Pte. May, W. (914), " B " Co.
2, Pte. Malgas, A. (3303), " A " Co.

Event 16.—V.C. RACE.
1, Pte. Jonathan, J. (3834), " C " Co.
2, Pte. Ward, P. (1249), Headquarters.

Event 17.—CAMEL RACE, 880 Yards.
1, Zubidar, Camel Scout Corps.
2, Jamidar, Camel Scout Corps.
3, Zheak, Camel Scout Corps.

Event 18.—MULE RACE.
(Special prize presented by Lt.-Colonel C. N. Hoy, D.S.O.)
1, Pte. Marthinus, H. (1631), Headquarters.
2, Pte. Meyer, H. (476), " B " Co.
3, Corpl. Group, J. (1087), " D " Co.

Event 19.—VISITORS' RACE.
First and second places were taken by men of the 204th Calcutta Battery.

In June we played the British West India team at cricket. Our eleven included six Currie Cup players, of whom two were also Internationals, but on a very dangerous wicket we were beaten by 13 runs. Our opponents were a good side and had won several matches. We were very much out of practice.

The scores were :—

British West India Regt. 86
1st Cape Corps 73

For us Captain Ivor Difford and Lieutenant Gordon White scored 20 apiece and Lieutenant S. V. Samuelson, M.C., took 7 wickets for 40 runs.

On October 21st, 1918, in Palestine, the third anniversary of the Battalion's mobilisation was celebrated by an all-day sports meeting at Ramleh, near Jerusalem.

Another very successful day may be recorded, and the visitors from our Brigade and Division were numerous.

The events open to officers and men of other units of the Brigade attracted very good entries.

After the Armistice, when the Battalion were located at Mustapha, near Alexandria, from 1st November, 1918, to 15th July, 1919, officers and men found ample time to indulge in athletics and games to the top of their bent, except during the six or seven weeks when the local unrest and disturbances occupied all our time and attention.

On November 20th, 1918, the Battalion Rugby fifteen drew with the Royal Welsh Fusiliers after a very keen game in which there was no score.

On November 22nd our Signallers beat the Royal Welsh Fusiliers Drummers at Soccer by 4 goals

On December 3rd our " C " Company were beaten at Soccer by " C " Company Royal Welsh Fusiliers by 2 goals to 1.

On December 19th teams picked respectively from Western Province and Griqualand West men of the Battalion played a very keen Rugby match in which inter-centre rivalry was intense. The Westerns won by 3 points to nil.

On December 25th a Soccer match between Officers and Sergeants resulted in a draw, 1 goal all.

On Boxing Day a Battalion sports meeting took place at Mustapha. A good programme and music by the Divisional Band was much enjoyed by all ranks and by a number of visitors.

The results were :—

100 yards.—L.-Corporal Bethanie (3778), " C " Company.
220 yards.—L.-Corporal Hopley (5160), " A " Company.
440 yards.—Private Abrahams, " A " Company.
One mile.—Private Clark (3443), Transport.
Long jump.—Private Kay (2154), Provost (Headquarters)
High jump.—Corporal Fitz (3143), " C " Company.
Tug-of-War.—" A " Company.
Officers' 100 yards (handicap).—Captain W. P. Anderson.
Officers' Relay Race.—" B " Company.

On January 2nd, 1919, the R.F.A. beat a Battalion team (officers and men) at Soccer by two goals to one after a very keen struggle.

The same evening our Concert Party, trained by Captain Edwards and L.-Corporal Oram of the " Welsh Rabbits " Concert Party (R.W.F.), and known as the " Peach Blossoms," gave their initial performance.

Major-General Mott and Brig.-General Borthwick and several of their Staff Officers were present, also a number of nurses.

The programme was very much appreciated by a crowded house.

Second Lieutenant Lambe and Corporals Frost and Martin were very good, also Sergeant Yon as a female impersonator.

The Concert Party gave several concerts during the next few months in Alexandria and in various camps.

During the period December 25th to January 5th a series of inter-company competitions were held in drill and other military exercises and events. The results were :—

Best turned out Lewis gun section.—" B " Company Lewis Gun Section.
Lewis gun—stripping and assembling—(blindfold).—Private Lawrence (756), " B " Company.
Best turned out Man.—1, Private Sampie (584), " A " Company; 2, Privates Hogart (3064), " A " Company, and Carrie (3646), " C " Company; 3, Privates Klink (3431), " B " Company, and Matthys (3235), " B " Company.
Best turned out Squad.—1, No. 7, Platoon, " B " Company; 2, No. 3 Platoon, " A " Company; 3, No. 13 Platoon, " D " Company.
Regimental Cable-laying Competition (teams of 4).—" C " Company.
Squad Drill Competition (teams of 1 Sergeant and 20 men).—No. 16 Platoon, Sergeant Drury, H. (1703).

On January 12, Machine Gunners beat Signallers at Soccer, one goal to nil.

On January 15, Machine Gunners and Signallers beat Rest of the Battalion at Soccer by three goals to nil.

On January 19, a return Soccer Match between Officers and Sergeants was won by the former by 4 goals to 2.

On January 24, a Soccer Match between our Officers and those of the 21st Punjabis resulted in a victory for us by three goals to nil.

On January 25, a Squad Drill Competition (one Sergeant and twenty men) resulted as follows :—

1. " C " Company Squad, Sergeant Augustus (204).
2. " B " Company Squad, Sergeant Wilkinson (1253).
3. " D " Company Squad, Sergeant Drury (1703).

THE STORY OF THE 1st CAPE CORPS.

As the result of the 160th Brigade Assault at Arms Eliminating Competitions the Battalion represented the Brigade at the Divisional Assualt at Arms (held 28th January) in the following Competitions, viz. :—

Best turned out Squad.—Nos. 3 " C " Company and 13 " D " Company Platoons.
Squad Arms Drill.—No. 10 Platoon " C " Company, and No. 5 Platoon " B " Company.
Bivouac and Alarm Race.—No. 13 Platoon " D " Company.
Best turned out Lewis Gun Team.—The Lewis Gun Section of No. 5 Platoon.
Lewis Gun In and Out of Action.—The Lewis Gun Section of No. 4 Platoon.
Tug-of-War.—" A " Company Team.
Our representatives did very well, taking the following prizes, viz. :—
Bayonet Fighting.—2, " D " Company ; 3, " B " Company.
Arms Drill.—1, No. 10 Platoon " C " Company, Sergeant Augustus' Squad (204) ; 2, No 5 Platoon " B " Company. Sergeant Wilkinson's (1253) Squad
Best Dressed Squad.—2, Composite (M.G.) Company.
Best turned out man.—2, Private Sampie (584).
Wrestling on Mules.—1st Prize.
Obstacle Race.—2, L.-Corpl. Hopley (5160) " A " Company.
Lewis Gun Stripping.—2, Private Lawrence, C. (756), " B " Company.
Lewis Gun In and Out of Action.—2, No. 4 Platoon " A " Company.
Best turned out Lewis Gun.—2, No. 5 Platoon " B " Company.
Officers Tent Pegging.—2, Lieutenant W. Wigman.
Officers Musical Chairs (Mounted).—1, Lieutenant E. P. Stubbs, M.C.
Best turned out L.G.S. Wagon.—4, 1st Cape Corps.

Our Brigade (160th) earned most points at the above Assualt At Arms and took 1st (Brigade) Prize.

Owing to some misunderstanding our Other Ranks did not compete at the Divisional Athletic meeting, but Second-Lieutenant M. S. Davies did so successfully. He won the 440 yards race and was placed 2nd in the 100 yards.

On the 18th February at Rond Point the Battalion beat the R.E. at Rugby Football by eight points to nil.

On February 22nd, in a Military Race Meeting held at the Sporting Club, Alexandria, Lieutenant G. Horseman, on Desert Queen, was placed second in a mile and a half race.

In the Steeplechase, Lieutenant Gibson had a nasty fall which fortunately was not as serious as it appeared to be.

On March 3rd, in the final tie of the Inter-Company Rugby Football Competition played at Rond Point, " A " Company beat " B " Company by eight points to six after a very keen match in which Sergeants Jansen and Fredericks were injured.

On March 10th another Battalion sports meeting took place at Mustapha, of which the results are appended :—

LONG JUMP.
1, Pte. Bailey, T (3180), " A " Co.

PLACE KICKING.
1, Pte. Bailey, T. (3180), " A " Co.

100 YARDS OPEN.
1, L.-Corpl. Hopley, J. (5160), " A " Co
2, L.-Corpl. Bethanie (3778), " C " Co.
3, Corpl. Sasse (3772), " A " Co.

TUG-OF-WAR.
Winning Team, " A " Co.

220 YARDS FLAT RACE
1, L.-Corpl. Hopley, J. (5160), " A " Co.
2, Corpl. Sasse (3772), " A " Co.
3, L.-Corpl. Bethanie (3778), " C " Co.

POTATO RACE.
1, Pte. Klassen (3353), " A " Co.

THROWING THE CRICKET BALL
1, Pte. Bailey, T. (3180), " A " Co.

COMPANY RELAY RACE.
1, " A " Company.
2, " B " Company.

440 YARDS RACE.
1, L.-Corpl. Hopley, J. (5160), " A " Co.
2, Corpl. Sasse (3772), " A " Co.
3, Pte. Frazenberg (4714), " B " Co.

100 YARDS HANDICAP.
1, Pte. Johnston (2246), " B " Co.
2, Pte. Frazenberg (4714), " B " Co.
3, Pte. Jaftha (725), " A " Co.

WHEEL BARROW RACE.
1, Pte. Abrahams (1161), " B " Co.
2, Pte. Engelbrecht (762), " B " Co.

880 YARDS RACE.
1, Sgt. Adams (48), " B " Co.
2, Pte. Visagie (4525), " C " Co.
3, Sgt. Carelse, D.C.M. (688), Composite Co.

MILE RACE.
1, Pte. Clarke (3443), " B " Co.
2, Pte. Jansen (2798), Composite Co.
3, Pte. Erasmus (3953), " C " Co.

THREE-LEGGED RACE.
1 Pte. Siebritz (2918), " C " Co. and Pte. Davids (3823), " C " Co.

HIGH JUMP.
1, Sgt. Fitz (3143), " C " Co.
2, Corpl. McLear (1486), Composite Co.

OBSTACLE RACE.
1, Pte. Arendolph (2385), " C " Co.
2, Pte. Less (3915), " B " Co.

BOLSTER BAR.
1, Pte. Martinus (1621), " D " Co.

SERGEANTS 100 YARDS
1, Sgt. Drury (1703), " D " Co.
2, Sgt. Fitz (3143), " C " Co.

OFFICERS 100 YARDS.
1, Lieut. M. S. Davies, Composite Co

OFFICERS RELAY RACE.
1, Composite Company.

VETERAN RACE (over 35 years).
1, Sgt. Samuels (504), Composite Co.
2, Pte Kay (2154), " A " Co.

WATERLOO RACE.
1, Composite Company.

COOKS RACE.
1, Sgt. February, S. (1357), Headquarters.

Cricket commenced on April 9th with a match against the Stationery Depot, at Mustapha, who won by 6 runs.

On April 19th the Battalion Officers, assisted by S.M. Hendericks, A. J., Sergeant Alies, J. H., and Corporal Fredericks, H. J., easily beat the Alexandria C.C.

Scores :—
    1st Cape Corps 247
    (Second-Lieutenant Lambe, 96.)
    Alexandria C.C. ... ... 137 and 80 for 8 Wickets.

On April 24th we easily beat 3rd Echelon, Alexandria.

Scores :—
    1st Cape Corps ... ... 253 for 5 Wickets, declared
    (Captain D. K. Pearse 130.)
    3rd Echelon 92

Lieutenant S. V. Samuelson took 6 wickets for 33 runs, and Captain Tandy 4 for 52. Our fielding in this match was very good.

THE STORY OF THE 1st CAPE CORPS.

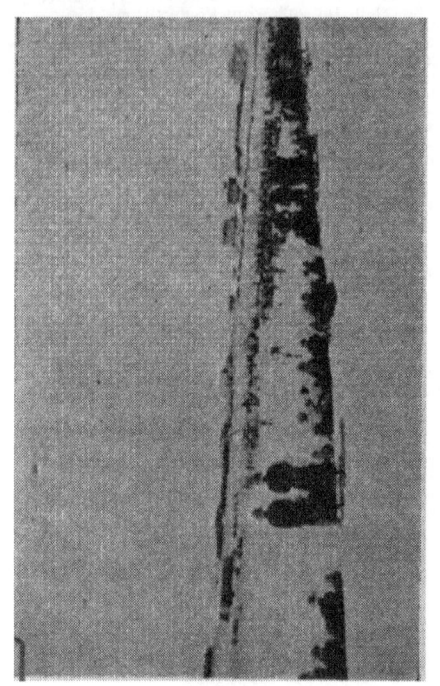

Photo by] [Sergeant Alies.
Garrison Sports at Mustapha. April, 1919.

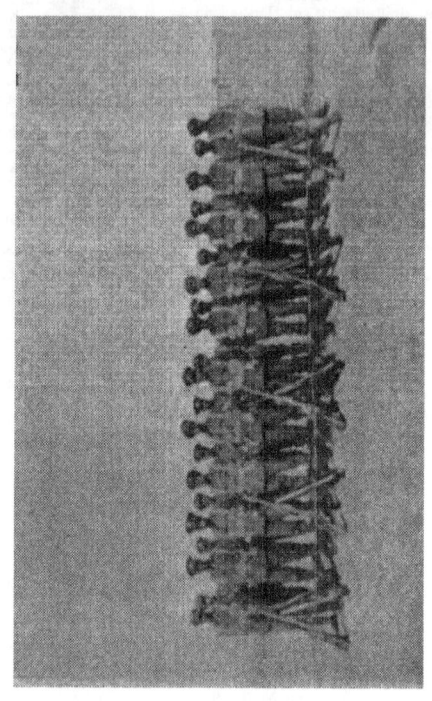

Photo by] [S. H. Rose-Innes.
No. 10 Platoon, "C" Company, Winners Arms Drill, 53rd Division Assault-at-Arms, Alexandria.

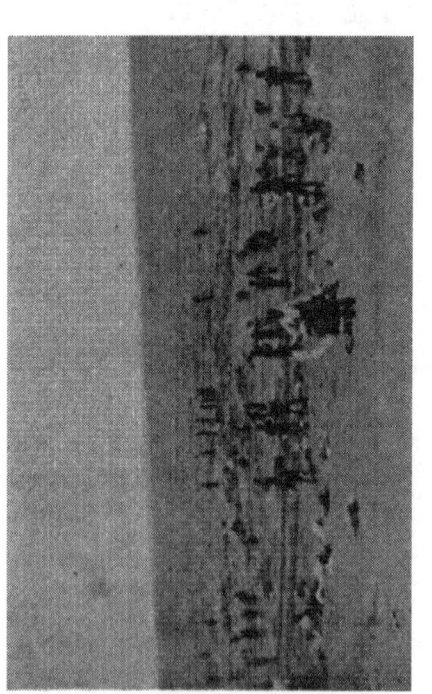

Photo by] [Sergeant Alies.
A Dip in the Mediterranean at Mustapha.

Photo by] [Sergeant Alies.
Men on Short Leave at the Pyramids, Cairo.

THE STORY OF THE 1st CAPE CORPS.

On April 27th, at Rond Point, the 158th Brigade Headquarters were no match for us.
Scores :—

    158th Brigade Headquarters 34
    1st Cape Corps ... ... 45 for 0 Wickets.
    (Lieutenant S. V. Samuelson took 7 wickets for 9 runs.)

On the same day Lieutenant M. S. Davies won the Singles Lawn Tennis Championship of Alexandria, beating the local Champion for six years, M. Zerlindi.

On May 1st a Divisional Cricket Championship commenced; not more than three Officers were allowed to play for any of the competing teams.

We lost our first match to 158th Brigade Headquarters. Scores :—

    158th Brigade Headquarters 50
    1st Cape Corps 26

A narrow Mat and bad wicket was responsible for the low scoring.

In our second match on May 6th we beat 266th Battery, R.F.A., by 155 runs to 63.

For us, Private Lothering (699) scored a good 49, and Sergeant Alies took 6 wickets for 24 runs.

On May 8th our Officers beat Alexandria District Officers.
Scores :—

    1st Cape Corps 173
    (Lieutenant Davies, 53; Captain Pearse, 44; and Lieutenant Reunert, 32.)
    Alexandria District Officers ... ... 97 and 103.

Our fielding was very good.

On May 3rd, in our next Divisional Championship Game, we easily routed the Divisional Train.
Scores :—

    1st Cape Corps ... ... 253 for 4 wickets.
    (Sergeant Alies, 97; Second-Lieutenant Adamson, 90.)
    Divisional Train ... ... 23 and 31

Sergeant Alies captured 12 wickets for 29 runs and Corporal Fredericks 5 for 9 runs.

On May 16th, at the Alexandria Club Ground, "South Africa" beat "England" very easily.
Scores :—

    "South Africa" 248
    "England" ... 81 and 88 for 6 wickets.

In this match Captain Pearse, 57; Lieutenant Davies, 31; Second-Lieutenant Adamson, 29; and Sergeant Alies, 26; of ours did well with bat, and Captain Pearse took 5 wickets for 15 runs and Lieutenant Samuelson 4 wickets for 37.

On May 19th, in the Semi-Final of the Divisional Championship, we carried too many guns for the 158th Brigade Headquarters.
Scores :—

    1st Cape Corps 190
    (Sergeant Alies, 65; Sergeant S. Fredericks, 29; Private De Kock, 20.)
    158th Brigade Headquarters 39
    (Sergeant Alies took 6 wickets for 15 runs and Private Damons (1100) 3 for 1 run.)

On May 22nd, in a return match between "South Africa" and "England" on the Alexandria Sporting Club's Ground, the scores were :—

    "South Africa" ... ... 265 for 7 wickets declared.
    "England" ... ... 261 for 6 wickets.

England were allowed an extension of 15 minutes to score 25 runs but did not quite succeed.

For S.A., Captain Pearse scored 86 and Lieutenant Davies 111.

For England, Lieutenant Gold scored 66; Captain Biss, 52 not out; Corporal Cook, 37; Major Dryland, 33; and Corporal V. C. W. Jupp (Sussex), 30.

South Africa's fielding was unusually faulty.

On May 23rd, in the final of the Divisional Championship, 1st Cape Corps beat 436 Company R.E. by 27 runs : 122 to 95.

For us S.M. Hendericks scored 27; Sergeant Fredericks, 25; and Sergeant Alies, 17. The last-named took 5 wickets for 49, and Corporal Fredericks 4 for 28.

On May 26th our Team, which had just won the above match, visited our detachment at Teh-El-Barud and were beaten by 6 runs.

On June 10th and 11th Alexandria beat Cairo, at Cairo, by an innings and 5 runs.

    Alexandria 319
    Cairo ... ... 140 and 174

For Alexandria, Captain Pearse scored 74 and Lieutenant Davies 62. The former also took 3 wickets for 17 runs in Cairo's first innings, and the latter 4 for 22 and 3 for 18.

On June 24th the 2nd Australian M.G. Squadron beat 1st Cape Corps Officers by 8 wickets.
Scores :—

    Australians ... ... 190 and 51 for 2 wickets.
    1st Cape Corps Officers ... ... 83 and 155

For us Second-Lieutenant Hirsch scored 26 and 52 and Second-Lieutenant Adamson 11 and 40.

The next day in a return match we took an ample revenge, winning by an innings and 121 runs.

We scored 347 (Lieutenant Davies, 99; Lieutenant Max Davison, 86; and Sergeant Alies, 45).

The Australians scored 99 and 127. In their first innings Lieutenant Davies took 7 wickets for 40 runs, and Lieutenant Samuelson 3 for 28.

On June 27th a Cape Corps eleven vanquished the 54th Division Signallers by an innings and 54 runs.
Scores :—

    1st Cape Corps ... ... 109 for 4 wickets, declared.
    (Sergeant Alies, 45; Corporal Fredericks, 30 not out.)

Our opponents found the bowling of C.Q.M.S. Reagon and S/Sergeant Cairns, M.M., too much for them and could only manage totals of 37 and 18.

On July 3rd an Inter-Company Cricket Competition commenced. (Teams to consist of one Officer and ten other ranks).

This competition commenced at Mustapha and was concluded after arrival of the Battalion at Suez, having extended over three weeks.

The results, in brief, were :—

    Headquarters (152) beat "C" Company (68).
    Composite Company (81) beat "C" Company (61).
    Headquarters (101 for 4 wickets) beat "B" Company (25).
    Composite Company (78 for 6) beat "A" Company (51).
    Headquarters beat Composite Company by 6 wickets.
    "A" Company (88) beat "B" Company (54).
    "C" Company (81) beat "B" Company (31).
    "A" Company (123) beat "C" Company (99).
    Headquarters (39 for 4) beat "A" Company (34) by 6 wickets.

THE STORY OF THE 1st CAPE CORPS.

This match decided the Competition in favour of Headquarters who beat all four Company Teams. Each member of the winning team received an engraved Cigarette Case.

On July 11th, at Alexandria, Sergeant Alies and Corporal Fredericks, M.M. were selected to play for the 3rd Echelon vs. Zeitoun School of Instruction. The match was won by the former.

On July 19th the Battalion met the Staff of the British Transit Camp at Suez. This was one more soft thing for the 1st Cape Corps who scored 190 for 6 wickets and then outed their opponents for 76. Four of the latter were run out by our men's smart fielding.

Second-Lieutenant Adamson scored 52; Sergeant Alies, 48; C.S.M. Hendericks, 45; and Private Luiters, 33. The first two named also bowled well.

On July 23rd the Somerset Light Infantry proved no match for the Battalion. We scored 185 for 7 wickets (Lieutenant Davies, 74; Lieutenant Rose-Innes, 38; Second-Lieutenant Adamson, 32). The Somersets could do no better than 57 all out.

On July 31st a return match between the Battalion (Divisional Championship Team) and our Teh-El-Barud Detachment Team took place.

The Divisional Champions took an ample revenge for their narrow defeat at Teh-El-Barud on May 26th, the scores being:—

Divisional Champions 136
Detachment 41

For the former Sergeant Alies and Corporal Fredericks, M.M., once more came off with bat and ball, Alies getting 36 runs and 6 wickets for 9 runs, and Fredericks 21 runs and 4 wickets for 30.

On August 1st our last Cricket match in Egypt gave us another win over the Somerset Light Infantry, this time by 42 runs on the 1st innings.

Scores:—

1st Cape Corps 129
Somerset Light Infantry 87

Private De Kock with 28 was our highest scorer. Lieutenant Davies had 5 wickets for 20, Lieutenant Samuelson 2 for 33 and Sergeant Alies 2 for 12.

The Somerset Light Infantry scored 144 in their second knock in which Sergeant Alies had 4 wickets for 36 runs.

On August 1st an inter-company drill competition took place at Suez. This was very keenly contested as the winning company were promised that they should lead the Battalion in the final marches at Durban and Cape Town prior to demobilisation.

"C" Company were adjudged the winners, but there were many good judges amongst the lookers on who would have given a different verdict.

Whilst on signal instruction course at Zeitoun (Cairo) in October, 1918, at the annual assault-at-arms, Sergeant Alies and three Australians won first prize in the visual signalling relay race (teams of four); each man received a prize of an engraved bronze medal.

Sergeant Alies was also one of a winning team of four in a team relay race (drill order), teams to consist of one officer, one instructor, and two students.

The race was won by the signal wing, and the prizes were a silver cup to the team and an engraved silver medal to each individual.

Prior to the Armistice officers and men at the Depôt had certainly no more, if anything less, time to devote to games and sport than the Battalion.

After the cessation of hostilities, however, everyone had plenty of leisure for football and athletics.

On October 21st, 1918, the third anniversary of the mobilisation of the Battalion was celebrated by a most successful all-day sports meeting. The sports were attended by practically every officer, man, and nursing sister in the area, and a most enjoyable day was spent by all ranks. The results are appended:—

1ST CAPE CORPS DEPOT ANNIVERSARY SPORTS HELD AT EL-ARISH (SINAI PENINSULA) ON MONDAY, 21st OCTOBER, 1918.

Event 1.—BEST TURNED OUT N.C.O.
1, Sgt. Bredenkamp (979).
2, Sgt. Meyer (1064).

Event 2.—100 YARDS (HEATS).
Heat 1.—1, Pte. Abrahams (5008).
    2, Pte. Lakey (4420).
Heat 2.—1, Pte. Swartz (4440).
    2, Pte. Petersen (4228).
Heat 3.—1, Pte. Keet (2866).
    2, Pte. Benjamin (4651).
Heat 4.—1, Pte. Gosling (3214).
    2, Pte. Abrahams (5007).
Heat 5.—1, Sgt. Parkins (3179).
    2, Pte. Wales (5053).
Heat 6.—1, Pte. Hopley (5160).
    2, L.-Corpl. Aspeling (639).

SEMI FINAL.
Heat 1.—1, Pte. Abrahams (5008).
    2, Pte. Keet (2866).
Heat 2.—1, Pte. Hopley (5160).
    2, Sgt. Parkins (3179).

FINAL.
1, Sgt. Parkins (3179).
2, Pte. Hopley (5160).
3, Pte. Keet (2866).

Event 3.—TENT PITCHING COMPETITION
(Teams of one N.C.O. and six men.)
1, Corpl. Fatman's Team.—Corpl. Fatman (385), Pte. Gebers (1233), Pte. Hackett (1276), Thomas (419), Downing (234), Julies (1592), and Pte. Dunbar (2829).
2, Corpl. Meiring's Team.—Corpl. Meiring (1983), Pte's. Adams (2203), Nelson (5036), Davids (4870), van Deventer (3765), Gosling (3214), and van Niekerk (4422).

Event 4.—BOMB THROWING (Accuracy).
(Team of four.)
1, Corpl. Strydom's Team (M.G.C.).—Corpl. Strydom (311), Pte. Petersen (1243), Pte. Le Bruin, M.M. (1179), and Pte. Petersen (5228)

Event 5.—440 YARDS (HEATS).
Heat 1.—1, Pte. Joshua (4757).
    2, Pte. Addinal (3086).
Heat 2.—1, Pte. Daniels (2273).
    2, Pte. Gosling (3214).
Heat 3.—1, Pte. Keet (2866).
    2, Pte. Batman (3056).
Heat 4.—1, Pte. Louw (4194).
    2, Pte. Lewis (1693).
Heat 5.—1, Pte. Wales (5053).
    2, Pte. Johnson (4242).
Heat 6.—1, Sgt. Madella (365).
    2, Pte. Johnson (5307).

FINAL.
1, Sgt. Madella (365).
2, Pte. Daniels (2273).
3, Pte. Wales (5053).

Event 6.—BOMB THROWING (Long Distance).
1, Corpl. Strydom (311), 47½ yards.
2, Sgt. Adonis (2859).
3, Pte. Langerveldt (3552).

Event 7.—HIGH JUMP
1, Pte. Smith (4927), 4 feet 11 inches.
2, Pte. Benjamin (4651).
3, Pte. Ziervogel (1432).

Event 8.—WAGON (L.G.S.) RACE (150 yds. open)
1, Cape Corps Team.—Bartman (4384), and Smith (3291).

Event 9.—BEST TURNED OUT (L.G.S.) WAGON (Open).
1, 204th Calcutta Battery, R.G.A

THE STORY OF THE 1st CAPE CORPS.

Photo by] [I.D.D.
BUFFALOES, NEAR PYRAMIDS, CAIRO.

Photo by] [I.D.D.
CRICKET—CAIRO vs. ALEXANDRIA AT SPORTING CLUB, CAIRO, JUNE, 1919.

Photo by] [I.D.D.
ALEXANDRIA HARBOUR, FROM RAS-EL-TIN HOSPITAL.

Photo by] [E. W. Templer.
IN THE MOSQUE OF EL ASKA IN SOLOMON'S TEMPLE AREA JERUSALEM.

THE STORY OF THE 1st CAPE CORPS

On December 26th another all-day sports meeting took place and proved even more successful and enjoyable than the previous one. Unfortunately the results of this meeting were mislaid at the time and cannot be given.

On New Year's Day (1919) an inter-company Marathon race was a great success and caused great keeness and enthusiasm. Ten individual cash prizes were given and a seventy-gallon barrel of beer to the winning Company. Excluding men on duty and others not available as starters owing to illness, etc., there were five hundred and twenty-two men possible starters in the Depôt at the time. Of these no less than four hundred and eighty-four started and four hundred and forty-four finished. " G " Company won the company prize, and the individual prize winners were :—

1, Private Jimson, J. (1738), " G " Company.
2, Private Grootboom, G. (4953), " G " Company.
3, Private Davids, A. (445), " G " Company.
4, Private Morkel, A. (5297), " F " Company.
5, Private Europa, J. (5326), " F " Company.
6, Private Bennett, D. (3091), Headquarters.
7, Private Oliver, J. (4432), " E " Company.
8, Private Jackson, H. (5267), " E " Company.
9, Private October, A. (4767), " F " Company.
10, Corporal Fatman, G. (385), " G " Company.

During October and November, 1918, two or three athletic meetings took place at the School of Instruction at El Arish. At these meetings several of the Reserve Half Battalion men competed and won a number of prizes.

At the School farewell sports meeting after the final classes several men of the Reserve Half Battalion distinguished themselves Lance-Corporal Hopley (5160) won the 100 yards and the obstacle race and was second in the mile. Corporal Sass (3772) was second in the 100 yards, and Private Africa (517) second in the obstacle race. Lieutenant Moin, on " The Bint," was second in the officers' jumping competition.

During January and February, 1919, inter-platoon Rugby and Association football leagues were played. These were the cause of the keenest rivalry and afforded equal enjoyment to players and onlookers. The results were :—

Winners Rugby—17 Platoon, " E " Company.
Winners Association—17 Platoon, " E " Company.
Both teams were captained by Sergeant M. J. Abrahamse (318).

Photo by] [*J.H.T.*
SERGEANT BEZUIDENHOUT'S SQUAD (NO. 11 PLATOON), " C " COMPANY, WINNERS OF BATTALION COMPETITION.

THE STORY OF THE 1st CAPE CORPS

Event 10.—REVEILLE RACE (50 Yards).
1, Pte Le Brun, M.M. (1179).
2, Sgt. Bredenkamp (979).
3, Pte. Vester (4026).

Event 11.—LONG JUMP.
1, Pte. Sturman (5273), 14 ft. 9 in.
2, Sgt. Thompson (1826).
3, Sgt. Carelse (916).

Event 12.—OBSTACLE RACE (250 Yards).
1, Pte. Nell (3368).
2, Pte. Melkers (4950).
3, Sgt. Carelse (916).

Event 13.—PONY SCURRY (OFFICERS).
(3 Furlongs, Open.)
1, Major Neave, 204th Calcutta Battery, R.G.A.
2, Lieut. Wallis, M.C., M.G.C. 1st Cape Corps.

Event 14.—MACHINE GUN COMPETITION.
(Vickers vs. Lewis.)
1, Lewis Guns (Officer i/c., Lieut. Hayton).
2, Vickers Guns (Officer i/c., Lieut. Moin).

Event 15.—POTATO RACE.
1, Sgt. Bredenkamp (979).
2, Sgt. Koetenberg (5178).
3, L.-Corpl. Aspeling (639).

Event 16.—CAMEL RACE (Open).
1, L.-Corpl. Ismail Mabrouk, Imp. Camel Corps.
2, Pte. Jadisit Gheyer, Imp. Camel Corps.
3, L.-Corpl. Hassim Ferad Ali, Imp. Camel Corps.

Event 17.—THREAD THE NEEDLE AND LIGHT THE CIGARETTE RACE (Mounted).
(Open)—(Sisters and Officers.)
1, Sister Davis and Lieut. Botha.
2, Sister Clark and Lieut. Moin.

Event 18.—RELAY RACE (880 Yards—Teams of 4)
1, Sgt. Koetenberg's Team.—Sgt. Koetenberg (5178), L.-Corpl. Aspeling (639), Pte November (1555), Pte. Hopley (5160).
2, Sgt. Carelse's Team.—Sgt. Carelse (916), Sgt. Hendricks (4061), Sgt. Daniels (321), Sgt. Adams (5182).

Event 19.—MULE RACE (BAREBACK).
(3 Furlongs—Open.)
1, Driver Cook, 204th Calcutta Battery, R.G.A.
2, Pte. Bartman (4384), 1st Cape Corps.

Event 20.—CATCH THE TENNIS BALL RACE.
(Officers mounted—Sisters dismounted.)
1, Sister Mansell and Major Neave, 204th Calcutta Battery, R.G.A.

Event 21.—SISTERS' EGG AND SPOON RACE
(50 Yards.)
1, Sister Clark.
2, Sister Swan.
3, Sister Patrick.

Event 22.—JUMPING COMPETITION, MOUNTED
(Open)—OFFICERS.
1, Lieut.-Col. Synnott, Inniskilling Dragoons.
2, Major Swan, School of Instruction.

Event 23.—VISITORS' RACE (Open)—100 Yards—ALL RANKS.
1, L.-Corpl. Hassim Ferad Ali, Imp. Camel Corps.
2, Bdr. Wilson, 204th Calcutta Battery, R.G.A.
3, Pte. Hirahim Belal, Imp. Camel Corps.

Event 24.—TUG-OF-WAR (Team of 8).
(REINFORCEMENTS VS. EAST AFRICAN TEAM.)
Winners : Reinforcements.—L.-Cpl. Hankin (4527), Pte. Joubert (4981), Pte. Smith (3291), Pte. Hendricks (4772), Pte. Daniels (3759), Pte. Oliver (5183), Pte. Kamis (5165), Pte. van Niekerk (4422) ; Coach, Sgt. Carelse (916).

Event 25.—OFFICERS BATMAN'S RACE
(100 Yards).
1, Pte. Louw (4194).
2, Pte Abrahams (4062).
3, Pte. Williams (2196).

Photo by]   [*I.D.D.*
H.H. THE SULTAN'S BODY-GUARD AT THE E.E.F. SPORTS AT CAIRO, 28TH FEBRUARY, 1919.

Photo by]   [*I.D.D.*
H.H. THE SULTAN'S BODY-GUARD AT THE E.E.F. SPORTS AT CAIRO, 28TH FEBRUARY, 1919.

CHAPTER XXI.

AFTERWORD.

THE CAPE CORPS GIFTS AND COMFORTS COMMITTEE.—COLOURED TROOPS REST HOUSE, CAPE TOWN.—THE VOCATIONAL TRAINING INSTITUTE, CAPE TOWN.—THE GOVERNOR-GENERAL'S FUND.—THE CAPE CORPS MEMORIAL FUND.—THE REGIMENTAL BAND.—PENSIONS.—THE FUTURE.

PRACTICALLY every incident and happening, whether of major or minor importance, in the career of the Battalion has been dealt with in the foregoing chapters and very little remains to be written by way of " Finis."

THE CAPE CORPS GIFTS AND COMFORTS COMMITTEE.

Tribute has already been paid to the splendid work done on behalf of the men by the Cape Corps Gifts and Comforts Committee, whose headquarters were at Cape Town. What was done from October, 1915, to September, 1919, certainly deserves the most generous appreciation.

As soon as there were a couple of hundred men in the Camp at Simonstown the need was felt of a responsible body to look after the welfare and comfort of the men.

The meeting of a number of the Corps' well wishers at once resulted in the formation of a strong Committee, viz.: Chairman, Mr. H. Hartog; Vice-Chairman, Mrs. N. Wyngard; Hon. General Secretary, Mr. A. S. Williams; Hon. Treasurer, Mr. H. Hartog; Committee: Rev. Canon Lavis, Rev. G. Robson, Mr. P. Smeda, Mr. P. C. Ryan, Mr. D. Swartz, Mr. R. Hoedemaker, Mr. H. J. Gordon, Mr. S. Reagon, Mr. R. W. Wooding, Mr. A. J. Desmore (Secretary). Later on Mrs. R. W. Wooding, the Rev. F. M. Gow, and Mr. C. J. Carelse joined this Committee.

The name " Cape Corps Gifts and Comforts Committee " was decided upon, and the purpose of the Committee was to provide comforts of every kind for the men and generally to look after their welfare. From the outset the Committee received the whole hearted support of public spirited men, led by the Mayor of Cape Town (Harry Hands Esq.), and official recognition was at once given by the Military Authorities. Operations were commenced on a small scale. The Cape Peninsula was canvassed systematically and several branches formed therein, and followed very shortly by branches at Stellenbosch, Paarl, Wellington, Worcester, etc., etc.

The first work was to organise a Christmas (1915) entertainment. Gifts were received from all parts of the Cape Province and several indefatigable members of the Committee went out to Simonstown to entertain the men. Shortly afterwards weekly concerts were organised and numbers of willing artistes came forward.

THE STORY OF THE 1st CAPE CORPS.

It was soon realised that to continue the good work a much larger fund would be required than the coloured community could themselves raise. At first only local entertainment had been necessary, but drafts would shortly be leaving for the front and others would be invalided home, and it would fall to the lot of the Committee to send off the former and care for the latter. It was then that the South African Gifts and Comforts Organisation came to the rescue and affiliated the Cape Corps Gifts and Comforts Committee, and from then onwards helped them by liberal cash grants. As the work of the Committee extended branches came into being throughout the Union.

After a time Mr. A. J. Desmore left for the front and handed over the secretarial duties to Mr. A. S. Williams.

CHRISTMAS TREAT TO CHILDREN OF COLOURED SOLDIERS.

On December 26th, 1917, a Christmas treat to all children of Coloured soldiers took place at the Groot Schuur Estate, Rondebosch. The Mayor of Cape Town heartily took the matter up with the result that two thousand children had a great time and were well looked after by the lady members of the Comforts Committee under the supervision of Mrs. N. Wyngard and Mrs. James Currey.

The treat was repeated the following year at the Rosebank Show Ground, and was a more pronounced success than that of the previous year. The Mayor of Cape Town (Mr. W. J. Thorne), the Dean of Cape Town, The Very Rev. Dean C. H. Rolt, and Canon S. W. Lavis were present and addressed the children.

Another matter which the Comforts Committee took up was the payment of allotments to dependents. Towards the end of 1917 dissatisfaction arose at delays and it was found that the Pay Staff could not possibly deal with matters. The Command Paymaster was sympathetic but shorthanded, and on the 17th June, 1918, at his request the Cape Corps Gifts and Comforts Committee undertook the work. They carried it out to the entire satisfaction of the Command Paymaster, and to the relief of the dependents, who freely expressed their delight at the new arrangement. The work was carried on under the supervision of Mr. A. S. Williams, assisted by Messrs. W. Willemburg and H. Hartog and Mrs. A. F. Dowman, with occasional help from Misses H. and A. Williams, Messrs. S. Reagon and C. J. Carelse, the late Mr. H. J. Carelse, and later by ex-Sergeant J. H. Alies. In all a sum in excess of £35,000 passed through the hands of the abovenamed workers, and the Command Paymaster expressed to them the thanks and appreciation of the General Officer Commanding in South Africa and also added his own very high compliments on the manner in which the work was performed.

The Comforts Committee was also entrusted with the distribution of Pension Vouchers to wounded and invalided men and the arrangement worked so well that it was extended to the Port Elizabeth Comforts Committee as well.

GENERAL COMFORTS.

In addition to the quarterly supply of comforts sent to each Regiment, i.e., the 1st and 2nd Cape Corps, the Cape Auxiliary Horse Transport and the Cape Labour Corps, comforts were also provided for drafts going forward to all of them. Each member of a draft going forward received a bag containing tobacco, cigarettes, soap, matches, balaclava cap, socks, dried fruit, pencil, handkerchiefs, housewife, etc. Men in Hospital were provided with comforts under medical direction and weekly entertainments were given to men in Hospitals. The lady workers of the Comforts Committee from time to time visited the Hospitals and distributed such articles as sweets, tobacco, fruits, handkerchiefs, as well as liberal supplies of eggs, which latter were sent by various branches, by schools and private individuals. Special appeals were made to all coloured Schools throughout the Union and the response was very satisfactory. The poorer schools made great efforts and their support was continuous and liberal, particularly in view of the fact that the majority were also contributing to the Red Cross and other patriotic funds.

CASH CHRISTMAS GIFTS.

At Christmas time, 1917, a special effort realised £1,250 and the following amounts were sent to the Officers Commanding the various Regiments to purchase gifts for the men or to distribute in cash, viz. :—

£150 to the Cape Coloured Labour Regiment in France.
£362 10s. to the Cape Auxiliary Horse Transport Corps in France (2s. 6d. per man).
£250 to the 2nd Cape Corps in Central Africa.
£246 to the 1st Cape Corps; these men were on recuperative leave in the Union at the time and the money was distributed to them later on in Egypt.
£25 7s. 6d. to men in local Hospitals and Camps.

In December, 1918, the following amounts were sent to the Officers Commanding for distribution, viz. :—

£250 to 1st Cape Corps in Egypt.
£200 to Cape Auxiliary Horse Transport Corps.
£150 to the Cape Coloured Labour Regiment.

To provide the above substantial amounts the community responded most liberally. Of the £1,250 raised at Christmas time (1917) £660 was the result of a Bazaar in the City Hall, Cape Town, on November 3rd, 1917.

In addition to all of the above, Branches and Work Parties all over the Union and as far afield as Rhodesia, kept in close touch with the Cape Town Committee and constantly forwarded gifts in money and in kind. The splendid results achieved were not a little due to the untiring efforts of the Branch Secretaries.

All the Hospitals where coloured men were patients were visited weekly and comforts and delicacies distributed.

In 1916 the Coloured community were not contributing to the funds as liberally as had been hoped. That, however, was probably due to lack of thorough organisation, as renewed efforts made in 1917 met with success beyond expectation. The Coloured Schools throughout the Union contributed over £250 in 1917.

At Christmas time (1917 and 1918) all officers of the Battalion received a present of ten shillings, " as a small Christmas gift " from the South African Gifts and Comforts Organisation. Though intrinsically small the gift was none the less greatly appreciated by every officer, and more welcome than the gift was the hearty Christmas greeting which accompanied it. That happy reminder that we were in the thoughts of friends far away at home had a stimulating and very cheering effect upon us, one and all.

Of the Branches the heaviest work and the greatest efforts were demanded and forthcoming from the Kimberley Branch. Kimberley contributed a large number of recruits to the Cape Corps in 1915/1916, and their friends in Kimberley were not slow to realise their responsibilities to those men and made great efforts.

The removal of our Depôt and a large number of Hospital patients to Kimberley in December, 1917, threw a heavy additional tax upon the resources of the small but energetic band of loyal hardworkers of Diamondopolis. There were at one time over two thousand Coloured troops in the Depôts at Kimberley, and nearly a thousand in No. 5 General Hospital.

The Coloured Community of the City was very small to minister to the needs of such a large number of men. They worked nobly, however, and did wonderful work. A dinner was given to the inmates of No. 5 General Hospital on Christmas Day (1917). Concerts were given and refreshments served on the two succeeding days in the Cape Corps and C.A.H.T. Depôts.

St. John's Hall, Clarence Street, was hired and opened as a Rest Room and free tea provided every afternoon and free cakes and fruit once or twice a week. Writing materials and games also were supplied. Later on a small charge had to be made for refreshments. The men in the Hospital were provided with cigarettes, matches, and other small comforts. Sporting gear was purchased and presented to the Depôts. Several concerts were given in the Camp and men leaving by train were given a hearty send off and a parcel of Comforts. All the money spent on the above good work was raised in Kimberley. The Coloured Community subscribed liberally and received much support from Europeans. Of the latter the following who contributed gifts in money or in kind and helped in many other ways should be mentioned, viz. :—The Directors of De Beers Consolidated Mines, Ltd.; Sir David Harris, K.C.M.G., V.D., M.L.A.; The Mayor (Councillor J. Orr, M.B.E.) and Mrs. Orr; The Deputy Mayor and Mrs. Colin Lawrence; The Rt. Rev. Gore Browne, Bishop of Kimberley; Mr. W. Pickering, D.S.O.; Mr. H. E. Clarke, M.B.E.; Mrs. Fynn; Mr. J. C. Looney; Mr. Hyam; Rev. W. and Mrs. Prescod; The Very Rev. Dean Robson; The Rev. E. Ramsden; Mr. J. G. and Mrs. Boyes. Mr. H. E. Clarke, M.B.E., who was at one time Secretary to the Kimberley Governor-General's Fund Committee, was always a good friend to the Coloured soldier— when his committee were unable to assist dependents Mr. Clarke personally interviewed the Governor-General on the subject with satisfactory results.

The European Section of the Gifts and Comforts Committee donated £25 and a piano for the Rest Room.

Bazaars got up by the Coloured Communities of Kimberley and Beaconsfield realised respectively £82 17s. 8d. and £52 2s. 10d.

Of the Coloured Community, one of the most indefatigable and unselfish workers in the interests of the Cape Corps was Mr. H. J. Tobin. He was first Secretary of the Cape Corps Recruiting Committee there and worked like a Trojan. When the local executive of the Governor-General's Fund intimated that they could not assist dependents of the men, Mr. Tobin, with Mr. J. W. Kay, interviewed the Secretary of the Governor-General's Fund in Cape Town and succeeded in obtaining that assistance in special cases. Mr. Tobin was a member of the Kimberley Executive of the Governor-General's Fund, as representing the Coloured man's interests, and did so with much vigour and success.

He was too old to enlist, but he devoted much time, and is still doing so to the sacrifice of his own business, to furthering the legitimate claims of Coloured soldiers and to promoting their welfare in every possible way.

Mr. J. J. Herman nobly supported Mr. Tobin's efforts, especially towards the end when the enthusiasm of more lukewarm helpers began to evaporate. Mr. Herman did very good work as a member of the Cape Corps Gifts and Comforts Committee and as Treasurer of the Welcome Home Committee.

The Ladies' Committee at Kimberley were as energetic and thorough as their menfolk. The late Mrs. A. Greef, Mrs. K. Mostert, and Mrs. J. J. Joshua were especially untiring in their efforts. They were in charge of the

Coloured Troops Rest House and were hospitality itself. They were always at the Station to provide refreshments for men passing through, to welcome men arriving, and to speed men leaving.

Others of the Coloured Community who were always to the fore were: Mrs. D. M. Africa, Mr. H. Van Rooyen (Chairman Comforts Committee), Messrs. C. J. Van Wyk and M. J. Krull, who in turn undertook the Secretarial (Honorary) duties, Mr. Ernest Samuels (Assistant Hon. Secretary), the late Mr. John Sasse, Mr. J. C. September, ex-C.S.M. W. T. McLeod, Mr. J. W. E. Janjes, and Mr. T. C. Amsterdam; and last, but a very long way from least, Mr. Isaac P. Joshua (Hon. Treasurer of the Cape Corps Gifts and Comforts Committee).

Mr. Joshua by no means confined his activities to his duties in the capacity named. In fact, he shared with Mr. H. J. Tobin the honour of doing the hardest and most persistent work in Kimberley on behalf of Coloured soldiers throughout and after the War period.

Special mention must also be made of the undermentioned, who rendered sterling service in the country districts, viz.: Mr. J. West, Mrs. B. Sylvester, Miss E. Engledoe, Mr. F. Weber, Mr. J. Phillips, (late) Mr. J. van Bloemmestein, Mr. C. Stewart, Mr. H. Rorich, Mr. J. Daniels, Rev. Zeeman, Rev. Sainsbury, Mr. A. Less, Mr. J. Petersen, Miss V. Abbott, Deaconess Florence, Rev. Figland, Miss P. Whitebooi, Miss Hendricks (Elim).

The Church Lads Brigade also rendered valuable assistance, when the invalided men were entertained. All school teachers and scholars splendidly organised functions and contributed gifts for the men in hospitals.

At Durban excellent work was done by a hard-working Committee of ladies, who had occasional assistance from a few men. Much of the success of the work was due to the energetic efforts of Mr. and Mrs. J. Crowley and their strong Committee, which were greatly appreciated by the men on their several journeys through Durban to and from the East.

At Port Elizabeth, a strong Committee did good work, and there ex-Sergeant Lovy Benjamin, as Secretary of the non-European Comrades, with a strong Committee looked after the welfare of the returned soldiers.

At Johannesburg a strong branch of the same organisation under the Secretaryship of ex-C.S.M. J. Abrahams was equally indefatigable.

At Pietermaritzburg every troop train passing to or fro was met by members of the Committee and the men regaled with tea, etc., and provided with comforts, and Mrs. and the Misses Pearse and other lady friends always entertained the officers.

It is regretted that lack of space precludes mention by name of many other splendid workers, men as well as ladies, who never tired of serving their compatriots who were " doing their bit."

The foregoing completes a tale of splendid and long continued unselfish endeavour upon which Mr. A. S. Williams, and the whole army of collectors, workers and helpers must be most deservedly congratulated and complimented. That their efforts and work were appreciated by the Officers and men of the various Coloured Regiments is to put it mildly. The writer can certainly speak for the 1st Cape Corps and emphatically assure all concerned that the Battalion will be for ever grateful to them for their magnificent work.

COLOURED TROOPS REST HOUSE, CAPE TOWN.

In 1917 when the Troops Rest House erected on the Grand Parade, Cape Town, had proved its value as a veritable haven of refuge to thousands of Europeans wearing the King's Uniform, and particularly to Oversea Troops passing to and fro, it was realised that a similar home from home was desirable and necessary for Coloured Troops. The S.A. Gifts and Comforts Committee accordingly erected, at a cost of approximately £1,000, a Coloured Troops Rest House on a site on the Castle Glacis just beyond the Grand Parade, Cape Town, which was very kindly placed at the disposal of the Committee by Brigadier-General Cavendish, C.M.G., G.O.C., South Africa. The cost of erection of the Rest House was considerably lessened by the generous manner in which the Architects (Messrs. Black & Fagg) and the builders (Messrs. Morris & Co.) met the S.A. Gifts and Comforts Committee. The Rest House was opened on October 10th, 1917. Sir James Rose-Innes, Chief Justice of the Union and President of the S.A. Gifts and Comforts Organisation, presided at the opening ceremony. He was supported by Brig.-General Cavendish, C.M.G., G.O.C. South Africa and by His Worship the Mayor, Harry Hands Esq., and by many members of the Gifts and Comforts Committee, the Cape Corps Recruiting Committee, leading Citizens and Officers of the Cape Garrison, etc. Sir James, in his opening address, mentioned that the S.A. Gifts and Comforts Committee forwarded gifts to the value of £300 monthly to the Cape Corps Gifts and Comforts Committee for the benefit of the Cape Corps and other coloured units. At the Opening Ceremony the 1st Cape Corps furnished the Guard of Honour, the smartness of which was the subject of comment by Sir James Rose-Innes.

The Rest House for Coloured Troops remained open from the 10th October, 1917, for close on two years and proved a veritable godsend to the numbers of coloured troops who visited Cape Town on duty or on leave or who passed to and fro going or coming from the various war theatres. The catering arrangements at the Rest House were in the hands of the Ladies Section of the Comforts Committee and were all that could have been desired.

ASSISTANCE FROM THE GOVERNOR-GENERAL'S FUND.

The very generous and much needed assistance which a substantial number of ex-Cape Corps and other Coloured soldiers have received since demobilisation from the Governor-General's Fund must certainly not be overlooked in this chapter. No man in need of temporary financial assistance, or of a loan or cash grant to enable him to start in business or trade or to resume a business or trade interrupted by his period of active service, or to rehabilitate himself in civil life, has appealed in vain to the Governor-General's Fund, and many who have already thoroughly re-established themselves have ample reason to be grateful for assistance rendered. The Returned Soldiers' Advisory Board (Coloured Branch) was established in Cape Town in November, 1918, with offices on the Grand Parade. There every Coloured soldier after demobilisation was enabled to register himself with a view to obtaining employment or re-instatement in any employment engaged in prior to enlistment. The Advisory Board is still carrying on the good work and is composed of prominent Cape Town Citizens. The majority of the Committee are business men with heavy calls on their time, but they have nevertheless most unselfishly devoted much valuable time to Advisory Board work by meeting at least once a week. Men unable to obtain immediate employment and in need of assistance have their cases gone into. Enquiries are made and each case treated on its merits. If the case is genuine relief by way of financial assistance from the Governor-General's Fund is recommended. Recommendations are made under the following headings, viz.:—

    (a) No employment—money grant made.
    (b) Employment secured—grant made pending receipt of first wages.
    (c) Certified medically unfit—money grant made.
    (d) Clothing required—granted.
       In the case of men with dependents grants of clothing are made to the latter in genuine and deserving cases.

(e) In the event of illness the Committee has the individual medically examined, and should it be ascertained that the illness is not due to or aggravated by military service, which prevents him receiving treatment in a Military Hospital, steps are taken to have the patient admitted to a Civil Hospital.

(f) Men suffering from illness or disease which cannot be conveniently treated in their homes have also, on the recommendation of the Committee, been handed over to the Corporation Medical Authorities for treatment in one or other of the local institutions.

(g) In the case of men unable to carry on their present occupation, but not so ill as to require medical treatment, they are, on the recommendation of the Honorary Medical Officer, handed over by the Committee to be taught a trade at the Vocational Training Institution (Coloured Branch) to which reference is presently made.

(h) In cases where pay, allowances or gratuity are due and not yet paid by the Authorities to men whilst still inmates of Hospitals, grants against stop orders are recommended by the Committee by advances from the Governor-General's Fund to the dependents of the detail concerned.

(i) In the event of illness of a serious nature of dependents, such as confinement cases, the payment of a Maternity Grant from the Governor-General's Fund is recommended.

(j) In the case of men in the advanced stages of tuberculosis and similar illnesses requiring removal from the coast, as a result of strong recommendations to the Government, such details are transferred to the Military Hospital at Tempe, near Bloemfontein.

Up to the present more than one thousand men and also a considerable number of dependents have been dealt with by the Advisory Board, and a very large sum of money has been disbursed. It is satisfactory to be able to record on the assurance of the Board that in the large majority of cases the ex-soldiers have appreciated the efforts made on their behalf, and that to the knowledge of the Committee rarely has the treatment meted out to the men been abused.

There cannot be the slightest doubt that men who have fought and suffered as many have during the past four or five years are entitled by every moral and legal right to consideration and treatment on their return from service such as above set forth. In fact in many cases even such kindness, assistance, and consideration as has been their reward falls short of what the men have deserved, as no possible reward can repay what some men have given. Nevertheless on behalf of the returned men of the 1st Cape Corps at least one may and must take this opportunity of expressing the most cordial and heartfelt thanks for all that has been done for them by a large number of those in Cape Town, in particular, and in other parts of the Union in general, who, being for one reason or another unable to take up arms themselves, have worked, many for more than five years, so hard, so ungrudgingly, and so unselfishly to do whatever lay in their power to help the men whilst in the field and to lighten their lot on their return.

The members of the Returned Soldiers' Advisory Board (Coloured Branch) who have been certainly not the least hard-working of Cape Town War Workers are: Canon S. W. Lavis (Chairman); Messrs. C. M. Gibbs, J.P., M.P.C.; J. W. Mushet, M.L.A.; the Revs. W. L. Clementson, R. P. Smart, and Caradoc Davies; Dr. R. D. A. Douglas (Honorary Medical Officer); Messrs. M. J. Fredericks, Henry Hartog, and A. S. Williams; Major Wm. Jardine (an ex-Officer of the 1st Cape Corps); Major N. A. N. Black (Secretary); D. Hodemaker (ex-Sergeant 1st Cape Corps) late Assistant Secretary, and Mr. M. J. Abrahamse (ex-Sergeant 1st Cape Corps) present Assistant Secretary.

Canon Lavis was the representative of the above Board on the General Advisory Board, and in addition he was a member of the Rest House Committee and also Chaplain to the Cape Corps Depôt whilst the same was at Woltemade III.

The above Board also constitutes the Committee of the Coloured Vocational Training Institute.

VOCATIONAL TRAINING.

The question of Vocational Training of disabled ex-members of Coloured Units has received the most sympathetic treatment. When vocational training was commenced for disabled European details no provision was made for Coloured men, but since April, 1919, that omission has been rectified, and to-day most successful efforts are being made to deal with disabled Coloured men and to fit with a new trade men unable to follow their pre-War occupations owing to disability caused through active service.

Some difficulty was experienced at the outset in finding a suitable building, but in April, 1919, a beginning in a small way was made. Very soon the Committee were compelled to look around to find a larger building. In October, 1919, much bigger premises, capable of accommodating one hundred learners, were found in Muir Street, off Sir Lowry Road, Cape Town, and there satisfactory work is being accomplished.

The trades taught under capable instructors are bootmaking and repairing, saddlery and harness making, and leather work generally. The men have settled down to their new work and are very anxious to become efficient and to launch out on their own and make a fresh start in life. The men in the bootmaking section, when their training is complete and the instructor is satisfied that they are capable of commencing work for themselves, are given a start by receiving an outfit of tools, which, if they continue their work, they are allowed to retain as their own property. Several have already been trained and placed and, the Committee have every reason to believe, are doing well.

The Leatherwork Section naturally requires a longer period of training, and care has to be taken by the Committee in choosing suitable men for this work. While undergoing training they are taught bag and suit case making and harness stitching. When their training is complete they obtain employment in one of the factories in the town. Here a word must be said in regard to the employers, who have been always willing to take these men and have shown them every consideration. The Vocational Training Committee is constantly in touch with the men and meets once a week. Frequent visits are also made to the Institute. The valuable time spent by the Committee is only a secondary consideration with them where the welfare of the learners is concerned.

In addition to the above named the Rev. George Robson is now also a Member of the Committee, the Secretary to which is Mr. L. Evans. The Superintendent of the Institution is Mr. J. F. Mason, himself an ex-Officer who saw service during the War. Mr. Mason is very keen on the men and pleased with their progress.

In concluding this brief reference to the good work done by the Advisory Board and the Vocational Training Institution, it may be said in a word that no deserving man in need has appealed in vain to the Advisory Board and through them to the Committee of the Governor-General's Fund.

THE REGIMENTAL BAND.

The Regimental Band was formed early in March, 1918, at Kimberley. A valuable set of instruments was presented by the Cape Corps Gifts and Comforts Committee. Mr. C. Linsell of Cape Town, an old bandsman of that splendid body the Royal Irish Constabulary, was attested as a member of the

THE STORY OF THE 1st CAPE CORPS.

Photo by] [*Aziz & Dores, Alexandria, Egypt.*
LIEUT.-COLONEL MORRIS, C.M.G., D.S.O., AND CAPTAIN H. EDWARDS WITH THE REGIMENTAL BAND TAKEN AT MUSTAPHA CAMP, ALEXANDRIA, EGYPT, JUNE, 1919.

THE STORY OF THE 1st CAPE CORPS.

Corps and appointed Bandmaster with the rank of Acting first-class Warrant Officer. Mr. Linsell soon licked promising material into something like preliminary shape, and good progress had been made before the Band embarked from Durban for Egypt with the Reserve Half Battalion in June, 1918. On arrival in the land of the Pharoahs the Band very soon proceeded to the front, where they contributed to the enjoyment of our Brigade and others when behind the line. After the Armistice the Band returned to Mustapha with the Battalion, and there during the ensuing eight months, Bandmaster Linsell was able to rapidly advance the skill of his musicians, who became in time quite useful performers. The cost of maintenance of the Band and the pay of the Bandmaster was borne by the Officers, and when demobilisation came about in September, 1919, the Band Fund was sufficient to enable the Bandmaster's services to be retained for one year.

During the past twelve months Mr. Linsell has been busy continuing the training of his men, practices taking place in the evening after the men have done their day's work.

The Band has appeared in public in Cape Town on several occasions, and is expected to do so more frequently in the near future now that they have attained quite an average measure of proficiency. A visit to Kimberley is on the *tapis*, and within the next six months it is hoped that the Band will obtain frequent engagements in Cape Town and the Peninsula. They are certainly efficient enough to contribute much to the enjoyment of Europeans as well as their compatriots in the Cape Peninsula. Quite recently, thanks to the courtesy of the Minister of Defence, Colonel Mentz, and to the good offices of Lieut.-Colonel Blew, District Staff Officer, Cape Town, uniforms have been issued to the Bandsmen by the Union Defence Department. Lieut.-Colonel Blew and Major Hodgson, Staff Adjutant, U.D.F., Cape Town, have both taken much interest in the Band since their return from Egypt, and their assistance has been much appreciated by all concerned.

Major William Jardine, of Cape Town, in addition to his activities as a member of the Returned Soldiers' Advisory Board and as a member of the Vocational Training Institution Committee is also Band President and Honorary Treasurer.

CAPE CORPS MEMORIAL FUND.

Very shortly after the first heavy casualties sustained by the Battalion (in East Africa in November, 1917), it was decided to inaugurate a Cape Corps Memorial Fund. Practically every Officer and man demobilised during 1919 contributed a day's pay to the Fund. At a Meeting of Officers held on board H.M.T. "Tambov" on September 1st, 1919, a few days before arrival at Cape Town for demobilisation, the balance standing to the credit of the Regimental Fund was voted to the Memorial Fund, and similarly the balance to credit of Officers' Mess Fund.

Shortly after arrival at Cape Town the Cape Corps Concert Party gave a most successful Concert in the City Hall, Cape Town, in aid of the Memorial Fund, which realized the useful amount of over £100, thanks to the energetic work and advertising of Mr. A. S. Williams. Soon afterwards the Concert Party visited Port Elizabeth and gave two concerts there, which realized a substantial amount. The sum total of the above efforts and subscriptions is that approximately £700 stands to the credit of the Memorial Fund and is in the hands of the Trustees, Colonel Sir W. E. M. Stanford and Major Wm. Jardine.

THE STORY OF THE 1st CAPE CORPS.

The site and form of the proposed Memorial remains to be decided. The Mayor of Cape Town was approached some months ago, but, owing to the number of memorials which it is desired to erect, and the limited amount of suitable space, His Worship could not offer an acceptable site. It is hoped, however, that when the Castle at Cape Town is handed over by the Imperial Authorities to the Union Government, as it is shortly to be, a suitable site may then be forthcoming within the Castle Grounds.

Over four hundred and fifty Officers and men of the 1st Cape Corps laid down their lives, and it is therefore certainly meet and fitting that a satisfactory site should be found and that a handsome and entirely worthy, appropriate and abiding Memorial should be erected.

PENSIONS.

It is very satisfactory to be able to record that during the Session of Parliament of the Union which closed a few months ago, a Pensions Bill was passed to increase the pensions of South Africans disabled during the late War and also the pensions to dependents of men killed. Under that Bill disabled men of the Cape Corps and the next of kin or dependents will benefit to some extent. That is as it should be, as the previous scale of pensions was by no means adequate or just. Our thanks are due to the Members of both Houses for that act of tardy justice.

MEMORIAL SERVICES.

Memorial Services to the fallen men of the Cape Corps have been held annually for the past three years in the City Hall, Cape Town. It is to be hoped that these services will be continued yearly for all time, not only as a tribute to the brave men who fell, but also as a reminder to succeeding generations of the coloured community of South Africa of the splendid sacrifice and service rendered by their kinsfolk for King and Country during the Great War.

THE FUTURE.

The positively last word of this Afterword must be an expression of the very greatest regret that it has not been found possible to perpetuate the Cape Corps in some form or other of Military Service.

When the Battalion returned for final demobilisation shortly over a year ago, their smartness, military bearing and discipline, etc., was the subject of general and favourable comment. Many who remembered the men when they came to the Recruiting Stations in 1915 could not but express the greatest surprise at the contrast provided by the same men in 1919. The result of discipline and training and an ordered life was remarkable. It is the greatest of pities that the result of so much sustained endeavour and that such promising material cannot be utilised.

Every able bodied man in the far flung dominions of the British Empire has, if he feels so disposed, the opportunity of military training and service, either in the regular or auxiliary forces of the Empire or of the particular dominion of his domicile. Why not then the Coloured men of the Union of South Africa? It may be urged that there are practical and academic objections to the maintenance of a Cape Coloured Regiment as a Volunteer Corps or as a Unit of the Union Defence Force. If that be granted, which it is not, then surely it should be possible to recruit the men in the Union and ship them away to some portion of the Empire where the colour bar or any similar objection does not obtain.

THE STORY OF THE 1st CAPE CORPS.

There the Unit could be maintained, and through its medium most valuable training imparted to the young Coloured men of the Union. The period of service could be from three to five years and the service compulsory (as it is in the Active Citizen Force, U.D.F.), between the ages of say 18 and 25. The men could be taught trades or handicrafts as well as military duties and exercises. The effect of such a scheme would certainly be most marked upon the rising generation of Cape Coloured men and, through them, upon the whole Coloured community. Physically, morally and mentally the men would benefit to an astounding degree.

That much must be obvious to all those who saw the Cape Corps recruits between 1914/17, and the finished article in 1919. When the 1st Cape Corps was demobilised, over one thousand strong, at Cape Town in September, 1919, not one man found his way into the Police Courts, although a large majority had drawn substantial amounts of arrear pay, and might well have been excused "a jamboree." More need not be said.

Photo by] [*Payne's Studios, Cape Town.*
MR. A. S. WILLIAMS.
Hon. Secretary, Cape Corps Gifts and Comforts Committee.

MR. P. C. RYAN.
Member of Cape Corps Recruiting Committee

Explanation of Abbreviations.

A.A.G.	Assistant Adjutant-General.
A.C.F.	Active Citizen Force.
A.D.C.	Aide-de-Camp.
A.G.	Adjutant-General.
A.D.M.S.	Assistant Director of Medical Services.
A.P.M.	Assistant Provost-Marshal.
A.T.	Ammunition Transport.
A./C.S.M.	Acting Company Sergeant-Major.
A./R.Q.M.S.	Acting Regimental Quartermaster Sergeant.
A./Q.M.S.	Acting Quartermaster Sergeant.
Bde.	Brigade.
Brig.	Brigadier.
Brig. Gen.	Brigadier-General.
B.E.A.	British East Africa.
B.G.G.S.	Brigadier-General—General Staff
Bt.	Brevet.
Bn. Btn.	Battalion.
B.W.I.	British West India.
C.A.H.T.C.	Cape Auxiliary Horse Transport Corps.
C.B.	Companion of the Bath.
C.C.L.R.	Cape Coloured Labour Regiment.
C.E.	Civil Engineer.
C. in C.	Commander-in-Chief.
C.G.A.	Cape Garrison Artillery.
C.O.	Commanding Officer.
Co.	Company.
C.M.G.	Companion of the Most Distinguished Order of St. Michael and St. George.
C.M.R.	Cape Mounted Rifles.
C.M.P.	Cape Mounted Police.
C.R.A.	Commanding Royal Artillery.
C.T.	Camel Transport.
C.Q.M.S.	Company Quartermaster Sergeant.
C.S.M.	Company Sergeant-Major.
C.V.O.	Commander of the Royal Victorian Order.
D.A.G.	Deputy Adjutant-General.
D.A.A.G.	Deputy Assistant Adjutant-General.
D.A.D.M.L.	Deputy Assistant Director of Military Labour.
D.C.M.	Recipient of Distinguished Conduct Medal.
D.L.I.	Durban Light Infantry.
D.E.O.V.R.	Duke of Edinburgh's Own Volunteer Rifles.
D.M.T.	District Mounted Troops.
D.O.R.E.	Divisional Officer, Royal Engineers.
D.P.O.	District Political Officer.
D.S.O.	Companion of the Distinguished Service Order
D.Q.M.G.	Deputy Quartermaster General.
E.A.M.T.C.	East African Mechanical Transport Corps.
E.A.P.F.	East African Protectorate Forces.
E.E.F.	Egyptian Expeditionary Force.
E.M.R.	Eastern Mounted Rifles.
E.S.O.	Embarkation Staff Officer.
F.A.M.P.	Frontier Armed Mounted Police.
F.O.O.	Forward Observation Officer.

G.B.D.	General Base Depôt.
G.C.B.	Knight Grand Cross of the Bath.
G.C.M.G.	Knight Grand Cross of the Most Distinguished Order of St. Michael and St. George.
G.E.A.	German East Africa.
G.H.Q.	General Headquarters.
G.O.C.I.C.	General Officer Commanding in Chief.
G.O.C.	General Officer Commanding.
G.S.	General Staff.
G.S.O.	General Staff Officer.
G.R.O.	General Routine Officer.
G.S.W.A.	German South-West Africa.
H.M.	His Majesty's.
H.M.T.	His Majesty's Troopship.
H.M.A.T.	His Majesty's Australian Troopship.
H.E.	His Excellency.
I.D.	Intelligence Department.
i/c.	In charge.
I.F.A.	Indian Field Ambulance.
I.G.C.	Inspector-General of Communications.
I.L.H.	Imperial Light Horse.
I.M.S.	Indian Medical Service.
I.Y.	Imperial Yeomanry.
J.M.R.	Johannesburg Mounted Rifles.
J.P.	Justice of the Peace.
K.A.R.	King's African Rifles.
K.B.E.	Knight Commander of the British Empire.
K.C.	King's Counsel.
K.C.B.	Knight Commander of the Most Honourable Order of the Bath.
K.C.M.G.	Knight Commander of St. Michael and St. George.
K.A.R.M.I.	King's African Riflemen Mounted Infantry.
K.O.S.B.	King's Own Scottish Borderers.
Lieut.-Col.	Lieutenant-Colonel.
L.Corpl.	Lance-Corporal.
L.N. Lancs.	Loyal North Lancashire.
M.B.E.	Member of Order of the British Empire.
M.B.F.A.	Mounted Brigade Field Ambulance.
M.C.	Recipient of Military Cross.
M.D.	Motor Depatch (Riders).
M.G.	Machine Gun.
M.M.	Recipient of Military Medal.
M.O.	Medical Officer.
M.P.C.	Member of Provincial Council (South Africa).
M.R.	Mounted Rifles.
M.L.A.	Member of the Legislative Assembly (South Africa).
M.L.B.	Military Labour Bureau.
M.I.	Mounted Infantry.
M.T.	Mechanical Transport.
M.V.O.	Member of the 4th or 5th Class of the Royal Victorian Order.
Maj.-Gen.	Major-General.
N.C.O.	Non-Commissioned Officer.
N.M.R.	Northern Mounted Rifles.

O.C.	Officer Commanding.
O.T.C.	Officers' Training Corps.
P.E.A.	Portuguese East Africa.
P.L. of C.	Palestine Lines of Communication.
P.O.W.	Prisoner of War.
Pte.	Private.
Q.R.V.	Queenstown Rifle Volunteers.
Q.M.S.	Quartermaster Sergeant.
Q.M.R.	Quartermaster.
R.A.F.	Royal Air Force.
R.A.O.C.	Royal Army Ordnance Corps.
R.A.M.C.	Royal Army Medical Corps.
R.F.C.	Royal Flying Corps.
R.G.A.	Royal Garrison Artillery.
R.H.B.	Reserve Half Battalion.
R.A.S.C.	Royal Army Service Corps.
R.E.	Royal Engineers.
R.M.O.	Regimental Medical Officer.
R.O.D.	Railway Operations Department.
R.Q.M.S.	Regimental Quartermaster Sergeant.
R.S.M.	Regimental Sergeant-Major.
R.W.F.	Royal Welsh Fusiliers.
R.N.A.S.	Royal Naval Air Service.
R.T.O.	Railway Transport Officer.
R.F.A. (T.F.)	Royal Field Artillery (Territorial Force).
S.A.E.C.	South African Engineer Corps.
S.A.F.A.	South African Field Artillery.
S.A.H.	South African Horse.
S.A.H.A.	South African Heavy Artillery.
S.A.C.	South African Constabulary.
S.A.S.C. (T. & R.)	South African Service Corps (Transport and Remounts).
S.A.M.R.	South African Mounted Riflemen.
S.O.	Signalling Officer.
S.A.I.	South African Infantry.
S.A.M.C.	South African Medical Corps.
S.A.M.D.R.	South African Motor Despatch Riders.
S.A.N.L.C.	South African Native Labour Corps.
S.A.S.C.M.T.	South African Service Corps Mechanical Transport.
S.R.C.	Southern Rhodesian Constabulary.
S.W.A.	South-West Africa.
Sgt.	Sergeant.
S.A.S.M.	South African Stokes Mortars.
T.D.	Territorial Decoration.
T.F.	Territorial Forces.
U.D.F.	Union Defence Force.
U.K.	United Kingdom.
V.D.	Volunteer Officer's Decoration.
W.H.	Western Horse.
W.O.	Warrant Officer.
W.P.M.R.	Western Province Mounted Rifles.

OFFICERS—NOMINAL ROLL OF.

Below is the Nominal Roll of all officers who served with the Battalion at one time or another between the periods of mobilisation and demobilisation of the Unit. The names appear in order of seniority and/or date on which officers were gazetted to the Battalion.

MORRIS, G. A., C.M.G., D.S.O., Lieut.-Colonel, Commanding Officer, joined 5/10/15, demobilised 5/10/19.
HOY, C. N., D.S.O. and Bar, Senior Major, Second in Command, joined 1/11/15, Acting Lieut.-Colonel 30/10/17 to 9/11/17, 6/12/17 to 21/12/17, 13/4/18 to 10/8/18, 8/10/18 to 9/11/18, granted rank of Lieut.-Colonel on demobilisation 17/6/19.
COWELL, W. R., D.S.O., Captain, joined 6/10/15, Major 16/5/17, killed in action at Kh. Jibeit, near Jerusalem, Palestine, 20/9/18.
DURHAM, C. G., D.S.O., Captain, joined 18/10/15, Major 15/1/16, transferred to the King's African Rifles in East Africa in May, 1917.
GUNNINGHAM, W. G., Captain (Adjutant), joined 18/10/15, transferred to Political Department, East Africa 21/9/16.
CAMPBELL, L., Captain (O.C. Machine Gun Section), joined 18/10/15, transferred to S.A. Native Labour Corps 21/4/17, was demobilised 20/1/20, died at Usakos, S.W.A. 21/7/20.
BAGSHAWE, F. J., Captain, joined 30/10/15, transferred to Political Department, East Africa, 14/11/16.
BRADSTOCK, F. E., D.S.O., M.C. and Bar, Lieutenant, joined 18/10/15, Captain 1/11/15, Major 26/6/17, transferred to King's African Rifles in East Africa 16/12/17.
WARR, H.G., Lieutenant, joined 18/10/15, Captain 1/12/15, medically boarded and released 17/7/17.
ROBINSON, J. E., Lieutenant, joined 18/10/15, Captain 18/12/15, medically boarded and released 8/4/19.
STEVENS, C. E., Lieutenant, joined 18/10/15, Captain 1/1/16, medically boarded and released 27/3/18.
ROBERTSON, D. W. Lieutenant, joined 18/10/15, Captain 21/9/16, demobilised 27/6/19.
MICHAU, J. M., Lieutenant, joined 18/10/15, Captain 6/11/16, demobilised 22/9/19.
YOUART, S., Lieutenant, joined 18/10/15, Captain 11/12/16, demobilised 25/6/19.
DENNISON, J. E., Lieutenant (Signalling Officer), joined 18/10/15, Captain 27/9/16, medically boarded and released 17/7/17.
ANDERSON, W. P., Lieutenant, joined 30/10/15, Captain 5/11/15, granted local rank of Major 2/7/17 whilst O.C. Cape Corps Depôt at Woltemade III., Major 16/12/17, transferred to Union Defence Forces 15/2/18, retransferred to 1st Cape Corps with rank of Captain 1/8/18, Major 21/9/18, demobilised 11/7/19.
BURGER, F., Lieutenant, joined 1/11/15, Captain 21/9/16, demobilised 6/10/19.
ASHLEY, S., Lieutenant, joined 22/11/15, Captain 16/5/17, medically boarded and released 30/4/18.
TANDY, J. H., M.C., Lieutenant, joined 1/12/15, Captain 27/9/16, demobilised 22/9/19.
CUNINGHAM, W. J. R., Lieutenant, joined 3/12/15, Captain 14/9/16, Major 25/3/18, demobilised 26/9/19.
PROCTER, W. W., Lieutenant, joined 10/12/15, transferred to 2nd/2nd King's African Rifles in East Africa 1/6/16.
HARRIS, J. V., M.C., Lieutenant, joined 16/12/15, Captain 7/2/17, killed in action at Kh. Jibeit, near Jerusalem, Palestine, 20/9/18.
ARNOTT, J., D.C.M., Lieutenant (Transport Officer), joined 20/12/15, Acting Captain 17/4/17, Captain 20/7/17, medically boarded and released 31/3/18.
HALLIER, F. C., Lieutenant, joined 24/12/15, Acting Captain 9/7/17, Captain 16/12/17, seconded to Political Department in East Africa 20/10/17.
ALEXANDER, W. W., Lieutenant, joined 24/12/15, medically boarded and released 12/6/18.
MACINTOSH, G. C., 2nd Lieutenant, joined 18/10/15, Lieutenant 18/4/16, transferred to Royal Flying Corps 31/12/16, demobilised 4/3/20.
WHITAKER, S. W., 2nd Lieutenant, joined 18/10/15, Lieutenant 18/4/16, transferred to King's African Rifles in East Africa 16/6/16.
PEARSE, D. K., 2nd Lieutenant, joined 22/11/15, Lieutenant 25/5/16, Acting Captain 18/6/17, Captain 16/12/17, demobilised 6/10/19.
STANFORD, F. W. C., 2nd Lieutenant, joined 22/11/15, Lieutenant 25/5/16, Acting Captain 18/6/17, Captain 25/3/18, medically boarded and released 12/4/18.
MURCHIE, F., 2nd Lieutenant, joined 1/12/15, Lieutenant 16/6/16, Acting Captain 25/9/17, Captain 25/3/18, transferred to Post Bellum Army at Alexandria, Egypt, 12/7/19.
EDWARDS, H., 2nd Lieutenant, joined 7/12/15, Lieutenant 7/6/16, Acting Captain 18/6/17, Captain 25/3/18, demobilised 17/10/19.
ROSE-INNES, T. P., 2nd Lieutenant, joined 20/12/15, Lieutenant 20/6/16, Acting Captain 22/11/17, Captain 25/3/18, demobilised 5/9/19.
WILSON, R., 2nd Lieutenant, joined 11/1/16, Lieutenant 26/7/16, medically boarded and released 22/6/17.

THE STORY OF THE 1st CAPE CORPS.

RACKSTRAW, E. J., M.C., 2nd Lieutenant, joined 27/1/16, Lieutenant 27/7/16, demobilised 28/6/19.
BELL, HARLAND S., Lieutenant, joined 7/4/16, transferred to Political Department in East Africa 16/6/16.
CLOKE, R. A., Staff Sergeant, joined 4/12/15, C.Q.M.S. 9/1/16, C.S.M. 17/4/16, R.Q.M.S. 3/5/16, 2nd Lieutenant 16/6/16, Lieutenant 16/12/16, demobilised 14/9/19.
HOSACK, J. C., R.Q.M.S., joined 29/10/15, 2nd Lieutenant 4/12/15, reverted at own request to R.Q.M.S. 14/12/15, 2nd Lieutenant 16/6/16, killed in action at Masinga, near Kangata, in East Africa on 20/7/16.
GARDNER, C. S. H., Platoon Sergeant, joined 1/3/16, 2nd Lieutenant 16/6/16, Lieutenant 16/12/16, demobilised 23/6/19.
HAYTON, A. A., Staff Sergeant, seconded from U.D.F. in November, 1915, transferred to Cape Corps 30/6/16, 2nd Lieutenant 1/7/16, Lieutenant 1/1/17, demobilised 6/7/19.
WIGMAN, W. T., Staff Sergeant, joined 1/1/16, 2nd Lieutenant 21/7/16, Lieutenant 21/1/17, demobilised 17/9/19.
WHITE, G. C., Captain, joined 1/8/16, reverted at own request to Lieutenant 10/12/16, died at 47th Stationary Hospital at Gaza on 17/10/18 (of wounds received in action at Kh. Jibeit, near Jerusalem, on 20/9/18).
COATES, H., Lieutenant, joined 3/8/16, medically boarded and released 25/3/18.
HEATON, W. S., M.C., 2nd Lieutenant, joined 11/8/16, Lieutenant 11/2/17, rejoined Loyal North Lancashire Regiment 21/8/18.
POTGIETER, M., Lieutenant, joined 20/8/16, medically boarded and released 20/7/18.
JAMES, T. E., Lieutenant, joined 20/8/16, Captain 27/6/18, demobilised 10/7/19.
JARDINE, WILLIAM, Capt., joined 28/8/16, demobilised 27/5/19.
FEETHAM, R. M.L.A., 2nd Lieutenant, joined 28/8/16, Lieutenant 28/2/17, demobilised 30/12/19.
LESLIE, A., 2nd Lieutenant, joined 28/8/16, Lieutenant 28/2/17, Captain 5/10/18, demobilised 6/10/19.
DE VILLIERS, G. W., 2nd Lieutenant, joined 28/8/16, Lieutenant 29/4/17, transferred to A.C.F., U.D.F., 14/2/18.
GUEST, I. A. M., 2nd Lieutenant, joined 30/8/16, Lieutenant 28/2/17, killed in action at Mkungu, Lindi area, East Africa, on 6/11/17.
THORNTON, H. R., 2nd Lieutenant, joined 21/8/16, medically boarded and released 7/6/17.
HOWE-BROWNE, N F., 2nd Lieutenant, joined 14/9/16, Lieutenant 14/3/17, seconded to Political Department in East Africa 2/3/18.
THOMPSON, R. A., 2nd Lieutenant, joined 18/10/16, Lieutenant 18/4/17, transferred to Political Department in East Africa 23/12/17.
BAIN, T., 2nd Lieutenant, joined 30/10/16, Lieutenant 30/4/17, released from service 6/5/18.
STUBBS, E. P., M.C., 2nd Lieutenant, joined 31/10/16, Lieutenant 30/4/17, demobilised 7/9/19.
WALTON, H., Lieutenant, joined 30/10/16, medically boarded and released 19/3/18.
HORSEMAN, G., 2nd Lieutenant, joined 4/11/16, Lieutenant 4/5/17, demobilised 3/12/19.
BOURHILL, A. F., 2nd Lieutenant, joined 13/11/16, Lieutenant 15/5/17, medically boarded and released 26/7/18.
BROWNE, E. H., 2nd Lieutenant, joined 15/11/16, Lieutenant 15/5/17, released from service 1/5/18.
HOFFE, T. M., 2nd Lieutenant, joined 26/12/16, Lieutenant 26/6/17, Acting Captain 1/7/17, died of pneumonia at Dodoma, East Africa, 23/9/17.
DIFFORD, A. N., 2nd Lieutenant, joined 10/1/17, Lieutenant 10/7/17, killed in action at Kh. Jibeit, near Jerusalem, Palestine, 20/9/18.
BARNARD, G. R., 2nd Lieutenant, joined 15/1/17, Lieutenant 15/7/17, died of malaria near Rham Alla, Palestine, on 22/7/18.
ABBOTT, C. F., 2nd Lieutenant, joined 29/3/17, Lieutenant 29/9/17, killed in action at Mkungu, East Africa, on 6/11/17.
ROSE-INNES, S. H., 2nd Lieutenant, joined 30/3/17, Lieutenant 30/9/17, demobilised 10/9/19.
POWER, W., Lieutenant, joined 10/4/17, killed in action at Mkungu, Lindi area, East Africa, 6/11/17.
BOTHA, D. F., Lieutenant, joined 10/5/17, transferred to Army of Occupation in Egypt 17/5/19, and promoted Captain, demobilised 12/4/20.
McNEIL, J., 2nd Lieutenant, joined 10/5/17, died 7/11/17 of wounds received in action at Mkungu, East Africa 6/11/17.
PILLANS, C. S. M., Lieutenant, joined 23/6/17, relinquished commission 15/2/18.
COLSON, R., 2nd Lieutenant, joined 2/7/17, Lieutenant 2/1/19, demobilised 6/7/19.
SAMUELSON, S. V., M.C., 2nd Lieutenant, joined 2/7/17, Lieutenant 2/1/19, demobilised 21/10/19.
DREYER, J. S., 2nd Lieutenant, joined 16/7/17, killed in action at Kh. Jibeit, near Jerusalem, Palestine, 20/9/18.
ROSENEL, E., 2nd Lieutenant, joined 16/7/17, medically boarded and released 11/3/18.
WARE, G. L., 2nd Lieutenant, joined 16/7/17, medically boarded and released 5/3/18.
GIRDWOOD, F. I., 2nd Lieutenant, joined 17/7/17, Lieutenant 17/1/19, demobilised 10/9/19.
BLOXAM, E. B., 2nd Lieutenant, joined 17/7/17, medically boarded and released 28/1/20.
DAVIES, M. S., 2nd Lieutenant, joined 21/7/17, Lieutenant 21/1/19, demobilised 10/9/19.
TEMPLER, E. W., 2nd Lieutenant, joined 7/11/17, transferred to Army of Occupation in Egypt 25/6/19.
VIPAN, C. A., 2nd Lieutenant, joined 7/11/17, killed in action at Kh. Jibeit, near Jerusalem, Palestine, 20/9/18.
GIBSON, A. S., 2nd Lieutenant, joined 17/11/17, Lieutenant 17/5/18, medically boarded and released 3/2/20.
MOIR, B. H. Lieutenant, joined 21/2/18, demobilised 8/10/19.
MANLEY, H. C., Lieutenant, joined 16/3/18, demobilised 30/6/19.
ROSS, A. S., Lieutenant, joined 28/3/18, demobilised 4/7/19.
LAMBE, C. R., 2nd Lieutenant, joined 28/3/18, demobilised 10/9/19.
WOODS, G. A., M.C., Lieutenant, joined 28/3/18, demobilised 22/9/19.

THE STORY OF THE 1st CAPE CORPS.

ANTILL, A. E. J., 2nd Lieutenant, joined 25/4/18, died on 21/9/18 (of wounds received in action at Kh. Jibeit, near Jerusalem, Palestine, on 20/9/18).
WALLIS, H., M.C., Lieutenant, joined 30/4/18, demobilised 4/10/19
MOSENTHAL, B. P., 2nd Lieutenant, joined 30/4/18, demobilised 8/9/19.
SOLOMON, R. R., 2nd Lieutenant, joined 1/5/18, demobilised 5/5/19.
JEPPE, O. R., Lieutenant, joined 9/5/18, Captain 21/9/18, demobilised 25/6/19.
BUCHANAN, W. J., 2nd Lieutenant, joined 28/5/18, demobilised 5/8/19.
HILLARY, C. A., Lieut., joined 1/6/18, demobilised 15/11/19.
MACKENZIE, A., 2nd/Lieut., joined 1/6/18, demobilised 6/8/19.
HIRSCH, J. G., 2nd/Lieut., joined 5/6/18, demobilised 7/9/19.
MACFARLANE, P., 2nd/Lieut., joined 10/6/18, demobilised 6/8/19.
HOLLINS, J. L., 2nd Lieutenant, joined 1/7/18, died of wounds at Alexandria, Egypt, on 15/10/18.
ADAMSON, F. C., 2nd/Lieut., joined 2/7/18, demobilised 8/9/19.
VAN DIGGELEN, H. C., Lieutenant, joined in July, 1918, demobilised 20/10/19.
WHITFIELD, Geo., D.C.M., 2nd/Lieut., joined 2/7/18, medically boarded and released 13/3/20.
BUCHANAN, D. H. F., 2nd/Lieut., joined 6/7/18, demobilised 8/10/19.
HALL, R. L., 2nd/Lieut., joined 6/7/18, Lieut. 6/1/20, demobilised 16/2/20.
JOHNSON, L. C., Lieut., joined 8/7/18, demobilised 20/8/19.
BROWN, W. I., 2nd/Lieut., joined 9/7/18, transferred to Army of Occupation in Egypt, 25/6/19.
LOUW, H., 2nd/Lieut., joined 11/7/18, demobilised 8/9/19
SMITH, W. R., Lieutenant, joined 20/9/18, died in Hospital, Kimberley, 22/10/18.
RAINIER, H. A., Lieutenant, joined 2/10/18, died in Hospital, Kimberley, 10/10/18.

REGIMENTAL QUARTERMASTER:
DIFFORD, I. D., Capt., joined 25/9/15, medically boarded and released 29/12/19.

MEDICAL OFFICERS ATTACHED FOR DUTY:
ROBB, R. M., S.A.M.C., Captain, attached from 24/11/15, resigned commission 20/6/16.
McNEIL, R. P., M.C., S.A.M.C., Captain, attached from 13/5/16, resigned commission 15/2/18.
DREW, D. W., S.A.M.C., Captain, attached from 1/3/18, demobilised 24/6/19.
BOUWER, J. W., S.A.M.C., Captain, attached from 25/3/18, demobilised 23/6/19.
DALGLIESH, M. C., R.A.M.C., Captain, attached from 24/3/19, left Cape Town for England for demobilisation, December, 1919, demobilised 5/1/20

PAYMASTERS:
LEVER, C. J., Lieutenant, joined 18/10/15, resigned 16/12/15.
BOAM, B., Lieut., joined 21/12/15, Temporary Capt. 21/9/16, Capt. 1/4/18, resigned commission 10/1/19.
SMITH, W. H., Captain, joined 11/1/19, still on service.

REGIMENTAL CHAPLAIN:
EARP-JONES, ALAN, Captain, joined 28/12/15, demobilised 19/9/19.

The below named Officers were seconded from 2nd to 1st Cape Corps about July, 1918, and proceeded to Egypt with Captain Anderson's reinforcements in August, 1918, viz.:—

REUNERT, CLIVE, Lieutenant, demobilised 8/9/19.
WHEELWRIGHT, W. D., 2nd Lieutenant, transferred to Army of Occupation in Egypt 25/6/19, demobilised 12/7/20.

Captains Difford and Rose-Innes at the Pyramids, Cairo.

Photo by] [I.D.D.
Major W. J. R. Cuningham, O.C. R.H.B. at El Arish, October, 1918.

Photo by] [Sergeant Alles.
In the Lines at Mustapha.

Photo by] [I.D.D.
Dar-es-Salaam Harbour.

OFFICERS, 1st CAPE CORPS.

Record of Active Service other than with the Battalion.

NOTE.—The names appear in order of seniority and/or date of joining the 1st Cape Corps.

It has not been possible to obtain the full and complete record of each and every officer, which fact is regretted.

MORRIS, GEORGE ABBOTT, Lieut.-Colonel, C.M.G., D.S.O., Lieutenant, Glen Grey Native Levies, 1899; Lieutenant, Queenstown Rifle Volunteers, 1900; promoted Captain, Q.R.V., 1901; commanded Q.R.V. in Colonel Charles Crewe's Column, 1902; Captain, N.W. Provincial Police, July-September, 1902. Total Anglo-Boer War service, two years. Sub-Inspector, Swaziland Police, 1906-1909; assisted in recruiting Rand Rifles, 1914; Captain, Special Service Squadron 2nd M.R. (Natal Carbineers), October, 1914; promoted Major, November, 1914; and to command Special Service Squadron 2nd M.R. served through Rebellion and in G.S.W.A. from December 12th, 1914, to July 15th, 1915. Mentioned in Despatches in G.S.W.A.; gazetted to command 1st Cape Corps, 5th October, 1915.

HOY, CHARLES NORMAN, Major, D.S.O. and Bar, served during Anglo-Boer War from December, 1899, to 30th June, 1902; started as a Trooper, ended as 1st Lieutenant; units, Royal Canadian Dragoons and Canadian Scouts; medals: Queen's (five clasps) and King's; served with 1st M.R. (Natal Carbineers) as Squadron Commander (Captain) during Rebellion and in G.S.W.A., 1914-15; gazetted to 1st Cape Corps, 1st November, 1915; rank, Senior Major (acted as Commanding Officer for ten months in all).

COWELL, WILLIAM RALPH (Late), Major, D.S.O., had fourteen months' service with Queensland Imperial Bushmen prior to Anglo-Boer War; served for twenty months (1901-1902) with Queensland Imperial Bushmen during Anglo-Boer War; was six months at Army Headquarters, Pretoria, in 1902; final rank, Lieutenant; Queen's and King's medals (three clasps); was on Anglo-German Boundary Commission in East Africa, 1904-5; served during Zululand Rebellion, 1906; joined 2nd M.R. (Natal Carbineers) in 1914, rank Lieutenant, and saw Service during Rebellion and in G.S.W.A. to July, 1915; gazetted to 1st Cape Corps, 6/10/15, rank Captain

DURHAM, CORNEY GEORGE, Major, D.S.O., served throughout Anglo-Boer War 1899-1902; from October, 1899, to January, 1901, with 1st I.L.H.; commissioned in Rand Rifles February, 1901; Queen's and King's medals; Captain and 3rd Field Officer in R.L.I. in G.S.W.A. 8th August, 1914, to 9th July, 1915; Mentioned in Despatches in G.S.W.A.; seconded to 1st Cape Corps 18/10/15, rank Captain; transferred from 1st Cape Corps to 1st/3rd K.A.R. in G.E.A. May, 1917, as Second in Command, promoted Lieut.-Colonel in March, 1918; was promoted to be a Column Commander in P.E.A. (August-October, 1918); received prompt award of D.S.O. for conspicuous gallantry whilst commanding 1st/3rd K.A.R. in G.E.A., July 19th, 1917; Mentioned in Despatches in P.E.A. about October, 1918.

GUNNINGHAM, WILLIAM GREIG, Captain, served throughout Anglo-Boer War 1899-1902 with Thornycroft's Mounted Infantry; promoted Captain 1901; medals: Queen's (six Bars), King's (two Bars); served during Zululand Rebellion, 1906, with Royston's Horse, rank, Captain, medal and clasp; Lieutenant in I.L.H. in G.S.W.A. 1914-1915; gazetted to 1st Cape Corps, 18th October, 1915, rank Captain and Adjutant; transferred from 1st Cape Corps to Political Service in East Africa in September, 1916, and promoted Honorary Major 17th March, 1917.

CAMPBELL, LINDSAY (Late), Captain, served with 16th (Queen's) Lancers 1888-1894 and had three and a half years Foreign Service (India), rank Corporal; served with C.M.R. (Artillery Troop) 1894 to 1898, rank Corporal; was Staff Sergeant Major Cape Police 1898 to 1902 and with Western Light Horse 1901/1902; saw service during Anglo-Boer War; was on Headquarters Staff, Transvaal Volunteers 1903 to 1912, rank Staff Sergeant-Major and Instructor in Musketry, Mounted Drill, and Machine Gunnery; Lieutenant Transvaal Cadets 1913/1914; gazetted Captain in Machine Gun Corps (U.D.F.) 7th October, 1914, and saw service in G.S.W.A., attached to 1st Eastern Rifles; released from service 30th September, 1915; gazetted to 1st Cape Corps 18th October, 1915, rank, Captain and Machine Gun Officer; transferred from Cape Corps, 21st April, 1917, to S.A. Native Labour Corps and proceeded to Flanders where placed in charge of a Prisoner of War Camp at Boulogne; demobilised 20th January, 1920; died at Usakos (S.W.A. Protectorate) of erysipelas and double pneumonia, 21st July, 1920.

BRADSTOCK, FRANK EDGAR, Major, D.S.O., M.C. and Bar, joined C.M.R in 1896, served with them during Anglo-Boer War from 1899 to 1902 as N.C.O., Queen's medal (four clasps), King's (two clasps); joined 1st M.R. (Natal Carbineers) in September, 1914, promoted Lieutenant January, 1915, and served with them during the Rebellion and in G.S.W.A until July, 1915; gazetted to 1st Cape Corps as Lieutenant, 18th October, 1915; transferred from 1st Cape Corps to 2nd K.A.R. in G.E.A., December 16th, 1917, rank, Major; awarded M.C. and mentioned in Despatches whilst serving with 1st Cape Corps in G.E.A.; awarded D.S.O. and Bar to M.C. and Mentioned in Despatches whilst serving with 2nd K.A.R. in G.E.A. and P.E.A., 1918; severely wounded, January, 1917; severely wounded, September, 1918; is still serving with 2nd K.A.R. and is 2nd in command.

BAGSHAWE, FRANCIS JOHN, Captain, served in Matabeleland, 1896, and Mashonaland, 1897, Campaigns (medals and 1897 Bar); served throughout Anglo-Boer War with Roberts' Horse and later with S.A. Constabulary in all ranks to 1st Lieutenant, Queen's and King's medals, Mentioned in Despatches; served as Burgher and afterwards as Assistant Field Cornet with Brand from 21st October, 1914, during Rebellion; served with 5th Mounted Brigade as Captain in 6th Regiment in G.S.W.A. in 1914-1915; released from services 30th July, 1915; Mentioned in Despatches; gazetted to 1st Cape Corps, 30th October, 1915, rank, Captain; transferred to Political Service in East Africa, 14th November, 1916

THE STORY OF THE 1st CAPE CORPS.

WARR, HENRI GEORGE, Captain, enrolled in C.M.R. in 1894; joined C.M.P. (Division II.) in 1896; served in Bechuanaland Campaign 1896/1897, medal and clasp; was detailed for special duty to Langeberg, Korranberg and in Kalahari Desert, 1898; appointed Acting Lieutenant Cape Police (Division II.) in 1901; acted as Recruiting Officer for Western Light Horse and Queenstown and District, May and June, 1901, then seconded for service to Western Light Horse (Lord Metheun's Command) as Captain and Acting Adjutant until conclusion of hostilities in 1902 when gazetted Lieutenant in C.P. (Division II.); Anglo-Boer War, Queen's (four Bars) and King's (two Bars) medals; transferred with rank of Captain (Inspector) to Southern Rhodesian Constabulary in November, 1902 (also J.P.); was at one time O.C., S.R.C. at Salisbury; resigned from S.R.C. in 1908; gazetted Captain, N.M. Rifles and to 1st Cullinans Horse (13th December, 1914); saw service during Rebellion in G.S.W.A., and after cessation of hostilities was for a time Chief of Police at Windhuk; released from service, 10th August, 1915; gazetted to 1st Cape Corps, 18th October, 1915, rank, Lieutenant; served as Assistant Political Officer at Morogoro and Kilossa, East Africa, November, 1916, to February, 1917; released from service with 1st Cape Corps, 17th July, 1917, and proceeded to England, where joined 4th S.A.I. (S.A. Scottish) and served with S.A. Brigade in France from September, 1917, to October, 1918, and was wounded at Beaurevoir, 8th October, 1918; after discharge from hospital was transferred to the Mercantile Marine Reserve and with them was engaged in relief work at Archangel (North Russia) from May, 1919; finally demobilised about December, 1919.

ROBINSON, JOHN EBENEZER, Captain, served throughout Anglo-Boer War (1899-1902), first as a Trooper in 2nd Brabant's Horse and afterwards as Lieutenant in O.R.V. Scouts, Queen's and King's medals (with five clasps in all); joined 1st Imperial Light Horse in 1914 and was promoted from Trooper to Lieutenant one month later; saw service in G.S.W.A. for nine months in 1914-1915; gazetted to 1st Cape Corps as Lieutenant, 18th October, 1915.

STEVENS, CECIL ERNEST, Captain, served in the Gaika (1878) and Zululand (1879) Campaigns, South African General Service medal and clasp; served in Matabele Campaigns, 1893 and 1896; served in Anglo-Boer War, 1900-1902, with French's Scouts, Queen's and King's medals (seven clasps in all); served with S.A.S.C. Transport and Remounts (U.D.F.), October, 1914, to October, 1915, rank, Lieutenant gazetted to 1st Cape Corps, 18th October, 1915, rank, Lieutenant.

ROBERTSON, DONALD WALTER, Captain, joined C.M.R. in 1895 and took part in Pondoland Campaign; left C.M.R. in 1898; served throughout Anglo-Boer War, 1899-1902, first with Remington's Guides, 1899-1900, and afterwards with W.P.M.R., 1901-1902, rank, Lieutenant, Queen's medal (seven Bars), King's medal (two Bars); was one of three selected to represent Remington's Guides on Commander-in-Chief's Bodyguard, with which served until same was disbanded on return of Lord Roberts to England, when transferred to W.P.M.R., final rank, Lieutenant; wounded in 1901; gazetted to 1st Cape Corps, 18th October, 1915, rank, Lieutenant.

MICHAU, JACOBUS MALAN, Captain, Trooper, Special Service Squadron Natal Carbineers in G.S.W.A., 1914-1915; gazetted to 1st Cape Corps, 18th October, 1915, rank, Lieutenant.

YOUART, STEPHEN, Captain, gazetted to 1st Cape Corps, 18th October, 1915, rank, Lieutenant; had no other War Service

DENNISON, JAMES EDWARD, Captain, gazetted to 1st Cape Corps, 18th October, 1915, rank, Lieutenant; further information unobtainable.

ANDERSON, WILLIAM PRITCHARD, Major, served during the Anglo-Boer War for two years and three months, first as Captain and Officer Commanding Imperial Yeomanry Scouts; after the occupation of Pretoria was appointed Assistant Commissioner of Police there; was subsequently attached to the Field Intelligence Department on General Babington's Staff with rank of Major, graded as D.A.A.G., Queen's and King's medals; saw service with the 2nd I.L.H. in G.S.W.A. from October, 1914, to July, 1915, rank, Lieutenant; gazetted to 1st Cape Corps, 30th October, 1915, rank, Lieutenant.

BURGER, FRANCOIS, Captain, served in Anglo-Boer War during 1902, first with Colonel Defence Force as Sergeant then with Graaff-Reinet D.M. Troops; was for some months Superintendent of Burgher Camp at Krugersdorp; Lieutenant, Imperial Light Horse Volunteers, 1st April, 1904, to 30th July, 1908, and was Assistant Adjutant for Musketry for two years; Lieutenant, Rand Rifles in G.S.W.A., 23rd October, 1914, to 1st November, 1915; seconded to 1st Cape Corps, 1st November, 1915, rank, Lieutenant.

ASHLEY, SIDNEY, Captain, served during Anglo-Boer War with Army Service Corps (Transport), Queen's medal; served as Gunner with S.A.F.A. from October to November 22nd, 1915, when transferred to 1st Cape Corps with rank of Lieutenant.

TANDY, JOHN HUBERT, Captain, M.C., Trooper, Special Service Squadron 2nd M.R. (Natal Carbineers) 1st November, 1914; was in G.S.W.A. from 5th December, 1914; promoted Lieutenant Native Labour Corps in G.S.W.A., March 14th, 1915; seconded to 1st Cape Corps, 1st December, 1915, rank, Lieutenant.

CUNINGHAM, WILLIAM JOHN ROLLAND, Major, Private in Lothian and Berkwickshire Yeomanry, 19th Co., 6th Regt. I.Y., 15th January, 1900, to 26th February, 1901; Lieutenant Imperial Light Horse "B" Squadron, 27th February, 1901, to 30th June, 1902, Queen's and King's medals; Lieutenant I.L.H. Volunteers, 1903 to 1904; Lieutenant 2nd I.L.H. in G.S.W.A., 26th October, 1914, to 1915; gazetted to 1st Cape Corps, 3rd December, 1915, rank, Lieutenant.

PROCTER, WILLIAM WILFRED, has General Service medal for service with C.M.P. in Bechuanaland, 1896; served throughout Anglo-Boer War, 1899 to 1902, in Cape Mounted Police; in seige of Kimberley was Trumpeter to Machine Gun Section, Corporal 1901, Sergeant 1902, Queen's and King's medals; gazetted to 1st Cape Corps, rank, Lieutenant, 10th December, 1915; transferred from 1st Cape Corps to 2nd/2nd K.A.R. in G.E.A., 1st June, 1916; later transferred to S.A. General List; was A.P.M. at Dodoma in July, 1917, and at Port Amelia in December, 1917; promoted Captain, December, 1917; demobilised, 19th February, 1919.

HARRIS, JAMES VAUGHAN (Late), Captain, M.C., was 1st Class Trooper in Cape Mounted Police prior to Anglo-Boer War; in Anglo-Boer War was Squadron Sergeant-Major in Bethune's Mounted Infantry, 1899 to 1902, Queen's medal (three clasps) King's medal (2 clasps), King Edward's Coronation Medal, 1902; served as Trooper with Special Service Squadron 2nd M.R. (Natal Carbineers) in G.S.W.A. Campaign, 1914/15; gazetted to 1st Cape Corps, 16th December, 1915, rank, Lieutenant.

ARNOTT, JOSEPH, Captain, D.C.M., served in Anglo-Boer War, October 19th, 1899, to May 31st, 1902, first as Sergeant, Thornycroft's Mounted Infantry, later Sergeant, afterwards promoted Lieutenant in Queenstown Rifle Volunteers, Queen's medal (six Bars) King's medal (two Bars); awarded D.C.M. at Helpmakaar whilst Sergeant in Q.R.V.; gazetted to 1st Cape Corps, rank, Lieutenant, and Transport Officer, 20th December, 1915.

HALLIER, FRANK COLLINGS, Captain, served in G.S.W.A. as Lieutenant, Cradock Commando, 19th October, 1914, to 15th September, 1915; gazetted to 1st Cape Corps, 24th December, 1915, rank, Lieutenant; transferred from 1st Cape Corps to Political Service in G.E.A., 20th October, 1917.

THE STORY OF THE 1st CAPE CORPS.

ALEXANDER, WILLIAM WATKIN, Lieutenant, served during Anglo-Boer War from October, 1899, to July, 1902, first as Private in French's Scouts and afterwards as Intelligent Agent, Queen's and King's medals; joined Brand's Horse in October, 1914, with rank of Lieutenant and was promoted Captain a month later; saw service in G.S.W.A. with 5th Mounted Brigade; gazetted to 1st Cape Corps, 24th December, 1915, rank, Lieutenant.

MACINTOSH, GEORGE CHEYNE, Lieutenant, served as a Trooper in Graaff Reinet Commando, 19th October, 1914, to 7th June, 1915, and saw service in G.S.W.A. in April and May, 1915; gazetted to 1st Cape Corps, 18th October, 1915, rank, 2nd Lieutenant; transferred from 1st Cape Corps at Morogoro, G.E.A., on 31st December, 1916, to 26th Squadron R.F.C. as Observer; proceeded to Egypt, 4th September, 1917, arrived there 5th October, 1917; obtained "wings" 16th February, 1918, and posted next day to 111th Squadron R.F.C. (R.A.F from 1st April, 1918) in Palestine; joined No. 2 African Survey Party R.A.F., 20th November, 1918, and proceeded through the Sudan to Uganda; engaged on Cape to Cairo Air Route at Nimule (Sudan) and Jinja (Uganda) until December, 1919; reached England (via Cairo) January 29th, 1920; demobilised at Winchester, March 4th, 1920.

WHITAKER, SAMUEL WHIELEY, Lieutenant, attested in 2nd Imperial Light Horse, Private (No. 561), 6th November, 1914, and saw service in G.S.W.A.; released 12th June, 1915; gazetted to 1st Cape Corps, 18th October, 1915, rank, 2nd Lieutenant; transferred to K.A.R. in East Africa, 16th June, 1916; relinquished commission on transfer to Ministry of Munitions in England, 11th July, 1917; later rejoined army and was in Egypt and Mesopotamia.

PEARSE, DUDLEY KENNETH, Captain, served as Trooper 1st M.R (Natal Carbineers) during Rebellion and G.S.W.A. Campaign, 9th October, 1914, to 27th July, 1915; gazetted to 1st Cape Corps, 22nd November, 1915, rank, Lieutenant.

STANFORD, FREDERICK WILLIAM CHARLES, Captain, enlisted in D.E.O.V.R., 20th December, 1914, rank, Private, and saw service in G.S.W.A.; released from service 30th July, 1915; gazetted 2nd Lieutenant in 1st Cape Corps, 22nd November, 1915.

MURCHIE, FINDLAY, Captain, served as Private in D.E.O.V.R. from 15th September, 1914, to 21st October (about) 1915, and was in G.S.W.A.; gazetted to 1st Cape Corps, 1st December, 1915, rank, 2nd Lieutenant; transferred from 1st Cape Corps to Post Bellum Army in Egypt, July 12th, 1919

EDWARDS, HUGH, Captain, joined as Private in 2nd Transvaal Scottish, 17th October, 1914; saw service during Rebellion and in G.S.W.A., October, 1914, to August, 1915; promoted Lieutenant (on the field) April, 1915; gazetted to 1st Cape Corps, 7th December, 1915, rank, 2nd Lieutenant.

ROSE-INNES, TREVOR PALMER, Captain, was Corporal in D.E.O.V.R. from August, 1914, to July, 1915, and saw service in G.S.W.A.; gazetted to 1st Cape Corps, 20th December, 1915, rank, 2nd Lieutenant.

WILSON, ROBERT, Lieutenant, served during Anglo-Boer War from 1900 to 1902 with Northumberland Fusiliers, Queen's and King's medals; served in G.S.W.A., 1914/1915, with S.A.M.R. Artillery (Gunner); gazetted to 1st Cape Corps, 11th January, 1916, rank, 2nd Lieutenant; was attached to the Road Corps for some months in G.E.A.

RACKSTRAW, ERNEST JAMES, Lieutenant, M.C., Sub-Lieutenant Cape Town Naval Cadet Corps, 1st September, 1913; Private, S.A.S.C. (1st Infantry Brigade Train) Cape Town, 8th August, 1914; was promoted C.S.M. 15th December, 1914, and transferred to 1st Cape Corps, with rank of 2nd Lieutenant, 27th January, 1916.

BELL, HARLAND SHINGLETON, Lieutenant, served in Anglo-Boer War, 5th October, 1899, to 30th July, 1900; Sergeant in Bechuanaland Rifles to July, 1900; was in siege of Mafeking, later Lieutenant in Field Intelligence Department; served as Intelligence Officer to General's Douglas, Babington, Kekewich, Raleigh, Grey, Fetherstonhaugh, Fortescue and Williams; Queen's and King's medals; Lieutenant 1st I.L.H., August, 1914, to March, 1916; saw service during Rebellion and in G.S.W.A. and was on special Native affairs duty for some time in Ovamboland; gazetted to 1st Cape Corps, 7th April, 1916, rank, Lieutenant; transferred from 1st Cape Corps to Political Service in East Africa, 16th June, 1916, with rank of Captain; promoted Honorary Major, March, 1917; Mentioned in Despatches in East Africa whilst in Political Service.

CLOKE, ROBERT ANDREW. Lieutenant; Private, 2nd D.L.I. during Rebellion and G.S.W.A. Campaign, August, 1914, to 3rd December, 1915; enlisted in 1st Cape Corps, rank, Sergeant, 4th December, 1915, and promoted 2nd Lieutenant and Transport Officer, 16th June, 1916.

HOSACK, JAMES CHARLES (Late), 2nd Lieutenant, served with Special Service Squadron, Natal Carbineers, first as Trooper, later as R.Q.M.S. in G.S.W.A., January to July, 1915; enlisted in 1st Cape Corps, 29th October, 1915, rank, R.Q.M.S.; promoted 2nd Lieutenant, 4th December, 1915, reverted to R.Q.M.S. at own request, 14th December, 1915; again promoted 2nd Lieutenant, 16th June, 1916.

GARDNER, COLLIER SAMUEL HYLTON, Lieutenant, served with Witwatersrand Rifles as Corporal and Sergeant, August, 1914, to July, 1915, and was in G.S.W.A.; Corporal with 9th S.A.I. in G.E.A., December, 1915, to February 29th, 1916; transferred to 1st Cape Corps at Moshi, G.E.A., with rank of Staff Sergeant, 1st March, 1916, and promoted 2nd Lieutenant, 16th June, 1916.

HAYTON, ALEXANDER ARTHUR, Lieutenant, saw service during the Rebellion, 1914, as Sergeant and Battery Q.M. Sergeant in Z Battery, Cape Garrison Artillery, and was in G.S.W.A. March to June, 1915; full period of service from 7th August, 1914, to 3rd July, 1915; seconded for duty as Sergeant Instructor to Cape Corps, November, 1915, and transferred to Cape Corps with rank of Staff Sergeant, 30th June, 1916; promoted 2nd Lieutenant 1st July, 1916.

WIGMAN, WILLIAM THOMAS, Lieutenant, saw service during Anglo-Boer War; proceeded to England with S.A. Coronation Contingents, 1902 and 1911; attested in 2nd M.R. (Natal Carbineers) as Squadron Sergeant-Major (No. 2895), 19th October, 1914; saw service in G.S.W.A.; released 23rd July, 1915; attested to 1st Cape Corps, rank, Staff Sergeant, 1st January, 1916, later Company Sergeant-Major; promoted 2nd Lieutenant, 21st July, 1916.

WHITE, GORDON CHARLES, Lieutenant, enrolled as a Trooper in Colonial Scouts (Natal), 28th November, 1899; discharged on disbandment of Corps, 19th March, 1900; enrolled as Trooper in Natal Carbineers, 24th March, 1900, Queen's medal (two Bars); saw service with Colonial Scouts in Zululand Rebellion, 1906; gazetted to 1st Cape Corps, 1st August, 1916, rank, Captain, later reverted to Lieutenant at his own request in order to correct a Staff blunder.

COATES, HENRY, Lieutenant, served as Private in Kimberley Town Guard (during Seige of Kimberley) October, 1899, to February, 1900; Queen's medal; gazetted to 1st Cape Corps, 3rd August, 1916, rank, Lieutenant.

HEATON, WILLIAM SMITH, Lieutenant, M.C., served in East Africa with L.N. Lancashire Regiment as C/Sergeant, R.Q.M.S. and R.S.M. from 1914 to August, 1916, and was present at first landing at Tanga, 3rd November, 1915; transferred from L.N. Lancashire Regiment to 1st Cape Corps, 11th August, 1916, rank, 2nd Lieutenant; invalided to England and rejoined Loyal North Lancashire Regiment in July, 1918, and still serving with that Unit.

POTGIETER, MARTIN, Lieutenant, proceeded to England with 3rd S.A.I. in November, 1915; later joined Officers Training Corps and promoted Lieutenant in July, 1916; returned to South Africa and transferred to 1st Cape Corps, 20th August, 1916, rank, Lieutenant.

THE STORY OF THE 1st CAPE CORPS.

JAMES, THOMAS EVANS, Captain, served with Cape Colonial Defence Force (when aged 16 years) as Corporal for six months, 1901-1902, Queen's medal; served in Zululand Rebellion, 1906, medal and Bar; joined 2nd Transvaal Scottish as Private, 14th October, 1914; transferred to Pretoria Regiment as Col. Sergeant, 27th October, 1914; was acting R.S.M. 30th December, 1914; joined Railway Regiment after occupation of Aus, G.S.W.A., in April, 1915, as R.S.M. and promoted 2nd Lieutenant, 24th May, 1915; was sent to Cape Town and Johannesburg to recruit staff for the South-West African Railways; released from service October, 1915; permission to rejoin withheld until 13th March, 1916, when joined Reserve of Officers at Potchefstroom and was attached to 3rd S.A.I.; was sent to G.E.A. in charge of a Draft, April, 1916; recalled six weeks later to resume duty as Training Officer (Instructor) at Potchefstroom; seconded to 1st Cape Corps, 20th August, 1916, rank, Lieutenant.

JARDINE, WILLIAM, Captain, joined Cape Town Highlanders, 1st July, 1886, promoted Lieutenant, 1st January, 1887; Captain, 8th July, 1888; and Major, April, 1903; on Active Service during Anglo-Boer War from 16th October, 1899, to January, 1901, Queen's medal; Major and Field Cornet in C.T. Defence Rifles, 1913; on War Service in England and Cape Town, January, 1915, to August, 1916; prevented by ill health from joining in August, 1914; gazetted to 1st Cape Corps, 28th August, 1916, with rank of Captain.

FEETHAM, RICHARD, M.L.A., Lieutenant, gazetted to 1st Cape Corps 28th August, 1916; rank 2nd Lieutenant. Had no other war service.

LESLIE, ALEXANDER, Captain, served during Anglo-Boer War in 1900 as Private in 1st Battalion Gordon Highlanders; Queen's medal; Corporal, Pretoria Town Guard, August to November, 1914; Inspector of Accounts (Transport and Remounts) in German South-West Africa, November, 1915, to March, 1916; gazetted to 1st Cape Corps 28th August, 1916, with rank of 2nd Lieutenant.

DE VILLIERS, GEORGE WARREN, Lieutenant, gazetted to 1st Cape Corps 28th August, 1916; rank, 2nd Lieutenant; was Depôt Adjutant (Woltemade and Kimberley) from November 25th, 1916, to February 14th, 1918, when transferred to Active Citizen Force (U.D.F.).

GUEST, IVOR ARTHUR MELVILLE (Late), Lieutenant, joined Victoria College Volunteers, Stellenbosch, in 1898; promoted Lieutenant 1899; obtained leave and joined Railway Pioneer Regiment in November, 1899; promoted Lieutenant in 2nd Battalion, December, 1900; served throughout Anglo-Boer War; Queen's and King's medals; was at Sand River fight and acted for some time as Commandant of Meyerton; enrolled in Wit. Rifles, 30th August, 1906; proceeded on active service with Wit. Rifles to G.S.W.A. as Lieutenant, 29th October, 1914, and was released 24th July, 1915, with rank of Captain; joined U.D.F. upon its inception and held rank of Captain and Quartermaster, De la Rey's Rifles; gazetted to 1st Cape Corps with rank of 2nd Lieutenant, 30th August, 1916.

THORNTON, H. R. H., 2nd Lieutenant; in 1914-1915, prior to release from Government service, served in the Pretoria Town Guard during the Rebellion; gazetted to 1st Cape Corps, 21st August, 1916; rank, 2nd Lieutenant; was discharged from 1st Cape Corps medically unfit, 7th June, 1917; joined S.A.N.L.C., 29th September, 1917; later transferred to Administrative Staff of the Controller of Labour as an Assistant Labour Superintendent; demobilised, 27th March, 1919; rank throughout, 2nd Lieutenant.

HOWE-BROWNE, NOEL FRANK, Lieutenant, gazetted to 1st Cape Corps from S.A.S.C. (Motor Despatch Riders) in East Africa, 14th September, 1916; rank, 2nd Lieutenant; remained in German East Africa on special duty when Battalion left there, 20th December, 1917, and was seconded to Political Service, 2nd March, 1918. No other information obtainable.

THOMPSON, ROBERT ANDREW, Lieutenant, served during Anglo-Boer War from October, 1899, to 31st May, 1902, with C.M.P., Division II.; rank, Lance-Corporal; medals, Queen's (four bars), King's (two bars), and Kimberley Siege Star; served in German East Africa as Signaller Corporal, Divisional Signal Company attached to 5th S.A.H. from April to October, 1916; transferred to 1st Cape Corps with rank of 2nd Lieutenant and Signalling Officer at Morogoro, 18th October, 1916; transferred to Political Service in German East Africa, 23rd December, 1917.

BAIN, THOMAS, Lieutenant, transferred from 9th S.A. Horse (Private No. 4921) to 1st Cape Corps, 30th October, 1916; rank, 2nd Lieutenant. No further information obtainable.

STUBBS, EDGAR PERCIVAL, Lieutenant, M.C., enlisted in 6th S.A. Infantry at end of 1915, rank, Private, later Lance-Corporal, and proceeded to East Africa early in 1916; transferred to 1st Cape Corps at Morogoro, 31st October, 1916; rank, 2nd Lieutenant.

WALTON, HERBERT, Lieutenant, proceeded from South Africa to German East Africa in 1916 as a draft conducting officer; transferred to 1st Cape Corps on 30th October, 1916, with rank of Lieutenant.

HORSEMAN, GEORGE, Lieutenant, saw service during Anglo-Boer War with S.A.C. (C Division) rank, Trooper; period March, 1901, to May, 1902; Queen's medal; served with 4th S.A.H. in G.E.A., 8th December, 1915, to 3rd November, 1916, first as Trooper (No. 246) then as Corporal; transferred to 1st Cape Corps with rank of 2nd Lieutenant, 4th November, 1916; from 5th November to 8th December, 1917, was acting Staff Captain to Brigadier General O'Grady, commanding Column 3 during Lindi operations in German East Africa.

BOURHILL, ARTHUR FRASER, Lieutenant, served during Rebellion and in G.S.W.A. with 1st M.R. (Natal Carbineers), 1914-15; rank, Trooper; served in G.E.A. in 1916 with 8th S.A.H. (Trooper No. 5363); transferred to 1st Cape Corps at Morogoro, 13th November, 1916; rank, 2nd Lieutenant.

BROWNE, ERNEST HENRY, Lieutenant, attested as No. 18 in Bloemhof Commando, 14th October, 1914, for service during Rebellion; discharged, 15th December, 1914; later was Trooper (No. 534) in 4th S.A. Horse and saw service in G.E.A.; transferred to 1st Cape Corps, 15th November, 1916; rank, 2nd Lieutenant. Further information unobtainable.

HOFFE, THOMAS MITCHELL (Late), Captain, served during Anglo-Boer War, 10th February, 1901, to 31st May, 1902, with S.A. Constabulary; joined as 3rd class Trooper and promoted Lance-Corporal, 25th April, 1901; 1st class Trooper, 21st June, 1901; Corporal, 17th July, 1901; Lance Sergeant, 11th December, 1901; 2nd class Sergeant, 12th March, 1902; Cornet, 1st July, 1902; 2nd Lieutenant, 2nd January, 1903; and Sub-Inspector, 1st July, 1906; Queen's medal (five bars); was awarded the Special Badge of Gallantry which was awarded to a certain few of the S.A. Constabulary during the Anglo-Boer War; joined Special Service Squadron, 2nd M.R. (Natal Carbineers) as Trooper, October, 1914, promoted Lieutenant a few days afterwards and served to July 17th, 1915, in Rebellion and G.S.W.A.; was acting Adjutant for some months; worked in Messrs. Kynoch's Munition Factory from September 1st, 1915, to November 30th, 1916; gazetted 2nd Lieutenant in 1st Cape Corps, 26th December, 1916.

DIFFORD, ARCHIBALD NEWCOMBE (Late), Lieutenant, gazetted to 1st Cape Corps, 10th January, 1917; rank, 2nd Lieutenant. Had no other war service.

BARNARD, GILBERT RICHARD (Late), Lieutenant, gazetted to 1st Cape Corps, 15th January, 1917; rank, 2nd Lieutenant. Had no other war service.

ABBOTT, CHARLES FREDERICK (Late), Lieutenant; Lieutenant during Burmese War, 1887-1889; Queen Victoria's medal with one bar; was Sergeant during Mashonaland Rebellion, 1897; medal and bar; served during Anglo-Boer War with B.S.A. Police, 1899 to 1902; medals: Queen's (four bars), King's (two bars); proceeded to German East Africa as Conductor, S.A.S.C. (T. and R.), January, 1917; transferred to 1st Cape Corps with rank of 2nd Lieutenant, March 29th, 1917.

THE STORY OF THE 1st CAPE CORPS.

ROSE-INNES, SAMUEL HOWARD, Lieutenant, was Staff Sergeant 3rd S.A.F. Ambulance (S.A.M.C.), 24th January, 1916, to 29th March, 1917, in German East Africa, when transferred to 1st Cape Corps with rank of 2nd Lieutenant.

POWER, WALTER (Late), Lieutenant, received Temporary Imperial Commission as Lieutenant, S.A. Reinforcements (East Africa), 11th July, 1916; assumed duty at Maktau, G.E.A., 5th August, 1916; and was (1) O.C. Segregation Camp, 12th August, 1916; (2) O.C. S.A. Horse Details, 12th October, 1916; (3) attached Stokes Gun Brigade, 12th January, 1917; (4) Adjutant B.W.I. Details, 1st March, 1917; transferred to 1st Cape Corps at Morogoro, 10th April, 1917; rank, Lieutenant.

BOTHA, DOUGLAS FREDERICK, Captain, was Machine Gun Officer with the Midland Horse when War broke out in August, 1914; was transferred on September 19th, 1914, to "B" Force under Lieut.-Colonel Maritz at Upington as Machine Gun Officer; was handed over to the Germans at Van Rooyen's Vlei as prisoner of war on October 8th, 1914, by Maritz, because he would not go into Rebellion; released by British Forces at Tsumeb, G.S.W.A., on July 8th, 1915; joined 5th S.A.I. in October, 1915; rank, Sergeant; promoted to Machine Gun Officer, 3rd S.A.H., on December 23rd, 1915; proceeded to East Africa, 29th February, 1916; left East Africa per Hospital Ship, December 19th, 1916; was transferred to 1st Cape Corps, 1st May, 1917, with rank of Lieutenant; transferred from 1st Cape Corps to Army of Occupation in Egypt, 17th May, 1919, and posted to Embarkation Staff at Suez with rank of Captain.

McNEIL, J. (Late), 2nd Lieutenant, served with the Rand Rifles, Johannesburg Mounted Rifles and as a Sergeant in the Mine Guard during the Anglo-Boer War; gazetted to 1st Cape Corps, 10th May, 1917, with rank of 2nd Lieutenant.

PILLANS, CHARLES STUART MORTIMER, Lieutenant, enlisted in 6th S.A.H. on 4th April, 1916; rank, Trooper (No. 2879); was subsequently promoted to Squadron Sergeant-Major; arrived in East Africa on 23rd May, 1916; granted local rank of 2nd Lieutenant on 6th June, 1916; promoted 2nd Lieutenant from unattached list E.A.P.F. on 11th May, 1917, and attached for duty to the Rufiji River Transport Column; transferred to 1st Cape Corps with rank of Lieutenant on 23rd June, 1917.

COLSON, RICHARD, Lieutenant, served as Sergeant in 2nd Brigade Reinforcements at Dar-es-Salaam, G.E.A., and was later transferred to 6th S.A.I. (period September, 1916, to June, 1917); transferred to 1st Cape Corps with rank of 2nd Lieutenant, 2nd July, 1917.

SAMUELSON, SIVERT VAUSE, Lieutenant, M.C., saw service in Zululand Rebellion in 1906; enlisted in Natal Carbineers (1st M.R.) as Trooper on 28th September, 1914, and was promoted Sergeant the following month and gazetted to commissioned rank (1st Lieutenant) on 7th November, 1914; saw service during the Rebellion in Northern Transvaal and Upington District in 1914; landed in G.S.W.A. with 1st M.R., 14th December, 1914; returned to Union at end of G.S.W.A. Campaign, July, 1915; gazetted to 1st Cape Corps, rank 2nd Lieutenant, 2nd July, 1917.

DREYER, JACOBUS STEPHANUS (Late), 2nd Lieutenant, saw service in the Zululand Rebellion in 1906; enlisted in Natal Light Horse in October, 1914; rank, Trooper; saw service during Rebellion and in G.S.W.A., 1914/15; was a prisoner for a few hours at Gibeon (G.S.W.A.) in April, 1915; joined 4th S.A. Horse and proceeded to East Africa in 1916; gazetted to 1st Cape Corps with rank of 2nd Lieutenant, 16th July, 1917.

ROSE-NEL, EWALD, 2nd Lieutenant, gazetted to 1st Cape Corps, 16th July, 1917; rank, 2nd Lieutenant. No other information obtainable.

WARE, GEORGE LAWRENCE, 2nd Lieutenant, had two and a half years' service during Anglo-Boer War, 1899-1902; Queen's and King's medals (three bars); joined 6th S.A.H. as Trooper for service in East Africa, January, 1916; promoted Regimental Sergeant Major towards the end of the same year; returned to South Africa and demobilised, January, 1917; gazetted to 1st Cape Corps as 2nd Lieutenant, 16th July, 1917.

GIRDWOOD, FRANK INGLIS, Lieutenant, served during the Rebellion and in G.S.W.A. with 1st Imperial Light Horse, 6th October, 1914, to July, 1915; served with 5th S.A.H. in G.E.A., May, 1916, to February, 1917; ranks, Trooper and Sergeant; gazetted to 1st Cape Corps as 2nd Lieutenant, 17th July, 1917.

BLOXAM, EDWARD BERNEY, Lieutenant, saw service during Rebellion and in G.S.W.A. with Krugersdorp Commando in 1914; was Trooper in 4th S.A.M.R. in G.S.W.A., 1914/15; was Trooper in 4th S.A.H. in G.E.A., 1916; gazetted to 1st Cape Corps as 2nd Lieutenant, 17th July, 1917.

DAVIES, MARCHANT STARR, Lieutenant, enlisted in 1st S.A. Horse in December, 1915; rank, Trooper; and was in East Africa from January, 1916, to February, 1917; gazetted to 1st Cape Corps, 21st July, 1917; rank, 2nd Lieutenant.

TEMPLER, ERNEST WILLIAM, 2nd Lieutenant, enlisted in 2nd S.A. Infantry Brigade Reinforcements, 5th April, 1916, and posted to 6th S.A.I. in G.E.A., 21st May, 1916; transferred to 1st Cape Corps, 7th November, 1917, at Hatia, G.E.A., with rank of 2nd Lieutenant; transferred to Army of Occupation in Egypt, 25th June, 1919, and posted to 1st/4th Essex Regiment; transferred to 2nd/22nd London Regiment, 5th January, 1920; returned to South Africa and demobilised about July, 1920.

VIPAN, CECIL ARTHUR (Late), 2nd Lieutenant, joined 6th S.A.I., 8th August, 1914; rank, Private (No. 1455); discharged 28th January, 1915; reattested in 6th S.A.I., 17th April, 1916; rank, Private No. 11332); served in East Africa, 8th June, 1916, to 14th April, 1917; returned to East Africa, 17th October, 1917; transferred from 6th S.A.I. to 1st Cape Corps at Hatia, G.E.A., with rank of 2nd Lieutenant, 7th November, 1917.

GIBSON, ARTHUR SARGENT, Lieutenant, joined C.M.P., Division II., in October, 1899; served in defence of Kuruman; joined Dennison's Scouts (Kimberley Column), August, 1900, became R.S.M. 1901; commissioned to Johannesburg Mounted Rifles in August, 1901, and served with General Bruce Hamilton's Brigade until June, 1902; medals: Queen's (one bar), King's (two bars); had continuous Volunteer service, 1902 to 1912, in J.M.R., E.M.R., and I.L.H.; was one of five selected to represent I.L.H at King George's Coronation in 1911; served in G.S.W.A. as Trooper and Sergeant, I.L.H., and captured a German sergeant at Kolmanskop in September, 1914—the first enemy prisoner captured in G.S.W.A.; later took part in advance to Otavi; served in G.E.A. at Dar-esSalaam as Staff Sergeant, A.G.'s Office from April, 1917; ransferred to 1st Cape Corps with rank of 2nd Lieutenant, 17th November, 1917.

MOIN, BASIL HOWARD, Lieutenant, joined 12th Royal Lancers, November 21st, 1897, at Aldershot and served with them throughout Anglo-Boer War as Corporal, 1899 to 1902; Queen's medal (five clasps), King's medal (two clasps); served in C.M.P. and S.A.M.R. from September, 1902, to August, 1914; took part in "Ferreira Raid" in 1906 on G.S.W.A. border and operations in Damaraland against Marengo in 1907, and also on North-West Border during German "Herero" Campaign; holds Permanent Oversea's Forces Long Service medal; crossed G.S.W.A. Border as Machine Gun Sergeant, 5th S.A.M.R., under General Lukin in September, 1914; saw service during the Rebellion, and later was with the Desert Column (Kalahari) under Colonel Berrange; returned from G.S.W.A. in November, 1915, and was seconded for Imperial Service; served in G.E.A. from 16th January, 1916, as Lieutenant and Machine Gun Officer, 10th S.A.I. (3rd S.A.I. Brigade); Mentioned in Despatches for action at "Rast Haus" (Himo River), 19th March, 1916; returned from G.E.A. in October, 1917; transferred to 1st Cape Corps with rank of Lieutenant, 21st February, 1918. Total service, twenty-two years.

THE STORY OF THE 1st CAPE CORPS.

MANLEY, HERBERT CHARLES, Lieutenant, was Sapper in Royal Engineers, December, 1900, to 31st May, 1901; joined 1st Mounted Brigade as Signaller, 14th December, 1915; promoted Corporal, 12th August, 1917; promoted Acting Sergeant in 10th S.A.H., 18th November, 1917; and saw service in German East Africa; gazetted to 1st Cape Corps as Signalling Officer, 16th March, 1918; rank, Lieutenant. Fuller information unobtainable.

ROSS, ANDREW STEWART, Lieutenant, prior to Anglo-Boer War was in 1st Cameron Highlanders Volunteers, served during Anglo-Boer War with 1st Scottish Horse; rank, Sergeant; during Zululand Rebellion, 1906, was Sergeant in 1st Transvaal Mounted Rifles; has been a member of 1st I.L.H. since 1911, and is now a Lieutenant in that unit; served during the Rebellion and in G.S.W.A. with 1st I.L.H., 22nd August, 1914, to 30th August, 1915; R.Q.M.S., 22nd August, 1914, to 31st October, 1914; Lieutenant, 1st November, 1914, to 30th August, 1915; joined 4th S.A.H. as Trooper, 28th November, 1915, and was later Squadron S.M. to June, 1917, in G.E.A.; Lieutenant, 9th July, 1917, and Acting Captain, 10th S.A.H., 19th November, 1917, to 25th February, 1918, in G.E.A., and was Mentioned in Despatches; Private, S.A.I., March 18th to 28th, 1918, when transferred to 1st Cape Corps with rank of Lieutenant.

LAMBE, CHARLES RUTHERFORD, 2nd Lieutenant, gazetted to 1st Cape Corps, 28th March, 1918; rank, 2nd Lieutenant. No other information obtainable.

WOODS, GEORGE ARTHUR, Lieutenant, M.C., Private, 2nd Battalion Transvaal Scottish, September, 1914, to end of G.S.W.A. Campaign, August, 1915; took part in the Battle of Trekkoppies; enlisted in 7th S.A.I., November, 1915; rank, Private; promoted in turn Lance-Corporal, Corporal, Sergeant, and then to Commissioned Rank; was in every engagement the regiment took part in and was never away on account of sickness or any other cause during the whole campaign—a most remarkable record when a very large number of officers and men were so frequently *hors re combat* from fever, dysentery, etc.; returned from East Africa with 7th S.A.I. in January, 1918; awarded M.C. in East Africa; gazetted to 1st Cape Corps with rank of Lieutenant, 28th March, 1918.

ANTILL, ALFRED EDWIN JOHN (late), 2nd Lieutenant, joined South African Motor Cycle Corps as No. C.M. 385, 3rd March, 1916; embarked for East Africa, 7th April, 1916; transferred to S.A.S.C. as No. M.T. 3501 in G.E.A., 19th May, 1917; promoted Corporal, 1st November, 1917, and Mechanic, 8th January, 1918; disembarked from East Africa, 19th February, 1918; discharged medically unfit, 10th April, 1918; gazetted to 1st Cape Corps with rank of 2nd Lieutenant, 25th April, 1918.

WALLIS, HAROLD, Lieutenant, M.C., served during Anglo-Boer War with the Worcestershire Yeomanry, 1st Division, 1901 to 1902, Queen's medal; attested as Sergeant in Cullinan's Horse Machine Gun Section Eastern Force, 27th October, 1914, and was in G.S.W.A.; discharged 18th July, 1915; joined O.T.C. at Potchefstroom towards end of 1915; gazetted Lieutenant in 11th S.A.I., 17th January, 1916; transferred to 8th S.A.I., 5th April, 1917, and promoted Captain, 13th April, 1917; was Machine Gun Officer in both units; was in G.E.A. with 11th S.A.I., 20th February, 1916, to 21st December, 1916, and with 8th S.A.I., 19th June, 1917, to 14th December, 1917; taken prisoner of war at Narumgombe, 19th July, 1917; released by 1st Cape Corps, 18th November, 1917, on the Makonde Plateau; awarded M.C. for gallantry in action when in Command of a Machine Gun Section at Kondoa Irangi, 9th May, 1916; Mentioned in Despatches, 8th February, 1917; released from service, 28th February, 1918; gazetted to 1st Cape Corps with rank of Lieutenant, 30th April, 1918; permitted to retain rank of Captain on demobilisation, 4th October, 1919.

MOSENTHAL, BERTHOLD PHILLIP, 2nd Lieutenant, saw service during Anglo-Boer War from December, 1900, to March, 1902, first as Transport Conductor and later as Assistant Press Censor at Krugersdorp; gazetted to 1st Cape Corps, 30th April, 1918, with rank of 2nd Lieutenant.

SOLOMON, REGINALD ROSS, 2nd Lieutenant, served with 5th S.A.I., rank Private, from 10th April, 1916, to 3rd June, 1917, and saw service in East Africa; gazetted to 1st Cape Corps, 1st May, 1918; rank, 2nd Lieutenant.

JEPPE, OTTO RICHARD, Captain, served in G.S.W.A. with 1st I.L.H. as Trooper, August, 1914, to July, 1915; joined O.T.C. (Potchefstroom) November, 1915; served with 7th S.A.I. as Lieutenant, 11th December, 1915, to January, 1918; was in G.E.A. and wounded at Salaita Hill, 12th February, 1916; gazetted to 1st Cape Corps with rank of Lieutenant, 9th May, 1918.

BUCHANAN, W. J., 2nd Lieutenant, Private S.A. Motor Cycle Corps in G.E.A., February, 1916, to April, 1918; gazetted to 1st Cape Corps as 2nd Lieutenant, 28th May, 1918.

HILLARY, CECIL AUBREY, Lieutenant, enlisted in S.A. Field Telegraph Corps in December, 1914; gazetted Lieutenant and Signalling Officer to 20th Mounted Rifles, 15th March, 1915, and served in G.S.W.A. until July, 1915; served with the Union Defence Forces in South Africa to December, 1915; proceeded to East Africa as Signalling Officer to 9th S.A.I. in March, 1916, and served with 2nd East African Division; invalided to South Africa in March, 1917, and owing to ill-health served in the Union for some twelve months on the staff at Robert's Heights and was promoted Captain; boarded fit for tropical or semi-tropical service early in 1918 and gazetted to 1st Cape Corps, 1st June, 1918; rank, Lieutenant.

MACKENZIE, ALEXANDER, 2nd Lieutenant, Sergeant Cape Cyclists (U.D.F.) 8th August, 1914, to October, 1915; Staff Sergeant Instructor 1st Cape Corps Depôt, October, 1915, to 31st May, 1918; gazetted to 1st Cape Corps with rank of 2nd Lieutenant, 1st June, 1918.

HIRSCH, JOHN GAUNTLETT, 2nd Lieutenant, served in G.E.A. with S.A.S.C. (M.T.) as Driver (No. 2780), 1916/1917; gazetted to 1st Cape Corps with rank of 2nd Lieutenant, 5th June, 1918.

MACFARLANE, PETER, 2nd Lieutenant, served in Colonial Defence Force, 27th February, 1901, to 29th December, 1901; rank, Private; served with Port Alfred Imperial Mounted Police, 28th March, 1902, to 30th June, 1902; rank, Corporal; served with 8th S.A.I., 20th November, 1915, to 2nd August, 1917; rank, Sergeant; gazetted to Cape Corps, 10th June, 1918; rank, 2nd Lieutenant. Fuller information unobtainable.

ADAMSON, FRERE CAMPBELL, 2nd Lieutenant, gazetted to 1st Cape Corps, 2nd July, 1918, as 2nd Lieutenant (then aged 18). Had no other war service.

VAN DIGGELEN, HARRY CORNELIS, Lieutenant, attested in Transvaal Horse Artillery, 11th August, 1914, rank Corporal (No. 3065); captured at Sandfontein 26th September, 1914, released July, 1915; provisionally released from service, 11th September, 1915; taken on strength of 1st Mounted Brigade Signallers, Private (No. 1607), 28th December, 1915; embarked for East Africa, 31st December, 1915; promoted Corporal, 25th January, 1916, and later Sergeant Signaller; promoted to S.A. Signal Coy. Western Division), 14th February, 1917; disembarked at Durban on return from East Africa, 30th March, 1917; posted to 1st S.A. Horse, 28th June, 1917; transferred to Divisional Signal Coy. as No. 1367, 30th June, 1917; discharged, 9th July, 1917; gazetted Lieutenant and Signalling Officer 2nd Cape Corps, 10th July, 1917; appointed Transport Officer, 31st July, 1917; left Woltemade III. for Central Africa, 1st August, 1917; returned to Pretoria from Central Africa, 3rd May, 1918; transferred to 1st Cape Corps in July, 1918.

WHITFIELD, GEORGE, 2nd Lieutenant, D.C.M., attested 16th February, 1915; rank, Armourer Sergeant; discharged 31st August, 1915; gazetted to 1st Cape Corps, 2nd July, 1918; rank, 2nd Lieutenant. Fuller information unobtainable.

THE STORY OF THE 1st CAPE CORPS.

BUCHANAN, DOUGLAS HUGH FRASER, 2nd Lieutenant, served in G.E.A. with S.A.S.C. (M.T.), 1915 to 1918; Driver, 1915; Mechanic, 1916; Sergeant Mechanic 1916/18, during which period was attached to K.A.R. i/c M.T. and later to 20th Squadron R.F.C. as Driver; gazetted to 1st Cape Corps as 2nd Lieutenant, 6th July, 1918.

HALL, ROBERT LANCELOT, Lieutenant, served in G.S.W.A., 19th December, 1914, to 30th July, 1915, as Staff Sergeant G.H.Q., Northern Force, first with Brigadier General Skinner's Staff and later with General Botha's Staff; joined S.A. Wireless Co. (attached R.E.) 3rd February, 1916; served in G.E.A., 12th April, 1916, to 4th June, 1917, rank, Sapper; discharged medically unfit, 29th November, 1917; gazetted to 1st Cape Corps as 2nd Lieutenant, 6th July, 1918; proceeded from Egypt to England on leave, 23rd May, 1919, and was taken on Staff of S.O. for Demobilisation (South African Forces) in London, 4th July, 1919; promoted Lieutenant, 6th January, 1920; demobilised at Cape Town, 16th February, 1920.

JOHNSON, LYNN CHARLES, Lieutenant, enlisted as Trooper, 1st S.A. Horse, 10th January, 1916; promoted Corporal, 12th February, 1916; Sergeant, 11th June, 1916; Staff Sergeant, 12th September, 1916; and Lieutenant, 9th December, 1916, promoted Record and Attesting Officer for 1st Cape Corps, 2nd Cape Corps, C.C.L.R. and C.A.H.T.C., 8th January, 1917; attested over 6,700 men for above units between 8th January, 1917, and 7th July, 1918; transferred to 1st Cape Corps, 8th July, 1918; rank, Lieutenant.

HOLLINS, JOHN LEWIS (Late), Lieutenant, joined 9th S.A.I., 1st December, 1915, rank Private (No. 6047); saw service in G.E.A. from 7th February, 1916, to 12th December, 1916; released from service, 20th March, 1917; gazetted 2nd Lieutenant in 2nd Cape Corps, 8th November, 1917; transferred to 1st Cape Corps in July, 1918.

BROWN, WILLIAM INGLIS, 2nd Lieutenant, served in Anglo-Boer War with 1st and 3rd Royal Welsh Fusiliers, 1900-2; served with Royston's Horse in Zululand Rebellion (1906) and was in Natal Carbineers in 1907; attested in Natal Light Horse, 1st September, 1914; rank, Provost Sergeant; discharged 10th January, 1915; gazetted to 1st Cape Corps, 9th July, 1918; rank, 2nd Lieutenant, transferred from 1st Cape Corps to 1st/4th Essex Regiment at Cairo, 25th June, 1919; later transferred to 2nd/22nd London Regiment; demobilised at Cape Town about July, 1920.

LOUW, HENRY, 2nd Lieutenant, joined 3rd S.A.H., 30th November, 1915; served in G.E.A. first as Trooper and later as Q.M.S.; transferred to K.A.R. with rank of 2nd Lieutenant, August, 1917; transferred to 1st Cape Corps with rank of 2nd Lieutenant, 11th July, 1918.

SMITH, WALTER RALPH (Late), Lieutenant, attested (No. 683) in 2nd S.A. Rifles, 9th November, 1915; promoted Sergeant shortly afterwards and C.Q.M.S. on 14th May, 1916; transferred to 2nd Cape Corps and gazetted 2nd Lieutenant on 3rd September, 1917; promoted Lieutenant, 3rd March, 1918; transferred to 1st Cape Corps, 20th September, 1918; died in Hospital of influenza at Kimberley, 22nd October, 1918.

RAINIER, HENRY AUBREY (Late), Lieutenant, attested (No. A6355) in D.E.O.V.R., 2nd October, 1914; discharged 31st July, 1915; attested (No. 10972) in 5th S.A.I., 10th April, 1916; promoted A/Sergeant, 6th May, 1916; promoted A/Sergeant-Major, 2nd June, 1916; discharged 31st January, 1917; attested (No. M.T. 4147) in S.A.S.C. (M.T.), 20th February, 1917; discharged 23rd April, 1917; gazetted to 2nd Cape Corps as 2nd Lieutenant, 24th April, 1917; promoted Lieutenant 24th October, 1917; transferred to 1st Cape Corps, 2nd October, 1918; died in Hospital at Kimberley of influenza, 10th October, 1918.

Quartermaster :—

DIFFORD, IVOR DENIS, Captain, Trooper W.P.M.R. January to April, 1901 (Anglo-Boer War), Queen's medal; Assistant Supply Officer, Docks Depôt, Cape Town, rank Lieutenant, 22/8/14 to 13/11/14; Supply Officer, Carnarvon, C.P., 14/11/14 to 13/12/14; promoted Captain and O.C. 3rd Infantry Brigade Train, 13/12/14; served in G.S.W.A., 23/12/14 to 8/8/15; on duty in South Africa with S.A. Service Corps, 9/8/15 to 25/9/15, when transferred to 1st Cape Corps with rank of Captain and Quartermaster.

Medical Officer's Attached :—

ROBB, ROBERT M. (S.A.M.C.), Captain, attached to 1st Cape Corps, 24th November, 1915, and was in German East Africa, 16th February to May, 1916; resigned commission, 20th June, 1916.

McNIEL, ROBERT PATRICK (S.A.M.C.), Captain, M.C., was attached to 1st M.R. (Natal Carbineers) during Rebellion and in G.S.W.A., October, 1914, to July, 1915; attached to 1st Cape Corps for duty from 13th May, 1916, and was in German East Africa from end May, 1916, to December 20th, 1917; resigned commission, 15th February, 1918.

DREW, DESMOND (S.A.M.C.), Captain, served in G.S.W.A., August, 1914, to July, 1915, with 1st M.B.F.A., and attached to S.A.M.R. and Wit. Rifles; served with Ovamboland Expeditionary Force, November, 1916, to April, 1917; attached to 1st Cape Corps for duty from 1st March, 1918.

BOUWER, JOHANNES WILLEM (S.A.M.C.), Captain, received commission in S.A.M.C., 23rd October, 1915; served in Central Africa with General Northey's Force from December, 1915, to January, 1918; acted as R.M.O., M.O. i/c. Field, Advanced Base, and Base Hospitals; Mentioned in Despatches in Central Africa, 25th September, 1917; invalided to South Africa, January, 1918; attached 1st Cape Corps for duty from 23rd March, 1918.

DALGLEISH, JOHN W., Captain, M.C., joined Glasgow University O.T.C. in September, 1914; gazetted Lieutenant in R.A.M.C., 4th August, 1916; embarked from United Kingdom, 24th August, 1916; arrived in Mesopotamia, 29th September, 1916, and detailed to 113th Indian Combined Field Ambulance, 25th October, 1916; promoted Captain, 5th February, 1917; present at capture of Kut and advance to Bagdhad, 11th March, 1917; mentioned in Sir Stanley Maude's despatches, 2nd November, 1917; awarded Military Cross, February 5th, 1918; embarked from Mesopotamia, 12th April, 1918, arrived at Suez 27th April, 1918; served with 53rd Division in Egypt and Palestine, May, 1918 to August 6th, 1919; attached for duty to 1st Cape Corps from 24th March, 1919, and returned to South Africa with them on August 6th, 1919; arrived at Cape Town, 4th September, 1919; proceeded to England in December, 1919; demobilised January 5th, 1920.

THE STORY OF THE 1st CAPE CORPS

Paymasters :—

LEVER, CHARLES JOHN, Lieutenant, served in Anglo-Boer War with 1st Scottish Horse as Trooper, February to 29th May, 1901, when demobilised owing to severe wound received at Vlakfontein; Queen's medal; joined Rand Rifles as Private, 13th October, 1914; transferred to 2nd M.R. (Natal Carbineers) in November, 1914, and served in G.S.W.A., December, 1914, to July, 1915; promoted Sergeant, April, 1915; appointed Paymaster (rank Lieutenant) 1st Cape Corps, 18th October, 1915; resigned December 16th, 1915; was Lieutenant at S.A.I. Depôts, Potchefstroom and Durban, 22nd February, 1916, to April, 1917; was two weeks in the field in G.E.A., in October, 1916; joined S.A.N.L.C. 4th May, 1917; rank, Corporal; landed in France 1st July, 1917; transferred to Labour Corps, August, 1918; demobilised 28th March, 1919. Is Lieutenant on Supernumerary List A.C.F. (U.D.F.).

BOAM, BARNETT, Captain (acting), was Paymaster 1st Cape Corps from December 21st, 1915, to January 10th, 1919; rank, Lieutenant; promoted Captain (acting) later. No further information obtainable.

SMITH, W. H., Captain, joined Union Imperial Service Contingent (Oversea Infantry) in 1915; transferred to Union Pay Department in December, 1915; promoted Staff Sergeant, December, 1915; Staff Sergeant-Major, March, 1916; Lieutenant, 1st May, 1916; Captain, July, 1917; succeeded Captain Boam as Paymaster 1st Cape Corps, 11th January, 1919, and is still on duty.

Regimental Chaplain :—

EARP-JONES, ALAN, Captain, served during Anglo-Boer War for eighteen months as Private in Mossel Bay Town Guard; appointed Chaplain 1st Cape Corps, 28th December, 1915; rank, Captain.

The following is the record of service of the below named Officers who were seconded from 2nd to 1st Cape Corps in July, 1918, and proceeded to Egypt with Captain Anderson's reinforcements in August, 1918.

REUNERT, CLIVE, Lieutenant, served with S.A.S.M. (attached S.A.E.C.) (Armoured Train No. 1) as Machine Gunner from 27th September, 1914, to 31st March, 1915; Gunner S.A.H.A. 1st April, 1915, to 6th August, 1915; was in G.S.W.A. 12th December, 1914, to 6th August, 1915; Machine Gunner 7th S.A.I. from 19th April, 1916, to 22nd March, 1917, in G.E.A.; 2nd Lieutenant, 2nd Cape Corps, 23rd March, 1917, to 30th June, 1918; saw service in Central Africa; seconded to 1st Cape Corps, 1st July, 1918; rank, Lieutenant.

WHEELWRIGHT, WILLIAM DOUGLAS, 2nd Lieutenant, served in Anglo-Boer War, 1899 to 1902; rank, Lieutenant; Queen's and King's medals; gazetted 2nd Lieutenant, 2nd Cape Corps, 23rd March, 1917; served in Nyasaland and Portuguese East Africa with 2nd Cape Corps in 1917/1918; seconded to 1st Cape Corps in July, 1918; transferred from 1st Cape Corps to 1st/4th Essex Regiment (Army of Occupation) in Egypt, 25th June, 1919; promoted Captain and Company Commander, 10th July, 1919, and subsequently transferred to 2nd/22nd London Regiment; admitted to hospital in Syria, 13th December, 1919, and invalided to United Kingdom; demobilised at Cape Town, 12th July, 1920.

NOMINAL ROLL (OTHER RANKS).
1st BATTALION CAPE CORPS.

NOTE.—The rank after each detail is the final rank held by him. The number after each detail is his regimental number.

KEY TO ABBREVIATIONS HEREIN.

R.S.M. : Regimental Sergeant-Major.
C.S.M. : Company Sergeant-Major.
R.Q.M.S. : Regimental Quartermaster-Sergeant.
C.Q.M.S. : Company Quartermaster-Sergeant.
Sgt. : Sergeant.
L./Sgt. : Lance-Sergeant.
Cpl. : Corporal.

L./Cpl. : Lance-Corporal.
a/ : Acting.
Pte. : Private
D.C.M. : Awarded the Distinguished Conduct Medal.
M.M. : Awarded the Military Medal
S.N.L.R. : Services no longer required.
N.C.O. : Non-Commissioned Officer.

DANIELS, P. A., C.S.M. (1), attested 25/10/15, Sgt. 25/10/15, C.S.M. 8/10/17, demobilised 7/10/19, passed general N.C.O.'s course
REINSBERG, J., Pte. (2), attested 25/10/15, demobilised 7/10/19.
COTTON, R., Pte. (3), attested 25/10/15, died of malaria 23/5/16.
SCHOLTZ, M., Cpl. (4), attested 25/10/15, Cpl. 25/10/15, released medically unfit 25/8/17.
JACOBS, I., Cpl. (5), attested 25/10/15, Sgt. 25/10/15, reverted to own request to Pte. 29/3/17, a/Cpl. 5/7/18, Cpl. 1/11/18, demobilised 30/7/19, was first battalion Cook Sgt.
DENNIS, J. R., Cpl. (6), attested 25/10/15, L./Cpl. 15/10/17, Cpl. 1/4/18, demobilised 27/8/19, passed grenade discharging and gas courses.
DE VRIES, A,, Pte. (7), attested 25/10/15, Sgt. 25/10/15, accidentally shot at Simonstown on 22/12/15.
SAMPSON, E., Pte. (8), attested 25/10/15, demobilised 11/7/19, qualified Lewis gunner.
BROWN, D. J. (D.C.M.), C.S.M. (9) attested 25/10/15, Cpl. 25/10/15, Sgt. 1/10/16, C.S.M. 30/6/17, demobilised 8/9/19.
ANTONELSE, J., Pte. (10), attested 25/10/15, demobilised 7/10/19.
WATSON, R., Pte. (11), attested 25/10/15, died of wounds 18/10/18.
SCHALKWYK, C., Pte. (12), attested 25/10/15, rejected 25/10/15.
DANIELS, A. J., C.Q.M.S. (13), attested 25/10/15, C.Q.M.S. 25/10/15, died of malaria on 24/12/16.
DE VOS, A., Pte. (14), attested 25/10/15, rejected 25/10/15.
MANUEL, Wm., Pte., (15), attested 25/10/15, demobilised 7/10/19.
VAN ROOI, I., L./Cpl. (16), attested 25/10/15, L./Cpl. 25/10/15, reverted to Pte. 11/4/17, L./Cpl. 5/7/18, demobilised 10/7/19, qualified Lewis gunner.
HEEGERS, P., Pte. (17), attested 25/10/15, released medically unfit 8/2/16.
RUDOLPH, L., Pte. (18), attested 25/10/15, L./Cpl. 30/6/17, reverted to Pte. at own request on 25/4/19, demobilised 21/7/19
TETYANA, E., Pte. (19), attested 25/10/15, released medically unfit 26/11/15.
ERASMUS, W., Pte. (20), attested 25/10/15, S.N.L.R., 3/2/16
HEEGER, P. F., C.Q.M.S. (21), attested 25/10/15, C.Q.M.S .25/10/15, released medically unfit 18/5/18, mentioned in despatches East Africa.
JACOBS, J., Pte. (22), attested 25/10/15, released medically unfit 8/8/17.
DAWSON, J., Pte. (23), attested 25/10/15, released medically unfit 12/11/17.
HAAS, G., Pte. (24), attested 25/10/15, demobilised 16/7/19.
HENDRICKS, J., Pte. (25), attested 25/10/15, released medically unfit 5/3/18.
KOOPMAN, J. G., L./Cpl. (26), attested 25/10/15, L./Cpl. 25/10/15, died of blackwater 26/9/17.
HOCHSCHIELD, J., Pte. (27), attested 25/10/15, rejected 13/11/15.
DANIELS, A. J., Sgt. (28), attested 25/10/15, Sgt. 25/10/15, released medically unfit 16/11/17.
HUMAN, A., Pte. (29), attested 25/10/15, rejected 15/12/15.
JOHANNES, A., Pte. (30), attested 25/10/15, demobilised 9/9/19.
DAMANT, L., Pte. (31), attested 25/10/15, rejected 15/12/15.
ARANTJIES, J., Pte. (32), attested 25/10/15, released medically unfit 24/9/17.
JACKSON, W., Pte. (33), attested 25/10/15, demobilised 7/9/19.
JACOBS, I., Pte. (34), attested 25/10/15, died of malaria 11/8/16.
COTTON, F., Pte. (35), attested 25/10/15, released medically unfit 20/11/17.
THOMPSON, W. E., Pte. (36), attested 25/10/15, released medically unfit 31/12/17
HODSKINS, J., Cpl. (37), attested 25/10/15, Cpl 25/10/15, released medically unfit 24/7/17.
SOLOMON, H., Pte. (38), attested 25/10/15, released medically unfit 6/7/17.
KOETENBERG, W. S., Sgt. (39), attested 25/10/15, Sgt. 25/10/15, released medically unfit 21/12/17, rejoined later under No. 5178.
JONES, P. W., Sgt. (40), attested 25/10/15, Cpl. 25/10/15, Sgt. 15/10/17, released medically unfit 19/4/18.
JOHNSON, M., Pte. (41), attested 26/10/15, released medically unfit 27/4/17.
PETERSEN, A. C., Pte. (42), attested 26/10/15, Pte. 10/11/17, regimental bugler.
McCRAIG, A. F., Staff-Sgt. (43a), attested 26/10/15, released medically unfit 6/10/17.
SCHOLTZ, M., Pte. (43), attested 26/10/15, released medically unfit 8/12/15
GOODALL, W. C., Pte. (44), attested 26/10/15, released medically unfit 8/12/15.
PHILLIPS, J., Pte. (45), attested 26/10/15, S.N.L.R. 16/5/18.
WILFORDT, J., Sgt. (46), attested 26/10/15, Cpl. 26/10/15, Sgt. 14/12/16, demobilised 11/7/19, passed physical and bayonet courses.
PRINCE, P., Pte. (47), attested 26/10/15, S.N.L.R. 28/2/16.

THE STORY OF THE 1st CAPE CORPS.

ADAMS, A., a/Sgt. (48), attested 26/10/15, Cpl. 1/10/17, L./Sgt. 25/10/17, a/Sgt. 1/8/18, demobilised 7/10/19, passed physical and bayonet courses.
CLARKE, J. H., Pte. (49), attested 26/10/15, Cpl. 26/10/15, reverted to Pte. 30/3/18, released medically unfit 3/1/19.
BLOEMESTEIN, F., Pte. (50), attested 26/10/15, died of influenza 8/10/18.
BIRD, H., Pte. (51), attested 26/10/15, died of abscess on liver 27/9/18.
VAN DER POEL, M., Pte. (52), attested 26/10/15, released medically unfit 3/12/18.
RHODA, W., Pte. (53), attested 26/10/15, released medically unfit 7/12/15.
SOLOMON, C. J. H., L./Cpl. (54), attested 26/10/15, L./Cpl. 26/10/15, released medically unfit 15/8/17.
McQUYA, I., Pte. (55), attested 26/10/15, rejected 29/10/15.
SAMSON, P., Pte. (56), attested 26/10/15, released medically unfit 8/7/17.
WILLIAMS, H., Pte. (57), attested 26/10/15, rejected 28/10/15.
GROENEWALD, A., Pte. (58), attested 26/10/15, released medically unfit 27/7/17.
JONKERS, H., Pte. (59), attested 26/10/15, demobilised 7/9/19.
FREDERICKS, J., Pte. (60), attested 26/10/15, demobilised 26/8/19.
ADAMS, S., Pte. (61), attested 26/10/15, released medically unfit 25/8/17.
ADAMS, J., Pte. (62), attested 26/10/15, demobilised 16/7/19.
PIETERSEN, H., Pte. (63), attested 26/10/15, S.N.L.R. 31/1/16.
STEENBERG, C., Pte. (64), attested 26/10/15, S.N.L.R. 6/12/15.
FREDERICKS, A., Pte. (65), attested 26/10/15, rejected 28/10/15.
BOSMAN, G., Pte. (66), attested 25/10/15, S.N.L.R. 7/12/15.
SCHOLTZ, H., Pte. (67), attested 25/10/15, demobilised 7/9/19.
KLEIN, P., Pte. (68), attested 25/10/15, died of influenza 16/10/18.
PETERSEN, J., Pte. (69), attested 25/10/15, released medically unfit 13/9/17.
MENTOOR, B., Pte. (70), attested 25/10/15, rejected 28/10/15.
MANUEL, P., a/Sgt. (71), attested 25/10/15, L./Cpl. 24/6/17, Cpl. 15/10/17, a/Sgt. 1/2/19, demobilised 7/9/19, awarded Belgian decoration "Chevalier Ordre de Leopold," bronze medal.
KRUGER, H., Pte. (72), attested 25/10/15, demobilised 7/9/19.
GROVEL, H., Pte. (73), attested 25/10/15, S.N.L.R. 6/12/15.
DE KOCK, J., Pte. (74), attested 25/10/25, L./Cpl. 5/7/18, Cpl. 1/11/18, reverted to Pte. 28/3/19, demobilised 4/9/19, passed physical and bayonet training course.
HARZENBERG, B., Pte. (75), attested 25/10/15, rejected 28/10/15.
JACKSON, W., Pte. (76), attested 25/10/15, rejected 28/10/15.
MANKMAN, J., Pte. (77), attested 25/10/15, rejected 28/10/15.
FARO, P., Pte. (78), attested 25/10/15, died of influenza 8/10/18.
JEFTHA, N., Pte. (79), attested 25/10/15, released medically unfit 13/7/17.
CORNELIUS, A., Pte. (80), attested 25/10/15, demobilised 7/9/19.
DEMOS, J., Pte. (81), attested 25/10/15, S.N.L.R. 6/12/15.
LE ROUX, C., Pte. (82), attested 25/10/15, S.N.L.R. 28/2/16.
BOOYSEN, E., Pte. (83), attested 25/10/15, released medically unfit 13/12/15.
AFRICA, B., Pte. (84), attested 25/10/15, S.N.L.R. 6/12/15.
ADAMS, J., Pte. (85), attested 25/10/15, S.N.L.R. 7/12/15.
PAULSE, A., L./Sgt. (86), attested 25/10/15, L./Cpl. 25/10/15, Cpl. 25/9/17, L./Sgt. 15/10/17, demobilised 13/1/19.
DANIELS, A., Pte. (87), attested 25/10/15, released medically unfit 21/12/15.
JEFTHA, C., Cpl. (88), attested 25/10/15, Cpl. 9/2/16, released medically unfit 12/11/17.
ADAMS, L., Pte. (89), attested 25/10/15, released medically unfit 29/11/15.
ABRAHAMS, I., Pte. (90), attested 25/10/15, demobilised 7/10/19.
FRANZMAN, S., Pte. (91), attested 25/10/15, released medically unfit 15/10/17.
FEBRUARY, M. (D.C.M.), Sgt. (92), attested 25/10/15, Cpl. 25/10/15, Sgt. 30/9/16, a/C.S.M. 11/9/17, Sgt. 11/10/17, demobilised 27/8/19, passed bombing course, mentioned in despatches (East Africa).
MARTHINUS, A., Pte. (93), attested 25/10/15, rejected 28/10/15.
ADRIAANSE, A., Pte. (94), attested 25/10/15, released medically unfit 6/6/18.
ABRAHAMS, M., Pte. (95), attested 25/10/15, released medically unfit 9/3/17.
SMITH, J., Pte. (96), attested 26/10/15, released medically unfit 7/6/16.
DAVIDS, J., C.Q.M.S. (97), attested 26/10/15, C.Q.M.S. 21/4/17, demobilised 31/12/19, twice mentioned in despatches (East Africa and Egypt).
DRISCOLL, J. J., Cpl. (98), attested 26/10/15, Cpl. 1/10/17, demobilised 5/2/19.
BURTS, J., Pte. (99), attested 26/10/15, released medically unfit 20/11/17.
BEUKES, E., Pte. (100), attested 26/10/15, L./Cpl. 29/6/17, reverted to Pte. 12/3/18, demobilised 7/9/19, mentioned in despatches (East Africa), awarded Belgian decoration "Chevalier Ordre de Leopold," bronze medal.
HAGER, M. A., Pte. (101), attested 26/10/15, released medically unfit 29/10/17.
AYLIFF, C., Pte. (102), attested 26/10/15, rejected 28/10/15.
SKONDIAS, J., Pte. (103), attested 26/10/15, S.N.L.R. 7/7/17.
JASSEN, H., Pte. (104), attested 26/10/15, demobilised 25/12/18.
LAKEY, S. F., Sgt. (105), attested 26/10/15, Sgt. 1/11/15, released medically unfit 14/6/18.
CROSS, M. W., Pte. (106), attested 30/10/15, released medically unfit 3/12/17, regimental bugler.
MILLER, J., Pte. (107), attested 30/10/15, L./Cpl. 29/6/17, reverted to Pte. 12/3/18, demobilised 15/1/19.
DE BRUIN, C., Pte. (108), attested 30/10/15, demobilised 11/7/19, mentioned in despatches (East Africa).
DANIELS, D., Pte. (109), attested 30/10/15, released medically unfit 6/1/17.
BAGLEY, B. C., Pte. (110), attested 30/10/15, demobilised 11/7/19, regimental bugler.
McLEOD, W. T. (M.M. French), C.S.M. (111), attested 27/10/15, Sgt. 25/10/15, C.S.M. 18/9/16, released medical unfit 24/9/17, did provost and transport duties, mentioned in despatches (East Africa).
PEAKE, H. E., Pte. (112), attested 27/10/15, demobilised 7/9/19.
JACOBS, A., Pte. (113), attested 27/10/15, released medically unfit 8/7/17.
JACOBS, H., Pte. (114), attested 27/10/15, released medically unfit 25/8/17.
GOODHEART, W., Pte. (115), attested 27/10/15, released medically unfit 27/7/17.
DREYER, P., Pte. (116), attested 27/10/15, demobilised 7/9/19.
AUGUST, J., Pte. (117), attested 27/10/15, died of pneumonia 21/11/17.
SAMSON, C., Pte. (118), attested 27/10/15, released medically unfit 27/7/17.
DU TOIT, P., Cpl. (119), attested 27/10/15, L./Cpl. 18/6/18, Cpl. 1/11/18, demobilised 7/9/19, passed grenade discharging course.
HOLLAND, C., Cpl. (120), attested 27/10/15, L./Cpl. 24/6/17, Cpl. 15/10/17, demobilised 7/9/19, passed scout course.
BARKLEY, H., Pte. (121), attested 27/10/15, demobilised 7/9/19, qualified machine gunner.
MILTON, S., a/L./Cpl. (122), attested 27/10/15, a/L./Cpl. 1/2/19, demobilised 7/9/19, qualified Lewis gunner.
SEFIER, K., Pte. (123), attested 27/10/15, demobilised 23/10/19.
WHITTEN, W., Pte. (124), attested 27/10/15, demobilised 7/9/19.

THE STORY OF THE 1st CAPE CORPS.

SMITH, W., Pte. (125), attested 27/10/15, S.N.L.R. 26/11/15.
MILLER, C. I., Sgt. (126), attested 27/10/15, Cpl. 27/10/15, Sgt. 1/4/18, demobilised 7/9/19, 1st class machine gunner.
MAY, H., Sgt. (127), attested 27/10/15, Sgt. 27/10/15, released medically unfit 19/6/17
VOEGT, C., L./Cpl. (128), attested 27/10/15, L./Cpl. 17/1/16, released medically unfit 16/8/17.
MYBURGH, C. J., Pte. (129), attested 27/10/15, released medically unfit 11/5/17.
THYNSMA, F. P., Pte. (130), attested 27/10/15, demobilised 7/9/19.
ADAMS, A., Pte. (131), attested 27/10/15, S.N.L.R. 2/12/15.
RUITERS, C. A., C.S.M. (132), attested 27/10/15, Sgt. 25/10/15, C.S.M. 10/12/16, demobilised 9/10/19. mentioned in despatches (East Africa), passed general course.
MILTON, J. C., Pte. (133), attested 27/10/15, demobilised 7/9/19.
BARNES, G., Pte. (134), attested 27/10/15, released medically unfit 29/10/17.
WALKER, A. C., Pte. (135), attested 27/10/15, L./Cpl. 17/1/16, reverted to Pte. 17/2/17, released medically unfit 18/9/17.
LEWIS, C. G. I., Pte. (136), attested 27/10/15, released medically unfit 11/11/15.
DU PLESSIS, E., Pte. (137), attested 27/10/15, Sgt. 27/10/15, reverted to Pte. 12/4/17, S.N.L.R. 4/11/18.
PEAKE, J. W., Sgt. (138), attested 27/10/15, Sgt. 27/10/15, released medically unfit 24/12/17.
VISAGIE, S., L./Cpl. (139), attested 27/10/15, L./Cpl. 15/10/17, passed grenade discharging course, killed in action 18/9/18.
VOEGT, A., Pte. (140), attested 27/10/15, released medically unfit 27/11/15.
TRIEGAARDT, L., Pte. (141), attested 27/10/15, S.N.L.R. 6/2/17.
ABRAHAMS, A., Pte. (142), attested 27/10/15, released medically unfit 12/7/18.
LE GRANGE, C., Sgt. (143), attested 27/10/15, Sgt. 27/10/15, demobilised 7/9/19.
STOKES, W., Pte. (144), attested 27/10/15, demobilised 7/9/19.
HEBER, H. J., Sgt. (145), attested 27/10/15, Sgt. 27/10/15, died of blackwater 22/3/17.
SMITH, H. E., Pte. (146), attested 27/10/15, Sgt. 27/10/15, reverted to Pte. 31/12/18, demobilised 21/7/19, passed physical and bayonet courses.
RUSSEL, J. C., a/L./Cpl. (147), attested 27/10/15, a/L./Cpl. 18/6/18, killed in action 20/9/18.
HOPLEY, J., Cpl. (148), attested 27/10/15, Cpl. 16/10/16, released medically unfit 27/7/17.
WILLIAMS, J., Pte. (149), attested 27/10/15, S.N.L.R. 8/12/15.
KESTER, J., Pte. (150), attested 27/10/15, released medically unfit 16/11/17.
DUSART, J. A., Cpl. (151), attested 27/10/15, L./Cpl. 27/10/15, reverted to Pte. 17/11/16, Cpl. 15/10/17, demobilised 27/8/19.
CALVERT, C. (D.C.M.), a/R.S.M. (152), attested 27/10/15, C.S.M. 18/9/16, a/R.S.M. 23/9/19, demobilised 21/10/19, mentioned in despatches (East Africa), passed N.C.O.'s general course.
DIXON, J., a/L./Sgt. (153), attested 27/10/15, L./Cpl. 18/12/16, a/Cpl. 4/5/17, Cpl 30/6/17, a/L./Sgt. 16/10/18, demobilised 21/7/19, passed musketry and grenade discharging courses.
BROOKS, R., Pte. (154), attested 27/10/15, demobilised 11/7/19.
VOSLOO, J., Pte. (155), attested 27/10/15, released medically unfit 3/10/17.
VOSLOO, A., Cpl. (156), attested 27/10/15, Cpl. 18/12/16, a/L./Sgt 16/10/18, Cpl. 20/12/18, demobilised 21/7/19, passed scout course.
AFRICA, S., Pte. (157), attested 27/10/15, released medically unfit 26/2/17.
WIENAND, C., Pte. (158), attested 27/10/15, released medically unfit 6/11/17.
ERENTZEN, A. G., Sgt. (159), attested 27/10/15, Cpl. 27/10/15, Sgt. 8/12/16, released medically unfit 6/11/17.
JOHAR, G., Sgt. (160), attested 27/10/15, Cpl. 21/10/16, Sgt. 11/12/16, demobilised 21/7/19, qualified machine gunner
LE ROUX, M. (M.M.), L./Cpl. (161), attested 27/10/15, Cpl. 1/4/18, reverted to L./Cpl. 18/1/19, demobilised 21/7/19.
MARTIN, G., Pte. (162), attested 27/10/15, released medically unfit 31/7/16.
LANDSMAN, A., Pte. (163), attested 27/10/15, demobilised 21/7/19.
BENJAMIN, A. G., Sgt. (164), attested 27/10/15, Cpl. 27/10/15, Sgt. 1/4/18, demobilised 8/8/19, passed musketry course.
GEORGE, A., Pte. (165), attested 27/10/15, died of wounds 27/11/17.
CLARKE, A., Pte. (166), attested 27/10/15, demobilised 7/10/19, qualified Lewis gunner.
HARTWICK, F., Pte. (167), attested 27/10/15, released medically unfit 23/8/17.
ABRAHAMS, H. G., Sgt. (168), attested 27/10/15, L./Cpl. 27/10/15, L./Sgt. 14/12/16, Sgt. 15/10/17, died of pneumonia 30/10/18.
FELTON, A. C., Pte. (169), attested 27/10/15, Sgt. 27/10/15, died of malaria 2/11/16.
CAMPBELL, T., Pte. (170), attested 27/10/15, demobilised 28/10/19
JOHNSTON, H., L./Cpl. (171), attested 27/10/15, L./Cpl. 21/11/17, demobilised 16/7/19.
GREEN, S., Pte. (172), attested 27/10/15, L./Cpl. 10/5/18, a/Cpl. 7/2/19, reverted to Pte. 10/3/19, demobilised 21/7/19.
ARENDSE, A., Pte. (173), attested 27/10/15, released medically unfit 14/8/17.
DE VILLIERS, P., Pte. (174), attested 27/10/15, demobilised 21/7/19.
ARRISON, A., Cpl. (175), attested 27/10/15, Cpl. 1/4/18, demobilised 12/12/19, passed gas course.
MULLER, E., Pte. (176), attested 27/10/15, S.N.L.R. 26/11/15.
BAHRENSE, W., Pte. (177), attested 27/10/15, released medically unfit 15/4/18.
FEBRUARY, S., Pte. (178), attested 27/10/15, demobilised 8/9/19.
JOSEPHS, J., Pte. (179), attested 27/10/15, died at Stellenbosch Hospital 4/9/17.
GORDON, J. H., Pte. (180), attested 27/10/15, demobilised 25/12/18.
PETERSEN, J., Pte. (181), attested 27/10/15, S.N.L.R. 7/6/17.
OLIESLAGER, A., Sgt. (182), attested 27/10/15, Sgt. 29/10/15, died of celebral malaria 6/3/17.
PRETORIUS, I. C., Pte. (183), attested 27/10/15, released medically unfit 3/10/17.
WITBOOI, G., Pte. (184), attested 27/10/15, released medically unfit 13/12/15
JAFTHA, F., L./Cpl. (185), attested 27/10/15, L./Cpl. 1/4/18, died of wounds 20/9/18, passed gas course.
PRETORIUS, J., Pte. (186), attested 27/10/15, released medically unfit 28/12/15.
NAMGOE, K., Pte. (187), attested 27/10/15, demobilised 25/12/18.
VAN ROOYEN, C., Pte. (188), attested 27/10/15, released medically unfit 12/11/17.
WAGNER, J., Pte. (189), attested 27/10/15, released medically unfit 25/8/17.
AFORD, A., Pte (190), attested 27/10/15, released medically unfit 2"/12/15.
ARMSTRONG, J. W., Pte. (191), attested 27/10/15, released medically unfit 6/11/17.
MATTHEWS, J., L./Cpl. (192), attested 27/10/15, L./Cpl. 27/10/15, released medically unfit 24/9/17.
CUPIDO, D., Pte. (193), attested 27/10/15, demobilised 21/7/19, passed trench warfare and bombing courses.
CARELSE, J., Pte. (194), attested 27/10/15, demobilised 11/7/19, pioneer plumber.
BEZUITENHOUT, A., Pte. (195), attested 27/10/15, released medically unfit 14/2/18
VAN BEULEN, D., Pte. (196), attested 27/10/15, demobilised 11/7/19.
WITBOOI, H., Cpl. (197), attested 27/10/15, Cpl. 27/10/17, demobilised 21/7/19.
PHILLIPS, D., Pte. (198), attested 27/10/15, demobilised 4/1/20.
BEZUIDENHOUT, J., Pte. (199), attested 27/10/15, released medically unfit 28/6/18.

THE STORY OF THE 1st CAPE CORPS.

BOOYSEN, J., Pte. (200), attested 27/10/15, demobilised 16/7/19, passed field cookery.
OLIVER, J., Pte. (201), attested 27/10/15, released medically unfit 17/1/16.
JARENS, A., Pte. (202), attested 27/10/15, demobilised 26/12/18
POUCKY, P., L./Cpl. (203), attested 27/10/15, L./Cpl 14/7/18, demobilised 16/7/19, passed physical and bayonet courses.
AUGUSTUS, W., Sgt. (204), attested 27/10/15, Cpl. 28/10/15, Sgt. 24/6/17, demobilised 7/10/19, passed gas course.
ARENDSE, A. J., Pte. (205), attested 28/10/15, released medically unfit 11/8/17
BIEL, S., Pte. (206), attested 28/10/15, released medically unfit 26/9/17.
ADAMS, I. M., Pte. (207), attested 28/10/15, demobilised 7/9/19, C.O.'s chauffeur.
AMSTERDAM, W., Pte (208), attested 28/10/15, released medically unfit 27/7/17.
SASSE, C. D., R.Q.M.S. (209), attested 28/10/15, C.Q.M.S. 28/10/15, a/R.Q.M.S. 25/3/17, R.Q.M.S. 15/3/18, to United Kingdom on leave 3/1/19, demobilised 30/9/19, mentioned in despatches (East Africa).
RUSSEN, W. J., L./Cpl. (210), attested 28/10/15, L./Cpl. 1/4/18, demobilised 7/9/19
DAVIDS, I., Pte. (211) attested 28/10/15, released medically unfit 23/2/18.
COETZE, A., Sgt. (212), attested 28/10/15, Sgt. 1/8/16, died of pneumonia 26/8/18, mentioned in despatches (East Africa), passed physical and bayonet courses.
VILJOEN, A., Cpl. (213), attested 28/10/15, Cpl. 28/10/15, released medically unfit 24/9/17.
OPPERMAN, A., Pte. (214), attested 28/10/15, S.N.L.R. 2/12/15.
DU TOIT, B., Pte. (215), attested 28/10/15, released medically unfit 6/11/17.
BISHOP, H., Pte. (216), attested 28/10/15, demobilised 21/7/19.
JOHNSON, G., Cpl. (217), attested 28/10/15, L./Cpl. 7/12/16, Cpl. 14/12/16, died of fever and diarrhœa 19/2/17.
GROENEWALD, J., Pte. (218), attested 28/10/15, demobilised 25/12/18.
SAMPSON, J., Sgt. (219), attested 28/10/15, Sgt. 28/10/15, released medically unfit 6/11/17.
DEMOS, D. (M.M.), Pte. (220), attested 28/10/15, L./Cpl. 1/4/18, reverted to Pte. 6/4/19, demobilised 7/9/19, mentioned in despatches (East Africa).
WALTERS, N., L./Sgt. (221), attested 28/10/15, Cpl. 15/10/17, L./Sgt. 1/4/18, passed bombing course, killed in action 20/9/18.
PETERSEN, J., Pte. (222), attested 28/10/15, demobilised 21/7/19.
HENDRICKS, P., Sgt. (223), attested 28/10/15, Sgt. 28/10/15, released medically unfit 6/12/18, mentioned in despatches (East Africa).
HENDRICKS, C., Pte. (224), attested 22/11/15, released medically unfit 24/2/18.
JANSEN, L., Pte. (225), attested 22/11/15, demobilised 16/7/19.
KIVIDO, J., Pte. (226), attested 22/11/15, released medically unfit 25/1/16.
KLEIN, J., Pte. (227), attested 22/11/15, rejected 21/12/15.
BROWN, J. G., Pte. (228), attested 22/11/15, released medically unfit 3/3/17, bugler.
McLAREN, D. D., Pte. (229), attested 22/11/15, demobilised 30/12/18.
JOSEPH, H., Pte. (230), attested 22/11/15, released medically unfit 26/9/17.
HERRING, C., L./Cpl. (231), attested 22/11/15, L./Cpl. 22/11/15, released medically unfit 16/11/17.
STAPLER, W., Pte. (232), attested 22/11/15, S.N.L.R. 3/2/16.
JACOBS, J., Pte. (233), attested 22/11/15, demobilised 7/9/19.
DOWNING, G., Pte. (234), attested 28/10/15, demobilised 27/10/19.
FORBES, E., Pte. (235), attested 28/10/15, demobilised 7/10/19.
SOLOMON, C., Cpl. (236), attested 28/10/15, Cpl. 1/3/17, demobilised 31/12/18.
DANKERS, W., Pte. (237), attested 28/10/15, died of wounds 24/9/18.
ROBERTSON, W., Pte. (238), attested 28/10/15, S.N.L.R. 31/1/16.
COLLINS, A., Pte. (239), attestation cancelled.
DULLISEAR, J. N., a/C.Q.M.S. (240), attested 28/10/15, Cpl. 28/10/15, Sgt. 30/6/17, a/C.Q.M.S. 23/9/18, demobilised 21/7/19, passed bombing course.
SIMMONS, D. F., Cpl. (241), attested 29/10/15, L./Cpl. 23/3/17, Cpl. 15/10/17, demobilised 1/1/19.
JANTJES, G., Pte. (242), attested 29/10/15, demobilised 28/10/19.
BURGERS, J., Pte. (243), attested 29/10/15, released medically unfit 10/2/18.
BURGER, T., Pte. (244), attested 29/10/15, demobilised 21/7/19.
WERNERS, H., Pte. (245), attested 29/10/15, released medically unfit 14/8/17.
PIETERSEN, J., Cpl. (246), attested 29/10/15, Cpl. 17/2/17, demobilised 7/9/19
PINETON, H., Pte. (247), attested 29/10/15, S.N.L.R. 7/12/15
DONOGHUE, H., Pte. (248), attested 29/10/15, S.N.L.R. 7/12/15.
BENJAMIN, H., Pte. (249), attested 29/10/15, L./Cpl. 1/4/18, reverted to Pte. 25/10/18, demobilised 7/9/19
ADAMS, G., Cpl. (250), attested 29/10/15, Cpl. 5/7/17, released medically unfit 29/10/17.
WILSON, A., Pte. (251), attested 29/10/15, died of influenza 12/10/18.
JACOBS, W. J., L./Cpl. (252), attested 29/10/15, L./Cpl. 29/10/16, released medically unfit 13/9/17.
NIEKERK, J., Pte. (253), attested 29/10/15, died of wounds 6/11/17.
LEVENDAL, L., Pte. (254), attested 29/10/15, demobilised 11/7/19.
FREDERICKS, S. J., Sgt. (255), attested 30/10/15, Sgt. 30/10/15, demobilised 8/10/19, passed physical and bayonet courses.
KYZER, C. R., Sgt. (256), attested 30/10/15, L./Cpl. 1/3/17, Cpl. 16/4/17, Sgt. 24/6/17, died of influenza 10/10/18.
KYZER, D. A., Pte. (257), attested 30/10/15, demobilised 7/9/19.
JACOBS, R. A., Cpl. (258), attested 30/10/15, Cpl. 30/10/15, released medically unfit 11/5/17
JACOBS, D. F., Pte. (259), attested 30/10/15, demobilised 5/1/19.
KINNEAR, D. J., Pte. (260), attested 30/10/15, demobilised 21/7/19.
CORNS, R., L./Cpl. (261), attested 30/10/15, L./Cpl. 16/11/18, demobilised 7/9/19, passed bombing and trench warfare courses.
TURNER, P., Pte. (262), attested 30/10/15, demobilised 7/9/19.
FRANCES, D., Pte. (263), attested 30/10/15, died of malaria 27/5/16.
ALEXANDER, D., Pte. (264), attested 30/10/15, demobilised 25/12/18.
MILLS, D., Pte. (265), attested 30/10/15, released medically unfit 27/7/17.
AUGUSTINE, G., Pte. (266), attested 30/10/15, demobilised 21/7/19.
APPOLLIS, J., Pte. (267), attested 30/10/15, demobilised 7/9/19.
MOODY, J., Pte. (268), attested 30/10/15, died of malaria 15/6/16.
RUITERS, J. (M.M.), Cpl. (269), attested 30/10/15, Cpl. 15/10/17, demobilised 6/8/19, passed scout and sniping courses.
UITHALDER, G., Pte. (270), attested 30/10/15, demobilised 7/9/19
FREEMAN, W., Pte. (271), attested 30/10/15, demobilised 22/7/19, passed bombing and trench warfare courses, qualified Lewis gunner.
SMITH, W., Pte. (272), attested 30/10/15, released medically unfit 29/5/18.
HAUPT, C., Pte. (273), attested 30/10/15, released medically unfit 30/9/18
DE KOCK, C., Pte. (274), attested 30/10/15, S.N.L.R. 3/8/18.
JOHNSON, M., Pte. (275) attested 30/10/15, released medically unfit 9/3/17.
WINDFORD, H., Pte. (276), attested 30/10/15, demobilised 16/9/19.

THE STORY OF THE 1st CAPE CORPS.

SIMPSON, J., Pte. (277), attested 1/11/15, demobilised 11/7/19.
ABRAHAMS, H. W. (D.C.M., M.M.), Sgt. (278), attested 1/11/15, L./Cpl. 15/10/17, Cpl. 25/10/17, Sgt. 25/3/18, demobilised 7/10/19.
JOSEPH, C. J., Pte. (279), attested 1/11/15, died of malaria 19/0/16.
CARROLLISSEN, J., Sgt. (280), attested 1/11/15, Sgt. 1/11/15, a/C.S.M. 22/11/17, Sgt. 2/8/18, demobilised 31/12/19, mentioned in despatches (East Africa).
ROBERTSON, F., Pte. (281), attested 1/11/15, S.N.L.R. 11/12/15.
PETERSEN, J., Pte. (282), attested 1/11/15, demobilised 7/10/19.
JONATHAN, W. M., L./Cpl. (283), attested 1/11/15, L./Cpl. 30/6/17, demobilised 11/7/19, machine gun section.
VELDSMAN, C., Sgt. (284), attested 1/11/15, Sgt. 1/11/15, killed in action 20/9/18, passed musketry course.
OCTOBER, C. H., Pte. (285), attested 1/11/15, demobilised 6/1/19.
PHILIPS, F., Pte. (286), attested 1/11/15, released medically unfit 7/6/17.
WINDVOL, I., Pte. (287), attested 1/11/15, S.N.L.R. 31/1/16.
PETERSEN, G., Pte. (288), attestation cancelled.
ISAACS, J., Pte. (289), attested 1/11/15, released medically unfit 3/10/17.
BARBIER, L., Pte. (290), attested 1/11/15, released medically unfit 23/1/18.
HAUPT, W., Pte. (291), attested 2/11/15, released medically unfit 23/2/16.
ASPELING, E., Pte. (292), attested 2/11/15, released medically unfit 17/1/16.
FORTUIN, P., Pte. (293), attested 2/11/15, S.N.L.R. 28/2/16.
HARRISON, C., Pte. (294), attested 2/11/15, demobilised 7/10/19, passed trench warfare and bombing courses.
OCTOBER, C., Pte. (295), attested 2/11/15, demobilised 6/1/19.
BASSON, F., Pte. (296), attested 2/11/15, demobilised 16/7/19.
WYNGAARD, G., Pte. (297), attested 2/11/15, released medically unfit 7/12/15.
SCHALKWYK, P., Pte. (298), attested 2/11/15, demobilised 7/10/19.
VAN WYK, P., L./Cpl. (299), attested 2/11/15, a/L./Cpl. 25/10/17, a/Cpl. 19/10/18, L./Cpl. 23/1/19, demobilised 7/10/19.
KAMES, J., Pte. (300), attested 2/11/15, released medically unfit 13/9/17.
GREYBE, J., Pte. (301), attested 2/11/15, released medically unfit 8/7/17.
MINAAR, D., Pte. (302), attested 2/11/15, released medically unfit 30/9/18.
SMITH, A., Sgt. (303), attested 2/11/15, Cpl. 3/11/15, Sgt. 2/11/17, demobilised 24/8/19.
MIENTJES, J., Pte. (304), attested 2/11/15, released medically unfit 30/4/18.
KROTZEN, S., Pte. (305), attested 2/11/15, released medically unfit 13/10/16.
LOTTERING, H, Pte. (306), attested 2/11/15, demobilised 3/12/18.
VAN HEERDEN, G., Pte. (307), attested 2/11/15, demobilised 21/7/19.
MEYERS, G., Pte. (308), attested 2/11/15, released medically unfit 25/2/18.
FRANKS, R, Cpl. (309), attested 2/11/15, L./Cpl. 3/11/15, Cpl. 1/10/16, demobilised 30/11/19, qualified first-class signaller.
HUTCHINSON, K. (D.C.M.), C.S.M. (310), attested 2/11/15, Cpl. 3/11/15, Sgt. 1/10/16, C.S.M. 30/6/17, demobilised 21/7/19, passed general N.C.O.'s course second-class.
STRYDOM, T., a/L./Sgt. (311), attested 2/11/15, a/Sgt 1/2/17, Cpl. 1/4/18, reverted to Pte. 31/3/18, a/L./Sgt. 7/2/19, demobilised 21/7/19, machine gun section.
DREYER, P., Sgt. (312), attested 2/11/15, L./Cpl. 3/11/15, Cpl. 18/12/16, a/Sgt. 1/4/18, Sgt. 1/7/18, demobilised 21/7/19, passed bombing, musketry and grenade discharging courses.
DAVIS, T., Pte. (313), attested 2/11/15, released medically unfit 27/7/17.
PITT, W., Pte (314), attested 2/11/15, died of malaria 1/8/16.
HAYNES, J., L./Cpl. (315), attested 2/11/15, L./Cpl. 3/11/15, released medically unfit 20/11/17.
PLAATJES, C., Pte. (316), attested 2/11/15, released medically unfit 20/11/17.
STOWMAN, J. C., Pte. (317), attested 2/11/15, demobilised 7/9/19.
ABRAHAMSE, M. J. Sgt. (318), attested 2/11/15, Sgt. 3/11/15, demobilised 21/7/19, passed physical and bayonet courses.
McPHERSON, H., Pte (319), attested 4/11/15, demobilised 25/12/18, medical orderly.
ISAACS, W., Pte. (320), attested 4/11/15, demobilised 15/10/19.
DANIELS, C., Cpl. (321), attested 4/11/15, Cpl. 15/10/17, a/Sgt. 5/7/18, Cpl. 1/11/18, demobilised 21/7/19, passed gas course, second-class.
VAN WELLIEGH, C., Pte. (322), attested 4/11/15, released medically unfit 13/9/17.
KOCK, C., Pte. (323), attested 4/11/15, demobilised 8/9/19.
ADAMS, C., Pte. (324), attested 4/11/15, demobilised 8/9/19.
DU TOIT, J., Pte. (325), attested 4/11/15, released medically unfit 3/9/17.
PHILANDER, W., Pte. (326), attested 4/11/15, demobilised 16/7/19.
HENRY, R. E., Sgt. (327), attested 4/11/15, Sgt. 20/12/15, released medically unfit 27/7/17.
JACOBS, W., Pte. (328), attested 4/11/15, S.N.L.R. 26/7/18
BROWN, J., L./Cpl. (329), attested 4/11/15, L./Cpl. 1/9/18, demobilised 12/11/19.
RICHARDS, A., L./Cpl. (330), attested 4/11/15, L./Cpl. 4/11/15, released medically unfit, 29/10/17.
SWARTZ, J. (D.C.M.), Sgt. (331), attested 4/11/15, Cpl. 30/6/17, Sgt 15/10/17, released medically unfit 16/5/18.
SOULS, J., Pte. (332), attested 4/11/15, S N.L.R. 8/2/18.
BEZUIDENHOUT, M., Pte. (333), attested 4/11/15, died of dysentery 23/2/17.
LOUW, H J., Sgt. (334), attested 4/11/15, Cpl. 4/11/15, Sgt. 10/2/16, demobilised 7/0/19.
JONES. J., Pte. (335), attested 4/11/15, released medically unfit, 3/9/17.
PETERSEN, P., Pte. (336), attested 4/11/15, released medically unfit 25/8/17.
DE VRIES, S., Pte. (337), attested 4/11/15, released medically unfit 19/8/16.
TERBLANCHE, S., Pte. (338), attested 4/11/15, released medically unfit 4/4/17.
PORTER, W., Pte. (339), attested 5/11/15, released medically unfit 13/12/15.
DE WAAL, J., Pte. (340), attested 5/11/15, demobilised 25/12/18.
LE ROUX, P., Pte. (341), attested 5/11/15, demobilised 25/12/18.
DE KOOKER, I., Pte. (342), attested 5/11/15, demobilised 11/7/19.
MICHAELS, A., Pte., (343), attested 5/11/15, S.N.L.R. 26/11/15.
JAGERS, A., Pte. (344), attested 5/11/15, released medically unfit 13/9/17.
JANSEN, R., Cpl. (345), attested 5/11/15, L./Cpl. 5/11/15, Cpl. 15/10/17, released medically unfit 7/7/18.
BLOUW, F., Pte. (346), attested 5/11/15, released medically unfit 24/9/17.
BAATJES, J., Pte. (347), attested 5/11/15, demobilised 16/7/19.
JULIES, S., Pte. (348), attested 5/11/15, released medically unfit 13/7/17.
SILJEUR, H., Sgt. (349), attested 5/11/15, Cpl. 15/1/16, Sgt. 1/4/16, demobilised 7/10/19.
PETERSEN, J., Pte. (350), attested 5/11/15, demobilised 7/9/19.
PONTAC, F., Pte. (351), attested 5/11/15, demobilised 7/9/19.
MUNNIK, H., Pte. (352), attested 5/11/15, demobilised 28/9/19.
AFRICA, A., Pte. (353), attested 5/11/15, demobilised 16/7/19, qualified Lewis gunner.
ABRAHAMS, E., Pte. (354), attested 5/11/15, demobilised 8/9/19.

THE STORY OF THE 1st CAPE CORPS.

MUNNIK, D., Pte. (355), attested 5//11/15, died of blackwater 2/4/17.
KOERT, F., Pte. (356), attested 5/11/15, demobilised 8/9/19.
CAROLUS, J., Pte. (357), attested 5/11/15, released medically unfit 3/12/17.
GOLIATH, M., L./Cpl. (358), attested 5/11/15, L./Cpl. 17/1/16, released medically unfit 29/7/16.
CUPIDO, G., Pte. (359), attested 5/11/15, released medically unfit 3/10/17.
VELDSMAN, H., Pte. (360), attested 5/11/15, demobilised 16/7/19.
SMITH, J., Pte. (361), attested 5/11/15, demobilised 2/1/19.
GOODWIN, J., Pte. (362), attested 5/11/15, released medically unfit 9/12/15.
MADELLA, D., Pte. (363), attested 5/11/15, demobilised 25/12/18.
WILLIAMS, M., Pte. (364), attested 5/11/15, released medically unfit 3/9/17.
MADELLA, I., Sgt. (365), attested 5/11/15, Cpl. 24/6/17, L./Sgt. 15/10/17, Sgt. 10/5/19, demobilised 21/7/19.
THOMAS, M., Sgt. (366), attested 5/11/15, Cpl. 4/11/15, Sgt. 29/5/16, demobilised 7/10/19, passed bombing course.
THOMAS, A., Pte. (367), attested 5/11/15, released medically unfit 25/8/17.
WILKINSON, J., Pte. (368), attested 5/11/15, demobilised 7/9/19.
SINFORD, E., Pte. (369), attested 5/11/15, demobilised 21/7/19.
AGULHAS, I., Pte. (370), attested 5/11/15, released medically unfit 20/7/17.
GLOVER, W., L./Sgt. (371), attested 5/11/15, Cpl. 5/11/15, L./Sgt. 24/4/16, released medically unfit 27/11/17.
MAART, S. D., a/Sgt. (372), attested 5/11/15, Cpl. 1/4/18, a/Sgt. 19/10/18, demobilised 7/9/19.
SYKES, W. C., Sgt. (373), attested 5/11/15, L./Cpl. 5/11/15, Cpl. 1/10/16, Sgt. 8/12/16, released medically unfit 12/11/17.
JACOBS, P., Pte. (374), attested 5/11/15) released medically unfit 1/5/18.
LODWICK, F., Pte. (375), attested 5/11/15, released medically unfit 15/10/17.
KLEINBOOI, M., Pte. (376), attested 5/11/15, demobilised 1/1/19.
LOURENCE, I., Pte. (377), attested 5/11/15, released medically unfit 20/7/17.
ATKINSON, C., Pte. (378), attested 6/11/15, demobilised 16/7/18.
LUITERS, W., Pte. (379), attested 6/11/15, demobilised 21/7/19.
WILLIAMS, E., L./Cpl. (380), attested 6/11/15, L./Cpl. 5/7/18, demobilised 7/9/19, machine gun section.
AHRENSON, W., Pte. (381), attested 6/11/15, unsuitable 26/11/15.
VAN WYK, C., Pte. (382), attested 6/11/15, released medically unfit 4/3/17.
VISAGIE, J., Pte. (383), attested 6/11/15, died of malaria 8/4/16.
MARTIN, A., Pte. (384), attested 6/11/15, died of enteric fever 26/3/17
FATMAN, J., Pte. (385), attested 6/11/15, demobilised 12/7/19, passed trench warfare and bombing elementary courses.
PETERSEN, C., Pte. (386), attested 6/11/15, demobilised 16/7/19.
ADAMS, I., Pte. (387), attested 6/11/15, released medically unfit 31/1/16.
PETER, A., Pte. (388), attested 6/11/15, released medically unfit 29/11/15.
TITUS, M. J., Cpl. (389), attested 7/11/15, Cpl. 1/2/16, released medically unfit 6/11/17.
ADOLPH, H., Cpl. (390), attested 7/11/15, a/L./Cpl. 18/6/18, Cpl. 1/11/18, demobilised 7/9/19.
THEUNISSEN, E., Pte. (391), attested 8/11/15, demobilised 11/7/19
CASTER, B., C.Q.M.S. (392), attested 8/11/15, Cpl. 23/12/16, C.Q.M.S. 2/2/17, demobilised 16/7/19.
CAMPBELL, A. W., Pte. (393), attested 8/11/15, died of dysentery 13/11/17.
HERBERT, P., Pte. (394), attested 8/11/15, demobilised 10/7/19
VAN DER POEL, J., Pte. (395), attested 8/11/15, released medically unfit 30/11/15.
GOLIATH, J., Pte. (396), attested 8/11/15, demobilised 21/7/19.
LAMONT, H. R., Pte. (397), attested 8/11/15, died of influenza 6/10/18.
CALVERT, A., Pte. (398), attested 8/11/15, demobilised 7/9/19.
BROWNLEE, R., Pte. (399), attested 8/11/15, released medically unfit 17/1/16.
MATAWANA, P., Pte. (400), attested 8/11/15, demobilised 7/10/19, mentioned in despatches East Africa.
ABRAHAMS, C., Pte. (401), attested 8/11/15, released medically unfit 8/12/15.
SWARTBOOI, A., Pte. (402), attested 8/11/15, demobilised 1/1/19.
BENJAMIN, W., Pte. (403), attested 8/11/15, released medically unfit 13/9/17.
PARIS, P., Pte. (404), attested 9/11/15, demobilised 23/8/19.
JONATHAN, J., Pte. (405), attested 9/11/15, released medically unfit 25/8/17.
CUPIDO, D., Cpl. (406), attested 10/11/15, Cpl. 15/10/17, demobilised 21/7/19.
PRINS, S., Pte. (407), attested 10/11/15, demobilised 7/9/19.
GELDERBLOEM, J., Pte. (408), attested 10/11/15, died of enteric fever 27/3/17.
LEEN, W., Pte. (409), attested 10/11/15, released medically unfit 15/10/17.
HANSEN, W., Pte. (410), attested 10/11/15, demobilised 16/7/19, qualified Lewis gunner.
KOERIES, P., Pte. (411), attested 10/11/15, demobilised 7/9/19.
ABDULLAS, C., Pte. (412), attested 10/11/15, died of pneumonia 29/3/17.
LINEMAN, A., Pte. (413), attested 10/11/15, demobilised 16/7/19.
PERRING, A. G., Cpl. (414), attested 10/11/15, L./Cpl. 30/6/17, a/Cpl. 13/5/18, L./Cpl. 17/7/18, a/Cpl 16/10/18, Cpl. 1/11/18, demobilised 28/8/19.
SEVER, A. J., Pte. (415), attested 10/11/15, released medically unfit 14/4/18.
MARAIS, J., Pte. (416), attested 10/11/15, demobilised 7/9/19.
DANIELS, A., Pte. (417), attested 10/11/15, released medically unfit 25/1/18.
DE VRIES, F., Pte. (418), attested 11/11/15, S.N.L.R. 31/1/16.
THOMAS, H., Pte. (419), attested 11/11/15, demobilised 21/7/19.
IRWIN, W., Pte. (420), attested 11/11/15, released medically unfit 8/3/16.
RUDOLPH, P. J., Pte. (421), attested 11/11/15, unsuitable 26/11/15.
MARTINUS, A., Pte. (422), attested 11/11/15, demobilised 21/7/19.
BARLOW, D., Pte. (423), attested 11/11/15, demobilised 7/9/19.
SEPTEMBER, J. J., Pte. (424), attested 11/11/15, demobilised 21/7/19.
PEDRO, J., Pte. (425), attested 11/11/15, released medically unfit 24/2/18.
SCHOLTZ, M., Pte. (426), attested 11/11/15, released medically unfit 3/9/17.
ADAMS, N., Pte. (427), attested 11/11/15, demobilised 16/7/19.
UYS, M. J. J., Pte. (428), attested 11/11/15, demobilised 7/9/19.
CUPIDO, T. B. D., Pte. (429), attested 12/11/15, demobilised 16/7/19.
DEVEREAUX, R., Pte. (430), attested 13/11/15, released medically unfit 27/7/17.
KIEVITZ, S., Pte. (431), attested 13/11/15, demobilised 21/7/19.
PAULSEN, J. C. M., Sgt. (432), attested 13/11/15, L./Sgt. 31/12/15, Sgt. 18/6/17, demobilised 16/7/19. Pioneer Sgt. throughout, mentioned in despatches East Africa.
CARELSE, D. C., Sgt. (433), attested 13/11/15, Sgt 20/1/16, released medically unfit 14/8/17.
CARELS, Z. F., Pte. (434), attested 13/11/15, demobilised 12/11/19.
JAFTHA, J., Pte. (435), attested 13/11/15, died of small pox 14/8/17.
WILLIAMS, W. T., L./Cpl. (436), attested 13/11/15, L./Cpl. 1/11/18, demobilised 29/8/19, qualified signaller instructor.

THE STORY OF THE 1st CAPE CORPS.

KOERT, A., Pte. (437), attested 13/11/15, demobilised 6/10/19.
VALENTINE, B., Pte. (438), attested 13/11/15, demobilised 31/12/18.
TEMMEZ, H., Pte. (439), attested 13/11/15, L.Cpl. 1/10/16, Sgt. 11/12/16, reverted to Pte. 31/12/18, demobilised 8/9/19, qualified machine gunner.
OCTOBER, M., Pte. (440), attested 13/11/15, released medically unfit 10/8/17.
OCTOBER, D., L./Cpl. (441), attested 13/11/15, L./Cpl. 15/10/17, died of wounds 8/11/17.
ENGEL, W., Pte. (442), attested 13/11/15, released medically unfit 22/8/17.
TEMMERZ, J., Pte. (443), attested 13/11/15, demobilised 8/9/19.
SWARTZ, E., Pte. (444), attested 13/11/15, demobilised 25/3/19.
DAVIDS, A., Pte. (445), attested 13/11/15, demobilised 16/8/19.
REDDING, J., Pte. (446), attested 13/11/15, demobilised 10/10/19.
MANUEL, S. J., Pte. (447), attested 13/11/15, released medically unfit 29/11/15.
PEDRO, J., Pte. (448), attested 13/11/15, demobilised 8/9/19.
FEBRUARY, K., Pte. (449), attested 14/11/15, released medically unfit 6/11/17.
DAVIDS, D., Pte. (450), attested 14/11/15, released medically unfit 21/12/15.
OCTOBER, D., Pte. (451), attested 14/11/15, released medically unfit 27/7/17.
MANHO, A., Pte. (452), attested 14/11/15, demobilised 7/9/19.
WILSON, L., Pte. (453), attested 14/11/15, demobilised 26/12/18.
CRONJE, A., Pte. (454), attested 14/11/15, released medically unfit 16/11/17.
DOMINGO, A., Pte. (455), attested 14/11/15, released medically unfit 26/7/17.
BOOYSEN, D., Pte. (456), attested 14/11/15, released medically unfit 12/8/17.
WILLIAMS, W., Cpl. (457), attested 14/11/15, L./Cpl. 14/11/15, Cpl. 24/6/17, demobilised 5/2/19.
JOZAFFE, G., Pte. (458), attested 14/11/15, died of malaria 5/5/16.
GIBBS, H., Pte. (459), attested 14/11/15, released medically unfit 11/2/16.
BOSCH, A. P., Pte. (460), attested 15/11/15, released medically unfit 1/9/17.
ADAMS, A. L., Pte. (461), attested 15/11/15, demobilised 8/9/19.
MARINUS, C., Pte. (462), attested 15/11/15, demobilised 27/8/19.
PICK, B. D., Pte. (463), attested 15/11/15, released medically unfit 18/11/18.
DEBONKA, D., Pte. (464), attested 15/11/15, released medically unfit 1/9/17.
JENNETJE, T., Pte. (465), attested 15/11/15, rejected 29/11/15.
CLOETE, A., Pte. (466), attested 15/11/15, demobilised 2/1/19.
JENNETJE, B., Pte. (467), attested 15/11/15, unsuitable 26/11/15.
MENNE, A., Pte. (468), attested 15/11/15, demobilised 1/7/19.
MARTIN, J., Pte. (468a), attested 15/11/15, released medically unfit 10/5/18.
LAKEY, J., Pte. (469), attested 15/11/15, demobilised 8/9/19.
VALENTINE, J., Pte. (470), attested 15/11/15, demobilised 7/9/19.
ERASMUS, M., Pte. (471), attested 15/11/15, demobilised 21/7/19.
MONTSINGER, A., Pte. (472), attested 15/11/15, released medically unfit 23/6/17.
LE GRANGE, W., Pte. (473), attested 15/11/15, released medically unfit 24/9/17.
JOHNSON, H., L./Cpl. (474), attested 15/11/15, L./Cpl. 25/2/16, released medically unfit 15/8/17.
WALLER, W. M., Pte. (475), attested 15/11/15, demobilised 28/8/19.
MEYERS, H., Cpl. (476), attested 15/11/15, Cpl. 1/11/18, demobilised 7/10/19, qualified Lewis gunner.
APPOLLIS, J., Pte. (477), attested 15/11/15, S.N.L.R. 28/7/17.
PETERSEN, A., Pte. (478), attested 15/11/15, S.N.L.R. 5/5/17.
HOOPT, J., Pte. (479), attested 15/11/15, released medically unfit 9/12/15.
SCHOOR, P. D. (D.C.M.), Sgt. (480), attested 15/11/15, Sgt. 15/11/15, demobilised 7/10/19, passed musketry course 2nd class.
MOLONEY, A., Pte. (481), attested 15/11/15, demobilised 8/10/19.
DAVIDSE, J., Pte. (482), attested 15/11/15, released medically unfit 8/12/15.
PHILLIPS, D. J. W., Pte. (483) attested 17/11/15, S.N.L.R. 23/2/16.
GIDEON, M., Pte. (484), attested 17/11/15, demobilised 28/8/19.
JAMES, M., Pte. (485), attested 17/11/15, demobilised 16/7/19, passed bombing and trench warfare courses.
CORNELIUS, R., Pte. (486), attested 17/11/15, demobilised 21/7/19, complimented by Commander-in-Chief, E.E.F., for gallantry in trying to save a comrade from drowning at Gaza, Egypt.
RAAS, N., Pte. (487), attested 17/11/15, demobilised 26/12/18.
WANZA, A., Pte. (488), attested 17/11/15, died of mitral regurgitation 10/6/17.
APPOLLIS, D., Pte. (489), attested 17/11/15, demobilised 13/12/18.
BOWERS, E., Pte. (490), attested 17/11/15, released medically unfit 15/12/15.
GOLIATH, H., Pte. (491), attested 17/11/15, demobilised 8/0/19, qualified machine gunner.
LAWRENCE, A., Pte. (492), attested 17/11/15, released medically unfit 30/11/15.
FEBURARY, C., Pte. (493), attested 17/11/15, demobilised 8/9/19.
ROBAIN, T., Pte. (494), attested 17/11/15, released medically unfit 7/2/18.
ROBAIN, M., Pte. (495), attested 17/11/15, demobilised 8/9/19.
SCHIPPERS, J., Pte. (496), attested 17/11/15, demobilised 11/7/19.
SCHAFFES, J., Pte. (497), attested 17/11/15, S.N.L.R. 28/10/17.
ADAMS, P., Pte. (498), attested 17/11/15, demobilised 18/10/19.
ANTHONY, D., Pte. (499), attested 17/11/15, demobilised 11/7/19.
FEBRUARY, A., Pte. (500), attested 17/11/15, died of mitral stenosis 28/4/17.
VISSER, G., Pte. (501), attested 17/11/15, released medically unfit 30/11/17.
NIEMAND, J., Pte. (502), attested 17/11/15, demobilised 21/7/19.
FILLIS, R., Pte. (503), attested 18/11/15, released medically unfit 20/10/17.
SAMUELS, W. S., Sgt. (504), attested 18/11/15, Cpl. 21/10/16, Sgt. 30/6/17, demobilised 7/9/19, mentioned in despatches (East Africa), passed physical and bayonet courses.
FREDERICKS, D., Pte. (505), attested 19/11/15, demobilised 7/9/19.
PETRUS, D., Pte. (506), attested 19/11/15, released medically unfit 7/9/17.
PETERSEN, J., Pte. (507), attested 19/11/15, S.N.L.R. 31/1/16.
FILIES, J., Pte. (508), attested 19/11/15, released medically unfit 7/12/15.
ANDRIES, J., Pte. (509), attested 19/11/15, released medically unfit 26/11/15.
PETERSEN, P., Pte. (510), attested 19/11/15, died of malaria 19/10/16.
FAROE, D., Pte. (511), attested 19/11/15, released medically unfit 29/11/15.
MOURIES, H., Pte. (512), attested 19/11/15, released medically unfit 24/7/17.
JASON, H., Pte. (513), attested 19/11/15, S.N.L.R. 6/12/15.
CARLS, P., Pte. (514), attested 19/11/15, released medically unfit 22/12/15.
FEBRUARY, P., Pte. (515), attested 19/11/15, released medically unfit 8/2/16.
RAAS, G., Pte. (516), attested 19/11/15, released medically unfit 4/8/17.
AFRICA, D., L./Cpl. (517), attested 19/11/15, L./Cpl. 7/10/18, demobilised 7/9/19.
BENJAMIN, R., Pte. (518), attested 22/11/15, demobilised 16/7/19.
ABRAHAMS, N. J. D., Pte. (519), attested 22/11/15, died of dysentery 27/10/17.
JOHNSON, M., Pte. (520), attested 22/11/15, released medically unfit 8/2/16.
JOHANNES, S., Pte. (521), attested 22/11/15, demobilised 8/9/19.

THE STORY OF THE 1st CAPE CORPS.

ABRAMS, C., Pte. (522), attested 22/11/15, released medically unfit 3/10/17.
MAJOR, A., Cpl. (523), attested 22/11/15, Cpl. 14/12/16, released medically unfit 20/11/17.
JEFTHA, J., Pte. (524), attested 22/11/15, demobilised 16/7/19.
PIETERSEN, W., Pte. (525), attested 22/11/15, released medically unfit 30/11/15.
SEALE, E., Pte. (526), attested 23/11/15, released medically unfit 15/4/16, regimental bugler.
POMAN, C., Cpl. (527), attested 23/11/15, released medically unfit 15/6/16.
ALEXANDER, T. E., Pte. (528), attested 23/11/15, demobilised 1/1/19.
MATTHYS, C., Pte. (529), attested 23/11/15, released medically unfit 13/9/17.
GORDON, J., Pte. (530), attested 23/11/15, drowned in Pangani River, East Africa, 2/7/16.
PETERSEN, D. H. S., Pte. (531), attested 23/11/15, discharged 10/12/15.
ARENDS, D., Pte. (532), attested 23/11/15, released medically unfit 8/8/17.
GLOYNE, G., Pte. (533), attested 23/11/15, released medically unfit 7/12/15.
ABRAHAMS, J., Pte. (534), attested 23/11/15, demobilised 7/2/19.
WHITE, J. R., Pte. (535), attested 23/11/15, S.N.L.R. 28/2/16.
JULIE, D., Pte. (536), attested 23/11/15, died of malaria 1/7/16.
KIRBY, J., Pte. (537), attested 23/11/15, released medically unfit 5/1/16.
BOUKART, J., Pte. (538), attested 23/11/15, released medically unfit 19/3/18.
JOHNSON, A., Pte. (539), attested 23/11/15, released medically unfit 4/4/16.
BAILEY, J., Pte. (540), attested 23/11/15, released medically unfit 31/12/15.
ERASMUS, J., Pte. (541), attested 23/11/15, released medically unfit 7/6/17.
McGASKILL, P., Pte. (542), attested 23/11/15, demobilised 21/7/19, regimental bugler.
FORD, A., Pte. (543) attested 23/11/15, released medically unfit 14/11/17.
ARENDESE, D., Pte. (544), attested 23/11/15, demobilised 18/10/19.
DANIEL, C. J., Cpl. (545), attested 23/11/15, L./Cpl. 1/1/17, Cpl. 1/3/17, demobilised 14/1/19.
FERRIS, A., Pte. (546), attested 23/11/15, S.N.L.R. 10/4/17.
SOLOMON, F., Pte (547), attested 23/11/15, released medically unfit 24/7/17.
BESICK, J., Pte. (548), attested 23/11/15, released medically unfit 28/7/17, regimental bugler
DAVIDS, S., Pte. (549), attested 23/11/15, demobilised 16/7/19.
FORTUIN, D., a/L./Cpl. (550), attested 23/11/15, a/L./Cpl. 25/10/17, demobilised 16/7/19.
ABLES, J., Pte. (551), attested 23/11/15, released medically unfit 30/10/17.
BENJAMIN, T. P., Pte. (552), attested 23/11/15, released medically unfit 27/6/17.
PEREL, H., Cpl. (553), attested 23/11/15, Cpl. 18/9/17, demobilised 5/1/19.
THOMAS, A., Pte. (554), attested 24/11/15, released medically unfit 3/10/17.
MESSIAS, J., Pte. (555), attested 24/11/15, released medically unfit 15/8/17.
STEMMERTS, H., Pte. (556), attested 24/11/15, demobilised 11/6/19, transport driver.
DEDRICKS, C., Pte. (557), attested 24/11/15, released medically unfit 17/10/16.
DIERS, J. A., Pte. (558), attested 24/11/15, S.N.L.R. 31/1/16.
GERTZE, D., Pte. (559), attested 24/11/15, released medically unfit 3/10/17.
FISHER, W. C., L./Cpl. (560), attested 24/11/15, L./Cpl. 24/11/15, released medically unfit 22/8/16.
MATTHEWS, R., Pte. (561), attested 24/11/15, released medically unfit 12/11/17.
ANDREWS, I., Pte. (562), attested 24/11/15, S.N.L.R. 2/1/16.
BERRY, H., Pte. (563), attested 24/11/15, released medically unfit 6/7/18.
MANEVELDT, F., Pte. (564), attested 24/11/15, S.N.L.R. 31/1/16.
KRIEGER, A., Pte. (565), attested 24/11/15, demobilised 7/10/19.
MARIE, M., Pte. (566), attested 24/11/15, demobilised 7/10/19.
VIGLAND, J. A., Pte. (567), attested 24/11/15, released medically unfit 21/12/15.
WILLIAMS, T. C., Pte. (568), attested 24/11/15, released medically unfit 3/12/15.
MARSTON, J. W., Pte. (569), attested 24/11/15, demobilised 7/10/19.
HARKER, R., Pte. (570), attested 24/11/15, released medically unfit 7/12/15.
ADAMS, J., Pte. (571), attested 25/11/15, released medically unfit 19/4/18.
JACOBS, H., Pte. (572), attested 25/11/15, S.N.L.R. 31/1/16.
BENTING, I., Pte. (573), attested 25/11/15, released medically unfit 30/4/18.
JOYCE, A. J., Cpl. (574), attested 25/11/15, Cpl. 1/4/18, demobilised 27/10/19, qualified signaller.
BOER, A., Pte. (575), attested 25/11/15, killed in action 20/9/18.
JANAKER, B. S., Pte. (576), attested 25/11/15, killed in action 16/11/17.
WAGNER, J. R., Pte. (577), attested 25/11/15, released medically unfit 24/9/17.
OAKES, W., Pte. (578), attested 25/11/15, released medically unfit 29/11/15.
BROWN, A., Pte. (579), attested 25/11/15, released medically unfit 27/7/16.
JACOBS, G., Pte. (580), attested 25/11/15, demobilised 29/7/19.
THOMAS, A., Pte. (581), attested 25/11/15, S.N.L.R. 31/1/16.
EVANS, L., Pte. (582), attested 25/11/15, released medically unfit 3/12/15.
KILLOW, M., a/Sgt (583), attested 25/11/15, Cpl. 1/3/17, L./Sgt. 1/11/18, a/Sgt. 10/5/19, demobilised 21/7/19, passed N.C.O.'s general course.
SAMPIE, G. C., Pte. (584), attested 25/11/15, demobilised 7/10/19.
DE BLEQUY, W., Pte. (585), attested 25/11/15, S.N.L.R. 30/12/15.
HOUTSAMMER, J., Pte. (586), attested 25/11/15, killed in action 6/11/17.
JOSEPHS, J., Pte. (587), attested 25/11/15, released medically unfit 27/7/16.
ABLES, J., Pte. (588), attested 25/11/15, demobilised 7/10/19.
JEPPES, J., Pte. (589), attested 25/11/15, released medically unfit 18/8/16.
BERRY, A., Pte. (590), attested 25/11/15, demobilised 7/9/19.
ADAMS, M., Pte. (591), attested 25/11/15, released medically unfit 16/11/17.
FORTUIN, A., Pte. (592), attested 25/11/15, deserted 2/7/18, mentioned in despatches East Africa.
McKAY, G. D., Pte. (593), attested 25/11/15, L./Cpl. 23/11/15, reverted to Pte. 6/4/16, Cpl. 30/6/17, Sgt. 15/10/17, reverted to Pte. 2/11/18, demobilised 15/1/19
CHARLES, G., Pte. (594), attested 26/11/15, L./Cpl. 30/6/17, Cpl. 21/11/17, reverted to Pte. 6/4/18, demobilised 2/1/19, mentioned in despatches, East Africa.
HENDRICKS, J., Pte. (595), attested 26/11/15, demobilised 16/7/19.
BARINDS, C., Pte. (596), attested 26/11/15, demobilised 15/10/19.
WILLIAMS, W., Cpl. (597), attested 26/11/15, Cpl. 1/4/18, demobilised 9/1/20.
KARELS, W., Pte. (598), attested 26/11/15, released medically unfit 17/12/15.
JACOBUS, D. C., C.Q.M.S. (599), attested 26/11/15, Cpl. 26/11/15, Sgt. 1/10/16, C.Q.M.S. 30/6/17, demobilised 7/10/19, did extra transport duty, machine gunner
PRETORIUS, C., Pte. (600), attested 26/11/15, released medically unfit 2/5/18.
HOHENKERK, J. G., Pte. (601), attested 26/11/15, released medically unfit 28/7/17.
KEMP, F., Pte. (602), attested 26/11/15, S.N.L.R. 28/2/16.
HILDERBRAND, N., Pte. (603), attested 26/11/15, released medically unfit 25/1/16.
CLOETE, J., Pte. (604), attested 26/11/15, died of influenza 10/10/18.
HUSSEY, E., a/Cpl. (605), attested 26/11/15, a/Cpl. 14/5/18, demobilised 21/7/19, passed gas course.
DORRIS, J., Pte. (606), attested 26/11/15, demobilised 7/10/19.

THE STORY OF THE 1st CAPE CORPS.

ARENDSE, I. W. (D.C.M.), Sgt. (607), attested 26/11/15, L./Cpl. 30/6/17, Cpl. 1/4/18, Sgt. 23/8/18, demobilised 7/10/19, passed scout course 1st class and 1st class machine gunner.
VAN EYSSEN, J., Pte. (608), attested 26/11/15, demobilised 16/9/19.
LOCK, J., Cpl. (609), attested 26/11/15, Sgt. 27/11/15, reverted to Cpl. 27/11/18, demobilised 7/10/19.
ABRAHAMS, J., Pte. (610), attested 26/11/15, demobilised 16/7/19
KONING, J., Pte. (611), attested 26/11/15, demobilised 7/10/19.
BROPHY, H. A., Cpl. (612) attested 26/11/15, Cpl. 27/11/15, released medically unfit 8/8/17.
LECHAT, J. G., Cpl. (613), attested 26/11/15, Cpl. 27/11/15, released medically unfit 3/2/17
KONING, R., Pte. (614), attested 26/11/15, released medically unfit 2/12/15.
SMITH, M., Pte. (615), attestation cancelled.
HOEDEMAKER, D. W., a/Sgt. (616), attested 26/11/15, Sgt. 3/12/15, reverted to Cpl. 13/2/16, a/Sgt. 26/6/16, released medically unfit 26/2/17.
ROSS, W., Pte. (617), attested 26/11/15, demobilised 25/2/18.
GAIN, J. J., Cpl. (618), attested 26/11/15, L./Cpl. 27/11/15, Cpl. 1/1/16, killed in action 20/9/18, passed gas course.
WILLIAMS, A., Pte. (619), attested 27/11/15, released medically unfit 4/2/16.
PETERSEN, D., Pte. (620), attested 27/11/15, released medically unfit 7/1/16.
TITUS, P., Pte. (621), attested 27/11/15, died of influenza 8/10/18.
PLAATJES, C., Pte. (622), attested 27/11/15, demobilised 11/7/19, pioneer saddler.
SCHROEDER, W., Pte. (623), attested 27/11/15, Cpl. 15/10/17, reverted to Pte. 7/3/18, demobilised 7/10/19.
SCHOLTZ, H., Pte. (624), attested 27/11/15, released medically unfit 7/6/17.
PAULSE, I., Cpl. (625), attested 27/11/15, L./Cpl. 11/12/17 Cpl. 1/4/18, demobilised 16/7/19.
MATTHEWS, J., Pte. (626), attested 27/11/15, released medically unfit 17/1/16.
ARENDS, A., Pte. (627), attested 27/11/15, demobilised 12/8/19.
SEPTEMBER, A., Pte. (628), attested 27/11/15, released medically unfit 12/11/17.
VAN WYK, A., Pte. (629), attested 27/11/15, killed in action 20/9/18.
DIXIE, R., Pte. (630), attested 27/11/15, demobilised 12/7/19.
MARAIS, L., Pte. (631), attested 27/11/15, demobilised 21/7/19.
LABANS, L., L./Cpl. (632), attested 28/11/15, L./Cpl. 1/4/18, demobilised 7/9/19.
HOFFMAN, J., Cpl. (633), attested 28/11/15, L./Cpl. 28/11/15, Cpl. 30/6/17, demobilised 26/2/18.
COLERIDGE, R., Pte. (634), attested 28/11/15, released medically unfit 30/12/15.
HARDTS, G., Pte. (635), attested 28/11/15, demobilised 1/11/19.
KNIGHT, G., Pte. (636), attested 28/11/15, S.N.L.R. 8/12/15.
EDWARDS, J., Pte. (637), attested 28/11/15, released medically unfit 3/2/16.
WILLIAMS, J., Pte. (638), attested 28/11/15, S.N.L.R. 8/12/15.
ASPELING, J., L./Cpl. (639), attested 28/11/15, L./Cpl. 15/10/17, demobilised 12/7/19, qual. Lewis gunner.
ABRAHAMS, W., Pte. (640), attested 28/11/15, demobilised 12/7/19.
FREECE, F., Pte. (641), attested 28/11/15, released medically unfit 13/12/15.
BUTLER, G., L./Cpl. (642), attested 28/11/15, L./Cpl. 2/11/17, released medically unfit 11/4/18.
JULIES, H. A., Pte. (643), attested 28/11/15, released medically unfit 11/11/18.
VAN ROOYEN, J. H., Pte. (644), attested 29/11/15, released medically unfit 7/1/16.
MEYER, R., L./Cpl. (645), attested 29/11/15, L./Cpl. 29/11/15, released medically unfit 28/2/18.
PANNEWITZ, L., Pte. (646), attested 29/11/15, released medically unfit 15/12/15.
ALLISON, J., Sgt. (647), attested 29/11/15, Cpl. 21/10/16, Sgt. 11/12/16, released medically unfit 25/9/18.
ABRAHAMS, C., Pte. (648), attested 29/11/15, S.N.L.R. 17/6/18.
BOYSE, F., Pte. (649), attested 29/11/15, died of malaria 24/7/16.
CLAYTON, J. P., Pte. (650), attested 29/11/15, demobilised 6/1/19.
PETERSEN, D. D., Pte. (651), attested 29/11/15, released medically unfit 27/7/16.
REID, H. F. W., Pte. (652), attested 29/11/15, released medically unfit 1/5/18.
MORGENDAL, T. F., Sgt. (653), attested 29/11/15, L./Cpl. 29/11/15, Sgt. 30/6/17, demobilised 11/7/19, qualified Lewis gunner.
DANIELS, L., Pte. (654), attested 29/11/15, released medically unfit 21/3/16.
DANIELS, A., Pte. (655), attested 29/11/15, released medically unfit 24/9/17.
JACOBS, J., Pte. (656), attested 29/11/15, killed in action 20/9/18
BOOYCE, J., Pte. (657), attested 29/11/15, released medically unfit 27/4/17
PIENAAR, R., Pte. (658), attested 29/11/15, demobilised 26/12/18.
ROBERTS, I. D., Pte. (659), attested 29/11/15, demobilised 15/10/19
FORTUIN, A., Pte. (660), attested 29/11/15, demobilised 8/9/19.
BRICKERS, D., Pte. (661), attested 29/11/15, S.N.L.R. 5/8/18.
DYASON, R., Pte. (662), attested 29/11/15, demobilised 16/7/19, regimental bugler.
DAVIES, J., Pte. (663), attested 29/11/15, S.N.L.R. 7/6/17.
SWINTON, W., Pte. (664), attested 29/11/15, demobilised 23/7/19.
LENDERS, G. N., Pte. (665), attested 29/11/15, rejected 15/12/15.
WILLIAMS, J., Pte. (666), attested 29/11/15, released medically unfit 22/12/15.
ABRAHAMS, J., Pte. (667), attested 29/11/15, released medically unfit 29/11/18.
ADAMS, J., Pte. (668), attested 29/11/15, released medically unfit 2/12/15.
GUNN, J., Pte. (669), attested 29/11/15, released medically unfit 13/12/15.
GROVERS, D., Pte. (670), attested 29/11/15, released medically unfit 24/9/17.
BURNS, J., Pte. (671), attested 29/11/15, released medically unfit 9/12/15.
SOLOMON, I. C., Pte. (672), attested 29/11/15, missing, death accepted 6/6/16.
OCTOBER, I., Pte. (673), attested 29/11/15, demobilised 7/10/19.
HEUVEL, H. M., L./Cpl. (674), attested 29/11/15, L./Cpl. 29/11/15, demobilised 7/10/19.
AFRICA, A., Pte. (675), attested 29/11/15, S.N.L.R. 8/6/18.
JACOBS, N. D., Pte. (676), attested 29/11/15, rejected 27/12/15.
McKINNON, H., Pte. (677), attested 29/11/15, released medically unfit 16/11/17.
MEIRING, S., Pte. (678), attested 29/11/15, released medically unfit 30/11/17.
LOSPER, J., Pte. (679), attested 29/11/15, demobilised 16/7/19, regimental butcher.
LESAR, J., Pte. (680), attestation cancelled.
ABRAHAMS, J., Pte (681), attested 29/11/15, demobilised 10/2/19.
BREAR, F. W., Pte. (682), attested 29/11/15, demobilised 8/9/19.
LEE, C., Pte. (683), attested 29/11/15, demobilised 5/1/19.
WILLIAMS, J. H., Pte. (684), attested 29/11/15, demobilised 11/7/19, signaller and regimental bugler.
COX, C., Pte (685), attested 29/11/15, released medically unfit 17/10/16, signaller.
KOEPSTADT, F., Pte. (686), attested 29/11/15, demobilised 7/10/19.
FEDER, H. A. G., Cpl. (687), attested 29/11/15, L./Cpl. 29/6/17, Cpl. 1/4/18, qualified Lewis gunner, killed in action 20/9/18.
CARELSE, C. (D.C.M.), Cpl. (688), attested 29/11/15, Cpl. 23/8/18, a/Sgt. 24/8/18, Cpl. 12/11/18, demobilised 7/10/19, 1st class machine gunner.
HENRY, J., Cpl. (689), attested 29/11/15, L./Cpl. 15/10/17, Cpl. 5/7/18, demobilised 11/7/19, passed gas course.

THE STORY OF THE 1st CAPE CORPS.

HENDRICKS, J., Pte. (690), attested 29/11/15, released medically unfit 15/8/17, rejoined again under No. 4061.
PONTAC, F., Pte. (691), attested 29/11/15, released medically unfit 16/11/17.
VALENTINE, P., Pte. (692), attested 29/11/15, S.N.L.R. 31/1/16.
CHARLES, J., Pte. (693), attested 29/11/15, released medically unfit 27/7/17.
SCHIPPERS, J., Pte. (694), attested 29/11/15, demobilised 8/9/19.
FORTUIN, P., Pte. (695), attested 29/11/15, demobilised 7/10/19, regimental tailor.
O'CONNOR, J., Pte. (696), attested 29/11/15, demobilised 16/7/19.
COETZEE, A., Pte. (697), attested 29/11/15, released medically unfit 6/11/17.
FRISKIN, C. G., Pte. (698), attested 29/11/15, died of influenza 14/10/18.
LOTTERING, A. H., Pte. (699), attested 29/11/15, demobilised 21/7/19, signaller.
DAWSON, R. T., Pte. (700), attested 29/11/15, demobilised 3/1/19.
HUNTER, A., Pte. (701), attested 29/11/15, died of cerebro spinal meningitis 17/8/17, signaller.
SUSMAN, M., Pte. (702), attested 29/11/15, released medically unfit 3/12/15.
PERRY, G., Pte. (703), attested 29/11/15, released medically unfit 9/6/17.
VONDELING, T., Pte. (704), attested 29/11/15, S.N.L.R. 8/12/15.
APPOLLIS, J., Pte. (705), attested 30/11/15, demobilised 7/10/19.
SKIPPERS, W., Pte. (706), attested 30/11/15, demobilised 8/9/19, signaller.
KANNEMEYER, H., Pte. (707), attested 30/11/15, released medically unfit 16/8/17.
WANZA, A., Pte. (708), attested 30/11/15, demobilised 8/9/19.
ADOLPH, D., Pte. (709), attested 30/11/15, S.N.L.R. 29/9/17.
HANEKAM, J., Pte. (710), attested 30/11/15, released medically unfit 9/12/15.
GERTZE, G., Pte. (711), attested 30/11/15, demobilised 21/7/19.
JOHNSON, J. E., Pte. (712), attested 30/11/15, released medically unfit 7/2/17.
STANLEY, W. T., Cpl. (713), attested 30/11/15, Cpl. 14/12/16, discharged medically unfit 23/8/17.
ALFOS, J. C., Pte. (714), attested 30/11/15, released medically unfit 6/11/17.
HARDING, J. S., Pte. (715), attested 30/11/15, died of dysentery 13/11/17.
ARENDS, J. J., Pte. (716), attested 30/11/15, released medically unfit 27/4/17.
NORRIS, E. C., Pte. (717), attested 30/11/15, L./Cpl. 30/11/15, reverted to Pte. 26/5/16, passed Grenade Discharging Course, killed in action 20/9/18.
ALEXANDER, J., Pte. (718), attested 30/11/15, released medically unfit 27/12/15.
WILLIAMS, F. A., Pte. (719), attested 30/11/15, demobilised 11/7/19.
THRUEBEN, J. T., Pte. (720), attested 30/11/15, signaller, died of heart failure 1/10/16.
SASSMAN, D., Pte. (721), attested 30/11/15, demobilised 7/10/19.
COETZE, D., Pte. (722), attested 30/11/15, released medically unfit 16/11/17.
SAMPSON, P., Pte. (723), attested 30/11/15, demobilised 5/1/19.
SCHIPPERS, H. S., Pte. (724), attested 30/11/15, released medically unfit 22/11/15.
JAFTA, A., Pte. (725), attested 30/11/15, demobilised 7/10/19.
VAN SCHOOR, B. P., a/Sgt. (726), attested 30/11/15, Cpl. 30/11/15, a/Sgt. 14/12/16, died of cerebro malaria 28/3/17.
FASSEN, C. S., Pte. (727), attested 30/11/15, released medically unfit 23/8/17.
LOUW, J., Pte. (728), attested 30/11/15, released medically unfit 21/6/18.
NEFDT, H. A. J., Pte. (729), attested 30/11/15, released medically unfit 27/8/16.
APPOLLIS, D., Pte. (730), attested 30/11/15, released medically unfit 6/11/17.
KELLY, M., Cpl. (731), attested 30/11/15, Cpl. 1/4/18, demobilised 7/10/19.
LENDERS, C., Pte. (732), attested 30/11/15, demobilised 11/7/19, cook.
ALLEN, A., Pte. (733), attested 30/11/15, demobilised 11/7/19, passed bombing and trench warfare courses.
KELLY, F., Pte. (734), attested 30/11/15, released medically unfit 24/7/17.
SMITH, J., L./Cpl. (735), attested 30/11/15, L./Cpl. 1/4/18, passed grenade discharging course, killed in action 20/9/18.
PATMORE, W., Pte. (736), attested 30/11/15, demobilised 30/12/18.
RAMUS, W., Pte. (737), attested 30/11/15, released medically unfit 20/3/18.
ACKERMAN, F., Pte. (738), attested 30/11/15, L./Cpl. 15/10/17, reverted to Pte. 7/4/18, demobilised 25/12/18.
MARCUS, J. J., L./Cpl. (739), attested 30/11/15, L./Cpl. 30/11/15, demobilised 5/2/19.
SOLOMON, P., Pte. (740), attested 30/11/15, S.N.L.R. 1/5/17.
THOMAS, W. A., Pte. (741), attested 30/11/15, released medically unfit 3/10/17.
ALEXANDER, L. W., Pte. (742), attested 30/11/15, released medically unfit 6/7/17.
BUTLER, M. H., Pte. (743), attested 1/12/15, S.N.L.R. 20/12/16.
HANMER, F. W., Pte. (744), attested 1/12/15, released medically unfit 1/11/17, signaller.
ROBERTS, J., Pte. (745), attested 1/12/15, released medically unfit 31/8/17, died at Durban 15/10/18.
VAN WYK, J. W., Pte. (746), attested 30/11/15, released medically unfit 22/8/16.
LE FLEUR, M. A., Sgt. (747), attested 1/12/15, Cpl. 1/12/15, Sgt. 6/12/16, demobilised 29/7/19, mentioned in Despatches, East Africa.
MOSES, B., Pte. (748), attested 1/12/15, demobilised 11/7/19.
BENJAMIN, M., Pte. (749), attested 1/12/15, released medically unfit 16/11/17.
ZACHARIAS, N., Pte. (750), attested 1/12/15, released medically unfit 4/2/16.
HENDRICKS, J., Pte. (751), attested 1/12/15, released medically unfit 22/12/15.
MAGGON, J. H., Pte. (752), attested 1/12/15, demobilised 11/7/19.
LESAR, H. M., Pte. (753), attested 1/12/15, released medically unfit 24/1/16.
SOLOMON, W., Pte. (754), attested 1/12/15, demobilised 11/7/19.
HIEBNER, I. J., Pte. (755) attested 1/12/15, released medically unfit 6/11/17.
LAWRENCE, C., Pte. (756), attested 1/12/15, demobilised 7/10/19.
STEVENS, R. E., Sgt. (757), attested 1/12/15, Cpl. 16/10/16, Sgt. 1/5/17, released medically unfit 6/11/17.
LA FLEUR, L., Sgt. (758), attested 1/12/15, Sgt. 1/12/15, released medically unfit 12/9/17.
FRENCHMAN, C. A., Pte. (759), attested 1/12/15, released medically unfit 8/12/15.
RAATZ, J. J., Pte. (760), attested 1/12/15, released medically unfit 1/7/18.
NICHOLSON, J. W., Pte. (761), attested 1/12/15, S.N.L.R. 7/12/15.
ENGELBRECHT, C., Pte. (762), attested 1/12/15, demobilised 11/7/19.
DANIEL, J., Pte. (763), attested 1/12/15, released medically unfit 17/12/15.
DAVIDS, I., Pte. (764), attested 1/12/15, demobilised 8/9/19.
FISHER, D. J., a/Sgt. (765), attested 1/12/15, Cpl. 15/10/17, a/Sgt. 10/5/19, demobilised 16/7/19.
JACOBS, J. C., Pte. (766), attested 1/12/15, released medically unfit 8/7/17.
SOLOMON, A., Sgt. (767), attested 1/12/15, Cpl. 1/12/15, Sgt. 23/12/16, released medically unfit 12/11/17, rejoined.
McKINNON, R. H. W., Pte. (768), attested 1/12/15, demobilised 8/10/19.
ABELS, I., Pte. (769), attested 1/12/15, S.N.L.R. 21/6/17.
HARRIS, A. H., Pte. (770), attested 1/12/15, demobilised 11/10/19.
MORRIS, J., Pte. (771), attested 1/12/15, released medically unfit 13/8/17.
WILDSCHUT, N., Pte. (772), attested 1/12/15, released medically unfit 6/12/18.

THE STORY OF THE 1st CAPE CORPS.

FEBRUARY, C., Pte. (773), attested 1/12/15, S.N.L.R. 6/12/18.
OLKERS, M. J., Pte. (774), attested 1/12/15, released medically unfit 8/3/16.
NICHOLSON, P. T., Pte. (775), attested 1/12/15, demobilised 7/10/19.
PADUA, E., Pte. (776), attested 1/12/15, released medically unfit 10/12/15.
THERON, K., Pte. (777), attested 1/12/15, released medically unfit 22/8/17.
CASPER, J. J., Pte. (778), attested 1/12/15, demobilised 29/12/18.
KEMMY, Pte. (779), attested 1/12/15, released medically unfit 6/6/18, signaller.
TISSONG, W., Pte. (780), attested 1/12/15, demobilised 2/1/19
FELIX, C., Pte. (781), attested 1/12/15, died of appendicitis 19/9/16.
SASS, D., Pte. (782), attested 1/12/15, S.N.L.R 11/10/17.
SPORT, T., Pte. (783), attested 1/12/15, died of maralia 29/4/16.
GREENWOOD, D., Pte. (784), attested 1/12/15, released medically unfit 13/12/15.
JOSEPH, G., Pte. (785), attested 1/12/15, died of blackwater 30/1/17.
GORDON, H., Pte. (786), attested 1/12/15, demobilised 29/7/19.
HEYNES, G., Pte. (787), attested 1/12/15, released medically unfit 3/9/17.
GORDON, E., Pte. (788), attested 1/12/15, released medically unfit 28/11/18.
HENDRICKS, A., Pte. (789), attested 1/12/15, died of malaria 25/10/16.
VAN WYK, J., Pte. (790), attested 1/12/15, released medically unfit 20/11/17.
WHITEBOOI, H., Pte. (791), attested 1/12/15, released medically unfit 27/1/16.
BLANKENBERG, J., Pte. (792), attested 1/12/15, released medically unfit 4/2/16.
PAULSE, T., Pte. (793), attested 1/12/15, released medically unfit 11/12/15.
SOLDAAT, W., Pte. (794), attested 1/12/15, demobilised 16/7/19.
LAKEY, J., Pte. (795), attested 1/12/15, S.N.L.R. 30/1/17.
JOHNSON, J., Pte. (796), attested 1/12/15, released medically unfit 25/8/17.
STEPHEN, A., Pte. (797), attested 1/12/15, killed in action 20/9/18.
CARELSE, C., Pte. (798), attested 1/12/15, released medically unfit 3/9/17.
MAART, E., Pte. (799), attested 1/12/15, released medically unfit 28/4/18.
JACOBUS, J., Pte. (800), attested 1/12/15, demobilised 7/9/19.
VAN ZYL, K., Pte. (801), attested 1/12/15, demobilised 7/9/19.
ABRAHAMS, S., Pte. (802), attested 1/12/15, demobilised 10/10/19.
ADRIAANSE, E. H., Pte. (803), attested 2/12/15, released medically unfit 6/12/15
SAMPSON, W. S., Pte. (804), attested 2/12/15, released medically unfit 24/7/17.
PEARSON, F., Pte. (805), attested 2/12/15, demobilised 25/12/18.
DAVIDS, D., Pte. (806), attested 2/12/15, demobilised 29/7/19.
MENTOR, D., Cpl. (807), attested 2/12/15, Cpl. 1/4/18, demobilised 7/10/19, qualified Lewis gunner.
PORTHEN, F., Pte. (808), attested 2/12/15, released medically unfit 25/8/17.
DE VILLIERS, I. J., Cpl. (809), 2/12/15, Cpl. 3/12/15, died of dysentery 2/12/16.
JONES, A., Pte. (810), attested 2/12/15, released medically unfit 17/12/15.
MEYER, J., Pte. (811), attested 2/12/15, released medically unfit 8/8/17.
BAILEY, D. H., Pte. (812), attested 2/12/15, released medically unfit 24/2/18.
DANIELS, M., Pte. (813), attested 2/12/15, demobilised 7/10/19.
THEUNIS, C. A., Pte. (814), attested 2/12/15, demobilised 11/7/19.
WILLIS, H. J., Pte. (815), attested 2/12/15, released medically unfit 16/11/17.
BURNS, J., Pte. (816), attested 2/12/15, demobilised 16/7/19.
WATKINS, J., Pte. (817), attested 2/12/15, demobilised 11/7/19.
BRINKHUIS, J., Pte. (818) attested 2/12/15, demobilised 7/10/19.
DAVIDS, P., Pte. (819), attested 2/12/15, demobilised 13/9/17.
PAULSEN, A., Pte. (820), attested 2/12/15, discharged 9/1/18.
PAYNE, P., Pte. (821), attested 2/12/15, demobilised 21/7/19.
THOMAS, T., Pte. (822), attested 2/12/15, demobilised 28/8/19.
SMITH, F., Pte. (823), attested 2/12/15, demobilised 7/10/19.
SCHOLTZ, J. J., Pte. (824), attested 2/12/15, killed in action 20/9/18.
ALIES, J. H., Sgt. (825), attested 2/12/15, Cpl. 11/4/16, a/Sgt. 11/4/17, Sgt. 1/4/18, demobilised 8/10/19, qualified first-class signalling instructor, mentioned in despatches, East Africa.
McLACHLAN, J. H., Pte. (826), attested 2/12/15, S.N.L.R. 29/2/16.
SCHROEDER, T., Pte. (827), attested 2/12/15, died of typhoid 18/8/18.
WATSON, A., Pte. (828), attested 2/12/15, released medically unfit 25/1/16.
FREDERICKS, H. J. (M.M.), Cpl. (829), attested 2/12/15, Cpl. 23/3/17, demobilised 8/9/19, regimental bugler and medical corporal.
APPOLLIS, F., Pte. (830), attested 2/12/15, demobilised 11/7/19.
FISHER, J., Pte. (831), attested 2/12/15, released medically unfit 13/7/18.
WILLIAMS, A., Pte. (832), attested 2/12/15, released medically unfit 28/11/17.
ROBERTS, J., Pte. (833), attested 2/12/15, killed in action 20/9/18.
BAGLEY, A., Pte. (834), attested 2/12/15, released medically unfit 27/7/17.
DAVIDS, F. C., Pte. (835), attested 2/12/15, released medically unfit 3/9/17.
ERASMUS, C., Pte. (836), attested 2/12/15, demobilised 7/9/19.
MUNROE, P., Pte. (837), attested 2/12/15, S.N.L.R. 29/2/16.
WILLIAMS, C., L./Cpl. (838), attested 2/12/15, L./Cpl. 30/6/17, released medically unfit 17/1/19.
FOURIE, I., Pte. (839), attested 2/12/15, S.N.L.R. 31/1/16.
FORBES, A. J., Pte. (840), attested 2/12/15, released medically unfit 5/1/16.
McPHERSON, N., Pte. (841), attested 2/12/15, demobilised 2/1/19.
SYMES, H., Pte. (842), attested 2/12/15, demobilised 7/10/19, qualified first-class signaller, mentioned in despatches, East Africa.
SMITH, P., Pte. (843) attested 2/12/15, released medically unfit 10/3/16.
SLINGER, J., Pte. (844), attested 2/12/15, died of dystentery 20/6/16
SMITH, P., Cpl. (845), attested 2/12/15), Cpl. 7/12/15, died of influenza 11/10/18.
OLIVER, J., Cpl. (846), attested 2/12/15, L./Cpl. 19/1/16, Cpl 1/11/18, demobilised 16/7.19, passed trench warfare and bombing courses.
CARELS, D. A., Pte. (847), attested 2/12/15, demobilised 27/12/18.
GELDENHUIS, J., Pte. (848), attested 2/12/15, released medically unfit 25/1/16.
APLOON, T., Pte. (849), attested 2/12/15, demobilised 8/9/19.
FREDERICKS, N. J., Pte. (850), attested 3/12/15, released medically unfit 20/11/17.
CHRISTIANS, W., Pte. (851), attested 3/12/15, released medically unfit 6/7/17.
STANDLEIT, T., Pte. (852), attested 3/12/15, released medically unfit 4/2/16.
FREDERICKS, K., Pte. (853), attested 3/12/15, released medically unfit 18/8/17.
ADAMS, J., Pte. (854), attested 3/12/15, released medically unfit 6/12/15.
NORMAN, D., Pte. (855), attested 3/12/15, demobilised 11/7/19.
McCALLUM, W., Pte. (856), attested 3/12/15, S.N.L.R. 31/1/16.
BAILEY, J., Pte. (857), attested 3/12/15, demobilised 9/10/19.
CUPIDO, L., Pte. (858), attested 3/12/15, demobilised 16/7/19.

THE STORY OF THE 1st CAPE CORPS.

HANS, S., Pte. (859), attested 3/12/15, released medically unfit 3/9/17.
BULL, F. P., Pte. (860), attested 3/12/15, released medically unfit 28/11/17.
HOFFMAN, F. W., C.Q.M.S. (861), attested 3/12/15, C.Q.M.S. 1/2/17, killed in action 20/9/18
HANMER, P., Sgt. (862), attested 3/12/15, Cpl. 14/7/16, Sgt. 11/12/16, released medically unfit 24/9/17, signaller, awarded Italian bronze medal.
ALEXANDER, P., Pte. (863), attested 3/12/15, released medically unfit 11/5/17.
SIMPSON, E., L./Cpl. (864), attested 3/12/15, L./Cpl. 15/10/17, demobilised 7/9/19
ERBACK, E., Pte. (865), attested 3/12/15, released medically unfit 3/12/17.
JULIES, J., Pte. (866), attested 3/12/15, demobilised 5/1/19.
KAY, R. F., Pte. (867), attested 4/12/15, demobilised 4/9/19, passed trench warfare and bombing courses.
WILLIAMS, C. R., Sgt. (868), attested 4/12/15, L./Cpl. 4/12/15, Cpl. 5/7/17, Sgt. 15/10/17, released medically unfit 16/5/18.
WATERWICH, J. C., Sgt. (869), attested 4/12/15, Sgt. 5/12/15, demobilised 6/1/19.
GERTZEN, G., L./Cpl. (870), attested 4/12/15, L./Cpl. 1/11/18, demobilised 7/10/19.
PETERSEN, J. F., Pte. (871), attested 4/12/15, S.N.L.R. 13/2/17.
ELLIOTT, W., Pte. (872), attested 4/12/15, S.N.L.R. 13/2/17.
DE JONGH, F. N., Sgt. (873), attested 4/12/15, Sgt. 4/12/15, died of dysentery 2/10/16.
TWYNAM, E., Cpl. (874), attested 4/12/15, reverted to Pte. 18/2/18, a/Sgt. 20/4/18, Cpl 1/11/18, demobilised 7/10/19, passed general N.C.O.'s course.
BARBIER, W. F., Sgt. (875), attested 4/12/15, Sgt. 4/12/15, demobilised 8/8/19.
SMIT, J., Cpl. (876), attested 4/12/15, Cpl. 1/3/17, demobilised 11/10/19
SEPTEMBER, M., Pte. (877), attested 4/12/15, demobilised 7/9/19.
STANDER, J., Pte. (878), attested 4/12/15, released medically unfit 18/8/17.
CHRISTOFFEL, D., Pte. (879), attested 4/12/15, released medically unfit 9/8/17.
PINTO, J., Pte. (880), attested 5/12/15, released medically unfit 6/7/17.
MARTIN, F., Pte. (881), attested 5/12/15, S.N.L.R. 31/1/16.
LAVIGRE, A. A., Cpl. (882), attested 5/12/15 Cpl. 7/10/16, released medically unfit 18/8/17, pioneer.
FLUSK, W., Pte. (883), attested 5/12/15, released medically unfit 20/11/17.
RUITERS, D., Pte. (884), attested 5/12/15, released medically unfit 14/6/17.
PEFFER, A., Sgt. (885), attested 5/12/15, L./Cpl. 5/12/15, Cpl. 4/10/16, Sgt. 5/12/16, released medically unfit 27/7/17.
PEFFER, G., Pte. (886), attested 5/12/15, demobilised 1/1/19, signaller.
LOTTERING, H., Pte. (887), attested 5/12/15, demobilised 13/1/19.
PHILLIPS, D., Cpl. (888), attested 6/12/15, Cpl. 17/2/16, released medically unfit 25/4/18.
HANSEN, F., Pte. (889), attested 6/12/15, released medically unfit 23/12/15.
DANIELS, S., Pte. (890), attested 6/12/15, died of wounds 22/9/18.
BENJAMIN, J., Pte. (891), attested 6/12/15, S.N.L.R. 8/8/17.
ADAMS, A., Pte. (892), attested 6/12/15, released medically unfit 28/7/16.
PETERSEN, J., Pte. (893), attested 6/12/15, demobilised 11/7/19.
HENDRICKS, C., Cpl. (894), attested 6/12/15, L./Cpl. 24/6/17, Cpl. 18/6/18, demobilised 11/7/19.
SYLVESTER, J., Pte. (895), attested 6/12/15, S.N.L.R. 31/1/16.
JAFTHA, J., Pte. (896), attested 6/12/15, released medically unfit 23/9/17, regimental bugler.
WILSON, C. H., Pte. (897), attested 6/12/15, released medically unfit 6/1/17.
BRAZER, W., Pte. (898), attested 6/12/15, released medically unfit 27/7/17.
ABRAHAMS, J. W., Pte. (899), attested 6/12/15, demobilised 6/1/19.
JOSHUA, C., Pte. (900), attested 6/12/15, demobilised 7/10/19.
ROOZA, P., Pte. (901), attested 6/12/15, released medically unfit 12/11/17.
HOFMEISTER, H., a/Sgt. (902), attested 6/12/15, Cpl. 1/4/18, a/Sgt. 19/10/18, demobilised 7/10/19, passed scout course.
EAVES, I., Pte. (903), attested 6/12/15, released medically unfit 23/7/17.
LE ROUX, H. D., Sgt. (904), attested 6/12/15, Sgt. 6/12/15, released medically unfit 24/7/17, rejoined under No. 4285.
LANGFORD, W., Pte. (905), attested 6/12/15, Sgt. 6/12/15, reverted to Pte. 30/3/17, demobilised 25/12/18.
EMMETT, G. H., Pte. (906), attested 6/12/15, released medically unfit 14/11/17.
HOLLOWAY, P., Pte. (907), attested 6/12/15, demobilised 17/1/19.
ADONIS, F., Pte. (908), attested 6/12/15, demobilised 30/12/19.
QUINTON, C. H., a/Sgt. (909), attested 6/12/15, Cpl. 6/12/15, a/Sgt. 15/10/17, released medically unfit 6/6/18.
WALSH, J. M., Pte. (910), attested 6/12/15, released medically unfit 12/5/17.
SOESMAN, J. W., Pte. (911), attested 6/12/15, demobilised 11/7/19.
BELFORD, G. S., Pte. (912), attested 6/12/15, demobilised 7/10/19.
HENDERSON, J., Pte. (913), attested 6/12/15, demobilised 5/2/19.
MAY, W., L./Cpl. (914), attested 6/12/15, L./Cpl. 2/11/17, killed in action 20/9/18.
MARNITZ, A. I., L./Cpl. (915), attested 6/12/15, L./Cpl. 1/11/18, demobilised 8/9/19, signaller.
CARELSE, J., a/Sgt. (916), attested 6/12/15, Cpl. 20/4/18, a/L./Sgt. 10/5/19, demobilised 29/7/19.
HECTOR, A. S., Pte. (917), attested 6/12/15, released medically unfit 8/8/17.
DESMORE, F., Pte. (918), attested 6/12/15, released medically unfit 4/4/16.
PETERSEN, J., Pte. (919), attested 6/12/15, released medically unfit 8/8/17.
ABRAMS, G., Pte. (920), attested 6/12/15, demobilised 6/10/19.
DE VOS, J., Pte. (921), attested 6/12/15, demobilised 22/7/19.
CHITTER, C., Pte. (922), attested 6/12/15, demobilised 7/10/19.
CROY, J., Pte. (923), attested 6/12/15, released medically unfit 27/4/17.
JOHANSEN, J. S., Cpl. (924), attested 6/12/15, Cpl. 6/12/15, released medically unfit 20/11/17.
VYFER, P., Pte. (925), attested 6/12/15, died of pulmonary phthisis 21/5/16.
LOMBARD, C., L./Cpl. (926), attested 6/12/15, L./Cpl. 6/12/15, died of tuberculosis 30/9/16.
MORRIS, J., Pte. (927), attested 6/12/15, died of malaria 8/6/16.
MATHEWS, D., Pte. (928), attested 6/12/15, released medically unfit 24/9/17.
CUPIDO, J., Pte. (929), attested 6/12/15, released medically unfit 7/12/15.
DU PREEZ, G., Pte. (930), attested 6/12/15, died of influenza 14/10/18.
JACOBUS, D., Pte. (931), attested 6/12/15, demobilised 16/7/19.
WILLIAMS, W., Pte. (932), attested 6/12/15, released medically unfit 7/12/15.
JACOBS, S., Pte. (933), attested 6/12/15, released medically unfit 7/12/15.
SEPTEMBER, W., Pte. (934), attested 6/12/15, released medically unfit 17/6/18.
ABRAHAMS, C., Pte. (935), attested 6/12/15, released medically unfit 26/9/17.
CORNEILSEN, E., Pte. (936), attested 6/12/15, released medically unfit 7/12/15.
JAFTHA, A., Pte. (937), attested 6/12/15, S.N.L.R. 23/4/17.
AVONTUUR, D., Pte. (938), attested 6/12/15, rejected 15/12/15.
STEADY, J., Pte. (939), attested 6/12/15, Cpl. 2/11/17, was Transport Sergeant for some time, reverted to Pte. 31/12/18, demobilised 7/9/19.
CLARKE, T. F., Pte. (940), attested 6/12/15, S.N.L.R. 31/1/16.

THE STORY OF THE 1st CAPE CORPS.

JORDAAN, J. M., Pte. (941), attested 6/12/15, demobilised 21/7/19.
VAN WYK, R., Pte. (942), attested 6/12/15, demobilised 5/2/19.
PETERSEN, J. J., Sgt. (943), attested 6/12/15, Sgt. 6/12/15, demobilised 21/7/19, Shoemaker Sgt., passed general N.C.O.'s course.
JORDAAN, H. J., L./Cpl. (944), attested 6/12/15, L./Cpl. 23/3/17, released medically unfit 12/5/18.
MEYERS, W. F., Pte. (945), attested 6/12/15, released medically unfit 22/12/15.
ORPEN, B., L./Cpl. (946), attested 6/12/15, L./Cpl. 6/12/15, released medically unfit 30/9/16.
STEYN, J., L./Sgt. (947), attested 6/12/15, L./Cpl. 1/4/18, a/Cpl. 2/4/18, Cpl. 1/7/18, L./Sgt. 1/11/18, demobilised 12/8/19, qualified Lewis gunner.
ARNOLDUS, A., Pte. (948), attested 6/12/15, demobilised 7/9/19.
DEVEREAUX, H., Pte. (949), attested 6/12/15, demobilised 7/9/19.
BAUMAN, A., Pte. (950), attested 6/12/15, died of dysentery 30/8/17.
CARELSON, M., Pte. (951), attested 6/12/15, released medically unfit 13/9/17.
DAVIS, C., Pte. (952), attested 6/12/15, released medically unfit 24/2/18.
JOHNSON, J., Pte. (953), attested 6/12/15, released medically unfit 23/12/15.
GORDON, J., Pte. (954), attested 6/12/15, demobilised 11/7/19.
DANIELS, J. J., Pte. (955), attested 6/12/15, released medically unfit 17/1/16.
ARENDSE, G., Pte. (956), attested 7/12/15, killed in action 6/11/17.
SAMUELS, I., Pte. (957), attested 7/12/15, rejected 27/12/15.
JACOBS, H., Pte. (958), attested 7/12/15, demobilised 29/12/18.
ABRAHAMS, J., Pte. (959), attested 7/12/15, released medically unfit 23/2/16
LIDDLE, J., Pte. (960), attested 7/12/15, demobilised 7/10/19.
PETERSEN, J., Pte. (961), attested 7/12/15, released medically unfit 15/3/17.
PLAATJES, A., Pte. (962), attested 7/12/15, died of blackwater 26/4/17.
ABRAHAMS, F., Pte. (963), attested 7/12/15, demobilised 7/10/19, qualified Lewis gunner.
ECKSTRIN, W., Pte. (964), attested 7/12/15, S.N.I.R. 31/1/16.
ROSS, J., Pte. (965), attested 7/12/15, rejected 15/12/15.
FAIRLING, W., L./Cpl. (966), attested 7/12/15, L./Cpl. 30/6/17, demolilised 27/12/18.
SHELDON, E., Pte. (967), attested 7/12/15, demobilised 11/7/19.
FRENCHMAN, J., Pte. (968), attested 7/12/15, released medically unfit 23/5/18.
OCTOBER, J., a/Sgt. (969), attested 7/12/15, Cpl. 1/4/18, a/Sgt. 19/10/18, demobilised 21/7/19.
JANUARY, H., Pte. (970), attested 7/12/15, demobilised 7/10/19.
ZIEDEL, J., Pte. (971), attested 7/12/15, died of malaria 4/10/16.
FREDERICKS, P., Pte. (972), attested 7/12/15, released medically unfit 20/11/17.
HARTZENBERG, H., Pte. (973), attested 7/12/15, released medically unfit 24/7/17.
GERTZE, J., Pte. (974), attested 7/12/15, released medically unfit 13/9/17.
JAFTHAS, S., Pte. (975), attested 7/12/15, died of malaria 3/8/16.
GROSS, F., Pte. (976), attested 7/12/15, rejected 15/12/15.
HECTOR, D., Sgt. (977), attested 7/12/15, Cpl. 7/12/15, Sgt. 11/12/16, released medically unfit 22/3/18.
HERMAN, H. W., Pte. (978), attested 7/12/15, Sgt. 7/12/15, reverted to Pte. 14/6/18, demobilised 5/2/19.
BREDEKAMP, J. B., Sgt. (979), attested 7/12/15, L./Cpl. 7/12/15, Cpl. 1/4/18, a/Sgt. 27/10/18, Sgt 1/11/18, demobilised 7/10/19.
SCHROEDER, F. (M.M.), L./Cpl. (980), attested 7/12/15, L./Cpl. 7/12/15, killed in action 6/11/17.
RHODA, R., L./Cpl. (981), attested 7/12/15, L./Cpl. 7/12/15, released medically unfit 27/7/17.
FILIES, J. J., Pte. (982), attested 7/12/15, missing, death accepted 15/4/17.
MARAIS, M., L./Cpl. (983), attested 7/12/15, L./Cpl. 20/5/18, demobilised 8/9/19.
LEWIS, D., Pte. (984), attested 7/12/15, released medically unfit 13/5/18.
PIENAAR, F., Pte. (985), attested 7/12/15, demobilised 16/7/19, qualified signaller.
FREDERICKS, C., Pte. (986), attested 7/12/15, demobilised 7/10/19.
WEBSTER, F. W., Pte. (987), attested 7/12/15, released medically unfit 12/11/17
DAVIDS, C., Pte. (988), attested 7/12/15, demobilised 8/9/19.
PLAATJES, J., Pte. (989), attested 7/12/15, demobilised 24/2/19.
SKIPPERS, F., L./Sgt. (990), attested 7/12/15, L./Cpl. 7/12/15, Cpl. 11/1/17, a/Sgt. 5/7/18, L./Sgt. 1/11/18, demobilised 16/7/19.
DU PLOOY, H., Pte. (991), attested 7/12/15, S.N.L.R. 17/7/17.
HILL, R., Pte. (992), attested 7/12/15, released medically unfit 4/8/17.
MINORDS, H., Pte. (993), attested 7/12/15, released medically unfit 31/8/17.
LEWIS, C., Pte. (994), attested 7/12/15, died of malaria 7/5/18.
DE VILLIERS, F., L./Cpl. (995), attested 7/12/15, demobilised 21/7/19.
DIEDERICKS, G., Pte. (996), attested 7/12/15, demobilised 21/7/19, passed scout course.
WICK, H., Pte. (997), attested 7/12/15, rejected 21/12/15.
ADONIS, H., Pte. (998), attested 7/12/15, demobilised 16/4/19.
EVERTS, E., Pte. (999), attested 7/12/15, demobilised 15/11/19
THEUNIS, J. J., Pte. (1000), attested 7/12/15, released medically unfit 23/2/16.
LEVINE, L., Pte. (1001), attested 7/12/15, demobilised 26/8/19.
ARENDSE, S. I., Pte. (1002), attested 7/12/15, released medically unfit 30/9/18.
RAYNARDT, C. W., L./Cpl. (1003), attested 7/12/15, L./Cpl. 7/12/15, released medically unfit 16/8/17.
WILLIAMS, J. E., Pte. (1004), attested 7/12/15, released medically unfit 30/11/17.
MOSES, D., Pte. (1005), attested 7/12/15, demobilised 28/10/19.
STEVENS, T., L./Cpl. (1006), attested 7/12/15, L./Cpl. 5/1/17, demobilised 2/1/19.
DE FARSE, F., Pte. (1007), attested 7/12/15, demobilised 7/10/19, qualified Lewis gunner.
JOHNSTON, W., Cpl. (1008), attested 7/12/15, L./Cpl. 7/12/15, Cpl. 14/12/16, demobilised 27/10/19.
LANDSMAN, C., Pte. (1009), attested 7/12/15, Cpl. 9/12/15, reverted to Pte. 28/9/17, released medically unfit 20/10/17.
SHELDON, C., L./Cpl. (1010), attested 7/12/15, L./Cpl. 1/7/18, demobilised 11/7/19.
FORTUIN, D., Pte. (1011), attested 7/12/15, demobilised 7/10/19.
SEPTEMBER, J., Pte. (1012), attested 7/12/15, released medically unfit 25/8/17
PETERSEN, J., Pte. (1013), attested 7/12/15, demobilised 8/9/19.
MARTHINUS, S., Pte. (1014), attested 7/12/15, demobilised 11/7/19
CUPIDO, J., Pte. (1015), attested 7/12/15, released medically unfit 14/8/17.
OSBORNE, J., Pte. (1016), attested 7/12/15, died of enteritis 18/1/17.
PETERSEN, A., Pte. (1017), attested 7/12/15, S.N.L.R. 31/1/16.
WEBBER, K., Pte. (1018), attested 7/12/15, released medically unfit 15/8/17.
MARTHINUS, H., Pte. (1019), attested 7/12/15, demobilised 16/7/19.
DANIELS, M., Pte. (1020), attested 7/12/15, S.N.L.R. 2/7/18.
OCTOBER, C., Pte. (1021), attested 7/12/15, demobilised 7/9/19, qualified 1st class signaller.
DE WET, J., Pte. (1022), attested 7/12/15, released medically unfit 27/7/17.
STAINER, F., Pte. (1023), attested 7/12/15, released medically unfit 18/8/17.
VAN DER WESTHUISEN, H., Pte. (1024), attested 7/12/15, released medically unfit 17/12/15.
VAN WYK, T., Pte. (1025), attested 7/12/15, released medically unfit 27/6/17.

THE STORY OF THE 1st CAPE CORPS.

HULL, C., Pte. (1026), attested 7/12/15, released medically unfit 26/9/17.
KOLBEE, D. G., Pte. (1027), attested 8/12/15, demobilised 7/10/19.
MATTHEWS, M., Pte. (1028), attested 8/12/15, released medically unfit 29/10/17.
POOLE, A., Pte. (1029), attested 8/12/15, released medically unfit 25/9/18.
JURY, A., Pte. (1030), attested 8/12/15, S.N.L.R. 13/5/17.
KARSTEN, P., Sgt. (1031), attested 8/12/15, Sgt. 8/12/15, released medically unfit 13/9/17
GOLIATH, F., Cpl. (1032), attested 8/12/15, L./Cpl. 1/4/18, Cpl. 1/11/18, demobilised 21/7/19, qualified Lewis Gun Instructor.
ARMSTRONG, J., Pte. (1033), attested 8/12/15, demobilised 1/1/19.
PRETORIUS, J., Pte. (1034), attested 8/12/15, released medically unfit 13/9/17.
VAN REENEN, E., Pte. (1035), attested 8/12/15, released medically unfit 2/8/17.
HYDE, J., Pte. (1036), attested 8/12/15, S.N.L.R. 31/1/16.
DAVIDS, J., Pte. (1037), attested 8/12/15, killed in action 6/11/17.
KARELE, J., Sgt. (1038), attested 8/12/15, Sgt. 8/12/15, reverted to Pte 20/8/16, a/Sgt. 7/7/17, Sgt. 1/4/18, demobilised 10/10/19, passed physical and bayonet courses.
THOMPSON, J., Cpl. (1039), attested 8/12/15, Cpl. 9/12/15, died of malaria 13/9/16.
RENSBURG, A., Pte. (1040), attested 8/12/15, released medically unfit 5/2/17.
VELKERS, P., Pte. (1041), attested 8/12/15, released medically unfit 2/2/17.
ANDRIES, J., Pte. (1042), attested 8/12/15, released medically unfit 27/12/15.
SAAISE, J., Pte. (1043), attested 8/12/15, demobilised 7/9/19.
UITHALDER, B., Pte. (1044), attested 8/12/15, demobilised 28/8/19.
ANDREWS, C., Pte. (1045), attested 8/12/15, released medically unfit 22/8/16.
BIRCHAM, R., R.S.M. (1046), attested 8/12/15, R.S.M. 8/12/15, transferred to U.D.F. 31/12/15, European personnel.
GREY, R.Q.M.S. (1047), attested 8/12/15, transferred to U.D.F. 12/12/15, European personnel.
MILLS, W. T., Staff Sgt. (1048), attested 8/12/15, released medically unfit 8/2/16, European personnel.
BETTS, F. W. E. (D.C.M.), R.S.M. (1049), attested 8/12/15, R.Q.M.S. 22/9/16, R.S.M. 1/1/17, released medically unfit 29/12/17, European personnel.
CASSIDY, C.S.M. (1050), attested 8/12/15, released medically unfit 4/5/17. European personnel.
WIGMAN, W. T., C.S.M. (1051), attested 8/12/15, commissioned to Cape Corpe 21/7/16, European personnel
PATERSON, D. A., C.S.M. (1052), attested 8/12/15, to S.A.L. Corps 29/11/16. European personnel.
CLENNEL, I., C.S.M. (1053), attested 8/12/15, released medically unfit 14/2/18, European personnel.
KLASSEN, C., Pte. (1054), attested 9/12/15, released medically unfit 22/8/17.
SYLVESTER, H., L./Cpl. (1055), attested 9/12/15, L./Cpl. 15/10/17, demobilised 23/7/19, N.C.O. i/c. Drum and Fife Band.
COURT, E., Cpl. (1056), attested 9/12/15, Cpl. 1/3/17, S.N.L.R. 17/2/18.
ST. CLAIR, S., Pte. (1057), attested 9/12/15, released medically unfit 13/8/17.
NEFDT, J., Cpl. (1058), attested 9/12/15, L./Cpl. 9/12/15, Cpl. 15/10/17, demobilised 23/9/19, passed grenade discharging and scout courses.
LYNX, A., Pte. (1059), attested 9/12/15, released medically unfit 16/6/16.
JOSHUA, F., Pte. (1060), attested 9/12/15, demobilised 7/10/19.
ISAACS, A., Pte. (1061), attested 9/12/15, demobilised 31/12/18.
SMITH, M., Pte. (1062), attested 9/12/15, demobilised 11/7/19.
GREEN, H., Pte. (1063), attested 9/12/15, released medically unfit 27/12/15.
MEYER, J., Sgt. (1064), attested 9/12/15, Cpl. (a/Sgt.) 9/12/15, Sgt. 25/3/18, demobilised 21/7/19, qualified 1st class machine gunner.
LANGEVELDT, C. J., Pte. (1065), attested 9/12/15, released medically unfit 27/12/15.
LOUIS, A. M., Sgt. (1066), attested 9/12/15, Sgt. 25/12/15, released medically unfit 1/5/18.
HENDRICKS, A. J. (D.C.M.), a/R.Q.M.S. (1067), attested 9/12/15, C.Q.M.S. 9/12/15, a/C.S.M. 23/9/18, a/R.Q.M.S. 3/3/19, demobilised 10/10/19, passed general N.C.O.'s course, mentioned in despatches, East Africa and Palestine.
HARDING, W. J., Pte. (1068), attested 9/12/15, released medically unfit 20/11/17.
HENDRICKS, P., Pte. (1069), attested 9/12/15, demobilised 2/1/19.
BARTLETT, H. R., Pte. (1070), attested 9/12/15, S.N.L.R. 18/10/18.
PHILIPS, H. R., Pte. (1071), attested 9/12/15, released medically unfit 18/8/17.
DE VOS, A. P., Sgt. (1072), attested 9/12/15, a/Sgt. 13/3/18, Sgt. 29/9/18, demobilised 8/9/19, Shoemaker Sgt. 1918/19.
WILLIAMS, J., Pte. (1073), attested 9/12/15, released medically unfit 25/8/17.
VYFER, F. J., Pte. (1074), attested 9/12/15, released medically unfit 26/1/16.
CELENTO, N. J., Pte. (1075), attested 9/12/15, released medically unfit 8/2/18.
ABDOL, A., Pte. (1076), attested 9/12/15, released medically unfit 27/12/15.
WHITEMAN C., Pte. (1077), attested 9/12/15), released medically unfit 28/7/16.
RAMUS, J., Pte. (1078), attested 9/12/15, released medically unfit 23/8/17.
ADAMS, G., Pte. (1079), attested 10/12/15, released medically unfit 12/11/17.
VALENTINE, J., Pte. (1080), attested 10/12/15, S.N.L.R. 6/1/16.
VAN HAARTE, M., Pte. (1081), attested 10/12/15, died of malaria 24/3/16.
ANTHONY, J., Pte. (1082), attested 11/12/15, demobilised 8/9/19.
RUDOLPH, J., Pte. (1083), attested 11/12/15, released medically unfit 27/6/17
VALENTINE, A., Pte. (1084), attested 11/12/15, released medically unfit 8/2/16.
WILLIAMS, J., Pte. (1085), attested 11/12/15, released medically unfit 21/7/18.
ROSE, R., Pte. (1086), attested 11/12/15, released medically unfit 27/12/15.
GROEP, J., L./Sgt. (1087), attested 11/12/15, Cpl. 18/12/16, a/Sgt. 6/10/18, L./Sgt. 1/11/18, demobilised 21/7/19, qualified Lewis gunner.
SWARTZ, W., a/Cpl. (1088), attested 11/12/15, L./Cpl. 1/4/18, a/Cpl. 2/4/18, demobilised 21/7/19, passed scout and grenade discharging courses.
WILLIAMS, T., L./Cpl. (1089), attested 12/12/15, L./Cpl. 5/7/18, demobilised 7/9/19.
CROWIE, H., Pte. (1090), attested 12/12/15, demobilised 7/9/19, signaller.
CROWIE, G. E., Pte. (1091), attested 12/12/15, released medically unfit 4/1/16.
TWYNHAM, D. F., (D.C.M.), a/R.S.M. (1092), attested 12/12/15, C.S.M. 18/9/16, a/R.S.M. 11/10/17, discharged 12/8/18, mentioned in despatches, East Africa.
KNIPE, T. J., Cpl. (1093), attested 12/12/15, L./Cpl. 1/6/17, Cpl. 1/4/18, died of malaria 12/8/19, qualified 1st class signaller.
THOMPSON, F. W., Pte. (1094), attested 12/12/15, released medically unfit 15/12/15.
GOODSELL, A., Pte. (1095), attested 12/12/15, released medically unfit 4/1/16
STEVENS, J., Pte. (1096), attested 12/12/15, demobilised 21/7/19.
ABRAHAMS, J., Pte. (1097), attested 13/12/15, demobilised 2/1/19.
ABEL, J., Pte. (1098), attested 13/12/15, released medically unfit 23/12/15.
BENJAMIN, P., Pte. (1099), attested 13/12/15, demobilised 7/10/19.
DAMONS, H., Pte. (1100), attested 13/12/15, demobilised 8/9/19, signaller.
DAVIDS, J., Pte. (1101), attested 13/12/15, demobilised 8/9/19.

THE STORY OF THE 1st CAPE CORPS.

HERMANUS, J., a/Cpl. (1102), attested 13/12/15, a/Cpl. 1/3/19, demobilised 8/9/19, Lewis gunner.
WALHUTER, C., Pte. (1103), attested 13/12/15, demobilised 16/7/19, drum and fife band.
VAN DER REEDE, F., Pte. (1104), attested 13/12/15, demobilised 31/12/18.
KOLBEE, F. J., Pte. (1105), attested 13/12/15, died of influenza 3/10/18.
SMITH, C., L./Cpl. (1106), attested 13/12/15, L.Cpl. 16/11/18, demobilised 8/9/19, qualified Lewis gunner
WELCOME, I., Pte. (1107), attested 13/12/15, demobilised 2/1/19.
BURMAN, R., Pte. (1108), attested 13/12/15, demobilised 7/9/19, qualified 1st class signaller.
GOLIATH, J., Cpl. (1109), attested 14/12/15, Cpl. 15/12/15, released medically unfit 3/3/17.
PHILLIPS, J., Pte. (1110), attested 14/12/15, released medically unfit 7/1/16.
JACOBS, C., Pte. (1111), attested 14/12/15, demobilised 21/11/19.
KRIEL, C. D., Pte. (1112), attested 14/12/15, released medically unfit 23/12/15.
OCKHUIS, J., Pte. (1113), attested 14/12/15, released medically unfit 27/4/17.
TOBIAS, P., Pte. (1114), attested 14/12/15, released medically unfit 12/6/16.
ADAMS, A., Pte. (1115), attested 15/12/15, released medically unfit 3/12/17.
GREENFIELD, J. W., Pte. (1116), attested 15/12/15, S.N.L.R. 28/1/17.
MASON, J. W., a/Cpl. (1117), attested 15/12/15, L./Cpl. 24/6/17, a/Cpl. 1/11/18, demobilised 29/7/19, qualified Lewis Gun Instructor.
JANSEN, J., Pte. (1118), attested 16/12/15, released medically unfit 25/1/16.
VAN ROOY, J., Pte. (1119), attested 16/12/15, released medically unfit 28/11/17.
DE VOS, W., Pte. (1120), attested 16/12/15, released medically unfit 7/1/16.
VAN WYK, R., Pte. (1121), attested 17/12/15, released medically unfit 3/10/17.
THOMAS, M. P., L./Sgt. (1122), attested 17/12/15, Cpl. 24/6/17, L./Sgt. 18/6/18, demobilised 7/10/19, passed grenade discharging course.
ROSE, F., Pte. (1123), attested 17/12/15, released medically unfit 20/7/17.
MUNNICK, J., Pte. (1124), attested 17/12/15, released medically unfit 20/4/16.
FREDERICKS, F., Pte. (1125), attested 17/12/15, S.N.L.R. 31/1/16.
POULTON, A. J., Pte. (1126), attested 17/12/15, demobilised 28/8/19.
LA VITA, H. W., C.Q.M.S. (1127), attested 17/12/15, L./Cpl. 1/1/16, Sgt. 1/4/16, C.Q.M.S. 13/12/18, demobilised 10/10/19, mentioned in despatches, East Africa.
CAMPBELL, W., Pte. (1128), attested 20/12/15, demobilised 19/2/19.
PETERSEN, C. J., Cpl. (1129), attested 21/12/15, Cpl. 21/12/15, released medically unfit 24/9/17.
PETERS, R. E., Pte. (1130), attested 21/12/15, released medically unfit 29/10/17, bugler.
MAVELA, M., Pte. (1131), attested 16/12/15, released medically unfit 13/2/16.
LANDSMAN, F., Pte. (1132), attested 22/12/15, died of malaria and blackwater 19/2/18
LYNERS, I., Pte. (1133), attested 22/12/15, demobilised 28/4/19
DUNN, S. W. (D.C.M.), Pte. (1134), attested 23/12/15, Sgt. 23/12/15, reverted to Pte. 17/9/16, Cpl. 26/12/16, Sgt. 11/2/17, reverted to Pte. at own request 8/12/17, discharged 19/4/18.
BERRY, J. G., Col. Sgt. (1135), attested 23/12/15, Cpl. 23/12/15, O.R. Sgt. 26/7/16, Col. Sgt. 27/7/18, demobilised 3/12/19, awarded Italian bronze medal.
HEMMING, I. A., Pte. (1136), attested 23/12/15, demobilised 7/9/19.
HOSACK, J. C., R.Q.M.S. (1137), attested 29/10/15, R.Q.M.S. 29/10/15, commissioned to 1st Cape Corps 4/12/15, reverted at his own request 14/2/16, commissioned 16/6/16, killed in action 20/7/16, European personnel.
CLOKE, R. A., R.Q.M.S. (1138), attested 4/12/15, a/C.Q.M.S. 4/12/15, C.Q.M.S. 9/1/16, C.S.M. 17/4/16, R.Q.M.S. 19/6/16, commissioned to 1st Cape Corps 30/6/16, European personnel.
ADAMS, T. C., Sgt. (1139), attested 29/11/15, Sgt. Cook—officers'—died of septicancinia 8/7/16, European personnel.
BAM, J. J., Pay Sgt. (1140), attested 26/12/15, discharged 19/3/17, European personnel.
FORSYTHE, G., R.S.M. (1141), attested 13/12/15, R.S.M. 1/1/16, transferred 26/10/17, European personnel
GOLIATH, M., Pte. (1142), attested 2/1/16, demobilised 8/10/19.
REAGON, A. J., C.Q.M.S. (1143), attested 4/1/16, Cpl. 29/12/16, a/C.Q.M.S. 8/10/17, C.Q.M.S. 23/3/18, demobilised 18/10/19, mentioned in despatches, Egypt.
CAIRNS, F. J. (M.M.), Staff Sgt. (1144), attested 4/1/16, L./Cpl. 4/10/16, Sgt. 29/12/16, Staff Sgt. 15/3/18, demobilised 10/10/19, Medical Staff Sgt.
VAN ZYL, F., Pte. (1145), attested 4/1/16, demobilised 10/10/19.
JACOBS, D. M., L./Cpl. (1146), attested 4/1/16, L./Cpl. 1/11/18, demobilised 7/10/19, qualified first-class signaller.
KRIEL, C. J., Cpl. (1147), attested 4/1/16, L./Cpl. 4/1/16, Sgt. 17/9/16, reverted to Cpl. 26/3/18, demobilised 7/10/19, medical section.
STEMMERS, F., L./Cpl. (1148), attested 4/1/16, L./Cpl. 1/9/18, demobilised 7/10/19, qualified Lewis gunner.
ROBERTS, R., Pte. (1149), attested 5/1/16, demobilised 22/7/19.
ADRIAANSE, P. J., Sgt. (1150), attested 5/1/16, Sgt. 20/1/16, demobilised 1/1/19.
THOMPSON, E. G., Pte. (1151), attested 5/1/16, released medically unfit 15/8/17.
SMIT, J., Pte. (1152), attested 5/1/16, demobilised 11/7/19.
GOODMAN, A., Pte. (1153), attested 5/1/16, demobilised 21/7/19.
SCHOLTZ, J., Pte. (1154), attested 5/1/16, released medically unfit 10/5/18.
GOLIATH, A., Pte. (1155), attested 5/1/16, released medically unfit 6/11/17.
JOHNSON, L., Pte. (1156), attested 5/1/16, died of influenza 14/10/18
DE WET, A., Pte. (1157), attested 5/1/16, demobilised 7/10/19.
GIBSON, J., L./Cpl. (1158), attested 5/1/16, L./Cpl. 23/8/18, a/Cpl. 24/8/18, reverted to L./Cpl. 12/12/18, demobilised 8/9/19, qualified machine gunner.
ADAMS, P., Pte. (1159), attested 5/1/16, released medically unfit 13/3/19.
JORDAN, J. Pte. (1160), attested 5/1/16, demobilised 2/1/19.
ABRAHAMS, J., a/L./Cpl. (1161), attested 5/1/16, a/L./Cpl. 1/3/19, demobilised 8/10/19.
STEPHENSON, J., Pte. (1162), attested 5/1/16, released medically unfit 16/11/17.
SPILANDER, A. J., Pte. (1163), attested 5/1/16, released medically unfit 6/11/17, bugler.
BOYES, J., Pte. (1164), attested 5/1/16, demobilised 11/7/19.
STADLER, W., Pte. (1165), attested 5/1/16, demobilised 11/7/19.
HERMANUS, R., Pte. (1166), attested 5/1/16, released medically unfit 17/1/16.
HERMANUS, I., Pte. (1167), attested 5/1/16, released medically unfit 17/1/17
FOWLER, W., Pte. (1168), attested 5/1/16, S.N.L.R. 31/1/16.
ASHBURY, J., Pte. (1169), attested 5/1/16, rejected, under age, 8/1/16.
BREDENKAMP, J., Cpl. (1170), attested 5/1/16, Cpl. 11/12/16, released medically unfit 20/11/17.
MATTHEWS, J. Pte. (1171), attested 5/1/16, released medically unfit 14/4/18.
McLEAN, D., Pte. (1172), attested 5/1/16, died of malaria 14/6/16.
CYSTER, A., Pte. (1173), attested 5/1/16, demobilised 8/9/19.
KLASSEN, P., Pte. (1174), attested 5/1/16, demobilised 30/12/18.
ROSSLANDS, L., Pte. (1175), attested 5/1/16, released medically unfit 20/11/17.
WILLIAMS, E. J., L./Cpl. (1176), attested 6/1/16, L./Cpl. 10/2/16, released medically unfit 29/6/17.

THE STORY OF THE 1st CAPE CORPS.

CAROLUS, P., Pte. (1177), attested 6/1/16, demobilised 31/12/19.
FLANDERS, C., Pte. (1178), attested 6/1/16, released medically unfit 28/7/16.
LE BRUIN, E., Pte. (M.M.), (1179), attested 6/1/16, demobilised 8/9/20, qualified machine gunner.
VISAGIE, J., Pte. (1180), attested 6/1/16, released medically unfit 4/2/16.
GOMBARD, J., Pte. (1181), attested 6/1/16, demobilised 7/10/19, Lewis gunner
PARKS, J., Pte. (1182), attested 6/1/16, demobilised 11/7/19.
HESS, G., Pte. (1183), attested 6/1/16, released medically unfit 7/6/18
GERTZEN, M., Pte. (1184), attested 6/1/16, demobilised 16/7/19.
TITUS, J., Pte. (1185), attested 6/1/16, released medically unfit 29/10/17.
ABLES, J., Pte. (1186), attested 7/1/16, demobilised 10/8/19.
WOLMARANS, W., Pte. (1187), attested 7/1/16, demobilised 11/7/19, passed trench warfare and trench mortar course.
SEBASTIAN, S., Cpl. (1188), attested 7/1/16, L./Cpl. 24/6/17, Cpl. 18/6/18, demobilised 24/10/19.
THOMAS, J., Pte. (1189), not attested.
ROBERTS, P., Pte. (1190), attested 7/1/16, L./Cpl. 15/10/17, reverted to Pte. 20/9/18, demobilised 6/1/19.
ARENDS, P., Pte. (1191), attested 7/1/16, released medically unfit 12/10/17.
DAVIS, J., Pte. (1192), attested 7/1/16, released medically unfit 23/2/16.
SUTTON, F., Pte. (1193), attested 7/1/16, released medically unfit 3/10/17.
ADRIAANSE, A., Pte. (1194), attested 7/1/16, Sgt. 20/1/17, reverted to Pte. 12/8/18, demobilised 20/1/19.
HARICOMBE, R. D., Pte. (1195), attested 7/1/16, released medically unfit 11/5/17.
ABRAHAMS, A., Pte. (1196), attested 7/1/16, demobilised 28/10/19.
TRANTRALL, W., Pte. (1197), attested 7/1/16, killed by mine explosion 21/1/17.
RAFFERTY, J., Pte. (1198), attested 7/1/16, released medically unfit 12/11/17.
SMITH, H., Pte. (1199), attested 7/1/16, demobilised 7/10/19.
MARTIN, M., Pte. (1200), attested 10/1/16, released medically unfit 15/8/17.
KUHN, S., Pte. (1201), attested 10/1/16, demobilised 7/10/19.
McLACHLAN, A., Pte. (1202), attested 10/1/16, released medically unfit 3/10/17.
DE YOUNG, G., Pte. (1203), attested 10/1/16, died of malaria 11/7/16.
SMIT, J., Sgt. (1204), attested 10/1/16, Cpl. 11/12/16, Sgt. 1/4/18, demobilised 7/10/19, 1st class machine gunner.
PHILANDER, J., Pte. (1205), attested 10/1/16, released medically unfit 28/7/16
ECKSTEIN, W., Pte. (1206), attested 10/1/16, released medically unfit 23/8/17.
GEORGE, M., Pte. (1207), attested 10/1/16, released medically unfit 6/11/17.
APPOLIS, F. S., Pte. (1208), attested 10/1/16, released medically unfit 18/12/18.
EDWARDS, J., Pte (1209), attested 10/1/16, released medically unfit 18/9/18.
JANUARY, J., Pte. (1210), attested 10/1/16, demobilised 28/10/19
PRESTON, G. H., L./Cpl. (1211), attested 10/1/16, L./Cpl. 25/4/19, demobilised 21/7/19, passed advanced army cookery.
PARIS, M., Pte. (1212), attested 10/1/16, demobilised 10/10/19
DE VREE, F., Pte. (1213), attested 10/1/16, died of dysentery 7/11/16.
FISHER, J., Pte. (1214), attested 10/1/16, released medically unfit 6/11/17.
CARELSE, L., Pte. (1215), attested 10/1/16, demobilised 7/10/19.
HENDRICKS, K., Pte. (1216), attested 10/1/16, released medically unfit 25/2/18.
FELIX, A., Pte. (1217), attested 10/1/16, released medically unfit 5/3/18.
RYAN, P., Pte. (1218), attested 10/1/16, released medically unfit 23/8/17.
WILLIAMS, P., Pte. (1219), attested 10/1/16, released medically unfit 7/3/17.
ADAMS, J., a/Cpl. (1220), attested 10/1/16, a/Cpl. 25/10/17, demobilised 21/7/19, passed physical and bayonet training course.
WILLIAMS, W., Pte. (1221), attested 10/1/16, released medically unfit 24/7/17.
FISHER, P., Pte. (1222), attested 11/1/16, released medically unfit 3/10/17.
WALLY, G., Pte. (1223), attested 11/1/16, demobilised 26/9/19, Lewis gunner.
CUPIDO, M., Pte. (1224), attested 11/1/16, Cpl. 1/1/17, reverted to Pte. 11/1/17, released medically unfit 3/8/18.
THOMAS, A., Pte. (1225), attested 11/1/16, still serving.
VAN DER POEL, D., Pte. (1226), attested 11/1/16, released medically unfit 27/7/17.
LANGEVELDT, C. P., Pte. (1227), attested 11/1/16, demobilised 7/10/19.
ARENDSE, W., Pte. (1228), attested 11/1/16, demobilised 16/7/19.
VELDSMAN, R., Pte. (1229), attested 11/1/16, released medically unfit 13/8/17.
WILLIAMS, J. J., Pte. (1230), attested 11/1/16, released medically unfit 13/9/17.
SAMUELS, J., Pte. (1231), attested 11/1/16, rejected 11/1/16.
LAWRENCE, I., Pte. (1232), attested 11/1/16, S.N.L.R. 6/12/17.
GEBERS, F., Pte. (1233), attested 11/1/16, demobilised 16/7/19.
NEETHLING, J., Pte. (1234), attested 11/1/16, demobilised 28/10/19.
KLASSEN, J., Pte. (1235), attested 11/1/16, demobilised 16/7/19.
OPPEL, F., Pte. (1236), attested 11/1/16, demobilised 22/7/19.
SASS, M., Pte. (1237), attested 11/1/16, released medically unfit 11/3/16.
BLOWS, J., Pte. (1238), attested 11/1/16, demobilised 25/12/18.
DU TOIT, G. P., Pte. (1239), attested 11/1/16, demobilised 7/10/19.
HERMAN, J., Pte. (1240), attested 12/1/16, released medically unfit 15/8/17.
FREDERICKS, R., Pte. (1241), attested 12/1/16, died of malaria 31/12/17.
BEACH, J., Pte. (1242), attested 12/1/16, Cpl. 1/7/16, reverted to Pte. 4/12/18, demobilised 28/4/19.
PETERSEN, J., Pte. (1243), attested 12/1/16, demobilised 8/11/19.
THEYS, G., Pte. (1244), attested 12/1/16, released medically unfit 27/4/18.
BEERWINKLE, S., Pte. (1245), attested 12/1/16, died of cerebral malaria 4/9/17.
REID, J., Pte. (1246), attested 12/1/16, a/Cpl. 29/7/17, reverted to Pte. 15/3/18, demobilised 6/2/19.
PETERSEN, W., Pte. (1247), attested 12/1/16, S.N.L.R. 20/6/17.
TRUTER, W. J., Cpl. (1248), attested 12/1/16, Cpl. 25/2/16, a/Sgt. 5/7/18, Cpl. 10/9/18, demobilised 10/10/19.
WARD, P., Pte. (1249), attested 12/1/16, demobilised 7/9/19, pioneer, transport driver.
QUICKFALL, C V., a/L./Cpl. (1250), attested 12/1/16, a/L./Cpl. 19/10/18, reverted to Pte. 30/3/19, a/L./Cpl. 7/4/19, demobilised 7/10/19.
SPIELMAN, B., Pte. (1251), died of malaria 13/5/16.
DREYER, A., Pte. (1252), attested 12/1/16, released medically unfit 4/2/16.
WILKINSON, D. A., Sgt. (1253), attested 13/1/16, Cpl. 1/2/16, Sgt. 1/5/16, a/C.S.M. 24/9/18, Sgt. 27/10/18, demobilised 7/10/19, passed general N.C.O.'s and musketry courses.
CUPIDO, L., Cpl. (1254), attested 13/1/16, Cpl. 18/12/16, demobilised 23/8/19.
BLOWS, A., Pte. (1255), attested 13/1/16, demobilised 16/7/19, drum and fife band.
SNYERS, F., Pte. (1256), attested 13/1/16, released medically unfit 24/9/17.
ADAMS, C., Pte. (1257), attested 13/1/16, released medically unfit 22/4/18.
PRINCE, S., Pte. (1258), attested 13/1/16, demobilised 11/7/19, Lewis gunner.
JOOSTE, I., Pte. (1259), attested 14/1/16, demobilised 11/7/19.

THE STORY OF THE 1st CAPE CORPS.

WATNEY, J., Pte. (1260), attested 14/1/16, released medically unfit 31/8/17.
BOWERS, H., Pte. (1261), attested 14/1/16, died of phthisis 22/7/16.
ABRAHAMS, J., Pte. (1262), attested 14/1/16, released medically unfit 14/3/17.
JONES, H., Pte. (1263), attested 14/1/16, demobilised 31/12/18.
DENNIS, C., Pte. (1264), attested 14/1/16, released medically unfit 24/9/17.
ISAACS, J., Pte. (1265), attested 14/1/16, released medically unfit 24/9/17.
ABRAHAMS, A., Pte. (1266), attested 14/1/16, demobilised 8/9/19.
FLUSK, P., Pte. (1267), attested 14/1/16, demobilised 7/9/19.
GROEP, M., Pte. (1268), attested 14/1/16, died of malaria 26/5/16.
ABRAHAMS, J., Pte. (1269), attested 14/1/16, released medically unfit 24/3/16.
VAN ROOYEN, J., Pte. (1270), attested 14/1/16, Sgt. 28/10/16, reverted to Pte. 10/11/18, demobilised 7/9/19, did duty as Armourer Sgt. (East Africa).
SALES, G., Pte. (1271), attested 15/1/16, released medically unfit 17/1/16.
DRURY, F., Pte. (1272), attested 15/1/16, killed in action 8/11/17, mentioned in despatches East Africa, signaller.
ARENDSE, A., Pte. (1273), attested 15/1/16, released medically unfit 6/11/17.
HARRISON, J., Pte. (1274), attested 15/1/16, S.N.L.R. 17/12/17.
HART, J., C.Q.M.S. (1275), attested 15/1/16, C.Q.M.S. 15/1/16, transferred to S.A Pay Corps 25/9/16, European personnel.
HACKETT, G. W., Pte. (1276), attested 15/1/16, demobilised 3/8/19.
JACOBS, A. B., Pte. (1277), attested 15/1/16, released medically unfit 17/3/16.
SIBLEY, R., Pte. (1278), attested 15/1/16, released medically unfit 8/3/16.
LANGEVELDT, J., Pte. (1279), attested 15/1/16, released medically unfit 11/8/17.
VAN SCHOOR, B. A., Pte. (1280), attested 15/1/16, released medically unfit 30/9/16.
HAYES, T., Pte. (1281), attested 15/1/16, demobilised 21/7/19.
MARTIN, H., Sig. Sgt. (1282), attested 10/1/16, Sig. Sgt. 10/1/16, released medically unfit 16/7/17, extra proficiency pay of 2/- per day. European personnel.
ALEXANDER, P., Pte. (1283), attested 16/1/16, demobilised 16/7/19, medical orderly.
ALEXANDER, T., Pte. (1284), attested 16/1/16, demobilised 14/10/19.
ANTONIE, C., Pte. (1285), attested 16/1/16, released medically unfit 19/1/16.
ANTONIE, J., Pte. (1286), attested 16/1/16, rejected 16/1/16
LIVERS, A., Pte. (1287), attested 16/1/16, released medically unfit 16/8/17.
CUPIDO, J., Pte. (1288), attested 16/1/16, released medically unfit 19/1/16.
LEWIS, W., Pte. (1289), attested 16/1/16, released medically unfit 29/10/17.
NOBLE, J., Pte. (1290), attested 16/1/16, S.N.L.R. 16/2/18.
VAN JAAREVELDT, J., Pte. (1291), attested 16/1/16, released medically unfit 4/3/16.
JACOBUS, A., Pte. (1292), attested 16/1/16, demobilised 11/7/19.
WHITE, J. (1293), attested 10/1/16, released medically unfit 1/9/17.
NORTON, W., Pte. (1294), attested 17/1/16, released medically unfit 30/11/17.
JACOBS, D., Pte. (1295), attested 17/1/16, killed in action 20/9/18.
ERNS, N., Pte. (1296), attested 17/1/16, released medically unfit 27/4/17.
AUGUST, J., Pte. (1297), attested 17/1/16, discharged medically unfit 6/11/17.
PETERSEN, G. (1298), attested 17/1/16, discharged on compassionate grounds 5/11/18.
ABRAHAMS, G., Pte. (1299), attested 17/1/16, L./Cpl. 7/10/18, reverted to Pte. 28/1/19, demobilised 11/7/19.
ANTHONY, J. Pte. (1300), attested 17/1/16, died of malaria 25/5/16.
MAPOMIE, R., Pte. (1301), attested 17/1/16, demobilised 16/7/19.
ANTHONY, H., Pte. (1302), attested 17/1/16, demobilised 7/10/19.
ARMSTRONG, J., Cpl. (1303), attested 17/1/16, Cpl. 1/4/18, demobilised 30/10/19, 1st class machine gunner, Orderly Room Clerk M.G. Coy.
SMITH, H., Pte. (1304), attested 17/1/16, demobilised 7/10/19.
LAMB, D. W., Pte. (1305) attested 17/1/16, released medically unfit 3/2/17.
KERSPAY, A., a/L./Cpl. (1306), attested 17/1/16, a/L./Cpl. 19/10/18, demobilised 7/9/19.
ADAMS, P., Pte. (1307), attested 17/1/16, released medically unfit 9/8/17.
KIEVIDO, D., Pte. (1308), attested 17/1/16, demobilised 18/11/19.
RYAN, T., Pte. (1309), attested 17/1/16, released medically unfit 31/8/17.
PETERSEN, J. H., Pte. (1310), attested 17/1/16, demobilised 30/12/18.
HOVEN, M. S., Pte. (1311), attested 17/1/16, released medically unfit 3/2/16.
AUGUSTUS, J., Pte. (1312), attested 17/1/16, demobilised 11/7/19, qualified signaller.
BLOEM, J., Pte. (1313), attested 17/1/16, demobilised 7/10/19.
JAFTHA, A., Pte. (1314), attested 17/1/16, released medically unfit 12/11/17.
BROWN, T., a/Cpl. (1315), attested 17/1/16, a/Cpl. 1/3/19, demobilised 7/10/19.
CROSBY, W., Pte. (1316), attested 17/1/16, demobilised 11/7/19.
JACOBUS, W. Pte. (1317), attested 17/1/16, released medically unfit 23/8/17.
VALENTINE, H., Pte. (1318), attested 17/1/16, released medically unfit 13/12/18.
GROENEWALD, C., Pte. (1319), attested 17/1/16, released medically unfit 6/7/17.
JAFTHA, J., Pte. (1320), attested 17/1/16, released medically unfit 19/4/18.
CAMPBELL, J., Pte. (1321), attested 17/1/16, released medically unfit 23/2/16.
JANSEN, J. F., Pte. (1322), attested 17/1/16, released medically unfit 6/6/18.
SCHOLTZ, C., Pte. (1323), attested 17/1/16, S.N.L.R. 31/1/16.
THOMAS, P., Sgt. (1324), attested 17/1/16, Sgt. 22/1/18, demobilised 21/10/19, passed general N.C.O.'s course.
VITALINGUM, J., Pte. (1325), attested 17/1/16, released medically unfit 7/2/16.
TROMPETER, W., Pte. (1326), attested 17/1/16, released medically unfit 24/12/17.
MATHYSE, C., Pte. (1327), attested 17/1/16, demobilised 21/7/19.
SEPTEMBER, P., L./Cpl. (1328), attested 17/1/16, L./Cpl. 1/10/18, demobilised 7/9/19.
SCHOLTZ, M. C., a/Sgt. (7329), attested 18/1/16, a/Sgt. 1/2/17, demobilised 5/1/19.
ROBERTS, E., Pte. (1330), attested 18/1/16, released medically unfit 25/8/17.
BENEFELDT, J., Pte. (1331), attested 18/1/16, released medically unfit 11/8/17.
BLOSSOPLES, H., a/Cpl. (1332), attested 18/1/16, a/Cpl. 1/7/17, Pte. 22/3/18, a/Cpl. 7/7/18, Pte. 30/7/18, a/Cpl. 31/1/19, demobilised 21/3/19, Pioneer Corps.
ABRAHAMS, A., Pte. (1333), attested 18/1/16, demobilised 8/9/19.
ERASMUS, F., Pte. (1334), attested 19/1/16, released medically unfit 9/3/16.
PRINS, W., Pte. (1335), attested. 19/1/16, died of pneumonia 25/1/17.
LUCKAS, D., Pte. (1336), attested 19/1/16, demobilised 7/9/19.
POWELL, E. J., Pte. (1337), attested 19/1/16, released medically unfit 13/8/17.
GREENHEAD, J., Staff-Sgt. (1338), attested 19/1/16, transferred to K.A. Rifles 21/7/16, European personnel
LAURIE, G. C., Staff-Sgt. (1339), attested 19/1/16, discharged 6/2/16, European personnel.
OGILVIE, D. R., Staff-Sgt. (1340), attested 19/1/16, discharged 31/12/17, European personnel.
MICHAELS, A., Pte. (1341), attested 19/1/16, released medically unfit 24/2/16.

ETSON, J., Pte. (1342), attested 19/1/16, demobilised 8/9/19.
BOOYSEN, W., Pte. (1343), attested 19/1/16, released medically unfit 20/1/16.
DU PLESSIS, A., L./Cpl. (1344), attested 19/1/16, L./Cpl. 10/4/16, released medically unfit 27/7/17, signaller.
GODFREY, D., Pte. (1345), attested 20/1/16, released medically unfit 23/2/16
DAVIDS, D., Pte. (1346), attested 20/1/16, demobilised 11/7/19
FORTUIN, W., Pte. (1347), attested 20/1/16, demobilised 27/12/18
CARELSE, C., Pte. (1348), attested 20/1/16, demobilised 11/7/19, pioneer bootmaker.
FORREST, T. A., Staff Sgt. (1349), attested 20/1/16, discharged 22/4/18, European personnel, S.A.M.C.
SHIPP, F. G., Medical Sgt. (1350), attested 16/12/15, Medical Sgt. 16/12/15, owing to illness of R.S.M. and R.Q.M.S. acted as R.S.M. December 16 to March, 1917, and also as R.Q.M.S. January to March, 1917, on proceeding to Egypt 3/4/18 was granted rank of acting 1st class W.O., demobilised 9/10/19. European personnel.
CUPIDO, H., Sgt. (1351), attested 21/1/16, Sgt. 30/6/17, released medically unfit 26/2/18.
CHARLES, J., Pte. (1352), attested 21/1/16, released medically unfit 30/11/17.
GROVERS, J., Pte. (1353), attested 21/1/16, demobilised 25/12/18.
GALLANT, D., Pte. (1354), attested 21/1/16, released medically unfit 13/9/17.
HAYMAN, P., Pte. (1355), attested 21/1/16, demobilised 7/9/19.
McKINNON, P. H., Pte. (1356), attested 22/1/16, demobilised 7/9/19, qualified machine gunner.
FEBRUARY, S., Sgt. (1357), attested 22/1/16, Sgt. 19/1/16, demobilised 7/10/19, did duties as Cook Sgt.
FEBRUARY, S., Sgt. (1357), attested 22/1/16, Sgt. 19/1/16, demobilised 7/10/19, was Transport Sgt. in East Africa and Sgt. Cook in Egypt and Palestine.
HARTZENBERG, A. A., Pte. (1358), attested 22/1/16, released medically unfit 24/9/17.
SKIPPERS, J., Pte. (1359), attested 22/1/16, L./Cpl. 25/2/16, reverted to Pte. 28/5/17, released medically unfit 28/11/17.
CADERBERG, D., Pte. (1360), attested 22/1/16, released medically unfit 27/1/16.
HERVEY, N. O., Staff Sgt. (1361), attested 22/1/16, released medically unfit 3/9/17, M.G. Sgt. with extra duty pay of 1/- per day, European personnel.
PEPPER, G. H., Staff Sgt. (1362), attested 26/1/16, returned to U.D.F. 5/3/18, Armourer Sgt., European personnel.
SCULLARD, J., a/C.S.M. (1363), attested 28/1/16, L./Cpl. 10/2/16, Cpl. 25/2/16, Sgt. 8/12/16, a/C.S.M. 7/7/17, Sgt. 1/4/18, a/C.S.M. 25/1/19, demobilised 7/10/19, mentioned in despatches, Palestine, passed musketry course.
HOPKINS, O., Staff Sgt. (1364), attested 28/1/16, transferred to U.D.F. 28/7/17, European personnel.
RICHARDSON, C., Staff Sgt. (1365), attested 28/1/16, transferred to U.D.F. 28/7/17, European personnel.
BROWN, J., Pte. (1366), attested 25/1/16, discharged 25/1/18
COLERIDGE, E., Pte. (1367), attested 25/1/16, released medically unfit 26/2/16.
KOOPMAN, J., Pte. (1368), attested 25/1/16, demobilised 11/7/19.
HARTZ, A., Pte. (1369), attested 25/1/16, killed in action 30/12/16.
SAMUELS, A., Pte. (1370), attested 25/1/16, released medically unfit 13/9/17.
LEE, A. H. B., Sgt. (1371), attested 29/1/16, released medically unfit 28/10/16, European personnel.
MOSES, W., Pte. (1372), attestation cancelled.
BAILEY, C., Pte. (1373), attested 2/2/16, demobilised 8/9/19, pioneer, mentioned in despatches, East Africa
JACOBS, J., Pte. (1374), attested 2/2/16, demobilised 16/7/19.
FORTUIN, C., Pte. (1375), attested 2/2/16, released medically unfit 25/1/17.
TITUS, C., Pte. (1376), attested 2/2/16, released medically unfit 1/9/17.
BAKER, J., Pte. (1377), attested 2/2/16, released medically unfit 6/7/17.
AGULHAS, A., L./Cpl. (1378), attested 2/2/16, L./Cpl. 5/7/18, demobilised 8/9/19.
RENSBURG, P., Pte. (1379), attested 2/2/16, released medically unfit 23/12/17.
WILLIAMS, A., Pte. (1380), attested 15/2/16, released medically unfit 12/10/17.
SANTOS, A., Pte. (1381), attested 4/3/16, S.N.L.R. 25/5/17.
BULL, C., Pte. (1382), attested 15/2/16, demobilised 7/10/19.
KUUN, D., a/Sgt. (1383), attested 15/2/16, Cpl. 5/7/17, L./Sgt. 1/11/18, a/Sgt. 10/5/19, demobilised 21/7/19.
SYFFERS, A., Pte. (1384), attested 7/2/16, demobilised 8/9/19.
WAGNER, J. H., Pte. (1385), attested 15/2/16, released medically unfit 25/8/17.
OCTOBER, A., Pte. (1386), attested 4/3/16, demobilised 16/7/19.
BAILEY, D., Pte. (1387), attested 16/2/16, demobilised 1/1/19.
FORTUIN, A., Pte. (1388), attested 16/2/16, demobilised 21/7/19.
FORTUIN, J., Pte. (1389), attested 16/2/16, died of influenza 9/10/18.
LUGGETT, J., Pte. (1390), attested 16/2/16, released medically unfit 24/9/17.
BOSCH, J., Pte. (1391), attested 4/3/16, released medically unfit 16/8/17.
CUPIDO, A., Pte. (1392), attested 16/2/16, demobilised 2/1/19.
TRUTER, J., Pte. (1393), attested 16/2/16, demobilised 8/9/19.
CAROLLISSEN, J., Pte. (1394), attested 16/2/16, demobilised 8/9/19.
VAN AARDT, J., Pte. (1395), attested 16/2/16, accidentally killed 29/8/17.
ROUX, S., Pte. (1396), attested 16/2/16, demobilised 8/9/19
SCHOLTZ, J. G., Pte. (1397), attested 4/3/16, demobilised 5/1/19
ADAMS, P., Pte. (1398), attested 4/3/16, died of malaria 18/10/16.
SCHOLTZ, C., Pte. (1399), attested 4/3/16, demobilised 8/9/19.
HIEBNER, J., Pte. (1400), attested 16/2/16, released medically unfit 14/8/17.
CUPIDO, D., Pte. (1401), attested 16/2/16, demobilised 16/7/19.
JOHANNES, D., Pte. (1402), attested 16/2/16, released medically unfit 27/4/17.
DU PLESSIS, J., Pte. (1403), attested 16/2/16, released medically unfit 15/6/18.
BOSCH, A., Pte. (1404), attested 4/3/16, released medically unfit 16/8/17.
ZIERS, E., Pte. (1405), attested 16/2/16, released medically unfit 28/11/17.
HULLETT, H., Pte. (1406), attested 16/2/16, released medically unfit 13/9/17.
STEMMET, J., Pte. (1407), attested 16/2/16, demobilised 15/1/19.
GEZWIND, P., Pte. (1408), attested 21/2/16, demobilised 15/1/19.
WYNGAARD, H., Pte. (1409), attested 21/2/16, demobilised 7/10/19, qualified signaller.
FORTUIN, P., Pte. (1410), attested 4/3/16, demobilised 8/9/19.
CUPIDO, M., Pte. (1411), attested 24/2/16, demobilised 11/7/19.
ADRIAANSE, D., Pte. (1412), attested 24/2/16, died of meningitis 3/9/18.
PEREGRINO, T. J., Pte. (1413), attested 24/2/16, released medically unfit 3/10/17.
TIMMINS, W., Cpl. (1414), attested 24/2/16, Cpl. 26/3/19, demobilised 11/7/19, qualified machine gunner
HENDRICKS, P. J., Pte. (1415), attested 23/2/16, demobilised 10/4/19, qualified machine gunner
MATTHEWS, J., Pte. (1416), attested 4/3/16, released medically unfit 30/7/19.
JOSEPHS, J., Pte. (1417), attested 4/3/16, released medically unfit 20/11/17.
SWARTZ, L. W., Pte. (1418), attested 4/3/16, released medically unfit 11/9/17.
POGGENPOEL, P., Pte. (1419), attested 24/2/16, demobilised 7/10/19

THE STORY OF THE 1st CAPE CORPS.

PLAATJES, W., Pte. (1420), attested 24/2/16, released medically unfit 3/5/16.
HOVEN, M., Pte. (1421), attested 24/2/16, released medically unfit 11/8/16.
CAMBELL, J., L./Cpl. (1422, attested 24/2/16, L./Cpl. 5/7/18, a/Cpl. 1/3/19, L./Cpl. 7/4/19, demobilised 7/10/19.
ZIERVOGEL, D., Pte. (1423), attested 23/2/16, demobilised 11/7/19, qualified machine gunner
FRANZ, J., Pte. (1424), attested 24/2/16, released medically unfit 8/8/17
MILLER, B., Pte. (1425), attested 24/2/16, demobilised 7/10/19.
GRIFFINS, R., Pte. (1426), attested 4/3/16, released medically unfit 31/8/17.
SOLOMON, M., Pte. (1427), attested 4/3/16, demobilised 16/7/19.
CORDOM, A., Pte. (1428), attested 21/2/16, released medically unfit 29/5/18.
RILEY, D. F., Pte. (1429), attested 4/3/16, demobilised 11/7/19.
QUIMPO, M., Pte. (1430), attested 29/2/16, demobilised 6/1/19.
PLAATJES, W., Pte. (1431), attested 26/2/16, demobilised 7/9/19, 1st class machine gunner
PETERS, R., Cpl. (1432), attested 28/2/16, Cpl. 1/10/18, demobilised 26/12/18.
MATTHEWS, T., Cpl. (1433), attested 28/2/16, Cpl. 21/9/18, demobilised 7/10/19.
PETERSEN, J. W., Pte. (1434), attested 28/2/16, demobilised 24/1/19.
ABRAHAMS, W., Pte. (1435), attested 28/2/16, released medically unfit 25/1/18.
ROODT, L. P., Pte. (1436), attested 4/3/16, demobilised 7/10/19.
JACOBS, A., Pte. (1437), attested 4/3/16, released medically unfit 30/11/17.
AKEHURST, R., Staff Sgt. (1438), attested 4/3/16, acted as R.S.M. December 14/26, 1916, discharged 26/10/17, European personnel.
CRAIGEN, W., C.S.M. (1439), attested 26/2/16, Sgt. 26/2/16, C.S.M. 25/5/16, to 2nd Cape Corps 18/4/17, European personnel.
OVIES, C., Pte. (1440), attested 26/2/16, died of heart failure 6/12/16.
LAVIN, H., Pte. (1441), attested 2/3/16, released medically unfit 28/4/16.
HARTRICK, W., Pte. (1442), attested 26/2/16, discharged 13/7/16.
WILKES, J., R.Q.M.S. (1443), attested 26/2/16, Sgt. 26/2/16, R.Q.M.S. 30/6/16, released medically unfit 6/3/17, European personnel.
DRAYCOTT (1444), attested 2/3/16, released medically unfit 28/4/16, European personnel.
FORTUIN, D. P., Pte. (1445), attested 27/2/16, released medically unfit 7/11/17.
FERGUSON, J., Pte. (1446), attested 27/2/16, demobilised 7/9/19.
RHODES, W., Pte. (1447), attested 27/2/16, S.N.L.R. 19/10/18.
DAVIDS, A., Pte. (1448), attested 27/2/16, released medically unfit 6/11/17.
VAN DER MUELEN, Pte. (1449), attested 10/3/16, died of dysentery 18/7/17
HEEGERS, P., Pte. (1450), attested 14/3/16, S.N.L.R. 23/9/17.
DE JAAR, J., Pte. (1451), attested 14/3/16, demobilised 15/1/19.
BILL, H., Pte. (1452), attested 14/3/16, L./Cpl. 12/11/17, reverted to Pte. 13/7/18, demobilised 21/7/19
DE BRUYNS, J., Pte. (1453), attested 14/3/16, demobilised 1/1/19.
VAN REENEN, R., Pte. (1454), attested 28/2/16, demobilised 11/7/19.
SOLOMON, J., Pte. (1455), attested 15/3/16, released medically unfit 12/4/16.
WILLIAMS, G., Pte. (1456), attested 29/2/16, died of wounds 23/9/18.
WILLIS, A., Pte. (1457), attested 15/3/16, released medically unfit 20/11/17.
SMITH, H. W., Pte. (1458), attested 15/3/16, demobilised 11/7/19.
BROWN, S., Pte. (1459), attested 15/3/16, died of malaria 9/8/16.
WILLIAMS, S. J., Pte. (1460), attested 15/3/16, released medically unfit 20/6/16.
ISAACS, J. J., Pte. (1461), attested 15/3/16, demobilised 20/10/19.
JULIES, D., Pte. (1462), attested 13/3/16, rejected 13/3/16.
DEERLING, D. W., Pte. (1463), attested 13/3/16, demobilised 21/7/19.
WICOMBE, A., Pte. (1464), attested 13/3/16, demobilised 21/7/19.
DAMON, H. P. (D.C.M.), Sgt. (1465), attested 16/3/16, Sgt. 1/5/16, demobilised 18/10/19, Transport Sgt. from 23/11/18, passed physical and bayonet courses.
SAMUELS, R., Pte. (1466), attested 21/3/16, demobilised 11/7/19, passed trench warfare and bombing courses, excellent.
JACOBS, J., Pte. (1467), attested 20/3/16, released medically unfit 25/8/17.
HENDRICKS, N., Pte. (1468), attested 17/3/16, demobilised 11/7/19.
MULLER, H. W., Cpl. (1469), attested 20/3/16, Cpl. 1/5/16, reverted to Pte. 7/10/17, released medically unfit 16/12/18.
WAGERSTROOM, G., Pte. (1470), attested 22/3/16, released medically unfit 9/8/17.
WILLIAMS, J., Pte. (1471), attested 17/3/16, demobilised 8/10/19, Lewis gunner.
YON, J. H., Sgt. (1472), attested 15/3/16, Cpl. 1/5/16, reverted to Pte. 27/7/16, Cpl. 18/12/16, Sgt. 30/6/17, demobilised 7/9/19.
JACOBS, A., Pte. (1473), attested 21/3/16, S.N.L.R. 1/1/18
KENNEDY, C., Pte. (1474), attested 16/3/16, released medically unfit 18/8/17.
ARENDSE, D. M., Pte. (1475), attested 17/3/16, released medically unfit 20/7/17.
DAVIDSON, W., Pte. (1476), attested 16/3/16, S.N.L.R. 3/9/17.
ANDREWS, P., Pte. (1477), attested 16/3/16, released medically unfit 26/2/17.
HENDRICKS, A., Pte. (1478), attested 19/3/16, demobilised 7/9/19
GOBEY, S., Pte. (1479), attested 11/3/16, demobilised 28/8/19.
REPHNAAR, H., Pte. (1480), attested 10/3/16, released medically unfit 18/8/17.
GARDINER, I., Pte. (1481), attested 18/3/16, released medically unfit 7/7/16.
JAGGERS, H., Pte. (1482), attested 20/3/16, demobilised 1/1/19.
ABRAHAMS, M. J., C.S.M. (1483), attested 15/3/16, Cpl. 1/6/16, Sgt. 1/10/16, a/C.S.M. 18/11/17, C.S.M. 9/8/18, demobilised 12/7/19, passed general N.C.O.'s course.
DE VOS, J., Pte. (1484), attested 20/3/16, released medically unfit 3/9/17.
FRANKS, P., Pte. (1485), attested 16/3/16, released medically unfit 29/10/17.
McLURE, L., Cpl. (1486), attested 20/3/16, Cpl. 11/12/16, demobilised 7/9/19.
HOLLOWAY, H., Pte. (1487), attested 16/3/16, released medically unfit 24/4/16.
JURGENS, J., Cpl. (1488), attested 15/3/16, Cpl. 1/6/16, released medically unfit 25/5/17
JAFTHA, A., Pte. (1489), attested 16/3/16, released medically unfit 6/11/17.
WILLIAMS, J., Pte. (1490), attested 17/3/16, demobilised 12/7/19.
BOK, C., Pte. (1491), attested 17/3/16, released medically unfit 3/8/17.
WATSON, W., Pte. (1492), attested 15/3/16, demobilised 2/1/19.
DE VOS, D., Pte. (1493), attested 17/3/16, released medically unfit 29/10/17.
DE CLARK, P., Pte. (1494), attested 16/3/16, demobilised 7/9/19.
VAN WYK, M., Pte. (1495), attested 17/3/16, released medically unfit 4/9/17.
DU PLESSIS, J., Pte. (1496), attested 17/3/16, demobilised 7/9/19.
JACOBS, P., Pte. (1497), attested 17/3/16, demobilised 21/7/19.
FEATHERS, H., Pte. (1498), attested 16/3/16, demobilised 7/9/19.
JASSON, J., Pte. (1499), attested 14/3/16, released medically unfit 3/10/17.
THOMAS, L., Pte. (1500), attested 15/3/16, released medically unfit 25/8/16.
AUGUST, P., Pte. (1501), attested 20/3/16, demobilised 3/1/19.

THE STORY OF THE 1st CAPE CORPS.

RECHTER, P., Pte. (1502), attested 20/3/16, demobilised 21/7/19.
CUPIDO, M. J., Pte. (1503), attested 20/3/16, released medically unfit 20/11/17.
LE KARP, J., Pte. (1504), attested 20/3/16, released medically unfit 16/5/16.
PHILANDER, M., Pte. (1505), attested 21/3/16, demobilised 16/7/19.
EVERSON, K., Pte. (1506), attested 20/3/16, released medically unfit 14/9/16.
BELL, J., Pte. (1507), attested 20/3/16, released medically unfit 14/4/16.
ADAMS, T., Pte. (1508), attested 21/3/16, released medically unfit 27/7/17.
VERLANDER, T., Pte. (1509), attested 20/3/16, released medically unfit 13/9/17.
ENGLE, T., Pte. (1510), attested 21/3/16, demobilised 21/7/19.
HARTZENBERG, T., Pte. (1511), attested 20/3/16, demobilised 26/12/18.
GOODWIN, W., Pte. (1512), attested 6/3/16, released medically unfit 24/12/17.
DANIELS, M., Pte. (1513), attested 6/3/16, released medically unfit 24/9/17.
STUURMAN, R., Pte. (1514), attested 20/3/16, died of wounds 9/11/17.
HAHN, W. D., Pte. (1515), attested 20/3/16, released medically unfit 29/10/17.
AFRICANDER, J., Pte. (1516), attested 21/3/16, demobilised 21/7/19.
ARENDS, A., Pte. (1517), attested 21/3/16, demobilised 8/9/19.
PETERS, F., Pte. (1518), attested 21/3/16, demobilised 11/9/19.
BOOYSEN, J., L./Cpl. (1519), attested 20/3/16, L./Cpl. 1/11/18, demobilised 7/9/19
FISHER, J., Pte. (1520), attested 21/3/16, released medically unfit 31/5/16.
PETERSEN, S., Pte. (1521), attested 21/3/16, demobilised 7/9/19.
SCORPIAN, J., Pte. (1522), attested 21/3/16, demobilised 1/1/19.
MITCHELL, C., Pte. (1523), attested 21/3/16, released medically unfit 26/6/16.
ANTHONIE, F., Pte. (1524), attested 21/3/16, demobilised 24/1/19.
CLEMMENTS, H., Pte. (1525), attested 21/3/16, released medically unfit 23/4/16.
MIDDLETON, W., Pte. (1526), attested 21/3/16, released medically unfit 18/4/16.
VAN ROOI, H., Pte. (1527), attested 21/3/16, demobilised 7/9/19.
BURTS, G., Cpl. (1528), attested 21/3/16, L./Cpl. 24/6/17, Cpl. 1/8/17, released medically unfit 12/12/18.
BAIN, J., Pte. (1529), attested 21/3/16, released medically unfit 20/5/17.
GREY, J., Pte. (1530), attested 21/3/16, demobilised 7/10/19.
PICK, P., Pte. (1531), attested 21/3/16, S.N.L.R. 22/5/17.
AKERS, P., Pte. (1532), attested 21/3/16, released medically unfit 27/7/17.
JOOSTE, F., Pte. (1533), attested 21/3/16, demobilised 16/7/19, pioneer carpenter.
ALLEN, E., Pte. (1534), attested 21/3/16, released medically unfit 24/5/16.
FEDER, W. H., Pte. (1535), attested 21/3/16, killed in action 6/11/17.
WILLIAMS, J., Pte. (1536), attested 21/3/16, S.N.L.R. 1/1/18.
JOHNSON, E., Pte. (1537), attested 21/3/16, released medically unfit 29/6/17.
ANDERSON, J., Pte. (1538), attested 21/3/16, demobilised 21/7/19.
PETERSEN, P. J., Pte. (1539), attested 21/3/16, released medically unfit 20/11/16.
JACOBS, H., Pte. (1540), attested 21/3/16, released medically unfit 20/11/16.
HATTINGH, A., Pte. (1541), attested 21/3/16, demobilised 7/9/19.
BOOYSEN, A., Pte. (1542), attested 21/3/16, released medically unfit 3/9/17.
DOLPH, H., Pte. (1543), attested 21/3/16, S.N.L.R. 18/7/17.
VAN NIEKERK, T., Pte. (1544), attested 21/3/16, released medically unfit 6/11/17.
MORRISON, S. H., Pte. (1545), attested 21/3/16, released medically unfit 18/11/18.
VAN DER WESTHUISEN, H., Pte. (1546), attested 21/3/16, released medically unfit 2/6/17.
LOUW, B., Pte. (1547), attested 21/3/16, released medically unfit 18/5/16.
HENDRICKS, W., Pte. (1548), attested 21/3/16, released medically unfit 26/1/17
HENDRICKS, J., Pte. (1549), attested 21/3/16, S.N.L.R. 8/4/18.
WELTS, S., Pte. (1550), attested 21/3/16, released medically unfit 28/9/16.
LENDERS, J., Pte. (1551), attested 21/3/16, released medically unfit 9/11/17.
HEYNS, J., Pte. (1552), attested 30/3/16, released medically unfit 20/5/16.
BALL, W., Pte. (1553), attested 31/3/16, rejected 31/3/16.
PETERS, N., Pte. (1554), attested 31/3/16, released medically unfit 7/11/17.
NOVEMBER, P., Pte. (1555), attested 3/4/16, demobilised 11/7/19, qualified Lewis gunner.
WHEATLY, J. J., Pte. (1556), attested 4/4/16, released medically unfit 7/11/17.
WILLIAMS, A., Sgt. (1557), attested 10/4/16, Cpl. 1/8/16, Sgt. 24/6/17, demobilised 5/1/19.
HANS, J., Pte. (1558), attested 10/4/16, released medically unfit 6/7/17.
ENGLEBRECHT, A., Pte. (1559), attested 10/4/16, demobilised 7/10/19.
BOTHA, P., Pte. (1560), attested 12/4/16, demobilised 7/10/19.
ABRAHAMS, H., Pte. (1561), attested 11/4/16, killed in action 20/9/18.
SMITH, J., Pte. (1562), attested 12/4/16, released medically unfit 10/5/16.
DU TOIT, A., Cpl. (1563), attested 11/4/16, Cpl. 24/6/17, demobilised 16/7/19, passed scout course 1st class.
HOOFDT, J., Pte. (1564), attested 12/4/16, released medically unfit 20/11/17.
WILLIAMS, A., Pte. (1565), attested 11/4/16, demobilised 7/10/19.
GEORGE, E. L. B., Sgt. (1566), attested 9/4/16, Cpl. 6/8/16, L./Sgt. 18/6/18, Sgt. 1/11/18, demobilised 8/10/19, passed topography course (distinguished).
HARVEY, T., Pte. (1567), attested 20/4/16, died of influenza 6/10/18.
UITHALDER, P., Pte. (1568), attested 19/4/16, released medically unfit 20/7/17.
DU PREEZ, N., Pte. (1569), attested 10/4/16, released medically unfit 3/9/17.
HUBBARD, D., Pte. (1570), attested 10/4/16, released medically unfit 20/5/16.
PETERSEN, C., Pte. (1571), attested 10/4/16, demobilised 26/2/19.
LUCAY, J., Pte. (1572), attested 10/4/16, demobilised 7/10/19.
McKENZIE, W., Pte. (1573), attested 10/4/16, demobilised 15/1/19.
BAATJES, M., Pte. (1574), attested 11/5/16, released medically unfit 20/11/17.
ADONIS, J. J., Pte. (1575), attested 11/5/16, released medically unfit 12/10/17.
ABRAHAMS, W., Pte. (1576), attested 12/5/16, died of malaria 27/3/17.
BAKER, J., Pte. (1577), attested 11/5/16, released medically unfit 26/2/17.
ADAMS, D., Pte. (1578), attested 15/5/16, released medically unfit 20/10/16.
ANTHONY, J. N., a/L./Cpl. (1579), attested 15/5/16, a/L./Cpl. 1/3/19, demobilised 16/7/19.
PLAATJES, P., Pte. (1580), attested 15/5/16, released medically unfit 14/8/17.
WOODS, C., Pte. (1581), attested 15/5/16, released medically unfit 10/7/18.
FORTUIN, J., Pte. (1582), attested 15/5/16, released medically unfit 16/5/18.
JONES, C., Pte. (1583), attested 15/5/16, released medically unfit 18/12/18.
ABRAHAMS, D., Pte. (1584), attested 18/5/16, demobilised 7/10/19.
WILLIAMS, W., Pte. (1585), attested 17/5/16, demobilised 7/9/19.
DANIELS, D., Pte. (1586), attested 18/5/16, demobilised 11/7/19.
JACOBS, J., Pte. (1587), attested 19/5/16, demobilised 25/10/20.
BLOUNT, E., Pte. (1588), attested 6/5/16, demobilised 31/12/18.
ISAACS, B., Pte. (1589), attested 10/5/16, S.N.L.R. 7/8/18.
TSUMANI, J., Pte. (1590), attested 16/5/16, released medically unfit 6/6/18.
HARTNICK, J., Pte. (1591), attested 17/5/16, S.N.L.R. 27/7/18.

THE STORY OF THE 1st CAPE CORPS.

ABRAHAMS, C. S., Pte. (1592), attested 17/5/16, released medically unfit 2/8/17.
JOHNSON, H., Pte. (1593), attested 23/5/16, demobilised 12/7/19, machine gunner.
CULLIS, H., Pte. (1594), attested 23/5/16, released medically unfit 8/2/18.
WENTZEL, A., Pte. (1595), attested 23/5/16, released medically unfit 3/10/17.
WILLIAMS, J. J., Sgt. (1596), attested 26/5/16, Sgt. 1/11/17, demobilised 11/7/19.
CURRY, J. C., Pte. (1597), attested 26/5/16, released medically unfit 20/5/17.
MAY, A., Pte. (1598), attested 26/5/16, released medically unfit 24/7/17.
STOFFELS, W., Pte. (1599), attested 26/5/16, released medically unfit 23/7/17.
VAN DER ROLL P., Pte. (1600), attested 26/5/16, released medically unfit 12/11/17.
JACOBS, P., Pte. (1601), attested 26/5/16, released medically unfit 28/11/17.
FILANDER, F., Pte. (1602), 27/5/16, demobilised 26/3/19.
FELIX, D., Pte. (1603), 26/5/16, died of influenza 12/10/18.
PETERS, P. J., Cpl. (1604), attested 29/5/16, Cpl. 1/4/18, demobilised 7/10/19, Lewis gunner.
HERBERT, C., Pte. (1605), attested 26/5/16, demobilised 7/9/19.
DE BRUYNS, H., Pte. (1606), attested 26/5/16, died 10/9/16.
WHITEMAN, P., Pte. (1607), attested 26/5/16, demobilised 22/7/19, passed army cookery course.
ANTONELSE C. F., Pte. (1608), attested 30/5/16, demobilised 25/12/18.
DERT, E. H., Pte. (1609), attested 30/5/16, died of cerebral malaria 12/3/17.
DE BLEQUY, H., Pte. (1610), attested 30/5/16, released medically unfit 20/11/17.
JOHANNES, J., Pte. (1611), attested 30/5/16, S.N.L.R. 25/11/16.
FORTUIN, W., Pte. (1612), attested 2/6/16, released medically unfit 27/7/17.
SMITH, W., Pte. (1613), attested 5/6/16, demobilised 7/10/19, Provost Staff.
JANSEN, S. D. (D.C.M.), Sgt. (1614), attested 5/6/16, Sgt. 1/8/16, a/C.S.M. 21/9/18, Sgt. 12/10/18, demobilised 7/10/19, passed physical and bayonet courses.
VAN AARDE, J., Pte. (1615), attested 5/6/16, demobilised 7/10/19.
SAMUELS, J., Pte. (1616), attested 5/6/16, demobilised 7/10/19.
WHITE, W., Pte. (1617), attested 22/5/16, died of nephritis 11/7/17.
REYNERS, P., Pte. (1618), attested 5/6/16, S.N.L.R. 2/7/17.
WILLIAMS, D.,Pte. (1619), attested 5/6/16, released medically unfit 12/11/17.
MULLINS, J., Pte. (1620), attested 2/6/16, demobilised 7/10/19.
LOUW, J. D., Sgt. (1621), attested 3/6/16, Sgt. 22/3/18, demobilised 7/10/19, Transport Sgt. for some time, passed general N.C.O.'s course.
CALVERT, G., Pte. (1622), attested 6/6/16, released medically unfit 21/12/17.
HENDRICKS, T., Pte. (1623), attested 6/6/16, died of malaria 10/12/16.
JULIES, C., Pte. (1624), attested 3/6/16, demobilised 10/4/20.
EDWARDS, J., Pte. (1625), attested 9/6/16, died of dysentery 22/4/17.
KAMIES, G., Pte. (1626), attested 9/6/16, released medically unfit 3/2/17.
WILLIAMS, A., Pte. (1627), attested 6/6/16, demobilised 27/7/19.
LEWIS, C., Pte. (1628), attested 7/6/16, demobilised 7/7/19.
DAVIDS, E., Pte. (1629), attested 12/6/16, demobilised 24/7/19.
ISAACS, I. J., Pte. (1630), attested 10/6/16, demobilised 7/10/19.
MARTHINUS, H., Pte. (1631), attested 13/6/16, demobilised 8/9/19.
VAN STEER, C., Pte. (1632), attested 12/6/16, released medically unfit 13/12/16.
WELLCOME, J., Pte. (1633), attested 14/6/16, released medically unfit 14/12/16.
CORDOM, Z., Sgt. (1634), attested 13/6/16, a/Sgt. 18/9/17, Sgt. 22/3/18, demobilised 7/1/19.
FEBRUARY, P., Pte. (1635), attested 13/6/16, demobilised 26/12/18.
DAMPIES, W., Pte. (1636), attested 14/6/16, Cpl. 15/10/17, reverted to Pte. 23/6/18, demobilised 3/1/19.
ROBUS, N., Pte. (1637), attested 13/6/16, released medically unfit 4/11/18.
VIRET, J., Pte. (1638), attested 14/6/16, demobilised 7/10/19.
DEAN, A., Pte. (1639), attested 12/6/16, released medically unfit 20/7/17.
MAGGOTT, R., Pte. (1640), attested 13/6/16, released medically unfit 13/9/17.
VAN ROOY, W., Pte. (1641), attested 15/6/16, drowned 16/9/18.
ABRAHAMS, J., Pte. (1642), attested 15/6/16, demobilised 7/10/19.
PHILANDER, A., Pte. (1643), attested 19/6/16, demobilised 11/7/19, Lewis gunner.
MANUEL, C., Pte. (1644), attested 19/6/16, released medically unfit 16/11/17.
PETERSEN, D., Pte. (1645), attested 19/6/16, demobilised 11/7/19.
GOLIATH, D., Pte. (1646), attested 19/6/16, demobilised 7/10/19.
ROBERTS, B., Pte. (1647), attested 26/6/16, released medically unfit 2/8/16.
REZERS, A., Pte. (1648), attested 20/6/16, released medically unfit 20/11/17.
FRANZEN, J., Pte. (1649), attested 26/6/16, released medically unfit 13/9/17.
BARENDS, J., Pte. (1650), attested 26/6/16, died of malaria 16/9/18.
CUPIDO, J., Pte. (1651), attested 22/6/16, released medically unfit 3/10/17.
THEUNIS, J., Pte. (1652), attested 23/6/16, S.N.L.R. 28/3/18.
ZACHARAIS, N., Pte. (1653), attested 23/6/16, demobilised 27/12/18.
FONDLING, T., Pte. (1654), attested 23/6/16, released medically unfit 18/8/17.
TITUS, J. W., Pte. (1655), attested 26/6/16, released medically unfit 20/11/17.
JOHNSON, P., Pte. (1656), attested 23/6/16, released medically unfit 3/10/17.
VAN NIEKERK, F., Pte. (1657), attested 26/6/16, released medically unfit 30/11/17.
DUNNING, P., Pte. (1658), attested 26/6/16, died of malaria 13/4/17.
JACOBS, N., Pte. (1659), attested 26/6/16, died from sunstroke 5/12/17.
ADONIS, W., Pte. (1660), attested 26/6/16, died of malaria 31/3/17.
ISAACS, J., Pte. (1661), attested 26/6/16, released medically unfit 15/9/16.
MARTIN, D., Pte. (1662), attested 26/6/16, released medically unfit 13/9/17.
THOMAS, K., Pte. (1663), attested 26/6/16, demobilised 7/10/19.
FRY, S., Pte. (1664), attested 27/6/16, released medically unfit 24/9/17.
SEPTEMBER, J., Pte. (1665), attested 27/6/16, demobilised 7/10/19.
FEBRUARY, D., Pte. (1666), attested 27/6/16, released medically unfit 22/1/17.
FORTUIN, D., Pte. (1667), attested 26/6/16, S.N.L.R. 25/11/16.
THOMAS, H., Pte. (1668), attested 1/7/16, demobilised 16/7/19, drum and fife band.
PALM, J. H., Cpl. (1669), attested 29/6/16, Cpl. 15/11/16, released medically unfit 3/10/17.
FELIX, C., Pte. (1670), attested 3/7/16, demobilised 7/10/19, qualified machine gunner.
CLAYTON, H., Pte. (1671), attested 3/7/16, released medically unfit 29/9/17.
FURNESS, W., Pte. (1672), attested 3/7/16, died of malaria 7/4/17.
ADAMS, D., Pte. (1673), attested 3/7/16, released medically unfit 31/8/17.
JANSEN, H., L./Cpl. (1674), attested 3/7/16, L./Cpl. 29/6/17, demobilised 21/3/19.
KOTZE, D., Pte. (1675), attested 3/7/16, released medically unfit 15/10/17.
EDWARDS, C., Pte. (1676), attested 5/7/16, demobilised 26/12/18.
SEPTEMBER, A., Pte. (1677), attested 5/7/16, demobilised 27/12/18.
DAVIS, A. F., Pte. (1678), attested 3/7/16, demobilised 1/1/19.
DYASON, T., Pte. (1679), attested 7/7/16, released medically unfit 29/6/17.
FEDER, J., Pte. (1680), attested 7/7/16, demobilised 7/10/19.

THE STORY OF THE 1st CAPE CORPS.

MICHAEL, D. P., Pte. (1681), attested 9/7/16, released medically unfit 27/11/17.
LEWIN, D., Pte. (1682), attested 10/7/16, demobilised 18/10/19, Lewis gunner.
MORRIS, B., Pte. (1683), attested 10/7/16, released medically unfit 16/11/17.
COFFIN, J. W., Cpl. (1684), attested 24/7/16, Cpl. 5/7/18, demobilised 16/7/19, medical Coporal.
OLIVER, J., Pte. (1685), attested 10/7/16, killed in action 20/9/18.
CANTERBURY, H., Pte. (1686), attested 10/7/16, released medically unfit 31/8/17.
WYNGAARD, G., Pte. (1687), attested 10/7/16, released medically unfit 1/12/16.
MATTHEWS, F., Pte. (1688), attested 11/7/16, released medically unfit 7/6/17.
LOOTS, P., Pte. (1689), attested 12/7/16, demobilised 7/9/19.
BANTAM, A., Pte. (1690), attested 12/7/16, released medically unfit 18/8/17.
DE CLARKE, A., Pte. (1691), attested 12/7/16, demobilised 7/9/19.
NICHOLLS, P., Pte. (1692), attested 24/7/16, released medically unfit 7/6/18, later died of influenza 11/10/18.
LEWIS, M., Pte. (1693), attested 24/7/16, demobilised 11/7/19.
BOOYSEN, E., Pte. (1694), attested 24/7/16, demobilised 7/9/19.
MULDER, W., Pte. (1695), attested 24/7/16, demobilised 29/12/18.
KANNEMEYER, H., Pte. (1696), attested 20/7/16, released medically unfit 14/6/18.
FORTUIN, J., Pte. (1697), attested 26/7/16, demobilised 21/7/19.
GROEPE, G., Pte. (1698), attested 27/7/16, killed in action 19/9/18.
VISAGIE, M., Pte. (1699), attested 27/7/16, released medically unfit 26/2/17.
WOOD, H., Pte. (1700), attested 29/7/16, released medically unfit 20/7/17.
JULIE, J. D., Pte. (1701), attested 27/7/16, released medically unfit 17/12/16.
ASCOTT, H., Pte. (1702), attested 28/7/16, released medically unfit 10/3/18.
DRURY, H., Sgt. (1703), attested 27/7/16, Cpl. 3/6/17, Sgt. 2/11/17, demobilised 22/7/19, passed general N.C.O.'s course.
TAYLOR, C., Pte. (1704), attested 29/7/16, S.N.L.R. 14/7/17.
LODEWICK, J., Pte. (1705), attested 28/7/16, released medically unfit 27/11/17.
STANLEY, J., Pte. (1706), attested 27/7/16, S.N.L.R. 10/1/17.
McLACHLAN, M., Pte. (1707), attested 31/7/16, released medically unfit 9/1/17.
THIPE, B., Pte. (1708), attested 26/7/16, demobilised 7/10/19.
McLACHLIN, J. H., Pte. (1709), attested 31/7/16, released medically unfit 12/10/17.
BRIELL, A., Pte. (1710), attested 31/7/16, released medically unfit 12/11/17.
DAVIDS, A., Pte. (1711), attested 27/7/16, demobilised 7/10/19.
WILLIAMS, J., Pte. (1712), attested 27/7/16, demobilised 11/7/19.
BAATJES, M., Pte. (1713), attested 27/7/16, demobilised 30/12/18.
JACKSON, E., Pte. (1714), attested 21/7/16, demobilised 16/7/19
SCHEEPERS, C., Pte. (1715), attested 27/7/16, demobilised 7/9/19.
SCHEEPERS, J. F., Pte. (1716), attested 27/7/16, demobilised 30/12/18.
BLANNO, N., Pte. (1717), attested 31/7/16, demobilised 7/10/19.
CITTO, A., a/Cpl. (1718), attested 31/7/16, a/Cpl. 7/2/19, demobilised 22/7/19.
LOCKE, R., Pte. (1719), attested 31/7/16, demobilised 7/10/19.
PETERSEN, H., Pte. (1720), attested 31/7/16, released medically unfit 4/2/17.
CUPIDO, F., Pte. (1721), attested 31/7/16, released medically unfit 6/11/17.
JANSEN, J., Pte. (1722), attested 27/7/16, released medically unfit 13/9/17.
ABRAHAMS, J., Pte. (1723), attested 27/7/16, released medically unfit 27/7/18.
FORTUIN, G., Pte. (1724), attested 31/7/16, demobilised 7/10/19
ANTONELSE, T., Pte. (1725), attested 31/7/16, demobilised 11/7/19.
ADAMS, J., Pte. (1726), attested 31/7/16, demobilised 7/10/19.
TELEMACHUS, A. H., Pte. (1727), attested 27/7/16, demobilised 10/10/19, 1st class signaller.
JACOBS, J., Pte. (1728), attested 1/8/16, released medically unfit 18/12/18.
COZETT, H. W., L./Cpl. (1729), attested 2/8/16, L./Cpl. 1/1/19, demobilised 7/10/19, bugler.
THOMPSON, H., Pte. (1730), attested 3/8/16, demobilised 21/7/19.
GALLANT, F., Pte. (1731), attested 3/8/16, demobilised 7/10/19, mentioned in despatches, East Africa.
WILLIAMS, J. D., Pte. (1732), attested 3/8/16, demobilised 31/12/18.
ESAU, J., Pte. (1733), attested 3/8/16, released medically unfit 1/5/18.
HARTNICK, H., Pte. (1734), attested 4/8/16, released medically unfit 20/11/17.
ADAMS, A., Pte. (1735), attested 4/8/16, demobilised 16/7/19, drum and fife band.
DAVIS, J., Pte. (1736), attested 7/8/16, released medically unfit 25/11/18
MAY, J., Pte. (1737), attested 8/8/16, released medically unfit 12/11/17.
JIMSON, J., Pte. (1738), attested 8/8/16, demobilised 16/7/19.
PEDRO, W., Pte. (1739), attested 8/8/16, S.N.L.R. 15/11/16.
MANAVELL, M., Pte. (1740), attested 8/8/16, killed in action 20/9/18.
FRANKS, J., Pte. (1741), attested 8/8/16, released medically unfit 27/11/17.
VILLOR, I., Pte. (1742), attested 8/8/16, released medically unfit 15/10/17.
DAVIDS, J., Pte. (1743), attested 8/8/16, released medically unfit 20/4/18.
ABSOLOM, P., Pte. (1744), attested 8/8/16, released medically unfit 20/4/18.
JOHANNES, A., Pte. (1745), attested 8/8/16, released medically unfit 30/12/18.
ARENDSE, H., Pte. (1746), attested 8/8/16, released medically unfit 31/8/17.
WILLIAMS, S., Pte. (1747), attested 8/8/16, demobilised 16/7/19, drum and fife band.
THOMAS, W., Pte. (1748), attested 8/8/16, died of malaria 2/2/17.
INGHAM, J., Pte (1749), attested 8/8/16, demobilised 7/10/19.
GOSMAN, S., Pte. (1750), attested 8/8/16, demobilised 15/1/19.
BENJAMIN, A. Pte. (1751), attested 8/8/16, demobilised 9/10/19.
ABRAHAMS, A., Pte. (1752), attested 8/8/16, released medically unfit 31/7/18
TITUS, A., Pte. (1753), attested 8/8/16, demobilised 7/10/19.
ADAMS, J, Pte. (1754), attested 8/8/16, died of malaria 9/7/17.
THOMAS, J., Pte. (1755), attested 8/8/16, demobilised 7/10/19.
SARDINE, A., Pte. (1756), attested 8/8/16, released medically unfit 25/1/18.
LEE, H., Pte. (1757), attested 8/8/16, demobilised 7/10/19.
DE BRUYN, H., Pte. (1758), attested 8/8/16, demobilised 26/12/18.
BAATJES, J., Pte. (1759), attested 8/8/16, released medically unfit 23/2/17
ABRAHAMS, A., Pte. (1760), attested 8/8/16, S.N.L.R. 31/1/17
POGGENPOEL, T., Pte. (1761), attested 8/8/16, died of malaria 23/3/18.
WILLIAMS, J., Pte. (1762), attested 8/8/16, released medically unfit 5/9/16.
JOHNSON, M., Pte. (1763), attested 8/8/16, demobilised 7/10/19, Lewis gunner.
ADAMS, D., Pte. (1764), attested 8/8/16, released medically unfit 27/4/17.
VAN REENEN, F., Pte. (1765), attested 8/8/16, demobilised 28/8/19.
KAMPHER, J. Pte. (1766), attested 8/8/16, released medically unfit 13/9/16.
JOUBERT, W., Pte. (1767) attested 8/8/16, demobilised 31/12/19.
ARENDSE, E., Pte. (1768), attested 9/8/16, S.N.L.R. 19/9/17.
APPOLIS, F., Pte. (1769), attested 9/8/16, demobilised 2/1/19.

THE STORY OF THE 1st CAPE CORPS.

BAILEY, F., Pte. (1770), attested 9/8/16, demobilised 11/7/19.
BEERWINKEL, M., Pte. (1771), attested 9/8/16, released medically unfit 20/7/17.
DAVIDS, D., Pte. (1772), attested 9/8/16, released medically unfit 29/8/16.
DAVIDS, J., Pte. (1773), attested 9/8/16, died of dysentery 18/2/17.
DE BRUYNS, M., Pte. (1774), attested 9/8/16, released medically unfit 30/12/18.
EVERTS, J., a/Cpl. (1775), attested 9/8/16, L./Cpl. 1/4/18, a/Cpl. 2/4/18, demobilised 7/10/19, Lewis gunner.
EMMANUEL, B., Pte. (1776), attested 9/8/16, released medically unfit 23/8/17.
FREDERICKS, J., Sgt. (1777), attested 9/8/16, Sgt. 11/1/17, demobilised 7/10/19.
JACOBS, D., Pte. 1778, attested 9/8/16, died of dysentery 29/3/17.
JACOBS, P. P., Pte. (1779), attested 9/8/16, released medically unfit 13/11/17.
JEFFRIES, J., Pte. (1780), attested 9/8/16, demobilised 7/10/19.
JACOBS, A., Pte. (1781), attested 9/8/16, released medically unfit 14/2/18.
COETZE, D., Pte. (1782), attested 9/8/16, demobilised 27/8/19.
LESSELS, J., Pte. (1783), attested 9/8/16, demobilised 7/10/19.
DAVIDS, M., Pte. (1784), attested 9/8/16, demobilised 8/9/19.
MITCHELL, B. J., Pte. (1785), attested 9/8/16, released medically unfit 12/11/17.
OOSTENDORP, Pte. (1786), attested 9/8/16, demobilised 7/10/19.
PETERSEN, L., Pte. (1787), attested 9/8/16, released medically unfit 8/7/18.
PETERSEN, J., Pte. (1788), attested 9/8/16, released medically unfit 21/9/18.
PARISH, G., Pte. (1789), attested 9/8/16, demobilised 11/7/19.
ROOKS, A., Pte. (1790), attested 9/8/16, released medically unfit 3/10/17.
REYNAARD, J., Pte. (1791), attested 9/8/16, released medically unfit 14/2/18.
SERANGE, A., Pte. (1792), attested 9/8/16, demobilised 22/7/19.
SAMUELS, H., Pte. (1793), attested 9/8/16, released medically unfit 6/9/17.
SAMUELS, M., Pte. (1794), attested 9/8/16, released medically unfit 27/10/16.
SOLOMON, G. E., Pte. (1795), attested 9/8/16, released medically unfit 15/8/17.
SCULLER, J., Pte. (1796), attested 9/8/16, died of acute enteritis 16/6/17.
SWARTS, W., Pte. (1797), attested 9/8/16, released medically unfit 12/3/17.
SEPTEMBER, F. G., Pte. (1798), attested 9/8/16, demobilised 27/12/18.
SOLOMON, G., Pte. (1799), attested 9/8/16, released medically unfit 12/11/17.
THERON, D., Pte. (1800), attested 9/8/16, released medically unfit 13/8/17.
WILLIAMS, H., Pte. (1801), attested 9/8/16, demobilised 7/10/19.
WILLIAMS, S. A., Pte. (1802), attested 9/8/16, demobilised 11/7/19.
WYNGAARD, A., Pte. (1803), attested 9/8/16, demobilised 11/7/19.
ALEXANDER, J., Pte. (1804), attested 10/8/16, released medically unfit 6/10/16.
ADONIS, W., Pte. (1805), attested 10/8/16, demobilised 11/7/19.
BAATJES, M., Pte. (1806), attested 10/8/16, demobilised 21/7/19.
CABLE, T. W., Pte. (1807), attested 10/8/16, released medically unfit 20/11/17.
CERFF, C., Pte. (1808), attested 18/8/16, demobilised 31/12/18.
DAMES, F., Pte. (1809), attested 18/8/16, released medically unfit 3/10/17.
DAVIDS, A., Pte. (1810), attested 10/8/16, released medically unfit 3/10/17.
GETTING, T., Pte. (1811), attested 10/8/16, released medically unfit 24/9/17.
HOLLAND, J., Pte. (1812), attested 10/8/16, demobilised 7/10/19, qualified machine gunner.
KEOWN, J. H., Pte. (1813), attested 10/8/16, released medically unfit 7/11/17.
LAWRENCE, D., Pte. (1814), attested 10/8/16, released medically unfit 15/8/17.
LE ROUX, D., Pte. (1815), attested 10/8/16, released medically unfit 6/11/17.
LIEDERMAN, J., Pte. (1816), attested 10/8/16, demobilised 8/9/19.
MARINES, C., Pte. (1817), attested 10/8/16, demobilised 7/9/19.
MANEVELDT, F., Pte. (1818), attested 10/8/16, released medically unfit 25/8/16.
PETERSEN, P., Pte. (1819), attested 10/8/16, demobilised 3/1/19.
PETERSEN, C., Pte. (1820), attested 10/8/16, released medically unfit 31/8/17.
PETERS, S., Pte. (1821), attested 10/8/16, demobilised 17/1/19.
PETERSEN, I., Pte. (1822), attested 10/8/16, released medically unfit 31/8/17.
PETERSEN, S., Pte. (1823), attested 10/8/16, S.N.L.R. 31/1/17.
STOFFELS, J., Pte. (1824), attested 10/8/16, demobilised 7/9/19.
SOLOMON, J., Pte. (1825), attested 10/8/16, demobilised 7/9/19.
THOMPSON, A. W., Sgt. (1826), attested 10/8/16, L./Sgt. 18/12/16, Sgt. 1/1/17, demobilised 7/10/19, passed physical and bayonet training courses.
TOBIAS, E., Pte. (1827), attested 10/8/16, demobilised 10/4/20.
WARD, M., Pte. (1828), attested 10/8/16, released medically unfit 9/11/16.
BAKERS, J., Pte. (1829), attested 11/8/16, released medically unfit 14/11/17.
WILLIAMS, M., Pte. (1830), attested 11/8/16, demobilised 26/12/18.
THOMAS, A., Pte. (1831), attested 11/8/16, demobilised 11/7/19.
ARENDSE, J., Pte. (1832), attested 11/8/16, released medically unfit 29/10/17.
GALLANT, A., Pte. (1833), attested 11/8/16, demobilised 8/9/19.
JACOBS, H., Pte. (1834), attested 11/8/16, released medically unfit 16/6/18.
SWARTZ, N., Pte. (1835), attested 11/8/16, demobilised 16/7/19.
RAS, B., Pte. (1836), attested 11/8/16, demobilised 2/12/19.
HENDRICKS, A., Pte. (1837), attested 11/8/16, demobilised 7/10/19, Lewis gunner.
ERICKSON, J., Pte. (1838), attested 11/8/16, released medically unfit 20/4/18.
STOFFELS, H., Pte. (1839), attested 11/8/16, died of malaria 30/6/17.
BLOW, C., Pte. (1840), attested 11/8/16, released medically unfit 15/10/17.
WILLIAMS, C., Pte. (1841), attested 11/8/16, released medically unfit 13/8/17.
SEDEMAN, H. M., a/Sgt. (1842), attested 11/8/16, L./Cpl. 2/11/17, a/Sgt. 20/4/18, demobilised 15/10/19.
HARTMAN, H., Pte. (1843), attested 10/8/16, demobilised 7/10/19, machine gunner.
LION, J., Pte. (1844), attested 11/8/16, released medically unfit 28/11/17.
CAMPBELL, J., Pte. (1845), attested 11/8/16, S.N.L.R. 30/12/16.
DE VOS, G., Pte. (1846), attested 11/8/16, released medically unfit 21/10/16.
KLEINHANS, H., Pte. (1847), attested 11/8/16, released medically unfit 8/8/17.
MEYERS, C., Pte. (1848), attested 12/8/16, released medically unfit 25/1/17.
NOBLE, N., Pte. (1849), attested 12/8/16, released medically unfit 6/11/17.
BURGER, J., Pte. (1850), attested 12/8/16, released medically unfit 31/8/17.
JACOBS, J. J., Pte. (1851), attested 12/8/16, released medically unfit 24/9/17.
MARSHALL, L., Pte. (1852), attested 12/8/16, demobilised 16/7/19.
STEVENS, A., Pte. (1853), attested 12/8/16, released medically unfit 13/10/16.
THEUNNISSEN, J., Pte. (1854), attested 12/8/16, died of malaria 10/6/17.
ABRAHAMS, M., Pte. (1855), attested 14/8/16, released medically unfit 6/11/17.
ARENDSE, A., Pte. (1856), attested 14/8/16, released medically unfit 20/11/17.
ABRAHAMS, H., Pte. (1857), attested 14/8/16, S.N.L.R. 26/10/18.

THE STORY OF THE 1st CAPE CORPS.

ARENDSE, J., Pte. (1858), attested 14/8/16, demobilised 18/7/19.
BREDENKAMP, J., Pte. (1859), attested 14/8/16, died of wounds 20/2/17.
BLANKENBERG, M., Pte. (1860), attested 14/8/16, demobilised 30/12/18
CLOETE, A., Pte. (1861), attested 14/8/16, demobilised 8/9/19.
CONGO, B., Pte. (1862), attested 14/8/16, released medically unfit 21/7/18.
DAVIDS, A., Pte. (1863), attested 14/8/16, released medically unfit 20/1/17.
DE BLEQUY, W., Pte. (1864), attested 14/8/16, released medically unfit 26/2/17.
DAVIDS, H. D., Pte. (1865), attested 14/8/16, demobilised 11/7/19, qualified Lewis gunner.
DAVIES, T., Pte. (1866), attested 14/8/16, demobilised 11/7/19.
FORTUIN, W., Pte. (1867), attested 14/8/16, died of influenza 19/10/18.
PHILANDER, I., Pte. (1868), attested 14/8/16, released medically unfit 3/8/18.
GEORGE, W., Pte. (1869), attested 14/8/16, released medically unfit 12/10/17.
HENDRICKS, D., Pte. (1870), attested 14/8/16, released medically unfit 21/10/16.
HENDRICKS, S., Pte. (1871), attested 14/8/16, released medically unfit 15/8/17.
ISAACS, D., Pte. (1872), attested 14/8/16, released medically unfit 12/11/17.
JEWELL, J. C., Pte. (1873), attested 14/8/16, released medically unfit 23/1/18.
CULLIS, A., Pte. (1874), attested 14/8/16, released medically unfit 3/10/17.
JEWELL, C. M., Pte. (1875), attested 14/8/16, released medically unfit 6/11/17.
JACOBS, J., Pte. (1876), attested 14/8/16, demobilised 7/9/19.
KLEINSMITH, C., Pte. (1877), attested 14/8/16, demobilised 16/7/19, tailor.
KING, M., Pte. (1878), attested 14/8/16, demobilised 8/10/19.
KEMP, J., Pte. (1879), attested 14/8/16, released medically unfit 16/12/17.
LAKEY, J., L./Cpl. (1880), attested 14/8/16, L./Cpl. 26/10/18, demobilised 28/10/19.
LEVENDAHL, G., Pte. (1881), attested 14/8/16, killed in action 20/9/18.
MATHEE, W., Pte. (1882), attested 14/8/16, S.N.L.R. 14/6/18.
MILLER, J., Pte. (1883), attested 14/8/16, died of pneumonia 5/4/17.
MITCHELL, J., Pte. (1884), attested 14/8/16, demobilised 11/7/19.
MEYER, A. S., Pte. (1885), attested 14/8/16, demobilised 7/10/19, signaller.
MANUEL, J., Pte. (1886), attested 14/8/16, released medically unfit 13/5/18.
OOSTEN, H., Pte. (1887), attested 14/8/16, demobilised 7/10/19.
POOLE, P. L./Sgt. (1888), attested 14/8/16, Cpl. 1/11/18, L./Sgt. 2/11/18, demobilised 7/10/19.
QUIMPO, M., Cpl. (1889), attested 14/8/16, Cpl. 19/11/16, released medically unfit 24/9/17.
RABIE, L., Pte. (1890), attested 14/8/16, S.N.L.R. 23/12/16.
ROSENBERG, J., Pte. (1891), attested 14/8/16, released medically unfit 6/9/17.
SHARPLEY, P., Pte. (1892), attested 14/8/16, demobilised 7/10/19.
SEPTEMBER, S., Pte. (1893), attested 14/8/16, released medically unfit 24/9/17.
STANFIELD, I., Pte. (1894), attested 14/8/16, demobilised 8/9/19.
SOLOMON, H., Pte. (1895), attested 14/8/16, rejected 14/8/16.
THOMAS, J., Pte. (1896), attested 14/8/16, demobilised 11/7/19, Lewis gunner.
TITUS, I. W., Pte. (1897), attested 14/8/16, demobilised 3/1/19.
THOMPSON, A., Pte. (1898), attested 14/8/16, demobilised 11/7/19.
VAN NOIE, E., Pte. (1899), attested 14/8/16, demobilised 7/10/19.
VAN REENEN, J., Pte. (1900), attested 14/8/16, demobilised 11/7/19.
HENDRICKS, J., Pte. (1901), attested 14/8/16, demobilised 11/7/19.
GREEN, R., Pte. (1902), attested 14/8/16, released medically unfit 26/2/17.
PETERSEN, W. F., Pte. (1903), attested 14/8/16, released medically unfit 13/8/1
MUNNIK, D., Pte. (1904), attested 14/8/16, died of dysentery 15/1/18.
ALLIE, A., Pte. (1905), attested 14/8/16, released medically unfit 21/9/18.
ADAMS, W., Pte. (1906), attested 15/8/16, demobilised 21/7/19.
ABRAHAMS, M., Pte. (1907), attested 15/8/16, released medically unfit 14/11/16.
ADAMS, W., Pte. (1908), attested 15/8/16, demobilised 7/10/19.
ABRAHAMS, W., Pte. (1909), attested 15/8/16, S.N.L.R. 16/9/17.
CAROLUS, P., Pte. (1910), attested 15/8/16, released medically unfit 7/11/17.
CROWE, J. L., Pte. (1911), attested 15/8/16, released medically unfit 12/11/17.
DIEDERICKS, A., Pte. (1912), attested 15/8/16, released medically unfit 13/9/17.
DIRKSE, J. M., Pte. (1913), attested 15/8/16, S.N.L.R. 25/9/18.
FLORIS, P., Pte. (1914), attested 15/8/16, released medically unfit 13/5/18
FORTUIN, G., Pte. (1915), attested 15/8/16, released medically unfit 15/10/17.
GEORGE, J., Pte. (1916), attested 15/8/16, demobilised 7/10/19.
HAROLD, J. E., Pte. (1917), attested 15/8/16, demobilised 2/12/19, qualified machine gunner, mentioned in despatches, East Africa.
HAMET, F., Pte. (1918), attested 15/8/16, died of pneumonia, 13/5/17.
ISAACS, J., Pte. (1919), attested 15/8/16, demobilised 16/7/19.
ISAACS, JOHN, Pte. (1920), attested 15/8/16, died of malaria 23/8/18.
JORDAN, A., Pte. (1921), attested 15/8/16, demobilised 1/1/19.
JACKSON, I., Pte. (1922), attested 15/8/16, released medically unfit 6/11/17.
JULIES, J., Pte. (1923), attested 15/8/16, released medically unfit 14/11/16.
JONKERS, J., Pte. (1924), attested 15/8/16, released medically unfit 31/8/16.
LUCAS, A., a/L./Cpl. (1925), attested 15/8/16, a/L./Cpl. 18/6/18, demobilised 7/9/19, passed scout course.
MILLER, C., Pte. (1926), attested 15/8/16, released medically unfit 21/8/16.
MANUEL, J., Pte. (1927), attested 15/8/16, died of influenza 11/10/18.
ROSS, A., Pte. (1928), attested 15/8/16, released medically unfit 20/11/17.
SOLOMON, J., Pte. (1929), attested 15/8/16, released medically unfit 20/4/18.
SNYMAN, J., Pte. (1930), attested 15/8/16, demobilised 11/7/19.
SKIPPERS, S., Pte. (1931), attested 15/8/16, S.N.L.R. 19/3/18.
SOLOMON, J., Pte. (1932), attested 15/8/16, S.N.L.R. 31/1/17.
THEUNIS, W., Pte. (1933), attested 15/8/16, released medically unfit 6/11/17.
WILLIAMS, J., Pte. (1934), attested 15/8/16, released medically unfit 2/3/17.
WILLIAMS, S., Pte. (1935), attested 15/8/16, demobilised 8/9/19.
WYNGAARD, J., Pte. (1936), attested 15/8/16, demobilised 7/10/19.
WILLIAMS, W., Pte. (1937), attested 15/8/16, demobilised 7/10/19.
APRIL, C., Pte. (1938), attested 16/8/16, released medically unfit 18/12/17.
ABRAHAMS, C., Pte. (1939), attested 16/8/16, released medically unfit 3/12/17.
ADRIAANSE, A., Pte. (1940), attested 16/8/16, released medically unfit 25/1/18.
CLASSEN, M., Pte. (1941), attested 16/8/16, released medically unfit 15/6/18.
CLARK, P., Pte. (1942), attested 16/8/16, demobilised 11/7/19.
CAMPHER, W., Pte. (1943), attested 16/8/16, demobilised 16/7/19.
CURREN, J., Pte. (1944), attested 16/8/16, released medically unfit 28/11/16.
DE BEER, P., Pte. (1945), attested 16/8/16, rejected 16/8/16.
GREY, J., Pte. (1946), attested 16/8/16, demobilised 11/7/19.
GEDULD, W., Pte. (1947), attested 16/8/16, demobilised 22/7/19

THE STORY OF THE 1st CAPE CORPS

HOCHSCHIELD, J., Pte. (1948), attested 16/8/16, released medically unfit 25/1/17.
HELLIG, D., Pte. (1949), attested 16/8/16, demobilised 7/9/19.
HOOFD, A., Pte. (1950), attested 16/8/16, released medically unfit 31/8/17.
HARTZENBERG, C., Pte. (1951), attested 16/8/16, died of malaria 14/2/17.
HENDRICKS, I., Pte. (1952), attested 16/8/16, demobilised 27/12/18.
ISAACS, J., Pte. (1953), attested 16/8/16, demobilised 26/12/18.
JACOBS, J., Pte. (1954), attested 16/8/16, demobilised 3/7/19.
JANSEN, J., Pte. (1955), attested 16/8/16, released medically unfit 20/11/17.
JACOBS, B., Pte. (1956), attested 16/8/16, released medically unfit 25/1/18.
JANSEN, L., Pte. (1957), attested 16/8/16, demobilised 7/9/19.
MANUEL, C., Pte. (1958), attested 16/8/16, S.N.L.R. 25/11/16.
MANUEL, C., Pte. (1959), attested 16/8/16, S.N.L.R. 25/11/16.
PRESENCE, J., Pte. (1960), attested 16/8/16, demobilised 8/4/19.
PRETORIUS, P., Pte. (1961), attested 16/8/16, released medically unfit 26/12/17.
PETERSEN, H., Pte. (1962), attested 16/8/16, demobilised 21/7/19.
TROUT, A. M., Pte. (1963), attested 16/8/16, released medically unfit 21/7/18.
TITE, F., Pte. (1964), attested 16/8/16, released medically unfit 26/6/18.
TROUT, F. D., Pte. (1965), attested 16/8/16, released medically unfit 6/11/17.
TEMBE, J. P., Sgt. (1966), attested 16/8/16, died of wounds 22/1/17.
WILLIAMS, F., Pte. (1967), attested 16/8/16, demobilised 25/12/18.
WHITEMAN, F., Pte. (1968), attested 16/8/16, demobilised 7/10/19.
ABRAHAMS, J., Pte. (1969), attested 16/8/16, released medically unfit 9/9/16.
ADONIS, T., Pte. (1970), attested 16/8/16, demobilised 2/1/19.
ARENDSE, J., Pte. (1971), attested 16/8/16, died of influenza 7/10/18.
ABRAHAMS, H. J., Pte. (1972), attested 17/8/16, S.N.L.R. 25/11/16.
BARGHUIS, H., Pte. (1973), attested 17/8/16, died of dysentery 4/4/17.
DANIELS, E., Pte. (1974), attested 17/8/16, demobilised 7/10/19.
DAVIDS, J., Pte. (1975), attested 17/8/16, died of malaria 16/4/17.
DE VRIES, J. A., Pte. (1976), attested 17/8/16, released medically unfit 27/5/18
DANIELS, P. W., Pte. (1977), attested 17/8/16, died of malaria 13/5/17.
DYASON, A., Pte. (1978), attested 17/8/16, released medically unfit 1/8/17.
HENDRICKS, W., Pte. (1979), attested 17/8/16, released medically unfit 20/11/17.
HENDRICKS, W., Pte. (1980), attested 17/8/16, S.N.L.R. 25/11/16.
JACOBS, A., Pte. (1981), attested 17/8/16, released medically unfit 19/9/16.
McKENNA, H., Pte. (1982), attested 17/8/16, died of dysentery 11/12/17.
MEIRING, D., Cpl. (1983), attested 17/8/16, Cpl. 15/10/17, demobilised 11/7/19.
PETERS, L. S., Pte. (1984), attested 17/8/16, S.N.L.R. 28/6/17.
ROSS, J. D., Cpl. (1985), attested 17/8/16, Cpl. 1/2/17, Sgt. 1/4/18, reverted to Cpl. 10/2/19, demobilised 7/9/19, Lewis gun course.
SCOTT, T., Pte. (1986), attested 17/8/16, released medically unfit 15/9/16.
VAN WEILING, A., Pte. (1987), attested 17/8/16, demobilised 7/9/19.
WALBRUGH, F. W., Pte. (1988), attested 17/8/16, demobilised 7/10/19, acted as Cpl.
ARENDSE, G., Pte. (1989), attested 17/8/16, released medically unfit 8/9/16.
ABRAHAMS, K., Pte. (1990), attested 18/8/16, released medically unfit 20/7/17.
BOMESTER, A. W., Pte. (1991), attested 18/8/16, released medically unfit 12/10/17.
DIXON, J., Pte. (1992), attested 18/8/16, died of malaria 18/7/17.
DE KOCK, G., Pte. (1993), attested 18/8/16, released medically unfit 13/9/17.
HILLBERG, J., Pte. (1994), attested 18/8/16, died of pneumonia 27/11/18.
HENDRICKS, F., Pte. (1995), attested 18/8/16, demobilised 16/7/19.
ISAACS, A., Pte. (1996), attested 18/8/16, released medically unfit 16/11/17.
JONATHAN, G., Pte. (1997), attested 18/8/16, demobilised 31/12/19
JOHNSTON, A., Pte. (1998), attested 18/8/16, S.N.L.R. 25/11/16.
JOUBERT, D., Pte. (1999), attested 18/8/16, demobilised 11/7/19.
JUTZEN, D., Pte. (2000), attested 17/8/16, demobilised 16/7/19, drum and fife band.
LOSPER, W., Pte. (2001), attested 18/8/16, released medically unfit 5/8/17.
LE ROUX, J., Pte. (2002), attested 18/8/16, released medically unfit 20/11/16.
MICHAEL, V., Pte. (2003), attested 18/8/16, released medically unfit 22/1/17.
MULLER, H., Pte. (2004), attested 18/8/16, demobilised 18/10/19.
STOUTZ, J. H., Pte. (2005), attested 18/8/16, released medically unfit 30/11/17.
TROUT, P., Pte. (2006), attested 10/8/16, released medically unfit 8/8/17.
LOTTS, W., Pte. (2007), attested 15/8/16, released medically unfit 25/9/16.
FEBRUARY, W., Pte. (2008), attested 17/8/16, released medically unfit 16/11/17.
CUPIDO, J., Pte. (2009), attested 17/8/16, released medically unfit 19/10/16.
DU TOIT, J., Pte. (2010), attested 17/8/16, released medically unfit 6/7/17.
FONTAINE, H., Pte. (2011), attested 17/8/16, released medically unfit 6/11/17.
LUCAS, P. P., Pte. (2012), attested 17/8/16, released medically unfit 20/11/17.
JANSEN, T., Pte. (2013), attested 18/8/16, demobilised 7/9/19.
STEFFENSEN, W. H., Pte. (2014), attested 19/8/16, released medically unfit 6/11/17.
ADONIS, S. J., Pte. (2015), attested 21/8/16, released medically unfit 31/8/17.
ADAMS, J., Pte. (2016), attested 21/8/16, released medically unfit 11/4/18.
ABRAHAMS, J., Pte. (2017), attested 21/8/16, demobilised 10/10/19.
AUGUST, F., Pte. (2018), attested 21/8/16, released medically unfit 5/3/18.
ADONIS, F., Pte. (2019), attested 21/8/16, released medically unfit 12/3/18.
ADAMS, S., Pte. (2020), attested 21/8/16, released medically unfit 15/2/17.
BARON, D. P., Pte. (2021), attested 21/8/16, demobilised 11/7/19.
BARDUS, W., Pte. (2022), attested 21/8/16, demobilised 7/10/19.
BOWERS, J., Pte. (2023), attested 21/8/16, released medically unfit 8/9/16.
BROWN, F., Pte. (2024), attested 21/8/16, demobilised 21/7/19.
BROOKS, W., Pte. (2025), attested 21/8/16, demobilised 11/7/19.
BARKLEY, P., Pte. (2026), attested 21/8/16, released medically unfit 13/12/18.
BURGESS, W., Pte. (2027), attested 21/8/16, demobilised 7/10/19.
COLLINS, E., Pte. (2028), attested 21/8/16, released medically unfit 12/11/17.
CAROLLISSEN, C., Pte. (2029), attested 21/8/16, demobilised 10/10/19, bugler.
DAMASO, G., Pte. (2030), attested 21/8/16, demobilised 8/9/19.
DU TOIT, A., Pte. (2031), attested 21/8/16, demobilised 11/7/19.
DE YOUNG, P., Pte. (2032), attested 21/8/16, demobilised 26/12/18.
DE BRUINS, J., Pte. (2033), attested 21/8/16, released medically unfit 15/8/17.
DAVIDS, G., Pte. (2034), attested 23/8/16, S.N.L.R. 23/12/16.
DEMPERS, D., Pte. (2035), attested 21/8/16, released medically unfit 3/12/17.
DELL, C., Pte. (2036), attested 21/8/16, released medically unfit 8/9/16.
ELY, F., Pte. (2037), attested 21/8/16, demobilised 11/7/19.

FORTUIN, W., Pte. (2038), attested 21/8/16, released medically unfit 27/7/17.
FRANKS, J., Pte. (2039), attested 21/8/16, killed in action 20/1/17.
FORD, F., Pte. (2040), attested 21/8/16, demobilised 10/7/19, qualified Lewis Gun Instructor
FORTUIN, D., Pte. (2041), attested 21/8/16, demobilised 11/7/19.
GRAHAM, D., Pte. (2042), attested 21/8/16, released medically unfit 24/9/17.
GREENFIELD, H., Pte. (2043), attested 21/8/16, released medically unfit 5/7/18.
HEYNES, H., Pte. (2044), attested 21/8/16, released medically unfit 13/9/17.
HUMAN G., Pte. (2045), attested 21/8/16 released medically unfit 18/8/17.
HARFILING, A., Pte. (2046), attested 21/8/16, released medically unfit 30/9/18.
ISAACS, H., Pte. (2047), attested 21/8/16, demobilised 11/7/19.
JACOBS, M., Pte. (2048), attested 21/8/16, released medically unfit 25/7/18.
KLOPPERS, A., Pte. (2049), attested 21/8/16, demobilised 14/11/19.
LE FLUER, J., Pte. (2050), attested 21/8/16, demobilised 8/10/19.
LEITH, R., Pte. (2051), attested 21/8/16, demobilised 3/8/19.
LEWIS, J., Pte. (2052), attested 21/8/16, demobilised 7/10/19.
LE FLUER, J., Pte. (2053), attested 21/8/16, demobilised 10/10/19.
MEIRING, J., Pte. (2054), attested 21/8/16, demobilised 21/7/19.
MENTOR, A., Pte. (2055), attested 21/8/16, demobilised 10/10/19.
MALLEP, J., Pte. (2056), attested 21/8/16, demobilised 26/12/18.
MULLER, C., Pte. (2057), attested 21/8/16, released medically unfit 23/3/17.
NICHOLSON, W., Pte. (2058), attested 21/8/16, released medically unfit 27/7/17.
MORRIS, J., Pte. (2059), attested 21/8/16, released medically unfit 19/9/16.
MANNISOW, H., Pte. (2060), attested 21/8/16, released medically unfit 20/7/17.
PETERSEN, J., Pte. (2061), attested 21/8/16, demobilised 7/10/19.
PETERS, H., Pte. (2062), attested 21/8/16, died of bronchitis 8/4/17.
PETERSEN, J., Pte. (2063), attested 21/8/16, demobilised 21/7/19.
PRESENCE, P., Pte. (2064), attested 21/8/16, died of malaria 18/2/17.
PETERSEN, A., Pte. (2065), attested 21/8/16, released medically unfit 20/11/17.
RHODES, S., Pte. (2066), attested 21/8/16, released medically unfit 31/8/17.
ROBUS, W., Pte. (2067), attested 21/8/16, demobilised 7/10/19.
RHODES, A., Pte. (2068), attested 21/8/16, S.N.L.R. 25/11/16.
SCOTT, T., Pte. (2069), attested 21/8/16, demobilised 7/10/19.
THOMAS, T., Pte. (2070), attested 21/8/16, released medically unfit 20/7/17.
THERON, I., Pte. (2071), attested 21/8/16, S.N.L.R. 9/9/17.
VAN EDEN, C., Pte. (2072), attested 21/8/16, demobilised 7/9/19.
VOLKWYN, W., L./Cpl. (2073), attested 21/8/16, L./Cpl. 21/9/18, demobilised 7/10/19.
WEINER, I., Pte. (2074), attested 21/8/16, released medically unfit 13/8/17.
YON, N., Pte. (2075), attested 21/8/16, demobilised 11/7/19.
COMBRINK, I., Pte. (2076), attested 18/8/16, released medically unfit 31/10/16.
PARKS, L., Pte. (2077), attested 18/8/16, released medically unfit 20/11/17.
CORNEILIUS, M., Pte. (2078), attested 18/8/16, released medically unfit 6/11/17.
BEHR, R., Pte. (2079), attested 18/8/16, S.N.L.R. 1/8/17.
AMANSURE, A., Pte. (2080), attested 22/8/16, demobilised 11/7/19.
BRAMBILL, H., Pte. (2081), attested 16/8/16, released medically unfit 3/10/18.
CALVERT, C., Pte. (2082), attested 22/8/16, released medically unfit 3/10/18.
DAVIDS, H., Pte. (2083), attested 22/8/16, released medically unfit 23/5/17.
EVANS, J., Pte. (2084), attested 22/8/16, S.N.L.R. 22/8/16.
FORBES, L., Pte. (2085), attested 22/8/16, released medically unfit 25/8/16.
HARTZENBERG, W., Pte. (2086), attested 22/8/16, demobilised 16/7/19.
HAMMAN, J., Pte. (2087), attested 22/8/16, released medically unfit 19/9/16.
JONES, F., Pte. (2088), attested 22/8/16, demobilised 11/7/19.
JACOBS, J., Pte. (2089), attested 22/8/16, died of malaria 16/10/17.
KNOOP, W., Pte. (2090), attested 22/8/16, demobilised 16/7/19.
LOVELOT, A., Pte. (2091), attested 22/8/16, demobilised 7/9/19.
LOTTER, F., Pte. (2092), attested 22/8/16, released medically unfit 6/11/17.
MARAIS, M., Pte. (2093), attested 22/8/16, demobilised 7/9/19.
MOORE, H., Pte. (2094), attested 22/8/16, demobilised 31/12/18.
PARENZEE, F., Pte. (2095), attested 22/8/16, released medically unfit 11/10/16.
PLAATJES, M., Pte. (2096), attested 22/8/16, demobilised 13/1/19.
PETERSEN, I., Pte. (2097), attested 22/8/16, demobilised 16/7/19.
RICKETTS, J., Pte. (2098), attested 21/8/16, died of dysentery 1/2/17.
REID, E. F. J., L./Cpl. (2099), attested 21/8/16, L./Cpl. 30/6/17, deserted 6/10/18.
SMOUSE, D., Pte. (2100), attested 21/8/16, died of wounds 10/11/17.
SLABBERT, G., Pte. (2101), attested 21/8/16, released medically unfit 26/8/16.
RUITERS, A., Pte. (2102), attested 21/8/16, released medically unfit 21/5/18.
SAULS, P., Pte. (2103), attested 21/8/16, died of influenza 11/10/18.
THOMAS, A., Pte. (2104), attested 21/8/16, demobilised 11/7/19.
WYMAN, P., Pte. (2105), attested 21/8/16, demobilised 7/10/19.
WILDSCHUT, A., Pte. (2106), attested 21/8/16, demobilised 7/9/19.
ARIES, J., Pte. (2107), attested 23/8/16, demobilised 7/10/19.
BASSON, N., Pte. (2108), attested 23/8/16, demobilised 8/10/19.
CODIES, G., Pte. (2109), attested 23/8/16, demobilised 21/7/19.
CONLAN, G., Pte. (2110), attested 23/8/16, demobilised 11/7/19.
DAVIDS, W., Pte. (2111), attested 23/8/16, released medically unfit 19/10/16.
ENGELBRECHT, G., Pte. (2112), attested 23/8/16, demobilised 11/7/19.
GRAIN, T., Pte. (2113), attested 23/8/16, released medically unfit 5/9/16.
JONES, H., Pte. (2114), attested 23/8/16, S.N.L.R. 25/11/16.
JOHNSTON, J., Pte. (2115), attested 22/8/16, demobilised 16/7/19.
GOOSEN J., Pte. (2116), attested 22/8/16, demobilised 16/7/19.
KLEINTJES, C., Pte. (2117), attested 23/8/16, died of dysentery 19/3/17.
MAY, S., Pte. (2118), attested 23/8/16, died of malaria 4/3/17.
MAZOO, M., Pte. (2119), attested 23/8/16, released medically unfit 31/8/16.
McCARTHY, P., Pte. (2120), attested 23/8/16, released medically unfit 15/9/16.
MITCHELL, S., Pte. (2121), attested 23/8/16, demobilised 16/7/19.
PRESENCE, F., Pte. (2122), attested 23/8/16, demobilised 11/7/19.
PATERSEN, F., Pte. (2123), attested 23/8/16, S.N.L.R. 25/11/16.
STOHRER, W., Pte. (2124), attested 22/8/16, demobilised 10/10/19, 1st class qualified signaller.
THOMPSON, E., Pte. (2125), attested 21/8/16, released medically unfit 24/7/17.
AVONTUUR, H., Pte. (2126), attested 24/8/16, demobilised 8/9/19.
ADAMS, J., Pte. (2127), attested 24/8/16, demobilised 7/9/19, machine gunner.
BRINK, J., Pte. (2128), attested 24/8/16, released medically unfit 30/9/16.

THE STORY OF THE 1st CAPE CORPS.

CORSTEN, H., Pte. (2129), attested 24/8/16, demobilised 22/7/19, machine gunner.
DANIELS, J., Pte. (2130), attested 16/8/16, S.N.L.R. 18/2/17.
DAMPIES, M., Pte. (2131), attested 24/8/16, died of dysentery 12/3/17.
DANIELS, J., Pte. (2132), attested 23/8/16, released medically unfit 12/11/16.
VAN WINKEL, J., Pte. (2133), attested 24/8/16, demobilised 25/12/18.
DE LEEUW, L., Pte. (2134), attested 23/8/16, S.N.L.R. 23/12/16.
GROEPE, D., Pte. (2135), attested 24/8/16, released medically unfit 13/9/17.
GORDON, J., Pte. (2136), attested 24/8/16, demobilised 1/1/19.
GROEPE, P., Pte. (2137), attested 24/8/16, released medically unfit 11/8/17.
HOPSEL, T., Pte. (2138), attested 24/8/16, demobilised 16/7/19, passed trench warfare and bombing courses.
IRVING, C., Pte. (2139), attested 24/8/16, released medically unfit 7/11/17.
JOHNSON, H., Pte. (2140), attested 24/8/16, released medically unfit 8/9/16.
JAPPIE, H. J., a/Sgt. (2141), attested 24/8/16, a/Sgt. 1/4/17, released medically unfit 20/11/17.
JACOBS, B., Pte. (2142), attested 24/8/16, released medically unfit 12/11/17.
JACOBS, A., Pte. (2143), attested 24/8/16, released medically unfit 25/8/17.
JACOBS, J., Pte. (2144), attested 24/8/16, released medically unfit 3/10/16.
RECKLIFF, C., Pte. (2145), attested 24/8/16, released medically unfit 13/9/17.
RECKLIFF, K., Pte. (2146), attested 24/8/16, released medically unfit 24/9/17.
SIPIKA, B., Pte. (2147), attested 24/8/16, demobilised 30/3/20.
ANDREWS, D., Pte. (2148), attested 24/8/16, demobilised 19/2/19.
CHAPEL, W., Pte. (2149), attested 23/8/16, released medically unfit 29/8/17.
DAVIDS, H. T., Pte. (2150), attested 24/8/16, released medically unfit 13/11/16.
FERNANDEZ, P. T., Pte. (2151), attested 24/8/16, released medically unfit 12/5/17.
GARRETT, W., a/L./Cpl. (2152), attested 24/8/16, a/L./Cpl. 1/3/19, demobilised 11/7/19.
JONKERS, P., Pte. (2153), attested 24/8/16, demobilised 16/7/19.
KAY, J., Pte. (2154), attested 24/8/16, demobilised 11/7/19.
PETERSEN, J. H., Pte. (2155), attested 24/8/16, S.N.L.R. 3/3/18.
ROBERTSON, J., Pte. (2156), attested 24/8/16, released medically unfit 23/8/17.
SIEGERS, J., Sgt. (2157), attested 23/8/16, Sgt. 11/1/17, released medically unfit 15/10/17.
SMITH, C. J., Pte. (2158), attested 23/8/16, released medically unfit 26/10/16.
WELLS, C., Pte. (2159), attested 23/8/16, demobilised 8/9/19.
CAROLUS, A., Pte. (2160), attested 23/8/16, released medically unfit 17/9/16.
DAVIDS, J., Pte. (2161), attested 23/8/16, released medically unfit 10/8/17.
HALTERS, A., Pte. (2162), attested 21/8/16, released medically unfit 15/9/16.
LOTTERING, C., Pte. (2163), attested 23/8/16, released medically unfit 10/11/17.
McPHERSEN, D., Pte. (2164), attested 23/8/16, released medically unfit 17/9/16.
PASCOE, J., Pte. (2165), attested 23/8/16, released medically unfit 11/10/16.
RANK, P., Pte. (2166), attested 21/8/16, demobilised 8/9/19.
SCHROEDER, M., Pte. (2167), attested 21/8/16, demobilised 13/1/19.
VAN WYK, J., Pte. (2168), attested 23/8/16, released medically unfit 12/11/17.
ABRAHAMS, P. R., Pte. (2169), attested 23/8/16, rejected 23/8/16.
DAVIDS, C., Pte. (2170), attested 23/8/16, released medically unfit 14/2/18.
ELLIS, J. T., Pte. (2171), attested 23/8/16, released medically unfit 16/5/17.
KLOOSMAN, J. A., Pte. (2172), attested 23/8/16, demobilised 7/10/19, qualified signaller.
LEWIS, J., Pte. (2173), attested 23/8/16, released medically unfit 31/8/16.
MAY, C., Pte. (2174), attested 23/8/16, released medically unfit 9/8/17.
MOSES, J., Pte. (2175), attested 23/8/16, demobilised 22/7/19.
MORRIS, W. F., Pte. (2176), attested 23/8/16, released medically unfit 7/11/17.
NICHOLSON, S., Pte. (2177), attested 23/8/16, demobilised 4/9/19.
PETERSEN, A., Pte. (2178), attested 23/8/16, released medically unfit 16/7/18.
SNYMAN, W., Pte. (2179), attested 23/8/16, S.N.L.R. 18/8/17.
SCHOLTZ, C., Pte. (2180), attested 23/8/16, released medically unfit 16/10/16.
WILLIAMS, J., Pte. (2181), attested 23/8/16, demobilised 11/7/19, transport driver
PETERSEN, P., Pte. (2182), attested 23/8/16, demobilised 7/9/19.
LOTTERING, J., Pte. (2183), attested 22/8/16, released medically unfit 8/6/18.
GOLDSMITH, A., Pte. (2184), attested 22/8/16, released medically unfit 12/8/18.
PETERSEN, S., Pte. (2185), attested 22/8/16, S.N.L.R. 17/5/18.
STERBEN, S., Pte. (2186), attested 22/8/16, released medically unfit 26/9/17.
CAROLUS, N., Pte. (2187), attested 26/8/16, demobilised 21/7/19.
JESSMAN, W., Pte. (2188), attested 26/8/16, demobilised 7/10/19.
OLIVER, J., Pte. (2189), attested 9/8/16, released medically unfit 15/1/17.
MOSES, M., Pte. (2190), attested 23/8/16, released medically unfit 3/12/17.
SCHOLTZ, C., Pte. (2191), attested 26/8/16, released medically unfit 9/1/18.
BELL, W., Pte. (2192), attested 25/8/16, demobilised 8/9/19.
MARLOW, A., Pte. (2193), attested 25/8/16, demobilised 10/4/20.
SPIRES, J., Pte. (2194), attested 28/8/16, demobilised 7/9/19.
WYNNE, G., Pte. (2195), attested 28/8/16, released medically unfit 25/9/18.
WILLIAMS, D., Pte. (2196), attested 28/8/16, demobilised 8/9/19.
GOLDING, W., Pte. (2197), attested 28/8/16, demobilised 28/8/19.
PETERS, K., Pte. (2198), attested 28/8/16, demobilised 8/11/19.
ABRAHAMS, I., Pte. (2199), attested 28/8/16, released medically unfit 29/10/17.
ADAMS, P., Pte. (2200), attested 28/8/16, demobilised 21/7/19.
ANTONY, D., Pte. (2201), attested 28/8/16, released medically unfit 7/11/17.
ABRAHAMS, J., Pte. (2202), attested 28/8/16, released medically unfit 16/11/17.
ADAMS, J., Pte. (2203), attested 28/8/16, demobilised 26/8/19.
ABRAHAMS, F., Pte. (2204), attested 28/8/16, released medically unfit 15/8/17.
ADAMS, S., Pte. (2205), attested 28/8/16, S.N.L.R. 17/2/17.
BAKERS, P., Pte. (2206), attested 28/8/16, released medically unfit 16/11/17.
BUCKTON H., Pte. (2207), attested 28/8/16, released medically unfit 6/11/17.
BASSON, A., Pte. (2208), attested 28/8/16, died of wounds 3/2/17.
CALVERT, H., Pte. (2209), attested 28/8/16, released medically unfit 7/11/17.
DAVIDS, L., Pte. (2210), attested 28/8/16, released medically unfit 16/8/17.
FELIX, A., Pte. (2211), attested 28/8/16, released medically unfit 26/9/17.
FREDERICKS, D., Pte. (2212), attested 22/8/16, did not report again 22/8/16.
FESTES, A., Pte. (2213), attested 28/8/16, demobilised 8/9/19.
GREEN, A., Pte. (2214), attested 28/8/16, demobilised 7/10/19.
HENDRICKS, T., Pte. (2215), attested 28/8/16, released medically unfit 23/8/17.
CHRISTIAN, J., Pte. (2216), attested 28/8/16, released medically unfit 30/6/18.
JACOBS, H. W., Pte. (2217), attested 28/8/16, released medically unfit 13/9/17.
JULIUS, R., Pte. (2218), attested 28/8/16, released medically unfit 29/6/17.

KEMP, M., Pte. (2219), attested 28/8/16, died of malaria 9/12/16.
LINEBOOM, F., Pte. (2220), attested 28/8/16, killed in action 20/9/18, passed grenade discharging course.
LE ROUX, A., Pte. (2221), attested 28/8/16, died of malaria and dysentery 1/3/17.
NAPOLEON, S., Pte. (2222), attested 28/8/16, demobilised 16/7/19.
OXFORD, S., Pte. (2223), attested 28/8/16, released medically unfit 24/9/17.
OLIVER, J., Pte. (2224), attested 28/8/16, demobilised 7/10/19.
OTTO, A., Pte. (2225), attested 28/8/16, released medically unfit 15/9/16.
PETERSEN, P., Pte. (2226), attested 28/8/16, demobilised 7/9/19.
RYLAND, J. S., Pte. (2227), attested 28/8/16, released medically unfit 29/10/17.
STEMMET, J., Pte. (2228), attested 28/8/16, demobilised 11/7/19.
SKIPPERS, H., Pte. (2229), attested 28/8/16, demobilised 7/9/19.
SAMUELS, W. J., a/Sgt. (2230), attested 23/8/16, Cpl. 1/4/18, a/Sgt. 2/4/18, Sgt. 1/11/18, reverted to Cpl. 9/7/19, a/Sgt. 1/8/19, demobilised 8/9/19, qualified Lewis gunner.
STUURMAN, F., Pte. (2231), attested 28/8/16, released medically unfit 11/8/17.
SAMUELS, J., Pte. (2232), attested 28/8/16, demobilised 7/10/19.
WILLIAMS, J., Pte. (2233), attested 28/8/16, released medically unfit 19/10/16
WILLIAMS, J., Pte. (2234), attested 28/8/16, died of appendicitis 12/9/16.
WILSCOTT, M., Pte. (2235), attested 28/8/16, released medically unfit 3/12/17
WILLIAMS, B., Pte. (2236), attested 28/8/16, killed in action 20/9/18.
ALBRECHT, J., Pte. (2237), attested 23/8/16, released medically unfit 17/9/16.
BROWN, J., Pte. (2238), attested 25/8/16, released medically unfit 22/10/16.
BARENDSE, J., Pte. (2239), attested 22/8/16, released medically unfit 8/6/18
BROWN, H., Pte. (2240), attested 24/8/16, released medically unfit 13/9/17.
CLASSEN, C., Pte. (2241), attested 24/8/16, died of influenza 9/10/18, machine gunner.
FORTUIN, A., Pte. (2242), attested 23/8/16, demobilised 7/9/19.
FILLANDER, S., Pte. (2243), attested 24/8/16, released medically unfit 25/8/17.
GRIFFIN, H., Pte. (2244), attested 22/8/16, released medically unfit 3/9/17.
HERWELL, P., Pte. (2245), attested 22/8/16, released medically unfit 30/3/18.
JANSEN, J., Pte. (2246), attested 23/8/16, demobilised 7/10/19.
JAFTHA, C., Pte. (2247), attested 22/8/16, released medically unfit 26/9/17.
KLEINHANS, A., Pte. (2248), attested 24/8/16, demobilised 7/9/19.
LE ROUX, J., Pte. (2249), attested 25/8/16, demobilised 1/1/19.
LANGEVELDT, A., Pte. (2250), attested 23/8/16, demobilised 16/7/19.
MORRIS, J., Pte (2251), attested 23/8/16, demobilised 22/7/19.
MEYER, W., Pte. (2252), attested 23/8/16, S.N.L.R. 31/1/17.
McKLEIN, I., Pte. (2253), attested 23/8/16, demobilised 29/7/19.
MINNIE, S., Pte. (2254), attested 22/8/16, demobilised 7/9/19, machine gunner.
OELSON, W., Pte. (2255), attested 22/8/16, demobilised 11/7/19.
OLIPHANT, M., Pte. (2256), attested 24/8/16, released medically unfit 24/9/18.
OLIVER, J., Pte. (2257), attested 24/8/16, released medically unfit 25/8/17.
OLIESLAGER, J., Pte. (2258), attested 22/8/16, demobilised 21/7/19.
OELSON, D., Pte. (2259), attested 23/8/16, demobilised 8/9/19.
PHILANDER, L., Pte. (2260), attested 23/8/16, released medically unfit 7/11/17.
RAMA, M., Pte. (2261), attested 23/8/16, demobilised 7/9/19.
SWIGELAAR, P., Pte. (2262), attested 23/8/16, released medically unfit 29/10/17.
SNYDERS, F., Pte. (2263), attested 23/8/16, demobilised 6/1/19.
TROMPETER, C., Pte. (2264), attested 23/8/16, died of malaria 6/4/17.
VALENTINE, F., Pte. (2265), attested 23/8/16, demobilised 7/9/19.
VISAGIE, M. A., Pte. (2266), attested 23/8/16, died of dysentery 24/1/17.
WYMAN, W., Pte. (2267), attested 24/8/16, demobilised 1/1/19.
WILDEMAN, H., Pte. (2268), attested 25/8/16, demobilised 7/9/19.
ARENDSE, C., Pte. (2269), attested 29/8/16, S.N.L.R. 16/10/18.
ADAMS, J., Pte. (2270), attested 29/8/16, demobilised 31/12/19.
AKKERMAN, A., Pte. (2271), attested 29/8/16, demobilised 7/10/19.
BERNICKOW, A., L./Cpl. (2272), attested 28/8/16, L./Cpl. 21/11/17, demobilised 13/1/19.
DANIELS, P., Pte. (2273), attested 28/8/16, demobilised 11/7/19.
DANIELS, L., Pte. (2274), attested 28/8/16, demobilised 8/9/19.
EXTEEN, P., Pte. (2275), attested 28/8/16, died of cerebro spinal meningitis 31/8/18.
GORDON, J., Pte. (2276), attested 28/8/16, demobilised 8/9/19.
HERMAN, A., Pte. (2277), attested 28/8/16, died of dysentery 13/2/17.
JOHNSTON, A., Pte. (2278), attested 28/8/16, died of influenza 11/10/18.
JAFTHA, J. D., Pte. (2279), attested 29/8/16, released medically unfit 31/8/17.
JOHNSON, R., Pte. (2280), attested 29/8/16, drowned at El Arish 2/11/18.
KATTS, J., Pte. (2281), attested 29/8/16, demobilised 8/9/19.
LOTTERING, G., Pte. (2282), attested 29/8/16, died of mitral regurgitation 1/5/18.
MARKHUIS, A., Pte. (2283), attested 29/8/16, released medically unfit 26/12/18.
MOSTERT, L. C., Pte. (2284), attested 26/8/16, released medically unfit 13/8/17.
OLIESLAGER, F., Pte. (2285), attested 28/8/16, released medically unfit 13/8/17
PETERSEN, F., Pte. (2286), attested 28/8/16, released medically unfit 29/10/17.
PAULSEN, S., Pte. (2287), attested 28/8/16, demobilised 11/7/19.
PETERSEN, C., Pte. (2288), attested 28/8/16, demobilised 7/10/19.
RENTZ, F., Pte. (2289), attested 29/8/16, demobilised 28/8/19.
RHODA, A., Pte. (2290), attested 29/8/16, released medically unfit 3/12/17.
RENTZ, W., Pte. (2291), attested 29/8/16, demobilised 5/2/19.
STRYDOM, C., L./Sgt. (2292), attested 24/8/16, L./Sgt. 5/7/17, demobilised 16/7/19, passed scout course 1st class.
SAMUELS, P., Pte. (2293), attested 28/8/16, demobilised 7/10/19, passed scout and sniping course.
VAN DER MERWE, A., Pte. (2294), attested 28/8/16, released medically unfit 11/4/18.
VAN BOOM, J. P W., Pte. (2295), attested 28/8/16, released medically unfit 18/8/17.
WILLIAMS, D. J., Pte. (2296), attested 28/8/16, died of malaria 11/3/17.
WILLIAMS, J. J., Pte. (2297), attested 28/8/16, demobilised 7/10/19. The G.O.C., Palestine, complimented him on his act of gallantry in trying to save a comrade from drowning in sea at Gaza.
ZWARTS, S., Pte. (2298), attested 29/8/16, released medically unfit 24/2/18.
FELL, P., Pte. (2299), attested 29/8/16, demobilised 2/1/19.
CORNELIUS, W., Pte. (2300), attested 26/8/16, demobilised 11/7/19.
SAULS, L., Pte. (2301), attested 29/8/16, demobilised 7/9/19.
ANTHONY, J., Pte. (2302), attested 28/8/16, demobilised 8/10/19.
ANDRIES, J. J., Pte. (2303), attested 28/8/16, demobilised 7/10/19.
BENJAMIN, P., Pte. (2304), attested 30/8/16, demobilised 31/12/18.
BARENDS, H., Pte. (2305), attested 28/8/16, released medically unfit 3/10/17
BAILEY, J., Pte. (2306), attested 30/8/16, demobilised 7/10/19.

THE STORY OF THE 1st CAPE CORPS.

CARELSON, J., Pte. (2307), attested 30/8/16, released medically unfit 30/9/18.
CALMEYER, C., Pte. (2308), attested 28/8/16, S.N.L.R. 12/9/17.
FRANCE, W., Pte. (2309), attested 30/8/16, S.N.L.R. 5/2/17.
GOODALL, W. C., Pte. (2310), attested 30/8/16, released medically unfit 18/11/16.
HARRIS, I., Pte. (2311), attested 28/8/16, released medically unfit 16/11/17.
JACOBS, J., Pte. (2312), attested 28/8/16, released medically unfit 15/8/17.
JOSEPHS, C., Pte. (2313), attested 29/8/16, released medically unfit 4/11/18.
JULIE, M., Pte. (2314), attested 30/8/16, still serving.
KING, C., Pte. (2315), attested 29/8/16, released medically unfit 29/10/17.
MANUEL, H., Pte. (2316), attested 28/8/16, S.N.L.R. 25/11/16.
PRINCE, C., Pte. (2317), attested 29/8/16, demobilised 7/9/19.
PARRY, J., Pte. (2318), attested 29/8/16, released medically unfit 11/4/18.
PARISH, J., Pte. (2319), attested 30/8/16, released medically unfit 22/1/17.
RODEWALD, J. C., Pte. (2320), attested 29/8/16, released medically unfit 8/9/16.
RODEWALD, J., Pte. (2321), attested 29/8/16, S.N.L.R. 31/1/17.
RODDHESQUE, R., Pte. (2322), attested 28/8/16, released medically unfit 7/11/16.
STEMMET, B., Pte. (2323), attested 29/8/16, died of enteritis 27/3/18.
SILVER, E., Pte. (2324), attested 29/8/16, S.N.L.R. 31/1/17.
SCHOLTZ, P., Pte. (2325), attested 30/8/16, demobilised 21/7/19.
VAN NIEKERK, A., Pte. (2326), attested 30/8/16, died of dysentery 12/1/18.
VAN REENEN, J. J., Pte. (2327), attested 30/8/16, demobilised 7/10/19, Lewis gunner.
TURNER, J., Pte. (2328), attested 28/8/16, demobilised 7/9/19.
BOOYSEN, W., Pte. (2329), attested 28/8/16, demobilised 12/7/19.
CAMPBELL, W., Pte. (2330), attested 28/8/16, released medically unfit 6/11/16.
BAILEY, F. J., Pte. (2331), attested 26/8/16, demobilised 6/1/19.
CHARLES, C., Pte. (2332), attested 26/8/16, released medically unfit 28/11/17.
ESAU, J., Pte. (2333), attested 24/8/16, released medically unfit 14/11/17.
ESAU, S., Pte. (2334), attested 24/8/16, released medically unfit 15/10/17.
JOSEPH, W., Pte. (2335), attested 29/8/16, demobilised 7/9/19.
JOHNSON, J. R., L./Cpl. (2336), attested 28/8/16, L./Cpl. 1/2/19, demobilised 18/10/19
MOUTON, D., Pte. (2337), attested 24/8/16, died of wounds 7/11/17.
MONTANUS, A., Pte. (2338), attested 28/8/16, demobilised 16/7/19.
SINDEN, H., Pte. (2339), attested 24/8/16, demobilised 7/9/19.
SMIT, W. J., Pte. (2340), attested 24/8/16, released medically unfit 14/2/17
STOFFBERG, I., Pte. (2341), attested 24/8/16, died of influenza 7/10/18.
TITUS, C., Pte. (2342), attested 26/8/16, demobilised 7/9/19.
ABRAHAMS, D., Pte. (2343), attested 31/8/16, released medically unfit 7/11/17.
APPOLLIS, A., Pte. (2344), attested 31/8/16, released medically unfit 15/1/17.
BRINKMAN, F., Pte. (2345), attested 31/8/16, demobilised 11/10/19, Lewis gunner, passed trench warfare and trench motar courses.
BREDA, P., Pte. (2346), attested 31/8/16, demobilised 28/8/19.
BUSH, R., Pte. (2347), attested 30/8/16, S.N.L.R. 12/7/18.
CARELSE, H., L./Cpl. (2348), attested 29/8/16, L./Cpl. 1/11/18, demobilised 8/9/19, 1st class signaller.
COFFIN, H., Pte. (2349), attested 31/8/16, demobilised 7/9/19.
CARSTEN, G., Pte. (2350), attested 31/8/16, released medically unfit 3/10/17.
DAVIDS, H., Pte. (2351), attested 29/8/16, S.N.L.R. 23/12/16.
DE VILLIERS, A., Pte. (2352), attested 29/8/16, demobilised 16/7/19, Lewis gunner.
DE VRIES, D., Pte. (2353), attested 30/8/16, demobilised 16/7/19.
EVERSON, F., Pte. (2354), attested 30/8/16, released medically unfit 6/10/16.
FORTUIN, J., Pte. (2355), attested 29/8/16, released medically unfit 19/8/18.
FARO, J., Pte. (2356), attested 29/8/16, released medically unfit 1/1/17.
FEBRUARY, W., Pte. (2357), attested 30/8/16, released medically unfit 22/8/17.
ABRAHAMS, W., Pte. (2358), attested 28/8/16, released medically unfit 3/8/18.
GERTZE, J., Pte. (2359), attested 29/8/16, released medically unfit 12/11/17.
GABRIELSE, B., Pte. (2360), attested 20/8/16, released medically unfit 13/11/17
HEUVEL, F., Pte. (2361), attested 31/8/16, demobilised 7/10/19.
HEYNEKE, S., Pte. (2362), attested 29/8/16, demobilised 28/8/19.
HAHMAN, D., Pte. (2363), attested 28/8/16, demobilised 16/7/19.
ISAACS, A., Pte. (2364), attested 30/8/16, demobilised 16/7/19.
JAGERS, P., Pte. (2365), attested 23/8/16, released medically unfit 8/7/18.
JACOBS, J., Pte. (2366), attested 31/8/16, released medically unfit 20/11/16.
MEYER, C., Pte. (2367), attested 31/8/16, released medically unfit 20/11/16.
NICHOLSON, E., Pte. (2368), attested 31/8/16, released medically unfit 21/7/18.
PHILANDER, A. W., Pte. (2369), attested 31/8/16, released medically unfit 30/6/18.
POOLE, D., Pte. (2370), attested 30/8/16, released medically unfit 20/11/17.
POOLE, W. M., Pte. (2371), attested 30/8/16, released medically unfit 16/8/17.
ABRAHAMS, J. A., Pte. (2372), attested 30/8/16, killed in action 6/11/17, machine gunner.
SCHEEPERS, G., Pte. (2373), attested 29/8/16, demobilised 28/8/19.
SYLVESTER, A., Pte. (2374), attested 30/8/16, released medically unfit 7/11/16.
SMIT, J., Pte. (2375), attested 29/8/16, released medically unfit 21/10/16.
STARK, H., Pte. (2376), attested 31/8/16, released medically unfit 26/9/17.
VAN REENEN, J., Pte. (2377), attested 31/8/16, released medically unfit 24/9/17.
WILLIAMS, C. J., Pte. (2378), attested 31/8/16, demobilised 7/10/19.
VAN DER WESTHUISEN, J., Pte. (2379), attested 29/8/16, demobilised 28/8/19
VAN ROY, J., Pte. (2380), attested 31/8/16, S.N.L.R. 11/2/18.
WOODING, D., Pte. (2381), attested 29/8/16, released medically unfit 5/10/19.
ABRAHAMS, J., Pte. (2382), attested 31/8/16, released medically unfit 13/8/17
YON, A., Pte. (2383), attested 31/8/16, demobilised 31/12/18.
DAVIDS, I., Pte. (2384), attested 30/8/16, released medically unfit 6/11/17
ARENDORF, A., Pte. (2385), attested 1/9/16, demobilised 21/7/19.
VALENTINE, J., Pte. (2386), attested 1/9/16, released medically unfit 31/1/17.
ABDULLA, A., Pte. (2387), attested 31/8/16, demobilised 11/7/19.
APPOLLIS, F., Pte. (2388), attested 1/9/16, demobilised 11/7/19.
CARELSE, A., Pte. (2389), attested 29/8/16, demobilised 29/8/19.
JULIE, M., Pte. (2390), attested 1/9/16, demobilised 15/1/19.
MALFENT, A., Pte. (2391), attested 31/8/16, released medically unfit 27/11/17.
MEYER, J., Pte. (2392), attested 1/9/16, released medically unfit 6/11/17.
RUTGERS, M., Pte. (2393), attested 1/9/16, demobilised 7/10/19, machine gunner.
SCHIPPERS, A., Pte. (2394), attested 31/8/16, demobilised 7/10/19.
LOUW, A., Pte. (2395), attested 2/9/16, released medically unfit 10/8/17.
VAN ROOYEN, J., Pte. (2396), attested 30/8/16, released medically unfit 13/9/17

LANGEVELDT, A., Pte. (2397), attested 29/8/16, released medically unfit 6/11/17.
CAMPHER, W. T., Pte. (2398), attested 29/8/16, released medically unfit 12/3/18.
CLASSEN, C., Pte. (2399), attested 29/8/16, demobilised 21/7/19.
HENDRICKS, P., Pte. (2400), attested 29/8/16, released medically unfit 17/11/16.
BLAUW, D., Pte. (2401), attested 29/8/16, released medically unfit 12/11/17.
PETERSEN, A., Pte. (2402), attested 29/8/16, released medically unfit 25/8/17.
ARIZON, J., Pte. (2403), attested 3/9/16, released medically unfit 16/8/17.
ABRAHAMS, D., Pte. (2404), attested 30/8/16, demobilised 7/9/19.
BAARTMAN, H., Pte. (2405), attested 30/8/16, demobilised 1/1/19.
IZAACS, J., Pte. (2406), attested 30/8/16, demobilised 22/7/19.
SALMONS, I., a/L./Cpl. (2407), attested 30/8/16, a/L./Cpl. 1/3/19, demobilised 21/7/19.
SWIGELAAR, F., Pte. (2408), attested 30/8/16, demobilised 7/9/19.
PEDRO, J., Pte. (2409), attested 29/8/16, demobilised 28/8/19.
ROBAIN, A., Pte. (2410), attested 2/9/16, released medically unfit 3/9/17.
PHILLIPS, M., Pte. (2411), attested 29/8/16, demobilised 10/4/20.
HENDRICKS, E., Pte. (2412), attested 1/9/16, released medically unfit 7/9/16.
APRIL, S., Pte. (2413), attested 2/9/16, released medically unfit 7/12/16.
KOOPMAN, F., Pte. (2414), attested 2/9/16, demobilised 6/10/19.
KATTS, T., Pte. (2415), attested 4/9/16, released medically unfit 5/11/18.
WILLIAMS, J. H., Pte. (2416), attested 4/9/16, Lewis gunner, died of pneumonia 3/10/18.
GLOVER, H., Pte. (2417), attested 4/9/16, demobilised 7/9/19.
ADONIS, J., Pte. (2418), attested 4/9/16, demobilised 15/1/19.
BUCKTON, P., Pte. (2419), attested 4/9/16, released medically unfit 3/11/16.
BAKER, E. W., Pte. (2420), attested 4/9/16, released medically unfit 4/10/16.
BREDEVELDT, H., Pte. (2421), attested 31/8/16, released medically unfit 30/11/17.
COX, H., Pte. (2422), attested 4/9/16, released medically unfit 29/8/17.
GREEN, J., Pte. (2423), attested 29/8/16, S.N.L.R. 11/2/18.
DAVIDS, S., Pte. (2424), attested 4/9/16, demobilised 7/10/19.
DELOW, A., Pte. (2425), attested 4/9/16, released medically unfit 16/11/17.
DANIELS, S., Pte. (2426), attested 4/9/16, released medically unfit 23/9/16.
HENDRICKS, G., Pte. (2427), attested 4/9/16, demobilised 10/2/19.
HENDRICKS, GIDEON, Pte. (2428), attested 4/9/16, released medically unfit 9/8/17.
ISAACS, I., Pte. (2429), attested 31/8/16, released medically unfit 31/8/17.
JACOBS, J., Pte. (2430), attested 4/9/16, S.N.L.R. 25/11/16.
JOHNSON, S., Pte. (2431), attested 4/9/16, died of dysentery 28/1/17.
JULIES, W., Pte. (2432), attested 4/9/16, died of malaria 16/3/17.
JASON, J. S., Pte. (2433), attested 4/9/16, released medically unfit 13/9/17.
JOHNSON, J., Pte. (2434), attested 4/9/16, accidentally killed 30/8/17.
LENDERS, H., Pte. (2435), attested 4/9/16, released medically unfit 26/9/17.
LODEWYKS, J., Pte. (2436), attested 4/9/16, demobilised 21/7/19.
LE FLEUR, I., Pte. (2437), attested 4/9/16, released medically unfit 31/8/17.
MEAS, D., Pte. (2438), attested 4/9/16, released medically unfit 12/10/17.
MANCHEST, A., Pte. (2439), attested 1/9/16, released medically unfit 20/3/17.
MILLER, A., Pte. (2440), attested 4/9/16, L./Cpl. 7/10/18, reverted to Pte. 7/2/19, demobilised 11/7/19, Lewis gunner.
MAARMAN, J. A., Pte. (2441), attested 31/8/16, released medically unfit 20/11/17.
PETERSEN, J., Pte. (2442), attested 4/9/16, released medicaly unfit 15/8/17.
PETERSEN, JOHN, Pte. (2443), attested 4/9/16, demobilised 7/10/19.
RHODA, A., Pte. (2444), attested 4/9/16, demobilised 15/1/19.
RICH, T., Pte. (2445), attested 4/9/16, released medically unfit 27/11/17.
STOLTENKAMP, J., Pte. (2446), attested 4/9/16, released medically unfit 15/8/17.
SOLOMON, C., Pte. (2447), attested 4/9/16, S.N.L.R. 22/7/17.
STONE, E., Pte. (2448), attested 4/9/16, demobilised 11/7/19, bootmaker.
STEWART, J. C., Pte. (2449), attested 4/9/16, released medically unfit 13/9/16.
VAN DER SCHYFF, C., Pte. (2450), attested 31/8/16, died of pneumonia 7/10/17.
VIGLAND, S., Pte. (2451), attested 1/9/16, demobilised 7/10/19.
WILLIAMS, J., Pte. (2452), attested 4/9/16, demobilised 6/10/19.
ABRAHAMS, T., Pte. (2453), attested 21/8/16, released medically unfit 20/7/17.
BEUKES, J., Pte. (2454), attested 31/8/16, demobilised 7/9/19.
BEUKES, R., Pte. (2455), attested 31/8/16, demobilised 21/7/19.
GAMBA, F., a/L./Cpl. (2456), attested 5/9/16, a/L./Cpl. 19/4/19, demobilised 21/7/19, signaller.
GOODMAN, J., Cpl. (2457), attested 5/9/16, a/L./Cpl. 21/11/17, a/Cpl. 19/10/18, Cpl. 1/11/18, demobilised 6/10/19.
HOLMES, J. C., Pte. (2458), attested 18/9/16, demobilised 11/7/19.
JOSEPH, A., Pte. (2459), attested 5/9/16, died of pneumonia 10/7/18.
JACK, M., Pte. (2460), attested 31/8/16, demobilised 7/9/19, signaller.
MORALLIE, F., Pte. (2461), attested 5/9/16, demobilised 8/9/19.
MANUELS, D., Pte. (2462), attested 5/9/16, released medically unfit 31/1/17.
MURPHY, J., Pte. (2463), attested 5/9/16, died of malaria 15/5/17.
MEINTJES, P., Pte. (2464), attested 5/9/16, died of dysentery 26/4/17.
ROELF, G., Pte. (2465), attested 5/9/16, released medically unfit 1/9/17.
SOLOMON, A., Pte. (2466), attested 4/9/16, demobilised 11/7/19, passed trench warfare and bombing courses.
SANDERSON, J. J., Pte. (2467), attested 5/9/16, S.N.L.R. 30/7/17.
WILLIAMS, C., Pte. (2468), attested 31/8/16, released medically unfit 1/9/17.
WHITE, J., Pte. (2469), attested 5/9/16, released medically unfit 27/11/18.
WILLIAMS, L., Pte. (2470), attested 5/9/16, died, mauled by lion 22/8/17.
VAN STEER, T., Pte. (2471), attested 5/9/16, demobilised 31/12/19.
WILLIAMS, P., Pte. (2472), attested 5/9/16, demobilised 11/7/19.
AFRICA, J., Pte. (2473), attested 1/9/16, released medically unfit 3/12/17.
BOESAAK, K., Pte. (2474), attested 1/9/16, demobilised 7/9/19.
CLOETE, A., Pte. (2475), attested 1/9/16, demobilised 21/7/19.
DANIELS, F., Pte. (2476), attested 1/9/16, released medically unfit 25/8/17.
HOPLEY, J., Pte. (2477), attested 1/9/16, demobilised 16/7/19.
HANS, P., Pte. (2478), attested 1/9/16, demobilised 8/9/19.
KNOLL, L., Pte. (2479), attested 1/9/16, demobilised 18/8/19.
KAPOT, T., Pte. (2480), attested 1/9/16, demobilised 8/9/19.
KING, P., Pte. (2481), attested 1/9/16, demobilised 8/9/19.
MOSES, F., Pte. (2482), attested 1/9/16, released medically unfit 16/7/18.
MARTIN, H., L./Sgt. (2483), attested 1/9/16, L./Cpl. 4/8/18, Cpl. 21/9/18, a/Sgt. 7/10/18, L./Sgt. 1/11/18, demobilised 8/9/19, passed physical and bayonet course.

PHILIPS, C., Pte. (2484), attestd 1/9/16, demobilised 16/7/19.
TALLIARD, P., Pte. (2485), attested 1/9/16, released medically unfit 3/10/17.
VAN REYNGAARD, M., Pte. (2486), attested 1/9/16, S.N.L.R. 24/2/18.
SWARTZ, M., Pte. (2487), attested 1/9/16, demobilised 1/11/19.
VAN DER HEYDEN, A., Pte. (2488), attested 1/9/16, released medically unfit 16/11/17.
VAN RHEEDE, T., Pte. (2489), attested 1/9/16, died of dysentery 5/5/17.
WAGNER, C., Pte. (2490), attested 1/9/16, demobilised 7/9/19.
BARON, H., Pte. (2491), attested 6/9/16, released medically unfit 16/11/16.
CHRISTIAN, D., Pte. (2492), attested 6/9/16, died of malaria 4/12/16.
McKAY, W., Pte. (2493), attested 6/9/16, demobilised 27/8/19.
SLINGER, C., Pte. (2494), attested 6/9/16, released medically unfit 20/10/16.
WILLIAMS, D., Pte. (2495), attested 6/9/16, released medically unfit 15/5/17.
FYFER, J. H., Pte. (2496), attested 5/9/16, released medically unfit 15/11/16.
PRETORIUS, G., Pte. (2497), attested 5/9/16, released medically unfit 15/11/16.
VAN STEER, J., Pte. (2498), attested 7/9/16, released medically unfit 16/10/16.
TROMP, A., Pte. (2499), attested 5/9/16, demobilised 7/9/19.
STEENBERG, A., Pte. (2500), attested 5/9/16, released medically unfit 16/9/16.
DAWSON, W., Pte. (2501), attested 5/0/16, released medically unfit 14/11/17.
RHODA, J., Pte. (2502), attested 11/9/16, demobilised 16/10/19.
WITBOOI, J., Pte. (2503), attested 5/9/16, demobilised 11/7/19.
FILLIES, J., Sgt. (2504), attested 11/9/16, L./Cpl. 5/1/17, Cpl. 5/7/17, Sgt. 1/11/18, demobilised 7/9/19.
BOOYSEN, T., Pte. (2505), attested 7/9/16, released medically unfit 15/1/17.
FILLIES, H., Pte. (2506), attested 11/9/16, demobilised 7/9/19.
HESS, G., Pte. (2507), attested 11/9/16, released medically unfit 3/10/17.
MOSES, J., Pte. (2508), attested 11/9/16, died of typhoid 26/8/18.
MOSES, W., Pte. (2509), attested 11/9/16, demobilised 7/9/19.
MEYER, G., Pte. (2510), attested 11/9/16, released medically unfit 20/11/17.
MOSES, J., Pte. (2511), attested 11/9/16, demobilised 7/9/19.
PRICE, D., Pte. (2512), attested 11/9/16, released medically unfit 29/9/16.
SOLOMONS, J., Pte. (2513), attested 13/9/16, released medically unfit 8/8/17.
DANIELS, T., Pte. (2514), attested 14/9/16, released medically unfit 30/12/18.
TIPPENS, A., Pte. (2515), attested 14/9/16, released medically unfit 20/11/17.
WATMAN, J. A., Pte. (2516), attested 14/9/16, released medically unfit 22/9/16.
McKERIL, D., Pte. (2517), attested 14/9/16, S.N.L.R. 10/8/17.
JAMES, W., Pte. (2518), attested 14/9/16, released medically unfit 8/8/17.
AFRICA, G., Pte. (2519), attested 14/9/16, released medically unfit 16/10/16.
VAN SCHALDER, H. C., Pte. (2520), attested 14/9/16, released medically unfit 14/8/17.
KOCKS, J., Pte. (2521), attested 14/9/16, demobilised 11/7/19.
JOHNSON, J., Pte. (2522), attested 14/9/16, released medically unfit 31/8/17, transport driver
FELIX, J., Pte. (2523), attested 14/9/16, demobilised 31/12/19, Lewis gunner.
JANTJES, A., a/L./Cpl. (2524), attested 14/9/16, a/L./Cpl. 1/3/19, demobilised 11/7/19.
WITBOOI, P., Pte. (2525), attested 14/9/16, demobilised 15/1/19.
PETERSEN, A. E., Pte. (2526), attested 14/9/16, died of pneumonia 4/7/17.
ANDREWS, M., Pte. (2527), attested 14/9/16, released medically unfit 18/10/17.
VAN BLERK, J., Pte. (2528), attested 15/9/16, released medically unfit 6/11/17
VAN WYK, W., Pte. (2529), attested 15/9/16, demobilised 2/1/19.
ADONIS, W., Pte. (2530), attested 15/9/16, released medically unfit 3/12/17.
CLAYTON, P., Pte. (2531), attested 15/9/16, demobilised 21/7/19.
CREUR, J., Pte. (2532), attested 14/9/16, released medically unfit 6/11/17.
DAVIDS, J., Pte. (2533), attested 15/9/16, released medically unfit 8/9/18.
DU PREEZ, J., Pte. (2534), attested 14/9/16, died of pneumonia 3/6/17.
DU SART, G., Pte. (2535), attested 15/9/16, demobilised 7/9/19, passed scout and sniping course.
DAVIS, P., Pte. (2536), attested 14/9/16, demobilised 11/7/19.
FREEMAN, B., Pte. (2537), attested 15/9/16, demobilised 10/4/20.
GROENEWALD, D., Pte. (2538), attested 15/9/16, released medically unfit 27/5/18.
GRAY, C., L./Sgt. (2539), attested 15/9/16, Cpl. 5/7/18, L./Sgt. 1/11/18, demobilised 10/10/19.
JACOBS, D., Pte. (2540), attested 14/9/16, demobilised 7/10/19.
THOMASO, H., Pte. (2541), attested 14/9/16, released medically unfit 7/12/16.
BRILL, C., Pte. (2542), attested 15/9/16, released medically unfit 12/11/17.
JANUARY, A., Pte. (2543), attested 15/9/16, released medically unfit 29/10/17.
LYNERS, P., Pte. (2544), attested 15/9/16, released medically unfit 25/8/17.
THOMAS, E., Pte. (2545), attested 15/9/16, released medically unfit 8/8/17.
ADAMS, J., Pte. (2546), attested 15/9/16, released medically unfit 21/10/16.
CYSTER, H., Pte. (2547), attested 15/9/16, released medically unfit 12/1/18.
JACK, M., Pte. (2548), attested 16/9/16, demobilised 1/11/19.
SMITH, W. F., Sgt. (2549), attested 16/9/16, Sgt 15/10/17, a/C.Q.M.S. 15/10/18, Sgt. 12/12/18, demobilised 1/11/19.
AMOS, J., Pte. (2550), attested 8/9/16, demobilised 28/8/19.
EZAU, C., Pte. (2551), attested 8/9/16, demobilised 28/8/19.
FRANZ, Z., Pte. (2552), attested 8/9/16, killed in action 20/1/17.
KELLY, A., Pte. (2553), attested 8/9/16, demobilised 7/9/19.
ADAMS, P., Pte. (2554), attested 18/9/16, released medically unfit 20/7/17
ABRAHAMS, J., Pte. (2555), attested 18/9/16, released medically unfit 7/11/17
ADAMS, A., Pte. (2556), attested 18/9/16, demobilised 26/12/18.
ABRAHAMS, F., Pte. (2557), attested 18/9/16, demobilised 11/7/19.
BLAUW, M., Pte. (2558), attested 18/9/16, released medically unfit 31/1/18.
BULL, J., Pte. (2559), attested 18/9/16, demobilised 10/10/19, bugler.
DE BRUYNS, A., Pte. (2560), attested 18/9/16, demobilised 11/7/19.
ERASMUS, W., Pte. (2561), attested 15/9/16, released medically unfit 10/8/17.
FISHER, C., Pte. (2562), attested 15/9/16, released medically unfit 13/9/17.
FESTER, W., Pte. (2563), attested 18/9/16, released medically unfit 2/11/17
FARO, J., Pte. (2564), attested 18/9/16, demobilised 16/7/19, chauffeur.
FENTON, T., Pte. (2565), attested 15/9/16, released medically unfit 8/8/17.
GALLANT, G., Pte. (2566), attested 18/9/16, demobilised 21/7/19
GOLDING, J., Pte. (2567), attested 18/9/16, demobilised 16/7/19, tailor.
GILL, A., Pte. (2568), attested 18/9/16, released medically unfit 20/9/16.
HENDRICKS, J., Pte. (2569), attested 16/9/16, demobilised 7/10/19.
HIGGINS, J., Pte. (2570), attested 18/9/16, released medically unfit 15/8/17.
HARVEY, A., Pte. (2571), attested 18/9/16, released medically unfit 27/4/18.
INGRAM, J., Pte. (2572), attested 15/9/16, released medically unfit 11/8/17.
JONES, W., Pte. (2573), attested 18/9/16, released medically unfit 19/5/17.

THE STORY OF THE 1st CAPE CORPS.

JORDAAN, C., Cpl. (2574), attested 15/9/16, Cpl. 1/3/17, released medically unfit 24/2/18.
KING, J., Pte. (2575), attested 18/9/16, died of blackwater 16/1/18
LOUW, W., Pte. (2576), attested 18/9/16, demobilised 7/9/19.
LEWIS, J., Pte. (2577), attested 18/9/16, released medically unfit 12/12/16.
LE ROUX, J., Pte. (2578), attested 15/9/16, released medically unfit 20/10/16.
LEFRE, L., Pte. (2579), attested 15/9/16, demobilised 7/9/19.
MATTHEWS, N., Pte. (2580), attested 18/9/16, S.N.L.R. 25/11/16.
MARINES, J., Pte. (2581), attested 18/9/16, demobilised 2/1/19.
MISSELBROOK, F., Pte. (2582), attested 15/9/16, demobilised 7/9/19.
NOAH, R. Pte. (2583), attested 15/9/16, demobilised 31/12/19, qualified 1st class signaller.
PRINCE, J., Pte. (2584), attested 18/9/16, demobilised 24/1/19.
PIENAAR, F., Pte. (2585), attested 18/9/16, demobilised 11/7/19.
POTTS, J., Pte. (2586), attested 15/9/16, released medically unfit 13/9/17.
PETERSEN, K., Pte. (2587), attested 15/9/16, released medically unfit 11/8/17.
RICHARDSON, J., Pte. (2588), attested 18/9/16, demobilised 15/10/18.
KUITERS, W., Pte. (2589), attested 15/9/16, died of dysentery 8/6/17.
STEYNER, F., Cpl. (2590), attested 18/9/16, a/Cpl. 5/7/18, Cpl. 1/11/18, demobilised 7/9/19.
STEVENS, W., Pte. (2591), attested 18/9/16, released medically unfit 13/9/17.
STEPHENS, P. D., L./Cpl. (2592), attested 15/9/16, L./Cpl. 15/10/17, released medically unfit 1/7/18
SILVER, J., Pte. (2593), attested 18/9/16, released medically unfit 22/11/16.
WILLIS, C., Pte. (2594), attested 15/9/16, released medically unfit 6/11/17.
WILLIAMS, J., Pte. (2595), attested 15/9/16, demobilised 21/7/19.
ADAMS, P., Pte. (2596), attested 16/9/16, released medically unfit 11/4/18.
ADAMS, P., Pte. (2597), attested 19/9/16, released medically unfit 31/1/17.
BESTER, J., Pte. (2598), attested 17/9/16, released medically unfit 11/7/19.
BODDINGTON, R., Pte. (2599), attested 17/9/16, released medically unfit 18/11/16
BRITZ, A., Pte. (2600), attested 16/9/16, released medically unfit 12/11/17.
CREWE, S., Pte. (2601), attested 14/9/16, released medically unfit 7/11/17.
DANIELS, W., Pte. (2602), attested 19/9/16, demobilised 13/11/19.
DANIELS, J., Pte. (2603), attested 17/9/16, released medically unfit 25/1/18.
DANIELS, J. A., Pte. (2604), attested 14/9/16, demobilised 22/7/19.
EMMENS, T., Pte. (2605), attested 14/9/16, demobilised 11/7/19.
FILLIES, J., Pte. (2606), attested 16/9/16, died of influenza 10/10/18.
FREDERICKS, C., Pte. (2607), attested 19/9/16, released medically unfit 21/7/18.
FORTUIN, A., Pte. (2608), attested 16/9/16, demobilised 31/12/19.
FRITZ, L., Pte. (2609), attested 14/9/16, demobilised 1/1/19.
HANEKOM, J., Pte. (2610), attested 17/9/16, released medically unfit 13/4/17.
HARVEY, R., Pte. (2611), attested 25/9/16, S.N.L.R. 24/10/18.
HARTNICK, G., Pte. (2612), attested 16/9/16, released medically unfit 24/9/17.
JULIES, S., Pte. (2613), attested 16/9/16, released medically unfit 15/10/17.
JULIES, J., L./Cpl. (2614), attested 17/9/16, L./Cpl. 1/3/19, demobilised 17/6/19.
LOSPER, F., Pte. (2615), attested 17/9/16, died of nephritis 8/7/17.
McHALON, F., Pte. (2616), attested 19/9/16, released medically unfit 13/9/17.
PAULSE, T., Pte. (2617), attested 16/9/16, released medically unfit 19/10/16.
REID, A., Pte. (2618), attested 14/9/16, demobilised 8/4/19.
ROSS, J. I., Sgt. (2619), attested 19/9/16, Cpl. 23/3/17, a/Sgt. 21/11/17, Sgt. 1/4/18, died of wounds 20/9/18, passed physical and bayonet course.
SKIPPERS, A., Pte. (2620), attested 19/9/16, demobilised 11/7/19.
SMIT, H., Pte. (2621), attested 16/9/16, released medically unfit 3/9/17.
SAMUELS, J., Pte. (2622), attested 19/9/16, demobilised 8/9/19.
SMITH, W., Pte. (2623), attested 19/9/16, released medically unfit 7/11/17.
VAN GRAAN, M., Pte. (2624), attested 17/9/16, released medically unfit 15/8/17.
VAN WYK, H., Pte. (2625), attested 19/9/16, released medically unfit 24/9/17.
VISSER, H., Pte. (2626), attested 19/9/16, released medically unfit 25/5/18.
VAN DER WESTHUIS, T., Pte. (2627), attested 18/9/16, demobilised 11/7/19.
ADAMS, F., Pte. (2628), attested 18/9/16, released medically unfit 26/2/17.
ADAMS, M., Pte. (2629), attested 19/9/16, demobilised 7/9/19.
CUPIDO, H., Pte. (2630), attested 19/9/16, demobilised 5/1/19.
COLLISON, D., Pte. (2631), attested 19/9/16, released medically unfit 24/7/17.
COMBRINK, J., Pte. (2632), attested 19/9/16, released medically unfit 26/9/18.
FAROA, D., Pte. (2633), attested 18/9/16, demobilised 15/7/19.
HECTOR, P., Pte. (2634), attested 19/9/16, demobilised 21/7/19.
JACOBS, A., Pte. (2635), attested 19/9/16, released medically unfit 24/7/18.
KING, J., Pte. (2636), attested 19/9/16, released medically unfit 7/11/17.
LOUW, J., Pte. (2637), attested 18/9/16, released medically unfit 16/11/17.
LESAR, A., Pte. (2638), attested 18/9/16, released medically unfit 28/11/17.
RICKETTS, C. H., Pte. (2639), attested 18/9/16, released medically unfit 26/10/16.
SOLOMON, F. C., Pte. (2640), attested 18/9/16, released medically unfit 20/11/16.
JACOBS, N., Pte. (2641), attested 14/9/16, released medically unfit 3/12/17.
ARRIES, T., Pte. (2642), attested 14/9/16, released medically unfit 27/12/18.
ANDERSON, D., Pte. (2643), attested 20/9/16, released medically unfit 3/10/17.
BAATJES, M., Pte. (2644), attested 19/9/16, died 21/10/18.
JOHANNES, S., Pte. (2645), attested 20/9/16, released medically unfit 31/8/17.
PEASE, J. C., Pte. (2646), attested 19/9/16, released medically unfit 7/11/16.
PAPAYANI, C., Staff Sgt. (2647), attested 20/9/16, Staff Sgt. 20/9/16, released medically unfit 23/6/17, European personnel.
DAVIES, T., Pte. (2648), attested 19/9/16, released medically unfit 31/1/17.
JANUARY, H., Pte. (2649), attested 19/9/16, released medically unfit 27/7/17.
JAANTJES, M., Pte. (2650), attested 19/9/16, demobilised 7/9/19.
JAFTHA, J., Pte. (2651), attested 19/9/16, released medically unfit 21/10/16
OERSON, C. Pte. (2552), attested 20/9/16, demobilised 16/7/19.
ABRAHAMS, P., Pte. (2653), attested 21/9/16, demobilised 11/7/19.
PETERSEN, I., Pte. (2654), attested 20/9/16, demobilised 8/9/19.
RIZANT, E., a/Cpl. (2655), attested 19/9/16, a/Cpl. 1/2/17, S.N.L.R. 14/6/18.
ROBERTS, M., Pte. (2656), attested 18/9/16, died of dysentery at sea 28/3/17.
SAFIERS, S., Pte. (2657), attested 20/9/16, demobilised 8/9/19.
WILLIAMS, G., Pte. (2658), attested 16/9/16, demobilised 21/7/19, passed scout and sniping course.
CHRISTIANS, J., Pte. (2659), attested 21/9/16, released medically unfit 31/8/17.
CONRADIE, J., Pte. (2660), attested 21/9/16, released medically unfit 8/2/18.
DOUGLAS, P., Pte. (2661), attested 18/9/16, released medically unfit 21/12/16.
FISHER, M., Pte. (2662), attested 21/9/16, released medically unfit 7/11/17.

THE STORY OF THE 1st CAPE CORPS.

HERMAN, A., Pte. (2663), attested 20/9/16, released medically unfit 23/10/16.
KORREMAN, A., Pte. (2664), attested 21/9/16, demobilised 5/1/19.
LIEDEMAN, J., Pte. (2665), attested 21/9/16, found dead on railway line at Woltemade, Cape, 21/7/17
LIVERS, J. A., Cpl. (2666), attested 19/9/16, Cpl. 15/10/17, demobilised 21/7/19, pioneer.
MILLER, P., Pte. (2667), attested 21/9/16, released medically unfit 28/9/16.
MITCHELL, W., Pte. (2668), attested 21/9/16, released medically unfit 6/11/17.
MULLER, J., Pte. (2669), attested 18/9/16, demobilised 25/12/18.
PETERS, G., Pte. (2670), attested 16/9/16, released medically unfit 3/10/17.
PAULSEN, D., Pte. (2671), attested 21/9/16, released medically unfit 31/1/17.
ROODER, J., Pte. (2672), attested 20/9/16, released medically unfit 6/11/17.
SAMPSON, J. V. C., Pte. (2673), attested 19/9/16, released medically unfit 20/7/17
VAN DYKE, A., Pte. (2674), attested 18/9/16, released medically unfit 5/2/17.
VAN DYKE, R., Pte. (2675), attested 18/9/16, released medically unfit 1/12/16.
HENDRICKS, D., Pte. (2676), attested 22/9/16, released medically unfit 15/12/16.
MILLER, A., Pte. (2677), attested 21/9/16, demobilised 10/12/19.
NORRIS, A., Pte. (2678), attested 22/9/16, demobilised 11/7/19.
SYLVESTER, L., Pte. (2679), attested 21/9/16, demobilised 1/1/19.
VAN NIEKERK, F., Pte. (2680), attested 21/9/16, demobilised 7/10/19, Lewis gunner.
WILLIAMS, C., Pte. (2681), attested 22/9/16, released medically unfit 13/8/17.
BARDIEN, T., Pte. (2682), attested 20/9/16, released medically unfit 20/10/16.
BAILEY, P., Pte. (2683), attested 20/9/16, released medically unfit 16/11/17.
BOEZAK, J., Pte. (2684), attested 20/9/16, released medically unfit 7/6/18.
CEDRASS, R., Pte. (2685), attested 20/9/16, demobilised 30/8/19.
CUYLER, P., Pte. (2686), attested 20/9/16, released medically unfit 29/10/17.
DANIELS, C., Pte. (2687), attested 20/9/16, released medically unfit 29/10/17
DU PLESSIS, M., Pte. (2688), attested 20/9/16, died of malaria 4/1/17.
FORBES, D., Pte. (2689), attested 20/9/16, demobilised 21/7/19.
FIFE, J., Pte. (2690), attested 20/9/16, demobilised 8/9/19.
FORBES, D., Pte. (2691), attested 19/9/16, released medically unfit 25/8/17.
HORN, J., Pte. (2692), attested 20/9/16, released medically unfit 16/11/17.
LANGEVELDT, H., Pte. (2693), attested 20/9/16, released medically unfit 17/10/16.
LANGEVELDT, J., Pte. (2694), attested 20/9/16, S.N.L.R. 16/2/18.
PETERSEN, H., Pte. (2695), attested 20/9/16, released medically unfit 27/7/17.
PETRUS, M., Pte. (2696), attested 19/9/16, demobilised 1/1/19.
PEARCE, A., Pte. (2697), attested 20/9/16, demobilised 11/7/19.
ROMAN, C., Pte. (2698), attested 20/9/16, released medically unfit 6/9/17.
ROBENHEIMER, W., a/Sgt. (2699), attested 18/9/16, Cpl. 1/3/17, a/Sgt. 26/6/17, Sgt. 29/6/17, reverted to Cpl. 9/7/17, a/Sgt. 1/8/19, demobilised 7/9/19.
VAN RENSBURG, M., Pte. (2700), attested 20/9/16, released medically unfit 15/11/16.
KARELSE, J., Pte. (2701), attested 23/9/16, released medically unfit 26/9/16.
MOWRIES, J., Pte. (2702), attested 21/9/16, released medically unfit 12/11/17.
BIRD, E., Pte. (2703), attested 22/9/16, rejected 22/9/16.
CLARKE, F., Pte. (2704), attested 23/9/16, released medically unfit 15/1/19.
FRANCE, H., Pte. (2705), attested 23/9/16, demobilised 11/7/19, complimented by G.O.C., Palestine, for act of gallantry in trying to save a comrade from drowning in sea at Gaza
BOWMAN, J., Pte. (2706), attested 22/9/16, demobilised 4/11/20.
BAILEY, J., Pte. (2707), attested 20/9/16, demobilised 7/10/19.
DUNN, T., Pte. (2708), attested 20/9/16, demobilised 23/7/19, pioneer.
DIAS, S. Pte. (2709), attested 18/9/16, demobilised 26/8/19.
ALIAS, D., Pte. (2710), released medically unfit 13/8/17.
AFRICANDER, A., Pte. (2711), attested 25/9/16, released medically unfit 10/10/16.
BENJAMIN, M., Pte. (2712), attested 25/9/16, released medically unfit 24/7/17.
BROWN, A., Pte. (2713), attested 25/9/16, demobilised 16/7/19, drum and fife band.
FREDERICKS, W., Pte. (2714), attested 25/9/16, demobilised 27/8/19.
GALLANT, M. J., Pte. (2715), attested 18/9/16, demobilised 8/9/19, passed scout and sniping course.
GOLIATH, J., Pte. (2716), attested 18/9/16, demobilised 21/7/19.
GERTZE, C., Pte. (2717), released medically unfit 28/2/18.
HENDRICKS, J., Pte. (2718), attested 25/9/16, released medically unfit 13/10/17
JULIUS, D., Pte. (2719), attested 25/9/16, demobilised 11/7/19.
JOHNSON, F., Pte. (2720), attested 25/9/16, demobilised 7/10/19
JACOBS, S., Pte. (2721), attested 25/9/16, demobilised 7/10/19, qualified signaller.
JALES, C. J., Pte. (2722), attested 25/9/16, released medically unfit 31/1/18.
KELLY, J., Pte. (2723), attested 25/9/16, released medically unfit 9/3/17.
KING, H., Pte. (2724), attested 25/9/16, released medically unfit 3/10/17.
MEYER, G., Pte. (2725), attested 25/9/16, S.N.L.R. 24/12/16.
OCTOBER, J., Pte. (2726), attested 25/9/16, released medically unfit 8/2/18.
OLKERS, I., Pte. (2727), attested 22/9/16, released medically unfit 8/7/17.
OELSON, D., Pte. (2728), attested 22/9/16, released medically unfit 24/5/18.
POTGIETER, J., Pte. (2729), attested 25/9/16, demobilised 7/9/19.
PAULSE, F., Pte. (2730), attested 25/9/16, demobilised 1/1/19.
VAN ROMBERG, P., Pte. (2731), attested 25/9/16, demobilised 11/1/19.
ROODT, C. M., Pte. (2732), attested 25/9/16, released medically unfit 7/11/17.
SKEDOW, D., Pte. (2733), attested 25/9/16, demobilised 21/7/19.
SOLOMON, C., Pte. (2734), attested 25/9/16, killed in action 20/9/18.
SIMONS, S., Pte. (2735), attested 25/9/16, demobilised 13/1/19
TIPPENS, M. D., Pte. (2736), attested 25/9/16, released medically unfit 19/2/17
VALLEY, A. H., Pte. (2737), attested 25/9/16, released medically unfit 26/3/17.
WILLIAMS, E., Pte. (2738), attested 25/9/16, released medically unfit 16/11/17.
CARSTEN, V., Pte. (2739), attested 30/9/16, demobilised 8/9/19.
CAROLUS, C., Pte. (2740), attested 23/9/16, released medically unfit 18/8/17.
DAMMONSE, C., Pte (2741), attested 25/9/16, demobilised 11/7/19.
DENNIS, E., Pte. (2742), attested 23/9/16, released medically unfit 21/8/17, transport driver
DREYER, P., Pte. (2743), attested 24/9/16, demobilised 11/7/19.
GIDEONS, L., Pte. (2744), attested 25/9/16, released medically unfit 9/10/16.
HAYNES, H., Pte. (2745), attested 25/9/16, demobilised 21/7/19.
JACOBS, J., Pte. (2746), attested 25/9/16, demobilised 5/2/19.
KANNEMEYER, M., Pte. (2747), attested 23/9/16, released medically unfit 30/9/16.
LIBERTY, P., Pte. (2748), attested 23/9/16, demobilised 16/7/19.
McKAY, A., Pte. (2749), attested 25/9/16, released medically unfit 24/9/17.
MORTAR, J. D., Pte. (2750), attested 25/9/16, released medically unfit 12/11/17.
RHAGOSIN, M., Pte. (2751), attested 23/9/16, released medically unfit 19/12/18.

SAMUELS, S., Pte. (2752), attested 25/9/16, released medically unfit 20/11/17.
SKIPPERS, S., Pte. (2753), attested 25/9/16, rejected 25/9/16.
SNYERS, J., Pte. (2754), attested 25/9/16, S.N.L.R. 1/1/18.
VAN DER HORST, A., Pte. (2755), attested 25/9/16, released medically unfit 29/8/17.
VAN AARDE, J., Pte. (2756), attested 25/9/16, released medically unfit 21/10/16.
WEBBER, W., Pte. (2757), attested 25/9/16 released medically unfit 21/10/16.
WEBBER, E., Pte. (2758), attested 25/9/16, released medically unfit 21/10/16.
ABRAHAMS, M., Pte. (2759), attested 18/9/16, released medically unfit 26/1/17.
BEZUIDENHOUT, F., Pte. (2760), attested 18/9/16, released medically unfit 31/7/17.
DOE, L., Pte. (2761), attested 26/9/16, demobilised 7/9/19.
GAMBA, I. P., Pte. (2762), attested 25/9/16, released medically unfit 28/11/17.
GEDULD, J., Pte. (2763), attested 18/9/16, killed in action 20/1/17.
HERADIEN, L., Pte. (2764), attested 22/9/16, demobilised 7/9/19.
HERADIEN, J., Pte. (2765), attested 18/9/16, demobilised 3/4/19.
HERADIEN, L., Pte. (2766), attested 22/9/16, died of malaria 18/5/17.
JACOBS, J., Pte. (2767), attested 26/9/16, released medically unfit 28/9/17.
MAY, C., Pte. (2768), attested 18/9/16, released medically unfit 29/11/16.
SEPTEMBER, J., Pte. (2769), attested 26/9/16, released medically unfit 12/11/17.
SMITH, D., Pte. (2770), attested 26/9/16, died of malaria 9/5/17.
SAMUELS, C., Pte. (2771), attested 26/9/16, demobilised 11/7/19.
VISSER, W., Pte. (2772), attested 26/9/16, released medically unfit 10/6/17.
WALKER, W., Pte. (2773), attested 18/9/16, demobilised 16/7/19.
ANDREWS, F. K., Pte. (2774), attested 27/9/16, demobilised 31/12/18.
BEZUIDENHOUT, E., Sgt. (2775), attested 25/9/16, Cpl. 1/4/17, Sgt. 24/6/17, demobilised 7/9/19.
DAVIDS, S., Pte. (2776), attested 27/9/16, released medically unfit 3/12/17.
FRANCE, G., Pte. (2777), attested 27/9/16, released medically unfit 13/9/17.
HOSKINS, G., Pte. (2778), attested 27/9/16, demobilised 11/7/19.
JANSEN, A., Pte. (2779), attested 25/9/16, demobilised 1/1/19.
JONES, J., Pte. (2780), attested 27/9/16, demobilised 21/7/19.
KAMPHER, K., Pte. (2781), attested 25/9/16, demobilised 1/1/19.
KLUE, N., Pte. (2782), attested 25/9/16, released medically unfit 12/11/17.
MAREE, J. G., Pte. (2783), attested 23/9/16, released medically unfit 10/8/17.
MEYER, I., Pte. (2784), attested 27/9/16, released medically unfit 20/8/18.
MANNOW, M., Pte. (2785), attested 27/9/16, released medically unfit 29/6/17.
MALAN, J., Pte. (2786), attested 27/9/16, released medically unfit 18/8/17.
MURRAY, J., Pte. (2787), attested 27/9/16, released medically unfit 7/6/17.
MAREE, H., Pte. (2788), attested 27/9/16, released medically unfit 13/9/17.
PRITCHETT, G., Pte. (2789), attested 27/9/16, released medically unfit 22/11/16.
PAULSE, C., Pte. (2790), attested 27/9/16, released medically unfit 5/10/16.
PETERSEN, C., Pte. (2791), attested 27/9/16, demobilised 30/12/18.
SIMMONDS, B., Pte. (2792), attested 27/9/16, released medically unfit 28/5/17.
RUITERS, J., Pte. (2793), attested 23/9/16, released medically unfit 3/12/17.
BAARTMAN, D., Pte. (2794), attested 25/9/16, released medically unfit 14/2/17.
EXFORD, J., Pte. (2795), attested 25/9/16, released medically unfit 15/10/16.
HUTCHINSON, W. (D.C.M.), a/Cpl. (2796), attested 24/9/16, L./Cpl. 24/6/17, a/Cpl. 1/2/19, demobilised 7/9/19, Lewis gunner.
KOK, G., Pte. (2797), attested 25/9/16, released medically unfit 6/11/16.
JANSEN, W., Pte. (2798), attested 25/9/16, demobilised 7/9/19.
KYNOCK, T., Pte. (2799), attested 22/9/16, released medically unfit 27/11/17.
KIRK, J., L./Cpl. (2800), attested 19/9/16, L./Cpl. 1/4/18, demobilised 7/9/19, passed bombing and trench warfare courses.
LANDMAN, D., Pte. (2801), attested 25/9/16, released medically unfit 28/10/16.
ROWLAND, H., Pte. (2802), attested 25/9/16, released medically unfit 20/10/17.
SAMPSON, H., Pte. (2803), attested 25/9/16, demobilised 7/9/19.
STUURMAN, M., Pte. (2804), attested 19/9/16, demobilised 21/7/19.
WILLIAMS, B., Pte. (2805), attested 25/9/16, released medically unfit 19/2/17.
ENGELBRECHT, S., Pte. (2806), attested 29/9/16, released medically unfit 24/7/17.
HOSWELL, C., Pte. (2807), attested 28/9/16, released medically unfit 11/11/16.
PHILLIPS, B., Pte. (2808), attested 28/9/16, released medically unfit 25/7/17.
THOMASSO, T., Pte. (2809), attested 28/9/16, demobilised 7/10/19.
WALDUCK, R. W., Pte. (2810), attested 28/9/16, released medically unfit 1/3/18.
BREAKWELL, P., Pte. (2811), attested 25/9/16, released medically unfit 7/11/16.
CLARKE, B., Pte. (2812), attested 28/9/16, demobilised 11/7/19.
DU PREEZ, D., Pte. (2813), attested 28/9/16, demobilised 11/7/19, passed trench warfare and bombing course.
LOMBARD, C., Pte. (2814), attested 25/9/16, released medically unfit 6/11/17.
LOMBARD, J. L., Pte. (2815), attested 26/9/16, released medically unfit 24/9/17.
VOLLENHOVEN, E., Pte. (2816), attested 29/9/16, released medically unfit 17/11/16.
ADONIS, J., Pte. (2817), attested 30/9/16, S.N.L.R. 25/11/16.
ADAMS, J., Pte. (2818), attested 28/9/16, released medically unfit 17/11/16.
BOWERS, J., Pte. (2819), attested 25/9/16, demobilised 22/7/19.
BRUCE, J., Pte. (2820), attested 26/9/16, demobilised 22/7/19.
CLOETE, J., Pte. (2821), attested 25/9/16, released medically unfit 10/9/17.
CHIPPENDALE, H., Pte. (2822), attested 25/9/16, released medically unfit 22/6/17.
CLOETE, J., Pte. (2823), attested 25/9/16, released medically unfit 3/10/17.
CREWE, J., Pte. (2824), attested 26/9/16, released medically unfit 12/8/17.
CLOETE, P., Pte. (2825), attested 26/9/16, released medically unfit 30/8/17.
DE JONGH, A., Pte. (2826), attested 26/9/16, demobilised 9/10/19.
DIXON, J., Pte. (2827), attested 26/9/16, demobilised 22/7/19, transport driver.
DAMONS, J., Pte. (2828), attested 27/9/16, released medically unfit 15/10/17.
DUNBAR, W., Pte. (2829), attested 25/9/16, demobilised 21/7/19.
DE JONGH, H., Pte. (2830), attested 26/9/16, released medically unfit 16/11/17.
HAYES, H., Pte. (2831), attested 25/9/16, released medically unfit 12/11/17.
HERNE, A., Pte. (2832), attested 25/9/16, demobilised 22/7/19.
HAYES, J., Pte. (2833), attested 25/9/16, demobilised 7/9/19.
HENRY, E., Pte. (2834), attested 25/9/16, demobilised 7/9/19.
JULIE, F., Pte. (2835), attested 26/9/16, demobilised 7/9/19.
JOHNSON, W., Pte. (2836), attested 27/9/16, demobilised 16/7/19, pioneer.
JENKINS, J. H., Pte. (2837), attested 25/9/16, released medically unfit 3/10/16.
JULIE, W., Pte. (2838), attested 25/9/16, released medically unfit 20/12/18.
LOSPER, D., Pte. (2839), attested 25/9/16, demobilised 22/7/19, passed trench warfare and bombing course.

THE STORY OF THE 1st CAPE CORPS.

JOSPER, H., Pte. (2840), attested 25/9/16, S.N.L.R. 11/2/18.
PHILANDER, D., Pte. (2841), attested 25/9/16, demobilised 26/1/19.
MAY, J., Pte. (2842), attested 25/9/16, died of malaria 23/1/17.
MEYER, S., Pte. (2843), attested 27/9/16, released medically unfit 28/10/10.
NEL, J., Pte. (2844), attested 25/9/16, demobilised 7/9/19.
OSBORNE, T., Pte. (2845), attested 25/9/16, released medically unfit 18/8/17.
OSBORNE, J., Pte. (2846), attested 25/9/16, demobilised 22/7/19.
SOCHOP, B., Cpl. (2847), attested 26/9/16, L./Cpl. 5/7/18, Cpl. 1/11/18, demobilised 21/7/19, passed gas course, 2nd class.
SIMON, W., Pte. (2848), attested 25/9/16, demobilised 22/7/19.
SWARTBOOI, L., Pte. (2849), attested 25/9/16, released medically unfit 22/12/16.
SOLOMON, R., Pte. (2850), attested 25/9/16, released medically unfit 14/5/18.
VOLKWYN, A., Pte. (2851), attested 27/9/16, released medically unfit 23/11/17.
WEST, J., Pte. (2852), attested 25/9/16, demobilised 7/10/19.
WHITLOW, H., Pte. (2853), attested 26/9/16, released medically unfit 20/11/17.
ARENDS, C., Pte. (2854), attested 3/10/16, released medically unfit 8/8/18.
ADONIS, M., Pte. (2855), attested 3/10/16, a/Cpl. 27/10/18, Cpl. 3/11/18, reverted to Pte. 16/11/18, demobilised 8/9/19.
BROWN, J. W., Pte. (2856), attested 3/10/16, released medically unfit 24/9/17.
DE VRIES, D., Pte. (2857), attested 3/10/16, released medically unfit 31/8/17.
DE VRIES, D., Junior, Pte. (2858), attested 3/10/16, demobilised 11/7/19.
ERNSTZEN, J. W., Pte. (2859), attested 25/9/16, released medically unfit 6/11/17, acted as C.Q.M.S. at depôt at Woltemade.
ESAU, H., Pte. (2860), attested 3/10/16, released medically unfit 31/12/17.
ISAACS, H., Pte. (2861), attested 3/10/16, S.N.L.R. 23/12/16.
ISAACS, R., Pte. (2862), attested 3/10/16, S.N.L.R. 20/8/17.
JACOBS, J., Pte. (2863), attested 3/10/16, released medically unfit 29/12/16.
JOSEPH, A., Pte. (2864), attested 3/10/16, demobilised 7/10/19.
JANSEN, H., Pte. (2865), attested 3/10/16, demobilised 11/7/19.
KEET, J., Pte. (2866), attested 3/10/16, demobilised 11/7/19.
MEYER, N., Pte. (2867), attested 3/10/16, released medically unfit 18/11/17.
NELSON, M., Pte. (2868), attested 3/10/16, released medically unfit 3/10/17.
PADUA, M., Pte. (2869), attested 3/10/16, demobilised 29/10/19.
SEPTEMBER, P., Pte. (2870), attested 3/10/16, demobilised 31/12/18.
SCULLER, J., Pte. (2871), attested 3/10/16, released medically unfit 16/11/17.
SEGERS, W., Pte. (2872), attested 29/9/16, demobilised 11/7/19.
SOLOMON, A., Pte. (2873), attested 3/10/16, released medically unfit 6/11/17.
SERFONTEIN, A., Pte. (2874), attested 3/10/16, released medically unfit 12/11/17.
VAN BLERK, W., Pte. (2875), attested 3/10/16, released medically unfit 15/8/17.
VAN DER HORST, G., Pte. (2876), attested 3/10/16, demobilised 8/9/19.
WHEELER, D., Pte. (2877), attested 3/10/16, demobilised 7/10/19.
WEST, V., a/L./Cpl. (2878), attested 30/9/16, a/L./Cpl. 5/7/18, demobilised 16/7/19.
ABRAHAMS, C., Pte. (2879), attested 4/10/16, released medically unfit 13/8/17.
ARENDSE, J., Pte. (2880), attested 4/10/16, released medically unfit 12/11/17.
JOSEPH, R., Pte. (2881), attested 4/10/16, released medically unfit 13/9/17.
PETERSEN, W., Pte. (2882), attested 4/10/16, demobilised 8/9/19.
SINNETT, J., Pte. (2883), attested 4/10/16, released medically unfit, 20/12/17.
SEPTEMBER, D., Pte. (2884), attested 4/10/16, released medically unfit 6/7/17.
ALEXANDER, H., Pte. (2885), attested 4/10/16, released medically unfit 20/10/17.
ABRAHAMS, R. B., Pte. (2886), attested 4/10/16, released medically unfit 26/10/16.
ARENDSE, J., Pte. (2887), attested 4/10/16, released medically unfit 22/2/18.
APPEL, A., Pte. (2888), attested 3/10/16, released medically unfit 18/8/17.
BOSMAN, A., Pte. (2889), attested 30/9/16, released medically unfit 18/10/16.
CATO, E., Pte. (2890), attested 5/10/16, released medically unfit 21/7/18.
DU PLESSIS, C., Pte. (2891), attested 30/9/16, released medically unfit 20/11/17.
DAVIS, W. J., Pte., (2892), attested 30/9/16, released medically unfit 23/2/18.
JOHNSON, A., L./Cpl. (2893), attested 30/9/16, L./Cpl. 1/4/18, demobilised 7/10/19, passed gas course.
JOEMAT, F., Pte. (2894), attested 27/9/16, released medically unfit 31/10/16.
JANUARY, J. C., Pte. (2895), attested 3/10/16, a/Cpl. 1/2/17, reverted to Pte. 8/2/18, released medically unfit 7/6/18.
JOEMAT, M., Pte. (2896), attested 3/10/16, released medically unfit 30/6/18.
LODEWICKS, J., Pte. (2897), attested 5/10/16, released medically unfit 20/11/17.
LEWIS, S., Pte. (2898), attested 3/10/16, killed in action 16/11/17.
LOWRENS, M., Pte. (2899), attested 2/10/16, demobilised 25/12/18.
McKENZIE, H., Pte. (2900), attested 29/9/16, released medically unfit 29/10/17.
OLIVER, H., Pte. (2901), attested 3/10/16, released medically unfit 7/11/17.
PONTAC, J., Pte. (2902), attested 2/10/16, S.N.L.R. 25/11/16.
STANLEY, T., Pte. (2903), attested 3/10/16, released medically unfit 24/5/18.
THOMAS, G., Pte. (2904), attested 27/9/16, released medically unfit 19/10/16.
ALCASTER, A., Pte. (2905), attested 6/10/16, demobilised 11/7/19.
APRIL, J., Pte. (2906), attested 6/10/16, demobilised 16/7/19.
BESTER, F., Pte. (2907), attested 6/10/16, demobilised 7/10/19.
BRUNDERS, A. P., Pte. (2908), attested 3/10/16, released medically unfit 14/10/16.
BUSACK, W., Pte. (2909), attested 3/10/16, demobilised 25/12/18.
FARO, J., Pte. (2910), attested 6/10/16, demobilised 8/9/19.
HOLLAND, P., Pte. (2911), attested 13/9/16, released medically unfit 19/10/16.
JOOSTE, N., Pte. (2912), attested 27/9/16, released medically unfit 24/11/16.
JANTJES, J., Pte. (2913), attested 2/10/16, released medically unfit 24/11/16.
JANSEN, H., Pte. (2914), attested 6/10/16, demobilised 16/7/19.
LOTTERING, G., Pte. (2915), attested 26/9/16, released medically unfit 19/10/16.
MAY, J., Pte. (2916), attested 6/10/16, died of dysentery 7/6/17.
ROODE, C., Pte. (2917), attested 3/10/16, released medically unfit 14/2/18.
SIEBRITZ, J., Pte. (2918), attested 6/10/16, demobilised 8/9/19.
HENDRICKS, C., Pte. (2919), attested 6/10/16, demobilised 11/7/19.
SAMUELS, C., Pte. (2920), attested 22/9/16, released medically unfit 24/9/17.
STEVE, A., Pte. (2921), attested 6/10/16, demobilised 7/10/19.
SWANLOW, W., Pte. (2922), attested 5/10/16, L./Cpl. 15/10/16, reverted to Pte. 13/11/18, demobilised 13/10/19.
WILLIAMS, F., Pte. (2923), attested 5/10/16, demobilised 5/2/19.
VALTYN, A., Pte. (2924), attested 2/10/16, released medically unfit 25/8/17.
WATNER, W., Pte. (2925), attested 5/10/16, released medically unfit 29/10/17.

THE STORY OF THE 1st CAPE CORPS.

WILLIAMS, H., Pte. (2926), attested 29/9/16, released medically unfit 19/10/16.
MACAULEY, W., Pte. (2927), attested 6/10/16, died of malaria 7/7/17.
SEPTEMBER, N., Pte. (2928), attested 29/9/16, S.N.L.R. 10/8/17.
VAN WYK, H., Pte. (2929), attested 6/10/16, demobilised 13/1/19.
VAN DER HORST, A., Pte. (2930), attested 6/10/16, demobilised 26/8/19.
ADAMS, O., Pte. (2931), attested 7/10/16, released medically unfit 9/10/16.
DU TOIT, J., Pte. (2932), attested 4/10/16, demobilised 16/7/19.
JACOBS, H., Pte. (2933), attested 7/10/16, demobilised 11/7/19.
MORRIS, A., Pte. (2934), attested 30/9/16, released medically unfit 3/10/17.
WILTERS, J., Pte. (2935), attested 7/10/16, demobilised 7/10/19.
BEZUIDENHOUT, J., Pte. (2936), attested 6/10/16, demobilised 16/7/19.
CUPIDO, J., Pte. (2937), attested 7/10/16, died of malaria 6/4/17.
FILLIES, W., Pte. (2938), attested 4/10/16, demobilised 16/7/19, Lewis gunner.
LANGEVELDT, J., Pte. (2939), attested 5/10/16, released medically unfit 22/11/16.
LANGEVELDT, C., Pte. (2940), attested 5/10/16, died of dysentery 6/3/17.
LANGEVELDT, J. J. W., Pte. (2941), attested 5/10/16, released medically unfit 20/11/17
LOUW, J., Pte. (2942), attested 6/10/16, demobilised 2/1/19.
McDONALD, G., Pte. (2943), attested 25/9/16, demobilised 7/9/19.
NAMDOE, J., Pte. (2944), attested 5/10/16, demobilised 8/9/19.
OLIVER, A., Pte. (2945), attested 5/10/16, demobilised 7/9/19.
THORPE, H., Pte. (2946), attested 4/10/16, demobilised 7/9/19, machine gunner.
VAN HEERDEN, N., Pte. (2947), attested 4/10/16, died of influenza 11/10/18.
WITBOOI, P., Pte. (2948), attested 5/10/16, released medically unfit 15/11/16.
WYNGAARD, A., Pte. (2949), attested 9/10/16, demobilised 16/7/19.
WILLIAMS, W., Pte. (2950), attested 9/10/16, released medically unfit 15/7/18.
ADAMS, J., Pte. (2951), attested 28/9/16, released medically unfit 20/11/17.
BOLTMAN, W., Pte. (2952), attested 8/10/16, demobilised 8/10/19.
BARENCE, A., Pte. (2953), attested 9/10/16, released medidically unfit 25/1/18.
CUPIDO, W., Pte. 2954), attested 9/10/16, demobilised 7/10/19.
CARELSON, D., Pte. (2955), attested 9/10/16, released medically unfit 23/8/17.
DARLING, A., Pte. (2956), attested 9/10/16, released medically unfit 13/8/18.
EMMANUEL, A., Pte. (2957), attested 9/10/16, demobilised 5/10/19.
DE GOEDE, H., Pte. (2958), attested 28/9/16, died of wounds 13/1/17
JAMES, J., Pte. (2959), attested 9/10/16, demobilised 16/7/19, cook.
LANGEVELDT, J., Pte. (2960), attested 9/10/16, demobilised 7/9/19.
MORRIS, D., Pte. (2961), attested 9/10/16, demobilised 27/10/19.
MARTHINUS, A., L./Cpl. (2962), attested 9/10/16, L./Cpl. 5/7/18, demobilised 16/7/19.
PEARCE, D., Pte. (2963), attested 9/10/16, demobilised 26/8/19.
ROSS, D., Pte. (2964), attested 9/10/16, demobilised 7/10/19.
SOUTHGATE, P., Pte. (2965), attested 9/10/16, demobilised 11/7/19.
SICKEL, F., Pte. (2966), attested 9/10/16, demobilised 20/10/17.
SOLOMON, A., Pte. (2967), attested 9/10/16, demobilised 7/10/19.
KRAK, M., Pte. (2968), attested 9/10/16, released medically unfit 25/1/18.
APRIL, P., Pte. (2969), attested 9/10/16, released medically unfit 27/4/17.
ANDRIES, A., Pte. (2970), attested 9/10/16, demobilised 21/7/19.
APRIL, A., Pte (2971), attested 4/10/16, released medically unfit 26/10/16.
ADONIS, A., Pte. (2972), attested 10/10/16, died of dysentery 24/6/17.
ADAMS, B., Pte. (2973), attested 10/10/16, released medically unfit 14/2/17.
BLEEK, M., Pte. (2974), attested 7/10/16, released medically unfit 11/10/16
CORNELIUS, I., Pte. (2975), attested 29/9/16, demobilised 31/12/19.
COETZEE, G., Pte. (2976), attested 9/10/16, died of malaria 17/12/17.
DAVIDS, J., Pte. (2977), attested 9/10/16, released medically unfit 7/12/16.
FRANCISCUS, F., Pte. (2978), attested 10/10/16, released medically unfit 29/9/17.
GOLIATH, P., Pte. (2979), attested 9/10/16, demobilised 29/8/19.
HARTZENBERG, J., Pte. (2980), attested 27/9/16, demobilised 16/7/19.
HENDRICKS, A., Pte. (2981), attested 9/10/16, died of smallpox 31/7/17
HOLMES, A., Pte. (2982), attested 9/10/16, released medically unfit 16/7/17.
JAFTHA, J., Pte. (2983), attested 10/10/16, released medically unfit 13/3/17
LOUW, M., Pte. (2984), attested 10/10/16, demobilised 21/7/19.
LAGUS, M., Pte. (2985), attested 6/10/16, demobilised 8/9/19.
MATHEE, J., Pte. (2986), attested 10/10/16, died of pneumonia 29/8/18, Lewis gunner.
RENSBURG, F., Pte. (2987), attested 10/10/16, demobilised 11/7/19.
LIEBRANDT, W., Pte. (2988), attested 10/10/16, demobilised 7/9/19.
SEPTEMBER, A., Pte. (2928), attested 4/10/16, demobilised 7/9/19.
ARENDSE, A., Pte. (2990), attested 9/10/16, demobilised 7/10/19.
ADAMS, J., Pte. (2991), attested 9/10/16, demobilised 11/7/19.
ANDERSON, M., Pte. (2992), attested 10/10/16, demobilised 1/1/19.
BUTTERY, J., Pte. (2993), attested 3/10/16, died of dysentery 12/3/17.
BREDENKAMP, A., Pte. (2994), attested 11/10/16, S.N.L.R. 9/1/18.
BATHURST, B., Pte. (2995), attested 20/9/16, demobilised 11/7/19.
BOTHA, P., Pte. (2996), attested 9/10/16, S.N.L.R. 23/3/17.
CUPIDO, F., Pte. (2997), attested 9/10/16, demobilised 16/7/19.
COLLAR, W., Pte. (2998), attested 0/10/16, released medically unfit 10/4/18.
DANIELS, E. A., Pte. (2999), attested 7/10/16, died of influenza 11/10/18.
DE KOCK, J., Pte. (3000), attested 9/10/16, demobilised 7/9/19.
DANIELS, D., Pte. (3001), attested 9/10/16, released medically unfit 14/2/17.
FLORIST, E., Pte. (3002), attested 11/10/16, released medically unfit 27/11/17.
GALLANT, M., Pte. (3003), attested 9/10/16, released medically unfit 19/12/18.
AFRIKA, G., Pte. (3004), attested 9/10/16, demobilised 9/9/19.
FILIES, J., Pte. (3005), attested 9/10/16, released medically unfit 19/8/18.
KENNEDY, F., Pte. (3006), attested 9/10/16, released medically unfit 21/12/16.
MULLER, D. M., Pte. (3007), attested 9/10/16, released medically unfit 25/12/18.
ADAMS, M., Pte. (3008), attested 9/10/16, S.N.L.R. 27/8/17.
NOLTE, B., Pte. (3009), attested 10/10/16, released medically unfit 22/12/16.
FRANSMAN, N., Pte. (3010), attested 9/10/16, demobilised 7/9/19.
PAULSEN, J., Pte. (3011), attested 9/10/16, demobilised 7/10/19.
PHILANDER, J., Pte. (3012), attested 9/10/16, demobilised 21/7/19.
PETERSEN, H., Pte. (3013), attested 11/10/16, demobilised 27/12/18.
PLAATJES, C., Pte. (3014), attested 9/10/16, released medically unfit 8/1/17.
ROMAN, J., Pte. (3015), attested 9/10/16, released medically unfit 29/12/16.
STEENBERG, C., Pte. (3016), attested 9/10/16, demobilised 15/10/19.

THE STORY OF THE 1st CAPE CORPS.

SMITH, C., Pte. (3017), attested 11/10/16, demobilised 6/10/19.
STAHL, C., Pte. (3018), attested 9/10/16, released medically unfit 24/9/17.
SAAYMAN, A., Pte. (3019), attested 9/10/16, demobilised 16/7/19.
VAN EDEN, W., Pte. (3020), attested 9/10/16, released medically unfit 22/10/16.
VAN LICH, D., Pte. (3021), attested 10/10/16, demobilised 7/10/19.
VAN EDEN, A., Pte. (3022), attested 9/10/16, released medically unfit 28/11/16.
VAN DER BERG, J., Pte. (3023), attested 11/10/16, killed in action 20/9/18.
VAN EDEN, P., Pte. (3024), attested 9/10/16, released medically unfit 12/11/16.
VAN DER MERWE, F., Pte. (3025), attested 9/10/16, released medically unfit 21/11/16.
WILLIAMS, J., Pte. (3026), attested 10/10/16, demobilised 12/7/19.
ARRIES, S., Pte. (3027), attested 12/10/16, demobilised 21/7/19, drum and fife band.
JACOBS, T., Pte. (3028), attested 11/10/16, released medically unfit 2/11/16.
ROOKS, A., Sgt. (3029), attested 11/10/16, Sgt. 18/9/17, demobilised 26/1/19.
WILLEMSE, A., Pte. (3030), attested 11/10/16, released medically unfit 23/11/16.
ADONIS, P., Pte. (3031), attested 13/10/16, released medically unfit 6/11/17.
ADAMS, M., Pte. (3032), attested 13/10/16, released medically unfit 29/12/16.
ANTHONY, G., Pte. (3033), attested 13/10/16, demobilised 7/10/19, machine gunner.
ANDREWS, J., Pte. (3034), attested 13/10/16, S.N.L.R. 27/6/18.
BENJAMIN, C., Pte. (3035), attested 13/10/16, demobilised 16/7/19.
BENJAMIN, J., Pte. (3036), attested 13/10/16, released medically unfit 26/9/17.
BERGSTEDT, P. J., Pte. (3037), attested 13/10/16, released medically unfit 15/7/18.
CARELSON, P., Pte. (3038), attested 13/10/16, released medically unfit 3/10/17.
CUPIDO, A., Pte. (3039), attested 13/10/16, released medically unfit 9/3/17.
DE VOS, A., Pte. (3040), attested 13/10/16, released medically unfit 13/5/18.
DAMMIS, J., Pte. (3041), attested 13/10/16, released medically unfit 19/10/16.
ENGELBRECHT, P. J., Pte. (3042), attested 11/10/16, released medically unfit 20/11/17.
FRANCIS, G., Pte. (3043), attested 11/10/16, released medically unfit 22/12/16.
JACKS, W., Pte. (3044), attested 13/10/16, S.N.L.R. 17/7/17.
JULIES, M., Pte. (3045), attested 13/10/16, released medically unfit 6/11/17.
LAKEY, P., Pte. (3046), attested 9/10/16, demobilised 7/9/19.
OCTOBER, A., Pte. (3047), attested 10/10/16, demobilised 7/9/19.
OCTOBER, E., Pte. (3048), attested 9/10/16, released medically unfit 13/3/17.
ROBAIN, J., Pte. (3049), attested 13/10/16, released medically unfit 6/11/17.
ROBERTS, P., Pte. (3050), attested 13/10/16, demobilised 11/10/19.
SNYERS, G., Pte. (3051), attested 12/10/16, demobilised 5/1/19.
WILLIAMS, D., Pte. (3052), attested 13/10/16, demobilised 11/7/19.
BARLOW, P. J., Pte. (3053), attested 9/10/16, demobilised 14/1/19.
BOTHA, J., Pte. (3054), attested 10/10/16, demobilised 28/10/19.
BRUINTJES, K., Pte. (3055), attested 10/10/16, demobilised 7/9/19.
BOTMAN, J., Pte. (3056), attested 9/10/16, demobilised 16/7/19, machine gunner.
COETZEE, S., Pte. (3057), attested 9/10/16, demobilised 7/9/19.
CONRADIE, J., Pte. (3058), attested 9/10/16, demobilised 21/7/19.
DANIELS, J., Pte. (3059), attested 9/10/16, released medically unfit 24/9/17.
DANSTER, J., Pte. (3060), attested 10/10/16, released medically unfit 20/11/16.
FEBRUARIE, M., Pte. (3061), attested 10/10/16, demobilised 7/9/19.
FRANS, S., Pte. (3062), attested 9/10/16, demobilised 7/9/19.
FORTUIN, D., Pte. (3063), attested 10/10/16, demobilised 7/9/19.
HOGART, A., Pte. (3064), attested 10/10/16, demobilised 7/9/19.
JULIES, I., Pte. (3065), attested 10/10/16, released medically unfit 16/11/16.
JANSEN, T., Pte. (3066), attested 9/10/16, released medically unfit 3/10/17.
JULIES, P., Pte. (3067), attested 10/10/16, died of small pox 15/7/17.
LAMINI, A., Pte. (3068), attested 9/10/16, demobilised 7/9/19.
LANGEVELD, W., Pte. (3069), attested 10/10/16, died of dysentery 15/4/17.
LEONARD, D., Pte. (3070), attested 9/10/16, released medically unfit 29/11/16.
LEVENDAHL, G., Pte. (3071), attested 10/10/16, released medically unfit 9/1/17.
MULLER, D., Pte. (3072), attested 9/10/16, demobilised 16/7/19.
MARTIN, J., Pte. (3073), attested 10/10/16, died of malaria 15/1/18.
MAY, J., Pte. (3074), attested 10/10/16, released medically unfit 15/11/16.
MEYER, H., Pte. (3075), attested 10/10/16, released medically unfit 7/1/17.
MUNNIK, W., Pte. (3076), attested 13/10/16, died of malaria 30/6/17.
OLIVER, J., Pte. (3077), attested 10/10/16, died of tuberculosis 26/5/18.
PIETERSE, J., Pte. (3078), attested 10/10/16, demobilised 16/7/19.
SMITH, J. C., Pte. (3079), attested 13/10/16, released medically unfit 30/9/18.
SMITH, B., Pte. (3080), attested 10/10/16, demobilised 7/9/19.
TROMPETTER, C., Pte. (3081), attested 10/10/16, demobilised 7/9/19.
TARENTAAL, H., Pte. (3082), attested 10/10/16, died of malaria 14/6/17.
TITUS, F., Pte. (3083), attested 9/10/16, died of malaria 21/6/17.
VAN VUUREN, J., Pte. (3084), attested 9/10/16, demobilised 7/9/19.
WITBOOI, J., Pte. (3085), attested 9/10/16, released medically unfit 24/12/16.
ADDINALL, J., Pte. (3086), attested 14/10/16, demobilised 21/7/19.
BARNARD, H., Pte. (3087), attested 14/10/16, released medically unfit 21/7/19.
BARTMAN, W., Pte. (3088), attested 13/10/16, demobilised 16/7/19.
ERASMUS, E. R., Pte. (3089), attested 14/10/16, released medically unfit 21/7/18.
FREDERICKS, E. F., Pte. (3090), attested 14/10/16, demobilised 7/10/19.
BENNETT, T., Pte. (3091), attested 30/9/16, demobilised 22/7/19.
JACOBS, A., Pte. (3092), attested 29/9/16, S.N.L.R. 3/2/17.
LANGLEY, J., Pte. (3093), attested 14/10/16, demobilised 3/1/19.
TITUS, J. C., Pte. (3094), attested 14/10/16, released medically unfit 6/12/17.
LANGLEY, J., Pte. (3095), attested 14/10/16, demobilised 21/7/19.
MATHEE, R., Pte. (3096), attested 14/10/16, demobilised 16/7/19.
MILLER, J. W., Pte. (3097), attested 14/10/16, released medically unfit 19/3/17.
STEENBERG, A., Pte. (3098), attested 12/10/16, released medically unfit 14/4/17.
STAMMIT, W., Pte. (3099), attested 14/10/16, released medically unfit 31/10/16.
STARKEY, C., Pte. (3100), attested 14/10/16, died of wounds 16/11/17.
SAMUELS, J., Pte. (3101), attested 14/10/16, released medically unfit 20/10/16.
SEPTEMBER, R. J., Pte. (3102), attested 14/10/16, demobilised 7/10/19.
SANDERS, B., Pte. (3103), attested 11/10/16, demobilised 7/9/19, 1st class machine gunner.
VOLKWYN, W., Pte. (3104), attested 14/10/16, demobilised 7/10/19.
VISAGIE, P., Pte. (3105), attested 14/10/16, released medically unfit 9/3/17.
VAN DER BYL, F., Pte. (3106), attested 14/10/16, released medically unfit 20/4/17.
WESSELS, F., Pte. (3107), attested 13/10/16, released medically unfit 8/1/17.

THE STORY OF THE 1st CAPE CORPS.

WANZA, A., Pte. (3108), attested 13/10/16, demobilised 16/7/19, 1st class machine gunner.
WILLIAMS, A., Pte. (3109), attested 13/10/16, demobilised 8/9/19.
ANDREWS, J., Pte. (3110), attested 13/10/16, demobilised 16/7/19.
BEHR, W., Pte. (3111), attested 13/10/16, died of wounds 21/11/17.
DENNIKKER, G., Pte. (3112), attested 13/10/16, released medically unfit 30/11/17.
ENGELBRECHT, M., Pte.. (3113), attested 13/10/16, released medically unfit 26/5/17.
KAYSTER, M., Pte. (3114), attested 13/10/16, demobilised 7/10/19, 1st class machine gunner.
SAMUELS, F., Pte. (3115), attested 13/10/16, released medically unfit 2/3/17.
VAN DER POEL, G., Pte. (3116), attested 13/10/16, released medically unfit 20/11/17.
THORNE, J., Pte. (3117), attested 13/10/16, released medically unfit 29/5/18.
SOLOMON, F. M. J., Pte. (3118), attested 13/10/16, demobilised 26/10/19.
WILLIAMS, J., Pte. (3119), attested 13/10/16, demobilised 1/2/20.
CYSTER, C., Pte. (3120), attested 13/10/16, demobilised 7/10/19.
ERASMUS, N., Pte. (3121), attested 17/10/16, demobilised 8/9/19.
VAN GRAAN, R., Pte. (3122), attested 16/10/16, demobilised 7/10/19.
PETERS, J., Pte. (3123), attested 16/10/16, released medically unfit 13/3/17.
BAILEY, J., Pte. (3124), attested 16/10/16, released medically unfit 28/10/16.
PETERSEN, D. B., Pte. (3125), attested 16/10/16, released medically unfit 24/7/17.
ISAACS, J., Cpl. (3126), attested 14/8/16, L./Cpl. 24/6/17, Cpl. 18/6/18, demobilised 7/9/19.
JACOBS, J., Pte. (3127), attested 14/8/16, released medically unfit 19/3/17.
MANUEL, J., Pte. (3128), attested 23/10/16, a/L./Cpl. 25/10/17, reverted to Pte. 12/3/18, demobilised 18/10/19.
SMITH, A., Pte. (3129), attested 23/10/16, released medically unfit 11/1/17.
VAN DER POEL, J., Pte. (3130), attested 23/10/16, released medically unfit 12/3/17.
WILLIAMS, G., Pte. (3131), attested 23/10/16, demobilised 7/10/19, qualified machine gunner.
WALKER, J. H., Sgt. (3132), attested 15/10/16, Cpl. 1/4/17, Sgt. 24/6/17, demobilised 8/9/19, qualified Lewis gun instructor.
FRASER, J., L./Sgt. (3133), attested 15/10/16, Cpl. 5/7/18, L./Sgt. 1/11/18, demobilised 16/7/19.
GEORGE, J., Pte. (3134), attested 15/10/16, demobilised 7/10/19, qualified machine gunner.
HENDRICKS, J., Pte. (3135), attested 15/10/16, demobilised 7/10/19.
WILLIAMS, F., Pte. (3136), attested 15/10/16, released medically unfit 16/11/17.
SEPTEMBER, M., Pte. (3137), attested 15/10/16, demobilised 21/7/19.
CUSICK, G., Staff Sgt. (3138), attested 15/10/16, Staff Sgt. 15/10/16, released medically unfit 7/11/17, European personnel.
SAMPSON, J. A., Pte. (3139), attested 15/10/16, S.N.L.R. 1/10/17.
MARSH, F., Pte. (3140), attested 31/5/16, released medically unfit 15/6/18, mentioned in despatches, E.A.
CUPIDO, T., Pte. (3141), attested 31/5/16, released medically unfit 8/1/17.
ALLISON, C., Pte. (3142), attested 31/5/16, killed in action 20/1/17.
FITZ, J., a/Sgt. (3143), attested 31/5/16, L./Cpl. 3/7/17, Cpl. 18/6/18, a/Sgt. 1/2/19, demobilised 8/9/19, qualified Lewis gunner.
WILKINS, J., Pte. (3144), attested 31/5/16, demobilised 17/1/19.
PALM, A. C., Pte. (3145), attested 31/5/16, demobilised 16/7/19, cook, officers' mess.
IGLESBY, J. T., Staff Sgt. (3146), attested 27/1/17, ? European personnel.
BERGSTEDT, W. B., Pte. (3147), attested 27/2/17, S.N.L.R. 28/4/17.
DE WAAL, H., Pte. (3148), attested 27/2/17, demobilised 17/1/19.
ROSS, J. P., Pte. (3149), attested 27/2/17, demobilised 7/10/19, Lewis gunner.
ADAMS, J., Pte. (3150), attested 24/2/17, demobilised 21/7/19, Lewis gunner.
SWANLOW, I., Pte. (3151), attested 27/2/17, demobilised 29/12/18.
PABIER, J., Pte. (3152), attested 27/2/17, S.N.L.R. 20/3/17.
ARENDSE, J., Pte. (3153), attested 27/2/17, demobilised 6/1/19.
FITZ, J., Pte. (3154), attested 26/2/17, demobilised 28/8/19.
VOGES, M., Pte. (3155), attested 27/2/17, demobilised 7/10/19.
ABLES, J., Pte. (3156), attested 27/2/17, released medically unfit 12/3/17.
DANIELS, W., Pte. (3157), attested 27/2/17, released medically unfit 12/3/17.
ABRAHAMS, C., L./Cpl. (3158), attested 27/2/17, L./Cpl. 7/10/18, demobilised 7/10/19.
PETERSEN, P., Pte. (3159), attested 27/2/17, released medically unfit 12/3/17
SMITH, C. J., Sgt. (3160), attested 27/2/17, Sgt. 30/6/17, demobilised 2/1/19.
DOUGLAS, P., Pte. (3161), attested 23/2/17, demobilised 7/9/19.
ARRIES, W., Pte. (3162), attested 23/2/17, demobilised 21/7/19.
LE ROUX, J. D., Pte. (3163), attested 27/2/17, demobilised 21/7/19.
TRUSSELL, D., Pte. (3164), attested 27/2/17, demobilised 11/7/19, acted as L./Cpl. Lewis gun section, qualified Lewis gun instructor.
ARENDSE, C., Pte. (3165), attested 27/2/17, demobilised 11/7/19.
McCARTHY, P., Pte. (3166), attested 27/2/17, released medically unfit 4/4/17.
HENNICKSON, C., Pte. (3167), attested 27/2/17, released medically unfit 28/5/17.
DERKOP, K., Pte. (3168), attested 27/2/17, demobilised 7/9/19.
KEMP, W. G., Pte. (3169), attested 27/2/17, demobilised 11/7/19.
EOON, A. A., Pte. (3170), attested 27/2/17, demobilised 7/10/19.
VAN NOOI, J. R., Pte. (3171), attested 27/2/17, demobilised 31/12/18.
PELLY, D., Pte. (3172), attested 27/2/17, released medically unfit 6/3/17.
MULLINS, C., Pte. (3173), attested 27/2/17, released medically unfit 12/3/17.
GREFF, A. M., Pte. (3174), attested 27/2/17, released medically unfit 7/5/17.
FRANCIS, A., Pte. (3175), attested 27/2/17, demobilised 7/10/19.
ABRAHAMS, P. P., Pte. (3176), attested 27/2/17, released medically unfit 27/6/18.
PAYNE, J. D., Pte. (3177), attested 24/2/17, demobilised 21/7/19, regimental butcher, also transport driver.
PEARCE, J. D., Pte. (3178), attested 23/2/17, demobilised 17/1/19.
PARKINS, A. S., Sgt. (3179), attested 26/2/17, Sgt. 30/6/17, demobilised 5/10/19, qualified Lewis gunner.
BAILEY, T. R., Pte. (3180), attested 24/2/17, demobilised 7/9/19.
BARNES, P., Pte. (3181), attested 24/2/17, demobilised 21/7/19.
DE KLERK, J., Pte. (3182), attested 24/2/17, released medically unfit 21/5/17.
BARNES, P., Pte. (3183), attested 24/3/17, demobilised 7/9/19.
LEWIS, S. J., Pte. (3184), attested 24/2/17, demobilised 25/12/18.
HAMILTON, P. M., Pte. (3185), attested 24/2/17, released medically unfit 19/3/17.
PETERSEN, F. C., Pte. (3186), attested 24/2/17, demobilised 21/12/18.
TENNANT, D. W., Pte. (3187), attested 23/4/17, killed in action 6/11/17.
BOWLES, G., Pte. (3188), attested 23/4/17, demobilised 7/9/19.
DEERS, A., a/L./Cpl. (3189), attested 23/4/17, a/L./Cpl. 1/8/18, reverted to Pte. 28/9/18, a/L./Cpl. 1/1/19, demobilised 7/9/19, Lewis gunner.
PARKINS, W. M., a/L./Cpl. (3190), attested 24/2/17, a/L./Cpl. 7/2/19, demobilised 7/9/19, qualified Lewis gun instructor.
FREDERICKS, N., Pte. (3191), attested 24/2/17, drowned at sea 11/7/17.

SMITH, A., Pte. (3192), attested 24/2/17, demobilised 15/11/19.
SWARTZ, G., Pte. (3193), attested 24/2/17, died of influenza 9/10/18.
JOSHUA, S., Pte. (3194), attested 24/2/17, demobilised 7/9/19.
EBDEN, P. T., Pte. (3195), attested 24/2/17, demobilised 2/1/19.
JACOBS, C. R., Pte. (3196), attested 26/2/17, demobilised 7/9/19, Lewis gunner.
SEPTEMBER, P. J., Pte. (3197), attested 26/2/17, demobilised 6/1/19.
STEMMETT, F., Pte. (3198), attested 26/2/17, released medically unfit 12/3/17.
CLEOPHAS, H., Pte. (3199), attested 27/2/17, released medically unfit 20/3/17.
HULLETT, J., Pte. (3200), attested 27/2/17, released medically unfit 12/3/17.
BOTHA, J. C., Pte. (3201), attested 27/2/17, demobilised 7/9/19, pioneer.
TOBIN, H. C., Pte. (3202), attested 26/2/17, died of malaria 30/9/17.
CLEOPHAS, F., Pte. (3203), attested 27/2/17, released medically unfit 12/3/17.
ANDREWS, C., Pte. (3204), attested 26/2/17, missing, death accepted 6/11/17.
NOVEMBER, H., Pte. (3205), attested 26/2/17, released medically unfit 22/9/18.
JANTJES, C., Pte. (3206), attested 26/2/17, released medically unfit 12/3/17.
BUIS, K., Pte. (3207), attested 26/2/17, released medically unfit 12/3/17.
MAART, H., Pte. (3208), attested 26/2/17, demobilised 16/7/19.
BOER, C. M., Pte. (3209), attested 26/2/17, demobilised 7/9/19.
SMITH, C. J., Pte. (3210), attested 28/2/17, demobilised 21/7/19, qualified machine gunner.
HOPSELL, J. G., Pte. (3211), attested 25/2/17, released medically unfit 3/12/17.
KIVIDO, J., Pte. (3212), attested 25/2/17, released medically unfit 24/5/18.
VAN DER MERWE, D., Pte. (3213), attested 25/2/17, released medically unfit 26/6/18.
GOSLING, J. J., Pte. (3214), attested 25/2/17, demobilised 16/7/19.
HAYNES, G. M., Pte. (3215), attested 25/2/17, released medically unfit 4/8/18.
TENNANT, E., Pte. (3216), attested 27/2/17, released medically unfit 17/12/18.
PETERSEN, A., Pte. (3217), attested 27/2/17, died of malaria 10/2/18.
GOODHEART, D., Pte. (3218), attested 27/2/17, demobilised 25/12/18.
ARENS, E., Pte. (3219), attested 27/2/17, released medically unfit 16/5/17.
KOLBE, R., Pte. (3220), attested 27/2/17, released medically unfit 18/7/17.
PALM, E. J., Pte. (3221), attested 27/2/17, demobilised 7/9/19.
WYNGAARD, W. E., Pte. (3222), attested 27/2/17, died of enteritis 23/1/18.
CLOETE, Hy., Pte. (3223), attested 26/2/17, released medically unfit 23/3/17.
CAPES, J. L., Pte. (3224), attested 1/3/17, demobilised 7/10/19.
SAWYER, J. E. B., Pte. (3225), attested 1/3/17, demobilised 7/10/19.
MANUEL, D., Pte. (3226), attested 1/3/17, released medically unfit 17/4/17.
ARENDSE, M. A., Pte. (3227), attested 1/3/17, demobilised 11/7/19.
DAVIDS, F., Pte. (3228), attested 1/3/17, released medically unfit 25/5/17.
MATHYS, C., Pte. (3229), attested 1/3/17, demobilised 7/10/19.
VAN DER ROSS, A., Pte. (3230), attested 1/3/17, released medically unfit 18/8/17.
WINDVOGEL, J., Pte. (3231), attested 1/3/17, released medically unfit 4/8/18.
JACOBS, C., Pte. (3232), attested 1/3/17, demobilised 11/7/19.
ABRAHAMS, C., Pte. (3233), attested 1/3/17, demobilised 7/10/19.
WILLIAMS, L., Pte. (3234), attested 1/3/17, released medically unfit 18/11/18.
MATTHYS, A., Pte. (3235), attested 1/3/17, demobilised 7/10/19.
SIMON, J. J., Pte. (3236), attested 1/3/17, died of influenza 10/10/18.
TAYLOR, A., Pte. (3237), attested 1/3/17, demobilised 7/10/19.
PETERSEN, J. C., Pte. (3238), attested 1/3/17, S.N.L.R. 26/5/17.
MURRAY, F., Pte. (3239), attested 1/3/17, released medically unfit 17/6/18.
INGRAM, I., Pte. (3240), attested 2/3/17, demobilised 11/7/19.
CRESWELL, A. B., Pte. (3241), attested 1/3/17, demobilised 1/1/19.
BAATJES, M., Pte. (3242), attested 2/3/17, S.N.L.R. 25/3/17.
FORTUIN, H., Pte. (3243), attested 2/3/17, demobilised 11/7/19, passed trench warfare and trench mortar courses.
VAN SCHOOR, L., Pte. (3244), attested 2/3/17, demobilised 7/10/19.
ADAMS, N., Pte. (3245), attested 2/3/17, S.N.L.R. 25/5/17.
LAKEY, J., Pte. (3246), attested 2/3/17, released medically unfit 25/9/18.
FERNANDEZ, J., Pte. (3247), attested 2/3/17, demobilised 13/1/19.
ROODE, J., Pte. (3248), attested 2/3/17, demobilised 3/1/19.
BAILEY, J., Pte. (3249), attested 2/3/17, demobilised 16/7/19.
FREDERICKS, A., Pte. (3250), attested 2/3/17, demobilised 7/10/19.
BOOYSENS, C., Pte. (3251), attested 2/3/17, demobilised 11/7/19, qualified machine gunner.
WITTEN, W., Pte. (3252), attested 2/3/17, died of influenza 19/10/18.
RETIEF, P., Pte. (3253), attested 2/3/17, demobilised 16/7/19.
BAILEY, J., Pte. (3254), attested 2/3/17, demobilised 15/1/19.
DIEKOP, S., Pte. (3255), attested 28/2/17, released medically unfit 1/8/18.
SCHOLTZ, J., Pte. (3256), attested 28/2/17, demobilised 21/7/19.
WILLIAMS, E., Pte. (3257), attested 28/2/17, demobilised 7/9/19, qualified 1st class signaller.
LOUW, B., Pte. (3258), attested 28/2/17, S.N.L.R. 6/6/17.
TOBIN, J. J. G., Cpl. (3259), attested 28/2/17, Cpl. 20/6/17, demobilised 31/1/19.
HOPLEY, J., Pte. (3260), attested 28/2/17, demobilised 25/12/18.
ABRAHAMS, J. P., Pte. (3261), attested 28/2/17, released medically unfit 19/7/18.
PETERS, J., Pte. (3262), attested 28/2/17, released medically unfit 17/4/17.
DAVIDS, A. G., Pte. (3263), attested 28/2/17, demobilised 25/12/18.
EVERSON, J., Pte. (3264), attested 28/2/17, demobilised 28/12/18.
TAYLOR, J., Pte. (3265), attested 28/2/17, demobilised 1/3/19.
THOMAS, C., Pte. (3266), attested 28/2/17, demobilised 31/12/18.
MARTIN, J. H., Pte. (3267), attested 28/2/17, demobilised 15/1/19.
HOLMAN, H. C., Pte. (3268), attested 27/2/17, demobilised 23/7/19.
KLINK, J., Pte. (3269), attested 26/2/17, released medically unfit 12/12/18.
SOULS, A., Pte. (3270), attested 26/2/17, demobilised 1/1/20.
BUYS, P., Pte. (3271), attested 26/2/17, died of influenza 14/10/18.
WATNEY, J., Pte. (3272), attested 24/2/17, killed in action 6/11/17.
SWARTZ, J., Pte. (3273), attested 26/2/17, released medically unfit 8/12/18.
PIENAAR, H., Pte. (3274), attested 26/2/17, demobilised 27/8/19.
STEENKAMP, A., Pte. (3275), attested 26/2/17, demobilised 16/7/19.
KLAASTEN, N., Pte. (3276), attested 26/2/17, demobilised 7/9/19.
PRETORIUS, W., Pte. (3277), attested 26/2/17, demobilised 15/1/19.
KAMPER, B., Pte. (3278), attested 26/2/17, demobilised 7/9/19.
BOTES, C., Pte. (3279), attested 26/2/17, demobilised 21/7/19, passed trench warfare and bombing course.
PRETORIUS, J., Pte. (3280), attested 26/2/17, released medically unfit 19/5/17.
PATTERSON, J., Pte. (3281), attested 26/2/17, demobilised 21/7/19.

THE STORY OF THE 1st CAPE CORPS.

LUCAS, G., Pte. (3282), attested 26/2/17, demobilised 6/1/19.
STEENKAMP, S., Pte. (3283), attested 27/2/17, died of malaria 15/12/17.
LUBBE, J., Pte. (3284), attested 26/2/17, killed in action 20/9/18.
HASS, J., Pte. (3285), attested 26/2/17, demobilised 12/7/19.
BIRD, C. W., Pte. (3286), attested 5/3/17, released medically unfit 12/11/17.
LANGLEY, S., Pte. (3287), attested 5/3/17, demobilised 7/10/19.
FOURIE, A., Pte. (3288), attested 5/3/17, L./Cpl. 7/10/18, reverted to Pte. 21/1/19, demobilised 8/9/19.
SMIT, J., Pte. (3289), attested 28/2/17, demobilised 7/9/19.
PEDRO, B., Pte. (3290), attested 26/2/17, demobilised 8/9/19.
SMITH, H., Pte. (3291), attested 1/3/17, demobilised 21/7/19, transport driver, acted L./Cpl.
OERSON, A., Pte. (3292), attested 1/3/17, released medically unfit 27/6/18.
PRINCE, P., Pte. (3293), attested 1/3/17, demobilised 13/1/19.
BALIE, C., Pte. (3294), attested 1/3/17, demobilised 10/10/19.
KOUTER, C., Pte. (3295), attested 26/2/17, demobilised 16/7/19.
VAN DER MERWE, A., Pte. (3296), attested 26/2/17, released medically unfit 22/4/18.
WILLIAMS, T., Pte. (3297), attested 5/3/17, released medically unfit 16/3/17.
JACKSON, T., Pte. (3298), attested 1/3/17, released medically unfit 27/11/18.
McKENZIE, J. T., Pte. (3299), attested 5/3/17, demobilised 7/10/19.
WILLIAMS, M., Pte. (3300), attested 1/3/17, demobilised 7/9/19.
HELFRICH, C., Pte. (3301), attested 1/3/17, released medically unfit 9/5/17.
HAILS, W., Pte. (3302), attested 1/3/17, died of malaria 19/1/18.
MALGAS, A., Pte. (3303), attested 1/3/17, demobilised 7/9/19.
PAGE, R. J., Pte. (3304), attested 1/3/17, demobilised 14/1/19.
SMITH, J., Pte. (3305), attested 1/3/17, demobilised 22/7/19, transport driver, passed trench warfare and bombing course.
COETZEE, G. J., Pte. (3306), attested 1/3/17, died of influenza 8/10/18.
VAN WYK, C., Pte. (3307), attested 1/3/17, demobilised 7/10/19, Lewis gunner.
BROWN, T., Pte. (3308), attested 1/3/17, demobilised 13/1/19.
THOMAS, W. R., Pte. (3309), attested 1/3/17, released medically unfit 22/5/17.
McLEAN, R., Pte. (3310), attested 28/2/17, released medically unfit 29/10/17.
TOBIN, L. A., Pte. (3311), attested 2/3/17, demobilised 24/1/19.
ROSIER, M., Pte. (3312), attested 2/3/17, demobilised 7/9/19.
ROOI, A., Pte. (3313), attested 4/3/17, released medically unfit 18/5/17.
NORRIS, A., Pte. (3314), attested 5/3/17, released medically unfit 28/2/18.
PLAATJES, A., Pte. (3315), attested 5/3/17, demobilised 30/12/18.
ROBERTS, J., Pte. (3316), attested 5/3/17, released medically unfit 21/7/18.
DE BEER, G. A., Pte. (3317), attested 5/3/17, S.N.L.R. 20/3/17.
WILLIAMS, F., Pte. (3318), attested 5/3/17, demobilised 15/1/19.
OCTOBER, S., Pte. (3319), attested 1/3/17, S.N.L.R. 30/3/17.
VAN WILLING, I., Pte. (3320), attested 1/3/17, S.N.L.R. 28/3/18.
ANDERSON, F., Pte. (3321), attested 6/3/17, released medically unfit 18/5/17.
SCHOLTZ, H., Pte. (3322), attested 6/3/17, demobilised 18/5/17.
ELIAS, J., Pte. (3323), attested 6/3/17, L./Cpl. 15/10/17, reverted to Pte. 10/11/18, demobilised 3/1/19.
CHARLES, E., Pte. (3324), attested 6/3/17, demobilised 7/10/19.
MAJOR, A., Pte. (3325), attested 6/3/17, demobilised 7/10/19.
LOTTS, W., Pte. (3326), attested 6/3/17, released medically unfit 12/3/17.
SEPTEMBER, C., Pte. (3327), attested 6/3/17, demobilised 11/7/19, machine gunner.
GORDON, A., Pte. (3328), attested 6/3/17, released medically unfit 29/10/18.
WEST, S., Pte. (3329), attested 6/3/17, released medically unfit 28/6/18.
GREEN, A., Pte. (3330), attested 1/3/17, released medically unfit 26/2/18.
LEBRON, P., Pte. (3331), attested 1/3/17, released medically unfit 20/11/17.
KNOLE, F., Pte. (3332), attested 6/3/17, demobilised 6/1/19.
RICHARDS, R. W., Pte. (3333), attested 1/3/17, demobilised 21/7/19.
REITZENBERG, G., Pte. (3334), attested 1/3/17, demobilised 14/10/19.
WILLIAMS, M., Pte. (3335), attested 1/3/17, demobilised 5/8/19.
VAN ZYL, S., Pte. (3336), attested 26/2/17, demobilised 7/9/19.
LAGGENBERG, A., Pte. (3337), attested 1/3/17, released medically unfit 26/6/18.
ROSE, G., Pte. (3338), attested 1/3/17, S.N.L.R. 3/8/18.
LOMBARD, H., Pte. (3339), attested 6/3/17, demobilised 21/10/19.
JOHNSON, J. W., Pte. (3340), attested 6/3/17, demobilised 26/8/19.
LOVE, C., Pte. (3341), attested 27/2/17, demobilised 12/7/19.
PETERSEN, C., Pte. (3342), attested 28/2/17, demobilised 7/9/19.
SWARTZ, E., Pte. (3343), attested 2/3/17, demobilised 8/10/19.
SCHOLTZ, J., Pte. (3344), attested 2/3/17, released medically unfit 7/12/18.
BROWN, J., Pte. (3345), attested 2/3/17, demobilised 13/1/19.
ABSOLOM, P., Pte. (3346), attested 2/3/17, released medically unfit 14/3/17.
JOHNSON, J., Pte. (3347), attested 5/3/17, died of influenza 6/10/18.
CARVIE, E., Pte. (3348), attested 6/3/17, demobilised 2/1/19.
JOSEPHS, N., Pte. (3349), attested 5/3/17, released medically unfit 12/3/17.
HENDRICKS, J., Pte. (3350), attested 2/3/17, died of malaria 28/2/18.
GELDENHUYS, T., Pte. (3351), attested 2/3/17, released medically unfit 7/12/18.
ADAMS, C., Pte. (3352), attested 2/3/17, demobilised 8/9/19.
KLASSE, N., Pte. (3353), attested 2/3/17, demobilised 7/9/19.
VAN NEITUNG, T., Pte. (3354), attested 2/3/17, released medically unfit 12/3/17.
STEVENS, C., Pte. (3355), attested 2/3/17, S.N.L.R. 29/3/17.
SABELS, A., Pte. (3356), attested 2/3/17, demobilised 8/10/19.
JURIES, C., L./Cpl. (3357), attested 2/3/17, L./Cpl. 5/7/18, reverted to Pte. 18/9/18, L./Cpl. 1/3/19, demobilised 8/9/19.
FICK, A., Pte. (3358), attested 2/3/17, demobilised 11/7/19.
BOWERS, J., Pte. (3359), attested 6/3/17, released medically unfit 28/11/17.
SKIPPERS, H., Pte. (3360), attested 6/3/17, released medically unfit 25/9/18.
KAIZER, J., Pte. (3361), attested 6/3/17, demobilised 7/9/19.
HENDRICKS, J., Pte. (3362), attested 6/3/17, demobilised 16/7/19.
VALENTINE, A., Pte. (3363), attested 7/3/17, demobilised 11/7/19.
JOSEPHS, J., Pte. (3364), attested 7/3/17, released medically unfit 21/6/17.
PICK, J., Pte. (3365), attested 2/3/17, demobilised 30/7/19.
BAARTMAN, A., Pte. (3366), attested 5/3/17, demobilised 25/12/18.
DAVIDS, W., Pte. (3367), attested 6/3/17, released medically unfit 12/3/17.
NEL, M., Pte. (3368), attested 5/3/17, demobilised 16/7/19.
MARTHINUS, C., Pte. (3369), attested 5/3/17, demobilised 7/10/19.
DU PREEZ, I., Pte. (3370), attested 5/3/17, demobilised 16/7/19.

THE STORY OF THE 1st CAPE CORPS.

ANDREWS, S., Pte. (3371), attested 3/3/17, released medically unfit 30/3/18.
PAULSE, G., Pte. (3372), attested 5/3/17, released medically unfit 12/4/18.
JACOBS, T., Pte. (3373), attested 7/3/17, released medically unfit 21/7/18.
FARMIL, R., Pte. (3374), attested 5/3/17, demobilised 7/10/19.
VOLKWYN, P., Pte. (3375), attested 5/3/17, demobilised 17/4/19.
KOOPMAN, D., Pte. (3376), attested 5/3/17, demobilised 15/9/19.
BOER, W., Pte. (3377), attested 5/3/17, demobilised 7/9/19.
AFORD, J., Pte. (3378), attested 5/3/17, demobilised 7/9/19.
PHILLIPS, G., Pte. (3379), attested 5/3/17, demobilised 25/12/18.
CIERS, T., Pte. (3380), attested 5/3/17, released medically unfit 12/8/18.
ABLES, G., Pte. (3381), attested 5/3/17, S.N.L.R. 31/3/18.
SOLOMON, C., Pte. (3382), attested 5/3/17, demobilised 8/9/18.
SAMBIE, T., Pte. (3383), attested 5/3/17, released medically unfit 28/11/17.
JOHNSON, H., Pte. (3384), attested 11/3/17, demobilised 25/12/18.
GORDON, G., Pte. (3385), attested 5/3/17, demobilised 26/12/18.
GUSSIAN, B., Pte. (3386), attested 3/3/17, demobilised 3/1/19.
ANDREWS, C. J., Pte. (3387), attested 3/3/17, released medically unfit 23/2/18.
SAMPSON, J., Pte. (3388), attested 3/3/17, demobilised 7/9/19.
KEVIDO, A., Pte. (3389), attested 3/3/17, demobilised 7/9/19.
WILLIAMS, C., Pte. (3390), attested 3/3/17, released medically unfit 9/6/18.
DAVIDS, M., Pte. (3391), attested 3/3/17, demobilised 9/9/19, passed scout and sniping course.
WILLIAMS, P., Pte. (3392), attested 3/3/17, demobilised 21/7/19.
FROST, F., a/Cpl. (3393), attested 3/3/17, L./Cpl. 1/4/18, a/Cpl. 16/10/18, demobilised 7/9/19, passed scout and sniping course also topography course
WHITBOOI, F., Pte. (3394), attested 3/3/17, demobilised 21/7/19, passed course of cookery.
ZEALAND, J., Pte. (3395), attested 3/3/17, demobilised 21/7/19.
RUITERS, H., Pte. (3396), attested 3/3/17, released medically unfit 20/11/17.
DAMONS, G., Pte. (3397), attested 5/3/17, demobilised 22/7/19.
WILLIAMS, S., Pte. (3398), attested 5/3/17, released medically unfit 14/3/17.
APRIL, E., Pte. (3399), attested 3/3/17, released medically unfit 14/3/17.
HUMPHRIES, I., Pte. (3400), attested 6/3/17, released medically unfit 4/4/18.
STERMAN, J., Pte. (3401), attested 3/3/17, demobilised 1/1/19.
ADAMS, C., Pte. (3402), attested 3/3/17, released medically unfit 14/3/17
HUGHES, G., Pte. (3403), attested 3/3/17, demobilised 7/9/19.
MOSES, J., Pte. (3404), attested 6/3/17, demobilised 8/9/19.
MITCHELL, J., Pte. (3405), attested 3/3/17, demobilised 21/7/19, machine gunner
JACOBS, D., Pte. (3406), attested 3/3/17, demobilised 7/9/19.
LITTLE, B., Pte. (3407), attested 3/3/17, released medically unfit 22/7/18.
DOMINGO, J., Pte. (3408), attested 3/3/17, demobilised 7/9/19.
PETERSEN, K., Pte. (3409), attested 7/3/17, demobilised 7/10/19.
DAWSON, T., Pte. (3410), attested 3/3/17, died of malaria 8/1/18.
SMALL, S., Pte. (3411), attested 7/3/17, demobilised 11/7/19.
AUGUST, J., Pte. (3412), attested 7/3/17, demobilised 7/9/19.
MITCHELL, G., Pte. (3413), attested 3/3/17, released medically unfit 7/5/17
ATTWELL, H., Pte. (3414), attested 3/3/17, demobilised 21/7/19.
LAGOS, G., Pte. (3415), attested 6/3/17, demobilised 7/9/19.
MAY, F., Pte. (3416), attested 3/3/17, demobilised 21/7/19.
GARDINER, T. I., Pte. (3417), attested 3/3/17, released medically unfit 25/9/18.
LANGFORD, J. A., Pte. (3418), attested 3/3/17, demobilised 7/9/19.
WILLIAMS, C., Pte. (3419), attested 3/3/17, demobilised 7/10/19.
MIDINA, F., Pte. (3420), attested 3/3/17, released medically unfit 5/3/18.
McLEAN, W., Pte. (3421), attested 3/3/17, demobilised 7/9/19.
MARCHMAN, W., Pte. (3422), attested 5/3/17, demobilised 16/7/19.
GREEN, J., Pte. (3423), attested 3/3/17, died of influenza 7/10/18.
PETERS, T., Pte. (3424), attested 3/3/17, released medically unfit 30/5/18.
WILLIAMS, S., Pte. (3425), attested 3/3/17, released medically unfit 12/11/17.
HOUSEGOOD, S., Pte. (3426), attested 8/3/17, S.N.L.R. 24/2/18.
GROVES, T., Pte. (3427), attested 5/3/17, released medically unfit 6/4/17.
OPPERMAN, W., Pte. (3428), attested 8/3/17, released medically unfit 2/5/17.
VAN DER ZENDE, F., Cpl. (3429), attested 8/3/17, Cpl. 29/6/17, demobilised 20/12/18.
RENSBURG, F., Pte. (3430), attested 8/3/17, demobilised 11/7/19.
KLINK, G., Pte. (3431), attested 3/3/17, demobilised 7/9/19, passed Stokes course.
ISAACS, I., Pte. (3432), attested 5/3/17, demobilised 21/7/19, pioneer.
SMITH, J., Pte. (3433), attested 5/3/17, S.N.L.R. 24/9/18.
BERKINS, W., Pte. (3434), attested 5/3/17, released medically unfit 6/11/17.
WATSON, E. A., Pte. (3435), attested 5/3/17, demobilised 16/7/19.
TEE, A., Pte. (3436), attested 5/3/17, released medically unfit 2/3/18.
STUURMAN, N., Pte. (3437), attested 5/3/17, released medically unfit 12/11/17.
BASSON, J. M., a/L./Cpl. (3438), attested 5/3/17, a/L./Cpl. 18/6/18, demobilised 21/7/19, passed trench warfare and bombing courses.
HEREDIEN, T., Pte. (3439), attested 5/3/17, released medically unfit 17/4/17.
BLOEMETJE, P., Pte. (3440), attested 5/3/17, demobilised 7/9/19.
DEVINE, S., Pte. (3441), attested 5/3/17, released medically unfit 20/11/17.
DE KOCK, M., Pte. (3442), attested 7/3/17, demobilised 8/9/19.
CLARKE, M., Pte. (3443), attested 7/3/17, demobilised 8/9/19.
KLASS, W., Pte. (3444), attested 5/3/17, released medically unfit 28/11/17.
MESSIAHS, J., Pte. (3445), attested 7/3/17, released medicaly unfit 30/11/17.
VAN DER MERWE, S., Pte. (3446), attested 7/3/17, Sgt. 29/6/17, reverted to Pte. at own request 7/9/18, demobilised 2/1/19.
GLASBY, A., Pte. (3447), attested 5/3/17, released medically unfit 20/5/17.
LE ROUX, J. D., Pte. (3448), attested 5/3/17, demobilised 29/12/18.
CLASSEN, P., Pte. (3449), attested 5/3/17, demobilised 15/1/19.
WILLIAMS, D., Pte. (3450), attested 5/3/17, released medically unfit 7/6/18.
RABIE, J., Pte. (3451), attested 7/3/17, demobilised 8/9/19.
DE KOCK, J., Pte. (3452), attested 7/3/17, released medically unfit 13/12/18.
ISAACS, H., Pte. (3453), attested 8/3/17, demobilised 7/10/19.
CAROLUS, J. F., Pte. (3454), attested 5/3/17, S.N.L.R. 1/5/17.
FORTUIN, A., Pte. (3455), attested 7/3/17, demobilised 8/9/19.
BAILEY, D., Pte. (3456), attested 7/3/17, demobilised 7/10/19, Lewis gunner.
VAN SATTIS, C., Pte. (3457), attested 7/3/17, released medically unfit 27/4/18.
MATHEE, W., Pte. (3458), attested 7/3/17, released medically unfit 27/4/18.

LAMBLEY, H., Pte. (3459), attested 7/3/17, demobilised 21/7/19.
ABRAHAMS, H., Pte. (3460), attested 7/3/17, demobilised 7/10/19.
BENJAMIN, R., Pte. (3461), attested 7/3/17, released medically unfit 19/3/17.
KLUE, J., Pte. (3462), attested 5/3/17, demobilised 7/9/19.
CARELSON, S., Pte. (3463), attested 7/3/17, demobilised 20/10/19.
SOLOMON, J., Pte. (3464), attested 7/3/17, demobilised 16/7/19.
GOLIATH, C., Pte. (3465), attested 7/3/17, released medically unfit 6/6/18.
WILLIAMS, C., Pte. (3466), attested 7/3/17, demobilised 11/7/19.
MOSES, A., Pte. (3467), attested 7/3/17, released medically unfit 7/6/18.
FORTUNE, M., Pte. (3468), attested 7/3/17, demobilised 31/12/18.
JACK, M., Pte. (3469), attested 7/3/17, demobilised 7/9/19.
DAMONS, P., Pte. (3470), attested 5/3/17, demobilised 11/7/19.
SWANEPOEL, G., Pte. (3471), attested 5/3/17, released medically unfit 14/3/17.
FORTUIN, P. Pte. (3472), attested 7/3/17, demobilised 7/10/19.
WEITCH, D., Pte. (3473), attested 5/3/17, demobilised 21/7/19.
ROOKS, E., Pte. (3474), attested 7/3/17, demobilised 27/12/18.
WILLIAMS, M., Pte. (3475), attested 5/3/17, demobilised 7/9/19.
WEITS, C., Pte. (3476), attested 7/3/17, demobilised 7/9/19.
KIVADO, I., Pte. (3477), attested 5/3/17, demobilised 16/7/19.
CAROLUS, T., Pte. (3478), attested 7/3/17, released medically unfit 6/4/17.
FORTUIN, J., Pte. (3479), attested 7/3/17, released medically unfit 23/2/18.
SOLOMON, M., Pte. (3480), attested 5/3/17, demobilised 23/6/19.
DE VARTEK, Hy. V. C.Q.M.S. (3481), attested 5/3/17, a/Sgt. 19/5/17, Sgt. 18/9/17, C.Q.M.S. 1/11/18, demobilised 30/8/19, acted Battalion Q.M.S. for R.H. Battalion.
HAYWOOD, J., Pte. (3482), attested 30/4/17, demobilised 16/7/19, drum and fife band.
BEIT, G., Pte. (3483), attested 30/4/17, died of malaria at sea 23/12/17.
MILLER, B., Pte. (3484), attested 30/4/17, demobilised 10/4/20.
TINESON, A., Pte. (3485), attested 30/4/17, released medically unfit 21/6/18.
JAFTA, A., Pte. (3486), attested 30/4/17, released medically unfit 6/6/18.
NOELSON, A., Pte. (3487), attested 30/4/17, released medically unfit 20/7/17.
HANNEKAMP, T., Pte. (3488), attested 30/4/17, released medically unfit 11/7/17.
AFRICA, D., Pte. (3489), attested 30/4/17, killed in action 6/11/17.
VOEGT, D., Pte. (3490), attested 30/4/17, demobilised 2/1/19.
DANIELS, G., Pte. (3491), attested 30/4/17, S.N.L.R. 14/7/17.
PETERSEN, J. C., Pte. (3492), attested 30/4/17, released medically unfit 29/5/18.
CHRISTIAN, J., Pte. (3493), attested 30/4/17, died of phthisis 30/11/17.
DOMAN, A., Pte. (3494), attested 30/4/17, Cpl. 15/10/17, reverted to Pte. 16/8/18, demobilised 27/12/18.
RHENES, H., Pte. (3495), attested 30/4/17, S.N.L.R. 6/12/17.
DAVIDS, A., Pte. (3496), attested 1/5/17, killed in action 26/8/17.
DU TOIT, D., Pte. (3497), attested 1/5/17, S.N.L.R. 14/5/17.
THEUNISSEN, M., Pte. (3498), attested 1/5/17, demobilised 7/10/19, tailor.
PHEIFFER, J., Pte. (3499), attested 1/5/17, released medically unfit 21/6/18.
HULLEY, J. D., Pte. (3500), attested 1/5/17, demobilised 7/9/19.
SPANNEBURG, W., Pte. (3501), attested 1/5/17, released medically unfit 24/2/18.
ADONIS, C., Pte. (3502), attested 2/5/17, released medically unfit 24/2/18.
ADAMS, C. J., Pte. (3503), attested 2/5/17, released medically unfit 15/8/17.
HANSEN, W., Pte. (3504), attested 2/5/17, demobilised 11/7/19.
DU PLESSIS, O., Pte. (3505), attested 2/5/17, released medically unfit 19/4/18.
PETERS, R., Pte. (3506), attested 2/5/17, released medically unfit 24/6/17.
PAULSE, L., Pte. (3507), attested 2/5/17, demobilised 30/12/18.
OVIES, W., Pte. (3508), attested 2/5/17, released medically unfit 15/6/18.
ADONIS, R., Pte. (3509), attested 3/5/17, demobilised 16/7/19.
SWARTZ, P., Pte. (3510), attested 3/5/17, released medically unfit 25/6/17.
BURGESS, J., Pte. (3511), attested 3/5/17, demobilised 10/2/19.
CUPIDO, C., Pte. (3512), attested 3/5/17, demobilised 13/1/19.
VAN DER BERG, P., Pte. (3513), attested 3/5/17, demobilised 6/1/19.
ESAU, J., Pte. (3515), attested 3/5/17, demobilised 8/9/19.
WILLIAMS, A., Pte. (3515), attested 3/5/17, demobilised 16/7/19.
LEWIS, J., Pte. (3516), attested 3/5/17, S.N.L.R. 16/9/17.
SLABB, P., Pte. (3517), attested 3/5/17, S.N.L.R. 21/9/17.
DANIELS, J., Pte. (3518), attested 3/5/17, died of influenza 13/10/18.
MORRIS, J., Pte. (3519), attested 3/5/17, died of influenza 13/10/18.
DANIELS, T., Pte. (3520), attested 3/5/17, S.N.L.R. 1/6/17.
MOSES, A., Pte. (3521), attested 3/5/17, released medically unfit 9/7/17.
PHARO, A., Pte. (3522), attested 4/5/17, released medically unfit 25/5/17.
MARAIS, J., Pte. (3523), attested 4/5/17, released medically unfit 26/5/17.
LOUW, P., Pte. (3524), attested 4/5/17, released medically unfit 14/6/17.
GOLIATH, S. T., Pte. (3525), attested 4/5/17, demobilised 3/1/19.
MAGERMAN, J., Pte. (3526), attested 4/5/17, demobilised 10/10/19.
JANUARY, D., Pte. (3527), attested 4/5/17, released medically unfit 11/7/17.
VAN SOHNEN, J., Pte. (3528), attested 5/5/17, demobilised 8/9/19.
HERRING, G., a/Cpl. (3529), attested 5/5/17, L./Cpl. 23/8/18, a/Cpl. 24/8/18, demobilised 9/10/19.
BOTHA, S., Pte. (3530), attested 7/5/17, released medically unfit 24/9/17.
SMITH, J., Pte. (3531), attested 7/5/17, released medically unfit 23/5/17.
KASTEN, C., Pte. (3532), attested 7/5/17, demobilised 7/10/19.
ALEXANDER, H., Pte. (3533), attested 7/5/17, killed in action 20/9/18.
SAMUELS, J., Pte. (3534), attested 7/5/17, released medically unfit 23/5/17.
CHAIS, P., Pte. (3535), attested 7/5/17, demobilised 20/11/19.
McPORTLAND, P., Pte. (3536), attested 7/5/17, released medically unfit 13/2/18.
FARO, C., Pte. (3537), attested 7/5/17, demobilised 10/4/20.
SAMBABA, A., Pte. (3538), attested 7/5/17, demobilised 12/7/19.
JOHNSON, W., Pte. (3539), attested 7/5/17, demobilised 7/10/19.
DE KLERK, P., Pte. (3540), attested 7/5/17, released medically unfit 31/5/17.
LIEDERMAN, J., Pte. (3541), attested 7/5/17, demobilised 16/7/19.
MOSES, J., Pte. (3542), attested 8/5/17, S.N.L.R. 21/6/17.
ADAMS, P., Pte. (3543), attested 8/5/17, released medically unfit 25/2/18.
WILLIAMS, J., Pte. (3544), attested 8/5/17, released medically unfit 12/6/17.
ADAMS, B., Pte. (3545), attested 8/5/17, S.N.L.R. 14/8/17.
ROMAN, A., Pte. (3546), attested 8/5/17, demobilised 7/9/19.
JACOBS, F., Pte. (3547), attested 8/5/17, released medically unfit 15/5/17.
NORMAN, P., Pte. (3548), attested 8/5/17, demobilised 21/7/19.

SANDERS, H., Pte. (3549), attested 8/5/17, demobilised 7/9/19.
MARTIN, H., Pte. (3550), attested 8/5/17, released medically unfit 17/7/17.
MAW, W., Pte. (3551), attested 8/5/17, S.N.L.R. 15/5/17.
LANGEVELDT, A., Pte. (3552), attested 8/5/17, demobilised 16/7/19.
SAMPSON, F., Pte. (3553), attested 8/5/17, released medically unfit 27/7/18.
ASSAM, C., Pte. (3554), attested 8/5/17, demobilised 7/9/19.
BOTHA, D., Pte. (3555), attested 8/5/17, demobilised 10/10/19.
SEPTEMBER, F., Pte. (3556), attested 8/5/17, demobilised 8/10/19.
HOPS, J., Pte. (3557), attested 8/5/17, demobilised 8/9/19.
SEPTEMBER, L., Pte. (3558), attested 8/5/17, demobilised 14/1/19.
WILLIAMS, C., Pte. (3559), attested 9/5/17, S.N.L.R. 18/6/17.
DE GOEDE, J., Pte. (3560), attested 9/5/17, S.N.L.R. 10/5/17.
SOLOMONS, C., Pte. (3561), attested 9/5/17, S.N.L.R. 8/8/18.
MAYER, F., Pte. (3562), attested 9/5/17, released medically unfit 25/5/17.
DAVIDS, J., Pte. (3563), attested 9/5/17, demobilised 31/12/18.
ROMAN, C. A., Pte. (3564), attested 9/5/17, released medically unfit 20/6/17.
DICKSON, D., Pte. (3565), attested 9/5/17, released medically unfit 17/5/17.
SOLOMONS, C., Pte. (3566), attested 9/5/17, released medically unfit 21/5/17.
CUPIDO, C., Pte. (3567), attested 9/5/17, released medically unfit 29/10/17.
SMITH, P., Pte. (3568), attested 9/5/17, demobilised 8/10/19.
GULT, M., Pte. (3569), attested 7/5/17, S.N.L.R. 20/5/17.
JOOSTE, A., Pte. (3570), attested 7/5/17, demobilised 7/9/19.
VAN GERER, A., Pte. (3571), attested 7/5/17, S.N.L.R. 20/5/17.
BEZUIDENHOUT, W., Pte. (3572), attested 9/5/17, demobilised 16/7/19.
TURNER, F., Pte. (3573), attested 7/5/17, demobilised 2/1/19.
JOOSTE, J., Pte. (3574), attested 7/5/17, demobilised 7/10/19.
PAUL, J., Sgt. (3575), attested 10/5/17, a/Sgt. 15/10/17, L./Sgt. 1/7/18, Sgt. 1/11/18, demobilised 21/7/19, passed grenade discharging and trench warfare and bombing courses.
MAGAZAN, J. Pte. (3576), attested 10/5/17, released medically unfit 20/6/18.
TITUS, F., Pte. (3577), attested 8/5/17, demobilised 7/9/19.
KAMFER, D., Pte. (3578), attested 8/5/17, released medically unfit 24/5/17.
WILLIAMS, A., Pte. (3579), attested 8/5/17, released medically unfit 27/5/17.
MANEL, C., Pte. (3580), attested 8/5/17, demobilised 26/12/18.
VILJOEN, J., Pte. (3581), attested 8/5/17, released medically unfit 22/6/17.
KOOPMAN, G., Pte. (3582), attested 8/5/17, demobilised 7/9/19.
GUYMAN, H., Pte. (3583), attested 8/5/17, released medically unfit 27/5/17.
SIMONS, W., Pte. (3584), attested 8/5/17, demobilised 11/7/19.
CUPIDO, F., Pte. (3585), attested 8/5/17, demobilised 7/9/19.
LIEBRANDT, C., Pte. (3586), attested 11/5/17, demobilised 7/10/19.
CORNELIUS, P., Pte. (3587), attested 11/5/17, demobilised 15/1/19.
HUMAN, F., Pte. (3588), attested 11/5/17, released medically unfit 21/10/18.
KLINK, J., Pte. (3589), attested 11/5/17, demobilised 8/9/19.
WITBOOI, F., Pte. (3590), attested 11/5/17, demobilised 7/9/19.
BOSMAN, K., Pte. (3591), attested 11/5/17, demobilised 8/9/19.
ARENDS, S., Pte. (3592), attested 11/5/17, released medically unfit 27/4/18.
DAMON, J., Pte. (3593), attested 7/5/17, demobilised 7/9/19.
ZACHARIAS, D., Cpl. (3594), attested 7/5/17, a/Cpl. 5/7/18, Cpl. 1/11/18, demobilised 21/7/19, passed trench warfare and bombing course.
HENDRICKS, C., Pte. (3595), attested 7/5/17, demobilised 7/9/19.
GOODMAN, H., Pte. (3596), attested 7/5/17, demobilised 7/9/19, machine gunner.
MOORINGS, H., Pte. (3597), attested 7/5/17, died of malaria 20/12/17.
JAMES, H., Pte. (3598), attested 7/5/17, demobilised 11/7/19.
LOUW, J., Pte. (3599), attested 12/5/17, demobilised 30/12/18.
VAN DER PHOLL, H., Pte. (3600), attested 12/5/17, S.N.L.R. 20/5/17.
ROWLAND, P. Pte. (3601), attested 12/5/17, released medically unfit 21/5/17.
BOYCE, D., Pte. (3602), attested 8/5/17, demobilised 21/7/19.
BASSON, P., Pte. (3603), attested 12/5/17, released medically unfit 28/6/17.
BENT, M. M., Pte. (3604), attested 14/5/17, demobilised 26/12/18.
WATSON, W. F., Pte. (3605), attested 10/5/17, released medically unfit 16/11/17.
VELKERS, W., Pte. (3606), attested 11/5/17, demobilised 7/9/19.
GEDULT, C., Pte. (3607), attested 14/5/17, released medically unfit 25/9/18.
ANTONIE, A., Pte (3608), attested 14/5/17, released medically unfit 1/6/17.
SOLOMONS, W., Pte. (3609), attested 14/5/17, released medically unfit 24/9/17.
FORTUIN, P., Pte. (3610), attested 14/5/17, demobilised 8/9/19.
SEPTEMBER, M., Pte. (3611), attested 14/5/17, demobilised 8/9/19.
FORTUIN, F., Pte. (3612), attested 14/5/17, died of influenza 8/10/18.
MANNEKOUE, N., Pte. (3613), attested 14/5/17, released medically unfit 2/7/17.
MUFKE, K., Pte. (3614), attested 14/5/17, S.N.L.R. 18/6/17.
PETERSEN, C., Pte. (3615), attested 14/5/17, demobilised 29/12/18, bugler.
FISHER, F., Pte. (3616), attested 14/5/17, released medically unfit 1/1/18.
TAYLOR, A., Pte. (3617), attested 15/5/17, demobilised 31/12/18
MENTOR, J., Pte. (3618), attested 15/5/17, demobilised 31/12/18.
LAURENTJES, L., Pte. (3619), attested 15/5/17, released medically unfit 9/11/18.
SIMONS, S. C. J., Pte. (3620), attested 15/5/17, released medically unfit 14/6/17.
PRETORIUS, A., Pte. (3621), attested 15/5/17, killed in action 20/9/18.
KLOPPERS, A., Pte. (3622), attested 15/5/17, released medically unfit 21/5/17.
WILDSCHUT, D., Pte. (3623), attested 15/5/17, demobilised 9/10/19.
MAY, D., Pte. (3624), attested 15/5/17, released medically unfit 21/5/17.
LEWIS, J., Pte. (3625), attested 15/5/17, released medically unfit 6/7/17.
VANIEL, J., Pte. (3626), attested 15/5/17, released medically unfit 6/8/17.
JANEKER, J., Pte. (3627), attested 15/5/17, died of malaria 11/10/17.
CONRAD, W., Pte. (3628), attested 14/5/17, demobilised 16/7/19.
JACOBS, J., Pte. (3629), attested 16/5/17, demobilised 7/10/19.
MARSH, J. H., Pte. (3630), attested 13/5/17, demobilised 7/9/19, first-class machine gunner.
AMSTERDAM, J. W. L./Cpl. (3631), attested 13/5/17, L./Cpl. 5/7/18, demobilised 21/7/19.
HECTOR, A., Pte. (3632), attested 15/5/17, released medically unfit 22/6/17.
JOHNSON, J. W., Pte. (3633), attested 13/5/17, demobilised 21/7/19.
BOSCH, W., Pte. (3634), attested 16/5/17, demobilised 9/7/19.
TORIEN, F., Pte. (3635), attested 15/5/17, released medically unfit 13/6/17.
ADAMS, Z., Pte. (3636), attested 15/5/17, demobilised 8/9/19.
OKKERS, T., Pte. (3637), attested 14/5/17, demobilised 16/7/19.

THE STORY OF THE 1st CAPE CORPS.

SAMSON, S., Pte. (3638), attested 16/5/17, released medically unfit 20/6/17.
SKIPPERS, L., Pte. (3639), attested 16/5/17, demobilised 16/7/19.
KEUR, C., Pte. (3640), attested 16/5/17, demobilised 7/10/19, Lewis gunner.
ROSS, A., Pte. (3641), attested 16/5/17, released medically unfit 21/5/17.
RENTZ, A. A., Pte. (3642), attested 15/5/17, missing, death accepted 6/11/17.
VIGELAND, I., Pte. (3643), attested 15/5/17, released medically unfit 28/5/17.
ABLES, G. G., Pte. (3644), attested 16/5/17, released medically unfit 28/5/17.
FAWCUS, G. E., Pte. (3645), attested 16/5/17, demobilised 13/11/19, pioneer.
COURIE, G., Pte. (3646), attested 16/5/17, demobilised 7/10/19.
THOMPSON, S., Pte. (3647), attested 15/5/17, released medically unfit 27/4/18.
PORTER, J., Pte. (3648), attested 13/5/17, released medically unfit 11/7/19.
VAN BLERK, P., Pte. (3649), attested 16/5/17, released medically unfit 23/11/18.
PETERSEN, K., Pte. (3650), attested 17/5/17, released medically unfit 25/5/17.
ALEXANDER, W., Pte. (3651), attested 17/5/17, S.N.L.R. 26/5/17.
CLOETE, I., Pte. (3652), attested 17/5/17, released medically unfit 16/11/17.
GOLIATH, G., Pte. (3653), attested 16/5/17, released medically unfit 25/5/17.
RUITERS, G., Pte. (3654), attested 15/5/17, released medically unfit 21/5/17.
DAVIDS, A. A., Pte. (3655), attested 15/5/17, released medically unfit 12/11/18
ARENDSE, J., Pte. (3656), attested 16/5/17, released medically unfit 14/8/17.
HUMAN, A., Pte. (3657), attested 12/5/17, demobilised 31/12/18.
CARELSE, N., Pte. (3658), attested 16/5/17, demobilised 17/10/19.
BASSON, A., Pte. (3659), attested 12/5/17, demobilised 31/12/19.
ASIA, J., Pte. (3660), attested 16/5/17, demobilised 2/1/19.
TITUS, A., Pte. (3661), attested 16/5/17, demobilised 21/7/19.
BRANDT, J., Pte. (3662), attested 12/5/17, released medically unfit 21/5/17.
KLASSE, W. D. J., Pte. (3663), attested 12/5/17, released medically unfit 15/6/17.
SWARTZ, D., Pte. (3664), attested 12/5/17, demobilised 11/7/19.
FRANS, C., Pte. (3665), attested 15/5/17, demobilised 8/9/19.
BASSON, S., Pte. (3666), attested 12/5/17, demobilised 11/7/19
GREEN, T., Pte. (3667), attested 16/5/17, released medically unfit 6/7/17.
MITCHELL, H., Pte. (3668), attested 18/5/17, released medically unfit 29/10/17.
ABRAHAMS, H., Pte. (3669), attested 16/5/17, released medically unfit 8/8/17.
HEYNES, J. H., Pte. (3670), attested 18/5/17, released medically unfit 25/4/18.
KUYS, F., Pte. (3671), attested 16/5/17, released medically unfit 26/5/17.
DIEDERICKS, D., Pte. (3672), attested 16/5/17, demobilised 21/7/19.
BAARTJES, C., Pte. (3673), attested 16/5/17, released medically unfit 10/7/17
GORDON, P., Pte. (3674), attested 15/5/17, released medically unfit 1/8/17.
JOSHUA, W., a/L./Cpl. (3675), attested 18/5/17, a/L./Cpl. 20/1/19, demobilised 9/9/19.
ZIMMIE, A., Pte. (3676), attested 16/5/17, released medically unfit 3/6/17.
SASSE, W. J., Pte. (3677), attested 16/5/17, released medically unfit 11/6/17.
SCHOLTZ, K., Pte. (3678), attested 16/5/17, released medically unfit 14/6/17.
SEPTEMBER, G., Pte. (3679), attested 18/5/17, released medically unfit 26/5/17.
HEYNES, D., Pte. (3680), attested 18/5/17, released medically unfit 3/10/17.
VAN AARDE, A., Pte. (3681), attested 18/5/17, released medically unfit 1/8/17.
LANGHOVEN, D., Pte. (3682), attested 18/5/17, demobilised 11/7/19, passed field cookery course.
VALENTYNE, P., Pte. (3683), attested 16/5/17, released medically unfit 3/6/17
AFRICA, P., Pte. (3684), attested 16/5/17, released medically unfit 12/4/18.
GEORGE, F., Pte. (3685), attested 18/5/17, released medically unfit 1/6/17.
CONSTANCE, J. F., Pte. (3686), attested 17/5/17, demobilised 16/7/19.
DYERS, J. P., Pte. (3687), attested 17/5/17, released medically unfit 11/7/17
MOLEVELDT, J. P., Pte. (3688), attested 20/5/17, demobilised 10/10/19.
POLLMAN, A., Pte. (3689), attested 19/5/17, demobilised 11/7/19.
CONSTANT, G. E., Pte. (3690), attested 21/5/17, released medically unfit 11/7/17.
KENNEDY, P., Pte. (3691), attested 21/5/17, released medically unfit 14/7/17.
STEPHANS, A., Pte. (3692), attested 21/5/17, S.N.L.R. 22/5/17.
ADONIS, A., Pte. (3693), attested 21/5/17, released medically unfit 23/5/17.
DAVIDS, J., Pte. (3694), attested 21/5/17, released medically unfit 25/5/17.
ADAMS, J., Pte. (3695), attested 21/5/17, released medically unfit 26/5/17.
SOLOMONS, O., Pte. (3696), attested 21/5/17, S.N.L.R. 26/5/17.
MATHYSE, J., Pte. (3697), attested 21/5/17, demobilised 27/12/18.
JAMES, W., Pte. (3698), attested 21/5/17, released medically unfit 1/6/17.
VAN STEER, A., Pte. (3699), attested 21/5/17, S.N.L.R. 25/5/17.
ABLES, H., Pte. (3700), attested 21/5/17, released medically unfit 13/6/17.
BENJAMIN, N., Pte. (3701), attested 21/5/17, released medically unfit 13/6/17
DANIELS, M., Pte. (3702), attested 21/5/17, released medically unfit 13/8/17.
DANIELS, G., Pte. (3703), attested 22/5/17, released medically unfit 25/5/17.
JACOBS, M., Pte. (3704), attested 22/5/17, released medically unfit 6/12/18.
CLARK, F., Pte. (3705), attested 22/5/17, demobilised 11/7/19.
WILSON, H., Pte. (3706), attested 22/5/17, released medically unfit 1/5/18.
JANUARY, S., Pte. (3707), attested 23/5/17, released medically unfit 11/7/17
VAN DER MERWE, P., Pte. (3708), attested 23/5/17, demobilised 7/9/19.
VAN NIEKERK, G., Pte. (3709), attested 23/5/17, relased medically unfit 22/6/17.
GROVEL, J., Pte. (3710), attested 23/5/17, wounded, missing, death accepted 16/11/17.
GARNARD, A., Pte. (3711), attested 21/5/17, died of wounds 20/9/18.
JOSHUA, F., Pte. (3712), attested 23/5/17, demobilised 9/10/19.
THIMM, E. G., Cpl. (3713), attested 21/5/17, Cpl. 29/9/18, demobilised 8/9/19, qualified Lewis gunner.
BOTES, L., Pte. (3714), attested 21/5/17, killed in action 6/11/17.
COOK, W., Pte. (3715), attested 21/5/17, S.N.L.R 16/2/18.
SUMMER, C., Pte. (3716), attested 21/5/17, released medically unfit 26/2/18.
CAMPBELL, F. J., Pte. (3717), attested 24/5/17, released medically unfit 14/6/17.
ERASMUS, J., Pte. (3718), attested 24/5/17, demobilised 7/9/19.
PETERSEN, C., Pte. (3719), attested 24/5/17, released medically unfit 24/6/17.
MAKWE, W., Pte. (3720), attested 22/5/17, demobilised 7/9/19
SASS, J., Pte. (3721), attested 24/5/17, released medically unfit 14/6/17.
FAMMERS, A., Pte. (3722), attested 23/5/17, released medically unfit 3/6/17.
SAMSON, J., Pte. (3723), attested 23/5/17, S.N.L.R. 31/3/18.
JOACHIM, H., Pte. (3724), attested 25/5/17, demobilised 31/12/18.
BENTICK, B., Pte. (3725), attested 25/5/17, released medically unfit 1/6/17.
RUNDLE, A., Pte. (3726), attested 25/5/17, released medically unfit 8/2/18.
AFRICA, L., Pte. (3727), attested 28/5/17, released medically unfit 1/6/17.
WILLIAMS, J., Pte. (3728), attested 28/5/17, S.N.L.R. 1/6/17.

THE STORY OF THE 1ST CAPE CORPS.

VILANDER, S., Pte. (3729), attested 28/5/17, demobilised 8/9/19.
TILLING, A., Pte. (3730), attested 28/5/17, demobilised 8/9/19.
HENDRICKS, J., Pte. (3731), attested 28/5/17, demobilised 30/12/18.
BENJAMIN, R., Pte. (3732), attested 26/5/17, demobilised 5/1/19.
SLEE, J., Pte. (3733), attested 28/5/17, S.N.L.R. 31/5/17.
BURNESS, G. A., a/Sgt. (3734), attested 26/5/17, a/Sgt. 15/10/17, released medically unfit 14/7/18.
SMITH, A., Pte. (3735), attested 28/5/17, released medically unfit 10/7/17.
McDONALD, H., Pte. (3736), attested 28/5/17, demobilised 11/7/19.
KAM, J., Pte. (3737), attested 26/5/17, released medically unfit 23/6/17.
VAN REET, C., Pte. (3738), attested 29/5/17, released medically unfit 7/6/17.
ABRAHAM, B., Pte. (3739), attested 29/5/17, released medically unfit 1/6/17.
HENDRICKS, M., Pte. (3740), attested 1/6/17, demobilised 5/1/19.
JOHNSON, R., Pte. (3741), attested 1/6/17, demobilised 7/9/19.
ANDERSON, J., Pte. (3742), attested 28/5/17, demobilised 7/9/19.
STUURMAN, J., Pte. (3743), attested 1/6/17, S.N.L.R. 1/6/17.
COZYEN, H., Pte. (3744), attested 1/6/17, released medically unfit 9/7/17.
FORTUIN, J., Pte. (3745), attested 29/5/17, died whilst on leave 10/5/18.
LE FLEUR, J., Pte. (3746), attested 29/5/17, demobilised 12/7/19.
OERSEN, P., Pte. (3747), attested 30/5/17, released medically unfit 19/12/18.
VAN HEERDEN, I., Pte. (3748), attested 30/5/17, demobilised 3/1/19.
BRINKHUIS, J. J., Pte. (3749), attested 1/6/17, a/Sgt. 15/10/17, reverted to Pte. 31/3/18, demobilised 16/7/19, medical orderly.
MORRIS, F. W., Pte. (3750), attested 31/5/17, demobilised 21/7/19.
LAURENCE, J. S., Pte. (3751), attested 29/5/17, released medically unfit 7/12/18.
MYBURGH, H., Pte. (3752), attested 1/6/17, demobilised 21/7/19.
PRINGLE, C. J., Pte. (3753), attested 1/6/17, released medically unfit 15/6/17.
LOOTS, J., Pte. (3754), attested 1/6/17, released medically unfit 15/6/17.
BARNES, M., Pte. (3755), attested 4/6/17, S.N.L.R. 5/6/17.
SMITH, S. J., Pte. (3756), attested 4/6/17, released medically unfit 20/12/18.
MINTOR, J., Pte. (3757), attested 1/6/17, demobilised 8/9/19.
SEPTEMBER, W., Pte. (3758), attested 1/6/17, demobilised 8/9/19.
DANIELS, J., Pte. (3759), attested 4/6/17, demobilised 22/7/19.
ABRAHAMS, A., Pte. (3760), attested 1/6/17, released medically unfit 14/6/17.
CORDAM, G., Pte. (3761), attested 4/6/17, S.N.L.R. 4/4/18.
GOLIATH, A., Pte. (3762), attested 4/6/17, demobilised 7/10/19.
STOFFELS, D., Pte. (3763), attested 1/6/17, released medically unfit 14/6/17.
JACOBS, J., Pte. (3764), attested 4/6/17, demobilised 10/7/19.
VAN DER VENTER, J., Pte. (3765), attested 4/6/17, demobilised 16/7/19.
LEWIN, L. P., Pte. (3766), attested 4/6/17, died of influenza 6/10/18.
BAILEY, D., Pte. (3767), attested 4/6/17, released medically unfit 13/6/17.
BASTIAN, G., Pte. (3768), attested 4/6/17, demobilised 17/1/19.
SKIPPERS, J., Pte. (3769), attested 4/6/17, demobilised 16/7/19.
WILLIAMS, J., Pte. (3770), attested 4/6/17, demobilised 16/7/19.
STEENEKAMP, H., Pte. (3771), attested 1/6/17, demobilised 21/7/19.
SASS, J., Cpl. (3772), attested 5/6/17, Cpl. 1/11/18, demobilised 8/9/19.
COMMISSRE, S., Pte. (3773), attested 5/6/17, released medically unfit 9/7/17.
DANIELS, J., Pte. (3774), attested 5/6/17, released medically unfit 21/6/17.
MAARMON, G., Pte. (3775), attested 5/6/17, S.N.L.R. 16/3/18.
BAILEY, G., Pte. (3776), attested 4/6/17, demobilised 5/8/19.
PRICHARD, H., Pte. (3777), attested 4/6/17, released medically unfit 23/2/18.
BATHANIE, C., L./Cpl. (3778), attested 6/6/17, L./Cpl. 13/11/17, demobilised 7/10/19.
FREDERICKS, B., Pte. (3779), attested 4/6/17, demobilised 11/7/19.
JOSEPHS, S., Pte. (3780), attested 7/6/17, demobilised 26/12/18.
FRANCIS, A., Pte. (3781), attested 8/6/17, released medically unfit 3/12/18.
GLOVER, C., Pte. (3782), attested 7/6/17, demobilised 21/7/19.
BOYCE, T., Pte. (3783), attested 4/6/17, S.N.L.R. 2/9/17.
TERBLANCHE, H., Pte. (3784), attested 4/6/17, released medically unfit 8/9/17.
CUPIDO, J., Pte. (3785), attested 4/6/17, S.N.L.R. 17/6/17.
SEPTEMBER, M., Pte. (3786), attested 4/6/17, demobilised 16/7/19.
DE-CUBE, G., Pte. (3787), attested 12/6/17, released medically unfit 28/6/17.
BOND, A., Pte. (3788), attested 12/6/17, demobilised 31/7/18.
MEINTJES, C. J., Pte. (3789), attested 10/6/17, released medically unfit 30/6/17.
FISHER, P., Pte. (3790), attested 13/6/17, released medically unfit 20/6/17.
CUPIDO, J., Pte. (3791), attested 12/6/17, released medically unfit 9/7/17.
FORTUIN, C., Pte. (3792), attested 13/6/17, released medically unfit 21/6/17.
FREDERICKS, K., Pte. (3793), attested 13/6/17, released medically unfit 22/6/17.
JOHANNES, C., Pte. (3794), attested 12/6/17, released medically unfit 10/7/17.
EPHRAIM, D., Pte. (3795), attested 13/6/17, released medically unfit 6/6/18.
DIEDERICKS, J., Pte. (3796), attested 14/6/17, released medically unfit 16/7/17.
BOTHA, J., Pte. (3797), attested 12/6/17, released medically unfit 22/6/17.
LOUW, J., Pte. (3798), attested 12/6/17, demobilised 7/9/19.
PRETORIUS, G., Pte. (3799), attested 12/6/17, demobilised 16/7/19.
VAN DER MERWE, D., Pte. (3800), attested 14/6/17, released medically unfit 22/6/17.
PAULSEN, J., Pte. (3801), attested 12/6/17, released medically unfit 7/9/17.
ADAMS, J., Pte. (3802), attested 12/6/17, demobilised 8/9/19.
RAMPHA, A., Pte. (3803), attested 15/6/17, released medically unfit 12/7/17.
LOUW, H. J., Pte. (3804), attested 14/6/17, demobilised 8/9/19.
HENDRICKS, A., Pte. (3805), attested 15/6/17, demobilised 8/9/19.
PEDRO, F., Pte. (3806), attested 13/6/17, demobilised 8/9/19.
PLAATJES, F., Pte. (3807), attested 13/6/17, released medically unfit 9/7/17.
ADONIS, A., Pte. (3808), attested 18/6/17, released medically unfit 9/7/17.
MORRIS, A., Pte. (3809), attested 14/6/17, demobilised 7/9/19.
PULLEN, S., Pte. (3810), attested 14/6/17, S.N.L.R. 10/2/18.
PETERSEN, J., Pte. (3811), attested 18/6/17, demobilised 8/9/19.
JACKSON, G. C., Pte. (3812), attested 16/7/17, demobilised 11/7/19.
CLOETE, J., Pte. (3813), attested 19/6/17, released medically unfit 2/7/17.
GENNEKER, A. M., Pte. (3814), attested 19/6/17, S.N.L.R. 14/7/17.
CLOETE, J., Pte. (3815), attested 19/6/17, released medically unfit 2/7/17.
CLOETE, E., Pte. (3816), attested 19/6/17, demobilised 8/9/19.
KRAAK, A., Pte. (3817), attested 20/6/17, demobilised 7/10/19.
SEPTEMBER, J., Pte. (3818), attested 21/6/17, demobilised 7/10/19.

THE STORY OF THE 1st CAPE CORPS.

DAVIDS, F., Pte. (3819), attested 20/6/17, released medically unfit 14/7/17.
NIEKERK, F., Pte. (3820), attested 20/6/17, released medically unfit 25/9/18.
COTENHAM, J., Pte. (3821), attested 20/6/17, released medically unfit 1/8/17.
JACOBS, S., Pte. (3822), attested 20/6/17, released medically unfit 2/7/17.
DAVIDS, M., Pte. (3823), attested 20/6/17, demobilised 8/9/19.
DE KOCK, A., Pte. (3824), attested 20/6/17, released medically unfit 10/7/17.
McKIE, G. T., L./Cpl. (3825), attested 21/6/17, L./Cpl. 1/4/18, died of typhoid 22/8/1
DE BEERS, S., Pte. (3826), attested 20/6/17, released medically unfit 2/7/17.
JONES, P., Pte. (3827), attested 20/6/17, released medically unfit 10/7/17.
ESAU, P., Pte. (3828), attested 20/6/17, demobilised 8/9/19.
SYME, L., Pte. (3829), attested 20/6/17, demobilised 3/1/19.
JOHANNES, H., Pte. (3830), attested 20/6/17, demobilised 8/9/19.
TITUS, J., Pte. (3831), attested 20/6/17, released medically unfit 2/7/17.
PICK, C., Pte. (3832), attested 20/6/17, released medically unfit 10/7/17.
ALFOS, A., Pte. (3833), attested 20/6/17, demobilised 21/7/19.
JONATHAN, J., Pte. (3834), attested 20/6/17, demobilised 8/9/19, Lewis gunner.
BOTHA, J., Pte. (3835), attested 20/6/17, demobilised 8/9/19.
APPOLIS, J., Pte. (3836), attested 20/6/17, demobilised 3/1/19.
ADONIS, M., Pte. (3837), attested 20/6/17, demobilised 5/9/19.
VILANDER, J., Pte. (3838), attested 20/6/17, S.N.L.R. 3/7/17.
CARELSE, A., Pte. (3839), attested 20/6/17, died of malaria 30/12/17.
ALLIE, L., Pte. (3840), attested 20/6/17, demobilised 21/7/19.
PICK, W., Pte. (3841), attested 20/6/17, demobilised 16/7/19.
ROMAN, M., Pte. (3842), attested 20/6/17, released medically unfit 13/10/17.
APRIL, S., Pte. (3843), attested 20/6/17, demobilised 16/7/19, pioneer.
HARDENBERG, J., Pte. (3844), attested 20/6/17, released medically unfit 13/12/18.
ADAMS, Z., Pte. (3845), attested 20/6/17, demobilised 16/7/19.
ABRAHAMS, H., Pte. (3846), attested 20/6/17, released medically unfit 2/7/17.
AFRICA, J., Pte. (3847), attested 20/6/17, released medically unfit 2/7/17.
VILANDER, M., Pte. (3848), attested 20/6/17, S.N.L.R. 3/7/17.
ADAMS, A., Pte. (3849), attested 21/6/17, demobilised 16/7/19.
MARTHINUS, J., Pte. (3850), attested 21/6/17, released medically unfit 10/7/17.
SNYDERS, H. J., Pte. (3851), attested 21/6/17, demobilised 8/9/19.
JACOBS, H., Pte. (3852), attested 25/6/17, demobilised 31/12/19.
GOSSMAN, E., Pte. (3853), attested 25/6/17, demobilised 11/7/19.
ADAMS, T., Pte. (3854), attested 25/6/17, demobilised 16/7/19.
HARRIS, W., Pte. (3855), attested 26/6/17, released medically unfit 29/6/17.
TRUTER, I., Pte. (3856), attested 26/6/17, S.N.L.R. 21/7/17.
CLOETE, C., Pte. (3857), attested 26/6/17, demobilised 8/9/19.
PETERSEN, J., Pte. (3858), attested 26/6/17, S.N.L.R. 21/7/17.
JORDAN, M., L./Cpl. (3859), attested 26/6/17, L./Cpl. 1/4/18, demobilised 16/7/19.
JACKSON, A., Pte. (3860), attested 27/6/17, released medically unfit 14/7/17.
DANIELS, M., Pte. (3861), attested 26/6/17, released medically unfit 14/7/17.
DE KOCK, D., Pte. (3862), attested 27/6/17, released medically unfit 9/7/17.
FRITZ, A., Pte. (3863), attested 28/6/17, released medically unfit 10/7/17.
SEPTEMBER, G., Pte. (3864), attested 28/6/17, demobilised 11/7/19.
ROBERTS, J., Pte. (3865), attested 28/6/17, demobilised 8/9/19.
RONGANGER, B., Pte. (3866), attested 28/6/17, demobilised 16/7/19.
VAN DER HEYDE, J., Pte. (3867), attested 28/6/17, demobilised 8/9/19.
PIETERSEN, P., Pte. (3868), attested 28/6/17, S.N.L.R. 27/3/18.
PICK, A., Pte. (3869), attested 28/6/17, released medically unfit 10/7/17.
GRANT, H., Pte. (3870), attested 27/6/17, demobilised 7/9/19.
FARO, G., Pte. (3871), attested 2/7/17, demobilised 16/7/19.
VAN REENEN, H. R., Pte. (3872), attested 2/7/17, released medically unfit 10/7/17.
WILLIAMS, J., Pte. (3873), attested 2/7/17, demobilised 7/10/19.
LAND, B., Pte. (3874), attested 30/6/17, released medically unfit 18/7/17.
PORTER, L., Pte. (3875), attested 1/7/17, demobilised 7/9/19.
STEGLING, P., Pte. (3876), attested 30/6/17, demobilised 7/9/19.
HENNIGAN, H., Pte. (3877), attested 30/6/17, released medically unfit 25/7/17.
MOSES, D., Pte. (3878), attested 30/6/17, S.N.L.R. 23/7/17.
BETERS, A., Pte. (3879), attested 3/7/17, released medically unfit 13/7/17.
PETERS, D., Pte. (3880), attested 2/7/17, released medically unfit 15/7/17.
WILLIAMS, D., Pte. (3881), attested 3/7/17, released medically unfit 11/7/17.
MATCHLALA, T., Pte. (3882), attested 3/7/17, demobilised 7/9/19.
ARUNDELL, R., Pte. (3883), attested 4/7/17, released medically unfit 15/11/18.
JONES, M., Pte. (3884), attested 5/7/17, demobilised 21/7/19.
JONK, J., Pte. (3885), attested 5/7/17, released medically unfit 25/7/17.
CYSTER, H., Pte. (3886), attested 4/7/17, demobilised 7/9/19.
OSWELL, C., Pte. (3887), attested 9/7/17, demobilised 21/7/19.
JOHNSON, R., Pte. (3888), attested 5/7/17, released medically unfit 23/7/17.
STEVENS, W., Pte. (3889), attested 5/7/17, demobilised 7/9/19.
SWARTZ, H., Pte. (3890), attested 9/7/17, demobilised 26/12/18.
JONKERS, J., Pte. (3891), attested 9/7/17, killed in action 19/9/18.
ROBYN, M., Pte. (3892), attested 9/7/17, demobilised 22/7/19.
GERTZE, M., Pte. (3893), attested 9/7/17, released medically unfit 25/7/17.
REYNARD, J., Pte. (3894), attested 10/7/17, released medically unfit 25/7/17.
VAN ROOY, H. C., Pte. (3895), attested 11/7/17, released medically unfit 6/6/18
PYOOS, D., Pte. (3896), attested 9/7/17, released medically unfit 20/7/17.
LUCAS, R., Pte. (3897), attested 9/7/17, released medically unfit 20/7/17.
JOHNSON, D., Pte. (3898), attested 8/7/17, released medically unfit 20/7/17.
HENDRIK, P., Pte. (3899), attested 9/7/17, released medically unfit 20/7/17.
DUARTE, J., Pte. (3900), attested 8/7/17, released medically unfit 4/11/18.
MEYERS, H., Pte. (3901), attested 7/7/17, demobilised 7/9/19.
STEVENS, J., Pte. (3902), attested 12/7/17, S.N.L.R. 18/7/17.
HUMAN, J., Pte. (3903), attested 9/7/17, demobilised 7/9/19, Lewis gunner.
RADIEN, E., L./Cpl. (3904), attested 13/7/17, L./Cpl. 21/5/18, killed in action 20/9/18, passed Stokes course.
ENGLEBERG, K., Pte. (3905), attested 14/7/17, released medically unfit 20/7/17.
BOOYSEN, S., Pte. (3906), attested 14/7/17, demobilised 7/10/19.
ADAMS, H., Pte. (3907), attested 17/7/17, released medically unfit 20/7/17.
SOLOMON, I., Pte. (3908), attested 17/7/17, S.N.L.R. 21/8/17.

AFRICA, J. M., Pte. (3909), attested 17/7/17, demobilised 10/10/19.
PETERSEN, M., Pte. (3910), attested 17/7/17, S.N.L.R. 22/7/17.
WITBOOI, A., Pte. (3911), attested 17/7/17, demobilised 10/10/19.
GOODALL, T., Pte. (3912), attested 17/7/17, released medically unfit 27/4/18.
WILLIAMS, J., Pte. (3913), attested 17/7/17, released medically unfit 25/7/17.
SASS, J., Pte. (3914), attested 17/7/17, demobilised 11/7/19.
BACHUS, W. J., Pte. (3915), attested 17/7/17, demobilised 16/7/19.
WITBOOI, S., Pte. (3916), attested 17/7/17, released medically unfit 6/6/18.
LESS, W., Pte. (3917), attested 18/7/17, demobilised 27/10/19.
ERASMUS, J., Pte. (3918), attested 19/7/17, released medically unfit 1/9/17.
ROSSOUW, J., Pte. (3919), attested 23/7/17, demobilised 7/9/19.
HENDRICKS, W., Pte. (3920), attested 16/7/17, demobilised 21/7/19.
NEFF, H., Pte. (3921), attested 16/7/17, demobilised 28/9/19.
ABRAHAMS, A., Pte. (3922), attested 23/7/17, S.N.L.R. 6/8/17.
LE ROUX, H., Pte. (3923), attested 22/7/17, died of malaria 4/4/18.
WILLIAMS, J., Pte. (3924), attested 24/7/17, S.N.L.R. 6/5/18.
HEUGH, D., Pte. (3925), attested 28/7/17, demobilised 16/7/19.
FRASER, J., Pte. (3926), attested 28/7/17, demobilised 7/10/19.
ABRAHAMS, J., Pte. (3927), attested 1/8/17, demobilised 11/7/19.
KROUTZ, M., Pte. (3928), attested 1/8/17, S.N.L.R. 16/2/18.
GELDENHUYS, H., Pte. (3929), attested 30/7/17, demobilised 8/9/19.
VERMUELEN, P., Pte. (3930), attested 31/7/17, released medically unfit 13/12/18.
OOSTEHUISEN, J., Pte. (3931), attested 30/7/17, demobilised 21/7/19.
JACKSON, J., Pte. (3932), attested 2/7/17, released medically unfit 14/8/17.
KAMAS, T., Pte. (3933), attested 2/7/17, released medically unfit 14/8/17.
VAN RENSBERG, P., Pte. (3934), attested 30/7/17, demobilised 7/9/19.
CANNON, J. H., Pte. (3935), attested 30/7/17, released medically unfit 25/9/18.
SOULS, C., Pte. (3936), attested 1/8/17, released medically unfit 26/10/17.
VAN WYNGAARD, S., Pte. (3937), attested 31/7/17, demobilised 13/8/19.
MOURITZ, J., Pte. (3938), attested 31/7/17, released medically unfit 14/8/17.
WILLIAMSON, S., Pte. (3939), attested 26/7/17, released medically unfit 14/6/18.
McCLINTON, E., Pte. (3940), attested 30/7/17, released medically unfit 14/8/17.
MAKOWYN, W., Pte. (3941), attested 1/8/17, released medically unfit 14/8/17.
PATIENCE, A., Pte. (3942), attested 2/8/17, demobilised 16/7/19.
ERASMUS, G., Pte. (3943), attested 2/8/17, released medically unfit 15/8/17.
JACOBS, S., Pte. (3944), attested 2/8/17, released medically unfit 14/8/17.
ADONIS, J., Pte. (3945), attested 2/8/17, demobilised 7/10/19.
DIPPENAAR, K., Pte. (3946), attested 2/8/17, demobilised 31/12/19.
MITAS, C., Pte. (3947), attested 2/8/17, demobilised 16/7/19.
EDENS, J., Pte. (3948), attested 2/8/17, released medically unfit 14/8/17.
CAROLUS, F., Pte. (3949), attested 2/8/17, demobilised 11/7/19.
ERASMUS, G., Pte. (3950), attested 2/8/17, released medically unfit 17/8/17.
RONEY, J., Pte. (3951), attested 2/8/17, demobilised 8/9/19.
DANSTER, S., Pte. (3952), attested 1/8/17, demobilised 21/7/19.
ERASMUS, S., Pte. (3953), attested 1/8/17, demobilised 7/9/19.
HENDRICKSE, H., Pte. (3954), attested 2/8/17, demobilised 8/10/19, machine gunner.
DE BRUIN, J., Pte. (3955), attested 2/8/17, released medically unfit 14/8/17.
HENDRICKS, J., Pte. (3956), attested 2/8/17, released medically unfit 14/8/17.
ERASMUS, C., Pte. (3957), attested 2/8/17, released medically unfit 6/9/17.
THYS, A., Pte. (3958), attested 1/8/17, demobilised 16/7/19.
ADAMS, R., Pte. (3959), attested 1/8/17, released medically unfit 17/8/17.
ADAMS, C., Pte. (3960), attested 1/8/17, demobilised 16/7/19.
LEE, J., Pte. (3961), attested 4/8/17, demobilised 16/7/19.
TORRENT, A., Pte. (3962), attested 4/8/17, demobilised 16/7/19.
SWART, J., Pte. (3963), attested 4/8/17, released medically unfit 6/9/17.
VARIE, A., Pte. (3964), attested 4/8/17, released medically unfit 14/8/17.
EVERSON, D., Pte. (3965), attested 4/8/17, released medically unfit 14/8/17.
DU TOIT, C., Pte. (3966), attested 6/8/17, released medically unfit 17/8/17.
PIENAAR, G., Pte. (3967), attested 4/8/17, demobilised 7/9/19.
MILFORD, W., Pte. (3968), attested 30/7/17, demobilised 22/7/19.
MORTLOCK, G., Pte. (3969), attested 7/8/17, demobilised 11/7/19.
BOER, C., Pte. (3970), attested 7/8/17, demobilised 8/9/19.
FIELDMAN, I., Pte. (3971), attested 7/8/17, released medically unfit 14/8/17.
BOOYSEN, P., Pte. (3972), attested 9/8/17, released medically unfit 17/8/17.
COETZEE, C., Pte. (3973), attested 13/8/17, released medically unfit 17/8/17.
ABRAHAMS, J. T., Pte. (3974), attested 9/8/17, released medically unfit 22/8/17.
WESTERMAN, G., Pte. (3975), attested 13/8/17, released medically unfit 6/9/17.
VAN DER POEL, E., Pte. (3976), attested 15/8/17, released medically unfit 17/8/17.
ADAMS, A., Pte. (3977), attested 15/8/17, demobilised 7/10/19.
BLOUMIT, J., Pte. (3978), attested 22/8/17, released medically unfit 29/8/17.
HENDRICKS, C., Pte. (3979), attested 22/8/17, released medically unfit 24/9/17.
EDWARDS, A., Pte. (3980), attested 27/8/17, released medically unfit 6/9/17.
FARO, F., Pte. (3981), attested 27/8/17, released medically unfit 6/9/17.
WITBOOI, J., Pte. (3982), attested 1/9/17, demobilised 16/7/19.
WILLIAMS, H., Pte. (3983), attested 7/9/17, released medically unfit 24/9/17.
ADAMS, F., Pte. (3984), attested 8/9/17, demobilised 11/7/19.
SMITH, J., Pte. (3985), attested 13/9/17, released medically unfit 24/9/17.
MICHAEL, T., Pte. (3986), attested 15/9/17, released medically unfit 16/9/17.
CLASSEN, W., Pte. (3987), attested 16/9/17, released medically unfit 27/4/18.
FEINHOLS, H., Staff Sgt. (3988), attested 21/9/17, Staff Sgt. 21/9/17, transferred to U.D.F. 1/6/18, European personnel.
McCALLUM, H., Staff Sgt. (3989), attested 19/9/17, Staff Sgt. 19/9/17, released medically unfit 13/4/18, European personnel.
SYLVESTER, F. D., Pte. (2990), attested 12/10/17, S.N.L.R. 15/10/17.
MICHAEL, S. D., Pte. (3991), attested 22/10/17, demobilised 8/9/19.
SCHIPPERS, G., Pte. (3992), attested 22/10/17, released medically unfit 12/11/17.
SCHIPPERS, G. A., Pte. (3993), attested 22/10/17, demobilised 8/9/19.
LE BRETON, J. T., Pte. (3994), attested 25/10/17, demobilised 7/9/19.
VAN WYK, J., Pte. (3995), attested 25/10/17, killed in action 20/9/18.
CLOETE, J., Pte. (3996), attested 25/10/17, demobilised 22/7/19.
HAYES, R., Pte. (3997), attested 25/10/17, died of pneumonia 28/8/18.

LOUW, G., Pte. (3998), attested 25/10/17, demobilised 7/9/19.
PRINS, I., Pte. (3999), attested 26/10/17, released medically unfit 15/11/17.
COMBRINK, J., Pte. (4000), attested 26/10/17, released medically unfit 13/11/17.
HICKLEY, S., Pte. (4001), attested 29/10/17, released medically unfit 9/11/17.
CROY, W., Pte. (4002), attested 31/10/17, released medically unfit 12/11/17.
NEWMAN, J., Pte. (4003), attested 26/10/17, released medically unfit 15/11/17.
SWART, J., Pte. (4004), attested 26/10/17, released medically unfit 15/11/17.
VAN DER RAHT, H. A., Pte. (4005), attested 29/10/17, released medically unfit 15/11/17.
FAROR, N., Pte. (4006), attested 29/10/17, released medically unfit 15/11/17.
EUROPA, J., Pte. (4007), attested 26/10/17, released medically unfit 13/11/17.
MINTOOR, G., Pte. (4008), attested 29/10/17, released medically unfit 15/11/17.
MURTZ, J., Pte. (4009), attested 26/10/17, demobilised 12/7/19.
STEGMAN, W., Pte. (4010), attested 29/10/17, demobilised 7/9/19.
HOFFMAN, S., Pte. (4011), attested 29/10/17, released medically unfit 12/11/17
MEAS, R., Pte. (4012), attested 30/10/17, demobilised 3/12/19.
MEAS, C., L./Cpl. (4013), attested 30/10/17, a/L./Cpl. 13/6/18, L./Cpl. 5/7/18, demobilised 21/7/19.
VAN DER MERWE, J., Pte. (4014), attested 10/11/17, released medically unfit 14/12/17.
BYMAN, J., Pte. (4015), attested 3/12/17, demobilised 7/9/19.
PLAATJES, J., Pte. (4016), attested 3/12/17, demobilised 7/9/19.
MORRIS, G., Pte. (4017), attested 4/12/17, released medically unfit 24/12/17.
MILLER, W., Pte. (4018), attested 18/12/17, released medically unfit 23/12/17.
BARTMAN, J., Pte. (4019), attested 18/12/17, released medically unfit 24/12/17.
BOOYSENS, J., Pte. (4020), attested 18/12/17, released medically unfit 23/12/17.
RUITERS, G., Pte. (4021), attested 18/12/17, released medically unfit 25/12/17.
BROWN, W., Pte. (4022), attested 14/1/18, demobilised 11/7/19.
DAVIDS, A., Pte. (4023), attested 11/1/18, demobilised 7/10/19.
HARRISON, J., Pte. (4024), attested 17/1/18, demobilised 7/9/19.
JOB, S., Pte. (4025), attested 15/1/18, demobilised 7/10/19.
FESTER, I., Pte. (4026), attested 11/1/18, demobilised 21/7/19.
KAMPSHALL, J., Pte. (4027), attested 15/1/18, released medically unfit 25/1/18
JOHNSON, H., Pte. (4028), attested 19/1/18, demobilised 21/7/19.
TITUS, J., Pte. (4029), attested 19/1/18, demobilised 7/9/19.
GEDULD, M., Pte. (4030), attested 17/1/18, demobilised 7/10/19.
CAROLUS, D., Cpl. (4031), attested 19/1/18, L./Cpl. 5/7/18, Cpl. 1/11/18, demobilised 16/7/19, machine gunner, passed physical and bayonet training course.
ARENDSE, J. T., Pte. (4032), attested 19/1/18, rejected 19/1/18.
MORRIS, H., Pte. (4033), attested 17/1/18, released medically unfit 30/1/18.
CAROLUS, F., Pte. (4034), attested 18/1/18, demobilised 7/9/19.
WILSON, C., L./Cpl. (4035), attested 23/1/18, L./Cpl. 5/7/18, killed in action 20/9/18
GREGORY, J., Pte. (4036), attested 25/1/18, demobilised 7/9/19.
HARRY, D., Pte. (4037), attested 11/1/18, demobilised 21/7/19.
JASSON, E. A., Pte. (4038), attested 11/1/18, released medically unfit 31/1/18.
LOUW, A., Pte. (4039), attested 25/1/18, released medically unfit 31/1/18.
BOOYSEN, D., Pte. (4040), attested 24/1/18, rejected 24/1/18.
PAULSE, A., Pte. (4041), attested 29/1/18, demobilised 21/7/19.
PETERSEN, T., Pte. (4042), attested 28/1/18, released medically unfit 20/3/18.
PIENAAR, W., Pte. (4043), attested 28/1/18, demobilised 21/7/19.
CAROLUS, J., Pte. (4044), attested 28/1/18, demobilised 8/9/19.
SIEBRITS, J., Pte. (4045), attested 28/1/18, demobilised 7/10/19.
THEUNNISSEN, K., Pte. (4046), attested 28/1/18, released medically unfit 5/3/18.
WESSELS, T., Pte. (4047), attested 29/1/18, demobilised 3/1/19.
MAY, H., Pte. (4048), attested 31/1/18, released medically unfit 1/3/18.
DE KOCK, L., Pte. (4049), attested 28/1/18, released medically unfit 7/2/18.
SCHOLTZ, N. F., Pte. (4050), attested 1/2/18, released medically unfit 5/6/18.
MORGENDAL, N., Pte. (4051), attested 30/1/18, demobilised 11/9/19.
FORTUIN, W., Pte. (4052), attested 29/1/18, demobilised 7/10/19, passed gas course.
MATHEE, T., Pte. (4053), attested 29/1/18, demobilised 8/9/19.
DE ROOCK, J., Pte. (4054), attested 29/1/18, demobilised 7/10/19.
FORTUIN, P., Pte. (4055), attested 30/1/18, S.N.L.R. 7/5/18.
VAN WYK, S., Pte. (4056), attested 1/2/18, released medically unfit 7/3/18.
ISAACS, L., Pte. (4057), attested 31/1/18, released medically unfit 5/3/18.
DANIELS, T., Pte. (4058), attested 31/1/18, demobilised 16/7/19, machine gunner.
PETERSEN, A., Pte. (4059), attested 31/1/18, demobilised 7/10/19.
VAN WYK, J. W., Pte. (4060), attested 28/1/18, demobilised 31/12/19.
HENDRICKS, J., Sgt. (4061), attested 29/1/18, a/Sgt. 20/4/18, Sgt. 1/11/18, demobilised 16/7/19.
ABRAHAMS, M., Pte. (4062), attested 30/1/18, demobilised 16/7/19.
BOOYSEN, F., Pte. (4063), attested 15/1/18, demobilised 6/9/19.
PRESENCE, W., Pte. (4064), attested 4/2/18, demobilised 7/10/19.
MURPHY, F., Pte. (4065), attested 2/2/18, released medically unfit 23/3/18.
MAGELLAN, J., Pte. (4066), attestetd 5/2/18, demobilised 7/10/19, passed trench warfare and bombing courses.
THERON, K., Pte. (4067), attested 5/2/18, demobilised 7/10/19.
LAURENCE, C., Pte. (4068), attested 5/2/18, demobilised 31/3/19.
BRIKLES, J., Pte. (4069), attested 4/2/18, demobilised 7/9/19.
JOHNSTON, J., Pte. (4070), attested 7/2/18, S.N.L.R. 16/6/18.
PATIENCE, J., Pte. (4071), attested 7/2/18, demobilised 8/9/19.
HUGHES, J., Pte. (4072), attested 7/2/18, demobilised 8/9/19.
MCOMBRING, J., Pte. (4073), attested 8/2/18, demobilised 25/10/20, qualified signaller.
SOLOMON, D. G., Pte. (4074), attested 8/2/18, demobilised 8/9/19.
ADAMS, B., Pte. (4075), attested 5/2/18, killed in action 20/9/18.
WILLIAMS, A. J., a/Cpl. (4076), attested 11/2/18, a/Cpl. 1/3/19, demobilised 7/9/19.
AFRICA, P., Pte. (4077), attested 11/2/18, demobilised 21/7/19.
PERRY, D., Pte. (4078), attested 12/2/18, released medically unfit 2/4/18.
AFRICA, C., Pte. (4079), attested 11/2/18, demobilised 7/9/19.
WENTZEL, T. M., Pte. (4080), attested 12/2/18, demobilised 21/7/19, transport driver.
CHRISTIAN, M., Pte. (4081), attested 11/2/18, demobilised 21/7/19.
WILLIAMS, F., Pte. (4082), attested 11/2/18, released medically unfit 21/9/18.
BROWN, H., Pte. (4083), attested 11/2/18, released medically unfit 27/4/18.
MINNIES, F. J., Pte. (4084), attested 11/2/18, died of uræmia 24/2/19.
DYASON, R., Pte. (4085), attested 11/2/18, demobilised 7/10/19.

THE STORY OF THE 1st CAPE CORPS.

MARTIN, J., Cpl. (4086), atested 9/2/18, Cpl. 1/11/18, demobilised 7/9/19, passed scout and sniping course, also range finding course.
WILLIAMS, H., Pte. (4087), attested 11/2/18, demobilised 7/10/19.
DIETTERICH, J., Pte. (4088), attested 7/2/18, rejected 23/2/18.
DIEDERICKS, C., Pte. (4089), attested 8/2/18, rejected 23/2/18.
GOLIATH, M., Pte. (4090), attested 8/2/18, rejected 23/2/18.
WILLIAMS, A., Pte. (4091), attested 12/2/18, rejected 23/2/18.
PETERSEN, J., Pte. (4092), attested 11/2/18, rejected 23/2/18.
ISAACS, M., Pte. (4093), attested 11/2/18, rejected 23/2/18.
MEYER, W., Pte. (4094), attested 12/2/18, demobilised 7/9/19.
JEPTHA, J., Pte. (4095), attested 11/2/18, demobilised 11/7/19.
FISH, J. W., L./Cpl. (4096), attested 12/2/18, L./Cpl. 5/7/18, demobilised 7/10/19.
ABRAMS, J., Pte. (4097), attested 12/2/18, demobilised 11/7/19.
SOLOMON, A., Sgt. (4098), attested 16/2/18, acted C.Q.M.S. paid 21/9/18 to 15/10/18, Sgt. 1/11/18, demobilised 7/10/19.
FRANCE, R., Pte. (4099), attested 16/2/18, released medically unfit 2/5/18.
MEAS, A., Pte. (4100), attested 16/2/18, rejected 4/3/18.
OAKS, W., Pte. (4101), attested 14/2/18, released medically unfit 30/3/18.
CONSTANT, J., Pte. (4102), attested 9/2/18, demobilised 22/7/19.
STOLLS, W., Pte. (4103), attested 15/2/18, demobilised 8/9/19.
VAN HEEVER, P., Pte. (4104), attested 9/2/18, released medically unfit 16/3/18.
VAN NEIL, H., Pte. (4105), attested 9/2/18, demobilised 22/7/19, machine gunner.
LINKS, P. J., Pte. (4106), attested 9/2/18, demobilised 22/7/19, passed cookery course.
VAN WYK, M., Pte. (4107), attested 9/2/18, released medically unfit 16/3/18.
AMAN, P., Pte. (4108), attested 9/2/18, released medically unfit 16/3/18.
ESSEX, J., Pte. (4109), attested 9/2/18, demobilised 21/7/19, passed trench warfare and trench mortar course.
CONSTANT, D., Pte. (4110), attested 9/2/18, released medically unfit 16/3/18.
HENRY, W., Pte. (4111), attested 9/2/18, demobilised 7/9/19.
JULES, H., Pte. (4112), attested 9/2/18, demobilised 16/7/19.
VAN WYK, S., Pte. (4113), attested 9/2/18, demobilised 7/9/19.
DE JONG, J., Pte. (4114), attested 9/2/18, released medically unfit 16/3/18.
CLOETE, J., Pte. (4115), attested 9/2/18, released medically unfit 23/4/18.
CAROLUS, J., Pte. (4116), attested 9/2/18, released medically unfit 16/3/18.
LOSPER, C., Pte. (4117), attested 7/2/18, demobilised 7/9/19.
LANNEY, B., Pte. (4118), attested 9/2/18, demobilised 7/9/19, machine gunner.
ALEXANDER, J. J., Pte. (4119), attested 9/2/18, demobilised 7/9/19.
VAN WYK, H., Pte. (4120), attested 9/2/18, demobilised 7/9/19, machine gunner.
VAN WYK, P., Pte. (4121), attested 9/2/18, demobilised 22/7/19.
CUPIDO, L., Pte. (4122), attested 13/2/18, demobilised 16/7/19.
PETERS, J., Pte. (4123), attested 11/2/18, released medically unfit 16/3/18.
LOWE, F., Pte. (4124), attested 15/2/18, demobilised 28/8/19.
ROMAN, J., Pte. (4125), attested 15/2/18, demobilised 21/7/19.
LAMS, J., Pte. (4126), attested 12/2/18, demobilised 11/7/19.
HERADIEN, J., Pte. (4127), attested 15/2/18, released medically unfit 12/8/18.
BREDEVELDT, M., Pte. (4128), attested 20/2/18, demobilised 16/7/19.
BARTMAN, A., Pte. (4129), attested 15/2/18, released medically unfit 2/3/18.
BEZUIDENHOUT, J., Pte. (4130), attested 9/2/18, released medically unfit 16/3/18.
BRITTEN, B., Pte. (4131), attested 15/2/18, released medically unfit 1/3/18.
CAMERON, C., Pte. (4132), attested 19/2/18, released medically unfit 16/3/18.
JANSEN, F., Pte. (4133), attested 14/2/18, released medically unfit 1/3/18.
KLOPPERS, A., Pte. (4134), attested 14/2/18, released medically unfit 1/3/18.
LODEWYK, J., Pte. (4135), attested 15/2/18, released medically unfit 2/3/18.
PETERS, G., Pte. (4136), attested 9/2/18, released medically unfit 16/3/18.
PETERS, H., Pte. (4137), attested 15/2/18, released medically unfit 1/3/18.
SEALS, J., Pte. (4138), attested 9/2/18, released medically unfit 16/3/18.
LEVENDAL, C., Pte. (4139), attested 20/2/18, demobilised 7/10/19, machine gunner.
THOMPSON, T., Pte. (4140), attested 12/2/18, released medically unfit 1/3/18.
WILLIAMS, J., Pte. (4141), attested 14/2/18, released medically unfit 1/3/18.
ZAL, J., Pte. (4142), attested 9/2/18, released medically unfit 16/3/18.
STAAL, B., Pte. (4143), attested 14/2/18, demobilised 16/7/19.
LINKS, J., Pte. (4144), attested 11/2/18, released medically unfit 16/3/18.
VENTER, I., Pte. (4145), attested 18/2/18, demobilised 22/7/19.
DE LA HARPE, F., Pte. (4146), attested 15/2/18, demobilised 29/3/20.
CLOETE, W., Pte. (4147), attested 15/2/18, released medically unfit 18/6/18.
REAGANS, D., Pte. (4148), attested 11/2/18, demobilised 7/9/19.
ALEXANDER, I., Pte. (4149), attested 13/2/18, released medically unfit 16/3/18.
DE JAAR, F., Pte. (4150), attested 13/2/18, demobilised 7/9/19, machine gunner.
DE JONGH, W., Pte. (4151), attested 11/2/18, demobilised 14/1/19.
RICHARDS, A., Pte. (4152), attested 16/2/18, released medically unfit 11/3/18.
PIPLOW, J. D., Pte. (4153), attested 11/2/18, released medically unfit 16/3/18.
VAN NEIL, A., Pte. (4154), attested 11/2/18, released medically unfit 15/4/18.
BUKIE, P., Pte. (4155), attested 11/2/18, released medically unfit 16/3/18.
JACOBS, A., Pte. (4156), attested 11/2/18, released medically unfit 16/3/18.
PETERS, J., Pte. (4157), attested 11/2/18, demobilised 7/9/19.
MALANZA, D., Pte. (4158), attested 15/2/18, demobilised 18/10/19.
VERMEULEN, J., Pte. (4159), attested 16/2/18, demobilised 3/1/19.
GEORGE, W., Pte. (4160), attested 19/2/18, demobilised 11/7/19.
JACOBS, B., Pte. (4161), attested 19/2/18, demobilised 1/11/19.
DANIELS, J., Pte. (4162), attested 19/2/18, demobilised 7/10/19.
MILLER, J., Pte. (4163), attested 19/2/18, released medically unfit 18/12/18.
BURGHER, J., Pte. (4164), attested 19/2/18, demobilised 20/10/19.
PETERSEN, C., Pte. (4165), attested 19/2/18, demobilised 11/7/19, passed trench warfare and trench mortar course.
VAN TORA, F., Pte. (4166), attested 19/2/18, demobilised 7/10/19.
SNYMAN, H., Pte. (4167), attested 21/2/18, demobilised 7/9/19.
RHODA, C., Pte. (4168), attested 18/2/18, released medically unfit 12/11/18.
VISAGIE, P., Pte. (4169), attested 19/2/18, demobilised 31/12/19.
DYASON, A., Pte. (4170), attested 19/2/18, released medically unfit 1/3/18.
DE KOCK, N. J., Pte. (4171), attested 19/2/18, released medically unfit 1/3/18.
ROODT, C., Pte. (4172), attested 19/2/18, released medically unfit 1/3/18.

FISHER, C., Pte. (4173), attested 19/2/18, released medically unfit 1/3/18.
STUBBS, T., Pte. (4174), attested 19/2/18, released medically unfit 1/3/18.
BLANKENBERG, J., Pte. (4175), attested 19/2/18, released medically unfit 1/3/18.
ZENK, H., Pte. (4176), attested 19/2/18, released medically unfit 1/3/18.
VISAGIE, P., Pte. (4177), attested 19/2/18, released medically unfit 1/3/18.
PAULSE, J. D., Pte. (4178), attested 18/2/18, demobilised 8/9/19, machine gunner.
FREDERICKS, J., Pte. (4179), attestd 19/2/18, demobilised 7/10/19.
THOMAS, W. G., Pte. (4180), attested 18/2/18, demobilised 11/7/19, qualified signaller
FORTUIN, I., Pte. (4181), attested 18/2/18, released medically unfit 1/3/18.
VAN REENEN, J., Pte. (4182), attested 15/2/18, released medically unfit 16/3/18.
VAN REENEN, J., Pte. (4183), attested 14/2/18, released medically unfit 16/3/18.
VAN ROOYEN, C. C. L., Pte. (4184), attested 19/2/18, S.N.L.R. 3/8/18.
WILLIAMS, S., Pte. (4185), attested 20/2/18, demobilised 11/7/19.
WHITEBOOI, M., Pte. (4186), attested 20/2/18, demobilised 21/7/19.
KLEINBOOI, M., Pte. (4187), attested 20/2/18, demobilised 7/9/19.
MEYER, D. J., Pte. (4188), attested 21/2/18, demobilised 10/4/20.
KYNOCH, T., Pte. (4189), attested 21/2/18, demobilised 21/7/19.
HEFKA, P., Pte. (4190), attested 19/2/18, demobilised 11/10/19.
POKBAAS, A., Pte. (4191), attested 18/2/18, released medically unfit 30/3/18.
REDLINKHUIS, A., Pte. (4192), attested 22/2/18, demobilised 7/10/19, machine gunner.
GROEP, J., Pte. (4193), attested 20/2/18, demobilised 7/9/19.
LOUW, J., Pte. (4194), attested 25/2/18, demobilised 21/7/19.
MYBURG, F. C., Pte. (4195), attested 25/2/18, demobilised 7/9/19, qualified first-class signaller.
WILLIAMS, N., Pte. (4196), attested 19/2/18, released medically unfit 11/3/18.
VAN NEEVER, G., Pte. (4197), attested 13/2/18, demobilised 7/9/19
SWART, K., Pte. (4198), attested 14/2/18, demobilised 31/12/19.
ABRAHAMS, N., Pte. (4199), attested 13/2/18, released medically unfit 30/8/18.
BEZUIDENHOUT, M., Pte. (4200), attested 23/2/18, demobilised 7/9/19.
FOURIE, B., Pte. (4201), attested 27/2/18, demobilised 7/9/19.
GAFFENY, P., Pte. (4202), attested 27/2/18, demobilised 7/9/19.
ROMAN, J., Pte. (4203), attested 25/2/18, released medically unfit 12/3/18.
DREYER, A., Pte. (4204), attested 20/2/18, demobilised 16/7/19.
COETZE, A., Pte. (4205), attested 21/2/18, released medically unfit 2/3/18.
ROSS, J., Pte. (4206), attested 20/2/18, released medically unfit 2/3/18.
FRANS, H., Pte. (4207), attested 16/2/18, released medically unfit 2/3/18.
BANTJES, J., Pte. (4208), attested 21/2/18, released medically unfit 2/3/18.
BREDENKAMP, H., Pte. (4209), attested 20/2/18, released medically unfit 2/3/18.
ARENDSE, J., Pte. (4210), attested 28/2/18, released medically unfit 2/3/18.
METHEWA, A., Pte. (4211), attested 14/2/18, released medically unfit 2/3/18.
VAN REENEN, W., Pte. (4212), attested 22/2/18, released medically unfit 2/3/18.
MEYERS, J., Pte. (4213), attested 19/2/18, released medically unfit 2/3/18.
O'MALLEY, H., Pte. (4214), attested 10/2/18, released medically unfit 2/3/18.
JOHNSON, J., Pte. (4215), attested 19/2/18, reeased medically unfit 2/3/18.
JOCHEMS, N., Pte. (4216), attested 15/2/18, released medically unfit 2/3/18.
FORTUIN, D., Pte. (4217), attested 20/2/18, released medically unfit 4/3/18.
WILLIAMS, L., Pte. (4218), attested 20/2/18, released medically unfit 4/3/18.
JONAS, F., Pte. (4219), attested 9/2/18, released medically unfit 16/3/18.
SEPTEMBER, S., Pte. (4220), attested 25/2/18, demobilised 1/1/19.
JONES, J., Pte. (4221), attested 25/2/18, demobilised 7/9/19.
DREYER, W., Pte. (4222), attested 25/2/18, demobilised 7/10/19, machine gunner.
POOLE, E., Pte. (4223), attested 25/2/18, demobilised 7/10/19.
SOMPIE, T., Pte. (4224), attested 25/2/18, demobilised 8/9/19.
NOBLE, P., Pte. (4225), attested 25/2/18, demobilised 16/7/19, qualified signaller.
APRIL, M., Pte. (4226), attested 27/2/18, released medically unfit 3/3/18.
SPENCELY, C., Pte. (4227), attested 25/2/18, demobilised 7/9/19.
HENDRICKS, J., Pte. (4228), attested 25/2/18, released medically unfit 23/3/18.
JOHNSON, H., Pte. (4229), attested 25/2/18, demobilised 26/12/18.
JOHNSON, J., Pte. (4230), attested 25/2/18, demobilised 9/9/19.
JOHNSON, HY., Pte. (4231), attested 25/2/18, demobilised 21/7/19.
VALENTINE, R., Pte. (4232), attested 25/2/18, demobilised 21/7/19.
ISHMAIL, J. J., Pte. (4233), attested 25/2/18, demobilised 7/9/19.
WAGNER, J., Pte. (4234), attested 26/2/18, demobilised 31/12/19.
BROWN, H. M., Pte. (4235), attested 1/3/18, demobilised 7/9/19, machine gunner.
IDAS, S., Pte. (4236), attested 26/2/18, demobilised 7/10/19, machine gunner.
DAVIDS, F., Pte. (4237), attested 26/2/18, demobilised 7/10/19.
SAMUELS, A., Pte. (4239), attested 26/2/18, demobilised 12/7/19.
PHILLIPS, F., Pte. (4240), attested 25/2/18, demobilised 21/7/19.
GELJOHN, F., Pte. (4241), attested 26/2/18, demobilised 11/7/19.
JOHNSON, D., Pte. (4242), attested 28/2/18, demobilised 11/7/19
DEVEREAUX, H., Pte. (4243), attested 28/2/18, released medically unfit 12/3/18.
VAN ROOI, A., Pte. (4244), attested 26/2/18, released medically unfit 12/3/18.
ELEY, J., Pte. (4245), attested 26/2/18, demobilised 30/7/19.
JOHNSON, P., Pte. (4246), attested 25/2/18, released medically unfit 12/3/18.
AUGUST, M. J., Pte. (4247), attested 23/2/18, released medically unfit 12/3/18.
BEZUIDENHOUT, J., Pte. (4248), attested 23/2/18, released medically unfit 12/3/18.
KLIENHANS, H., Pte. (4249), attested 23/2/18, released medically unfit 30/6/18.
WILLIAMS, J., Pte. (4250), attested 23/2/18, demobilised 7/9/19, machine gunner
DE KOCK, M., Pte. (4251), attested 6/3/18, demobilised 11/7/19.
PALM, J. H., Pte. (4252), attested 4/3/18, released medically unfit 13/1/19.
MARHOTA, C., Pte. (4253), attested 4/3/18, released medically unfit 30/3/18.
WILLS, J. H., Pte. (4254), attested 4/3/18, demobilised 16/7/19.
BAILEY, W., Pte. (4255), attested 4/3/18, demobilised 11/11/19.
LE ROUX, D., Pte. (4256), attested 4/3/18, demobilised 7/10/19.
ADAMS, A., Pte. (4257), attested 3/3/18, demobilised 7/10/19, machine gunner.
FREDERICKS, P., Pte. (4258), attested 2/3/18, demobilised 11/7/19, machine gunner.
CUPIDO, J., Pte. (4259), attested 28/2/18, demobilised 29/12/18.
ANDRIES, M., Pte. (4260), attested 4/3/18, demobilised 8/10/19.
SMITH, P. H., Pte. (4261), attested 5/3/18, S.N.L.R. 4/6/18.
SEAT, A., Pte. (4262), attested 6/3/18, demobilised 16/7/19.
JORDAN, W., Pte. (4263), attested 1/3/18, demobilised 7/9/19, machine gunner.
ARENDS, J., Pte. (4264), attested 2/3/18, demobilised 12/7/19.

THE STORY OF THE 1st CAPE CORPS.

STEVENS, H., Pte. (4265), attested 2/3/18, demobilised 7/9/19.
STENFLEIT, L., Pte. (4266), attested 26/2/18, demobilised 21/7/19.
SMIT, C., Pte. (4267), attested 5/3/18, died of malaria 21/8/18.
SAMPSON, P., Pte. (4268), attested 4/3/18, demobilised 21/10/19.
VAN ZITTERS, J., Pte. (4269), attested 5/3/18, killed in action 20/9/18.
RICHARDS, P., Pte. (4270), attested 5/3/18, demobilised 16/7/19.
VAN SCHALKWYK, K., Pte. (4271), attested 5/3/18, demobilised 8/10/19.
JACOBUS, W., Pte. (4272), attested 5/3/18, killed in action 20/9/18.
MARTIN, J., Pte. (4273), attested 4/3/18, demobilised 8/10/19.
SEMERIE, A., Pte. (4274), attested 5/3/18, released medically unfit 30/3/18.
ABRAHAMS, J., Pte. (4275), attested 5/3/18, demobilised 7/10/19.
LONDON, P., Pte. (4276), attested 5/3/18, demobilised 21/7/19.
JACOBUS, J., Pte. (4277), attested 5/3/18, demobilised 16/7/19.
ADAMS, J., Pte. (4278), attested 5/3/18, demobilised 7/10/19.
KANTO, J., Pte. (4279), attested 4/3/18, released medically unfit 11/3/18.
ARNOLDS, J. G., Pte. (4280), attested 5/3/18, released medically unfit 11/3/18.
JACOBS, M., Pte. (4281), attested 5/3/18, released medically unfit 11/3/18.
THOMAS, N., Pte. (4282), attested 5/3/18, released medically unfit 11/3/18.
ALBERTUIN, B., Pte. (4283), attested 8/3/18, released medically unfit 20/3/18.
WILLIAMS, A., Pte. (4284), attested 6/3/18, released medically unfit 20/3/18.
LE ROUX, H. D., Sgt. (4285), attested 8/3/18, Cpl. (a/Sgt.) 5/7/18, Sgt. 28/11/18, demobilised 16/7/19
GOMEZ, J., Pte. (4286), attested 6/3/18, released medically unfit 30/3/18.
DU PLESSIS, M., Pte. (4287), attested 8/3/18, demobilised 7/9/19.
SMITH, P., Pte. (4288), attested 9/3/18, released medically unfit 30/3/18.
SWAMLOW, W., Pte. (4289), attested 6/3/18, demobilised 7/9/19.
MARTINUS, W., Pte. (4290), attested 7/3/18, demobilised 21/7/19.
KLASSEN, S. R., Pte. (4291), attested 9/3/18, demobilised 21/7/19, first-class qualified scout.
DAVIDS, W., Pte. (4292), attested 6/3/18, released medically unfit 20/3/18.
VAN BLERK, J., Pte. (4293), attested 7/3/18, released medically unfit 20/3/18.
WILLIAMS, F., Pte. (4294), attested 8/3/18, released medically unfit 20/3/18.
ESAU, W., Pte. (4295), attested 6/3/18, released medically unfit 19/3/18.
MILTON, A., Pte. (4296), attested 2/3/18, released medically unfit 19/3/18.
SMITH, F., Pte. (4297), attested 26/2/18, released medically unfit 20/3/18.
SWARTBOOI, R., Pte. (4298), attested 2/3/18, released medically unfit 20/3/18.
DE WET, J., Pte. (4299), attested 2/3/18, released medically unfit 3/8/18.
CAMPBELL, H., Pte. (4300), attested 11/3/18, demobilised 7/9/19.
MILLER, H., Pte. (4301), attested 12/3/18, demobilised 21/7/19, passed trench warfare and bombing course
JANSEN, J., Pte. (4302), attested 9/3/18, demobilised 21/7/19, drum and fife band.
BEUKES, D., Pte. (4303), attested 12/3/18, demobilised 7/9/19.
DAVIES, B., Pte. (4304), attested 11/3/18, died of influenza 8/10/18.
DE VILLIERS, J., Pte. (4305), attested 11/3/18, demobilised 6/1/20.
NORMAN, P., Pte. (4306), attested 14/3/18, S.N.L.R. 15/7/18.
OOSTHUIZEN, D., Pte. (4307), attested 12/3/18, demobilised 28/8/19.
ABRAHAMS, J., Pte. (4308), attested 12/3/18, demobilised 7/9/19.
SWANEPOEL, D., Pte. (4309), attested 11/3/18, released medically unfit 6/6/18.
TISSONG, H., Pte. (4310), attested 13/3/18, S.N.L.R. 2/5/18.
FRANCIS, J., Pte. (4311), attested 11/3/18, demobilised 7/9/19.
KOCK, J., Pte. (4312), attested 13/3/18, demobilised 7/9/19.
KERN, S., Pte. (4313), attested 11/3/18, demobilised 2/11/19.
MARTIN, H., Pte. (4314), attested 11/3/18, demobilised 6/1/19.
JOSEPH, H., Pte. (4315), attested 12/3/18, demobilised 7/10/19.
EVERED, H., Pte. (4316), attested 12/3/18, demobilised 21/7/19.
VENTER, C., Pte. (4317), attested 11/3/18, released medically unfit 30/3/18.
PATTERSON, W., Pte. (4318), attested 12/3/18, demobilised 21/7/19.
PIETERSE, H., Pte. (4319), attested 13/3/18, demobilised 21/7/19.
ASHLEY, E., Pte. (4320), attested 11/3/18, demobilised 3/11/19.
JONES, D., Pte. (4321), attested 11/3/18, demobilised 8/9/19, qualified scout.
VAN WEST, K., Pte. (4322), attested 13/3/18, released medically unfit 7/6/18.
STEWART, J., Pte. (4323), attested 13/3/18, released medically unfit 27/4/18.
PARMER, S., Pte. (4324), attested 13/3/18, demobilised 6/9/19.
MATROSS, I., Pte. (4325), attested 13/3/18, demobilised 7/9/19.
LOUW, J., Pte. (4326), attested 13/3/18, demobilised 7/9/19.
PETERSEN, J., Pte. (4327), attested 13/3/18, released medically unfit 19/3/18.
ARENDS, P., Pte. (4328), attested 13/3/18, released medically unfit 19/3/18.
GWAMGWAM, H., Pte. (4329), attested 13/3/18, released medically unfit 19/3/18.
HANS, P., Pte. (4330), attested 13/3/18, released medically unfit 19/3/18.
STRUIS, J., Pte. (4331), attested 13/3/18, released medically unfit 19/3/18.
OLIFANT, I., Pte. (4332), attested 13/3/18, released medically unfit 19/3/18.
VIS, G., Pte. (4333), attested 13/3/18, released medically unfit 19/3/18.
JANUARY, J., Pte. (4334), attested 13/3/18, released medically unfit 19/3/18.
GOODMAN, J., Pte. (4335), attested 13/3/18, released medically unfit 19/3/18.
WILLIAMS, A., Pte. (4336), attested 13/3/18, released medically unfit 19/3/18
ARNOLDS, K., Pte. (4337), attested 12/3/18, released medically unfit 20/3/18.
ADAMS, T., Pte. (4338), attested 12/3/18, released medically unfit 14/3/18.
ADAMS, J., Pte. (4339), attested 12/3/18, released medically unfit 14/3/18.
OOSTEHUIZEN, S., Pte. (4340), attested 12/3/18, released medically unfit 14/3/18.
McCARTHY, J. R., Pte. (4341), attested 12/3/18, released medically unfit 14/3/18.
RANDALL, V., Pte. (4342), attested 16/3/18, demobilised 21/7/19.
BOLACE, A., Pte. (4343), attested 14/3/18, demobilised 7/9/19, 1st class signaller.
CAROLSE, A., Pte. (4344), attested 13/3/18, demobilised 7/10/19.
ISAACS, B., Pte. (4345), attested 15/3/18, demobilised 21/7/19.
PIETERSEN, O., Pte. (4346), attested 12/3/18, S.N.L.R. 23/4/18.
CORNELIUS, J., Pte. (4347), attested 14/3/18, demobilised 26/12/18.
BANNISTER, H., Pte. (4348), attested 18/3/18, demobilised 12/7/19, congratulated by G.O.C., E.E.F., for his gallant act in effort to save a comrade from drowning in sea at Gaza.
ADAMS, J., Pte. (4349), attested 18/3/18, demobilised 7/9/19.
BOTHA, J., Pte. (4350), attested 18/3/18, released medically unfit 21/6/18.
PETERSEN, A., Pte. (4351), attested 13/3/18, released medically unfit 23/4/18.
SIDNEY, J., Pte. (4352), attested 14/3/18, released medically unfit 23/4/18.
VAN WYK, Pte. (4353), attested 14/3/18, demobilised 29/12/18.
VAN DER MERWE, J., Pte. (4354), attested 13/3/18, released medically unfit 7/6/18.

THE STORY OF THE 1st CAPE CORPS.

THOMAS, S., Pte. (4355), attested 15/3/18, released medically unfit 22/3/18.
VANNER, D., Pte. (4356), attested 19/3/18, released medically unfit 22/3/18.
CHERRY, W. D., Pte. (4357), attested 13/3/18, released medically unfit 22/3/18.
BLAUW, C., Pte. (4358), attested 15/3/18, released medically unfit 22/3/18.
MOSES, J., Pte. (4359), attested 15/3/18, released medically unfit 24/3/18.
WESSELS, S., Pte. (4360), attested 15/3/18, released medically unfit 24/3/18.
ARENDSE, J., Pte. (4361), attested 15/3/18, released medically unfit 24/3/18.
MEYER, H., Pte. (4362), attested 15/3/18, released medically unfit 24/3/18.
DESAI, M. M., Pte. (4363), attested 15/3/18, released medically unfit 24/3/18.
LIEBENBERG, A., Pte. (4364), attested 15/3/18, released medically unfit 22/3/18.
LOOTS, A., Pte. (4365), attested 14/3/18, demobilised 21/7/19, passed trench warfare and trench mortar course.
STRYDOM, S., Pte. (4366), attested 18/3/18, released medically unfit 2/5/18.
IRWIN, Wm., L./Sgt. (4367), attested 13/3/18, Cpl. 31/10/18, L./Sgt. 1/11/18, demobilised 30/7/19.
CAROLUS, J., Pte. (4368), attested 11/3/18, released medically unfit 27/3/18.
SWANEPOEL, M., Pte. (4369), attested 11/3/18, released medically unfit 27/3/18.
EDWARDS, F., Pte. (4370), attested 11/3/18, released medically unfit 27/3/18.
MALAY, J., Pte. (4371), attested 11/3/18, released medically unfit 27/3/18.
TOM, J., Pte. (4372), attested 11/3/18, released medically unfit 27/3/18.
MASS, A., Pte. (4373), attested 11/3/18, released medically unfit 27/3/18.
KLASS, G., Pte. (4374), attested 11/3/18, released medically unfit 27/3/18.
ONION, J., Pte. (4375), attested 11/3/18, released medically unfit 27/3/18.
BROWN, J., Pte. (4376), attested 11/3/18, released medically unfit 27/3/18.
SCHROEDER, C., Pte. (4377), attested 19/3/18, demobilised 7/9/19.
KILIAN, J. T., a/Cpl. (4378), attested 16/3/18, a/Cpl. 5/7/18, demobilised 7/10/19.
SIMONS, J., Pte. (4379), attested 18/3/18, demobilised 26/12/18.
JONAS, T. W., Pte. (4380), attested 18/3/18, released medically unfit 2/5/18.
JONKERS, J. J., Pte. (4381), attested 20/3/18, released medically unfit 7/6/18.
DICKSON, T., Pte. (4382), attested 19/3/18, demobilised 12/7/19.
COTTLE, F., Pte. (4383), attested 22/3/18, demobilised 7/10/19.
BARTMAN, P., Pte. (4384), attested 22/3/18, demobilised 12/7/19, transport driver.
SHEPPARD, J. H., Pte. (4385), attested 22/3/18, demobilised 7/9/19.
TRUMPETER, W., Pte. (4386), attested 18/3/18, demobilised 31/12/19.
BURGHER, J., Pte. (4387), attested 18/3/18, demobilised 7/10/19.
CUPIDO, C., Pte. (4388), attested 19/3/18, demobilised 8/9/19.
HENDRICKS, P., Pte. (4389), attested 18/3/18, demobilised 12/11/19.
HENRY, J., Pte. (4390), attested 22/3/18, demobilised 22/7/19.
DE LANGE, P., Pte. (4391), attested 18/3/18, released medically unfit 14/5/18.
KANNEMEYER, H., Pte. (4392), attested 18/3/18, demobilised 11/7/19.
ERASMUS, W., Pte. (4393), attested 12/3/18, demobilised 7/10/19.
OLIVER, R., a/Cpl. (4394), attested 18/3/18, a/Cpl. 5/7/18, demobilised 16/7/19.
LOUBSER, J. P., Pte. (4395), attested 12/3/18, demobilised 10/10/19.
RAYNERS, J., Pte. (4396), attested 16/3/18, demobilised 12/7/19.
GELDERBLOEM, J., Pte. (4397), attested 11/3/18, released medically unfit 26/9/18.
DAVIDS, A., Pte. (4398), attested 21/3/18, released medically unfit 1/5/18.
MEYER, G., Pte. (4399), attested 20/3/18, demobilised 7/10/19.
MATTHEWS, F., Pte. (4400), attested 23/3/18, demobilised 21/7/19.
SAMPSON, C., Pte. (4401), attested 23/3/18, demobilised 21/7/19.
MATTHEWS, H., Pte. (4402), attested 18/3/18, rejected 26/3/18.
BOOYSENS, J., Pte. (4403), attested 18/3/18, rejected 26/3/18.
JACOBS, J., Pte. (4404), attested 18/3/18, rejected 26/3/18.
MITCHELL, T., Pte. (4405), attested 18/3/18, rejected 26/3/18.
OPPERMAN, P., Pte. (4406), attested 18/3/18, rejected 19/3/18.
ROSS, J., Pte. (4407), attested 15/3/18, rejected 17/3/18.
BROWN, J., Pte. (4408), attested 15/3/18, rejected 15/3/18.
STELLBLOOM, R., Pte. (4409), attested 16/3/18, rejected 17/3/18.
JACKSON, D., Pte. (4410), attested 15/3/18, rejected 15/3/18.
SERETTO, J., Pte. (4411), attested 18/3/18, rejected 20/3/18.
HENDRICKS, M., Pte. (4412), attested 23/3/18, rejected 30/3/18.
RARENDS, J., Pte. (4413), attested 23/3/18, rejected 30/3/18.
JOHNSON, J. C., Pte. (4414), attested 18/3/18, rejected 30/3/18.
WILLIAMS, J., Pte. (4415), attested 18/3/18, rejected 30/3/18.
NORRIS, A., Pte. (4416), attested 23/3/18, released medically unfit 13/3/19.
LODEWICK, A., Pte. (4417), attested 21/3/18, demobilised 10/10/19.
MARAIS, G., Pte. (4418), attested 22/3/18, demobilised 7/9/19.
SUIGERBROD, F., Pte. (4419), attested 23/3/18, released medically unfit 17/12/18.
LE KAY, D., Pte. (4420), attested 25/3/18, demobilised 7/10/19, 1st class machine gunner.
KRUGER, W., Pte. (4421), attested 25/3/18, demobilised 7/9/19.
VAN NIEKERK, E., Pte. (4422), attested 25/3/18, demobilised 21/7/19.
CHRISTIANS, J., Pte. (4423), attested 25/3/18, released medically unfit 17/9/18.
FORTUIN, F., Pte. (4424), attested 26/3/18, demobilised 7/9/19, 1st class machine gunner.
LYNCH, A. B., L./Cpl. (4425), attested 26/3/18, a/L./Cpl. 20/4/18, L./Cpl. 5/7/18, demobilised 7/9/19.
MYBURGH, I., Pte. (4426), attested 26/3/18, demobilised 21/7/19.
JORDAN, H., Pte. (4427), attested 25/3/18, released medically unfit 30/3/18.
DANIELS, T., Pte. (4428), attested 25/3/18, released medically unfit 30/3/18.
BOOYSEN, J., Pte. (4429), attested 25/3/18, released medically unfit 30/3/18.
PIENAAR, N., Pte. (4430), attested 25/3/18, released medically unfit 30/3/18.
PIENAAR, J., Pte. (4431), attested 26/3/18, released medically unfit 10/4/18.
OLIVER, J., Pte. (4432), attested 25/3/18, demobilised 21/7/19.
NORMAN, N., Pte. (4433), attested 26/3/18, demobilised 15/12/19.
WILSON, W., Pte. (4434), attested 27/3/18, demobilised 21/7/19.
STEENBERG, A., Pte. (4435), attested 18/3/18, demobilised 7/9/19.
SCHEEPERS, G., Pte. (4436), attested 25/3/18, demobilised 7/9/19.
ADAMS, J., Pte. (4437), attested 25/3/18, demobilised 7/9/19.
GRIFFITHS, F., Pte. (4438), attested 25/3/18, S.N.L.R. 14/6/18.
HARTNICK, C., Pte. (4439), attested 25/3/18, killed in action 20/9/18.
SWARTZ, C., Pte. (4440), attested 25/3/18, demobilised 12/7/19, qualified machine gunner.
McBRIDE, T., Pte. (4441), attested 25/3/18, released medically unfit 10/4/18.
OVERMEYER, I., Pte. (4442), attested 25/3/18, released medically unfit 16/5/18.
THOMAS, J., Pte. (4443), attested 18/3/18, demobilised 7/9/19.
CLOETE, P., L./Cpl. (4444), attested 18/3/18, L./Cpl. 5/7/18, demobilised 10/4/20.

HERNE, D., Pte. (4445), attested 18/3/18, demobilised 7/9/19.
DE JONGH, W., Pte. (4446), attested 18/3/18, demobilised 1/1/19.
CLOETE, G., Pte. (4447), attested 18/3/18, demobilised 7/9/19.
DIRKSE, J., Pte. (4448), attested 11/3/18, demobilised 7/9/19.
VAN TOURA, L., Pte. (4449), attested 18/3/18, demobilised 7/9/19.
VAN NEEVER, J., Pte. (4450), attested 18/3/18, demobilised 7/9/19.
HERMANS, J., Pte. (4451), attested 26/3/18, demobilised 12/7/19, qualified machine gunner
MARTIN, T., Pte. (4452), attested 26/3/18, demobilised 26/12/18.
SWARTZ, A., Pte. (4453), attested 26/3/18, demobilised 7/9/19.
DAVIDS, T., Pte. (4454), attested 26/3/18, demobilised 12/7/19.
NICHOLS, G., Pte. (4455), attested 26/3/18, demobilised 7/9/19.
ADRIAANSE, D., Pte. (4456), attested 23/3/18, demobilised 31/12/19.
FRANCIS, J., Pte. (4457), attested 24/3/18, demobilised 16/7/19.
FRANCIS, C., Pte. (4458), attested 27/3/18, released medically unfit 10/4/18
PENNEL, R., Pte. (4459), attested 29/3/18, released medically unfit 11/4/18.
LINDE, F., Pte. (4460), attested 29/3/18, released medically unfit 11/4/18.
KOSANE, J., Pte. (4461), attested 29/3/18, released medically unfit 11/4/18.
MUOTA, J., Pte. (4462), attested 29/3/18, released medically unfit 11/4/18.
GANSTHO, J., Pte. (4463), attested 29/3/18, released medically unfit 11/4/18.
BEZUIDENHOUT, Pte. (4464), attested 22/3/18, released medically unfit 11/4/18
FLOURES, F., Pte. (4465), attested 22/3/18, released medically unfit 11/4/18.
RHODA, J., Pte. (4466), attested 22/3/18, released medically unfit 11/4/18.
ROSSOUW, W., Pte. (4467), attested 21/3/18, released medically unfit 10/4/18
KNOLL, L., Pte. (4468), attested 24/3/18, released medically unfit 11/4/18.
MORAKE, J., Pte. (4469), attested 23/3/18, released medically unfit 11/4/18.
HEARN, H., Pte. (4470), attested 28/3/18, released medically unfit 11/4/18.
PALM, G., Pte. (4471), attested 26/3/18, demobilised 21/7/19.
ROBERTS, W., Pte. (4472), attested 26/3/18, demobilised 21/7/19.
LOUW, J., Pte. (4473), attested 27/3/18, demobilised 12/7/19.
KNOOP, J., Pte. (4474), attested 25/3/18, demobilised 7/10/19.
THYSON, F., Pte. (4475), attested 27/3/18, demobilised 12/7/19.
JORDAN, J., Pte. (4476), attested 26/3/18, demobilised 7/9/19.
DANIELS, H., Pte. (4477), attested 3/4/18, rejected 3/4/18.
PHILLIPS, H., Pte. (4478), attested 3/4/18, rejected 3/4/18.
HYMAN, G., Pte. (4479), attested 22/3/18, released medically unfit 15/4/18.
VISSER, W., Pte. (4480), attested 27/3/18, released medically unfit 15/4/18.
SEPTEMBER, J., Pte. (4481), attested 26/3/18, released medically unfit 15/4/18.
McDONALD, H., Pte. (4482), attested 22/3/18, released medically unfit 15/4/18
ADAMS, J., Pte. (4483), attested 29/3/18, released medically unfit 11/4/18.
ALFREDS, T., Pte. (4484), attested 29/3/18, released medically unfit 10/4/18.
MALGAS, K., Pte. (4485), attested 2/4/18, released medically unfit 10/4/18.
MALGAS, C., Pte. (4486), attested 2/4/18, released medically unfit 10/4/18.
KOOPMAN, J., Pte. (4487), attested 1/4/18, released medically unfit 15/6/18
THRING, A., Pte. (4488), attested 11/3/18, demobilised 7/9/19.
KOOPMAN, D., Pte. (4489), attested 1/4/18, demobilised 7/9/19.
PETERS, G., Pte. (4490), attested 2/4/18, released medically unfit 6/6/18.
MONTSINGER, J., Pte. (4491), attested 22/3/18, demobilised 7/9/19, pioneer.
DE BRUIN, P., Pte. (4492), attested 29/3/18, demobilised 7/9/19.
THOMAS, F., Pte. (4493), attested 30/3/18, demobilised 7/9/19.
LOUW, W., Pte. (4494), attested 30/3/18, demobilised 25/12/18.
JOB, W., Pte. (4495), attested 1/4/18, demobilised 21/7/19, qualified signaller
SWARTZ, E., Pte. (4496), attested 28/3/18, demobilised 1/1/19.
WILLIAMS, L., Pte. (4497), attested 22/3/18, demobilised 7/9/19.
MALAZZI, S., Pte. (4498), attestation cancelled.
GREEN, H., Pte. (4499), attested 29/3/18, demobilised 22/7/19, transport driver
BAATJES, T., Pte. (4500), attested 16/3/18, demobilised 30/7/19.
RICHARDS, R., Pte. (4501), attested 22/3/18, demobilised 16/7/19.
MAANS, C., Pte. (4502), attested 29/3/18, demobilised 11/7/19, transport driver.
BLOEM, J., Pte. (4503), attested 3/4/18, released medically unfit 13/4/18.
SASH, J., Pte. (4504), attested 27/3/18, released medically unfit 10/4/18.
WALTERS, F., Pte. (4505), attested 27/3/18, released medically unfit 10/4/18.
JAGGERS, N., Pte. (4506), attested 27/3/18, released medically unfit 10/4/18.
DU PLESSIS, J., Pte. (4507), attested 27/3/18, released medically unfit 10/4/18.
BOSCH, C., Pte. (4508), attested 27/3/18, released medically unfit 11/4/18.
BOWREN, H. C., Pte. (4509), attested 27/3/18, released medically unfit 11/4/18.
MAY, W., Pte. (4510), attested 27/3/18, released medically unfit 10/4/18.
CLOETE, S., Pte. (4511), attested 27/3/18, released medically unfit 15/4/18.
LOTTERING, W., Pte. (4512), attested 27/3/18, released medically unfit 11/11/18.
METHYSON, J., Pte. (4513), attested 25/3/18, demobilised 21/7/19.
TARR, J., Pte. (4514), attested 27/3/18, released medically unfit 10/4/18.
DAVIES, H., Pte. (4515), attested 27/3/18, released medically unfit 10/4/18.
ROSENBANK, L., Pte. (4516), attested 27/3/18, released medically unfit 10/4/18.
ELIAS, A., Pte. (4517), attested 27/3/18, released medically unfit 10/4/18.
JOHNSON, A., Pte. (4518), attested 28/3/18, released medically unfit 10/4/18
McLEAN, P., Pte. (4519), attested 28/3/18, demobilised 21/7/19.
BASSON, H., Pte. (4520), attested 2/4/18, S.N.L.R. 26/5/18.
VOLLMER, P., Pte. (4521), attested 18/3/18, demobilised 22/7/19.
JACOBS, D., Pte. (4522), attested 2/4/18, demobilised 21/7/19.
JACOBS, F., Pte. (4523), attested 2/4/18, demobilised 7/9/19.
VAN WYK, N., Pte. (4524), attested 2/4/18, demobilised 21/7/19.
VISAGIE, J., Pte. (4525), attested 22/3/18, demobilised 7/9/19.
LIKWE, J., Pte. (4526), attested 28/3/18, demobilised 7/9/19.
HANKINS, N., Cpl. (4527), attested 2/4/18, L./Cpl. 5/7/18, Cpl. 1/11/18, demobilised 12/7/19, was i/c Transport R.H. Bn.
KOFF, P., Pte. (4528), attested 25/3/18, demobilised 5/2/19.
BAARDMAN, A., Pte. (4529), attested 3/4/18, released medically unfit 10/4/18.
MATTHEWS, C., Pte. (4530), attested 3/4/18, released medically unfit 10/4/18.
MALEKE, P., Pte. (4531), attested 3/4/18, released medically unfit 10/4/18.
THANGANA, R., Pte. (4532), attested 3/4/18, released medically unfit 10/4/18.
DAVIES, P., Pte. (4533), attested 3/4/18, released medically unfit 10/4/18.
SMITH, S., Pte. (4534), attested 3/4/18, released medically unfit 10/4/18.

TITUS, S, Pte. (4535), attested 4/4/18, released medically unfit 10/4/18.
WINDVOGEL, H., Pte. (4536), attested 4/4/18, released medically unfit 10/4/18.
AMOED, J., Pte. (4537), attested 6/4/18, released medically unfit 10/4/18.
JACOBS, H., Pte. (4538), attested 3/4/18, released medically unfit 10/4/18.
STAMBLE, D., Pte. (4539), attested 3/4/18, released medically unfit 10/4/18.
MALGAS, H., Pte. (4540), attested 3/4/18, released medically unfit 10/4/18.
JACOBS, J., Pte. (4541), attested 3/4/18, released medically unfit 10/4/18.
SWARTZ, J., Pte. (4542), attested 3/4/18, released medically unfit 10/4/18.
VAN WYK, H., Pte. (4543), attested 3/4/18, released medically unfit 10/4/18.
KOOPMAN, M., Pte. (4544), attested 3/4/18, released medically unfit 10/4/18.
PETERSEN, H. C., Pte. (4545), attested 3/4/18, released medically unfit 10/4/18.
LEYMOUR, M., Pte. (4546), attested 2/4/18, demobilised 7/9/19.
VISAGIE, P. A., Pte. (4547), attested 3/4/18, demobilised 16/7/19.
RUITERS, W., Pte. (4548), attested 2/4/18, demobilised 7/10/19.
BURGERS, R., L./Cpl. (4549), attested 28/3/18, L./Cpl. 17/8/18, demobilised 31/12/19.
FORBES, D., Pte. (4550), attested 5/4/18, demobilised 7/9/19.
LOUW, J., Pte. (4551), attested 28/3/18, demobilised 5/2/19.
BENGAL, T., Pte. (4552), attested 25/3/18, released medically unfit 15/6/18.
MINAAR, J., Pte. (4553), attested 5/4/18, released medically unfit 25/4/18.
JOSEPH, D., Pte. (4554), attested 7/4/18, released medically unfit 15/4/18.
VESTER, G., Pte. (4555), attested 7/4/18, released medically unfit 15/4/18.
DOYLE, W., Pte. (4556), attested 25/3/18, released medically unfit 14/4/18.
ERASMUS, W., Pte. (4557), attested 5/4/18, released medically unfit 14/4/18.
BAILEY, G., Pte. (4558), attested 8/4/18, released medically unfit 16/4/18.
HARLEY, R., Pte. (4559), attested 3/4/18, released medically unfit 15/4/18.
FRIESLAND, D., Pte. (4560), attested 2/4/18, released medically unfit 14/4/18.
OSTRICH, E., Pte. (4561), attested 27/3/18, released medically unfit 16/4/18.
TARENTAAL, G., Pte. (4562), attested 26/3/18, released medically unfit 15/4/18.
DANIELS, I., Pte. (4563), attested 2/4/18, released medically unfit 15/4/18.
WILLIAMS, I., Pte. (4564), attested 26/3/18, released medically unfit 16/4/18.
PHILANDER, D., Pte. (4565), attested 25/3/18, released medically unfit 15/4/18.
ALEXANDER, J., Pte. (4566), attested 31/3/18, released medically unfit 16/4/18
NELL, F., Pte. (4567), attested 2/4/18, released medically unfit 14/4/18.
BOSMAN, T., Pte. (4568), attested 30/3/18, released medically unfit 15/4/18.
ROBERTSON, J., Pte. (4569), attested 2/4/18, released medically unfit 14/4/18.
KURUMAN, W., Pte. (4570), attested 2/4/18, released medically unfit 14/4/18.
FISHER, P., Pte. (4571), attested 27/3/18, released medically unfit 15/4/18.
SOLOMON, C., Pte. (4572), attested 27/3/18, released medically unfit 15/4/18.
ERNSTZEN, A. G., Pte. (4573), attested 8/4/18, released medically unfit 16/4/18.
ANDERSON, A., Pte. (4574), attested 3/4/18, released medically unfit 14/4/18.
SMITH, P., Pte. (4575), attested 28/3/18, released medically unfit 14/4/18.
CUPIDO, H., Pte. (4576), attested 4/4/18, demobilised 16/7/19.
DUNN, W., Pte. (4577), attested 3/4/18, released medically unfit 13/5/18.
JAFTHA, A., Pte. (4578), attested 4/4/18, demobilised 7/9/19.
RONDGANGER, J., Pte. (4579), attested 4/4/18, released medically unfit 7/6/18.
WITBOOI, F., Pte. (4580), attested 5/4/18, released medically unfit 6/6/18.
JOSHUA, A., Pte. (4581), attested 5/4/18, demobilised 16/7/19.
AFRIKANDER, J., Pte. (4582), attested 5/4/18, demobilised 26/12/18.
BRINK, S., Pte. (4583), attested 5/4/18, demobilised 16/7/19.
JACOBS, J., Pte. (4584), attested 4/4/18, demobilised 7/9/19.
SOLOMON, J., Pte. (4585), attested 4/4/18, demobilised 7/9/19.
WILLIAMS, P., Pte. (4586), attested 4/4/18, demobilised 5/10/19.
BARNES, J., Pte. (4587), attested 4/4/18, died of tuberculosis 2/8/19.
WILLIAMS, D., Pte. (4588), attested 4/4/18, released medically unfit 15/4/18.
MOSES, D., Pte. (4589), attested 4/4/18, released medically unfit 14/4/18.
LOMBARD, P., Pte. (4590), attested 8/4/18, released medically unfit 14/4/18.
STOGA, D., Pte. (4591), attested 8/4/18, released medically unfit 14/4/18.
BELLINGHAM, F., Pte. (4592), attested 3/4/18, released medically unfit 16/4/18.
GOLIATH, W., Pte. (4593), attested 28/3/18, released medically unfit 16/4/18.
KLASS, J., Pte. (4594), attested 28/3/18, released medically unfit 16/4/18.
TEMBANI, T., Pte. (4595), attested 28/3/18, released medically unfit 16/4/18.
RIJKIES, A., Pte. (4596), attested 28/3/18, released medically unfit 15/4/18.
WILLIAMS, A., Pte. (4597), attested 3/4/18, released medically unfit 15/4/18
OGLE, A., Pte. (4598), attested 3/4/18, demobilised 21/7/19.
FYNN, L., Pte. 4599), attested 3/4/18, demobilised 21/7/19.
RUDLING, R. W., Pte. (4600), attested 27/3/18, demobilised 7/9/19.
RADEMEYER, L., Pte (4601), attested 4/4/18, demobilised 7/9/19.
FORTUIN, J., Pte. (4602), attested 8/4/18, demobilised 10/4/20, qualified signaller.
MASTERIS, A., Pte. (4603), attested 8/4/18, demobilised 12/7/19, transport driver.
VAN DER ROSS, J., Pte. (4604), attested 4/4/18, machine gunner, killed in action 20/9/18.
COLMS, F., Pte. (4605), attested 4/4/18, demobilised 7/9/19, machine gunner.
KLINK, P., Pte. (4606), attested 4/4/18, machine gunner, killed in action 20/9/18.
MATOBAS, P., Pte. (4607), attested 8/4/18, demobilised 7/9/19, machine gunner.
ADAMS, H., Pte. (4608), attested 8/4/18, demobilised 10/4/20, qualified 1st class signaller.
JUTA, J., Pte. (4609), attested 4/4/18, demobilised 12/7/19.
FORTUIN, C., Pte. (4610), attested 6/4/18, demobilised 7/9/19.
FARO, D., Pte. (4611), attested 4/4/18, demobilised 29/12/18.
WILLIAMS, J., Pte. (4612), attested 4/4/18, S.N.L.R. 1/8/18
WILDSCHUT, N., Pte. (4613), attested 4/4/18, demobilised 7/9/19.
PLAATJES, S., Pte. (4614), attested 4/4/18, demobilised 21/7/19.
RENECKE, P., Pte. (4615), attested 4/4/18, released medically unfit 20/4/18.
PYOOS, H., Pte. (4616), attested 6/4/18, released medically unfit 19/4/18.
BEGBIE, W., Pte. (4617), attested 2/4/18, released medically unfit 20/4/18.
SELO, J., Pte. (4618), attested 8/4/18, released medically unfit 19/4/18.
ISAACS, J., Pte. (4619), attested 6/4/18, released medically unfit 20/4/18.
LOMBARD, J., Pte. (4620), attested 4/4/18, released medically unfit 4/5/18.
FRANCIS, J., Pte. (4621), attested 4/4/18, released medically unfit 20/4/18.
SCHOLTZ, M., Pte. (4622), attested 4/4/18, released medically unfit 20/4/18.
COLLER, W., Pte. (4623), attested 4/4/18, released medically unfit 20/4/18.
PLAATJES, H., Pte. (4624), attested 5/4/18, released medically unfit 19/4/18.
PETERSEN, H., Pte. (4625), attested 5/4/18, released medically unfit 19/4/18

THE STORY OF THE 1st CAPE CORPS.

CAMPBELL, J., Pte. (4626), attested 3/4/18, released medically unfit 18/4/18.
SOLOMON, G., Pte. (4627), attested 4/4/18, released medically unfit 20/4/18.
LATIEF, A., Pte. (4628), attested 5/4/18, released medically unfit 19/4/18.
VESTER, J., Pte. (4629), attested 4/4/18, released medically unfit 20/4/18.
DANIELS, W., Pte. (4630), attested 8/4/18, released medically unfit 14/4/18.
DAVIDS, J., Pte. (4631), attested 8/4/18, demobilised 7/10/19.
DAVIDS, A., Pte. (4632), attested 8/4/18, demobilised 7/10/19.
MARTIN, D., Pte. (4633), attested 10/4/18, died of influenza 11/10/18.
WILCOCKS, A., Pte. (4634), attested 9/4/18, demobilised 7/10/19.
BROWN, F., Pte. (4635), attested 9/4/18, demobilised 11/7/19.
STEYN, D., Pte. (4636), attested 8/4/18, demobilised 11/7/19, transport driver.
FOWLER, M., Pte. (4637), attested 9/4/18, demobilised 11/7/19.
VALENTINE, M., Pte. (4638), attested 9/4/18, demobilised 7/10/19, machine gunner.
VISAGIE, F., Pte. (4639), attested 9/4/18, demobilised 28/8/19, machine gunner.
MARITZ, G., Pte. (4640), attested 10/4/18, S.N.L.R. 21/11/18.
GROOTJE, R., Pte. (4641), attested 8/4/18, demobilised 8/9/19, machine gunner.
AFRICA, J., Pte. (4642), attested 10/4/18, killed in action 20/9/18.
PAULUS, G., Pte. (4643), attested 10/4/18, not yet demobilised.
McKECHNIE, N., Pte. (4644), attested 8/4/18, demobilised 11/7/19, machine gunner.
WILLIAMS, W., Pte. (4645), attested 8/4/18, released medically unfit 1/5/18.
HOLSTEN, C., Pte. (4646), attested 4/4/18, released medically unfit 14/5/18.
ELLIOTT, J., Pte. (4647), attested 8/4/18, demobilised 7/10/19.
MARAIS, S., Pte. (4648), attested 8/4/18, demobilised 7/9/19.
KRUGER, J., Pte. (4649), attested 9/4/18, demobilised 21/10/19., machine gunner.
PETERSEN, J., Pte. (4650), attested 9/4/18, machine gunner, killed in action 20/9/18.
BENJAMIN, W., Pte. (4651), attested 8/4/18, demobilised 7/10/19.
SMITH, C., Pte. (4652), attested 4/5/18, demobilised 31/12/19, machine gunner.
ROSSOUW, H., Pte. (4653), attested 10/4/18, released medically unfit 7/6/18.
EXTEEN, W., Pte. (4654), attested 8/4/18, demobilised 21/7/19.
CONSTABLE, J. P., Pte. (4655), attested 10/4/18, demobilised 10/10/19, qualified 1st class signaller.
VAN DER HEUVEL, L., Pte. (4656), attested 10/4/18, demobilised 16/7/19.
PETERSEN, H., Pte. (4657), attested 3/4/18, demobilised 7/10/19.
VAN ROOY, A., Pte. (4658), attested 8/4/18, demobilised 22/7/19, transport driver.
WILSON, M., Pte. (4659), attested 8/4/18, demobilised 7/9/19.
SIEVERS, W., Pte. (4660), attested 9/4/18, demobilised 11/7/19, machine gunner.
APPOLLIS, G., Pte. (4661), attested 8/4/18, demobilised 7/10/19.
MENTOR, H., Pte. (4662), attested 4/4/18, demobilised 7/9/19.
ABRAHAMS, D., Pte. (4663), attested 8/4/18, demobilised 11/7/19, machine gunner.
SALIE, A., Pte. (4664), attested 8/4/18, demobilised 7/10/19.
TRUSSELS, J., Pte. (4665), attested 8/4/18, demobilised 7/10/19.
ABRAHAMS, C., Pte. (4666), attested 8/4/18, demobilised 7/10/19, machine gunner.
WILLIAMS, K., Pte. (4667), attested 8/4/18, demobilised 7/9/19, machine gunner.
LIEBRANDT, F., Pte. (4668), attested 8/4/18, demobilised 7/10/19, machine gunner.
NELSON, C., Pte. (4669), attested 8/4/18, demobilised 7/9/19, machine gunner.
ABRAHAMS, F., Pte. (4670), attested 8/4/18, demobilised 7/10/19.
ADAMS, K., Pte. (4671), attested 4/4/18, released medically unfit 1/5/18.
WEPNER, M., Pte. (4672), attested 8/4/18, demobilised 7/10/19, machine gunner.
JEREMIAH, H., Pte. (4673), attested 25/3/18, demobilised 7/9/19.
AVONTEUR, F., Pte. (4674), attested 8/4/18, demobilised 7/10/19.
CUPIDO, D., Pte. (4675), attested 8/4/18, demobilised 7/9/19, machine gunner.
KOLOMBE, M., Pte. (4676), attested 4/4/18, demobilised 16/7/19, transport driver and groom.
GILPIN, W., Pte. (4677), attested 8/4/18, demobilised 7/9/19, machine gunner.
FORTUIN, I., Pte. (4678), attested 9/4/18, released medically unfit 7/6/18.
KEYSTER, L., Pte. (4679), attested 8/4/18, demobilised 7/9/19.
FEBRUARY, P., Pte. (4680), attested 9/4/18, demobilised 18/10/19, qualified 1st class signaller.
HENDRICKS, T., Pte. (4681), attested 11/4/18, released medically unfit 19/4/18.
FRIDAY, R., Pte. (4682), attested 12/4/18, released medically unfit 19/4/18.
PAIL, J., Pte. (4683), attested 15/4/18, released medically unfit 19/4/18.
FREDERICKS, J., Pte. (4684), attested 12/4/18, released medically unfit 19/4/18.
KING, A., Pte. (4685), attested 12/4/18, released medically unfit 19/4/18.
ADAMS, J., Pte. (4686), attested 10/4/18, released medically unfit 20/4/18.
WILLIAMS, J., Pte. (4687), attested 12/4/18, released medically unfit 20/4/18.
HILMAN, F., Pte. (4688), attested 11/4/18, released medically unfit 19/4/18.
FILLIES, D., Pte. (4689), attested 12/4/18, released medically unfit 20/4/18.
SAMPSON, W., Pte. (4690), attested 11/4/18, released medically unfit 19/4/18.
MORRIS, J., Pte. (4691), attested 11/4/18, released medically unfit 19/4/18.
LODEWYK, J., Pte. (4692), attested 11/4/18, released medically unfit 19/4/18.
DESFONTEIN, J., Pte. (4693), attested 11/4/18, released medically unfit 19/4/18.
BARNES, B., Pte. (4694), attested 11/4/18, released medically unfit 19/4/18.
ISAACS, J., Pte. (4695), attested 11/4/18, released medically unfit 19/4/18.
NOBLE, M., Pte. (4696), attested 9/4/18, released medically unfit 19/4/18.
BROWN, C. J., Pte. (4697), attested 11/4/18, released medically unfit 19/4/18.
THOMAS, A., Pte. (4698), attested 11/4/18, released medically unfit 19/4/18.
PETERSEN, T., Pte. (4699), attested 11/4/18, released medically unfit 19/4/18.
VLOTMAN, F., Pte. (4700), attested 11/4/18, released medically unfit 18/4/18.
KUMONI, S., Pte. (4701), attested 12/4/18, released medically unfit 18/4/18.
BROODY, C., Pte. (4702), attested 12/4/18, released medically unfit 18/4/18.
STABALALA, H., Pte. (4703), attested 11/4/18, released medically unfit 18/4/18.
HETZEROTH, A. J., Pte. (4704), attested 6/4/18, demobilised 21/7/19.
JENNEKER, D., Pte. (4705), attested 11/4/18, demobilised 21/7/19.
FAGO, G., Pte. (4706), attested 11/4/18, demobilised 21/7/19.
BOTES, H., Pte. (4707), attested 9/4/18, demobilised 16/7/19.
MARTHINUS, D., Pte. (4708), attested 8/4/18, demobilised 7/9/19.
JOHNSON, D., Pte. (4709), attested 12/4/18, demobilised 15/1/19.
DAVIS, A., Pte. (4710), attested 16/4/18, released medically unfit 25/4/18.
BROWN, T., Pte. (4711), attested 16/4/18, released medically unfit 25/4/18.
LUDWICK, P., Pte. (4712), attested 16/4/18, released medically unfit 25/4/18.
HECTOR, A., Pte. (4713), attested 12/4/18, demobilised 7/9/19.
FRASERBURG, C., Pte. (4714), attested 13/4/18, demobilised 31/12/19.
PFEEFER, N., Pte. (4715), attested 13/4/18, demobilised 1/1/19.
FOURIE, I. W., Pte. (4716), attested 8/4/18, demobilised 7/9/19.

SMITH, G., Pte. (4717), attested 13/4/18, demobilised 12/7/19.
FOSTER, D., Pte. (4718), attested 13/4/18, demobilised 21/7/19, qualified scout
BAILEY, J., Pte. (4719), attested 12/4/18, demobilised 27/10/19.
BRINKHUIS, C., Pte. (4720), attested 8/4/18, demobilised 8/9/19.
RUITERS, H., Pte. (4721), attested 8/4/18, demobilised 21/7/19.
MILLER, I., Pte. (4722), attested 11/4/18, demobilised 21/7/19.
HEYNES, J., Pte. (4723), attested 9/4/18, demobilised 14/1/19.
SAMDAK, W., Pte. (4724), attested 12/4/18, demobilised 12/7/19.
BROWN, G., Pte. (4725), attested 12/4/18, demobilised 12/7/19.
NCOKANA, J., Pte. (4726), attested 12/4/18, demobilised 21/7/19.
LOUW, J., Pte. (4727), attested 15/4/18, released medically unfit 1/5/18.
MALGAS, J., Pte. (4728), attested 15/4/18, demobilised 7/9/19.
SMITH, A., Pte. (4729), attested 15/4/18, demobilised 16/7/19.
MATTYS, J., Pte. (4730), attested 15/4/18, transport driver, run over and killed by train at Suez 7/5/19.
TOPLEY, J., Pte. (4731), attested 15/4/18, demobilised 12/7/19.
GLOVER, J., Pte. (4732), attested 13/4/18, demobilised 16/7/19.
JANSEN, C., Pte. (4733), attested 13/4/18, released medically unfit 21/6/18
SMITH, J., Pte. (4734), attested 15/4/18, demobilised 12/7/19.
MEYER, S., Pte. (4735), attested 15/4/18, demobilised 7/9/19.
DIEDERICKS, J., Pte. (4736), attested 13/4/18, demobilised 16/7/19, pioneer.
EITCHELS, J., Pte. (4737), attested 13/4/18, demobilised 7/9/19.
KLASTET, A., Pte. (4738), attested 11/4/18, released medically unfit 28/5/18.
PETERSEN, T., Pte. (4739), attested 15/4/18, demobilised 13/1/19.
PAILMAN, I., Pte. (4740), attested 15/4/18, demobilised 21/7/19.
MANUEL, E., Pte. (4741), attested 15/4/18, demobilised 28/10/19.
LEPPAN, R., Pte. (4742), attested 10/4/18, released medically unfit 28/4/18.
MASON, J., Pte. (4743), attested 12/4/18, released medically unfit 25/4/18.
WILLIAMS, J., Pte. (4744), attested 14/4/18, released medically unfit 25/4/18.
PRINS, M., Pte. (4745), attested 10/4/18, released medically unfit 25/4/18.
WILLIAMS, M., Pte. (4746), attested 16/4/18, released medically unfit 25/4/18.
KOK, J., Pte. (4747), attested 12/4/18, released medically unfit 28/4/18.
ABRAHAMS, W., Pte. (4748), attested 6/4/18, released medically unfit 25/4/18.
LEWIS, J., Pte. (4749), attested 5/4/18, released medically unfit 26/4/18.
MATHEE, J., Pte. (4750), attested 17/4/18, released medically unfit 26/4/18.
HILL, J., Pte. (4751), attested 12/4/18, demobilised 7/10/19.
ASHLEY, P., Pte. (4752), attested 15/4/18, demobilised 16/7/19.
SIMONS, P., Pte. (4753), attested 15/4/18, demobilised 11/7/19.
PRINSLOO, K. A., Pte. (4754), attested 13/4/18, demobilised 16/7/19.
YON, H. M., Pte. (4755), attested 15/4/18, demobilised 7/10/19.
CUPIDO, P., Pte. (4756), attested released medically unfit 1/5/18.
JOSHUA, A. D., Pte. (4757), attested 16/4/18, demobilised 16/7/19, drum and fife band.
GOERA, F., Pte. (4758), attested 13/4/18, demobilised 16/7/19, cook.
KOUTER, J., Pte. (4759), attested 16/4/18, released medically unfit 15/5/18.
THYS, A., Pte. (4760), attested 15/4/18, demobilised 21/7/19.
JACOBS, A., Pte. (4761), attested 16/4/18, demobilised 7/10/19.
JOHNSON, J., Pte. (4762), attested 15/4/18, demobilised 7/10/19.
SABLES, J., Pte. (4763), attested 15/4/18, demobilised 21/7/19.
SALIE, F., Pte. (4764), attested 14/4/18, demobilised 2/1/19.
RUSSOUW, A., Pte. (4765), attested 16/4/18, demobilised 16/7/19.
MUNNIK, J., Pte. (4766), attested 14/4/18, demobilised 16/7/19.
OCTOBER, A., Pte. (4767), attested 16/4/18, demobilised 16/7/19.
DAVIDS, J., Pte. (4768), attested 15/4/18, demobilised 11/7/19.
MENTOR, J., Pte. (4769), attested 8/4/18, demobilised 7/9/19.
DU PLESSIS, F., Pte. (4770), attested 11/4/18, released medically unfit 7/6/18
MART, G., Pte. (4771), attested 9/4/18, demobilised 11/7/19.
HENDRICKS, J., Pte. (4772), attested 15/4/18, demobilised 12/7/19.
STEENEKAMP, J., Pte. (4773), attested 12/4/18, demobilised 21/7/19.
SWARTZ, K., Pte. (4774), attested 16/4/18, released medically unfit 26/4/18.
GROEPE, C., Pte. (4775), attested 17/4/18, released medically unfit 28/4/18.
GYSMAN, P., Pte. (4776), attested 17/4/18, released medically unfit 28/4/18.
KENNELLY, E., Pte. (4777), attested 16/4/18, released medically unfit 30/4/18.
ARENDS, H. J., Pte. (4778), attested 17/4/18, released medically unfit 28/4/18.
PALEMAN, C., Pte. (4779), attested 17/4/18, released medically unfit 26/4/18.
PRESTON, W., Pte. (4780), attested 17/4/18, released medically unfit 26/4/18.
NOVEMBER, J., Pte. (4781), attested 13/4/18, released medically unfit 26/4/18
DU PREEZ, J., Pte. (4782), attested 8/4/18, released medically unfit 30/4/18.
SCOTT, W. B., Pte. (4783), attested 5/4/18, released medically unfit 30/4/18.
THAYSER, A., Pte. (4784), attested 12/4/18, released medically unfit 28/4/18.
DELPORT, J., Pte. (4785), attested 8/4/18, released medically unfit 26/4/18.
TITTIES, D., Pte. (4786), attested 11/4/18, released medically unfit 26/4/18.
STUURMAN, H., Pte. (4787), attested 9/4/18, released medically unfit 28/4/18.
SAWYERS, J. E., Pte. (4788), attested 8/4/18, released medically unfit 26/4/18
BEUKES, P., Pte. (4789), attested 8/4/18, released medically unfit 26/4/18.
SCHOEMAN, G., Pte. (4790), attested 11/4/18, released medically unfit 26/4/18
DELPORT, R., Pte. (4791), attested 10/4/18, released medically unfit 26/4/18.
HARTNICK, J., Pte. (4792), attested 14/4/18, released medically unfit 26/4/18
CLOETE, A., Pte. (4793), attested 8/4/18, released medically unfit 26/4/18.
BOTES, B., Pte. (4794), attested 8/4/18, released medically unfit 26/4/18.
MATROSS, F., Pte. (4795), attested 11/4/18, released medically unfit 26/4/18.
JEFFRIES, W., Pte. (4796), attested 8/4/18, released medically unfit 28/4/18.
MARNCE, F., Pte. (4797), attested 5/4/18, released medically unfit 30/4/18.
ARENDSE, P., Pte. (4798), attested 15/4/18, demobilised 11/7/19.
FURST, A. V., Pte. (4799), attested 15/4/18, demobilised 12/7/19.
SALMONS, F., Pte. (4800), attested 16/4/18, demobilised 21/7/19.
SCHUBART, F., Pte. (4801), attested 15/4/18, demobilised 12/7/19, machine gunner
STUTE, D., Pte. (4802), attested 19/4/18, S.N.L.R. 10/7/18.
INNES, J. E., Pte. (4803), attested 12/4/18, demobilised 26/12/18.
MOWERS, F., Pte. (4804), attested 13/4/18, demobilised 16/7/19.
LEWAK, S., Pte. (4805), attested 8/4/18, demobilised 16/7/19.
HADDEN, J., Pte. (4806), attested 9/4/18, released medically unfit 2/5/18.
SMITH, F., Pte. (4807), attested 17/4/18, died 10/10/18.

THE STORY OF THE 1st CAPE CORPS.

SYMON, E., Pte. (4808), attested 17/4/18, demobilised 12/7/19.
PETERSEN, W., Pte. (4809), attested 17/4/18, released medically unfit 1/5/18.
SASS, J., Pte. (4810), attested 12/4/18, demobilised 21/7/18.
SASS, J., Pte. (4811), attested 12/4/18, released medically unfit 27/4/18.
VAN ROOYEN, J., Pte. (4812), attested 16/4/18, released medically unfit 27/4/18.
BENJAMIN, P., Pte. (4813), attested 13/4/18, released medically unfit 27/4/18.
ANICHADE, C., Pte. (4814), attested 10/4/18, released medically unfit 4/5/18.
FRES, W., Pte. (4815), attested 13/4/18, released medically unfit 25/4/18.
MILLER, J., Pte. (4816), attested 8/4/18, released medically unfit 25/4/18.
GOLIATH, H., Pte. (4817), attested 13/4/18, released medically unfit 26/4/18.
FREEMAN, J., Pte. (4818), attested 15/4/18, released medically unfit 26/4/18.
NEWLAND, J., Pte. (4819), attested 13/4/18, released medically unfit 26/4/18.
SMITH, J., Pte. (4820), attested 15/4/18, released medically unfit 26/4/18.
CUPIDO, J., Pte. (4821), attested 15/4/18, released medically unfit 26/4/18.
DU PLESSIS, J., Pte. (4822), attested 12/4/18, released medically unfit 26/4/18.
OCTOBER, J., Pte. (4823), attested 12/4/18, released medically unfit 26/4/18.
NELSON, T., Pte. (4824), attested 15/4/18, released medically unfit 26/4/18.
PETERSEN, P., Pte. (4825), attested 16/4/18, released medically unfit 26/4/18.
DIRKSE, W., Pte. (4826), attested 17/4/18, released medically unfit 26/4/18.
ABRAHAMS, D., Pte. (4827), attested 10/4/18, released medically unfit 25/4/18.
LIBERTZ, F., Pte. (4828), attested 11/4/18, released medically unfit 27/4/18.
JACOBS, J., Pte. (4829), attested 11/4/18, released medically unfit 27/4/18.
HAGAS, W., Pte. (4830), attested 12/4/18, released medically unfit 25/4/18.
PRINS, C., Pte. (4831), attested 16/4/18, released medically unfit 27/4/18.
GOODMAN, W., Pte. (4832), attested 9/4/18, released medically unfit 30/4/18.
FOURIE, C., Pte. (4833), attested 11/4/18, released medically unfit 25/4/18.
PETERSEN, C., Pte. (4834), attested 10/4/18, released medically unfit 25/4/18.
SWARTZ, C., Pte. (4835), attested 10/4/18, released medically unfit 25/4/18.
MAY, B., Pte. (4836), attested 16/4/18, released medically unfit 26/4/18.
LEWIS, J., Pte. (4837), attested 18/4/18, S.N.L.R. 29/4/18.
HOMENE, T., Pte. (4838), attested 18/4/18, demobilised 16/7/19
KOPPER, S., Pte. (4839), attested 18/4/18, demobilised 7/9/19.
FRASER, J., Pte. (4840), attested 17/4/18, released medically unfit 16/7/18.
BLOOM, F., Pte. (4841), attested 19/4/18, demobilised 16/7/19.
MANTROSS, P., Pte. (4842), attested 18/4/18, demobilised 21/7/19.
KAMPHER, J., Pte. (4843), attested 16/4/18, released medically unfit 28/5/18.
ISAACS, L., Pte. (4844), attested 13/4/18, released medically unfit 15/6/18.
WILLIAMS, J. J., a/L./Cpl. (4845), attested 15/4/18, a/L./Cpl. 1/3/19, demobilised 7/10/19.
WILLIAMS, E., a/L./Cpl. (4846), attested 15/4/18, a/L./Cpl. 19/5/19, demobilised 16/7/19, qualified scout.
MARTHINUS, S., Pte. (4847), attested 15/4/18, demobilised 16/7/19, qualified scout.
FINGO, J., Pte. (4848), attested 22/4/18, demobilised 7/9/19.
WANZA, S., Pte. (4849), attested 19/4/18, demobilised 8/9/19.
CROUCH, J., Pte. (4850), attested 23/4/18, demobilised 21/7/19.
RANK, J., Pte. (4851), attested 15/4/18, demobilised 16/7/19.
DU PLESSIS, B., Pte. (4852), attested 19/4/18, demobilised 21/7/19, transport driver.
JACOBS, S., Pte. (4853), attested 17/4/18, demobilised 16/7/19.
WALSH, J., Pte. (4854), attested 17/4/18, demobilised 1/1/19.
BEUKES, J., Pte. (4855), attested 14/4/18, released medically unfit 27/6/18.
BLAZER, H., Pte. (4856), attested 22/4/18, released medically unfit 30/6/18.
ADAMS, M., Pte. (4857), attested 22/4/18, demobilised 11/7/19.
SNELL, J., Pte. (4858), attested 22/4/18, demobilised 16/7/19.
CONSTANCE, J., Pte. (4859), attested 23/4/18, released medically unfit 27/6/18
BARRON, S., Pte. (4860), attested 20/4/18, demobilised 14/1/19.
SNELL, G., Pte. (4861), attested 22/4/18, released medically unfit 29/5/18.
STEVENS, S., Pte. (4862), attested 22/4/18, demobilised 16/7/19.
McLEAN, A., Pte. (4863), attested 22/4/18, demobilised 7/10/19.
KLEINHANS, M., Pte. (4864), attested 24/4/18, demobilised 16/7/19.
DANIELS, S. F., Pte. (4865), attested 13/4/18, released medically unfit 27/6/18.
HARTZENBERG, J., Pte. (4866), attested 20/4/18, demobilised 16/7/19.
JOHNSON, I., Pte. (4867), attested 22/4/18, died of influenza 18/10/18
HENDRICKS, E., Pte. (4868), attested 20/4/18, demobilised 11/7/19
WILLIAMS, J., Pte. (4869), attested 22/4/18, released medically unfit 27/6/18.
DAVIES, J., Pte. (4870), attested 20/4/18, demobilised 7/9/19.
WILLIAMS, A., Pte. (4871), attested 22/4/18, demobilised 7/9/19.
WILLIAMS, J., Pte. (4872), attested 23/4/18, demobilised 12/7/19.
GALLANT, J., Pte. (4873), attested 19/4/18, S.N.L.R. 10/6/18.
PETERSEN, C., Pte. (4874), attested 22/4/18, demobilised 30/12/18.
JACOBS, H., Pte. (4875), attested 24/4/18, released medically unfit 2/5/18.
KONING, P., Pte. (4876), attested 23/4/18, released medically unfit 2/5/18.
BRANDER, A., Pte. (4877), attested 21/4/18, released medically unfit 1/5/18.
McPHERSON, J., Pte. (4878), attested 18/4/18, released medically unfit 1/5/18.
BUTLER, P., Pte. (4879), attested 17/4/18, released medically unfit 2/5/18.
LAKAY, S., Pte. (4880), attested 15/4/18, released medically unfit 1/5/18.
STROEBEL, J., Pte. (4881), attested 20/4/18, released medically unfit 2/5/18.
HENORANAGE, A., Pte. (4882), attested 18/4/18, released medically unfit 30/4/18.
JACOBS, J., Pte. (4883), attested 17/4/18, released medically unfit 1/5/18.
PETERSEN, A., Pte. (4884), attested 18/4/18, released medically unfit 1/5/18.
PETERSEN, S., Pte. (4885), attested 18/4/18, demobilised 7/9/19.
SEPTEMBER, H., Pte. (4886), attested 4/4/18, released medically unfit 1/5/18.
CALEMEYER, D., Pte. (4887), attested 18/4/18, demobilised 5/8/19.
VAN HEERDEN, W., Pte. (4888), attested 18/4/18, released medically unfit 30/4/18
FERRIER, W., Pte. (4889), attested 10/4/18, released medically unfit 1/5/18.
FOURIE, J., Pte. (4890), attested 18/4/18, released medically unfit 1/5/18.
CAPES, S. J., Pte. (4891), attested 18/4/18, demobilised 18/6/19.
TOMBOER, I., Pte. (4892), attested 22/4/18, released medically unfit 2/5/18.
BRUINERS, W., Pte. (4893), attested 31/4/18, demobilised 16/7/19.
NKATO, L., Pte. (4894), attested 24/4/18, released medically unfit 30/4/18.
BOWDEN, I., Pte. (4895), attested 18/4/18, demobilised 16/7/19.
ZEEKOE, J., Pte. (4896), attested 23/4/18, demobilised 2/1/19.
AMSTERDAM, D., Pte. (4897), attested 22/4/18, demobilised 16/7/19, machine gunner.
MOOLMAN, J., Pte. (4898), attested 22/4/18, demobilised 7/9/19.

JACOBS, H., Pte. (4899), attested 20/4/18, demobilised 21/7/19.
VAN EDEN, W., Pte. (4900), attested 20/4/18, demobilised 21/7/19, machine gunner
ADAMS, S., Pte. (4901), attested 18/4/18, released medically unfit 1/5/18.
JACOBS, J., Pte. (4902), attested 19/4/18, released medically unfit 1/5/18.
WICHMAN, J., Pte. (4903), attested 24/4/18, released medically unfit 29/5/18.
PITTS, J., Pte. (4904), attested 26/4/18, demobilised 21/7/19.
HENEKE, H., Pte. (4905), attested 24/4/18, demobilised 17/1/19.
HARTNICK, D., Pte. (4906), attested 24/4/18, demobilised 16/7/19.
JAFTHA, W., Pte. (4907), attested 24/4/18, demobilised 7/9/19.
JAFTHA, H., Pte. (4908), attested 24/4/18, demobilised 7/9/19.
BARNARD, W., Pte. (4909), attested 20/4/18, demobilised 7/9/19.
MAY, J., Pte. (4910), attested 20/4/18, demobilised 7/9/19.
WITBOOI, P., Pte. (4911), attested 20/4/18, released medically unfit 14/5/18.
SCHOLTZ, C., Pte. (4912), attested 20/4/18, released medically unfit 14/5/18.
VOEGT, W., Pte. (4913), attested 24/4/18, released medically unfit 13/5/18.
WILLIAMS, J., Pte. (4914), attested 20/4/18, released medically unfit 14/5/18.
STEMMET, J., Pte. (4915), attested 24/4/18, released medically unfit 13/5/18.
MARAIS, D., Pte. (4916), attested 15/4/18, released medically unfit 14/5/18.
MEYER, W. G., Pte. (4917), attested 20/4/18, released medically unfit 13/5/18.
SWARTZ, M., Pte. (4918), attested 20/4/18, released medically unfit 13/5/18.
VAN REENEN, W., Pte. (4919), attested 22/4/18, released medically unfit 13/5/18.
LANGHAN, H., Pte. (4920), attested 15/4/18, released medically unfit 14/5/18.
BAUMGART, H. C., Pte. (4921), attested 10/4/18, released medically unfit 14/5/18.
SOLOMON, J., Pte. (4922), attested 22/4/18, released medically unfit 13/5/18.
ABELS, W. G., Pte. (4923), attested 24/4/18, released medically unfit 29/5/18.
BOLTMAN, J., Pte. (4924), attested 29/4/18, demobilised 7/10/19.
VAN REENEN, J., Pte. (4925), attested 27/4/18, demobilised 7/9/19.
ISAACS, P., Pte. (4926), attested 29/4/18, released medically unfit 29/5/18.
SMITH, N., Pte. (4927), attested 25/4/18, demobilised 11/7/19.
SNYDER, W., Pte. (4928), attested 25/4/18, demobilised 20/7/19.
LAPOEK, D., Pte. (4929), attested 29/4/18, demobilised 21/12/19.
ALBRECHT, M., Pte. (4930), attested 27/4/18, demobilised 3/1/19.
LOTTERING, A., Pte. (4931), attested 25/4/18, demobilised 16/7/19.
BEATON, A., Pte. (4932), attested 25/4/18, released medically unfit 1/7/18.
WILLEMSE, J., Pte. (4933), attested 25/4/18, demobilised 16/7/19.
ALART, P., Pte. (4934), attested 25/4/18, demobilised 16/7/19.
MATROSS, A., Pte. (4935), attested 25/4/18, demobilised 14/1/19.
DORIS, I., Pte. (4936), attested 25/4/18, demobilised 21/7/19.
PETERSEN, H., Pte. (4937), attested 26/4/18, demobilised 21/7/19.
HARTNICK, J., Pte. (4938), attested 20/4/18, demobilised 7/9/19.
JANSE, J., Pte. (4939), attested 25/4/18, demobilised 21/7/19.
BRUINERS, F., Pte. (4940), attested 26/4/18, demobilised 16/7/19.
CLASSEN, C., Pte. (4941), attested 25/4/18, demobilised 7/9/19.
GERTZE, J., Pte. (4942), attested 26/4/18, demobilised 17/1/19.
OCTOBER, S., Pte. (4943), attested 25/4/18, demobilised 27/7/19.
HERMIS, F., Pte. (4944), attested 23/4/18, demobilised 16/7/19.
FORTUIN, O., Pte. (4945), attested 20/4/18, demobilised 1/1/19.
MEYER, D., Pte. (4946), attested 23/4/18, demobilised 16/7/19.
DU PLESSIS, J., Pte. (4947), attested 23/4/18, demobilised 21/7/19.
JAMES, J., Pte. (4948), attested 23/4/18, demobilised 16/7/19.
ZUISTER, J., Pte. (4949), attested 23/4/18, demobilised 16/7/19.
FRANCIS, D., Pte. (4950), attested 23/4/18, demobilised 28/8/19.
MALGAS, J., Pte. (4951), attested 23/4/18, demobilised 21/7/19.
WILLIAMS, P., Pte. (4952), attested 23/4/18, demobilised 21/7/19.
GROOTBOOM, J., Pte. (4953), attested 23/4/18, demobilised 16/7/19.
MICHAEL, M., Pte. (4954), attested 23/4/18, demobilised 21/7/19.
FILLIES, J., Pte. (4955), attested 23/4/18, demobilised 7/9/19.
GROENEWALD, J., Pte. (4956), attested 23/4/18, demobilised 7/9/19.
MICHAELS, W., Pte. (4957), attested 26/4/18, released medically unfit 16/6/18.
MEYER, I., Pte. (4958), attested 27/4/18, demobilised 21/7/19.
HENNIS, G., Pte. (4959), attested 23/4/18, released medically unfit 22/6/18.
JACOBS, A., Pte. (4960), attested 23/4/18, demobilised 21/7/19, pioneer.
LE ROUX, P., Pte. (4961), attested 23/4/18, demobilised 7/9/19.
ANTHONY, S., Pte. (4962), attested 23/4/18, demobilised 10/4/20.
BRUINTJES, F., Pte. (4963), attested 24/4/18, released medically unfit 16/6/18.
DAMON, P., Pte. (4964), attested 15/4/18, demobilised 21/7/19.
RUITERS, A., Pte. (4965), attested 22/4/18, released medically unfit 15/6/18.
VOLKWYN, J., Pte. (4966), attested 26/4/18, demobilised 7/9/19.
TURNER, H., Pte. (4967), attested 30/4/18, released medically unfit 28/5/18.
OVERMEYER, Pte. (4968), attested 30/4/18, released medically unfit 13/12/18.
FORTUIN, D., Pte. (4969), attested 30/4/18, demobilised 16/7/19.
SMIT, J., Pte. (4970), attested 24/4/18, demobilised 21/11/18.
ROBAIN, A., Pte. (4971), attested 29/4/18, demobilised 11/7/19.
MATHIE, P., Pte. (4972), attested 30/4/18, died of influenza 19/10/18.
SINGERS, W., Pte. (4973), attested 27/4/18, demobilised 16/7/19.
VISTER, P., Pte. (4974), attested 27/4/18, demobilised 10/8/19.
ARENDSE, J., Pte. (4975), attested 1/5/18, demobilised 26/12/18.
STOUT, J., Pte. (4976), attested 29/4/18, demobilised 11/7/19.
WILDS, J. P., Pte. (4977), attested 29/4/18, demobilised 7/10/19.
PHILANDER, D., Pte. (4978), attested 29/4/18, demobilised 16/7/19.
KIER, A., Pte. (4979), attested 1/5/18, demobilised 16/7/19.
WITTLE, J., Pte. (4980), attested 2/5/18, released medically unfit 23/5/18.
JOUBERT, L., Pte. (4981), attested 30/4/18, demobilised 11/7/19, transport driver.
BARRY, J., Pte. (4982), attested 27/4/18, demobilised 16/7/19.
WILLIAMS, A., Pte. (4983), attested 1/5/18, released medically unfit 16/7/18.
TERBLANCHE, S., Pte. (4984), attested 1/5/18, demobilised 21/7/19, pioneer.
SCHEEPERS, H., Pte. (4985), attested 29/4/18, demobilised 14/1/19.
TROMPETER, S., Pte. (4986), attested 29/4/18, died of influenza 8/10/18.
ISAACS, M., Pte. (4987), attested 29/4/18, transferred to C.A.H.T.C. 8/6/18.
KOEBERG, N., Pte. (4988), attested 20/4/18, died of heart failure 20/3/19.
WINDVOGEL, H., Pte. (4989), attested 30/4/18, demobilised 28/8/19.

THE STORY OF THE 1st CAPE CORPS.

HENDRICKS, F., Pte. (4990), attested 30/4/18, demobilised 21/7/19.
McBEAN, J., Pte. (4991), attested 30/4/18, demobilised 21/7/19.
LOWE, P., Pte. (4992), attested 29/4/18, demobilised 24/7/19.
HARTNICK, H., Pte. (4993), attested 29/4/18, transferred to C.A.H.T.C. 8/6/18.
LOTTERING, J., Pte. (4994), attested 1/5/18, demobilised 7/9/19.
UITHALDER, N., Pte. (4995), attested 13/5/18, demobilised 28/8/19.
MAART, W., Pte. (4996), attested 26/4/18, released medically unfit 13/5/18.
BATTY, L., Pte. (4997), attested 26/4/18, released medically unfit 13/5/18.
FAROE, H., Pte. (4998), attested 22/4/18, released medically unfit 14/5/18.
GRAY, A., Pte. (4999), attested 20/4/18, released medically unfit 13/5/18.
JOHNSON, W., Pte. (5000), attested 2/5/18, demobilised 1/1/19.
PETERS, S., Pte. (5001), attested 2/5/18, demobilised 1/1/19.
VAN WYK, H., Pte. (5002), attested 2/5/18, demobilised 22/7/19.
TELLING, J., Pte. (5003), attested 2/5/18, demobilised 26/12/18.
RENTZ, A., Pte. (5004), attested 3/5/18, released medically unfit 13/12/18.
ROMAN, N., Pte. (5005), attested 2/5/18, demobilised 15/7/19, passed scout course.
WELCOME, H., Pte. (5006), attested 3/5/18, demobilised 21/7/19.
ABRAHAMS, F., Pte. (5007), attested 2/5/18, demobilised 16/7/19.
ABRAHAMS, H., Pte. (5008), attested 2/5/18, demobilised 16/7/19.
GELDERBLOOM, P., Pte. (5009), attested 2/5/18, demobilised 16/7/19.
VAN WYK, T., Pte. (5010), attested 2/5/18, demobilised 26/12/18.
EDWARDS, H., Pte. (5011), attested 3/5/18, released medically unfit 20/6/18.
DUNKAN, J., Pte. (5012), attested 3/5/18, demobilised 12/7/19.
BANTAN, A., Pte. (5013), attested 2/5/18, died of pneumonia at sea 10/9/18.
MORRIS, S., Pte. (5014), attested 2/5/18, released medically unfit 20/6/18.
OERSON, T. P., Pte. (5015), attested 1/5/18, demobilised 12/7/19, acted Cpl. Orderly Room Clerk; R.H. Bn.
CORNELLISSEN, A., Pte. (5016), attested 30/4/18, demobilised 21/7/19.
DU PLESSIS, W., Pte. (5017), attested 3/5/18, released medically unfit 15/6/18.
HANNIE, H., Pte. (5018), attested 16/4/18, released medically unfit 23/6/18.
PETERS, J., Pte. (5019), attested 1/5/18, demobilised 10/4/20.
LEPHOI, J., Pte. (5020), attested 8/5/18, demobilised 5/10/19.
AUGUSTINE, J., Pte. (5021), attested 7/5/18, died of influenza 9/10/18.
ADAMS, A., Pte. (5022), attested 3/5/18, demobilised 21/7/19.
KEYSTER, P., Pte. (5023), attested 3/5/18, demobilised 21/7/19.
TITUS, B., Pte. (5024), attested 1/5/18, demobilised 16/7/19.
PETERS, F., Pte. (5025), attested 1/5/18, released medically unfit 16/6/18.
HEYNES, N., Pte. (5026), attested 1/5/18, demobilised 16/7/19.
DEYCE, D., Pte. (5027), attested 28/4/18, demobilised 7/9/19.
MEYER, G., Pte. (5028), attested 25/5/18, demobilised 7/9/19, qualified scout.
DE SILVA, J., Pte. (5029), attested 25/4/18, demobilised 16/7/19.
WILLIAMS, B., Pte. (5030), attested 23/4/18, demobilised 21/7/19.
BISSETH, D., Pte. (5031), attested 6/5/18, demobilised 7/9/19.
JAFTHA, C., Pte. (5032), attested 25/4/18, demobilised 16/7/19.
DE BRUIN, J., Pte. (5033), attested 26/4/18, demobilised 16/7/19.
BOTHA, J., Pte. (5034), attested 25/4/18, released medically unfit 16/6/18.
BRINKHUIS, H., Pte. (5035), attested 29/4/18, demobilised 16/7/19.
NELSON, A. J., Pte. (5036), attested 3/5/18, demobilised 21/7/19.
OKKERS, J., Pte. (5037), attested 30/4/18, demobilised 21/7/19.
BEVIE, A., Pte. (5038), attested 3/5/18, demobilised 21/7/19.
SMITH, D., Pte. (5039), attested 3/5/18, demobilised 16/7/19.
SAULS, S. G., Pte. (5040), attested 30/4/18, demobilised 7/9/19.
MEYERS, W., Pte. (5041), attested 9/5/18, released medically unfit 21/6/18.
MILLER, G., Pte. (5042), attested 6/5/18, demobilised 11/7/19.
COOKSON, T., Pte. (5043), attested 2/5/18, demobilised 7/9/19.
CLOETE, W., Pte. (5044), attested 18/4/18, transferred to C.A.H.T.C. 8/6/18.
LEO, J., Pte. (5045), attested 18/4/18, demobilised 22/7/19.
HAYES, H., Pte. (5046), attested 18/4/18, demobilised 7/9/19.
CLOETE, J., Pte. (5047), attested 18/4/18, demobilised 7/9/19.
VOLMER, J., Pte. (5048), attested 18/4/18, demobilised 21/7/19.
CLOETE, D., Pte. (5049), attested 18/4/18, demobilised 22/7/19.
LOMBARD, M., Pte. (5050), attested 6/5/18, S.N.L.R. 28/8/18.
BROWN, J., Pte. (5051), attested 6/5/18, demobilised 11/7/19, machine gunner, passed trench warfare and bombing course.
JORDAAN, A., Pte. (5052), attested 30/4/18, demobilised 7/9/19.
WHALES, J., Pte. (5053), attested 4/5/18, demobilised 16/7/19.
FOUNTAIN, J., Pte. (5054), attested 23/4/18, demobilised 21/7/19.
VISTER, H., Pte. (5055), attested 4/5/18, released medically unfit 15/6/18.
PETERSE, J., Pte. (5056), attested 4/5/18, demobilised 7/6/19.
CUPIDO, D., Pte. (5057), attested 4/5/18, demobilised 11/7/19.
FYFER, A., Pte. (5058), attested 6/5/18, demobilised 21/7/19.
ENDLEY, W. L., Pte. (5059), attested 30/4/18, demobilised 16/7/19, pioneer.
ABRAHAMS, J., Pte. (5060), attested 7/5/18, demobilised 16/7/19.
SMITH, A., Pte. (5061), attested 6/5/18, demobilised 7/10/19.
BAILEY, R., Pte. (5062), attested 7/5/18, demobilised 7/9/19.
BROWN, H., Pte. (5063), attested 7/5/18, demobilised 16/7/19.
FRANS, J., Pte. (5064), attested 23/4/18, demobilised 16/7/19.
LOUW, D., Pte. (5065), attested 1/5/18, demobilised 21/7/19.
SOLOMON, B., Pte. (5066), attested 27/4/18, demobilised 16/7/19.
AMAN, J., Pte. (5067), attested 1/5/18, demobilised 21/7/19.
HYMAN, J., Pte. (5068), attested 1/5/18, released medically unfit 17/5/18.
KEIZER, A., Pte. (5069), attested 1/5/18, released medically unfit 17/5/18.
CASPER, J., Pte. (5070), attested 8/5/18, released medically unfit 15/5/18.
JANSEN, J., Pte. (5071), attested 23/4/18, released medically unfit 17/5/18.
WILLIAMS, G., Pte. (5072), attested 23/4/18, released medically unfit 17/5/18.
JOUBERT, F., Pte. (5073), attested 23/4/18, released medically unfit 17/5/18.
GERT, J., Pte. (5074), attested 24/4/18, released medically unfit 16/5/18.
PIETERSEN, J., Pte. (5075), attested 30/4/18, released medically unfit 15/5/18.
DAMON, P., Pte. (5076), attested 10/5/18, released medically unfit 17/5/18.
JONES, F., Pte. (5077), attested 23/4/18, released medically unfit 17/5/18.
TOBIAS, A., Pte. (5078), attested 24/4/18, released medically unfit 17/5/18.
WAGENAAR, K., Pte. (5079), attested 29/4/18, released medically unfit 17/5/18.

THE STORY OF THE 1st CAPE CORPS.

MARTIN, J., Pte. (5080), attested 25/4/18, released medically unfit 17/5/18.
ARONTJES, J., Pte. (5081), attested 29/4/18, released medically unfit 17/5/18.
WITBOOI, J., Pte. (5082), attested 25/4/18, released medically unfit 17/5/18.
DE SILVA, B., Pte. (5083), attested 25/4/18, released medically unfit 17/5/18.
DU PREEZ, J., Pte. (5084), attested 25/4/18, released medically unfit 17/5/18.
SCHARNECK, A., Pte. (5085), attested 30/4/18, released medically unfit 16/5/18.
SMITH, L., Pte. (5086), attested 1/5/18, released medically unfit 17/5/18.
HOPSEL, J. G., Pte. (5087), attested 7/5/18, S.N.L.R. 29/7/18.
RUYTER, P., Pte. (5088), attested 6/5/18, demobilised 16/7/19.
HENDRICKS, W., Pte. (5089), attested 7/5/18, demobilised 16/7/19.
ISAACS, J., Pte. (5090), attested 6/5/18, demobilised 11/7/19.
THANNA, J., Pte. (5091), attested 8/5/18, demobilised 21/7/19.
JULIES, J., Pte. (5092), attested 6/5/18, demobilised 11/7/19.
LOTTERING, H., Pte. (5093), attested 6/5/18, demobilised 21/7/19.
PETERSEN, S., Pte. (5094), attested 7/5/18, demobilised 26/12/18.
APPLES, D., Pte. (5095), attested 27/4/18, demobilised 21/7/19.
OLKERS, D., Pte. (5096), attested 6/5/18, demobilised 16/7/19.
BROWN, J., Pte. (5097), attested 27/4/18, demobilised 16/7/19.
THORNE, H., Pte. (5098), attested 7/5/18, demobilised 21/7/19.
PRINSLOO, N., Pte. (5099), attested 9/5/18, demobilised 7/9/19.
DELPORT, P., Pte. (5100), attested 27/4/18, demobilised 16/7/19.
GOLDING, J., Pte. (5101), attested 7/5/18, demobilised 16/7/19.
NOVEMBER, A., Pte. (5102), attested 6/5/18, released medically unfit 31/8/18.
BAATJES, M., Pte. (5103), attested 6/5/18, demobilised 7/9/19.
BAATJES, J., Pte. (5104), attested 6/5/18, demobilised 7/9/19.
MILLER, J., Pte. (5105), attested 6/5/18, demobilised 16/7/19.
SWARTZ, C., Pte. (5106), attested 5/5/18, transferred to C.A.H.T.C. 8/6/18.
MEYER, I., Pte. (5107), attested 23/4/18, demobilised 16/7/19.
PETERSEN, J., Pte. (5108), attested 8/5/18, demobilised 12/7/19.
FRANSMAN, N., Pte. (5109), attested 11/5/18, demobilised 12/7/19.
STEYN, G., Pte. (5110), attested 22/4/18, demobilised 21/7/19.
JOHNSON, W., Pte. (5111), attested 11/5/18, demobilised 21/7/19.
VAN WYK, J., Pte. (5112), attested 15/5/18, demobilised 21/7/19.
SARS, F. W., Pte. (5113), attested 13/5/18, demobilised 21/7/19, machine gunner.
VOLTYN, B., Pte. (5114), attested 8/5/18, demobilised 21/7/19.
VOLTYN, A., Pte. (5115), attested 8/5/18, demobilised 21/7/19.
DAMONS, H., Pte. (5116), attested 7/5/18, released medically unfit 22/6/18.
LUITERS, J. W., Pte. (5117), attested 13/5/18, demobilised 7/9/19.
VERSTER, C., Pte. (5118), attested 11/5/18, demobilised 16/7/19.
DRAAINER, J., Pte. (5119), attested 11/5/18, demobilised 21/7/19.
PRESENCE, H., Pte. (5120), attested 11/5/18, demobilised 11/7/19.
CLOETE, D. W., Pte. (5121), attested 13/5/18, demobilised 11/7/19.
DE KOCK, P., Pte. (5122), attested 7/5/18, demobilised 11/7/19.
STEYN, W., Pte. (5123), attested 14/5/18, S.N.L.R. 31/7/18.
BUSH, J., Pte. (5124), attested 13/5/18, S.N.L.R. 27/5/18.
PETERSEN, C., Pte. (5125), attested 15/5/18, demobilised 6/1/19.
CAROLLISSEN, G., Pte. (5126), attested 16/5/18, demobilised 25/7/19.
ENSOR, D., Pte. (5127), attested 13/5/18, demobilised 7/9/19.
VAN WYK, C., Pte. (5128), attested 16/5/18, demobilised 16/7/19, pioneer.
DAVIDS, J., Pte. (5129), attested 17/5/18, demobilised 16/7/19.
PRINS, M., Pte. (5130), attested 20/4/18, released medically unfit 24/5/18.
KROTZ, G., Pte. (5131), attested 11/5/18, released medically unfit 28/5/18.
POPP, H., Pte. (5132), attested 6/5/18, released medically unfit 29/5/18.
THERON, J., Pte. (5133), attested 6/5/18, released medically unfit 29/5/18.
PETERSEN, S., Pte. (5134), attested 6/5/18, released medically unfit 29/5/18.
LOSPER, D., Pte. (5135), attested 6/5/18, released medically unfit 18/6/18.
MATHYSE, J., Pte. (5136), attested 16/5/18, transferred to C.A.H.T.C. 8/6/18.
CUPIDO, J., Pte. (5137), attested 16/5/18, demobilised 7/10/19.
FOURIE, A., Pte. (5138), attested 30/4/18, demobilised 21/7/19.
BROWN, J., Pte. (5139), attested 17/5/18, released medically unfit 16/7/18.
PRINCE, J., Pte. (5140), attested 13/5/18, demobilised 1/1/19.
BUIS, E., Pte. (5141), attested 11/5/18, transferred to C.A.H.T.C. 8/6/18.
JOHAR, H. V., Pte. (5142), attested 10/5/18, released medically unfit 21/9/18.
FRED, A., Pte. (5143), attested 18/5/18, demobilised 21/7/19.
KOUTER, M., Pte. (5144), attested 13/5/18, demobilised 26/12/18.
SOLOMON, J., Pte. (5145), attested 20/5/18, released medically unfit 15/6/18.
ROSENT, E., Pte. (5146), attested 18/5/18, demobilised 12/7/19.
BOOYSEN, W., Pte. (5147), attested 20/5/18, demobilised 16/7/19.
GORDON, I., Pte. (5148), attested 16/5/18, demobilised 11/7/19.
ROUX, A., Pte. (5149), attested 14/5/18, demobilised 12/7/19, machine gunner.
HARTNICK, J., Pte. (5150), attested 21/5/18, demobilised 16/7/19.
HENRY, J., Pte. (5151), attested 21/5/18, demobilised 11/7/19.
GREEN, C., Pte. (5152), attested 21/5/18, released medically unfit 21/6/18.
BAARTES, D., Pte. (5153), attested 21/5/18, demobilised 21/7/19.
HENRY, W., Pte. (5154), attested 17/5/18, demobilised 12/7/19.
CLASSE, J., Pte. (5155), attested 22/5/18, released medically unfit 27/6/18.
JONES, J., Pte. (5156), attested 18/5/18, demobilised 21/7/19.
HASSEN, M., Pte. (5157), attested 16/5/18, demobilised 21/7/19, machine gunner.
ALFRED, E., Pte. (5158), attested 16/5/18, demobilised 31/1/20.
BOK, H., Pte. (5159), attested 28/5/18, released medically unfit 26/6/18.
HOPLEY, J. D., a/L./Cpl. (5160), attested 28/5/18, a/L./Cpl. 1/1/19, demobilised 7/9/19, qualified Lewis Gun Instructor.
ALBERTS, J., Pte. (5161), attested 2/5/18, released medically unfit 6/6/18.
SOLOMON, C., Pte. (5162), attested 20/5/18, released medically unfit 6/6/18.
BRINKHUIS, F., Pte. (5163), attested 11/5/18, released medically unfit 6/6/18.
SCHIFFERS, J., Pte. (5164), attested 25/5/18, S.N.L.R. 1/6/18.
KAMMERS, A., Pte. (5165), attested 21/5/18, demobilised 21/7/19.
WALLACE, W., Pte. (5166), attested 22/5/18, demobilised 12/7/19.
DAWNLEY, A., Pte. (5167), attested 21/5/18, released medically unfit 28/6/18.
BOTHA, S., Pte. (5168), attested 25/5/18, demobilised 21/7/19.
CORDOM, J., Pte. (5169), attested 25/5/18, released medically unfit 30/6/18.

SEPTEMBER, N., Pte. (5170), attested 25/5/18, released medically unfit 28/6/18.
TROUTTER, C., Pte. (5171), attested 25/5/18, released medically unfit 22/6/18.
SILVER, J., Pte. (5172), attested 27/5/18, demobilised 10/11/19.
FREDERICKS, P., Pte. (5173), attested 24/5/18, demobilised 7/10/19.
SNYERS, J., Pte. (5174), attested 22/5/18, released medically unfit 15/6/18.
JOB, E. S. A., Pte. (5175), attested 25/5/18, demobilised 7/10/19.
BARON, J., Pte. (5176), attested 27/5/18, demobilised 21/7/19.
JACOBS, P., Pte. (5177), attested 25/5/18, demobilised 20/10/19.
KOETENBERG, W., Sgt. (5178), attested 28/5/18, Sgt. 1/11/18, demobilised 11/7/19.
ABRAHAMS, G., Pte. (5179), attested 30/5/18, demobilised 11/7/19, tailor.
THEUNIS, W., Pte. (5180), attested 30/5/18, demobilised 31/12/18.
STEMINCH, F., Pte. (5181), attested 30/5/18, released medically unfit 15/6/18.
ADAMS, G., Cpl. (5182), attested 30/5/18, Cpl. 5/7/18, demobilised 21/7/19.
OLIVER, H., Pte. (5183), attested 29/5/18, demobilised 12/7/19.
GELDENHUIS, J., Pte. (5184), attested 3/6/18, released medically unfit 15/6/18.
SIMON, D., Pte. (5185), attested 3/6/18, demobilised 7/7/19.
McCARTHY, J. R., Pte. (5186), attested 3/6/18, demobilised 30/7/19.
FORTUIN, C., Pte. (5187), attested 3/6/18, demobilised 11/7/19.
LINSELL, C., Bandmaster (5188), attested 3/6/18, promoted to the rank of acting first-class W.O. whilst acting as Bandmaster 10/6/18, demobilised 11/10/19, European personnel.
HORSE, T., Pte. (5189), attested 3/6/18, released medically unfit 29/6/18.
VERWEY, N., Pte. (5190), attested 31/5/18, demobilised 21/7/19.
VISAGIE, J., Pte. (5191), attested 30/5/18, released medically unfit 1/7/18.
LLOYD, R., Pte. (5192), attested 8/5/18, released medically unfit 1/7/18.
GILMORE, R., Pte. (5193), attested 5/6/18, demobilised 7/10/19.
HESS, N., Pte. (5194), attested 5/6/18, demobilised 1/1/19.
DAVIDS, E., Pte. (5195), attested 5/6/18, released medically unfit 30/6/18.
DAVIDS, C., Pte. (5196), attested 5/6/18, released medically unfit 27/6/18.
AFRIKANDER, A., Pte. (5197), attested 5/6/18, released medically unfit 27/6/18.
HERCLASS, J., Pte. (5198), attested 1/6/18, demobilised 21/7/19.
JACOBS, P., Pte. (5199), attested 1/6/18, released medically unfit 30/6/18.
RAY, W., Pte. (5200), attested 5/6/18, demobilised 21/7/19.
KLASS, W., Pte. (5201), attested 4/6/18, demobilised 21/7/19.
KANNEMEYER, F., Pte. (5202), attested 4/6/18, demobilised 16/7/19.
CUPIDO, O., Pte. (5203), attested 4/6/18, demobilised 11/7/19.
CROW, I. J., Pte. (5204), attested 4/6/18, released medically unfit 30/6/18.
TOM, T., Pte. (5205), attested 25/5/18, released medically unfit 15/6/18.
KLASSEN, K., Pte. (5206), attested 3/6/18, demobilised 21/7/19.
ADAMS, D., Pte. (5207), attested 5/6/18, demobilised 11/7/19.
DE LANGE, W., Pte. (5208), attested 15/5/18, demobilised 1/1/19.
KENNY, L., Pte. (5209), attested 15/5/18, released medically unfit 15/6/18.
ROUSTOFF, P., Pte. (5210), attested 23/5/18, demobilised 21/7/19.
DEVEREAUX, R., Pte. (5211), attested 10/6/18, demobilised 31/1/19.
KLASSE, A., Pte. (5212), attested 10/6/18, demobilised 11/7/19.
CAMPHOR, P., Pte. (5213), attested 1/6/18, demobilised 30/12/18.
CANA, D. R., Pte. (5214), attested 13/6/18, demobilised 11/7/19.
NAUDE, L., Pte. (5215), attested 13/6/18, demobilised 30/12/18.
FEBRUARY, M., Pte. (5216), attested 11/6/18, demobilised 21/7/19.
AFRICA, W., Pte. (5217), attested 11/6/18, demobilised 12/7/19.
ABDOL, C., Pte. (5218), attested 6/6/18, released medically unfit 27/6/18.
ROHAN, W. C., Pte. (5219), attested 17/6/18, demobilised 21/7/19.
GILBERT, A., Pte. (5220), attested 17/6/18, demobilised 12/7/19.
SMITH, J., Pte. (5221), attested 18/6/18, demobilised 7/9/19.
ENSOR, J., Pte. (5222), attested 11/6/18, demobilised 12/7/19.
WILSON, P., Pte. (5223), attested 11/6/18, released medically unfit 26/6/18.
WILLIAMS, N., Pte. (5224), attested 17/6/18, demobilised 10/8/19.
JACOBS, J., Pte. (5225), attested 17/6/18, demobilised 22/7/19.
PRITCHARD, H., Pte. (5226), attested 15/6/18, demobilised 21/7/19, drum and fife band.
WILLIAMS, W., Pte. (5227), attested 15/6/18, demobilised 3/9/19.
PETERSEN, M. J., Pte. (5228), attested 17/6/18, demobilised 11/7/19, machine gunner.
PETERSEN, J. B., Pte. (5229), attested 17/6/18, demobilised 7/10/19.
HARRISON, C., Pte. (5230), attested 17/6/18, demobilised 11/7/19.
PETERSEN, P., Pte. (5231), attested 17/6/18, demobilised 16/7/19.
RANSON, N., Pte. (5232), attested 15/6/18, demobilised 29/12/18.
PETERSEN, P., Pte. (5233), attested 19/6/18, demobilised 12/7/19.
WILSON, B., Pte. (5234), attested 18/6/18, released medically unfit 21/6/18.
DAVIDS, P., Pte. (5235), attested 17/6/18, demobilised 26/12/18.
LOTTER, F. J., Pte. (5236), attested 19/6/18, demobilised 7/10/19.
ABDULLAH, H., Pte. (5237), attested 19/6/18, demobilised 16/7/19.
KLEINSMITH, A., Pte. (5238), attested 17/6/18, demobilised 7/10/19.
HILL, R., Pte. (5239), attested 19/6/18, demobilised 11/7/19.
MARTIN, H., Pte. (5240), attested 29/5/18, demobilised 21/7/19.
WILLIAMS, K., Pte. (5241), attested 21/6/18, demobilised 12/7/19.
BENJAMIN, J., Pte. (5242), attested 21/6/18, demobilised 21/7/19.
WILLIAMS, C., Pte. (5243), attested 21/6/18, demobilised 16/7/19.
SIMPSON, J., Pte. (5244), attested 24/6/18, S.N.L.R. 31/8/18.
VAN WYK, J., Pte. (5245), attested 24/6/18, died of influenza 8/10/18.
SEFOOR, J., Pte. (5246), attested 26/6/18, demobilised 16/7/19.
SEPTEMBER, S., Pte. (5247), attested 26/6/18, demobilised 16/7/19.
VILANDER, I., Pte. (5248), attested 26/6/18, released medically unfit 3/8/18.
KELLY, E. F., Pte. (5249), attested 26/6/18, demobilised 16/7/19.
ROOKS, J., Pte. (5250), attested 26/6/18, demobilised 16/7/19.
CROWLEY, R. A., Pte. (5251), attested 24/6/18, demobilised 21/7/19.
BOTHA, C. S., Pte. (5252), attested 24/6/18, demobilised 21/7/19.
ADAMS, P., Pte. (5253), attested 13/6/18, demobilised 22/7/19.
APRIL, W., Pte. (5254), attested 13/6/18, demobilised 1/1/19.
JULIE, J. D. L./Cpl. (5255), attested 21/5/18, L./Cpl. 1/11/18, demobilised 22/7/19.
EDWARDS, J., Pte. (5256), attested 28/6/18, demobilised 12/7/19.
GALLANT, J., Pte. (5257), attested 27/6/18, demobilised 1/1/19.
BOTHA, H., Pte. (5258), attested 25/6/18, demobilised 21/7/19, passed course of field cookery.
BEUKES, J., Pte. (5259), attested 17/6/18, demobilised 30/7/19.

STEBLECKI, D. C., Pte. (5260), attested 26/6/18, demobilised 22/7/19, passed course of field cookery.
STEBLECKI, S. C., Pte. (5261), attested 26/6/18, demobilised 22/7/19.
VAN SCHALKWYK, O., Pte. (5262), attested 14/6/18 demobilised 10/8/19.
BOOYSEN, M., Pte. (5263), attested 27/6/18, demobilised 21/7/19.
CLARKE, G., Pte. (5264), attested 27/6/18, demobilised 16/7/19.
JORDAN, L., Pte. (5265), attested 1/7/18, released medically unfit 30/7/18.
FRASER, W., Pte. (5266), attested 29/6/18, demobilised 21/7/19.
JACKSON, W., Pte. (5267), attested 4/7/18, demobilised 7/9/19.
BRUINERS, J., Pte. (5268), attested 6/7/18, demobilised 12/7/19.
BRUINERS, W., Pte. (5269), attested 6/7/18, demobilised 12/7/19.
LAWRENCE, P., Pte. (5270), attested 1/7/18, demobilised 12/7/19.
ALEXANDER, W., Pte. (5271), attested 6/7/18, demobilised 31/12/19.
SASS, J., Pte. (5272), attested 6/7/18, demobilised 29/7/19.
STUURMAN, D., Pte. (5273), attested 1/7/18, demobilised 12/7/19.
OLMAN, T., Pte. (5274), attested 1/7/18, demobilised 25/7/19.
RATCLIFFE, C., Pte. (5275), attested 1/7/18, demobilised 21/7/19.
LAWRENCE, T., Pte. (5276), attested 9/7/18, demobilised 21/7/19.
ADONIS, I., Pte. (5277), attested 1/7/18, demobilised 1/1/19.
MICHAEL, J., Pte. (5278), attested 5/7/18, released medically unfit 20/7/18.
FERGUSON, F., Pte. (5279), attested 13/7/18, released medically unfit 21/7/18.
SARDINE, A., Pte. (5280), attested 11/7/18, released medically unfit 20/7/18.
COETZEE, S. A., Pte. (5281), attested 2/7/18, demobilised 13/8/19.
LIBERTY, P., Pte. (5282), attested 2/7/18, demobilised 21/7/19.
SWARTZ, J., Pte. (5283), attested 2/7/18, demobilised 11/7/19.
SORTELI, M., Pte. (5284), attested 2/7/18, released medically unfit 11/8/18.
BRUINTJES, A., Pte. (5285), attested 9/7/18, released medically unfit 13/7/18.
RAYNIE, J., Pte. (5286), attested 9/7/18, released medically unfit 13/7/18.
NAMDOE, S., Pte. (5287), attested 9/7/18, released medically unfit 13/7/18.
FRANCIS, G., Pte. (5288), attested 12/7/18, demobilised 7/9/19.
JORDAAN, J., Pte. (5289), attested 15/7/18, demobilised 11/7/19.
ARENDSE, A., Pte. (5290), attested 15/7/18, demobilised 16/7/19.
BARTMAN, C., Pte. (5291), attested 13/7/18, demobilised 21/7/19.
DAVIDS, A., Pte. (5292), attested 15/7/18, demobilised 16/7/19.
CYSTER, J., Pte. (5293), attested 15/7/18, demobilised 21/7/19.
JOHANNES, E., Pte. (5294), attested 15/7/18, demobilised 16/7/19.
KYSTER, B., Pte. (5295), attested 13/7/18, demobilised 16/7/19.
LEWIS, G., Pte. (5296), attested 13/7/18, demobilised 7/9/19.
MORKEL, A., Pte. (5297), attested 15/7/18, demobilised 16/7/19.
NATTERS, D., Pte. (5298), attested 15/7/18, demobilised 16/7/19.
SEPTEMBER, A., Pte. (5299), attested 15/7/18, demobilised 21/7/19.
SERFONTEIN, J., Pte. (5300), attested 15/7/18, demobilised 29/7/19.
VISTER, S., Pte. (5301), attested 18/7/18, demobilised 21/7/19.
VAN DER VENT, J., Pte. (5302), attested 17/7/18, demobilised 21/7/19.
WILLIAMS, J., Pte. (5303), attested 16/7/18, demobilised 12/7/19.
ZIAS, J., Pte. (5304), attested 15/7/18, demobilised 29/12/18.
ABRAHAMS, C., Pte. (5305), attested 17/7/18, demobilised 11/11/19.
FREDERICKS, A., Pte. (5306), attested 16/7/18, demobilised 16/7/19.
JOHNSON, P., Pte. (5307), attested 17/7/18, demobilised 12/7/19.
McDONALD, W., Pte. (5308), attested 11/7/18, demobilised 21/7/19.
SOLOMON, I., Pte. (5309), attested 17/7/18, demobilised 12/7/19.
ADRIAANSE, I., Pte. (5310), attested 20/7/18, demobilised 21/7/19.
MOSS, A., Pte. (5311), attested 20/7/18, demobilised 11/7/19.
ROUX, P., Pte. (5312), attested 17/7/18, released medically unfit 13/8/19.
SMITHWICK, S., Pte. (5313), attested 17/7/18, demobilised 21/7/19.
WILLIAMS, J., Pte. (5314), attested 16/7/18, released medically unfit 20/7/18.
JOSEPHS, G., Pte. (5315), attested 16/7/18, released medically unfit 20/7/18.
FRANKS, C. T., Pte. (5316), attested 24/7/18, released medically unfit 26/9/18.
PARKERS, D., Pte. (5317), attested 24/7/18, demobilised 31/7/19.
TROUT, P. A., Pte. (5318), attested 24/7/18, demobilised 16/7/19.
EKSTEEN, S. D., Pte. (5319), attested 26/7/18, demobilised 21/7/19.
ABRAHAMS, J., Pte. (5320), attested 22/7/18, demobilised 16/7/19.
AFRICA, J., Pte. (5321), attested 22/7/18, demobilised 8/9/19.
DUMENY, M., Pte. (5322), attested 22/7/18, demobilised 16/7/19.
DANIELS, A., Pte. (5323), attested 22/7/18, demobilised 16/7/19.
ENGEL, D., Pte. (5324), attested 22/7/18, demobilised 11/7/19.
ENGEL, A., Pte. (5325), attested 22/7/18, demobilised 11/7/19.
EUROPA, J., Pte. (5326), attested 23/7/18, demobilised 16/7/19.
GELDENHUIS, J., Pte. (5327), attested 22/7/18, demobilised 30/7/19.
GERTZE, D., Pte. (5328), attested 22/7/18, demobilised 11/7/19.
HANS, S., Pte. (5329), attested 22/7/18, demobilised 11/7/19.
JOZEF, A., Pte. (5330), attested 22/7/18, demobilised 16/7/19.
JANTJES, A., Pte. (5331), attested 23/7/18, demobilised 11/7/19.
McGREGOR, C., Pte. (5332), attested 26/7/18, demobilised 7/9/19.
NEWMAN, W., Pte. (5333), attested 23/7/18, demobilised 16/7/19.
OOSTENDORP, L., Pte. (5334), attested 25/7/18, demobilised 11/7/19.
OCTOBER, T., Pte. (5335), attested 22/7/18, demobilised 8/9/19.
PLAATJES, P., Pte. (5336), attested 22/7/18, demobilised 8/9/19.
SMIT, J., Pte. (5337), attested 22/7/18, demobilised 16/7/19.
HILL, J., Pte. (5338), attested 23/7/18, demobilised 14/1/19.
BOTHA, W., Pte. (5339), attested 23/7/18, released medically unfit 3/8/18.
VAN TURA, C., Pte. (5340), attested 23/7/18, released medically unfit 3/8/18.
AFRICA, P., Pte. (5341), attested 25/7/18, tranferred to C.A.H.T.C. 1/9/18.
ABERG, B., Pte. (5342), attested 25/7/18, demobilised 30/12/18.
BOOYSE, J., Pte. (5343), attested 29/7/18, demobilised 1/1/19.
DAMONS, C., Pte. (5344), attested 26/7/18, demobilised 19/12/18.
PLAATJES, J., Pte. (5345), attested 25/7/18, demobilised 29/12/18.
PONTAC, J., Pte. (5346), attested 25/7/18, demobilised 29/12/18.
RANK, C., Pte. (5347), attested 25/7/18, demobilised 1/1/19.
VALENTYNE, C., Pte. (5348), attested 25/7/18, demobilised 13/1/19.
ADAMS, A., Pte. (5349), attested 25/7/18, demobilised 30/12/18.
ABRAHAMS, S., Pte. (5350), attested 29/7/18, demobilised 27/12/18.

THE STORY OF THE 1st CAPE CORPS.

ADONIS, J. J., Pte. (5351), attested 29/7/18, demobilised 26/1/19.
ADOLF, A., Pte. (5352), attested 29/7/18, demobilised 24/2/19.
ABRAHAMS, C., Pte. (5353), attested 29/7/18, demobilised 30/12/18.
BOOIS, A., Pte. (5354), attested 29/7/18, demobilised 19/12/18.
BOYCE, C., Pte. (5355), attested 29/7/18, demobilised 30/12/18.
BASSON, F., Pte. (5356), attested 29/7/18, demobilised 26/12/18.
BARRON, S., Pte. (5357), attested 29/7/18, demobilised 30/12/18.
BOYES, A., Pte. (5358), attested 29/7/18, demobilised 30/12/18.
BOOIS, F., Pte. (5359), attested 29/7/18, demobilised 25/12/18.
BOOYSEN, W. N., Pte. (5360), attested 29/7/18, demobilised 26/12/18.
CORDON, A., Pte. (5361), attested 29/7/18, demobilised 19/12/18.
COETZEE, S., Pte. (5362), attested 29/7/18, died of influenza 8/10/18.
CONRADIE, C., Pte. (5363), attested 29/7/18, demobilised 30/12/18.
CARELSE, J., Pte. (5364), attested 30/7/18, demobilised 27/12/18.
CHRISTIANS, J. W., Pte. (5365), attested 29/7/18, demobilised 31/12/18.
DIRK, S., Pte. (5366), attested 29/7/18, demobilised 26/12/18.
DIRK, K., Pte. (5367), attested 29/7/18, demomilised 27/12/18.
DIETRICH, K., Pte. (5368), attested 29/7/18, demobilised 19/12/18.
DIETRICH, C., Pte. (5369), attested 29/7/18, demobilised 27/12/18.
DE VRIES, A., Pte. (5370), attested 30/7/18, demobilised 30/12/18.
ESAU, N., Pte. (5371), attested 29/7/18, demobilised 14/1/19.
ENGELBRECHT, D., Pte. (5372), attested 29/7/18, demobilised 31/12/18.
FISHER, T., Pte. (5373), attested 29/7/18, demobilised 25/12/18.
FARO, T., Pte. (5374), attested 29/7/18, demobilised 30/12/18.
HENDRIK, F., Pte. (5375), attested 29/7/18, demobilised 29/12/18.
GOLIATH, A., Pte. (5376), attested 29/7/18, demobilised 27/12/18.
GOLIATH, P., Pte. (5377), attested 29/7/18, demobilised 27/12/18.
HENDRICKS, H., Pte. (5378), attested 30/7/18, demobilised 3/1/19.
JULIES, E., Pte. (5379), attested 29/7/18, died of influenza 9/10/18.
JULIES, L. T., Pte. (5380), attested 29/7/18, died of influenza 13/10/18.
JULIES, P., Pte. (5381), attested 29/7/18, demobilised 14/1/19.
JOHNSON, J., Pte. (5382), attested 29/7/18, demobilised 30/12/18.
KASSER, F., Pte. (5383), attested 29/7/18, demobilised 6/1/19.
KAFFER, C., Pte. (5384), attested 29/7/18, demobilised 29/12/18.
KAFFER, B., Pte. (5385), attested 29/7/18, demobilised 29/12/18.
KLASSEN, W. C., Pte. (5386), attested 29/7/18, demobilised 15/1/19.
LESS, E., Pte. (5387), attested 29/7/18, demobilised 29/12/18.
LYKERT, J., Pte. (5388), attested 29/7/18, demobilised 3/1/19.
LESS, D., Pte. (5389), attested 29/7/18, demobilised 29/12/18.
LESS, D. C., Pte. (5390), attested 29/7/18, demobilised 29/12/18.
LESS, J., Pte. (5391), attested 29/7/18, demobilised 30/12/18.
LEWIS, S., Pte. (5392), attested 30/7/18, demobilised 14/1/19.
LESS, J., Pte. (5393), attested 29/7/18, demobilised 30/12/18.
LOTRING, B., Pte. (5394), attested 29/7/18, demobilised 29/12/18.
MAZIAS, H., Pte. (5395), attested 29/7/18, demobilised 26/12/18.
MORITZ, F., Pte. (5396), attested 29/7/18, demobilised 31/12/18.
MAURITS, D., Pte. (5397), attested 29/7/18, demobilised 29/12/18.
MAART, W., Pte. (5398), attested 29/7/18, demobilised 26/12/18.
MOORE, P., Pte. (5399), attested 29/7/18, released medically unfit 13/9/18.
MASCHULLA, J., Pte. (5400), attested 29/7/18, demobilised 26/12/18.
MANUEL, K., Pte. (5401), attested 29/7/18, demobilised 26/12/18.
NATHAN, J., Pte. (5402), attested 29/7/18, demobilised 29/12/18.
PETERSEN, J., Pte. (5403), attested 29/7/18, demobilised 1/1/19.
PIETERSEN, H., Pte. (5404), attested 29/7/18, released medically unfit 13/9/18.
PARSON, P., Pte. (5405), attested 29/7/18, demobilised 26/12/18.
PARISH, J., Pte. (5406), attested 30/7/18, demobilised 26/1/19.
ERASMUS, F., Pte. (5407), attested 29/7/18, demobilised 30/12/18.
ERASMUS, T., Pte. (5408), attested 29/7/18, demobilised 14/1/19.
ROMAN, A., Pte. (5409), attested 29/7/18, demobilised 29/12/18.
ROMAN, P., Pte. (5410), attested 29/7/18, demobilised 29/12/18.
SMITH, D., Pte. (5411), attested 29/7/18, demobilised 29/12/18.
STEPHANUS, W., Pte. (5412), attested 29/7/18, demobilised 1/1/19.
SALTMAN, A., Pte. (5413), attested 29/7/18, demobilised 30/12/18.
SMITH, H., Pte. (5414), attested 29/7/18, transferred to C.A.H.T.C. 1/9/18.
SMITH, P., Pte. (5415), attested 29/7/18, demobilised 26/12/18.
SMITH, H., Pte. (5416), attested 29/7/18, demobilised 26/12/18.
SANNEBERG, L., Pte. (5417), attested 29/7/18, demobilised 29/12/18.
SWARTZ, E., Pte. (5418), attested 29/7/18, demobilised 29/12/18.
STAALMEESTER, G., Pte. (5419), attested 29/7/18, demobilised 1/1/19.
STAALMEESTER, H., Pte. (5420), attested 29/7/18, demobilised 1/1/19.
SAMSON, A., Pte. (5421), attested 29/7/18, demobilised 27/12/18.
VAN WYK, J., Pte. (5422), attested 29/7/18, demobilised 30/12/18.
VAN ROOY, C., Pte. (5423), attested 29/7/18, demobilised 14/1/19.
VAN ROOY, J., Pte. (5424), attested 29/7/18, demobilised 31/12/18.
VAN ROOY, D., Pte. (5425), attested 29/7/18, demobilised 14/1/19.
VAN WYK, A., Pte. (5426), attested 29/7/18, demobilised 27/12/18.
VAN NIEL, A., Pte. (5427), attested 29/7/18, demobilised 26/1/19.
VLOTMAN, D., Pte. (5428), attested 29/7/18, died of influenza 22/10/18.
VIELAND, A., Pte. (5429), attested 29/7/18, transferred to C.A.H.T.C. 1/9/18.
WILLIAMS, D., Pte. (5430), attested 29/7/18, released medically unfit 17/1/19.
ZINCK, C., Pte. (5431), attested 29/7/18, demobilised 29/12/18.
ZINCK, T., Pte. (5432), attested 29/7/18, demobilised 29/12/18.
MANEVELDT, J., Pte. (5433), attested 1/8/18, demobilised 29/12/18.
OLIVER, J., Pte. (5434), attested 1/8/18, demobilised 27/12/18.
JOB, M., Pte. (5435), attested 29/7/18, died of influenza 8/9/18.
OATS, F., Pte. (5436), attested 29/7/18, died of influenza 11/10/18.
DIXON, H. B., Pte. (5437), attested 1/8/18, demobilised 1/1/19.
HUMPHRIES, T., Pte. (5438), attested 1/8/18, died of influenza 14/10/18.
JANSEN, W., Pte. (5439), attested 2/8/18, rejected 6/8/18.
MARTHINUS, B., Pte. (5440), attested 1/8/18, demobilised 15/1/19.
SLEY, J., Pte. (5441), attested 29/7/18, demobilised 31/12/18.

YOUNG, A., Pte. (5442), attested 2/8/18, demobilised 1/1/19.
ZEALAND, J., Pte. (5443), attested 1/8/18, demobilised 26/12/18.
BOSMAN, A., Pte. (5444), attested 29/7/18, demobilised 2/1/19.
DAST, F., Pte. (5445), attested 6/8/18, demobilised 19/12/18.
DE VRIES, J., Pte. (5446), attested 6/8/18, demobilised 14/1/19.
ERASMUS, A., Pte. (5447), attested 8/8/18, transferred to C.A.H.T.C. 1/9/18
HEYNES, T., Pte. (5448), attested 2/8/18, demobilised 26/12/18.
HENDRICKS, H. W., Pte. (5449), attested 6/8/18, demobilised 5/2/19.
JACK, D., Pte. (5450), attested 6/8/18, demobilised 31/12/18.
JOSEPH, W., Pte. (5451), attested 8/8/18, demobilised 14/1/19.
LEWIS, A., Pte. (5452), attested 1/8/18, demobilised 14/1/19.
MORRIS, F., Pte. (5453), attested 8/8/18, demobilised 31/12/18.
MOSES, M., Pte. (5454), attested 6/8/18, demobilised 6/1/19.
MOLOKOWLE, K., Pte. (5455), attested 1/8/18, died of influenza 9/10/18.
OSBORNE, B., Pte. (5456), attested 6/8/18, demobilised 1/1/19.
PRETORIUS, L., Pte. (5457), attested 7/8/18, released medically unfit 19/9/18.
POTGIETER, L., Pte. (5458), attested 6/8/18, demobilised 29/12/18.
ROODERS, J., Pte. (5459), attested 8/8/18, demobilised 2/1/19.
RAUTENBACH, A., Pte. (5460), attested 1/8/18, died of influenza 15/10/18.
SMITH, J., Pte. (5461), attested 7/8/18, released medically unfit 17/9/18.
SMITH, D., Pte. (5462), attested 8/8/18, demobilised 30/12/18
VASSEN, S. F., Pte. (5463), attested 6/8/18, demobilised 14/1/19.
WILLIAMS, P., Pte. (5464), attested 6/8/18, released medically unfit 19/9/18.
ABRAHAMS, J., Pte. (5465), attested 29/7/18, rejected 22/8/18, not Cape coloured.
HENDERSON, K., Pte. (5466), attested 26/7/18, rejected 22/8/18, not Cape coloured.
HENDRICKS, W., Pte. (5467), attested 7/8/18, rejected 22/8/18, not Cape coloured.
MITCHELL, E., Pte. (5468), attested 7/8/18, rejected 21/8/18, not Cape coloured.
MALORTER, E., Pte. (5469), attested 26/7/18, rejected 22/8/18, not Cape coloured
OLIPHANT, J., Pte. (5470), attested 29/7/18, rejected 22/8/18, not Cape coloured.
ABRAHAMS, H., Pte. (5471), attested 8/8/18, demobilised 2/1/19.
CAMMIES, J., Pte. (5472), attested 8/8/18, demobilised 19/12/18.
DE VOS, H., Pte. (5473), attested 6/8/18, demobilised 1/1/19.
FARO, P., Pte. (5474), attested 8/8/18, demobilised 30/12/18.
FARO, T., Pte. (5475), attested 8/8/18, demobilised 31/12/18.
BOTHA, J., Pte. (5476), attested 9/8/18, demobilised 14/1/19.
PLAATJES, C., Pte. (5477), attested 9/8/18, demobilised 14/1/19.
PETERS, J., Pte. (5478), attested 8/8/18, demobilised 14/1/19.
THOMPSON, E., Pte. (5479), attested 12/8/18, demobilised 30/12/18.
DYERS, J., Pte. (5480), attested 14/8/18, died of influenza 9/10/18.
HECTOR, M., Pte. (5481), attested 13/8/18, demobilised 2/1/19.
HENDRICKSEN, D., Pte. (5482), attested 14/8/18, demobilised 29/12/18.
HARTZENBERG, J., Pte. (5483), attested 12/8/18, died of influenza 10/10/18.
FLORRIS, W., Pte. (5484), attested 14/8/18, demobilised 30/12/18.
VAN REENEN, S., Pte. (5485), attested 8/8/18, demobilised 29/12/18.
PETERS, H., Pte. (5486), attested 9/8/18, rejected 30/8/18.
GEDDES, J., Pte. (5487), attested 19/8/18, died of influenza 9/10/18.
PHILLIPS, G. W., Pte. (5488), attested 19/8/18, demobilised 30/1/19.
RYAN, M., Pte. (5489), attested 16/8/18, demobilised 6/1/19.
SAMUELS, F., Pte. (5490), attested 29/8/18, released medically unfit 20/10/18.
KAYSER, J., Pte. (5491), attested 19/8/18, demobilised 30/12/18.
MEYER, W., Pte. (5492), attested 19/8/18, demobilised 26/1/19, acted Sgt.
SAMUELS, H., Pte. (5493), attested 23/8/18, demobilised 29/12/18.
THOMPSON, N., Pte. (5494), attested 23/8/18, demobilised 5/1/19
SALES, J., Pte. (5495), rejected 31/8/18, unattested.
NOAH, A., Pte. (5496), attested 14/8/18, demobilised 1/1/19.
TITUS, J. C., Pte. (5497), attested 21/8/18, demobilised 1/1/19.
CAPONG, F., Pte. (5498), attested 16/4/18, rejected 21/4/18.
AMERICA, C., Pte. (5499), attested 26/8/18, demobilised 1/1/19.
ANDREWS, J. F, Pte. (5500), attested 26/8/18, demobilised 19/12/18.
ALEXANDER, M., Pte. (5501), attested 26/8/18, died of influenza 6/10/18.
AMSTERDAM, A., Pte. (5502), attested 26/8/18, released medically unfit 18/9/18
LINKS, A., Pte. (5503), attested 27/8/18, demobilised 2/1/19.
MARTIN, M., Pte. (5504), attested 28/8/18, demobilised 29/12/18.
MANLEY, W., Pte. (5505), attested 10/8/18, died of influenza 23/10/18.
MULLER, J. M., Pte. (5506), attested 10/8/18, demobilised 1/1/19.
NIEMOND, J., Pte. (5507), attested 26/8/18, died of influenza 10/10/18.
SOULS, T., Pte. (5508), attested 26/8/18, demobilised 31/12/18.
SOLOMON, F., Pte. (5509), attested 27/8/18, demobilised 2/1/19.
BRANDT, F., Pte. (5510), attested 30/8/18, died of influenza 7/10/18.
BEUKES, M., Pte. (5511), attested 28/8/18, demobilised 1/1/19.
CARLES, C. J., Pte. (5512), attested 29/8/18, demobilised 1/1/19.
GERTSE, W., Pte. (5513), attested 28/8/18, released medically unfit 18/9/18.
GOLIATH, A., Pte. (5514), attested 28/8/18, demobilised 27/12/18.
GRANGER, J. C., Pte. (5515), attested 30/8/18, demobilised 30/12/18.
ISAACS, A., Pte. (5516), attested 29/8/18, demobilised 1/1/19.
KAIZER, F., Pte. (5517), attested 27/8/18, demobilised 29/12/18.
STEVENS, E., Pte. (5518), attested 29/8/18, demobilised 15/1/19
ZWART, J., Pte. (5519), attested 29/8/18, released medically unfit 18/9/18.
BRITAIN, B., Pte. (5520), attested 3/9/18, demobilised 1/1/19.
BRANDT, A., Pte. (5521), attested 31/8/18, demobilised 27/12/18
CONSTANT, D., Pte. (5522), attested 26/8/18, demobilised 14/1/19.
HENRY, R., Pte. (5523), attested 26/8/18, demobilised 1/1/19.
JACOBS, C., Pte. (5524), attested 2/9/18, demobilised 29/12/18.
JORDAAN, J., Pte. (5525), attested 31/8/18, demobilised 6/1/19.
JOHANNES, F., Pte. (5526), attested 2/9/18, demobilised 26/12/18.
JACOBS, J., Pte. (5527), attested 2/9/18, demobilised 13/1/19.
KRUGER, H., Pte. (5528), attested 30/8/18, demobilised 14/1/19.
LE ROUX, M., Pte. (5529), attested 1/9/18, demobilised 29/12/18.
MARTIN, S., Pte. (5530), attested 2/9/18, demobilised 29/12/18.
MEYER, D., Pte. (5531), attested 30/8/18, demobilised 14/1/19.
MOORE, D., Pte. (5532), attested 2/9/18, demobilised 31/12/18.

THE STORY OF THE 1st CAPE CORPS.

MARTLOUW, N., Pte. (5533), attested 31/8/18, demobilised 1/1/19.
PETERS, G., Pte. (5534), attested 28/8/18, demobilised 1/1/19.
PETERSEN, I., Pte. (5535), attested 28/8/18, demobilised 30/12/18.
SMITH, G., Pte. (5536), attested 2/9/18, demobilised 30/12/18.
WHITNEY, R., Pte. (5537), attested 31/8/18, demobilised 26/12/18.
WILDSCHUT, J., Pte. (5538), attested 28/8/18, demobilised 29/12/18.
WEST, F., Pte. (5539), attested 26/8/18, demobilised 14/1/19.
ZAHL, D., Pte. (5540), attested 26/8/18, demobilised 1/1/19.
ZAHL, D., Pte. (5541), attested 2/9/18, demobilised 14/1/19.
AFRICA, A., Pte. (5542), rejected 17/9/18, unattested.
KRON, G., Pte. (5543), attested 26/8/18, rejected 17/9/18, not Cape coloured.
MAY, J., Pte. (5544), attested 26/8/18, rejected 17/9/18, not Cape coloured.
PETERSEN, E., Pte. (5545), attested 26/8/18, rejected 17/9/18, not Cape coloured.
APRIL, D., Pte. (5546), attested 26/8/18, demobilised 30/12/18.
ADAMS, D., Pte. (5547), attested 26/8/18, demobilised 27/12/18.
DAVIDS, G., Pte. (5548), attested 26/8/18, demobilised 14/1/19.
DOMING, R., Pte. (5549), attested 26/8/18, demobilised 26/12/18.
FISHER, P., Pte. (5550), attested 26/8/18, demobilised 31/12/18.
HERMANS, H., Pte. (5551), attested 26/8/18, demobilised 13/1/19.
PIETERS, K., Pte. (5552), attested 2/9/18, rejected 5/9/18.
PELSTON, J., Pte. (5553), attested 2/9/18, demobilised 27/12/18.
RICH, A., Pte. (5554), attested 2/9/18, demobilised 2/1/19.
WILDSCHUT, J., Pte. (5555), attested 30/8/18, rejected 2/9/18.
BEZUIDENHOUT, W., Pte. (5556), attested 30/8/18, demobilised 30/12/18.
GRAHAM, H., Pte. (5557), attested 30/8/18, demobilised 15/1/19.
MOORE, J., Pte. (5558), attested 30/8/18, demobilised 1/1/19.
SMITH, P., Pte. (5559), attested 30/8/18, demobilised 1/1/19.
BALLIE, P., Pte. (5560), attested 3/9/18, died of influenza 21/10/18.
GILBERT, P., Pte. (5561), attested 9/9/18, demobilised 2/1/19.
JACOBS, S., Pte. (5562), attested 6/9/18, demobilised 1/1/19.
FORTUIN, T., Pte. (5563), attested 11/9/18, demobilised 30/12/18.
WILLIAMS, B., Pte. (5564), attested 10/9/18, demobilised 3/1/19.
ARRIES, F., Pte. (5565), attested 12/9/18, demobilised 30/12/18.
BRAAM, A., Pte. (5566), attested 12/9/18, demobilised 1/1/19.
FORTUIN, C., Pte. (5567), attested 10/9/18, demobilised 2/1/19.
MALGAS, H., Pte. (5568), attested 12/9/18, released medically unfit 3/12/18.
NORMAN, H., Pte. (5569), attested 12/9/18, demobilised 2/1/19.
VERNEK, J., Pte. (5570), attested 12/9/18, demobilised 1/1/19
VAN SCHALKWYK, J., Pte. (5571), attested 10/9/18, demobilised 2/1/19
BAATJES, R., Pte. (5572), attested 12/9/18, demobilised 19/12/18.
CLOETE, J., Pte. (5573), attested 12/9/18, demobilised 1/1/19.
GALLANT, G., Pte. (5574), attested 12/9/18, demobilised 30/12/18.
MARTHINUS, P., Pte. (5575), attested 13/9/18, demobilised 29/12/18.
MARTHINUS, I., Pte. (5576), attested 13/9/18, demobilised 30/12/18.
SIAS, G., Pte. (5577), attested 13/9/18, demobilised 30/12/18.
TITUS, J., Pte. (5578), attested 12/9/18, demobilised 31/12/18.
VAN VUUREN, C. R., Pte. (5579), attested 9/9/18, demobilised 1/1/19
BOOYSEN, W., Pte. (5580), attested 14/9/18, demobilised 1/1/19.
BUTLER, P., Pte. (5581), attested 13/9/18, demobilised 1/1/19.
CHARLES, F., Pte. (5582), attested 13/9/18, demobilised 1/1/19.
FORTUIN, B., Pte. (5583), attested 14/9/18, demobilised 7/2/19.
LAWLER, N., Pte. (5584), attested 13/9/18, demobilised 1/1/19.
LESSING, J., Pte. (5585), attested 14/9/18, demobilised 1/1/19.
MAARMAN, D., Pte. (5586), attested 14/9/18, demobilised 5/11/18.
ALEXANDER, N., Pte. (5587), attested 10/9/18, rejected 14/9/18
BANTOM, D., Pte. (5588), attested 13/9/18, rejected 17/9/18.
BARNARD, J., Pte. (5589), attested 10/9/18, rejected 14/9/18.
BOOYSEN, H., Pte. (5590), attested 10/9/18, rejected 14/9/18.
DE LANGE, I., Pte. (5591), attested 10/9/18, rejected 14/9/18.
KARLESTER, J., Pte. (5592), attested 13/9/18, rejected 17/9/18.
LOFANI, K., Pte. (5593), attested 13/9/18, rejected 17/9/18.
LOUIS, D., Pte. (5594), attested 10/9/18, rejected 14/9/18.
MAKASTER, T., Pte. (5595), attested 13/9/18, rejected 17/9/18.
MINTOR, A., Pte. (5596), attested 10/9/18, rejected 14/9/18.
MINTOR, H., Pte. (5597), attested 13/9/18, rejected 17/9/18.
MARMAN, J., Pte. (5598), attested 13/9/18, rejected 17/9/18.
MINTOR, F., Pte. (5599), attested 13/9/18, demobilised 17/9/18.
TISANE, B., Pte. (5600), attested 13/9/18, rejected 17/9/18.
KANON, J., Pte. (5601), attested 10/9/18, rejected 14/9/18.
WILLIAMS, G., Pte. (5602), attested 13/9/18, rejected 17/9/18.
ALFOS, J. C., Pte. (5603), attested 17/9/18, demobilised 5/2/19.
BAKER, C., Pte. (5604), attested 10/9/18, demobilised 15/1/19.
BRENELL, W., Pte. (5605), attested 10/9/18, demobilised 26/12/18.
DIRKSE, J., Pte. (5606), attested 10/9/18, demobilised 29/12/18.
DAVIDS, T., Pte. (5607), attested 10/9/18, demobilised 30/12/18.
GILLION, W., Pte. (5608), attested 10/9/18, demobilised 27/12/18.
GILLION, J., Pte. (5609), attested 10/9/18, demobilised 27/12/18.
HESS, E., Pte. (5610), attested 10/9/18, demobilised 2/1/19.
HULL, F., Pte. (5611), attested 10/9/18, demobilised 29/12/18.
NEWMAN, J., Pte. (5612), attested 10/9/18, demobilised 30/12/18.
PETERSEN, A., Pte. (5613), attested 10/9/18, demobilised 31/12/18.
RUDOLPH, M., Pte. (5614), attested 10/9/18, died of influenza 11/10/18.
SPANDIEL, N., Pte. (5615), attested 10/9/18, demobilised 26/12/18.
SMITH, S., Pte. (5616), attested 10/9/18, died of influenza 12/10/18.
SOULS, J., Pte. (5617), attested 17/9/18, demobilised 29/12/18.
ZUEM, J., Pte. (5618), attested 17/9/18, demobilised 20/12/18.
BUSH, J., Pte. (5619), attested 18/9/18, demobilised 20/12/18.
CLOETE, J., Pte. (5620), attested 18/9/18, demobilised 30/12/18.
ERASMUS, C., Pte. (5621), attested 18/9/18, died of influenza 9/10/18.
FARO, C., Pte. (5622), attested 16/9/18, demobilised 30/12/18.
HOOPIE, J., Pte. (5623), attested 16/9/18, died of influenza 12/10/18.

JOSEPH, P., Pte. (5624), attested 18/9/18, demobilised 29/12/18.
JAPTHA, A., Pte. (5625), attested 16/9/18, demobilised 1/1/19.
LOUW, J., Pte. (5626), attested 17/9/18, demobilised 2/1/19.
LEGGENBERG, D., Pte. (5627), attested 16/9/18, demobilised 1/1/19.
MICHAELS, A. D., Pte. (5628), attested 16/9/18, demobilised 30/12/18.
OCTOBER, S., Pte. (5629), attested 18/9/18, demobilised 27/12/18.
ROBERTS, W., Pte. (5630), attested 16/9/18, demobilised 1/1/19.
SEPTEMBER, J., Pte. (5631), attested 20/9/18, demobilised 29/12/18.
SHELTON, F., Pte. (5632), attested 17/9/18, demobilised 2/1/19.
VALENTYNE, W., Pte. (5633), attested 18/9/18, demobilised 1/1/19.
ADAMS, S., Pte. (5634), attested 23/9/18, demobilised 19/12/18.
DAVIDS, A., Pte. (5635), attested 23/9/18, demobilised 2/1/19.
SCHOLTZ, C., Pte. (5636), attested 23/9/18, died of influenza 10/10/18.
SEIBERG, A., Pte. (5637), attested 23/9/18, demobilised 30/12/18.
WILLIAMS, D., Pte. (5638), attested 23/9/18, died of influenza 8/10/18.
BRUINTJES, M., Pte. (5639), attested 24/9/18, demobilised 1/1/19.
MONDZINGER, A., Pte. (5640), attested 23/9/18, died of influenza 14/10/18.
VAN DER MATVEL, A., Pte. (5641), attested 25/9/18, demobilised 1/1/19.
ANTHONIE, J., Pte. (5642), attested 14/9/18, released medically unfit 3/10/18.
KLASS, M., Pte. (5643), attested 9/9/18, released medically unfit 3/10/18.
SIMONS, J., Pte. (5644), attested 16/9/18, released medically unfit 2/10/18.
ADAMS, C., Pte. (5645), attested 26/9/18, demobilised 27/12/18.
CLARKE, J., Pte. (5646), attested 26/9/18, died of influenza 11/10/18.
JANUARY, A., Pte. (5647), attested 25/9/18, demobilised 27/12/18.
LAKAY, H., Pte. (5648), attested 25/9/18, demobilised 1/1/19.
AAS, J., Pte. (5649), attested 28/9/18, rejected 28/10/18, not Cape coloured.
GILLIE, G., Pte. (5650), attested 28/9/18, rejected 28/10/18, not Cape coloured.
GREY, J., Pte. (5651), attested 28/9/18, rejected 28/10/18, not Cape coloured.
ABELS, T., Pte. (5652), attested 30/9/18, demobilised 21/11/18.
ANDERSON, W., Pte. (5653), attested 1/10/18, demobilised 1/1/19.
BROWN, H., Pte. (5654), attested 24/9/18, demobilised 1/1/19.
GORDON, R. C., Pte. (5655), attested 1/10/18, demobilised 29/12/18.
BOHN, G., Pte. (5656), attested 23/9/18, died of influenza 10/10/18.
DE KLERK, J., Pte. (5657), attested 4/10/18, demobilised 1/1/19.
DAVIDS, D., Pte. (5658), attested 28/9/18, demobilised 30/12/18.
DE KOCK, T., Pte. (5659), attested 21/9/18, demobilised 1/1/19.
DANIELS, D., Pte. (5660), attested 4/10/18, demobilised 1/1/19.
FRITZ, C., Pte. (5661), attested 1/10/18, demobilised 1/1/19.
FISHER, A., Pte. (5662), attested 30/9/18, demobilised 27/12/18.
JACOBS, C., Pte. (5663), attested 4/10/18, demobilised 6/1/19.
KLASSEN, D., Pte. (5664), attested 28/9/18, demobilised 30/1/19.
LEFFIR, T., Pte. (5665), attested 24/9/18, demobilised 1/1/19.
MORAT, M., Pte. (5666), attested 4/10/18, transferred to C.A.H.T.C. 1/11/18.
MULLER, J., Pte. (5667), attested 24/9/18, died of influenza 10/10/18.
VAN BLERK, J., Pte. (5668), attested 13/10/18, demobilised 2/1/19.
WILLIAMS, T., Pte. (5669), attested 28/9/18, demobilised 31/12/18.
BECK, W., Pte. (5670), attested 28/9/18, died of influenza 4/11/18.
THORNE, J., Pte. (5671), attested 1/10/18, demobilised 30/12/18.
WILLIAMS, F., Pte. (5672), attested 1/10/18, demobilised 29/12/18.
ADAMS, J., Pte. (5673), attested 9/10/18, demobilised 5/1/19.
ALBERT, T., Pte. (5674), attested 9/10/18, demobilised 14/1/19.

In March, 1918, it was decided to disband the 2nd Battalion, Cape Corps on completion of their East African Service and to transfer all N.C.O.'s and men as they returned to the Depôt, to the 1st Battalion.

During the period April, 1918 to August, 1918, the undermentioned ex N.C.O.'s and men of the 2nd Battalion were accordingly taken on the strength of the 1st Battalion.

CORDON, H., Pte. (5695), demobilised 19/12/18.
BOWMAN, J., Pte. (5706), demobilisation pending.
JACOBS, P., Pte. (5777), demobilised 20/10/19.
OPPERMAN, R., Cpl. (6001), L./Cpl. 18/4/17, Cpl. 20/5/17, demobilised 3/1/19.
BINGHAM, R., Pte. (6002), demobilised 3/1/19.
KERSPUY, S., Pte. (6003), demobilised 1/1/19.
MILLER, J., Pte. (6004), died of influenza 9/10/18.
PEDRO, A., L./Cpl. (6005), L./Cpl. 5/1/18, demobilised 13/1/19.
DU PREEZ, C., Pte. (6006), demobilised 1/1/19.
JORDAN, B., Pte. (6007), demobilised 5/1/19.
SAMUELS, J., Pte. (6009), demobilised 25/12/18.
NELL, A., Pte. (6011), demobilised 24/1/19.
BAILEY, S., Pte. (6012), demobilised 30/12/18.
SAMUELS, D., Pte. (6015), died of influenza 12/10/18.
ABRAHAMS, J. H., Pte. (6016), demobilised 30/12/18.
DOMBAS, A., Pte. (6017), demobilised 13/2/19.
CAMPHOR, H., Pte. (6020), demobilised 1/1/19.
HENDRICKS, F., Pte. (6023), demobilised 3/1/19.
VAN ZYL, J., Pte. (6025), demobilised 31/12/18.
WILLIAMS, J., Pte. (6029), demobilised 25/12/18.
OCTOBER, H., Pte. (6030), demobilised 26/12/18.

THE STORY OF THE 1st CAPE CORPS.

PHILLIPS, J., Pte. (6031), demobilised 17/1/19.
KLASSEN, C., Pte. (6032), died of influenza 10/10/18.
CROATES, J., Pte. (6033), demobilised 14/1/19.
MAART, A., L./Cpl. (6034), L./Cpl. 18/9/17, died of influenza 11/10/18.
DE MUNK, M., Pte. (6036), died of influenza 14/10/18.
DU PLESSIS, G., Pte. (6037), demobilised 20/1/19.
SMITH, S., Sgt. (6039), L./Cpl. 18/4/17, reverted to Pte. 26/6/17, pioneer Cpl. 16/7/17, Sgt. 25/9/17, demobilised 3/1/19.
PLAATJES, P., Pte. (6041), demobilised 5/1/19.
DAY, P., Cpl. (6042), L./Cpl. 18/4/17, Cpl. 10/7/17, demobilised 5/1/19.
MALGAS, J., L./Cpl. (6043), L./Cpl. 18/4/17, demobilised 26/12/18.
POTGIETER, J., Pte. (6044), demobilised 13/1/19.
MARTIN, G., Pte. (6045), demobilised 27/12/18, bugler.
MENTOR, C., Pte. (6046), died 30/7/18.
RUITERS, S., Pte. (6047), demobilised 1/1/19.
MEYER, W., Cpl. (6048), Cpl. 1/6/17, demobilised 1/1/19.
BROWN, N., Pte. (6049), demobilised 3/1/19.
CARLSE, S., Cpl. (6051), Cpl. 1/7/17, acted Sgt., demobilised 13/1/19.
JULIES, F., Pte. (6052), demobilised 30/12/18.
ISAACS, B., L./Cpl. (6054), L./Cpl. 5/11/17, demobilised 1/1/19.
STEENKAMP, F., Pte. (6055), demobilised 31/12/18.
DUNSTAN, W., L./Cpl. (6056), L./Cpl. 18/4/17, demobilised 13/1/19.
LOMBARD, J., Pte. (6059), demobilised 6/1/19.
ANDERSON, J., Pte. (6060), demobilised 26/12/18.
MATCALF, P., L./Cpl. (6061), L./Cpl. 23/6/17, demobilised 24/1/19.
FITTS, P., Pte. (6062), demobilised 27/12/18.
VAN DER MERWE, P., Pte. (6063), demobilised 31/12/18.
WILLIAMS, G., L./Cpl. (6064), L./Cpl. 18/4/17, demobilised 15/1/19.
VAN WYK, J., Pte. (6065), demobilised 3/1/19.
KLASSEN, J., Pte. (6066), demobilised 14/1/19.
VAN DER ROSS, J., Cpl. (6070), L./Cpl. 18/4/17, Cpl. 20/5/17, died of influenza 18/10/18.
CORDON, M., Pte. (6074), demobilised 31/12/18.
ABRAHAMS, S. D., Pte. (6075), L./Cpl. 18/4/17, Cpl. 14/5/17, reverted to Pte. 17/10/17, demobilised 27/12/18.
ISAACS, T., Pte. (6078), demobilised 29/12/18.
MULLER, C., Pte. (6079), demobilised 31/12/18.
FORTUIN, A., Pte. (6081), demobilised 24/1/19.
LAWLER, A., Pte. (6083), demobilised 1/1/19.
JAFTHA, J., Pte. (6084), demobilised 13/1/19, acted L./Cpl.
DE VOS, J., Pte. (6088), died of influenza 21/10/18.
JAGGERS, P., Pte. (6090), demobilised 9/4/19.
WILLIAMS, S., Pte. (6091), L./Cpl. 18/4/17, Cpl. 14/5/17, demobilised 1/1/19.
LEE, M., Pte. (6093), died 29/5/17.
RAMSEY, H., Pte. (6094), demobilised 3/1/19.
WEST, H., Pte. (6096), demobilised 1/1/19.
JAGGERS, J., Pte. (6098), demobilised 26/12/18.
BARTMAN, H., Pte. (6100), demobilised 7/9/19.
TAMBLYN, R., Pte. (6101), demobilised 14/1/19.
DISSEL, H., Pte. (6102), demobilised 13/1/19.
PETERSEN, J., Pte. (6103), demobilised 7/10/19.
SAM, L., Pte. (6104), demobilised 24/1/19.
WILLIAMS, W., Cpl. (6107), Cpl. 1/6/17, demobilised 2/1/19.
DE VRIES, W., Pte. (6109), demobilised 6/1/19.
TAMBLYN, R., Pte. (6111), demobilised 26/1/19.
DAVIDS, I., L./Cpl. (6113), L./Cpl. 5/1/18, demobilised 1/1/19.
DAMONS, H., Pte. (6114), demobilised 15/1/19.
PETERSEN, E., Pte. (6115), demobilised 15/1/19.
STUURMAN, A., Pte. (6117), demobilised 24/1/19.
ISAACS, J., Pte. (6120), released medically unfit 30/9/18.
SCHUBART, A., Pte. (6121), released medically unfit 24/1/19.
WILLIAMS, J., Pte. (6124), demobilised 29/12/18.
SAMUELS, J., Pte. (6129), demobilised 31/12/18.
HENDRICKS, A., Pte. (6130), demobilised 26/12/18.
ABRAHAMS, J., L./Sgt. (6133), L./Cpl. 18/4/17, Cpl. 14/5/17, L./Sgt. 1/8/17, demobilised 17/1/19.
BAAS, M., Pte. (6135), died of influenza 8/10/18.
DISSEL, J., Pte. (6136), demobilised 7/9/19.
ABSOLOM, J., Pte. (6137), demobilised 31/12/18.
RHOODE, M., Pte. (6138), demobilised 27/12/18.
LENFORD, W., Pte. (6139), demobilised 31/12/18.
ANDERSON, H. A., Pte. (6140), demobilised 29/12/18.
FESTER, W., Pte. (6141), demobilised 30/12/18.
LATEGAN, L., Pte. (6143), demobilised 5/2/19.
WHITBOOI, H., Pte. (6146), demobilised 26/12/18.
HEATON, F., Pte. (6148), demobilised 24/1/19.
LANGHOVEN, G., Pte. (6150), demobilised 30/12/18.
RUBIES, P., Pte. (6151), demobilised 24/1/19.
PETERSEN, J., Pte. (6152), demobilised 24/1/19.
STADLER, J., Pte. (6153), demobilised 26/1/19.
PETERSEN, F., Pte. (6154), died of influenza 11/10/18.
MAPELA, M., Pte. (6157), demobilised 1/1/19.
JACOBS, A., Pte. (6158), demobilised 27/12/18.
ADONIS, W., Pte. (6159), demobilised 30/12/18.
HENDRICKS, H., Pte. (6160), demobilised 31/12/18.
SCHUT, A., Pte. (6161), demobilised 27/12/18.
STORKEY, G. A., Cpl. (6162), L./Cpl. 18/4/17, Cpl. 20/5/17, acted Sgt., demobilised 13/1/19.
JACOBS, D., Pte. (6163), demobilised 16/1/19.
BURGERS, A., Pte. (6166), died of influenza 16/10/18.
MAJIKEBA, B., Pte. (6168), demobilised 1/1/19.
CHRISTIANS, M., Pte. (6170), demobilised 31/12/18.
EACHILL, J., Pte. (6171), died of influenza 7/10/18.

BUTTERSON, J. F., Pte. (6172), demobilised 26/12/18.
REID, J., Pte. (6174), demobilised 27/12/18.
CAROLUS, T., Pte. (6175), demobilised 31/12/18.
MARITZ, C., Pte. (6176), demobilised 29/12/18.
BOSCH, M., Pte. (6177), died of influenza 10/10/18.
VAN ROOY, W., Pte. (6178), demobilised 13/1/19.
WILLIAMS, P., Pte. (6181), demobilised 5/1/19.
MICHAEL, P., Pte. (6183), demobilised 13/1/19.
GOLIATH, P., Pte. (6184), died of influenza 11/10/18.
GUIDA, A., Pte. (6188), demobilised 2/1/19.
BASE, F., Pte. (6192), demobilised 2/1/19, acted Cpl.
ELDERS, C., Pte. (6193), demobilised 1/1/19.
ALBRECHT, F., Pte. (6194), demobilised 13/1/19.
HENDRICKS, A., Pte. (6195), demobilised 1/1/19.
ADAMS, A., Pte. (6196), demobilised 3/1/19.
WOODING, A., Pte. (6197), demobilised 13/1/19.
CARELSE, J., Pte. (6198), demobilised 31/12/18.
VERA, N., Pte. (6200), demobilised 27/12/18.
DIEDERICKS, C., Pte. (6202), demobilised 24/1/19.
JORDAAN, S., Pte. (6204), died of influenza 6/10/18.
JONKERS, D., Pte. (6205), demobilised 26/12/18.
ABRAHAMS, J., Pte. (6207), demobilised 1/1/19.
MATHER, G., Pte. (6208), demobilised 13/2/19.
CLARK, H., Cpl. (6209), L./Cpl. 11/7/17, Cpl. 5/11/17, demobilised 1/1/19.
MEYER, J. C., Pte. (6210), demobilised 3/1/19, acted L./Cpl.
VAN DER ROSS, J., Pte. (6211), demobilised 1/1/19.
GOLIATH, S. S., L./Cpl. (6212), L./Cpl. 18/4/17, demobilised 2/1/19.
BLOWS, I., Pte. (6213), demobilised 13/1/19.
DAVIS, T., Pte. (6215), demobilised 13/1/19.
BAARTMAN, J., Pte. (6216), demobilised 2/1/19.
VAN DER ROSS, A., Pte. (6218), demobilised 27/12/18.
MEYER, J., Pte. (6219), demobilised 1/1/19.
WILLIAMS, H., Pte. (6220), demobilised 5/1/19.
DAVIDS, H., Pte. (6223), demobilised 7/10/19.
PLAATJES, K., Pte. (6224), demobilised 26/1/19.
DAVIDS, A., Pte. (6226), demobilised 31/12/18.
DU PREEZ, K., Pte. (6227), demobilised 26/12/18.
DE BEER, M., Pte. (6229), demobilised 31/12/18.
BOWMAN, A., Pte. (6230), demobilised 24/1/19.
WILSON, R., Pte. (6231), demobilised 26/12/18.
CLOETE, J., Pte. (6233), demobilised 13/1/19.
PRINCE, N., L./Cpl. (6234), L./Cpl. 8/9/17, demobilised 1/1/19.
KAPP, E., Pte. (6235), demobilised 13/1/19.
BAGLEY, C., L./Sgt. (6236), Cpl. 20/5/17, L./Sgt. 1/8/17, demobilised 1/1/19
STROEBEL, J., Pte. (6240), demobilised 24/1/19.
ROSS, W., Pte. (6241), demobilised 31/12/18.
FERNDAL, M., Pte. (6242), demobilised 1/1/19.
OPPEL, S., L./Sgt. (6243), L./Cpl. 18/4/17, Cpl. 14/5/17, L./Sgt. 1/8/17, demobilised 13/1/19
DE JONG, J., Pte. (6244), demobilised 13/1/19.
VELDSMAN, F. W., Pte. (6246), demobilised 1/1/19.
MARTIN, J., Pte. (6247), demobilised 19/2/19.
SMITH, T., Pte. (6249), demobilised 17/1/19.
PETERS, J., Pte. (6251), demobilised 5/1/19.
DU PLOOY, J., Pte. (6254), demobilised 24/1/19.
KLEINSMITH, F., Pte. (6255), demobilised 26/12/18.
BARRY, E. R., Pte. (6256), demobilised 19/12/18.
BARRON, J., Pte. (6257), demobilised 30/12/18
LOUW, A., Pte. (6259), demobilised 1/1/19.
SCHRIKKER, G., Pte. (6260), died 10/10/18.
LEVENDAL, W., Pte. (6261), demobilised 21/7/19.
DE WAAL, J., L./Cpl. (6262), L./Cpl. 26/4/18, demobilised 13/1/19.
JENKINS, M., Pte. (6264), demobilised 13/1/19, bugler.
VAN LOUW, P., Pte. (6266), demobilised 30/12/18.
VAN DRIEL, J., Pte. (6267), demobilised 26/1/19.
NEWMAN, J., Pte. (6268), ?
PETERSEN, R., Pte. (6269), demobilised 26/12/18.
FICK, J., Pte. (6270), demobilised 31/12/18.
KROKAM, E., Pte. (6271), demobilised 31/12/18.
LE ROUX, J., Pte. (6272), demobilised 13/1/19.
WILLIAMS, S., Pte. (6274), demobilised 26/12/18.
ZUURVOGEL, C., Pte. (6275), demobilised 31/12/18.
CLASSEN, D., Pte. (6276), demobilised 31/12/18.
ABRAHAMS, J., Pte. (6278), demobilised 13/1/19.
PETERSEN, M., Pte. (6281), demobilised 17/1/19.
GERTZE, J., Pte. (6282), demobilised 26/12/18.
JACOBS, J., Pte. (6283), demobilised 2/1/19.
MITCHELL, E., Pte. (6286), demobilised 15/1/19.
OLKERS, H., Pte. (6289), demobilised 29/12/18.
FORTUIN, M., Pte. (6290), demobilised 26/12/18.
GARLAND, H., Pte. (6292), demobilised 3/1/19.
WITBOOI, A., Pte. (6293), demobilised 27/12/18.
ROSSOUW, F., Pte. (6294), demobilised 24/12/18.
THOMAS, A., Pte. (6295), demobilised 27/12/18.
MITCHELL, A., Pte. (6298), demobilised 24/1/19.
WILLIAMSON, W., Pte. (6302), demobilised 31/12/18.
DAMES, G., L./Cpl. (6304), L./Cpl. 5/1/18, demobilised 13/1/19.
PAULSE, D., Pte. (6306), demobilised 26/12/18.
JOHNSON, C., Pte. (6312), demobilised 13/1/19.
JACOBS, F. J., Pte. (6314), demobilised 13/1/19.
LEWIS, J., Pte. (6315), demobilised 13/1/19.

THE STORY OF THE 1st CAPE CORPS.

CASPER, J., Pte. (6316), demobilised 6/1/19.
WILLIAMS, J., Pte. (6317), demobilised 13/1/19.
BRUINERS, J., Pte. (6318), demobilised 3/1/19.
ADAMS, J., Pte. (6319), demobilised 15/1/19.
FEBRUARY, S., Pte. (6320), demobilised 24/1/19.
PETRUS, F., Pte. (6324), demobilised 2/1/19.
HERCLASS, J., Pte. (6325), demobilised 29/12/18.
BLOEMESTIEN, W., Pte. (6326), demobilised 1/1/19.
OOSTENDORP, J., Pte. (6329), demobilised 26/12/18.
PETERSEN, S., Pte. (6331), demobilised 3/1/19.
RUITERS, C., Pte. (6332), demobilised 24/1/19.
WHITBOOI, S., Pte. (6333), demobilised 27/12/18.
LAKEY, C., Pte. (6335), demobilised 13/1/19.
PETRUS, H., Cpl. (6336), Cpl. 1/7/17, demobilised 24/1/19.
LEBRON, M., Pte. (6337), demobilised 24/1/19.
JACOBS, G., Pte. (6339), demobilised 1/1/19.
McBRYANT, C., Pte. (6340), demobilised 5/1/19.
ADAMS, J., Pte. (6342), demobilised 13/1/19.
STEER, W., Pte. (6343), died of influenza 16/10/18.
TOBIN, P., Pte. (6344), demobilised 24/1/19.
CEASER, O., Pte. (6346), demobilised 24/1/19.
STRIKKER, J., Pte. (6347), demobilised 31/12/18.
STOFFBERG, R., Pte. (6349), demobilised 27/12/18.
VAN DER POEL, A., Pte. (6354), demobilised 13/1/19.
ESAU, H., Pte. (6355), demobilised 13/1/19.
VAN REENEN, A., Pte. (6357), died of malaria 5/8/18.
RUBEN, P., Pte. (6358), demobilised 23/1/19.
SWARTZ, A., Pte. (6361), demobilised 13/1/19.
DAVIS, J., L./Cpl. (6363), L./Cpl. 5/1/18, demobilised 24/1/19.
ROSSOUW, J., Pte. (6365), demobilised 2/1/19.
JACOBS, G., Pte. (6367), demobilised 27/12/18.
VAN DER BERG, I. H., Pte. (6369), demobilised 13/1/19.
LAWRENCE, A., Pte. (6371), demobilised 6/1/19.
TERRY, J., Pte. (6372), demobilised 5/1/19.
DIEDERICKS, A., Pte. (6373), demobilised 26/12/18.
ADAMS, F., Pte. (6375), died of influenza 12/10/18.
MARAIS, F., Pte. (6376), demobilised 24/1/19.
ADAMS, S., Pte. (6378), died of influenza 11/10/18.
MATTHEWS, W., Pte. (6381), demobilised 15/1/19.
DE VOS, L., Pte. (6382), demobilised 13/1/19.
VAN NELSON, J., Pte. (6384), demobilised 11/7/19
MIKKELSON, F., Pte. (6385), died of influenza 7/10/18.
IRWIN, J. D., L./Sgt. (6388), L./Cpl. 18/4/17, Cpl. 14/5/17, L./Sgt. 1/8/17, demobilised 27/11/18
RENSBERG, D., Pte. (6389), demobilised 13/1/19.
CUMMINGS, C., L./Cpl. (6390), L./Cpl. 23/6/17, demobilised 27/12/18.
HUGO, M., Pte. (6391), demobilised 24/1/19.
FERRY, W., Pte. (6394), demobilised 24/1/19.
ABRAHAMS, J., Cpl. (6395), L./Cpl. 10/7/17, Cpl 4/10/17, demobilised 11/7/19, acted C.Q.M.S. at R.H. Bn. depôt in Egypt.
LEWIS, L., Pte. (6397), demobilised 30/12/18.
BLOEM, D., Pte. (6398), demobilised 5/2/19.
ARMOED, A., Pte. (6399), demobilised 1/1/19.
APRIKANDER, K., Pte. (6401), died of influenza 9/10/18.
FORTUIN, A., Pte. (6402), demobilised 26/12/18.
ADAMS, A., Pte. (6403), demobilised 1/1/19.
VAN WYK, S., Pte. (6406), demobilised 26/12/18.
PRESSLIN, A., Pte. (6407), demobilised 1/1/19.
HAUPT, H., Pte. (6411), demobilised 31/12/18.
SIMONS, H., Pte. (6413), demobilised 30/12/18.
BAATJES, P., Pte. (6414), demobilised 7/9/19.
FRANKA, F., Pte (6416), died of influenza 13/10/18.
HILDERBRAND, N., L./Cpl. (6417), L./Cpl. 11/9/17, demobilised 13/12/18.
LAESON, C., Pte. (6419), demobilised 2/1/19.
STEVENS, W., Pte. (6421), demobilised 31/12/18.
MATTHYSE, J., Pte. (6422), demobilised 31/12/18.
PETERSEN, J., Sgt. (6423), L./Cpl. 18/4/17, Cpl. 20/5/17, Sgt. Shoemaker 12/7/17, died of influenza 13/10/18.
RANDALL, F., Pte. (6424), demobilised 24/1/19.
ABRAHAMS, H., Pte. (6425), demobilised 6/1/19.
FREDERICKS, C., Pte. (6427), demobilised 15/1/19.
MEYER, S., Pte. (6428), demobilised 29/12/18.
PAULSE, L., Pte. (6430), demobilised 27/12/18.
DANIELS, F., Cpl. (6431), Cpl. 1/7/17, demobilised 31/12/18.
NOLAND, J., Pte. (6433), demobilised 30/12/18.
IFFLEY, L., Pte. (6436), demobilised 1/1/19.
DAVIDS, J., Pte. (6437), demobilised 2/1/19.
EBENEZER, E., Pte. (6440), demobilised 2/1/19.
CUPIDO, C., Pte. (6441), demobilised 30/12/18
CURNOW, J., L./Cpl. (6442), L./Cpl. 23/6/17, demobilised 13/1/19.
MORKEL, J., Pte. (6445), demobilised 30/12/18.
BREDENKAMP, C., Pte. (6446), demobilised 17/1/19.
WESSELS, D., Pte. (6450), demobilised 13/1/19.
DAVIDS, J. F., Pte. (6452), demobilised 27/12/18, acted Sgt.
WALDECK, H., Pte. (6453), demobilised 2/1/19.
BURGERS, I., Pte. (6454), demobilised 26/12/18.
ABRAHAMS, P., L./Cpl. (6455), L./Cpl. 31/7/17, demobilised 3/2/19.
BROWN, J. C., Pte. (6456), demobilised 24/1/19, acted Cpl. bugler.
BREDEKAMP, F., Pte. (6457), demobilised 2/1/19.
NOKWE, H., Pte. (6458), demobilised 1/1/19.
APPIE, J., Pte. (6459), died of influenza 22/10/18.

STANLEY, R., Pte. (6460), demobilised 3/2/19.
LYONS, J., Pte. (6461), demobilised 24/1/19.
MATTHEWS, W., Pte. (6462), demobilised 13/1/19.
RODDESQUE, S., Pte. (6463), demobilised 29/12/18.
EDWARDS, J., Pte. (6464), died of influenza 10/10/18.
MAY, S., L./Cpl. (6465), L./Cpl. 11/9/17, demobilised 14/1/19.
SAMUELS, S., Pte. (6466), demobilised 29/12/18.
DREYER, L., Pte. (6467), demobilised 31/12/18.
CARELSE, A., Pte. (6468), demobilised 30/12/18.
PETRIE, J., Pte. (6469), demobilised 27/12/18.
SYLVESTER, J., Pte. (6471), demobilised 15/1/19.
KUBIE, D. B., Pte. (6472), demobilised 5/2/19.
FAROIE, J., Pte. (6474), demobilised 20/12/18.
WINDVOGEL, J., Pte. (6475), demobilised 31/12/18.
BINGLE, J., Pte. (6476), demobilised 24/1/19.
HENDRICKS, J., Pte. (6478), demobilised 3/1/19.
SWARTZ, J., Pte. (6479), demobilised 27/12/18.
FICK, W., Cpl. (6482), Cpl. 1/7/17, demobilised 5/2/19.
CORNELIUS, T., Pte. (6483), demobilised 26/12/18.
FILANDER, H., Pte. (6484), demobilised 30/12/18.
DAVIDS, J., Pte. (6485), demobilised 31/12/18.
DU PLESSIS, N., Pte. (6486), died of pneumonia 6/10/18.
WYNGAARD, A., Cpl. (6487), Cpl. 6/9/17, demobilised 30/12/18.
STACKLING, J., Pte. (6488), demobilised 2/1/19.
TITUS, G., L./Cpl. (6491), L./Cpl. 1/6/17, demobilised 31/12/18.
SOLOMON, D., Cpl. (6495), Cpl. 11/7/17, demobilised 1/1/19.
VAN BUELEN, S., Pte. (6498), demobilised 29/12/18.
AUGUST, J., Pte. (6501), demobilised 27/12/18.
MARTIN, J., Pte. (6502), demobilised 2/1/19.
SHELDON, A., Pte. (6504), demobilised 13/1/19.
LAGORIS, C., Pte. (6505), demobilised 29/12/18.
TALEB, A., Pte. (6506), died of influenza 8/10/18.
JONES, W., Pte. (6507), demobilised 2/1/19.
JONATHAN, J., Cpl. (6508), Cpl. 5/11/17, demobilised 27/12/18.
ANTONIE, D., Pte. (6511), demobilised 31/12/18.
ELLIOTT, D., Pte. (6512), demobilised 1/2/19.
FRAY, E., Pte. (6513), demobilised 5/1/19.
JANUARY, J., Pte. (6515), demobilised 27/12/18.
GESWIND, J., Pte. (6517), demobilised 27/12/18.
OOSTENDORP, D., Pte. (6518), demobilised 17/1/19.
JANTJES, A., Pte. (6520), demobilised 24/1/19.
MYBURGH, P. A., Pte. (6522), demobilised 30/12/18.
THOMPSON, J., Pte. (6524), demobilised 29/12/18.
PLAATJES, A., Pte. (6526), died of influenza 9/10/18.
LEONARDS, L., Pte. (6527), demobilised 31/12/18.
HICKLEY, F., Pte. (6528), demobilised 14/1/19.
PETERSEN, A., Pte. (6529), died of influenza 14/10/18.
FAIRLEY, P., Pte. (6530), demobilised 26/12/18.
VAN HALL, G., Pte. (6531), demobilised 17/1/19.
STOFFBERG, L., Pte. (6532), demobilised 29/12/18.
VALENTINE, A., L./Cpl. (6533), L./Cpl. 8/12/17, died of influenza 10/10/18.
PETERSEN, A., Pte. (6535), demobilised 24/1/19.
BARENDS, A., Pte. (6537), died of influenza 23/10/18.
JACOBS, B., Pte. (6539), died of influenza 16/10/18.
PLAATJES, A., Pte. (6539), died 1/11/18.
DU TOIT, P. D., Pte. (6540), demobilised 13/1/19.
MARNWICH, J., Pte. (6544), demobilised 6/1/19.
AFRICA, J., Pte. (6545), demobilised 19/12/18.
BOWLES, J., Pte. (6546), demobilised 5/1/19.
SKATE, R., Pte. (6547), demobilised 1/1/19.
PRINSLOO, J. O., Pte. (6548), demobilised 26/12/19.
SMITH, J., Pte. (6549), demobilised 1/1/19.
BAATJES, G., Cpl. (6550), L./Cpl. 23/10/17, Cpl. 14/12/17, died of influenza 10/10/18.
PETERSEN, J., Pte. (6551), demobilised 13/1/19.
MANIS, J. Pte. (6552), demobilised 5/1/19.
OCTOBER, D., Pte. (6555), demobilised 30/12/18.
STEYN, S., Pte. (6556), demobilised 29/12/18.
ADAMS, J., Pte. (6557), demobilised 26/12/18.
ERASMUS, J., Pte. (6559), demobilised 27/12/18.
THOMAS, J., Pte. (6561), demobilised 13/1/19.
GORDON, R., Pte. (6563), demobilised 24/1/19.
PETERSEN, D., Pte (6568), demobilised 27/12/18.
CASTOOR, D., Pte. (6569), demobilised 20/1/19.
SMIT, H., Pte. (6570), demobilised 24/1/19.
MARMON, M., Pte. (6571), demobilised 13/1/19.
ABRAHAMS, J., Pte. (6574), demobilised 31/12/18.
JANUARY, P., Pte. (6576), demobilised 31/12/18.
MASSERLEY, M., Pte. (6577), demobilised 1/1/19.
OBEY, E., Pte. (6579), demobilised 30/12/18.
ARENDSE, H., Pte. (6580), demobilised 27/12/18.
JOHNSON, J., Pte. (6581), died of influenza 10/10/18.
VAN DER BERG, A., Pte. (6582), demobilised 31/12/18.
ROSSOUW, P., Pte. (6583), demobilised 24/1/19.
ADONIS, H., Pte. (6586), demobilised 13/1/19.
CHANDLER, W. J., Cpl. (6587), Cpl. 20/5/17, demobilised 31/12/18.
BOOM, W., Pte. (6589), demobilised 31/12/18.
PETERSEN, I., Pte. (6590), demobilised 9/12/18.
CAROLUS, J., Pte. (6591), demobilised 30/12/18.
HAUPT, W. A., Pte. (6593), demobilised 24/1/19.
ORGILL, C., Sgt.(6594), Sgt. 9/10/17, demobilised 2/1/19.
ERISPE, C., Cpl. (6595), Cpl. 1/6/17, demobilised 13/2/19.

FERNANDEZ, M., Cpl. (6596), Cpl. 1/6/17, demobilised 13/1/19.
STEEDY, H., Pte. (6597), demobilised 26/12/18.
MAART, C., Pte. (6599), demobilised 26/12/18.
FORTUIN, G., Pte. (6600), demobilised 27/12/18.
VISAGIE, J., Pte. (6601), demobilised 29/12/18.
FRANKE, D., Pte. (6603), demobilised 27/12/18.
DAVIS, E., Pte. (6604), demobilised 13/1/19.
SMITH, A., Pte. (6606), demobilised 13/1/19.
MIKE, N., Pte. (6609), S.N.L.R. 26/10/18.
WILLIAMS, S., Pte. (6610), demobilised 1/1/19.
JACOBS, A., Pte. (6611), demobilised 30/12/18.
ALBERTS, A., Pte. (6612), demobilised 31/12/18.
MANUEL, J. Pte. (6617), died of influenza 14/10/18.
VISAGIE, H., Pte. (6618), demobilised 27/12/18.
PIENAAR, L., Pte. (6619), demobilised 26/12/18.
VIVIERS, J., Pte. (6620), demobilised 27/12/18.
JONATHAN, I., Pte. (6625), demobilised 13/1/19.
STUBBS, H. Pte. (6626), demobilised 13/1/19.
MOLIVELDT, P., Pte. (6629), released medically unfit 18/12/18.
JACOBS, C., Pte. (6633), demobilised 6/1/19.
VAN DER BERG, P., Pte. (6635), demobilised 31/12/18.
SMITH, W., Pte. (6637), demobilised 7/9/19.
STEVENS, J., Pte. (6638), demobilised 26/12/18.
LUNDALL, A., Pte. (6639), demobilised 24/1/19.
PRETORIUS, N., L./Cpl. (6640), L./Cpl. 14/2/17, demobilised 26/12/18.
APRIL, H., Cpl. (6642), Cpl. 20/5/17, demobilised 14/1/19.
MATTHYS, A. Pte. (6644), demobilised 31/12/18.
PETERSEN, T., Pte. (6645), demobilised 24/1/19.
WILLIAMS, D., Pte. (6646), demobilised 24/1/19.
GEORGE, A., Pte. (6647), demobilised 14/1/19.
DAVIDS, J., Pte. (6648), demobilised 27/12/18.
PRINGLE, A., Pte. (6650), demobilised 3/1/19.
BAARTIE, J., L./Cpl. (6651), L./Cpl. 16/9/17, demobilised 3/1/19.
KOERT, E., Pte. (6653), demobilised 5/1/19.
ADONIS, T., Pte. (6654), demobilised 13/1/19.
PHILANDER, E., Pte. (6655), demobilised 13/1/19.
DAVIDS, J., Pte. (6656), demobilised 27/12/18.
JAFTHA, H., Pte. (6657), died of influenza 17/10/18.
CLOETE, A., Pte. (6658), died of influenza 10/10/18.
PHILANDER, S., Pte. (6659), demobilised 29/12/18.
ABELS, E., Pte. (6660), demobilised 14/1/19.
PITTS, P., Pte. (6662), demobilised 19/12/18.
AFRICA, J., Pte. (6664), died of influenza 10/10/18.
APPOLIS, P., Pte. (6665), demobilised 14/1/19.
MENTOOR, J. Pte. (6666), demobilised 30/12/18.
APLOON, J., Pte. (6667), demobilised 30/12/18.
APPLE, J., Pte. (6668), died of influenza 18/10/18.
NEWMAN, M., Pte. (6670), demobilised 30/12/18.
PETERS, S., L./Cpl. (6671), L./Cpl. 6/1/18, demobilised 2/1/19.
SWARTZ, J., Pte. (6672), demobilised 31/12/18.
PETERS, W., Pte. (6673), demobilised 2/1/19.
ABRAHAMS, J., Pte. (6675), demobilised 6/1/19.
JOHNSON, H., Pte. (6676), demobilised 24/1/19.
STEMMERS, E., Pte. (6677), demobilised 29/12/18.
HYDE, J., Pte. (6678), demobilised 1/2/19.
AFRICA, B., L./Cpl. (6679), L./Cpl. 25/3/18, demobilised 27/12/18.
NEWMAN, D., Pte. (6681), demobilised 26/12/18.
ZAHL, D., Pte. (6683), demobilised 1/1/19.
HANMER, W., Pte. (6684), demobilised 1/1/19.
SHELDON, C., Pte. (6685), demobilised 1/1/19.
ANTHONEY, G., Pte. (6686), demobilised 1/1/19.
VAN WYK, C., Pte. (6688), demobilised 1/1/19.
TROY, W., Pte. (6689), demobilised 1/2/19.
SWARTBOOI, L., Cpl. (6693), Cpl. 8/1/18, demobilised 13/1/19.
CURNOW, J., Pte. (6694), demobilised 7/9/19.
BURKES, A., Pte. (6697), demobilised 3/2/19.
COON, J., Pte. (6699), died of influenza 9/10/18.
ESTERHUIZEN, J., Pte (6700), died of influenza 10/10/18.
BAGLEY, F., Pte. (6701), demobilised 13/1/19.
CLOETE, W., Pte. (6703), demobilised 14/1/19.
JARMAN, G., Pte. (6704), demobilised 5/1/19.
VAN WYK, J., Pte. (6705), demobilised 1/1/19.
CANNON, J., L./Cpl. (6708), L./Cpl. 6/1/18, demobilised 1/2/19.
VAN DER MERWE, D., Pte. (6710), demobilised 6/1/19.
KESTER, C. W., L./Cpl. (6711), L./Cpl. 13/7/17, demobilised 2/1/19.
LUMIS, G. Pte. (6712), demobilised 14/1/19.
ISAACS, C., Pte. (6714), demobilised 13/1/19.
JAFTHA, D., Pte. (6715), demobilised 31/12/18.
WILLIAMS, D., Pte. (6716), demobilised 5/1/19.
ARENDSE, M., Pte. (6717), demobilised 27/12/18.
ABELS, H., Pte. (6718), demobilised 30/12/18.
JAMES, F., Pte. (6719), demobilised 24/1/19.
PETERSEN, M., Pte. (6721), demobilised 31/12/18.
DAVIS, W., Pte. (6722), demobilised 13/1/19.
WILLIAMS, J., Pte. (6725), demobilised 29/12/18.
GEORGE, P., Pte. (6726), demobilised 27/12/18.
MEYER, C., Pte. (6728), demobilised 13/1/19.
JACOBS, A., Pte. (6729), demobilised 26/12/18.
ISAACS, F., Pte. (6730), demobilised 31/12/18.
WILLIAMS, J., Pte. (6731), died of influenza 14/10/18.

CORUM, J., Pte. (6732), demobilised 31/12/18.
HEUVEL, H., Pte. (6733), demobilised 2/1/19.
RABBIE, S., Pte. (6734), demobilised 26/12/18.
MULLER, T., Pte. (6735), demobilised 30/12/18.
FESTER, I., Pte. (6736), demobilised 2/1/19.
MAY, P., Pte. (6737), demobilised 31/12/18.
WATERLOO, N., Pte. (6738), demobilised 2/1/19
ALIES, G., Pte. (6742), demobilised 3/1/19.
DE VILLIERS, D., Pte. (6743), demobilised 27/12/18.
CONSUL, H., Pte. (6744), demobilised 13/1/19.
FESTERS, A., Pte. (6747), died of influenza 9/10/18.
FELIX, S., Pte. (6748), demobilised 24/1/19.
VAN REENEN, C., Pte. (6749), demobilised 13/1/19.
HENDERSON, B., Pte. (6750), died of influenza 12/10/18.
RICHARDS, J., Pte. (6751), demobilised 3/1/19.
JARDIEN, H., Pte. (6752), died of influenza 10/10/18.
SANDELEY, S., Pte. (6753), demobilised 11/7/19.
FRITZ, J., Pte. (6754), demobilised 27/12/18.
JONKERS, J., Pte. (6755), demobilised 27/12/18.
DU PREEZ, J., Pte. (6757), demobilised 5/1/19.
NURSE, J., Pte. (6759), died of influenza 6/10/18.
JONES, E., Pte. (6760), demobilised 31/12/18.
ANDREWS, J., Pte. (6762), died of influenza 21/10/18.
DOWLING, J., Pte. (6765), demobilised 3/1/19.
PRIESTLEY, W. H., Pte. (6766), demobilised 31/12/18.
KOOPMAN, F., Pte. (6768), died of influenza 7/10/18.
TITUS, T., Pte. (6770), demobilised 1/1/19.
ALEXANDER, J., Pte. (6772), demobilised 27/12/18.
HARDINE, D., Pte. (6776), demobilised 14/1/19.
ADONIS, C., Pte. (6778), demobilised 27/12/18.
BUFFEL, J., Pte. (6779), demobilised 24/1/19.
FIKKIES, J., Pte. (6781), demobilised 31/12/18.
DANIELS, W., Pte. (6782), demobilised 24/1/19.
WINDVOGEL, F., Pte. (6783), died of influenza 12/10/18.
CAROLUS, C., Pte. (6785), demobiised 30/12/18.
DANIELS, H., Pte. (6786), demobilised 15/1/19.
BESTEMBER, P., Pte. (6787), demobilised 17/1/19
FIKKIES, A., Pte. (6788), demobilised 26/12/18.
VISAGIE, S., Pte. (6790), demobilised 1/1/19.
DE WET, J., Pte. (6792), demobilised 31/12/18.
PRETORIUS, D., Pte. (6795), demobilised 1/1/19.
CORNELIS, J., Pte. (6798), demobilised 26/12/18.
CAMPHER, J., Pte. (6800), demobilised 31/12/18.
CAMPHER, G., Pte. (6802), demobilised 16/1/19.
JACOBS, M., Pte. (6803), demobilised 7/10/19.
LAMB, E., Pte. (6805), demobilised 24/1/19.
AUGUST, C., Pte. (6806), demobilised 26/12/18.
FELA, A., L./Cpl. (6808), L./Cpl. 23/10/17, demobilised 3/1/19.
DAVIDS, A., Pte. (6809), demobilised 14/1/19.
JULIES, L., Pte. (6810), demobilised 14/1/19.
JONES, H., Pte. (6812), demobilised 29/1/19.
WILLIAMS, H., Pte. (5813), demobilised 31/12/18.
OCTOBER, M., Cpl. (6814), L./Cpl. 31/7/17, Cpl. 20/2/18, demobilised 19/12/18.
SOLOMON, S., Pte. (6815), demobilised 27/12/18.
HENDRICKS, J., Pte. (6816), demobilised 7/9/19.
HESS, P., Pte. (6817), demobilised 24/1/19.
AREND, J., Pte. (6818), demobilised 27/12/19.
BREDEKAMP, B., Pte. (6821), demobilised 26/12/18.
JACOBS, W., Pte. (6822), demobilised 2/1/19.
ABDOL, M., Pte. (6824), demobilised 19/12/18.
BLOOMSTIEN, B., Pte. (6825), demobilised 13/1/19.
DE JONG, L., Pte. (6826), demobilised 5/1/19.
RAYNARD, E., Pte. (6827), demobilised 26/11/18.
VISAGIE, J., Pte. (6830), demobilised 1/1/19.
JULIES, J., Pte. (6832), demobilised 2/1/19.
GOLIATH, G., Pte. (6833), demobilised 24/1/19.
LINKS, H., Pte. (6835), demobilised 29/12/18.
DU PREEZ, P., Pte. (6838), demobilised 1/1/19.
VAN WYK, A., Pte. (6839), demobilised 27/12/18.
ABRAHAMS, D., Pte. (6840), demobilised 27/12/18.
RUDOLPH, C. S., L./Cpl. (6842), L./Cpl. 31/7/17, demobilised 2/1/19.
LE ROUX, P., Pte. (6843), demobilised 16/7/19.
MOULTRY, J., Cpl. (6844), L./Cpl. 19/5/17, Cpl. 1/6/17, demobilised 1/1/19.
MACDONALD, J., Pte. (6845), demobilised 26/12/18.
HENDRICKS, J., L./Cpl. (6849), L./Cpl. 11/9/17, demobilised 30/12/18.
GROENEWALD, B., Pte. (6850), died of Influenza 8/10/18.
LUCAS, E., Pte. (6851), demobilised 1/1/19.
OCTOBER, J., Pte. (6852), demobilised 29/12/18.
PAULSEN, C., Pte. (6854), demobilised 15/11/18.
CHRISTIE, A., Pte. (6858), demobilised 3/1/19.
JULIE, D., Pte. (6861), demobilised 1/1/19.
WILSON, W., L./Cpl. (6862), L./Cpl. 10/7/17, demobilised 5/2/19.
AFRICA, B., Pte. (6863), demobilised 13/1/19.
JOHANNES, J., Pte. (6868), demobilised 26/12/18.
SHARP, N., Pte. (6869), demobilised 27/12/18.
DARIES, E., Pte. (6870), demobilised 31/12/18.
FORD, S., Pte. (6872), demobilised 26/12/18.
LAKAY, H., Pte. (6875), demobilised 11/11/19.
CALVERT, A., Cpl. (6876), L./Cpl. 19/5/17, Cpl. 2/9/17, demobilised 1/1/19.
PETERS, J., Pte. (6877), demobilised 3/2/19.
HIDE, J., Pte. (6878), demobilised 1/1/19.

THE STORY OF THE 1st CAPE CORPS.

CARELSE, C., Pte. (6879), demobilised 2/1/19.
JANUARY, I., L./Cpl. (6880), L./Cpl. 6/1/18, demobilised 13/1/19.
McCALLUM, C., L./Cpl. (6881), L./Cpl. 23/6/17, demobilised 13/1/19.
BARNES, J., Pte. (6882), died of influenza 8/10/18.
OHLSSON, A., Pte. (6883), demobilised 6/1/19.
HEINEKE, J., Pte. (6884), demobilised 26/12/19.
ABRAHAMS, A., Pte. (6887), demobilised 13/1/19.
ANDREWS, A., Pte. (6888), demobilised 19/12/18.
ABRAHAMS, S., Pte. (6890), demobilised 13/1/19.
DAVIDSON, D., Pte. (6891), demobilised 3/1/19.
BOBBERT, N., Pte. (6892), demobilised 6/1/19
DE LILLY, W. M., L./Cpl. (6893), L./Cpl. 2/6/17, demobilised 5/2/19.
HARE, J., Pte. (6894), released medically unfit 4/12/18.
DE LILLY, N., Pte. (6895), demobilised 30/12/18.
WALTERS, I., Pte. (6896), demobilised 29/12/18.
BARTHUS, A., Pte. (6897), demobilised 5/1/19.
BAILEY, J., Pte. (6901), died of influenza 10/10/18.
OKKERS, J., Pte. (6902), demobilised 30/12/18
JOHNSON, W., Pte. (6903), demobilised 13/1/19.
SLINGER, R., Pte. (6904), demobilised 27/12/18.
FISHER, R., Pte. (6905), demobilised 24/1/19
MOSES, W., Pte. (6906), demobilised 14/1/19.
MEYER, J., Pte. (6907), died of influenza 9/10/18.
SIMET, J., Pte. (6909), demobilised 13/1/19.
KIEVIETS, P., Pte. (6911), demobilised 27/12/18.
MAY, E., Pte. (6912), demobilised 3/1/19.
DYASON, R., Pte. (6914), demobilised 26/12/18.
NIEKERK, G., Pte. (6915), demobilised 30/12/18.
SWARTZ, S., Pte. (6916), demobilised 31/12/18.
SAMPSON, C., Pte. (6918), demobilised 16/7/19.
KLEINSMIDT, A., Pte. (6919), demobilised 3/1/19.
COMBRINK, J., Pte. (6920), demobilised 31/12/18.
DANIELS, D., Pte. (6921), released medically unfit 17/1/19.
SOLOMON, I. G., Pte. (6925), demobilised 31/12/18.
COOK, G., Pte. (6927), demobilised 17/1/19.
JOSEPH, P., Pte. (6929), demobilised 13/1/19.
DIFFENDAL, J., Pte. (6930), demobilised 26/12/18.
ARENDSE, A., Pte. (6933), demobilised 27/12/18.
DESMORE, A. J., Sgt. (6934), L./Cpl. 14/5/17, Cpl. 19/5/17, Sgt. Cook 1/12/17, demobilised 30/12/18.
VAN GRAAN, J., Pte. (6935), died of influenza 11/10/18
SEEFORTH, P., Pte. (6936), demobilised 3/1/19.
HARLEY, J., Pte. (6937), demobilised 11/7/19.
CLASSEN, J., Pte. (6938), demobilised 30/12/18.
SPEILMAN, J., Pte. (6939), demobilised 29/12/18.
STOCKBRIDGE, H., Pte. (6940), demobilised 27/12/18.
PRETORIUS, W. H. J., Cpl. (6941), L./Cpl. 19/5/17, Cpl. 1/8/17, demobilised 30/12/18.
LAMBO, A., Pte. (6943), demobilised 24/1/19.
ESAU, I., Pte. (6944), demobilised 19/12/18.
FREDERICKS, A., Pte. (6945), demobilised 30/12/18.
BESTMAN, T., Pte. (6950), demobilised 13/1/19.
BREDA, H., Pte. (6951), demobilised 1/1/19.
BOCKSEN, J., (6952), demobilised 27/1/19.
JACOBS, N., Pte. (6953), released medically unfit 13/1/19.
LEWIS, H., Pte. (6934), demobilised 24/1/19.
VAN DER ROSS, J., L./Cpl. (6958), L./Cpl. 18/9/17, demobilised 1/2/19.
BARNES, T., Pte. (6959), demobilised 13/1/19.
VAN BLOEMESTIEN, W., Pte. (6960), demobilised 31/12/18.
PETERSEN, D., Pte. (6961), demobilised 2/1/19.
BRINK, M., Pte. (6962), demobilised 24/1/19.
FRANS, J., Pte. (6964), demobilised 27/12/18.
VILJOEN, D., L./Cpl. (6967), L./Cpl 10/7/17, died of influenza 12/10/18.
VAN NIEKERK, W., Cpl. (6969), Cpl. 20/5/17, demobilised 1/1/19.
BENJAMIN, E., Pte. (6971), demobilised 13/1/19.
BARTNICK, P., Pte. (6972), demobilised 13/1/19.
GABRIEL, L., Pte. (6973), demobilised 29/12/18.
ADAMS, F., Pte. (6974), died of influenza 9/10/18.
GALLANT, D., Pte. (6975), demobilised 24/1/19.
ISAACS, I., Pte. (6977), demobilised 3/1/19.
KEMM, A., Pte. (6978), demobilised 24/1/19.
MOSES, J., Pte. (6979), demobilised 13/1/19.
SMALL, J., Pte. (6981), demobilised 27/12/18.
GRIFFINS, W., Pte. (6982), demobilised 1/1/19.
JACOBS, W., Pte. (6983), demobilised 26/12/18.
WOODMAN, W., Pte. (6986), demobilised 3/1/19.
DAMONT, A., Pte. (6987), demobilised 26/12/18.
SAMUELS, G., Pte. (6988), demobilised 6/1/19.
SEPTEMBER, A., Pte. (6989), demobilised 2/1/19.
JOHNSON, E., Pte. (6990), demobilised 3/1/19.
PETERSEN, F., Pte. (6991), demobilised 13/1/19.
MATHEWS, T., Pte. (6992), died of influenza 8/10/18.
MARTIN, W., Pte. (6993), demobilised 2/1/19.
WHITE, H., Pte (6994), demobilised 27/12/18.
ROBERTS, S., Pte. (6996), demobilised 27/12/18.
PLATO, J., Pte. (6997), demobilised 2/1/19.
ADAMS, C., Pte. (6999), demobilised 30/12/18.
SMITH, I., Pte. (7001), demobilised 27/12/18.
TRUMP, W., Pte. (7002), demobilised 31/12/18.
JOHANNES, E., Pte. (7004), died of influenza 16/10/18
MARTINUS, M., Pte. (7005), demobilised 31/12/18.
BAILEY, C., L./Cpl. (7006), L./Cpl. 23/10/17, demobilised 17/12/18.
WILLENBERG, J., Pte. (7007), demobilised 31/12/18.

FORTUIN, S., Pte. (7009), demobilised 14/1/19.
FOX, F., Pte. (7010), demobilised 29/12/18.
SEAGULLS, S., Pte. (7012), demobilised 29/12/18.
DIPPENAAR, W., Pte. (7014), demobilised 1/1/19.
JACOBS, A., Pte. (7017), demobilised 31/12/18.
PLAATJES, C., Pte. (7018), demobilised 13/1/19.
McBULLEN, C., Pte. (7019), demobilised 13/1/19.
KEUR, C., Pte. (7020), demobilised 29/12/18.
LIEDERMAN, P., Pte. (7021), demobilised 16/7/19.
DE JONGH, W., Pte. (7024), demobilised 24/1/19.
JAMES, M., Pte. (7025), demobilised 14/1/19.
PETERSEN, A. J., Pte. (7026), demobilised 2/1/19.
NABEY, C., Pte. (7027), demobilised 24/1/19.
HENKEMAN, L., Pte. (7028), demobilised 30/12/18.
DE GOEDE, J. J., Pte. (7029), demobilised 2/1/19.
TELEMACHUS, J., Pte. (7031), demobilised 24/1/19.
SOLOMON, D., Pte. (7034), demobilised 13/1/19.
GRAINGER, P., Pte. (7035), demobilised 26/12/18.
BASTION, W., Pte. (7036), demobilised 13/1/19.
FREDA, W., Pte. (7037), demobilised 31/12/18.
ADAMS, B., Pte. (7038), demobilised 16/7/19, medical orderly.
PRINS, S. J., Pte. (7039), demobilised 2/1/19.
FISHER, S., Pte. (7040), demobilised 15/1/19.
VAN DYK, J., L./Cpl. (7041), L./Cpl. 25/6/17, demobilised 13/1/19.
CAPONNA, H. Pte. (7042), demobilised 13/1/19.
HENDRICKS, E., Pte. (7044), demobilised 13/1/19.
HARTOG, J., Cpl. (7045), Cpl. 18/7/17, died of influenza 7/10/18.
TAILOR, L., Pte. (7046), demobilised 31/12/18.
DUDGEON, S., Pte. (7047), demobilised 1/1/19.
WEE, W., Pte. (7049), demobilised 3/2/19.
O'REILLY, J., Cpl. (7050), L./Cpl. 18/6/17, Cpl. 31/7/17, demobilised 1/1/19.
ARENDS, W., Pte. (7051), died of influenza 12/10/18.
ELLIOTT, I., Pte. (7052), demobilised 1/1/19.
THOMAS, T., Pte. (7054), demobilised 15/1/19.
DREYER, S., Pte. (7056), demobilised 1/1/19.
JACOBS, J., Pte. (7058), demobilised 29/12/18.
LOTTS, C., Cpl. (7061), Cpl. 1/6/17, demobilised 27/12/18.
HENDRICKS, G., Pte. (7062), demobilised 30/12/18.
REYNARD, W., Pte. (7063), died of influenza 7/10/18.
SMITH, F., Pte. (7067), demobilised 24/1/19.
MACARTHY, M., Pte. (7068), demobilised 5/1/19.
FRENCH, D., Pte. (7069), demobilised 13/1/19.
FRANS, S., Pte. (7070), demobilised 14/1/19.
LEWIS, A., Pte. (7071), demobilised 30/12/18.
GREENTREE, J., Pte. (7072), demobilised 27/12/18.
ABRAHAMS, R., Pte. (7075), demobilised 31/12/18.
FACOLINE, J., Pte. (7076), demobilised 3/1/19.
SAMPSON, W., L./Sgt. (7077), Cpl. 3/7/17, L./Sgt. 1/12/17, died of influenza 9/10/18.
JACOBS, K., Pte. (7079), demobilised 27/12/18.
LOMBARD, E., Pte. (7080), demobilised 24/1/19.
CIAS, N., Pte. (7081), demobilised 13/1/19.
RHODES, J., Pte. (7083), demobilised 27/12/18.
JACOBS, J., Pte. (7084), demobilised 30/12/18.
WILLIAMS, P., Pte. (7089), demobilised 29/12/18.
VALENTYNE, R., Pte. (7091), demobilised 15/1/19.
FEBRUARY, J., Pte. (7092), demobilised 6/1/19.
VOLLENHOVEN, A., Pte. (7093), demobilised 1/1/19.
PETERSEN, J., Pte. (7095), demobilised 27/12/18.
DAVIDS, S., Pte. (7096), demobilised 2/1/19.
LEONARDS, N., Pte. (7101), demobilised 13/1/19.
MOSTERT, C., Pte. (7104), demobilised 30/12/18.
ROBERTSON, J., Pte. (7105), died of influenza 11/10/18.
LAWRENCE, S., Pte. (7106), demobilised 13/1/19.
SOLOMON, J., Pte. (7110), demobilised 24/1/19.
DE STADLER, G., Pte. (7112), demobilised 27/12/18.
SCHOLTZ, S. J., Pte. (7115), died of influenza 15/10/18.
VAN RHEEDE, R., Pte. (7116), demobilised 2/1/19.
ABRAHAMS, W., Pte. (7118), demobilised 27/12/18.
CAMPHER, M., Pte. (7120), demobilised 1/1/19.
MOSS, J., Pte. (7121), died of influenza 9/10/18.
NORMAN, H., Pte. (7122), demobilised 2/1/19.
NYHOFF, J., Pte. (7123), died of influenza 9/10/18.
SOULS, A., Pte. (7127), demobilised 15/1/19.
LEO, T. A., L./Sgt. (7128), Cpl. 1/6/17, L./Sgt. 14/12/17, demobilised 31/12/18.
JACOBS, E., Pte. (7129), died of influenza 12/10/18.
ADRIAANSE, F. L./Cpl. (7131), L./Cpl. 23/10/17, died of influenza 11/10/18.
FISHER, L., Pte. (7132), demobilised 3/1/19.
JAFTHA, G., Cpl. (7133), L./Cpl. 31/7/17, Cpl. 14/12/17, demobilised 26/12/18.
DAVIDS, D., Pte. (7135), demobilised 26/12/18.
DANIELS, C., Pte. (7136), demobilised 26/12/18.
CONRADIE, I., Pte. (7137), demobilised 22/12/18.
THEUNISSEN, P. E., Pte. (7138), demobilised 3/1/19.
ISAACS, J., Pte. (7141), demobilised 29/12/18.
OCTOBER, M., Pte. (7142), died of influenza 11/10/18.
LOUW, F., Pte. (7143), demobilised 17/1/19.
LOSPER, J., Pte. (7145), demobilised 13/1/19.
AUGUSTUS, M., Pte. (7146), demobilised 1/1/19.
CHIPPENDALE, A., Cpl. (7147), Cpl. 1/6/17, demobilised 13/1/19.
MAGGOT, A., Pte. (7148), demobilised 1/1/19.
JAGGERS, J., Pte. (7149), demobilised 27/12/18.
HEYNES, J., Pte. (7151), demobilised 13/1/19

THE STORY OF THE 1st CAPE CORPS.

STEWART, J., Pte. (7153), demobilised 30/12/18.
VAN WYK, J., Pte. (7156), demobilised 14/1/19.
ARROW, T., Pte. (7158), demobilised 31/12/18.
SMITH, B., Pte. (7159), demobilised 24/1/19.
CLOETE, T., Pte. (7163), demobilised 1/1/19.
AUGUST, W., Pte. (7164), demobilised 1/1/19.
JULY, S., Pte. (7165), demobilised 6/1/19.
SMITH, J., Pte. (7166), demobilised 1/1/19.
CLOETE, F., Pte. (7167), demobilised 1/1/19.
CAMERON, W., L./Cpl. (7169), L./Cpl. 23/6/17, demobilised 1/1/19.
BOTMAN, W., Pte. (7170), demobilised 1/1/19.
CLOETE, J., Pte. (7171), demobilised 1/1/19.
VAN ROOY, C., Pte. (7172), demobilised 1/2/19.
JANTJES, F., Pte. (7175), demobilised 13/1/19.
HARRIS, G., Pte. (7177), demobilised 14/1/19.
CUPIDO, A., Pte. (7178), demobilised 19/12/18.
BORE, H., Pte. (7179), demobilised 19/12/18.
SPANNEBERG, I., Pte. (7180), demobilised 27/12/18.
PETERSEN, A., Pte. (7182), released medically unfit 18/12/18.
WALTERS, T., Pte. (7184), demobilised 27/12/18.
CUPIDO, J., Pte. (7185), demobilised 30/12/18.
SAMUELS, M., Pte. (7186), demobilised 13/1/19.
LIEBRANDT, D., Pte. (7190), demobilised 17/1/19.
JANSEN, M., Pte. (7191), died of influenza 9/10/18.
BLOEM, J., L./Cpl. (7192), L./Cpl. 31/7/17, demobilised 24/1/19.
WILLIAMS, J., Pte. (7193), died of influenza 15/10/18.
JOHANNES, T., Pte. (7195), died of influenza 13/10/18.
CUPIDO, M., Pte. (7196), demobilised 30/12/18.
WENTZEL, I., Pte. (7197), demobilised 31/12/18.
JOSEPH, R., Pte. (7199), demobilised 13/1/19.
RAVENSCROFT, J., Pte. (7203), demobilised 5/1/19.
RUCIMELEU, V., Cpl. (7208), Cpl. 25/3/18, demobilised 19/12/18.
SAMUELS, J., Pte. (7209), S.N.L.R. 13/12/18.
JOHNSON, M., Pte. (7210), demobilised 13/1/19.
DICKSON, J., Pte. (7211), demobilised 27/11/18.
ROBYNTJES, C., Pte. (7212), demobilised 24/1/19.
MACDONALD, C., Pte. (7214), demobilised 13/1/19.
HENDRICKS, A., Pte. (7218), demobilised 1/1/19.
SEPTEMBER, J., Pte. (7220), demobilised 1/1/19, acted L./Cpl.
DE VERE, P., Pte. (7224), demobilised 21/7/19.
ARENDSE, K., Pte. (7226), demobilised 30/12/18.
FRANCIS, H., Pte. (7227), demobilised 29/12/18.
FOSTER, J., Pte. (7234), demobilised 13/1/19.
CHIKOKO, M., Pte. (7241), demobilised 13/1/19.
WILSON, D., Pte. (7242), died of influenza 8/10/18.
STEPHEN, J., Pte. (7245), died of influenza 15/10/18
KING, H., Pte. (7246), demobilised 30/12/18.
HARTZENBERG, S., Pte. (7247), demobilised 27/12/18.
COERT, J., Pte. (7251), demobilised 24/1/19.
ARMOED, P., Pte. (2256), demobilised 1/1/19.
STEVENS, T. P., Pte. (7257), demobilised 29/12/18.
DAVIDS, H., Pte. (7260), demobilised 24/1/19
SWARTZ, P., Pte. (7261), demobilised 13/1/19.
STEYN, A., Pte. (7264), demobilised 30/12/18.
WILLIAMS, M., Pte. (7265), demobilised 31/12/18.
FELIX, A., Pte. (7266), demobilised 31/12/18.
JENKINS, W., Pte. (7267), demobilised 31/12/18.
PETERSEN, J., Pte. (7268), demobilised 26/12/18.
WOODMAN, D., Pte. (7269), demobilised 6/1/19.
ARTHUR, J., Pte. (7271), demobilised 27/12/18.
JAVIS, M., Pte. (7274), demobilised 2/1/19.
PETERS, S., Pte. (7275), demobilised 27/12/18.
WILLIAMS, J., Pte (7276), demobilised 13/1/19.
PAULSEN, T., Pte. (7277), demobilised 1/1/19.
SWARTZ, L., Pte. (7280), demobilised 30/12/18.
MOOS, M., Pte. (7281), demobilised 2/1/19.
GREENFIELD, A., Pte., released medically unfit 13/1/19.
ALFRED, J., Pte. (7290), demobilised 1/1/19.
SOULS, G., Pte. (7291), died of influenza 11/10/18.
SHACKLE, C. E., C.S.M. (7293), demobilised 2/1/19, European personnel.
MANUEL, K., Pte. (7294), demobilised 14/1/19.
PETERSEN, D., Pte. (7301), demobilised 24/1/19.
LETOKA, I., Pte (7302), demobilised 6/1/19.
TUCKER, C., Cpl. (7305), demobilised 26/12/18.
WILLIAMS, P., Pte. (7306), died of influenza 12/10/18.
MESSALIE, S., Pte. (7307), demobilised 1/1/19.
DANIELS, P., Pte. (7309), demobilised 2/1/19.
MICHAEL, F., Pte. (7311), died of influenza 9/10/18.
JACOBS, D., Pte. (7314), died of influenza 20/10/18.
LEVENDAL, S., Pte. (7316), demobilised 13/1/19.
GOLIATH, M., Pte. (7317), demobilised 30/12/18.
KLASSEN, C. W., Pte. (7319), demobilised 15/1/19.
SAMPSON, J., Pte. (7326), demobilised 5/1/19.
SASS, J., Pte. (7327), demobilised 29/12/18.
FRANCIS, N., Pte. (7329), demobilised 14/1/19.
O'BRIEN, W., Pte. (7332), demobilised 7/9/19.
HOLMES, W., Pte. (7333), demobilised 24/1/19.
BOWERS, R., Pte. (7334), demobilised 3/2/19.
GERTZ, D., Pte. (7336), demobilised 1/1/19.
BRAK, J., Pte. (7337), died of Influenza 11/10/18.
GORDON, D., Pte. (7338), demobilised 26/12/18.
PRICE, J., Pte. (7340), demobilised 1/1/19.

ERASMUS, E., Pte. (7342), demobilised 1/2/19.
LE FLEUR, J., Pte. (7344), demobilised 31/12/18.
HARTZEN, S., Pte. (7345), demobilised 24/1/19.
SEPTEMBER, D., Pte. (7346), demobilised 29/12/18.
GEDULD, A., Pte. (7348), demobilised 2/1/19.
ROSSOUW, N., Pte. (7350), demobilised 26/1/19.
LEVENDAL, A., Pte. (7352), demobilised 30/12/18.
KAYZER, D., Pte. (7354), died of influenza 18/10/18.
DAVIDSON, N., Pte. (7356), demobilised 3/1/19.
MEYER, N., Pte. (7359), demobilised 13/1/19.
ARMOED, J., Pte. (7360), demobilised 1/1/19.
CUPIDO, C., Pte. (7362), demobilised 25/12/18.
SMITH, M., Pte. (7366), demobilised 29/12/18.
SEPTEMBER, N., Pte. (7367), demobilised 30/12/18.
MACTAVISH, J., Pte. (7369), demobilised 27/12/18.
HENDRICKS, H., Pte. (7370), demobilised 27/12/18.
PYOOS, H., Pte. (7371), demobilised 1/1/19.
LOUW, W., Pte. (7372), demobilised 21/7/19.
PETERSEN, I., Pte. (7373), demobilised 29/12/18.
MHINDA, H., Pte. (7378), demobilised 15/10/18.
KAM, Pte. (7380), demobilised 29/12/18.
CAPES, J., Pte. (7381), demobilised 13/1/19.
PLAATJES, D., Pte. (7382), demobilised 26/12/18.
QUITTE, N., Pte. (7383), demobilised 26/12/18.
FOURIE, A., Pte. (7384), died 2/7/18.
JACOBS, J., Pte. (7386), died of influenza 10/10/18.
MULLER, J., Pte. (7391), died of influenza 13/10/18.
MARTIN, A., Pte. (7400), demobilised 13/1/19.
BANTAM, J., Pte. (7402), released medically unfit 12/11/18.
SOLOMON, S., Pte. (7403), demobilised 27/12/18.
JACOBS, P., Pte. (7404), demobilised 27/12/18.
CUPIDO, F., Pte. (7407), demobilised 1/1/19.
MATJAU, T., Pte. (7409), demobilised 26/12/18.
PEKEUR, F., Pte. (7412), demobilised 30/12/18.
PLAATJES, T., Pte. (7413), demobilised 3/1/19.
MAHOMED, S., Pte. (7414), demobilised 31/12/18.
WILLIAMS, F., Pte. (7416), demobilised 3/1/19.
WENTZEL, J., Pte. (7417), died of influenza 11/10/18.
HENDRICKS, F., Pte. (7419), demobilised 31/12/18.
PETERSEN, G., Pte. (7420), demobilised 30/12/18.
PRATT, J., Pte. (7425), demobilised 13/1/19.
JOHNSON, H., Pte. (7426), demobilised 1/1/19.
COETZEE, J., Pte. (7428), demobilised 2/1/19.
THOMAS, I., Pte. (7432), demobilised 24/1/19.
SAMUELS, P., Pte. (7433), demobilised 13/1/19.
SWARTZ, P., Pte. (7434), demobilised 27/12/18.
JONES, A., Pte. (7437), demobilised 26/12/18.
BOOYSE, J., Pte. (7439), demobilised 27/12/18.
CROW, J., Pte. (7440), demobilised 27/12/18.
ADAMS, C., Pte. (7445), demobilised 1/1/19.
ANTHONY, A., Pte. (7446), demobilised 1/1/19.
VAN HEERDEN, J., Pte. (7447), demobilised 13/1/19.
ARRIES, S., Pte. (7449), demobilised 19/12/18.
ABRAHAMS, S., Pte. (7450), demobilised 27/12/18.
FORTUIN, J., Pte. (7451), demobilised 26/12/18.
STEENEVELDT, F., Pte. (7453), demobilised 27/12/18.
DAVIDS, J., Pte. (7455), demobilised 27/12/18.
NEL, S., Pte. (7456), demobilised 14/1/19.
BARENDSE, L., Pte. (7458), died 16/10/18.
BUSSACK, D., Pte. (7459), demobilised 13/1/19.
FISHER, G., Pte. (7460), demobilised 1/1/19.
PLAATJES, C., Pte. (7461), demobilised 1/1/19.
VAN STADER, I., Pte. (7462), demobilised 1/1/19.
KLEINSMITH, D., Pte. (7463), demobilised 11/7/19.
DE VOS, J., Pte. (7465), demobilised 1/1/19.
WITBOOI, S., Pte. (7470), demobilised 1/1/19.
FORTUNE, D., Pte. (7473), demobilised 1/1/19.
ERASMUS, E., Pte. (7542), demobilised 1/1/19.
PORTER, H., Pte. (7600), demobilised 27/12/18.

1st. CAPE CORPS ROLL OF HONOUR, 1915-1919.

"The muffled drums' sad roll has beat
  The soldier's last tattoo;
No more on Life's parade shall meet
  The brave and fallen few.
On Fame's eternal camping-ground
  Their silent tents are spread,
And Glory guards, with solemn round,
  The bivouac of the dead."

Theodore O'Hara.

"A death without fear, without self, whose renown shall not cease."

W. A. Way.

OFFICERS.

IN EAST AFRICA:

Killed in Action.

ABBOTT, C. F.	2nd.-Lieut.	At Mkungu (Lindi Area).	6/11/17.
GUEST, IVOR, A. M.	Lieut.	,, ,,	,,
HOSACK, J. C.	2nd.-Lieut.	At Massinga (near Kangata).	20/7/16.
POWER, WALTER	Lieut.	At Mkungu (Lindi Area).	6/11/17.

Died of Wounds.

McNIEL, JOHN	2nd.-Lieut.	At Mkungu (Lindi Area) of wounds received on 6/11/17.

Died of Disease.

HOFFE, T. M.	Capt. (acting)	At Dodoma of Lobar Pneumonia.	23/9/17.

IN EGYPT AND PALESTINE:

Killed in Action.

COWELL, W. R., D.S.O.	Major.	At Kh. Jibeit, near Jerusalem, Palestine.	20/9/18.
DIFFORD, A. N.	Lieut.	,, ,,	,,
DREYER, J. S.	2nd.-Lieut.	,, ,,	,,
HARRIS, J. V., M.C.	Captain.	,, ,,	,,
VIPAN, C. A.	2nd.-Lieut.	,, ,,	,,

Died of Wounds.

ANTILL, A. E. J.	2nd.-Lieut.	At Cheshire Ridge, near Jerusalem, Palestine, of wounds received 20/9/18.	21/9/18.
HOLLINS, J. L.	2nd.-Lieut.	At Alexandria, Egypt.	15/10/18.
WHITE, G. C.	Lieut.	At Gaza, of wounds received at Kh. Jibeit, near Jerusalem, Palestine, 20/9/18.	17/10/18.

IN EGYPT AND PALESTINE (Continued):
Died of Disease.

BARNARD, G. R.	... ...	Lieut.	At Ranger's Corner, near Rham Alla, Palestine, of Cerebral Malaria.	22/7/18.

IN THE UNION OF SOUTH AFRICA:

RAINIER, H. A.	... ...	Lieut.	Kimberley (Influenza).	10/10/18.
SMITH, W. R.	... ...	Lieut.	,, ,,	22/10/18.

OTHER RANKS.

IN EAST AFRICA:
Killed in Action.

Name.	Rank.	Regt. No.	Place.	Date.
ALLISON, C.	Pte.	3142	Mkindu (Rufiji River).	20/1/17.
ABRAHAMS, J.	,,	2372	Mkungu (Lindi area).	6/11/17.
ARENDS, G.	,,	956	,, ,,	,,
AFRICA, D.	,,	3489	,, ,,	,,
BOTES, L.	,,	3714	,, ,,	,,
DRURY, F.	,,	1272	,, ,,	8/11/17.
DAVIDS, J.	,,	1037	,, ,,	6/11/17.
DAVIDS, A.	,,	3496	Kwedihombo, near Morogoro.	26/8/17.
FEDER, W.	,,	1535	Mkungu (Lindi area).	6/11/17.
FRANS, Z.	,,	2552	Kibongo (Rufiji River).	20/1/17.
FRANKS, J.	,,	2039	,, ,,	,,
GEDULD, J.	,,	2763	,, ,,	,,
HOUTSAMMER, J. ...	,,	586	Mkungu (Lindi area).	6/11/17.
HARTZ, A.	,,	1369	Duthumi.	30/12/16.
JANAKER, S.	,,	576	Makonde Plateau (Lindi area).	16/11/17.
JOHNSON, J.	,,	2434	Sogosso Hill.	30/8/17.
LEWIS, S.	,,	2898	Makonde Plateau (Lindi area).	16/11/17.
SCHROEDER, F. ...	Cpl.	980	Mkungu (Lindi area).	6/11/17.
TRANTRALL, W. ...	Pte.	1197	Nyakisiki (Mine Explosion).	21/1/17
TENNANT, D. W. ...	,,	3187	Mkungu (Lindi area).	6/11/17.
VAN AARDE, J. ...	,,	1395	Sogosso Hill.	30/8/17.
WATNEY, J.	,,	3272	Mkungu (Lindi area).	6/11/17.

Died of Wounds.

BREDENKAMP, J. ...	Pte.	1859	Morogoro.	20/2/17.
BEHR, W.	,,	3111	Dar-es-Salaam.	21/11/17.
DE GOEDE, H. ...	,,	2958	Duthumi (accidental).	13/1/17.
GEORGE, A.	,,	165	Ndanda (Lindi area).	27/11/17.
MOUTON, D.	,,	2337	Mkware ,,	8/11/17.
NIEKERK, J.	,,	253	Mkungu. ,,	6/11/17.
OCTOBER, D.	,,	441	Mkware. ,,	8/11/17.
STUURMAN, R. ...	,,	1514	Mkware (Lindi area).	9/11/17.
SMOUSE, D.	,,	2100	,, ,,	10/11/17.
STARKEY, C.	,,	3100	Makonde Plateau (Lindi area).	16/11/17.
TEMBE, J. P.	Sgt.	1966	Mkindu (Rufiji River)	22/1/17.

IN EGYPT AND PALESTINE:
Killed in Action.

ABRAHAMS, H. ...	Pte.	1561	Kh. Jibeit, near Jerusalem, Palestine.	20/9/18.
AFRICA, J.	,,	4642	,, ,,	,,
ALEXANDER, H. ...	,,	3533	,, ,,	,,
ADAMS, B.	,,	4075	,, ,,	,,
BOER, A.	,,	575	,, ,,	,,
FEDER, H.	Cpl.	687	,, ,,	,,
GAIN, J. J.	,,	618	,, ,,	,,
GROEP, G.	Pte.	1698	Square Hill, Palestine.	19/9/18.
HOFFMAN, F.	C.Q.M.S.	861	Kh. Jibeit, near Jerusalem, Palestine.	20/9/18.
HARTNICK, C. ...	Pte.	4439	,, ,,	,,
JACOBS, D.	,,	1295	,, ,,	,,

THE STORY OF THE 1st CAPE CORPS.

IN EGYPT AND PALESTINE (Continued):

Killed in Action.

Name.	Rank.	Regt. No.	Place.	Date.
JONKERS, J.	Pte.	3891	Square Hill, Palestine.	19/9/18.
JACOBS, J.	,,	656	Kh. Jibeit, near Jerusalem, Palestine.	20/9/18.
JACOBUS, W.	,,	4272	,, ,,	,,
KLINK, P.	,,	4606	,, ,,	,,
LEVENDAHL, G.	,,	1881	,, ,,	,,
LUBBE, J.	,,	3284	,, ,,	,,
LINEBOOM, F.	,,	2220	,, ,,	,,
MAY, W.	,,	914	,, ,,	,,
MANAVELL, M.	,,	1740	,, ,,	,,
NORRIS, E.	L.-Cpl.	717	,, ,,	,,
OLIVER, J.	Pte.	1685	,, ,,	,,
PRETORIUS, A.	,,	3621	,, ,,	,,
PETERSEN, J.	,,	4650	,, ,,	,,
RUSSEL, J. C.	,,	147	,, ,,	,,
RADIEN, E.	L.-Cpl.	3904	,, ,,	,,
ROBERTS, J.	Pte.	833	,, ,,	,,
SCHOLTZ, J.	,,	824	,, ,,	,,
SMITH, J.	L.-Cpl.	735	,, ,,	,,
SOLOMON, C.	Pte.	2734	,, ,,	,,
STEPHENS, A.	,,	797	,, ,,	,,
VISAGIE, S.	L.-Cpl.	139	Square Hill, Palestine.	18/9/18.
VAN WYK, A.	Pte.	629	Kh. Jibeit, near Jerusalem, Palestine.	20/9/18.
VAN DER BERG, J.	,,	3023	,, ,,	,,
VAN DER ROSS, J.	,,	4604	,, ,,	,,
VAN SITTERS, J.	,,	4269	,, ,,	,,
VELDSMAN, C.	Sergt.	284	,, ,,	,,
VAN WYK, J.	Pte.	3995	,, ,,	,,
WALTERS, N.	L.-Sergt.	221	,, ,,	,,
WILLIAMS, B.	Pte.	2236	,, ,,	,,
WILSON, C.	,,	4035	,, ,,	,,

Died of Wounds.

Name	Rank	Regt. No.	Place.	Date.
DANIELS, S.	Pte	890	Wadi Samieh. ,,	22/9/18.
DANKERS, W.	,,	237	Nablus Road. ,,	24/9/18.
GARNARD, A.	,,	3711	Wadi Samieh. ,,	20/9/18.
JAFTHA, F.	L.-Cpl.	185	,, ,,	,,
ROSS, J. L.	Sgt.	2619	,, ,,	,,
WATSON, R.	Pte.	11	Cairo, Egypt.	18/10/18.
WILLIAMS, G.	,,	1456	Jerusalem.	23/9/18.

IN EAST AFRICA:

Died of Disease.

Name	Rank.	Reg. No.	Disease.	Place.	Date.
ADAMS, T. C.	Sergt.	1139	Septicæmia.	Moshi	8/7/16.
ABRAHAMS, N.	Pte.	519	Dysentery.	Lindi.	27/10/17.
ABDULLA, C.	,,	412	Pneumonia.	Duthumi.	29/3/17.
AUGUST, J.	,,	117	,,	Mtama.	21/11/17.
ANTHONY, J.	,,	1300	Malaria.	Muthaiga (B.E.A.)	25/5/16
ADAMS, P.	,,	1398	,,	Mbuyuni (B.E.A.)	18/10/16.
ADONIS, W.	,,	1660	,,	Morogoro.	31/3/17.
ADONIS, A.	,,	2972	Dysentery.	,,	24/6/17.
ADAMS, J.	,,	1754	Malaria.	,,	9/7/17.
BOYSE, F.	,,	649	,,	Kangata.	24/7/16.
BEZUIDENHOUT, M.	,,	333	Dysentery.	Duthumi.	23/2/17.
BAUMAN, A.	,,	950	,,	Morogoro.	30/8/17.
BROWN, S.	,,	1459	Malaria.	Korogwe.	9/8/16.
BARGHUIS, H.	,,	1973	Dysentery.	Duthumi.	4/4/17.
BUTTERY, J.	,,	2993	,,	Mkesse.	12/3/17.
BARENDS, J.	,,	1650	Malaria.	Utete.	19/5/17.

THE STORY OF THE 1ST CAPE CORPS.

IN EAST AFRICA (Continued):

Died of Disease.

Name.	Rank.	Reg. No.	Disease.	Place.	Date.
BEIT, G.	Pte.	3483	Cerebral malaria.	At Sea.	23/12/17.
CAMPBELL, A.	,,	393	Dysentery.	Dar-es-salaam.	13/11/17.
CHRISTIANS, D.	,,	2492	Malaria.	Morogoro.	4/12/16.
COETZEE, G.	,,	2976	Cerebral malaria.	Dar-es-salaam.	17/12/17.
CUPIDO, J.	,,	2937	Malaria.	Morogoro.	5/4/17.
COTTON, R.	,,	3	,,	Moshi.	23/5/16.
DANIELS, A.	C.Q.M.S.	13	,,	Dar-es-salaam.	24/12/16.
DE JONGH, F.	Sgt.	873	Dysentery.	Tanga.	2/10/16.
DE JONGH, G.	Pte.	1203	Malaria.	Mombo.	11/7/16.
DE VRIES, F.	,,	1213	Dysentery.	Korogwe.	7/11/16.
DAVIDS, J.	,,	1975	Malaria.	Morogoro.	16/4/17.
DAMPIES, M.	,,	2131	Dysentery.	Mkesse.	12/3/17.
DAVIDS, J.	,,	1773	,,	Dakawa.	18/2/17.
DU PREEZ, J.	,,	2534	Pneumonia.	Morogoro.	3/6/17.
DU PLESSIS, M.	,,	2688	Malaria.	Dar-es-salaam.	4/1/17.
DUMING, P.	,,	1658	,,	Morogoro.	13/4/17.
EDWARDS, J.	,,	1625	Dysentery.	,,	22/4/17.
FELTON, A.	Sgt.	169	Malaria.	Dar-es-salaam.	2/11/16.
FRANCIS, D.	Pte	263	,,	Moshi.	27/5/16.
FELIX, C.	,,	781	Appendicitis.	Korogwe.	19/9/16.
FURNESS, W.	,,	1672	Malaria.	Morogoro.	7/4/17.
FILLIES, J.	,,	982	Missing, death acpt.	,,	15/4/17.
GROVELL, J.	,,	3710	,,	,,	16/11/17.
GELDERBLOEM, J.	,,	408	Enteric fever.	Tulo.	27/3/17.
GORDON, J.	,,	530	Drowned.	Pangani River.	2/7/16.
FREDERICKS, M.	,,	3191	,,	At Sea.	11/7/17.
GROEP, M.	,,	1268	Malaria.	Moshi.	26/5/16.
HEBER, H.	Sgt.	145	Blackwater.	Morogoro.	22/3/17.
HARDING, J.	Pte.	715	Dysentery.	Dar-es-salaam.	13/11/17.
HENDRICKS, A.	,,	789	Malaria.	Korogwe.	25/10/16
HUNTER, A.	,,	701	C. spinal meningitis.	Dodoma.	17/8/17.
HERADIEN, L.	,,	2766	Malaria.	Morogoro.	18/5/17.
HARTZENBERG, C.	,,	1951	,,	Dakawa.	14/2/17.
HAMET, F.	,,	1918	Pneumonia.	At Sea.	13/5/17.
HERMAN, A.	,,	2277	Dysentery.	Wiransi.	13/2/17.
HENDRICKS, A.	,,	2981	Smallpox.	Morogoro.	31/7/17.
HENDRICKS, T.	,,	1623	Malaria.	Tanga.	10/12/16.
JULIE, D.	,,	536	,,	Taveta.	1/7/16.
JOSEPH, C.	Cpl.	279	,,	Morogoro.	19/9/16.
JACOBS, I.	Pte.	34	,,	Amani.	11/8/16.
JACOBS, N.	,,	1659	Sunstroke.	Morogoro.	5/12/17.
JAFTHAS, S.	,,	975	Malaria.	Amani.	3/8/16.
JOSEPH, G.	,,	785	Blackwater.	Dar-es-salaam.	30/1/17.
JOHNSON, G.	Cpl.	217	Fever and diarrhoea.	Mpangas.	19/2/17.
JOZAFFE, G.	Pte.	458	Malaria.	Moshi.	5/5/16.
JAFTHA, J.	,,	435	Smallpox.	Morogoro.	14/8/17.
JACOBS, J.	,,	2089	Cerebral malaria.	,,	16/10/17.
JACOBS, D.	,,	1778	Dysentery.	Duthumi.	29/3/17.
JULIES, W.	,,	2432	Malaria.	Mpangas.	16/3/17.
JOHNSON, S.	,,	2431	Dysentery.	Duthumi.	28/1/17.
JULIES, P.	,,	3067	Smallpox.	Morogoro.	15/7/17.
JANAKER, J.	,,	3627	Cerebral malaria.	Dodoma.	11/10/17.
KOOPMAN, G.	L.-Cpl.	26	Blackwater.	Morogoro.	26/9/17.
KLEINTJES, C.	Pte.	2117	Dysentery.	Dar-es-salaam.	19/3/17.
KEMP, M.	,,	2219	Malaria.	,,	9/12/16.
LOMBARD, C.	L.-Cpl.	926	Tuberculosis.	Mbuyuni (B.E.A.)	30/9/16.
LANGEVELDT, W.	Pte.	3069	Dysentery.	Beho Beho.	13/4/17.
LE ROUX, A.	,,	2221	Malaria & dysentery.	Duthumi.	1/3/17.
LOSPER, F.	,,	2615	Nephritis.	Dar-es-salaam.	8/7/17.
MUNNIK, D.	,,	355	Blackwater.	Utete.	2/4/17.
MOODY, J.	,,	268	Malaria.	Moshi.	16/5/16.
McLEAN, D.	,,	1172	Malaria.	Loldoloi.	14/6/16.
MARTIN, A.	,,	384	Enteric fever.	Dar-es-salaam.	26/3/17.

THE STORY OF THE 1st CAPE COR

IN EAST AFRICA (Continued):

Died of Disease.

Name.	Rank.	Reg. No.	Disease.	Place.	Date.
MULLER, J.	Pte.	1883	Pneumonia.	Duthumi.	5/4/17.
MAY, S.	,,	2118	Malaria.	Mpangas.	4/3/17.
MEINTJES, P.	,,	2464	Dysentery.	Morogoro.	26/4/17.
McKENNA, H.	,,	1982	,,	Ndanda.	11/12/17.
MURPHY, J.	,,	2463	Malaria.	Morogoro.	15/5/17.
MUNNIK, W.	,,	3076	,,	,,	30/6/17.
MAY, J.	,,	2916	Dysentery.	At Sea.	7/6/17.
MAY, J.	,,	2842	Malaria.	Duthumi.	23/1/17.
MACAULY, W.	,,	2927	,,	Morogoro.	7/7/17.
MOORINGS, H.	,,	3597	,,	Dar-es-salaam.	20/12/17.
OLIESLAGER, A.	Sgt.	182	Cerebral malaria.	Mpangas.	6/3/17.
OSBOURNE, J.	Pte.	1016	Enteritis.	Dar-es-salaam.	18/1/17.
OVIES, C.	,,	1440	Heart failure.	Morogoro.	6/12/16.
PLAATJES, A.	,,	962	Blackwater.	Utete.	26/4/17.
PETERSEN, P.	,,	510	Malaria.	Mbuyuni (B.E.A.)	19/10/16.
PITT, W.	,,	314	,,	Kangata.	1/8/16.
PRINCE, W.	,,	1335	Pneumonia & pleurisy.	Rufiji River.	25/1/17.
PETERS, H.	,,	2062	Bronchitis.	Duthumi.	8/4/17.
PRESENCE, P.	,,	2064	Cerebral malaria.	,,	18/2/17.
RICKETTS, J.	,,	2098	Dysentery.	Morogoro.	1/2/17.
ROBERTS, M.	,,	2656	,,	At Sea.	28/3/17.
SLINGERS, J.	,,	844	,,	Muthaiga (B.E.A.)	20/6/16.
SPORT, T.	,,	783	Malaria.	Unterer-Himo.	29/4/16.
SPIELMAN, B.	,,	1251	,,	Voi (B.E.A.)	13/5/16.
SMITH, D.	,,	2770	,,	,,	9/5/17.
STOFFELS, H.	,,	1839	,,	Utete.	30/6/17.
THOMPSON, J.	Cpl.	1039	,,	Korogwe.	13/9/16.
THRUEBEN, J.	Pte.	720	Heart failure.	Amani.	1/10/16.
THOMAS, W.	,,	1748	Malaria.	Kipenio.	2/2/17.
TROMPETTER, C.	,,	2264	,,	Morogoro.	6/4/17.
TITUS, F.	,,	3083	,,	Dar-es-salaam.	21/6/17.
TARENTAAL, H.	,,	3082	,,	Morogoro.	14/6/17.
TOBIN, H.	,,	3202	,,	Nairobi (B.E.A.)	30/9/17.
VAN SCHOOR, B.	Sgt.	726	Cerebral malaria.	Rufiji River.	28/3/17.
VISAGIE, J.	Pte.	383	Malaria.	Moshi.	8/4/16.
VAN HAARTE, M.	,,	1081	,,	,,	24/3/16.
VAN RHEEDE, T.	,,	2489	Dysentery.	Morogoro.	5/5/17.
VAN NIEKERK, A.	,,	2326	,,	Dar-es-salaam.	12/1/18.
VISAGIE, A.	,,	2266	,,	Duthumi.	24/1/17.
WILLIAMS, D.	,,	2296	Malaria.	Morogoro.	11/3/17.
WILLIAMS, L.	,,	2470	Mauled by lion.	Dodoma.	22/8/17.
ZIEDEL, J.	,,	971	Malaria.	Turiani.	4/10/16.

IN EGYPT AND PALESTINE:

Name	Rank	Reg. No.	Disease	Place	Date
ABRAHAMS, H.	Sgt.	168	Pneumonia.	Kantara.	30/10/18.
BIRD, H.	Pte.	51	Abscess on liver.	Alexandria.	27/9/18.
BANTAN, A.	,,	5013	Pneumonia.	At Sea.	10/9/18.
COETZEE, A.	Sgt.	212	,,	Jerusalem.	26/8/18.
ECKSTEIN, P.	Pte.	2275	C. spinal meningitis.	Nablus Road.	31/8/18.
HILLBERG, J.	,,	1994	Broncho pneumonia.	Alexandria.	27/11/18.
HAYES, R.	,,	3997	,,	Gaza.	28/8/18.
ISAACS, J.	,,	1920	Malaria.	Belah.	23/8/18.
JOSEPH, A.	,,	2459	Pneumonia.	At Sea.	10/7/18.
JOHNSON, R.	,,	2280	Drowned.	El Arish.	2/11/18.
KOEBERG, N.	,,	4988	Heart failure.	El Arish.	20/3/19.
KNIPE, T. J.	Cpl.	1093	Malaria.	Alexandria	12/8/19.
MATHEE, J.	Pte.	2986	Pneumonia.	Nablus Road.	29/8/18.
McKIE, G.	L.-Cpl.	3825	Typhoid fever.	Jerusalem.	22/8/18.
MOSES, J.	Pte.	2508	,,	Jerusalem.	26/8/18.
MINNIES, F.	,,	4084	Uræmia.	Alexandria.	24/2/19

THE STORY OF THE 1st CAPE CORPS.

IN EGYPT AND PALESTINE (Continued):
Died of Disease.

Name.	Rank.	Regt. No.	Disease.	Place.	Date.
MATTHYS, J.	Pte.	4730	Run over by train.	Arbain Camp, Suez	7/5/19.
SCHROEDER, T.	,,	827	Typhoid fever.	Jerusalem.	18/8/18.
SMIT, C.	,,	4267	Cerebral malaria.	At sea.	21/8/18.
VAN ROOY, W.	,,	1641	Drowned.	Kantara.	16/9/18.
WILLIAMS, J. H.	,,	2416	Pneumonia.	Belah.	3/10/18.

IN THE UNION OF SOUTH AFRICA.

Name.	Rank.	Reg. No.	Disease.	Place.	Date.
ADRIAANSE, J.	Pte.	1412	Meningitis.	Kimberley.	3/9/18.
ADAMS, F.	,,	6974	Influenza.	,,	9/10/18.
ADRIAANSE, F.	,,	7131	,,	,,	11/10/18.
ADAMS, S.	,,	6378	,,	,,	11/10/18.
ADAMS, F.	,,	6375	,,	,,	12/10/18.
ARENDS, W.	,,	7051	,,	,,	12/10/18.
APPLE, J.	,,	6668	,,	,,	18/10/18.
ARENDSE, J.	,,	1971	,,	,,	7/10/18.
AUGUSTINE, J. E.	,,	5021	,,	,,	9/10/18.
AFRICA, J.	,,	6664	,,	,,	10/10/18.
ANDREWS, J.	,,	6762	,,	,,	21/10/18.
AFRICANDER, K.	,,	6401	,,	,,	9/10/18.
ALEXANDER, M.	,,	5501	,,	,,	6/10/18.
BAILEY, J.	,,	6901	,,	,,	10/10/18.
BAATJES, G.	,,	6550	,,	,,	10/10/18.
BRAK, J.	,,	7337	,,	,,	11/10/18
BARENDS, A.	,,	6537	,,	,,	13/10/18.
BUYS, P.	,,	3271	,,	,,	14/10/18.
BURGERS, A.	,,	6166	,,	,,	16/10/18.
BRANDT, F.	,,	5510	,,	,,	7/10/18.
BARNES, J.	,,	6882	,,	,,	8/10/18.
BAAS, M.	,,	6135	,,	,,	8/10/18.
BOHN, G.	,,	5656	,,	,,	10/10/18.
BOSCH, M.	,,	6177	,,	,,	10/10/18.
BAATJES, M.	,,	2644	,,	,,	21/10/18.
BALLIE, P.	,,	5560	,,	,,	21/10/18.
BECK, W	,,	5670	,,	,,	4/11/18.
BLOEMSTEIN, F.	,,	50	,,	,,	8/10/18
COETZEE, G.	,,	3306	,,	,,	8/10/18.
COETZEE, S.	,,	5362	,,	,,	8/10/18.
CLASSEN, C.	,,	2241	,,	,,	9/10/18.
COON, J	,,	6699	,,	,,	9/10/18.
CLOETE, A.	,,	6658	,,	,,	10/10/18.
CLARKE, J.	,,	5646	,,	,,	11/10/18.
CLOETE, J.	,,	604	,,	,,	10/10/18.
CARELSE, A.	,,	3839	Malaria.	,,	30/12/17.
DAVIES, B.	,,	4304	Influenza.	,,	8/10/18.
DANIELS, E.	,,	2999	,,	,,	11/10/18.
DANIELS, J.	,,	3518	,,	,,	13/10/18.
DE MUNK, M.	,,	6036	,,	,,	14/10/18.
DU PREEZ, G.	,,	930	,,	,,	14/10/18.
DYERS, J.	,,	5480	,,	,,	9/10/18.
DE VOS, J.	,,	6088	,,	,,	21/10/18.
DAWSON, T.	,,	3410	Malaria.	,,	8/1/18.
ERASMUS, C.	,,	5621	Influenza.	,,	9/10/18.
EDWARDS, J.	,,	6464	,,	,,	10/10/18
ESTERHUIZEN, J.	,,	6700	,,	,,	10/10/18.
EACHILL, J.	,,	6171	,,	,,	7/10/18.
FESTEES, A.	,,	6747	,,	,,	9/10/18.
FILLIES, J.	,,	2606	,,	,,	10/10/18.
FELIX, D.	,,	1603	,,	,,	12/10/18.
FRANKA, F.	,,	6416	,,	,,	13/10/18.
FRISKIN, C.	,,	698	,,	,,	14/10/18.
FORTUIN, W.	,,	1867	,,	,,	19/10/18.
FORTUIN, F.	,,	3612	,,	,,	8/10/18.

THE STORY OF THE 1st CAPE CORPS.

IN THE UNION OF SOUTH AFRICA (Continued):

Died of Disease.

Name.	Rank.	Reg. No.	Disease.	Place.	Date.
FARO, P.	Pte.	78	Influenza.	Kimberley.	8/10/18.
FORTUIN, J.	,,	1389	,,	,,	9/10/18.
GROENEWALD, B.	,,	6850	,,	,,	8/10/18.
GOLIATH, P.	,,	6184	,,	,,	11/10/18.
GEDDES, J.	,,	5487	,,	,,	9/10/18.
GREEN, J.	,,	3423	,,	,,	7/10/18
HARTZENBERG, J.	,,	5483	,,	,,	10/10/18.
HOOPIE, J.	,,	5623	,,	,,	12/10/18.
HENDERSON, B.	,,	6750	,,	,,	12/10/18.
HUMPHRIES, T.	,,	5438	,,	,,	14/10/18.
HARTOG, J.	,,	7045	,,	,,	7/10/18.
HARVEY, T.	,,	1567	,,	,,	6/10/18
HENDRICKS, J.	,,	3350	Mal., pleur. & pneu.	,,	28/2/18.
HAILS, W.	,,	3302	Mal. & Heart failure.	,,	19/1/18.
JOB, M.	,,	5435	Influenza.	,,	8/10/18.
JULIES, E.	,,	5379	,,	,,	9/10/18
JANSEN, M. J.	,,	7191	,,	,,	9/10/18.
JARDIEN, H.	,,	6752	,,	,,	10/10/18.
JOHNSON, A.	,,	2278	,,	,,	11/10/18.
JACOBS, E.	,,	7129	,,	,,	12/10/18.
JULIUS, L. T.	,,	5380	,,	,,	13/10/18.
JOHANNES, T.	,,	7195	,,	,,	13/10/18.
JOHNSON, L.	,,	1156	,,	,,	14/10/18.
JACOBS, B.	,,	6539	,,	,,	16/10/18.
JOHANNES, E.	,,	7004	,,	,,	16/10/18.
JOHNSON, I.	,,	4867	,,	,,	18/10/18.
JACOBS, D.	,,	7314	,,	,,	20/10/18.
JOHNSON, J.	,,	3347	,,	,,	6/10/18.
JOHNSON, J.	,,	6581	,,	,,	10/10/18.
JACOBS, J.	,,	7386	,,	,,	10/10/18.
JAFTHA, H.	,,	6657	,,	,,	16/10/18.
JORDAN, S.	,,	6204	,,	,,	17/10/18.
KLASSEN, G.	,,	6032	,,	,,	6/10/18.
KYZER, C. R.	Sgt.	256	,,	,,	10/10/18.
KLEIN, P.	Pte.	68	,,	,,	10/10/18.
KAYZER, D.	,,	7354	,,	,,	18/10/18.
KOLBE, J.	,,	1105	,,	,,	3/10/18.
KOOPMAN, F.	,,	6768	,,	,,	7/10/18.
LAMONT, H. L. R.	,,	397	,,	,,	6/10/18.
LEWIN, L. P.	,,	3766	,,	,,	6/10/18.
LANDSMAN, F.	,,	1132	Malaria & blackwater.	,,	19/2/18.
LEWIS, C.	,,	994	Cereb'l embol. & mal.	,,	7/5/18.
LE ROUX, H.	,,	3923	Malaria.	,,	4/4/18.
MATHEWS, T.	,,	6992	Influenza.	,,	8/10/18.
MOSS, J.	,,	7121	,,	,,	9/10/18.
MICHAELS, F.	,,	7311	,,	,,	9/10/18.
MANUEL, J.	,,	1927	,,	,,	11/10/18.
MARTIN, D.	,,	4633	,,	,,	11/10/18.
MORRIS, J. R.	,,	3519	,,	,,	13/10/18.
MULLER, J.	,,	7391	,,	,,	13/10/18.
MANUEL, J.	,,	6617	,,	,,	14/10/18.
MONDZINGER, A.	,,	5640	,,	,,	14/10/18.
MATHIE, P.	,,	4972	,,	,,	19/10/18.
MULLER, J.	,,	5667	,,	,,	10/10/18.
MOLOKWELE, K.	,,	5455	,,	,,	9/10/18.
MILLER, J.	,,	6004	,,	,,	9/10/18.
MEYER, J.	,,	6907	,,	,,	11/10/18.
MAART, A.	,,	6034	,,	,,	23/10/18.
MANLEY, W.	,,	5505	,,	,,	7/10/18.
MIKKELSON, F.	,,	6385	,,	,,	10/10/18.
NIEMOND, J.	,,	5507	,,	,,	9/10/18.
NYHOFF, J.	,,	7123	,,	,,	6/10/18.
NURSE, J.	,,	6759	,,	,,	10/10/18.
OATS, F.	,,	5436	,,	,,	

THE STORY OF THE 1st CAPE CORPS.

IN THE UNION OF SOUTH AFRICA (Continued):
Died of Disease.

Name.	Rank.	Reg. No.	Disease.	Place.	Date.
OCTOBER, M.	Pte.	7142	Influenza.	Kimberley.	11/10/18.
OLIVER, J.	,,	3077	Tuberculosis.	,,	26/5/18.
PLAATJES, A.	,,	6526	Influenza.	,,	9/10/18.
PETERSEN, F.	,,	6154	,,	,,	11/10/18.
PETERSEN, A.	,,	6529	,,	,,	14/10/18.
PETERSEN, J. N.	,,	6423	,,	,,	13/10/18.
POGGENPOEL, S.	,,	1761	Malaria.	,,	23/3/18.
REYNARD, W.	,,	7063	Influenza.	,,	7/10/18.
RUDOLPH, M.	,,	5614	,,	,,	11/10/18.
ROBERTSON, J.	,,	7105	,,	,,	11/10/18.
ROUTENBACH, A.	,,	5460	,,	,,	15/10/18.
SWARTZ, G.	,,	3193	,,	,,	9/10/18.
SIMON, J.	,,	3236	,,	,,	10/10/18.
SCHOLTZ, C.	,,	5636	,,	,,	10/10/18.
SMITH, P.	,,	845	,,	,,	11/10/18.
SAULS, P.	,,	2103	,,	,,	11/10/18.
SAMUELS, D.	,,	6015	,,	,,	12/10/18.
STEER, W.	,,	6343	,,	,,	16/10/18.
SAMPSON, W.	,,	7077	,,	,,	9/10/18.
SOULS, G.	,,	7291	,,	,,	11/10/18.
SMITH, S.	,,	5616	,,	,,	12/10/18.
STEPHEN, J.	,,	7245	,,	,,	15/10/18.
SCHOLTZ, S. J.	,,	7115	,,	,,	15/10/18.
SMITH, F.	,,	4807	,,	,,	10/10/18.
STOFFBERG, I. A.	,,	2341	,,	,,	7/10/18.
TITUS, P	,,	621	,,	,,	8/10/18.
TALEB, A.	,,	6506	,,	,,	8/10/18.
TROMPETER, S.	,,	4986	,,	,,	8/10/18.
VAN WYK, J.	,,	5245	,,	,,	8/10/18.
VALENTINE, A.	,,	6533	,,	,,	10/10/18.
VAN GRAAN, J.	,,	6935	,,	,,	11/10/18.
VAN HEERDEN, N.	,,	2947	,,	,,	11/10/18.
VILJOEN, D.	,,	6967	,,	,,	12/10/18.
VAN DER ROSS, J.	,,	6070	,,	,,	18/10/18.
VLOTMAN, D.	,,	5428	,,	,,	22/10/18.
VAN REENEN, A.	,,	6357	Malaria.	,,	5/8/18.
WILLIAMS, P.	,,	7306	Influenza.	,,	12/10/18.
WILSON, A.	,,	251	,,	,,	12/10/18.
WINDVOGEL, F.	,,	6783	,,	,,	12/10/18.
WILLIAMS, J.	,,	6731	,,	,,	14/10/18.
WILLIAMS, J.	,,	7193	,,	,,	15/10/18.
WITTEN, W.	,,	3252	,,	,,	18/10/18.
WILSON, D.	,,	7242	,,	,,	8/10/18.
WILLIAMS, D.	,,	5638	,,	,,	8/10/18.
WENTZEL, J.	,,	7417	,,	,,	11/10/18.
WOODMAL, W.	,,	7074	,,	,,	29/10/18.
WESTHUISEN, v.d. H.	,,	7454	,,	,,	29/10/18.
ABRAHAMS, W.	,,	1576	Malaria.	Maitland.	27/3/17.
APPIE, J.	,,	6459	,,	Port Elizabeth	22/10/18.
BARENDS, L.	,,	7458	Influenza.	Wellington.	16/10/18.
BASSON, A.	,,	2208	Accident.	Kalabaskraal.	3/2/17.
BEERWINKEL, S.	,,	1245	Cerebral malaria.	Maitland	4/9/17.
BOWERS, H.	,,	1261	Phthisis.	,,	22/7/16.
BARNES, J.	,,	4587	Tuberculosis.	,,	2/8/19.
CHRISTIAN, J.	,,	3493	Phthisis.	,,	30/11/17.
DERT, E. H.	,,	1609	Cerebral malaria.	Cape Town.	12/3/17.
DANIELS, P. W.	,,	1977	Malaria.	Maitland	13/5/17.
DIXON, J.	,,	1992	,,	,,	18/7/17.
DU PLESSIS, N.	,,	6486	Pneumonia.	Genadendal.	6/10/18.
DE VRIES, A.	Sgt.	7	Accidentally shot.	Simonstown.	22/12/15.
DE VILLIERS, I. J.	,,	809	Empeyema & exh'st.	Durban	2/12/16.
FEBRUARY, A.	,,	500	Mitral stenosis.	Maitland	28/4/17.
FOURIE, A.	Pte.	7384	Malaria.	,,	2/11/18.
FREDERICKS, R. G.	a/C.Q.M.S.	1241	Blackwater.	Durban.	31/12/17.

THE STORY OF THE 1st CAPE CORPS.

IN THE UNION OF SOUTH AFRICA (Continued):

Died of Disease.

Name.	Rank.	Reg. No.	Disease.	Place.	Date.
JOSEPHS, J.	Pte.	179	Appendicitis.	Stellenbosch.	4/9/17
KING, J.	,,	2575	Blackwater.	Durban	16/1/18.
LEE, M.	,,	6093	Broncho pneumonia.	Cape Town	29/5/17.
LOTTERING, G.	,,	2282	Mitral regurgitation.	,,	1/5/17.
LANGEVELDT, C.	,,	2940	Dysentery.	,,	6/3/17.
LIEDEMAN, J.	,,	2665	Found dead on line.	Woltemade.	21/7/17.
MUNNICK, D.	,,	1904	Acute enteritis.	Cape Town.	15/1/18.
MARTIN, J.	,,	3073	Malaria & blackwater.	Potchefstroom.	15/1/18.
MORRIS, J.	,,	927	Malaria.	Maitland	8/6/16.
MENTOR, C.	,,	6046	Cerebral malaria.	Durban	30/7/18.
NICHOLLS, P.	,,	1692	Influenza.	Cape Town	11/10/18.
PLAATJES, A.	,,	6536	,,	Bredasdorp.	1/11/18.
PETERSEN, A. E.	,,	2526	Pneumonia.	Maitland	25/7/17.
PETERSEN, A. C.	,,	42	Celebral malaria.	,,	10/11/17.
PETERSEN, A.	,,	3217	Malaria.	Durban	10/2/18.
RUITERS, W.	,,	2589	Dysentery.	Cape Town	8/6/17.
SCHULLER, J.	,,	1796	Acute enteritis.	,,	16/6/17.
SCHRIKKER, G.	,,	6260	Influenza.	,,	10/10/18.
STEMMET, B.	,,	2323	Enteric fever.	Durban	27/3/18.
STEENEKAMP, S.	,,	3283	Malaria.	,,	15/12/17.
THEUNNISSEN, J.	,,	1854	Malaria.	Maitland.	19/6/17.
VYFER, P.	,,	925	Pulmonary phthisis.	Wynberg.	21/5/16.
VAN DER MULLEN, J.	,,	1449	Dysentery.	Maitland	18/7/17.
VAN DER SCHYFF, C.	,,	2450	Pneumonia.	,,	7/10/17.
WHITE, W.	,,	1617	Nephritis.	,,	11/7/17.
WILLIAMS, J.	,,	2234	Appendicitis.	,,	12/9/16.
WANZA, A.	,,	488	Mitral regurgitation.	Cape Town	10/6/17.

"They recked not of their promise lost,
They did not grudge the price.
More splendid beacons loomed for them:
Duty and Sacrifice."

W. A. Way.

IN EAST AFRICA:

WOUNDED.
OFFICERS.

HOY, C. N., D.S.O. and Bar	Major.	At Mahiwa (Lindi Area).	8/11/17.
BRADSTOCK, F. E., D.S.O., M.C. and Bar	Captain.	At Kibongo, Rufiji River.	20/1/17.
MICHAU, J. M.	Captain.	At Mahiwa (Lindi Area).	6/11/17.
McNEIL, R. P., M.C.	Captain.	,, ,,	,,
ASHLEY, S.	Lieut.	At Kibongo, Rufiji River.	20/1/17.
BOTHA, D. F.	,,	At Mahiwa (Lindi Area).	6/11/17.
COLSON, R.	,,	,, ,,	,,
GIRDWOOD, F. I.	,,	,, ,,	,,
SAMUELSON, S. V., M.C.	,,	,, ,,	,,
WIGMAN, W. T.	,,	,, ,,	8/11/17.
BARNARD, G. R.	,,	,, ,,	,,
ROSE-NEL, E.	,,		
GIRDWOOD, F. I.	,,	Makonde Plateau (Lindi Area)	16/11/17.

THE STORY OF THE 1st CAPE CORPS.

IN PALESTINE:

MORRIS, G. A., C.M.G., D.S.O.	Lieut.-Col.	At Kh. Jibeit, near Jerusalem, Palestine.	20/9/18.
RACKSTRAW, E. J., M.C.	Lieut.	,,	,,
CLOKE, R. A.	,,	,,	,,
BLOXAM, E. B.	,,	,,	,,
STUBBS, E. P., M.C.	,,	,,	,,
ROSS, A. S.	,,	,,	,,

IN EAST AFRICA:

Wounded.
OTHER RANKS.

Name.	Rank.	Regt. No.	Place.	Date.
ADAMS, A. M.	Sgt.	48	Hatia.	10/11/17.
APLOON, T.	Pte.	849	Mahiwa.	6/11/17.
ADAMS, S.	,,	2020	Duthumi.	10/2/17.
ABRAHAMS, M.	Sgt.	318	Kwahongo.	26/12/16.
AFRICA, A.	Pte.	353	near Mgere.	29/8/17.
ADRIAANSE, D	,,	1412	Mahiwa.	6/11/17.
ABLES, G.	,,	338	,,	,,
ABRAHAMS, J.	,,	1097	,,	,,
ALIES, J.	Sgt.	825	,,	,,
ADAMS, C.	Pte.,	1257	,,	,,
APPOLLIS, F.	,,	1769	,,	,,
ADAMS, P.	,,	2596	,,	,,
ADONIS, M.	,,	2855	Makonde Plateau	16/11/17.
ABRAHAMS, J.	,,	899	,, ,,	,,
BRINKHUIS, J.	,,	818	Mahiwa.	6/11/17.
BAATJES, M.	,,	347	,,	,,
BARRY, A.	,,	590	,,	,,
BENTING, J.	,,	573	,,	,,
BOTMAN, J.	,,	3056	Hatia.	9/11/17.
CORNEILIUS, A.	,,	80	Duthumi.	30/12/16.
CREWE, J.	,,	2884	Nyakisiku.	19/1/17.
CARELSON, J.	,,	2307	Mahiwa.	8/11/17.
CUPIDO, D.	,,	1401	Makonde Plateau	16/11/17.
CONRADIE, J.	,,	3058	,, ,,	,,
CARELSE, A.	,,	3839	,, ,,	15/11/17.
CARELSE, C.	,,	688	,, ,,	17/11/17.
DANIELS, P. A.	C.S.M.	1	Mahiwa.	6/11/17.
DAMPIES, P.	Pte.	1636	Hatia.	10/11/17.
DREYER, P.	Cpl.	312	Mahiwa.	6/11/17.
DIKKOP, S.	Pte.	3255	,,	,,
DANIELS, L.	L.-Cpl.	2274	,,	,,
DEVEREUX, H.	Pte.	949	,,	8/11/17.
DU PLESSIS, O.	,,	3505	Hatia.	9/11/17.
DIEDRICKS, J.	,,	996	Makonde Plateau.	16/11/17.
DANIELS, J.	,,	2604	,, ,,	17/11/17.
EVERTS, E.	,,	999	,, ,,	15/11/17.
ESAU, C.	,,	2551	Mahiwa.	6/11/17.
FORTUIN, G.	,,	1724	near Mgere.	29/8/17.
FRENCHMAN, J.	,,	968	Mahiwa.	6/11/17.
FORTUIN, F.	,,	3612	Makonde Plateau	16/11/17.
FISHER, D.	Cpl.	765	,, ,,	17/11/17.
GREEN, J.	Pte.	3423	Hatia.	10/11/17.
GROVELL, G.	,,	3710	Makonde Plateau	16/11/17.
HENDRICKS, N.	,,	1460	Nyakisiku.	19/1/17.
HAROLD, J.	,,	917	Mahiwa.	6/11/17.
HOPS, J.	,,	3557	,,	6/11/17.
HAUPT, C.	L.-Cpl.	273	,,	6/11/17.
HECTOR, D.	Sgt.	977	,,	8/11/17.
HANSEN, D.	Pte	3504	,,	,,
HEUVEL, H.	L.-Cpl.	674	Hatia.	9/11/17.
JACOBS, J.	Pte.	233	,,	10/11/17.

THE STORY OF THE 1st CAPE CORPS.

IN EAST AFRICA (Continued):

Wounded.

Name.	Rank.	Regt. No.	Place.	Date.
JAFTHA, J.	Pte.	1312	Njangalo.	21/9/17.
JACOBS, A.	,,	2143	Mkindu.	20/1/17.
JOHNSTON, L.	,,	1156	Mahiwa.	6/11/17.
JACOBS, P.	,,	374	Makonde Plateau.	16/11/17.
JANAKER, A.	,,	3814	,, ,,	17/11/17.
KLINK, G.	,,	3431	Njangalo.	21/9/17.
LANGEVELDT, A.	,,	2250	Nyakisiku.	26/2/17.
LANGEVELDT, J.	,,	1279	Mkindu.	20/1/17.
LIEDEMAN, J.	,,	3541	Mahiwa.	6/11/17.
LAKEY, J.	,,	3246	,,	,,
LE ROUX, M.	,,	161	,,	,,
LE ROUX, P.	Cpl.	340	,,	8/11/17.
LANGEVELDT, J.	Pte.	2960	,,	,,
MINAAR, L.	Pte.	302	Mahiwa.	6/11/17.
MALEVELD, J.	,,	3688	Makonde Plateau.	16/11/17.
MATAWANA, P.	,,	400	,, ,,	17/11/17.
NORMAN, D.	,,	855	,, ,,	16/11/17.
OCTOBER, J.	Cpl.	909	Mahiwa.	6/11/17.
PETERS, S.	Pte.	1821	Luita Berg.	9/10/17.
PETERS, T.	,,	3424	Njangalo.	21/9/17.
PETERSEN, C.	Cpl.	1129	Duthumi.	30/12/16.
PHILANDER, A.	Pte.	2593	Mkindu.	20/1/17.
PETERSEN, C.	,,	2388	,,	,,
POOLE, D.	,,	2375	,,	,,
PLAATJES, J.	,,	989	near Mgere.	29/8/17.
PAULSEN, J. C. M.	Sgt.	432	Mahiwa.	6/11/17.
PAULSEN, A.	,,	820	Mkindu (Rufiji River)	20/1/17.
PETERSEN, J.	Pte.	893	Mahiwa.	6/11/17.
PHILANDER, J.	,,	3012	Hatia.	10/11/17.
PATMORE, W.	,,	736	Makonde Plateau.	16/11/17.
ROOKS, E.	,,	3474	Hatia.	10/11/17.
RUITERS, A.	,,	2102	Mahiwa.	6/11/17.
ROSS, E.	,,	1836	Makonde Plateau.	16/11/17.
RENTZ, A.	,,	3642	Mahiwa.	6/11/17.
SMITH, C. J.	Sgt.	3160	Sogosso Hill	29/8/17.
SEPTEMBER, J.	Pte.	1612	Nyakisiku.	19/1/17.
STEENEKAMP, S.	,,	3283	Mahiwa.	6/11/17.
SOLOMON, J.	,,	1929	,,	,,
SIMON, J.	,,	3236	,,	,,
SMITH, A.	Sgt.	303	,,	,,
SAMPSON, J.	Pte.	3723	,,	,,
SMITH, J.	,,	1152	Makonde Plateau.	16/11/17.
SKIPPERS, W.	,,	706	,, ,,	,,
SIMONS, D.	,,	2735	,, ,,	,,
SCHOOR, P.	Sgt.	480	,, ,,	17/11/17.
SWARTBOOI, A.	Pte.	402	,, ,,	,,
SKIPPERS, J.	,,	3360	,, ,,	,,
TEE, A.	,,	3436	Mahiwa	6/11/17.
THOMPSON, S.	,,	3647	,,	,,
VAN HEERDEN, W.	,,	2947	Mahiwa.	6/11/17.
VAN SITTERS, C.	,,	3457	,,	,,
VAN WYK, R.	,,	942	,,	,,
VAN ROMBERG, J.	,,	2731	Makondo Plateau.	16/11/17.
WILLIAMS, J.	,,	684	Mahiwa.	6/11/17.
WITBOOI, J.	,,	2503	Makondo Plateau.	16/11/17.
WILLIAMS, J.	Cpl.	597	Mahiwa.	6/11/17.

IN PALESTINE:

ABRAHAMS, D	Pte.	4663	Kh. Jibeit, near Jerusalem, Palestine.	20/9/18
ADAMS, A.	,,	4257	,,	,,
ADAMS, J.	,,	3150	,,	,,
ADAMS, W.	,,	1906	,,	,,

THE STORY OF THE 1st CAPE CORPS.

IN PALESTINE (Continued):

Wounded.

Name.	Rank.	Regt. No.	Place.	Date.
ADAMS, Z.	Pte.	3845	Kh. Jibeit, near Jerusalem, Palestine.	20/9/18.
ARENDS, D.	,,	544	,,	,,
ARENDSE, A.	,,	1517	,,	,,
AMOES, J.	,,	2550	,,	,,
APPOLLIS, H.	,,	830	,,	,,
BARRON, D.	,,	2021	,,	,,
BREDENKAMP, J.	Cpl.	979	,,	,,
BETHANIE, C.	Pte.	3778	,,	,,
BRUCE, J.	,,	2820	,,	,,
CAMPBELL, J.	,,	1422	,,	,,
CARELSE, A.	,,	4344	,,	,,
DAMONDS, G.	,,	3397	,,	,,
DAVIDS, M.	,,	3823	,,	,,
DE KLERK, A.	,,	1691	,,	,,
DIPPENAAR, K.	,,	3946	,,	,,
DANIELS, M.	,,	813	,,	,,
DEERS, A.	,,	3189	,,	,,
DE KOCK, J.	,,	3452	,,	,,
DEERLING, D.	,,	1463	,,	,,
ENGEL, T.	,,	1510	,,	,,
FITZ, J.	Pte.	3154	,,	,,
FORTUIN, A.	,,	660	,,	,,
FORBES, D.	,,	2689	,,	,,
FREDERICKS, J.	,,	4179	,,	,,
GOBEY, S.	,,	1479	Square Hill, Palestine.	18/9/18.
HENDRICKS, F.	,,	1995	Kh. Jibeit, near Jerusalem, Palestine	20/9/18.
HUTCHINSON, K.	C.S.M.	310	,,	,,
HARRIS, A.	Pte.	770	,,	,,
HEYNECKE, S.	,,	2362	,,	,,
HAHMAN, D.	,,	2363	Square Hill, Palestine.	19/9/18.
JACK, M.	,,	2548	Kh. Jibeit, near Jerusalem, Palestine.	20/9/18.
JEPTHA, J.	,,	524	,,	,,
JUTA, J.	,,	4609	,,	,,
JALES, H.	,,	4112	,,	,,
JIMSON, J.	,,	1738	,,	,,
JACOBS, J.	,,	1587	,,	,,
KIEWITZ, S.	,,	431	,,	,,
LANGEVELDT, A.	,,	2250	,,	,,
LANGEVELDT, A.	,,	3552	,,	,,
LIEBRANDT, C.	,,	3586	,,	,,
LEWIN, L.	,,	1001	,,	,,
LOUW, F.	,,	4124	,,	,,
MAART, H.	,,	3208	,,	,,
MAJOR, A.	,,	3355	,,	,,
MALONEY, A.	,,	481	,,	,,
MARINUS, C.	,,	462	,,	,,
MILANZA, D.	,,	4158	,,	,,
MALGAS, A.	,,	3303	,,	,,
MANHO, A.	,,	452	,,	,,
MATOBOS, P.	,,	4607	,,	,,
MUNNIK, H.	,,	352	,,	,,
NEFDT, J.	Cpl.	1058	,,	,,
PEDRO, J.	Pte.	2409	,,	,,
PETERSEN, P.	,,	1645	,,	,,
PHILANDER, W.	,,	326	,,	,,
PRETORIUS, G.	,,	3799	,,	,,
PEARCE, D.	,,	2963	,,	,,
PHILANDER, W.	,,	3012	,,	,,
PHILLIPS, R.	,,	198	,,	,,
RAUBENHEIMER, W.	Sgt.	2699	,,	,,
RETIEF, P.	Pte.	3253	,,	,,
RUITERS, J.	Cpl.	269	,,	,,

THE STORY OF THE 1st CAPE CORPS.

IN PALESTINE (Continued):

Wounded.

Name.	Rank.	Regt. No.	Place.	Date.
RABBE, J.	Pte.	3451	Kh Jibeit, near Jerusalem, Palestine.	
RENTZ, F.	,,	2289	,,	20/9/18.
ROBERTS, W.	,,	4472	,,	,,
RICHARDSON, R.	,,	3333	,,	,,
SAMUELS, J.	,,	2622	,,	,,
SAWYER, J.	,,	3225	,,	,,
SCHOOR, P. D.	Sgt.	480	,,	,,
SKEDOW, D.	Pte.	2733	,,	,,
STEGLING, P.	,,	3876	,,	,,
SAMPSON, P.	,,	4268	,,	,,
SCHEEPERS, G.	,,	2373	,,	,,
SCHOLTZ, P.	,,	2325	,,	,,
SKIPPERS, J.	,,	3769	,,	,,
SKIPPERS, J.	,,	496	,,	,,
SAMUELS, J.	,,	1616	,,	,,
THOMAS, A.	,,	1225	,,	,,
THOMAS, M.	Sgt.	366	,,	,,
THOMAS, T.	Pte.	822	,,	,,
TROMPETTER, W.	,,	4386	,,	,,
THEUNNISSEN, E.	,,	391	,,	,,
UITHALDER, B.	,,	1044	,,	,,
VISAGIE, F.	,,	4639	,,	,,
VAN DER HORST, A.	,,	2930	,,	,,
VAN DER WESTHUIZEN, T.	,,	2379	,,	,,
WILLIAMS, A.	,,	3515	,,	,,
WILLIAMS, J.	,,	3873	,,	,,
WILLIAMS, M.	,,	3335	,,	,,
WILLIAMS, W.	,,	597	,,	,,
WALLIE, G.	,,	1223	,,	,,
WILLIAMS, J.	,,	3770	,,	,,
YON, J. H.	Sgt.	1472	,,	

NEAR JAFFA GATE, JERUSALEM, SHEWING TOWER AND CLOCK PRESENTED BY THE KAISER.

MOSQUE OF OMAR AT JERUSALEM.

THE HONOURS LIST.

THE FOLLOWING OFFICERS APPEARED IN THE HONOURS LISTS WHILST SERVING WITH THE 1st CAPE CORPS, VIZ. :—

MORRIS, G. A., Lieut.-Colonel, C.M.G., D.S.O., East Africa, 1917.
HOY, C. N., Major, D.S.O. and Bar to D.S.O., East Africa, 1917.
COWELL, W. R., Major, D.S.O., East Africa, 1917.
BRADSTOCK, F. E., Captain, M.C., East Africa, 1917.
TANDY, J. H., Captain, M.C., East Africa, 1917.
HARRIS, J. V., Captain, M.C., East Africa, 1917.
HEATON, W. S., Lieutenant, M.C. (prompt award), East Africa, 1917.
STUBBS, E. P., Lieutenant, M.C., East Africa, 1917.
SAMUELSON, S. V., Lieutenant, M.C. (prompt award), East Africa, 1917.
RACKSTRAW, E. J., Lieutenant, M.C., Palestine, 1918.
MCNEIL, R. P., Captain, M.C. (Medical Officer), East Africa, 1917.

The following appeared in the Honours Lists prior to joining the Battalion:

ARNOTT, J., Captain, D.C.M., Anglo-Boer War. (Then Sgt. in Queenstown Rifle Volunteers).
WOODS, G. A., Lieutenant, M.C., East Africa, 1917. (Whilst serving with 7th S.A. Infantry).
WALLIS, H., Lieutenant, M.C., East Africa, 1917. (Then Captain in 8th S.A. Infantry).

The following appeared in the Honours Lists after release from service with the Battalion :—

DURHAM, C. G., Major, D.S.O. (prompt award) 19/7/18. Whilst serving with 1st/3rd King's African Rifles in East Africa.
BRADSTOCK, F. E., Major, Bar to M.C. June 1918, D.S.O. December 1918. Whilst serving with 2nd King's African Rifles in East Africa.

The following were awarded Decorations by our Allies whilst serving with the Battalion :—

ROBINSON, J. E., Captain, Order of Crown of Italy (Silver Medal). Whilst serving in East Africa, 1916/17.
TANDY, J. H., Captain, Croix de Chevalier de l'Ordre de la Couronne and Diploma (Belgian). Whilst serving in East Africa, 1916/17.

MENTIONED IN DESPATCHES.

The following Officers, 1st Battalion Cape Corps, were Mentioned in Despatches whilst serving with the Battalion :—

MORRIS, G. A., Lieut.-Colonel (Mentioned four times), East Africa and Palestine.
HOY, C. N., Major (Mentioned twice), East Africa and Palestine.
BRADSTOCK, F. E., Major (Mentioned twice), East Africa.
DIFFORD, I. D., Captain, East Africa.

MICHAU, J. M., Captain (Mentioned twice), East Africa and Palestine.
BURGER, F., Captain, Palestine.
TANDY, J. H., Captain, East Africa.
HARRIS, J. V., Captain, East Africa.
EDWARDS, H., Captain, East Africa.
ROBERTSON, D. W., Captain, Palestine.
WIGMAN, W. T., Lieutenant, East Africa.
LESLIE, A., Captain, Palestine.
BAIN, T., Lieutenant, East Africa.
CLOKE, R. A., Lieutenant, Palestine.

The following Officers were Mentioned in Despatches prior to joining the Battalion:—

MORRIS, G. A., Lieut.-Colonel, then Major, whilst serving with 2nd M.R. (Natal Carbineers) in G.S.W.A., 1914/15.
DURHAM, C. G., Major, then Captain, whilst serving with R.L.I. in G.S.W.A., in 1915.
WALLIS, H., then Captain, whilst serving with 8th S.A.I. in East Africa, in 1917.
MOIN, B. H., then Lieut. and Machine Gun Officer, whilst serving with 10th S.A.I. at Rast-Haus (Himo River) East Africa, 10th March, 1916.
ROSS, A. S., then Lieut. (acting Captain), whilst serving with 10th S.A.H. in East Africa, 1917.
BOUWER, J. W., Captain S.A.M.C., whilst serving with General Northey's Force in Central Africa, 1916/17.
BAGSHAWE, F. J., Captain, during Anglo-Boer War, and also whilst serving with 6th Regiment in G.S.W.A., 1914/15.
JOHNSON, L. C., Lieutenant, whilst serving as Records and Attesting Officer (for Coloured Units) (U.D.F.) in 1916/18.

The following Officers were Mentioned in Despatches after release from service with the Battalion:—

DURHAM, C. G., D.S.O., Major (acting Lieut.-Colonel), whilst serving in Portuguese East Africa, October (about), 1918.
BRADSTOCK, F. E., Major, D.S.O., M.C., whilst Second in Command of 2nd K.A.R. in East Africa in February, 1918.
BELL, HARLAND, S., Lieutenant, whilst serving with Political Department in East Africa in 1917, rank Major.

OTHER RANKS 1ST CAPE CORPS

who, whilst on Active Service in the field, won the Distinguished Conduct Medal, Military Medal, or Decorations awarded by our Allies.

BETTS, F. W., R.S.M. (1049), D.C.M., East Africa.
BROWN, D. J., C.S.M. (9), D.C.M., East Africa.
CALVERT, C., C.S.M. (152), D.C.M., East Africa.
TWYNHAM, D., C.S.M. (1092), D.C.M., East Africa.
ABRAHAMS, H. W., Sergeant (278), D.C.M., East Africa.
SWARTZ, J., Sergeant (331), D.C.M., East Africa.
SCHOOR, P. D., Sergeant (480), D.C.M., East Africa.
ARENDSE, I. W., Sergeant (607), D.C.M., East Africa.
DUNN, S. W., Sergeant (1134), D.C.M., East Africa.
DAMON, H. P., Sergeant (1465), D.C.M., East Africa.
CARELSE, C., Corporal (688), D.C.M., East Africa.
HENDRICKS, A. J., C.S.M. (1067), D.C.M., Palestine.
HUTCHINSON, K., C.S.M. (310), D.C.M., Palestine.

FEBRUARY, M., Sergeant (92), D.C.M., Palestine.
JANSEN, D., Sergeant (1614), D.C.M., Palestine.
HUTCHINSON, W., L/Corporal (2796), D.C.M., Palestine.
CAIRNS, F. J. C., Staff-Sergeant (1144), M.M., East Africa.
ABRAHAMS, H. W., Sergeant (278), M.M., East Africa.
SCHROEDER, F., Corporal (980), M.M., East Africa (prompt award).
FREDERICKS, H. J., Corporal (829), M.M., East Africa (prompt award).
LE ROUX, M. C., L/Corporal (161), M.M., East Africa.
DEMOS, D., L/Corporal (220), M.M., East Africa.
LE BRUN, E., Private (1179), M.M., East Africa.
RUITERS, J., Corporal (269), M.M., Palestine.

DECORATIONS AWARDED BY OUR ALLIES.

MCLEOD, W. T., C.S.M. (111), Medaille Militaire (French). East Africa.
BERRY, J. G., Colour-Sergeant (1135), Order of Crown of Italy (Bronze Medal). East Africa.
HANMER, P., Sergeant (862), Order of Crown of Italy (Bronze Medal), E. Africa.
MANUEL, P., Corporal (71), Decoration Militaire (2nd Class Belgian). E. Africa.
BEUKES, E., L/Cpl. (100), Decoration Militaire (2nd Class Belgian). E. Africa.

OTHER RANKS 1ST CAPE CORPS

who were Mentioned in Despatches whilst on service with the Battalion :—

ADAMS, J., Private (1220), East Africa.
BAILEY, C., Private (1373), East Africa.
CALVERT, C., C.S.M. (152), East Africa.
CHARLES, G., L./Corporal (594), East Africa.
DAVIDS, J., C.Q.M.S. (97), twice mentioned, East Africa and Palestine.
DEMOS, D., Private (220), East Africa.
DRURY, F., Private (1272), East Africa.
FORTUIN, A., Private (592), East Africa.
GALLANT, F., Private (1731), East Africa.
HEEGER, P., C.Q.M.S. (21), East Africa.
HAROLD, J., Private (1917), East Africa.
HENDRICKS, A. J., C.Q.M.S. (1067), twice mentioned, East Africa and Palestine.
JOSEPH, C., Private (2133), East Africa.
LA VITA, W. H., C.Q.M.S. (1127), East Africa.
LE FLEUR, M., Sergeant (747), East Africa.
MC LEOD, W. T., C.S.M. (111), East Africa.
MATAWANA, P., Private (400), East Africa.
MARSH, A., Private (3140), East Africa.
PAULSEN, J. C. M., Sergeant (432), East Africa.
SYMES, H., Private (842), East Africa.
TWYNHAM, D., C.S.M. (1092), East Africa.
ALIES, J., Sergeant (825), East Africa.
BEUKES, E., L./Corporal (100), East Africa.
COETZEE, A., Sergeant (212), East Africa.
CAROLLISSEN, P., Sergeant (280), East Africa.
DE BRUYN, C., Private (108), East Africa.
FRENCHMAN, J., Private (908), East Africa.
FEBRUARY, M., Sergeant (92), East Africa.
HENDRICKS, P., Sergeant (223), East Afrcia.
RUITERS, C. A., C.S.M. (132), East Africa.
REAGON, A. J., C.Q.M.S. (1143), East Africa.
SAMUELS, W. S., Sergeant (504), East Africa.
SASSE, C. D., R.Q.M.S. (209), East Africa.
SCULLARD, J., A/C.S.M. (1363), Palestine.

COPIES OF LETTERS AND TELEGRAMS OF CONGRATULATION, ETC., RECEIVED BY THE OFFICER COMMANDING 1st BATTALION CAPE CORPS.

(1915-19.)

Copy of a letter, dated 16th June, 1916, from the late Hon. W. P. Schreiner, P.C., C.M.G., K.C., High Commissioner for the Union of South Africa in London, to an officer of the Battalion:—

MY DEAR................

Thank you for your long and interesting letter, dated 1st May, which reached me at the end of that month.

I am very pleased to have your graphic account of the training and experiences of your men. I fully expect to hear that they have rendered very effective and gallant service: for they will take full advantage of any opportunity they may receive to demonstrate that they are worthy of recognition as citizens ready to do their duty, whether in East Africa or elsewhere, in support of the cause and the flag. Mr. Nightingale read your letter with much interest, and unites with me in sending very kind regards. May you win through with honour and distinction in your arduous service.

Yours sincerely,

(Signed) W. P. SCHREINER.

Copy of Special Order by Brigadier-General W. F. S. Edwards, D.S.O., Inspector-General Communications, East Africa Force, dated New Moshi, 17/6/16:—

In bidding the Cape Corps farewell on transfer to the field formation the Inspector-General of Communications wishes to place on record his high appreciation of the invaluable services rendered by the Cape Corps on the Lines of Communication during the time the Regiment has been under his Command. He owes a special debt of gratitude to Lieut.-Colonel Morris, whose loyal support and unflagging zeal has assisted so materially in the overcoming of the many difficulties which are inseparable from a Campaign in a tropical country.

In wishing the Officers, Non-Commissioned Officers and men of the Cape Corps good-bye, the General Officer Commanding the Lines of Communication wishes one and all the best of good luck and success, while he is assured that the Regiment, whose doings he will always follow with the greatest interest, will at all times uphold the highest traditions of British Arms.

(Signed) J. S. MARSHALL, Major,
General Staff, Lines of Communication.

Extract from a speech of the Lord Bishop of Pretoria (the Right Reverend Michael B. Furse) on the 7th October, 1916:—

From all I heard and saw I formed a very good impression of the Cape Corps. They were as well disciplined and well set up a regiment as one could wish to see. To cover some hundred and fifty miles and come in singing at the end with heads high and swinging step and at full strength (less sixteen out of over a thousand) was no mean performance.

The pride of the officers in their men was good to see.

[NOTE.—When Bishop Furse made the above remarks he had just returned from a visit to the troops in East Africa.]

THE STORY OF THE 1st CAPE CORPS.

Extract from the *Cape Times*, dated 28th December, 1917:—

The following has been communicated to the Press by Defence Headquarters, Pretoria:—

The following telegram in connection with the return of the 1st Battalion Cape Corps from East Africa to the Union of South Africa has been received from the War Office:—

The experiment of forming a combatant force of the Coloured population of the Union of South Africa has been amply justified by the good opinion formed of the Cape Corps by the General Officer Commanding-in-Chief, East Africa, where this Unit has rendered constant and valuable service since taking the field early in 1916. The capacity of the officers and the zeal of the rank and file reflect the utmost credit on all concerned with the organisation and training of the Corps, and on the loyal population from which it was recruited.

It is the desire of the Army Council to afford the Cape Corps a further opportunity of service in another theatre, and the Union Government has been accordingly requested to re-organise the Corps with that object on its return from East Africa, after all ranks have had a period of rest and recuperation to which their services entitle them.

Copy of a telegram from Lieut.-General Sir J. L. Van Deventer, K.C.B., G.O.C. in East Africa, 1917/18, to the Minister of Defence, Union of South Africa, dated January, 1918:—

On the return of the South African Units at the conclusion of the Campaign in German East Africa I desire to express to you my appreciation of the services they have rendered. (References to different regiments follow) . . . . And the 1st Battalion Cape Corps has gained a high reputation for its good discipline, willingness, and good marching and fighting qualities.

Copy of a telegram from Major-General S. F. Mott, C.B., Commanding the 53rd Division, in Palestine, received by Brig.-General Commanding 160th Brigade, on 19th September, 1918:—

I congratulate you warmly on the complete success of your operations. Please convey my congratulations to all your Battalion Commanders on their very fine achievements.

Copy of a message received from Lieut.-General Sir Philip Chetwode, Bt., K.C.B., K.C.M.G., D.S.O., Commanding XXth Corps in Palestine, by Brig.-General Commanding 160th Brigade through G.O.C. 53rd Division, on September 21st, 1918:—

General Chetwode called on all ranks for a supreme effort and he cannot sufficiently admire the magnificent response by all ranks and departments.

Operations by the 53rd Division on the first night went almost without a hitch and their subsequent action was characterised by great gallantry and determination.

NOTE.—The 160th Brigade consisted of the 1/7th Battalion Royal Welsh Fusiliers, 1/17th Loyal (Indian) Infantry, 1/21st Punjabis, 1st Battalion Cape Corps, 160th Light Trench Mortar Battery.

Copy of a letter from Brig.-General J. W. Walker, Commanding the Royal Artillery of the 53rd Division in Palestine, to Brig.-General V. L. N. Pearson, Commanding 160th Infantry Brigade, dated 23/9/18:—

MY DEAR PEARSON,

Will you convey to all ranks under your command the congratulations of the Gunners of the 53rd Division to their comrades in the Infantry for the great gallantry and endurance displayed by them during the recent operations.

It gives the Gunners the greatest satisfaction to be able to support such magnificent Infantry.

Under your able leadership the 160th Infantry Brigade as at present formed has commenced to follow in the footsteps of the old 160th Brigade, which had such an excellent name for valour.

Regarding the Indian troops please inform them that the Gunners appreciate to the fullest extent that they are fighting behind men of excellent mettle and untiring zeal.

The gallantry displayed by the Cape Corps Battalion was of the highest order and beyond all praise.

Yours sincerely,
(Signed) JAMES W. WALKER,
Brig.-Gen. C.R.A. 53rd Division.

THE STORY OF THE 1st CAPE CORPS.

Copy of a Special Order issued by the G.O.C. 53rd Division in Palestine, 22nd September, 1918:—

I wish to congratulate all ranks of the 53rd Division on their share in the splendidly successful operations, just concluded, resulting in the destruction of the Turkish Army.

The capture of the Samieh Basin, which constituted such a formidable obstacle to our advance, fell chiefly to the lot of the 160th Infantry Brigade. By a brilliant night march across a ravine nearly 2,000 feet deep, it surprised, overwhelmed and captured the entire system of Turkish Defence on this flank.

On the left the 159th Infantry Brigade ably co-operated. Before dawn, thanks to bold leading, completely justified by results, Hindhead—the key to the whole Turkish position—was in our hands.

Then followed a pause in which we completed the first night's work and linked up our road system with that of the enemy. During this period, the 160th Infantry Brigade was called upon to withstand a determined counter attack by the enemy in an attempt to cover the retirement of his main body.

The main advance was carried out by the 158th Infantry Brigade, which, by a successful night march, cut the principal road by which the Turks could escape into the Jordan Valley, and the only one left for their heavy guns.

I am glad to be able again to congratulate my old friends the Welsh troops on their splendid performance throughout, which reflected the greatest credit on themselves and on the able Commanding Officers who led them.

It was the first time that I have commanded troops of the Indian Army, and I wish to express to them my admiration for the magnificent fighting and marching qualities they displayed, and my complete satisfaction with all that they have done.

To the 1st Battalion Cape Corps I make the same remarks. They have lived up to the fine reputation brought to Palestine from their African Campaigns.

As for the Artillery, perhaps the best way that I can express my thanks is to inform them that I have heard nothing but praise from their comrades, the Infantry, for the splendid support they gave.

To the R.E., Machine Gunners, and Cyclists, also to the Medical and Administrative Services I desire to express my thanks for the admirable work they have done.

(Signed) S. F. MOTT, Major-General,
Commanding 53rd (Welsh) Division.

Rham Alla, 22nd September, 1918.

Copy of telegram from the Mayor, Cape Town, to G.O.C. Egyptian Expeditionary Force, Palestine, on September 25th, 1918:—

On behalf of Cape Town desire express appreciation of special gallantry and push of Cape Corps capturing Square Hill reported in to-day's cables.

Copy of reply from General Allenby to the Mayor, Cape Town, dated 26th September, 1918:—

I have conveyed to Cape Corps your message of appreciation. They fought with the utmost bravery and rendered splendid service.

Copy of telegram from the Cape Corps Gifts and Comforts Committee to Lieut.-Colonel Morris, in Palestine, on the 27th September, 1918:—

Congratulate Regiment upon success achieved.

Extract from a telegram from Murray Bisset, Esq., K.C., M.L.A., Cape Town, to an Officer of the Battalion in Palestine on September 27th, 1918:—

Congratulations Corps Gallantry.

THE STORY OF THE 1st CAPE CORPS.

Copy of telegram from General Sir Edmund Henry Hynman Allenby, G.C.B., G.C.M.G., Commander-in-Chief in Egypt and Palestine, to the Corps Commanders, etc., of the Egyptian Expeditionary Force on the 26th September, 1918:—

I desire to convey to all ranks and all arms of the Force under my Command my admiration and thanks for their great deeds of the past week, and my appreciation of their gallantry and determination, which has resulted in the total destruction of the VIIth and VIIIth Turkish Armies.

Such a complete victory has seldom been known in all the history of war.

(Signed) E. H. H. ALLENBY, General,
Commander-in-Chief.

Copy of a telegram received by General Allenby from His Highness the Sultan of Egypt, published 28/9/18:—

I have heard with extreme pleasure the news of the brilliant success which has just been achieved by your troops, and which so happily coincides with the victory of the Allied Armies on the European fronts.

I sincerely congratulate you as well as officers and soldiers serving under your supreme Command, and wish you complete and definite success in your offensive for the triumph of Right and Liberty.

Copy of a letter received by Lieut.-Colonel Morris from Colonel W. E. M. Stanford, C.B., C.M.G., Honorary Colonel of the Battalion, on 10th December, 1918:—

Please accept for yourself and convey to your gallant officers and men my hearty congratulations on their splendid conduct in the fighting in Palestine. The Regiment may well be proud to have on its record this achievement in a land so full of great traditions and ancient glories.

Extract from a cable from Reuter's Agency in Palestine to South Africa describing the operations in Palestine, September 18/20, 1918:—

Supported by a Cape Coloured Regiment from South Africa who captured the first enemy gun on this sector and attacked with great gallantry and dash.

Extract from letter received by Lieut.-Colonel G. A. Morris, C.M.G., D.S.O., from Colonel W. E. M. Stanford, C.B., C.M.G., in 1918:—

Will you accept yourself and kindly convey to officers, non-commissioned officers, and men of the 1st Battalion Cape Corps my high appreciation of the honour conferred upon me in my appointment as Honorary Colonel of a Regiment which has gained so splendid a record in East Africa and Palestine. It is my hope that I shall be able personally to meet you all on your arrival in the Union for the purpose of demobilisation.

Copy of a letter from the G.O.C. Alexandria District to the G.O.C. 53rd Division in Egypt, 31st March, 1919:—

G.O.C. 53rd Division,

Will you please accept my best thanks for the great assistance you have given me during the present unrest by so readily supplying the necessary personnel to enable me to take the required steps to prevent any serious disturbances or riot in this district.

May I express my appreciation of the ready and cheerful manner in which all your officers and men responded to calls made on them.

(Signed) R. C. BOYLE, Brigadier-General,
G.O.C. Alexandria District

To Officers Commanding:
5/6th R.W. Fusiliers.
4/5th Welsh Regiment.
1st Battalion Cape Corps.
The attached letter is forwarded for information.

THE STORY OF THE 1st CAPE CORPS.

Copy of a letter, dated 28th April, 1919, from Lieut.-Colonel S. S. Taylor, C.M.G., D.S.O., Commanding S.A. Field Artillery in Palestine, to Major W. J. R. Cuningham, Commanding Reserve Half Battalion 1st Cape Corps:—

MY DEAR CUNINGHAM,

I must write you a line to thank you on behalf of my men and myself for the very warm hearted send off which your men gave us as we passed down the line to Suez. I cannot tell you how much we all appreciated it, and all the more so as we are returning before your men to South Africa. I should like you, if you think fit, to let your men know that we all admired the appearance of your people although, of course, a Corps which has earned such a high reputation as yours needs no praise from us.

Yours sincerely,
(Signed) S. S. TAYLOR.

Copy of a letter from Brig.-General A. H. O. Lloyd, Commanding Palestine Lines of Communication, to Major W. J. R. Cuningham, O.C. Reserve Half Battalion 1st Cape Corps, dated Ismailia, Egypt, 1st May, 1919:—

MY DEAR CUNINGHAM,

Had the Detachment of your Regiment concentrated for entrainment at Ismailia or Moascar rather than at Fayed I should of course have made a point of coming to the Station to say Good-bye to you all. As matters are, however, I have too much to do here to enable me even to fly down to you. To-morrow the L. of C. cease to exist and my official association with you ends. So all I can do is just to write you a line to wish you all good luck and a safe passage home. Your Regiment has made a great name in the Force as a splendid fighting Unit: I felt confident that such would be the case when I inspected the 1st Battalion at Kantara over a year ago.

My very best wishes to yourself and to every Officer and man who sails with you.

Yours sincerely,
(Signed) A. H. O. LLOYD, Brig.-General,
Commanding Palestine Lines of Communication.

Copy of telegram from H.E. the Governor-General (Viscount Buxton) to G.O.C. Egypt Force, dated 21/5/19:—

Your telegram 9th May, M.F.A. 37623 Cape Corps.

My ministry has made enquiries and have no reason to believe health of dependents is anything but good. Relatives and friends ceased writing in view of anticipated early return of Corps. Please advise whether letters can still be sent with prospect of delivery. Will be glad if you will communicate following message to Corps.
Begins:—

We have followed with lively interest the very creditable progress of your Battalion. I regret that your return to South Africa has been delayed temporarily. I learnt with great pleasure that you are doing excellent work in Egypt, and I feel sure that you have been glad to take the opportunity to add fresh distinction to your honourable record in the War. The people and the Government of the Union join me in sending you hearty good wishes.—BUXTON. Ends.

Copy of a letter from the G.O.C. 54th Division to Lieut.-Colonel Morris shortly before the final departure of the Battalion from Egypt in August, 1919:—

To Officer Commanding, 1st Cape Corps Regiment:

The Major-General Commanding, wishes to express to Colonel Morris, C.M.G., D.S.O., and to all ranks of the 1st Battalion, Cape Corps Regiment, his high appreciation of the excellent bearing, discipline, and conduct of the Battalion whilst serving under his Command in West Delta and 54th Divisional Areas.

The trying conditions during the recent Egyptian outbreak, equally with deferred demobilization, have been faced cheerfully by all ranks, and the Battalion has most loyally made the best of discomfort and hardship.

(Signed) S. H. KERSHAW, Lieut.-Colonel,
General Staff, 54th Division

THE STORY OF THE 1st CAPE CORPS.

Copy of a letter from Field Marshal Viscount Allenby, G.C.B., G.C.M.G., His Majesty's High Commissioner in Egypt, received by Dean Robson, of Kimberley, on 1st June, 1920 :—

MY DEAR DEAN ROBSON,

I hear that you are erecting a Roll of Honour containing Cape Corps Names. I had the honour of serving with many of the Cape Corps in Palestine, and I should like to add my tribute of appreciation. The record of those of the Cape Corps who fought under my Command is one that any troops might envy. Especially on September 19th and 20th, 1918, they covered themselves with glory, displaying a bravery and determination that have never been surpassed.

Photo by]   *[Sergeant Alies.*
AN EGYPTIAN BELLE.

SERGEANT D. W. HOEDEMAKER (616).

THE STORY OF THE 1st CAPE CORPS.

Depôt Battalion in Darling Street, Cape Town, 12th October, 1916. Major C. G. Durham marching at the head.

Kantara.

South Bridge, Kantara.

COURSES PASSED AT SCHOOLS OF INSTRUCTIONS.

Whilst the Battalion were in the Union (December 25th, 1917, to 3rd April, 1918) a number of officers, N.C.O.'s and men attended various courses at the Military School at Potchefstroom, and the majority passed well.

In Egypt and Palestine the majority of the officers and over two hundred N.C.O.'s and men passed one or more courses.

The courses comprised Trench Warfare and Bombing, Scouting and Sniping, Range Finding, Topography, Machine Gun, Stokes Gun, Lewis Gun, Musketry, and Transport Courses.

Senior Officers, Company Commanders, and Platoon Commanders Courses.

Handling of Machine Guns (Tactical and Technical combined).

Infantry Officers Tactical and N.C.O.'s General Course. Signalling, Physical Training and Bayonet Fighting, Gas Course, Advanced Cookery, and Cookery.

As it has not been possible to compile a complete and accurate list of passes the same cannot be given.

That is unfortunate as the general results were very satisfactory. Failures were few and the majority of those due only to the fact that men whose practical and technical knowledge was good were unable to do themselves justice at written examinations.

Two officers and one N.C.O. did exceptionally well and were classified as distinguished (over ninety-seven per cent. of marks).

Those were the late Lieutenant A. N. Difford (Trench Warfare and Bom), Lieutenant J. G. Hirsch (Platoon Officers Course), and Lieutenant ... ...orge (No. 1566), (Range Finding).

www.ingramcontent.com/pod-product-compliance
Lightning Source LLC
Chambersburg PA
CBHW080632230426
43663CB00016B/2842